Encouraging Positive Behaviors in Today's Kids

Encouraging Positive Behaviors in Today's Kids

A New Guide for Behavior Problems and Other Concerns for Counselors, Teachers, and Other School Personnel

Mary Lou McCormick

ROWMAN & LITTLEFIELD
Lanham • Boulder • New York • London

Published by Rowman & Littlefield
An imprint of The Rowman & Littlefield Publishing Group, Inc.
4501 Forbes Boulevard, Suite 200, Lanham, Maryland 20706
www.rowman.com

6 Tinworth Street, London SE11 5AL, United Kingdom

Copyright © 2020 by Mary Lou McCormick

All rights reserved. No part of this book may be reproduced in any form or by any electronic or mechanical means, including information storage and retrieval systems, without written permission from the publisher, except by a reviewer who may quote passages in a review.

British Library Cataloguing in Publication Information Available

Library of Congress Cataloging-in-Publication Data

Names: McCormick, Mary Lou, 1945- author.
Title: Encouraging positive behaviors in today's kids : a new guide for behavior problems and other concerns for counselors, teachers, and other school personnel / Mary Lou McCormick.
Description: Lanham, Maryland : Rowman & Littlefield, 2020. | Includes bibliographical references. | Summary: "This new practical handbook is not only meant to help manage negative behavior problems but assists the educator in discovering ways to encourage positive behaviors among young people"—Provided by publisher.
Identifiers: LCCN 2020006311 (print) | LCCN 2020006312 (ebook) | ISBN 9781475858020 (cloth) | ISBN 9781475858037 (paperback) | ISBN 9781475858044 (epub)
Subjects: LCSH: Behavior modification. | Classroom management. | Teacher-student relationships.
Classification: LCC LB1060.2 .M38 2020 (print) | LCC LB1060.2 (ebook) | DDC 370.15/28—dc23
LC record available at https://lccn.loc.gov/2020006311
LC ebook record available at https://lccn.loc.gov/2020006312

DEDICATIONS

To all the children who will shape the future of our world, for—
"All the flowers of all the tomorrows are in the
seeds of today."—Chinese Proverb

To all the educators—counselors, teachers, and other school
staff members—who shape the future of our nation one child
at a time, and whose influence will last an eternity.

Contents

Preface — xv

A New Guide for Behavior Problems
and Other Concerns — 1

1 Absenteeism — 3
   The Law — 3
   Refusal Behavior — 3
   The Snowball Effect — 4
   Kids' Basic Needs — 4
   Conflict of Values — 4
   Albert Three C's — 5
   Strategies and Activities for Absenteeism — 6
   References & Resources — 7

2 Anger and Aggression versus Self-Control — 9
   Discussion — 9
   Scenarios to Consider — 10
   Importance of Self-Control — 10
   Teaching Kids Self-Control — 11
   Problem-Solving Skills — 11
   Helping Kids with Anger and Aggression Issues — 12
   Strategies and Activities for Anger and Aggression versus
      Self-Control — 13
   References & Resources — 16

3 Anxieties and Fears ... 17
Discussion ... 17
Age-Related Fears ... 17
Differences between Anxiety and Fear ... 18
Symptoms of Anxiety and Fear ... 18
Common Types of Anxieties and Fears ... 19
When to Refer to a Professional ... 20
Strategies and Activities for Anxieties and Fears ... 21
References & Resources ... 22

4 Attention and Focusing Difficulties ... 23
Discussion ... 23
Types of Distractions ... 23
Questions to Ask ... 24
Teaching Attending and Focusing Skills ... 24
Strategies and Activities for Attention and Focusing Concerns ... 25
References & Resources ... 27

5 Attention-Seeking Behavior ... 29
Discussion ... 29
The Need to Belong ... 30
Strategies and Activities for Attention-Seeking Behavior ... 31
References & Resources ... 34

6 Bullying and Hate Crimes ... 35
Discussion ... 35
The Victim or "Target" ... 36
The Bystander: Another Victim ... 36
The Bully ... 37
A Case Story ... 39
Dealing with Bullying and Hate Crimes ... 39
School Bullying/Harassment Surveys ... 40
Summary ... 40
Strategies and Activities for Bullies and Bullying ... 41
References & Resources ... 44

7 Child Abuse Indicators ... 47
Emotional Abuse ... 47
Physical Abuse ... 49
Sexual Abuse ... 50
Helping Children Who Have Been Abused ... 51
What You Should Do If You Suspect Child Abuse ... 52
References & Resources ... 52

8	Cooperation versus Defiance	53
	Discussion	53
	Negative Ways to Get Recognition	53
	A Respectful Learning Environment	54
	Developing Social Interest	55
	Strategies and Activities for Cooperation versus Defiance	55
	References & Resources	58
9	Decision-Making Difficulties	61
	Discussion	61
	Glasser's Choice Theory	61
	Teaching Kids to Make Wise Decisions	62
	A Decision-Making Process	63
	Strategies and Activities for Decision-Making Difficulties	64
	References & Resources	66
10	Depression and Sadness	67
	Discussion	67
	Depression Defined	67
	Warning Signs of Depression	68
	Strategies and Activities for Depression and Sadness	70
	References & Resources	71
11	Divorce and Separation Issues	73
	Discussion	73
	Common Reactions	73
	Behavioral Changes at School	74
	"Red Flags" to Look For	74
	Normal Feelings and Concerns	76
	Strategies and Activities for Divorce and Separation Issues	76
	References & Resources	79
12	Empathy and Compassion Development	81
	Discussion	81
	Should Empathy and Compassion Be Taught in Schools?	82
	Implications for Developing Empathy and Compassion	82
	Strategies and Activities for Empathy and Compassion Development	83
	References & Resources	84
13	Following Directions	87
	Discussion	87
	Mistakes to Avoid	87
	Giving Effective Directions	88

Strategies and Activities for Following Directions	89
References & Resources	91

14 Following the Rules — 93
- Discussion — 93
- Model the Behavior You Want to See — 93
- Create a Caring and Respectful Climate — 94
- Developing a Class Code of Conduct — 94
- Consequences for Violating the Code — 95
- Sense of Belonging Encourages Compliance — 95
- Strategies and Activities for Following the Rules — 95
- References & Resources — 97

15 Goal Setting — 99
- Discussion — 99
- Benefits of Setting Goals — 100
- Teaching the Value of Setting Goals — 100
- How to Set Goals — 101
- Important Areas for Setting Goals — 102
- Strategies and Activities for Goal Setting — 103
- References & Resources — 105

16 Honesty Issues — 107
- Discussion — 107
- Influences on Honest Behavior — 107
- Teaching the Virtues of Honesty — 108
- Albert's Four R's of Logical Consequences — 109
- Strategies and Activities for Honesty Issues — 110
- References & Resources — 112

17 Listening Skills — 113
- Discussion — 113
- The Process of Listening — 113
- Importance of Listening Skills — 114
- Teaching Listening Skills — 114
- Strategies and Activities for Developing Listening Skills — 115
- References & Resources — 117

18 Motivation Concerns — 119
- Discussion — 119
- Intrinsic and Extrinsic Motivation — 120
- Glasser's Choice Theory — 120
- How Motivation Affects Kids' Attitudes — 121
- Nurturing Intrinsic Motivation — 121

Tips to Encourage Motivation 123
Strategies and Activities for Motivation Concerns 124
References & Resources 125

19 Organizational Skills 127
Discussion 127
The Benefits 127
Setting and Achieving Goals 128
Strategies and Activities for Organizational Skills 129
References & Resources 130

20 Personal-Social Issues 131
Discussion 131
Meeting Kids' Basic Needs 131
Fostering Positive Personal-Social Development 132
Different Strokes for Different Folks 132
Your Attitude Makes a Difference 133
Strategies and Activities for Personal-Social Issues 133
References & Resources 134

21 Problem-Solving Skills 135
Discussion 135
A Problem-Solving Process 136
The "Think Before You Act" Principle 136
Using Problem Solving to Settle Disputes 137
Strategies and Activities for Problem-Solving Difficulties 137
References & Resources 139

22 Respect for Authority 141
Discussion 141
Kids Learn from Adult Modeling 141
Tips for Encouraging Compliance 143
Creating a Mutually Respectful Climate 144
References & Resources 145

23 Respect for Self and Others 147
Discussion 147
Modeling Respect 147
Respectful Ways of Relating 148
Teaching Respect to Kids 148
References & Resources 150

24 Self-Discipline 151
Discussion 151
Developing Self-Discipline in Kids 152

	Strategies and Activities for Developing Self-Discipline	153
	References & Resources	155
25	**Self-Esteem**	**157**
	Discussion	157
	Factors That Contribute to Positive Self-Esteem	157
	Fostering Kids' Self-Esteem	158
	Strategies and Activities for Enhancing Self-Esteem	161
	References & Resources	163
26	**Separation Anxiety**	**165**
	Discussion	165
	Symptoms of Separation Anxiety	166
	Helping Kids Deal with Separation Anxiety	167
	References & Resources	168
27	**Sexual Harassment**	**169**
	Discussion	169
	Teaching Our Kids about Sexual Harassment	170
	Preventing Sexual Harassment	171
	Strategies and Activities for Sexual Harassment	172
	References & Resources	174
28	**Social Anxiety and Shyness**	**177**
	Discussion	177
	Avoidance Behaviors	178
	Symptoms of Social Anxiety	179
	Fear of Failure	180
	Overcoming Social Anxiety and Shyness	180
	Developing a Sense of Belonging	181
	Strategies and Activities for Social Anxiety and Shyness	181
	References & Resources	183
29	**Underachievement**	**185**
	Discussion	185
	Contributing Factors	186
	Characteristics of Underachievers	187
	Tips for Helping Underachievers	187
	Strategies and Activities for Underachievement	189
	References & Resources	190
30	**Work Completion**	**191**
	Discussion	191
	Why Assign Homework?	192
	Motivators for Doing Homework	192

Tips for Teachers	193
Strategies and Activities for Work Completion	194
References & Resources	195
Bibliography	197
About the Author	205

Preface

FROM THE AUTHOR

This new guide is provided to assist educators—counselors, teachers, administrators, and any other school staff members—in dealing effectively with the most common behavior problems and other concerns found among young people today. It presents various interventions, strategies, and activities compatible with the democratic principles of the larger society, to promote and encourage positive behaviors among young people as they become responsible, self-reliant, and self-managing individuals.

ABOUT PRONOUNS

It is not easy in the English language to refer to a child without indicating whether the child is a "he" or "she". To resolve this difficulty, the author has chosen to alternate the usage of the pronouns, although reference may be made to either sex. Please imagine that the child being referred to is the child you have in mind, even though the sex reference may not agree.

A New Guide for Behavior Problems and Other Concerns

INTRODUCTION

We often do not know what to do with our young people because many of the traditional methods of dealing with problematic behaviors are no longer effective in today's world.

Due to the decrease in educational funding, more and more school districts are appointing elementary school counselors to multiple-school assignments, and others are eliminating the elementary school counseling program from their districts altogether.

Teachers in middle schools are finding themselves in similar situations. School counselors are being assigned to multiple schools and their duties are often limited to scheduling and testing with very little time available for dealing with problem behaviors and student concerns. In these cases, the schools' teachers and other educators are left to their own resources to deal with disruptive behavioral problems and address student concerns.

Teachers are given very little training in their educational courses on how to deal with specific problematic behaviors found in the classroom, and frustration with the teaching experience is becoming more and more prevalent.

This new guide is provided to assist educators—counselors, teachers, administrators, and any other school staff members—in dealing effectively with the most common behavior problems and other concerns. Discussions, strategies, and activities to deal with the problems and concerns are offered to assist educators in training and educating healthy, successful, happy kids.

This practical handbook is not only meant to help deal with negative behavior problems but to assist the educator in discovering ways to encourage positive behaviors among young people as they become responsible, self-reliant, and self-managing individuals. It will equip educators with strategies not only to minimize misbehavior but to assist kids of all ages in developing skills in self-control, self-management, and self-discipline—gifts that will last a lifetime!

As it says in the book, "Sure it is important to learn to read, write, think, and do math, but if kids do not learn to love, respect, and accept themselves and each other, what difference does the rest really make for a successful future?" (Charles, 2013)

WHEN TO REFER A CHILD TO A PROFESSIONAL

The problematic situations presented in this practical guide for educators are based on common behavioral problems and concerns found in the school setting. In most cases, given the proper tools, educators will be equipped to deal with these problems and concerns effectively. However, if the problem is so severe and pervasive that it persists and continues to interfere with daily activities, professional intervention may be needed. The following are some criteria for making the decision to refer the child for professional intervention:

- if the behavioral problem is atypical for the child's age;
- if the problem is long-standing and does not seem to be improving;
- if the behavior is causing significant problems in the child's daily life in one or all of the following areas of development: personal, social, academic

If any of these conditions exist, it is advisable to talk with a professional, such as the school psychologist or counselor, who may recommend a referral to a community mental health professional. Individual counseling, or even group or family counseling, may be offered to help the child deal with school, family, or personal issues related to the presenting maladaptive behavior.

In some rare cases, the child may even be referred to a physician or child psychiatrist who might recommend medication, although the child would need to be closely monitored. In these instances, the professional would stay in close contact with the child's parents and may contact the child's teachers for behavioral reports as well.

Chapter 1

Absenteeism

It is not a matter of judging the "right or wrong" of it but understanding the "what is."

THE LAW

In the United States, every state and the District of Columbia have enacted Compulsory School Attendance Laws that date from the earliest adoption in Massachusetts in 1852 to the latest in Alaska in 1929. Clearly, by enacting these compulsory attendance laws, legislators have made a strong statement that school attendance is not a choice but rather is *mandatory*.

Unexcused absences often fall under the term of "truancy." Children who do not attend school regularly, and who exhibit patterns of extended absences, are in violation of the law and are, therefore, the focus of many public-school systems. If Child Protective Services (CPS) become aware of these excessive absences, parents could face charges of educational neglect.

REFUSAL BEHAVIOR

Another term used synonymously with absenteeism and truancy is "school refusal behavior," or SRB. Addressed by professionals, including educators, psychologists, and pediatricians, SRB is defined as "difficulty attending school or remaining in school for the entire day" (Strickney & Miltenberger, 1998). Included in the classification for SRB are the following: social phobia, school phobia, school anxiety, and truancy.

THE SNOWBALL EFFECT

Absenteeism is indeed a problem for many children in our schools, and it tends to exhibit a snowball effect. What we often see is the more a child is absent, the more he misses out on school work, which leads to missing out on learning skills, which leads to feelings of inadequacy and failure, which leads to increased levels of anxiety and depression, which leads to avoidance of the group in which he experiences these feelings, resulting in more absences.

Whatever precipitated the onset of this disturbing cycle, whether it be illness or parental irresponsibility, the end result is that the child is often simply avoiding being in a situation in which he or she feels inadequate and incompetent within the school group, and so the cycle of absenteeism continues.

KIDS' BASIC NEEDS

According to Glasser (1992), children's basic needs must be met before the spark for learning can even be lit. These needs include (1) *survival*—food, shelter, safety, (2) *belonging*—security, comfort, group membership, (3) *power*—sense of importance, consideration by others, (4) *fun*—having a good time emotionally and intellectually, and (5) *freedom*—of choices, having self-direction and responsibility.

If these needs are not met, children are not interested in going to school. It is as simple as that. The happier kids are at school, the more instilled they are with the desire to learn, the more they feel they belong to the group. In other words, the more their needs are met, the less likely they will have a problem with attendance.

CONFLICT OF VALUES

It is important to note that absenteeism is sometimes the result of a conflict of values within certain ethnic subcultures where the family's needs take priority over the school's needs or even over the student's needs—such as, keeping a child home to tend to younger siblings when mom is ill, or taking a child to an appointment to interpret for a non-English speaking parent. It is not a matter of judging whether this is right or wrong, but rather understanding there are differences in value systems—values which have been passed down for generations and are not easily changed (Blum, 1989).

Another example is what we often hear referred to as "the culture of poverty" (Lewis, 1998). People who are a part of this subculture pass certain attitudes and values down from generation to generation. Among the beliefs and values found in this group are strong feelings of helplessness, of dependency, of not belonging, of powerlessness, of inferiority, and personal unworthiness. They are a people who know only their own troubles, their own local conditions, and their own neighborhoods. They have very little sense of history, tend to live in the present moment, and have very little hope for a brighter future, thus they do not view education as a way of improving their condition.

These beliefs and values are passed on to their children, so they also do not view school as a priority in their lives. According to Abraham Maslow (1943) and his Hierarchy of Needs, until the needs of food, clothing and shelter are met, the parents in this group are not *capable* of being concerned with their children's educational needs. Again, it is not a matter of judging the "right or wrong" of it, but rather understanding the "what is."

In all of these home scenarios, parents must be led to understand the school's expectations for attendance, the possible legal consequences for failing to comply, as well as the adverse effects absenteeism have on their children's lives.

When parents are not capable of being concerned about their children's education, the school must assume the responsibility for the development of attitudes—how children feel about themselves, about others, about school, and the world around them. It is of paramount importance that these kids feel important, worthwhile, and valued in their social groups.

ALBERT THREE C's

Albert (1996) devised *the three c's* of helping kids feel they belong:

1. *Capable* or "I-can" level—helping kids feel they are capable of learning, achieving, and succeeding.
2. *Connect*—assisting kids in initiating and maintaining positive relationships with peers and teachers by using *the five A's* (Acceptance, Attention, Appreciation, Affirmation and Affection).
3. *Contribute*—making kids feel *needed* by the group by contributing to their class, their school, and their community, as well as helping out other students.

It is important to help kids feel secure about themselves, to help them to learn how to make every day positive decisions that affect their lives, and to be accountable for their own actions. This will serve as solid footing for making such decisions as *responsible school attendance* in the present and *reliable work ethics* in the future.

STRATEGIES AND ACTIVITIES FOR ABSENTEEISM

1. Communicate with the student, parents, agencies, or any other appropriate parties in order to determine the *causes* for the absenteeism.
2. Begin each day with a success-oriented activity which is likely to be enjoyable and fun.
3. Provide the student with his own Attendance Chart with reinforcers and/or initiatives for meeting expectations. Use a time frame appropriate for the child, such as one week, one month, a grading period. Using a system which gives special recognition for "Perfect Attendance" is often effective.
4. Assign the child a specific responsibility to be performed at the beginning of each day (e.g., being the "Teacher's Assistant," or TA, to get supplies and materials ready for the day, changing the daily calendar, feeding the classroom pet, and so forth). Let him or her know how important the task is to the group.
5. Ensure that the difficulty of the child's daily tasks and activities and the time allotted to perform them is appropriate to the child's ability, thus minimizing feelings of discouragement and inadequacy.
6. Provide packets (large manila envelopes work well) with the papers, seatwork, and homework assignments for each student absent in order to afford the opportunity to make up the work, thus avoiding lagging behind.
7. Provide positive and encouraging interactions with the child throughout the day. Remember, encouragement is not only saying *Good job*, but adding *I knew you could do it*.
8. Encourage students to help other students. Some suggestions are as follows:
    - Display a box labeled "Random Acts of Kindness" and give peer recognition for doing good deeds.
    - Provide *peer tutoring* for kids who are having difficulties with an activity. For the kids who often need help, make arrangements for them to tutor kids from a lower grade level.
    - Albert (1996) suggests establishing a *circle of friends* who make sure everyone has someone to talk with, to sit with during lunch, and to play with at recess.
9. Encourage students to contribute to the class. This is done by asking for opinions about such matters as routines, class projects, the class code of conduct, and the consequences for violations of the code.
10. Communicate to parents the expectations, policies, and laws regarding attendance and the consequences for failure to comply (such as making up school work, formal letter home after three absences, possible

educational neglect charges reported to Child Protective Services with the possibility of parents being charged in a court of law).

REFERENCES & RESOURCES

Albert, L. (1996). *Cooperative discipline.* Circle Pines, MN: American Guidance Service.
Blum, D. (1998). *The school counselor's book of lists.* San Francisco: Jossey-Bass.
Glasser, W. (1998). *The quality school: Managing students without coercion.* New York: Harper & Row.
Lewis, O. (1998, January). The culture of poverty. *Society, 35*(2), 7.
Maslow, A. (1943). A theory of human motivation. *Psychological Review, 50*(4), 370–96.
Stickney, M. & Miltenberger, R. (1998). School refusal behavior: Prevalence, characteristics, and schools' response. *Education & Treatment of Children, 21*(2), 160–70.

Chapter 2

Anger and Aggression versus Self-Control

Angry students are at risk for being left behind in school and in life.

DISCUSSION

Although anger is a natural and normal human emotion, some children have low impulse control to anger-provoking events. Aggressive, angry behavior is characterized by physical and/or verbal attacks on school staff, other students, property (as in breaking things), threatening remarks to others, and sometimes physical abuse to self.

Anger-related behavior is often unplanned and unintentional, related to delays in development and difficulties with skills of flexibility and the ability to tolerate frustration (McFadden & Cooper, 2004). Angry students are at risk for being left behind in school and in life. Educators and parents can provide useful learning experiences in anger control for those students who need healthier means of expressing themselves in anger-provoking situations.

Sometimes children do not have the social skills or self-control to manage their behavior. These must be modeled and taught. When children cannot find the words to deal with angry feelings, or are not encouraged to express themselves, they become frustrated and this can lead to aggressive behavior. Kids need to learn appropriate, acceptable ways to express their anger and coping skills to deal with frustration. This will help to minimize aggressive behavior and increase the chances of personal, social, and academic success.

SCENARIOS TO CONSIDER

In an attempt to understand the child who exhibits these negative behaviors, it may be helpful to consider the following scenarios:

- The child's parents and/or siblings use aggressive behavior to resolve conflicts at home, often ending in angry, abusive, even violent disputes. These are the child's role models. He may adhere to the belief that aggressive acts are the only options available to him.
- The child experiences a sense of powerlessness in the home environment but discovers that there is power in angry, aggressive behavior at school and in the community.
- The child's home environment is chaotic and family members are abusive toward each other and toward the child. The child carries his emotional pain to school. His way of coping with this emotional pain may be to create havoc at school by exhibiting aggressive behavior toward other students and/or the teacher, thus taking the focus of his mind off of the pain inflicted upon him at home.
- The child receives more attention (albeit *negative* attention) when he displays aggressive, deviant behavior than when he is well behaved and compliant; thus, he chooses the behaviors which award him the most attention.
- The child has a reputation for being mean and aggressive—a fighter. The child internalizes these views others have of him and is simply living up to their expectations, as well as his own self-perceptions.
- The child frequently displays angry, and sometimes aggressive, behavior when confronted with tasks he considers to be too difficult for him. He would rather be perceived as mean or bad, than dumb or stupid.
- All behavior has meaning and purpose within the child's social context. If the child lacks a *sense of belonging* within his social groups of home and school, he may lack confidence in himself to succeed by useful and positive means.

IMPORTANCE OF SELF-CONTROL

Self-control and self-discipline are enormously important attributes we must help our kids develop. They are learned skills that help kids take ownership and responsibility for their behavior. It gives them the ability to think before they act, enables them to perform better at school, and to become good problem-solvers. Teaching kids self-control will help them to get along with others, to control their impulses, to make good choices, and to stay safe. It means that an individual knows right from wrong. And when they do the right thing, they feel good about themselves, thus their self-esteem is also enhanced.

Kids who do not make good behavioral choices do not take responsibility for the consequences of their own actions. Instead, they rely on other kids, parents, teachers, or other adults to make choices for them, and if something goes wrong, they blame someone else for their poor choices. These kids may follow others' poor examples and get involved in ridiculing others, taking other's property, and making other inappropriate, risky, and unsafe choices.

TEACHING KIDS SELF-CONTROL

When teaching children self-control, respect for children's will and autonomy must be balanced with respect for the needs of others and the limitations placed on us to ensure safety and survival. Teaching kids self-control involves helping them to (1) think before they act, (2) control their impulses, (3) weigh the possible consequences, and (4) make safe and appropriate choices.

It is important that expectations and goals for self-control be age appropriate for each stage of development, thus it is essential for parents and educators to be familiar with what is normal and what is not when it comes to their children's lack of impulse control (Ericson, 1963).

Gordon (1998) maintains that self-control is the only true effective discipline. He also contends that teachers can strongly assist kids in developing such self-control. In order to help children control their own behavior and become self-reliant in making positive decisions, teachers must first give up their "controlling" power. Gordon says, "You acquire more influence with young people when you give up using your power to control them . . . and the more you use power to try to control people, the less real influence you'll have on their lives" (p. 7). In order for educators to effectively teach children how to develop self-control, they must first model self-control in their own lives.

PROBLEM-SOLVING SKILLS

One of the most effective ways of developing self-control in kids is to teach them problem-solving strategies. The process of problem solving should be taught in every classroom. This helps kids to clarify problems, come up with possible solutions, select solutions that are acceptable to all, put the solutions into action, and evaluate whether the solutions worked to solve their problem.

Coloroso (1994) asserts that they must also learn to distinguish between *reality* and *problem*, with reality being an accurate appraisal of what has occurred in a situation, and problem being the discomfort being caused by the reality. She contends that in learning to solve problems, "We accept (the) realities; (then) we solve the problems that come from them" (Charles, 1983, p. 31). She points out that as students make this distinction, they begin to see that there is no problem so great it cannot be solved.

Below are the steps to teach kids a plan of attack for solving their problems:

1) Identify and define the problem specifically until all persons involved understand it.
2) Brainstorm possible solutions to the problem.
3) Delete the options which are unsatisfactory, such as those that are unkind, unfair, dishonest, or hurtful.
4) Evaluate and examine the possible consequences of the remaining options.
5) Select one best option.
6) Make a plan for the selected option and agree to try it.
7) Evaluate and revise the plan as necessary.

What is important is that when children experience a problem, they have the skills to attack it. The approach they use should culminate in a plan, not an excuse.

Kids' frustration levels are greatly reduced when they have the tools to attack problems successfully and they are less likely to display anger and aggression. This gives them control over their problems and the way they choose to respond to them.

HELPING KIDS WITH ANGER AND AGGRESSION ISSUES

The following are some suggestions to consider when helping children who are having difficulties with anger and aggression:

- Give children responsibilities to help them feel they are *connected* and *contributing* to the good of the group. Frequently let them know how important their tasks are to the group.
- Provide the child with opportunities for *social and academic successes* and give frequent, positive feedback which indicates he or she is important and respected.
- Assess that the *difficulty of a given task* is within the child's ability to perform successfully, given the allotted amount of time for completion.

- Provide the children with as many *high-interest and "fun" activities* within the academic setting, thus increasing their level of happiness and sense of well-being.
- Give children *choices* whenever possible. For example, *Here are two papers which need to be completed. Which one would you like to do first?* Or, *This assignment needs to be completed because it gives you practice in multiplication. Would you like to use the yellow pencil or my mechanical pencil?* (Kids love using mechanical pencils so the child will probably choose it and get busy working on the assignment.)
- If necessary, provide a *quiet place* for the child to work independently, away from peer interactions. Include his opinion in determining where he might feel most comfortable. Allow him to rejoin the group during those times in which a quiet place is not necessary. Besides reducing frustrating distractions, this will lessen his need to "save face" if the task is difficult for him.

Self-control skills are among the most valuable tools that educators can help their kids develop. They are some of the most important skills for success, not only now when they are young, but throughout their lives.

STRATEGIES AND ACTIVITIES FOR ANGER AND AGGRESSION VERSUS SELF-CONTROL

1. Activity: *My Situations Journal* (grades 3 +)

    Allow the child to choose a name for his journal (such as *My Self-Control Journal, My Personal Journal, My Annoyance Journal, My Feelings Journal,* and so forth). Suggest writing the following information in his journal as a guide:
    1) What was happening *before* the incident?
    2) What happened *during* the incident?
    3) What happened *after* the incident? (Include the consequences of your actions.)
    4) What could you have *chosen* to do differently? Why?

    (Younger children might keep a picture journal of times when they showed self-control and times when they lost control. Then have them circle the times when they made good choices.)

2. Activity: *Solving Problems*

    Give children a variety of problematic scenarios, and using the problem-solving format below, have them practice resolving the issues.
    Instructions:
    1) Identify the problem. *In your own words, what is the problem?*
    2) Determine the goal. *What do you want to happen?*

3) List the options. *What are some ways you could choose to deal with the problem?*
4) Choose one option. *Choose the way you think would be best.* When dealing with a real-life problem, you would include
5) Carry out the plan.
6) Evaluate how successful the plan was in solving the problem.

3. Activity: *SODAS*

    One decision-making process to teach kids self-control uses the acronym *SODAS*, which stands for situation, options, disadvantages, advantages, and solution. This activity can be used with an individual and with groups. The purpose is to teach children to reason out a situation and evaluate the advantages and disadvantages of choices before making a decision. Provide various problematic scenarios and allow children to practice resolving the issue.

    Instructions for the five-step SODAS decision-making process:
    1) Identify the Situation. *What exactly is the decision to be made? Be specific about the issue to be decided. Answer the "who, what, where when and why" questions.* (Remind them to avoid being emotional, because emotion tends to cloud judgment.)
    2) List all of the Options. *What are the possible choices at hand? List both the good and bad options, even those that show out-of-control behavior.*
    3) List the Disadvantages of each option given above. The idea is to get kids to see the negative consequences of an option.
    4) List the Advantages of each option given above. By exploring both the advantages and disadvantages of an option, kids will be better prepared to see why an option might work or fail.
    5) Choose a Solution. Give kids some time to think about the solutions, then allow them to make the choice as to which option might be the best. It may not be the choice you want, but this is part of the learning process. As long as the choice is not immoral or illegal, let them make the choice and deal with the consequences.

4. Activity: *Anger Analysis* (analyze the anger-provoking situation with the child)
    1) Assist the child in *identifying the signs* that indicate anger, such as rapid heartbeat, shortness of breath, rapid breathing, face feels hot, hands clench up, stomach feels tight, and so on.
    2) Have the child *identify the event* that happened *prior* to the angry feeling.
    3) Encourage the child to *express his feelings* about the event by using the *"I Message"* format:

Anger and Aggression versus Self-Control 15

- I feel/felt _____ when _____ because _____ and I need/want_____.
- Example: I feel *angry* when *Carlos calls me Shorty* because *it embarrasses me in front of my friends,* and I want *him to stop.*

4) Discuss *alternative ways* to deal with situations which cause frustration and anger, for example, walking away, talking it out, taking "time out" to cool off, changing the game, counting to thirty, and so forth.

5) Have the child choose *one alternative way* he could have responded to the current situation being discussed and have him role-play the alternative choice.

6) If necessary and the child agrees, *formulate a behavior agreement*, based on the process of setting and achieving goals, and offer to assist him:
   a) State the Goal—*What do you want to happen?*
   b) The Plan of Action—*What are the steps you will need to take in order to reach your goal?*
   c) Evaluation—*How well did your plan work? Did you reach your goal? What changes might you make for next time?*

5. Activity: *My Remote Control* (all grade levels, with modifications). This exercise helps kids to identify opposing feelings and to understand what situations elicit those feelings (adapted from Wittner, Thompson & Loesch, 1997).

   Materials:
   Provide (1) construction-paper-replicas of remote controls with eight pairs of circles about the size of quarters, or have the children make their own; (2) pencils for drawing, and (3) a list of pairs of feelings/attitudes. (Be sure to make these developmentally appropriate; for younger children use fewer and the most familiar pairs of feelings.)

   Instructions:
   1) Say, *Imagine your mind is like a TV set with lots of different channels inside your head. You have sad and happy channels, angry and relaxed channels, worried and calm channels, scary and safe channels, bored and focused channels, noisy and quiet channels, unpleasant and agreeable channels and grumpy and cheerful channels. Now label your remote control buttons by drawing little pictures in the circles and writing the feeling words below them. You are ready to start playing "My Remote Control."*
   2) *Press one button on your remote control, close your eyes, and think of a situation that makes you feel that way—for example, press grumpy and imagine a situation which makes you feel grumpy, then change your channel to happy and imagine*

something that makes you feel happy. Do this for all your channels. (Students may want to share these situations with a partner or the group.)

3) *Right now, you have a remote control on your desk, but you also have a remote control in your head, in your mind, to your feelings channels. Just press your thumb to a finger and imagine the channel changing from a negative feeling or attitude into a positive one. You can decide what channel you want to be on anytime, anywhere.*

6. *Increasing a sense of Belonging*

Increase children's sense of belonging by giving them specific tasks with a title which provides a service to the class group. A few examples are as follows:
- The Class Attendance Clerk (e.g., make an unofficial classroom attendance card and have the student mark the students present each morning);
- The Chief Boys/Girls Restroom Monitor
- The Class Cafeteria Captain
- The Class Distributor (passes out papers, supplies, and other tasks).

Frequently let children know how important their task is to the group.

REFERENCES & RESOURCES

Albert, L. (1996). *A teacher's guide to cooperative discipline* (rev. ed.). Circle Pines, MN: American Guidance Service.

Charles, C. (1983). *Elementary classroom management.* New York: Longman.

Charles, C. (2013). *Building classroom discipline.* New York: Pearson.

Coloroso, B. (1994). *Kids are worth it! Giving your child the gift of inner discipline.* New York: William Morrow.

Gordon, T. (1989). *Discipline that works: Promoting self-discipline in children.* New York: Random House.

McFadden, A. & Cooper, K. (2004). *Leave no ANGRY child behind: The ABC's of anger management for grades K-12.* Chapin, SC: Youth Light, Inc.

Wittner, J., Thompson, D., & Loesch, L. (1997). *Classroom guidance activities: A sourcebook for elementary counselors.* Minneapolis: Educational Media Corporation.

Chapter 3

Anxieties and Fears

A certain amount of fear can be healthy. A child who fears falling will not get too close to the edge of a cliff.

DISCUSSION

Everyone, from the youngest child to the oldest adult, experiences anxieties and fears at one time or another. Anxiety and fear serve as a means of protection and can often enhance our performance in stressful situations. Young children have more fears and phobias than adults and experience the emotion of them more intensely. Such fears may start and stop for little apparent reason as the child develops.

It is important to point out that with children, such feelings of fear are not only normal, they are also necessary in learning to deal with life's challenges and experiences. They can be helpful because they make children behave in a safe manner. In other words, a certain amount of fear can be healthy. A child who fears falling will not get too close to the edge of a cliff, or a child who fears fire will not play with matches.

AGE-RELATED FEARS

Typical childhood fears change with age. They include fear of strangers, heights, darkness, animals, blood, insects, and being left alone. Children often learn to fear a specific object or situation after having an unpleasant experience, such as a dog bite or an accident. The following provides some guidelines to age-appropriate fears:

- *Ages four to six*: Children of these ages have anxieties about things that are not based in reality, such as fears of monsters, dragons, and ghosts.
- *Ages seven to twelve*: Children of these ages tend to have fears that reflect real circumstances that may happen to them, such as bodily injury, natural disasters, and death.
- *Adolescents*: These kids commonly experience anxieties and fears related to social acceptance and academic achievement.

Approximately, one out of ten children suffers from some type of anxiety disorder (Conner, 2008).

DIFFERENCES BETWEEN ANXIETY AND FEAR

The terms "fear" and "anxiety" are often used interchangeably, but it is generally agreed that "fear" refers to an emotional response toward a situation whereby an individual feels threatened, and the cause of the threat is *realistic in nature*. Oftentimes, fear toward a particular situation or event is brought about by a traumatic experience that the individual experienced earlier in life, such as being bitten by a dog or getting lost in a store.

Anxiety, on the other hand, is a psychological disorder that, unlike fear, the symptoms leading to anxiety occur *even though there is no apparent risk to the individual's well-being or cause for physical harm to occur* (Goldman, 2001). Even though anxiety is a state of uneasiness whereby the child experiences "apprehension without apparent cause," it is important to remember that the child *perceives* the threat as real. More often than not, the cause for the individual to feel anxious cannot be pinpointed. This is in stark contrast with fear, where individuals can readily determine the root cause of their fears.

SYMPTOMS OF ANXIETY AND FEAR

The experience of anxiety and fear typically has two components: emotional and physical sensations. The emotional symptoms include feelings of worry, apprehension, nervousness, and distress. Anxiety and fear have similar physical symptoms, to varying degrees, such as muscle tension, increased heart rate and blood pressure, "butterflies" in the stomach, restlessness, body perspiration, and shortness of breath, brought about by the body's *fight-or-flight* instinct—either *fight* for our lives or *flee* for our lives.

Anxiety and fear can cause a multitude of other complaints, such as nausea, vomiting, stomach pain, diarrhea, tingling, weakness, and headaches, to name a few. Over time, children who suffer from frequent anxiety and fear may become clingy, impulsive, depressed, easily distracted, and suffer from low self-esteem (American Academy of Child and Adolescent Psychiatrists, 2004).

They often worry about things before they happen, have constant worries or concerns about family, school, friends, or activities, and lack self-confidence. Anxiety disorders, when severe, can affect a child's thinking processes, decision-making ability, perceptions of the environment, learning capabilities, and level of concentration (Goldman, 2001).

COMMON TYPES OF ANXIETIES AND FEARS

Separation Anxiety: It is natural for young children ages eighteen months through four or five years of age to feel anxious when separated from a parent. Although it can be difficult, separation anxiety is a normal stage of development. With understanding, patience, and coping strategies, it can be relieved, and should fade as the child gets older.

In some children, however, fears about separation seem to only intensify as time passes or may suddenly reappear. Symptoms of separation anxiety include (1) constant thoughts and intense fears about the safety of parents or caregivers, (2) refusing to go to school, (3) panic or tantrums at times of separation from parents, and (4) frequent physical complaints, such as headaches, stomachaches, and so forth. If anxieties are persistent and excessive enough to get in the way of school or other activities, it is possible that the child has separation anxiety disorder. Unlike normal separation anxiety, this condition may require the support of a professional, but there is also a lot that you, as an educator, can do to help.

Social Anxiety. Social anxiety involves fear of varying degrees of certain social situations—especially unfamiliar situations in which the child will be watched or evaluated by others. There is nothing abnormal about a child being shy, but children with social anxiety disorder, or social phobia, experience extreme distress over everyday activities and situations such as playing with other kids, reading in class, speaking to adults, taking tests, or performing in front of others. These social situations may be so frightening that the child may get anxious just thinking about them and may go to great lengths to avoid them.

Underlying social anxiety disorder is the fear of being judged, scrutinized, or embarrassed in front of others. Children with extreme social anxiety often have a fear of meeting or talking to people, especially adults, they avoid social situations, have few friends outside of the family, and may not want to go to school.

Fear of Failure. The fear of failure among children in America today is at epidemic proportions (Taylor, 2005). The fear of failure may stop many children from achieving the success that they deserve for their efforts. Fear of failure causes children to experience debilitating anxiety before they take a test, compete in a sport, or perform in a recital. It causes them to give less than their best effort, not take risks, and, ultimately, never achieve complete success. Taylor suggests providing children with a new definition of failure which encourages them to *value success* rather than fear failure. The points are as follows:

- Failure means not giving your best effort, making poor decisions, and not doing what is in your best interest.
- Failure means lying, cheating, stealing, and not taking responsibility for yourself.
- Failure means taking the easy way out, being influenced by peer pressure, and acting in ways that can hurt you.
- Failure means being selfish, uncaring, and disrespectful to others.

Giving children a definition of failure that takes away the fear frees them to strive for success, to explore, to take risks, and to pursue their goals and dreams.

Fear of Success. Some children fear being ostracized by their peers if they are too successful in school, so they find ways to sabotage themselves. This is especially true for children who have friends who are not particularly successful in school. The following signs may indicate that a child has a fear of success (Blum, 1998):

- Does not perform near potential.
- Does not complete homework or study for tests.
- Spends time socializing rather than focusing on work.
- Seems overly concerned about being accepted by peers.

Educators can help students with a fear of success by being aware of peer pressure and influencing this pressure for positive outcomes when possible. Help the child to determine future goals, and to see the relationship between current academic success and the future achievement of desired goals.

WHEN TO REFER TO A PROFESSIONAL

As has been pointed out, many of the anxieties and fears that children have appear out of the blue, and then disappear with time. A certain amount of anxiety and fear is not only natural but necessary in learning to deal with the challenges of life, protecting oneself from harm, and beneficial for optimal performance. But when anxiety becomes excessive beyond what is expected for the circumstances and the child's developmental level, problems in social, personal, and academic functioning may occur, resulting in an anxiety disorder.

When anxiety and fear interfere with the child's ability to focus on activities at school or prevents the child from performing daily activities, then intervention may be warranted. Prompt treatment of school refusal is the key to shorten the course of the disorder. Without treatment, as many as 40 percent to 50 percent of these youths are at risk for not graduating from high school due to the intensity and chronic nature of their anxiety (Kearney, 2008).

When anxiety becomes severe and recurring, it can negatively impact a child's thinking, decision-making ability, perceptions of the environment, learning, and concentration. Without professional help to assist the child in facing and overcoming his or her anxieties and fears, the child will eventually end up making choices based on feared situations and not realities.

When kids' confidence suffers, they will fail to thrive at home, in school, or in the larger society. If the child's fear seems out of proportion to the causes of the stress, this may signal the need to seek an evaluation from a qualified mental health professional, such as a counselor, psychologist, or psychiatrist.

STRATEGIES AND ACTIVITIES FOR ANXIETIES AND FEARS

1. *Acknowledge that the fear is real.* As inconsequential as a fear may seem, it feels real to the child and is causing him or her to feel anxious and afraid. Provide empathetic understanding by saying something like, *I realize you are afraid of tornadoes whenever it is windy outside.* Being able to talk about the fear helps, because words often take some of the power away from the negative feelings.
2. *Never make fun of the fear.* Saying things like, *That is so ridiculous to be afraid of tornadoes when there aren't even any clouds in the sky. It is just windy outside!* does not make the fear go away and will most likely make the child feel embarrassed and guilty in addition to feeling fearful.
3. *Do not accommodate the fear.* For example, if the child is afraid of tornadoes on windy days, do not allow him to stay inside during recess, because this will reinforce that windy days should be feared and avoided.
4. *Teach coping skills.* Teaching children stress-management skills will often transfer to learning to overcome fears. The idea is to help the child change ways of thinking about the problem. The following guide might be useful to:

1) Identify the problem/fear.
2) Generate various solutions to responding to the fear.
3) Examine possible consequences of the various solutions.
4) Choose one best solution to put into action for coping with the fear.
5) Agree to try out the solution.
6) Evaluate the effectiveness of the solution for dealing with the fear and revise as necessary.

5. Activity: *Relax and Breathe Deep Exercise.* This activity will help kids to be able to relax when feeling frustrated, stressed, worried, angry, or scared.

Instructions:
1) Explain to the group or individual: *Your goal is to get so good at relaxing that you can do it whenever you feel frustrated, tense, stressed out, worried, upset, angry, or scared. You can learn to do this by practicing the Relax and Breathe Deep Exercise. This will put you in control of your mind, your body, your stress, and your relaxation. Let's start right now.*
2) *When I say, "Go," I want you to slowly breathe in, taking in one long, deep breath. As you breathe in, I want you to feel the air slowly filling your body with calmness. Hold the air in and count slowly to three. Then slowly breathe out, letting all your bad feelings flow out of your body with the air. Tell yourself, "Relax," and feel the stress leave your body. How did you do? Great!"* (Repeat)
3) *You can get really good at relaxing if you practice this exercise, especially when something upsets you—at home, on the playground, in a game, in the classroom, anywhere!*

REFERENCES & RESOURCES

American Academy of Child and Adolescent Psychiatry (AACAP). (2004). *Facts for families: The anxious child.* No. 47. Updated November 2004. http://aacap.org.

Blum, D. (1998). *The school counselor's book of lists.* San Francisco: Jossey-Bass.

Conner, M. (2008). Anxiety in children. *Crisis counseling.* http://crisiscounseling.com/Articles/AnxietyinChildren

Goldman, W. (2001). *Childhood and adolescent anxiety disorders.* Updated June 2001. Retrieved August 2011. http://www.keepkidshealthy.com/anxiety_disorders.html.

Kearney, C. (2008, March). School absenteeism and school refusal behavior in youth: A contemporary review. *Clinical Psychology Review, 28*(3), 451–71.

Taylor, J. (2005, April). *Fear of failure: A childhood epidemic.* http://www.keepkidshealthy.com/parenting_tips.

Watkins, C. (2004). *Separation anxiety.* Northern County Psychiatric Associates. http://www.baltimorepsych.com/separation_anxiety.

Chapter 4

Attention and Focusing Difficulties

Parents and teachers must share the responsibility of teaching kids the skills of attending and focusing, essential skills for academic success.

DISCUSSION

Every teacher has had students with limited attention spans who have difficulties focusing on assigned tasks. They range from students having minor focusing problems to children who have been diagnosed as having Attention Deficit Hyperactivity Disorder (ADHD). It is important to point out that many of the recent discoveries about ADHD show that these children can be motivated to remember, concentrate, and learn from the consequences of their actions (Fay & Cline, 2000).

Paying attention, focusing, and concentrating are the most important mental skills affecting learning—performance in particular and life experiences in general. The ability to focus and concentrate affects interpersonal relationships, playful adventures, physical activities, creative experiences, and joyful living.

TYPES OF DISTRACTIONS

Greenspan (1995) asserts that some children have difficulty paying attention because of the way they take in and interpret what they hear or see. They are easily distracted because sights and sounds do not have sufficient meaning to hold their attention.

Some children might be *visually* oversensitive, for example. They might be highly distracted by bright sunlight coming through a window or too much color on a bulletin board. Others who are oversensitive to *smells* might be distracted by the teacher's perfume or a pet cage nearby. *Auditory* sensitivity can be just as distracting. Some children are so sensitive to sounds that they could be distracted by a low-pitch sound coming from a motor, perhaps a boiler room next door, which most children would not even notice. Others are *under-reactive* and may not even focus when they hear a voice, and you might have to tap them on the shoulder to get their attention.

QUESTIONS TO ASK

The following questions might be useful to ask before devising a plan to help the child with focusing challenges:

- Does the child have emotional problems?
- Is the child experiencing problems at home which might be affecting her ability to concentrate, such as divorce, death, violence, abuse, and so on?
- Does the child have a fear of failing? Of making mistakes? Are there harsh consequences at home if she fails or makes mistakes?
- Has the child's hearing been checked recently?
- Is ADHD suspected? Has a referral been made for an evaluation?

TEACHING ATTENDING AND FOCUSING SKILLS

Parents and teachers must share the responsibility of teaching kids the skills of attending and focusing, essential skills for academic success. The following suggestions are provided for developing these skills:

1. Implement an individualized program and chart the progress and reinforce the child for attending and maintaining attention by providing the child with:
   - *Tangible* incentives (classroom privileges, class "bucks," passing out materials, line leading, class coupons for five minutes of free time, and so forth)
   - *Intangible* incentives (words of praise and encouragement, a smile, a pat on the back, a handshake). Always provide *choices* whenever possible.
2. Before delivering directions, explanations, and instructions, be certain the child is attending (making direct eye contact, hands free of objects, and so on).

3. Make sure that competing sounds are silenced while giving the child directions or explanations. These sounds might include talking, laughing, learning center recorders, public address announcements, and pencil tapping.
4. With the child's assistance, create a verbal cue and/or hand signal which denotes that you are about to deliver an instruction or explanation.
5. Use a timer to help students stay on task. They could be given an incentive for "beating the bell" with quality performance.
6. Initially, it may be important to stand directly in front of the child and call her by name before delivering directions. As the child becomes conditioned to focusing when she hears the verbal cue or sees the hand signal, try standing some distance away. Also, a peer seated close by might provide the information at this point.
7. Reduce distracting stimuli by allowing the child to choose where she might work and concentrate best (e.g., at the front of a row, in her own special carrel, or in her "office space" at the back of the room).
8. Give instructions in a variety of ways—verbally, written, have the child copy them, on a tape recorder. Use pictures, diagrams, gestures, and the chalk or white board.
9. Deliver directions one step at a time. Gradually increase the number of steps as the child demonstrates her ability to attend and maintain attention. When several steps are involved in an activity, provide the child with a checklist she can mark as she completes each task.
10. Ask the child questions about the instructions. Have her verbally repeat or paraphrase the information delivered.
11. Rephrase directions and explanations in order to increase the likelihood of the child's understanding of the information being presented.
12. Provide these children with a consistent schedule and a structured environment.

The bottom line is—children must learn to focus and concentrate effectively if they are to experience academic success. This is accomplished by providing these children with appropriate guidance and practice at connecting fully with essential tasks in the present moment, in the here and now.

STRATEGIES AND ACTIVITIES FOR ATTENTION AND FOCUSING CONCERNS

1. Activity: Play games designed to teach listening skills. A couple of examples are *Simon Says* and *Mother/Father May I?*
2. Activity: *The Leaf Pile.*

The purpose of this activity is to develop the skills of focusing and attending to enhance learning and performance.

Instructions:
1) Divide the class into groups (the smaller the group, the easier the activity is).
2) Give each child a leaf and ask them to examine it carefully. Then have them put their leaves in a pile in the middle, mix them up, and see if they can find their leaf.
3) Have the children tell what it was about their leaves that let them know it was theirs.
4) Exchange leaves and play the game again.

3. Activity: *Posing Partners*

   Instructions:
   1) Divide the class into pairs so everyone has a partner. (Three children in a group works, too.)
   2) Partner A turns his back and closes his eyes while Partner B makes a pose.
   3) Partner B says, "ready," and Partner A turns around and looks at him carefully.
   4) Then Partner A turns back around, and Partner B changes his pose in some way. When he says, "ready," Partner A turns back around and looks for the change in his partner's pose (such as arms up or down, feet together or apart, head straight or turned, shoes on or off, sweater on or off, face smiling, angry, or sad).
   5) Then switch positions, and Partner B turns his back and closes his eyes while Partner A makes a pose, and repeats steps 3 and 4.
   6) Then have the partners try two changes, then do it again with three changes.

4. Activity: *Do You See What I See?*

   Instructions:
   1) Divide the class into groups of two to five.
   2) Give each child a picture to hold so no one else can see it.
   3) Then have one child at a time be the Speaker and describe her picture in detail.
   4) The Listeners are asked to imagine what the picture looks like.
   5) When the Speaker has finished, she shows her picture to the Listeners and they:
      • tell whether the picture looked like they had imagined, and
      • find details the Speaker left out.
   6) A fun variation of this game is after the Speaker describes her picture, have the Listeners of her group draw what they imagine the picture to look like. Then compare the drawn pictures with the actual picture.

5. Paxton (2006) suggests doing the following activities with kids to increase their attention span:
   1) Get kids involved in high-interest projects in creative or expressive arts. They might use drawing, painting, sketching, or sculpting with clay for their projects.
   2) Other options might include activities such as cross-stitch or latch-hook. Some kids may enjoy putting model cars or airplanes together. These activities will usually hold their interest for extended periods of time.
   3) Provide kids with recorded stories, and let them get comfortable, close their eyes, and listen to it. Have them tell the story to you or ask them questions about it.

REFERENCES & RESOURCES

Blum, D. (1998). *The school counselor's book of lists.* San Francisco: Jossey-Bass.

Fay, J., Cline, F., & Sornson, B. (2000). *Meeting the challenge: Using love and logic to help children develop attention and behavior skills.* Golden, CO: The Love and Logic Press, Inc.

Greenspan, S. (1995). *Challenging child: How to understand, raise, and enjoy your "difficult child."* Cambridge, MA: Perseus Books.

Paxton, J. (2006, August). Fun ways to increase your child's attention span. *Garden & Hearth Magazine.*

Chapter 5

Attention-Seeking Behavior

A child would rather receive negative, reprimanding attention, than no attention at all.

DISCUSSION

Most students receive enough attention in the classroom to keep them happy and satisfied. There are those students, however, we might term "attention-seekers," and they tend to disrupt the class and annoy the teacher. In an attempt to understand the child who seeks attentions, it may be helpful to consider the following scenarios:

- A child comes from a large family with multiple siblings and in his attempt to meet his need to belong, has found his "place" in this social group as the "family clown," "family troublemaker," or "family loafer" (as in having to be continually reminded to do his chores). He is simply transferring those behaviors which elicit attention within the family structure to the class setting.
- Both parents work outside of the home and the child spends most of his waking hours with a babysitter, an older sibling, or a nanny. During the times when the parents are with the child, they tend to dote on her, showering her with attention. She has been conditioned to expect the undivided attention from the important adults in her life. Within the class setting, this means the teacher.
- Parents are either too busy with their careers, or too busy just trying to make ends meet, to show the child much attention at all. Since attention is crucial for a sense of belonging, and since belonging is a universal psychological need (Glasser, 1986), and in this scenario if the need is not

being sufficiently met within the family structure, it is logical the child will attempt to seek the attention he so desperately needs in order to feel he belongs in the second most important place in his world—at school. There are many ways he might seek this attention, including clinginess, constantly asking for help, hanging around the teacher's desk, wanting to stay after school or get there early to help the teacher, tattling, pencil tapping, making annoying sounds, and blurting out in class, to mention a few.

- As a school counselor, I had the following situation: A child is reported to exhibit disturbing attention-seeking behaviors in the classroom setting. However, he is reported by his parents to be happy, cooperative, and well behaved at home. They are shocked by his behavior at school, and the child's teacher is just as surprised by his good behavior at home. The mother was questioned about how she dealt with misbehavior in the family setting. She related that the child was sent to his room for "time-out" and no one in the family was allowed to talk to him during this time. There was no spanking, no yelling, basically very little attention was given to him at all for the so-called bad behavior—just "time-out" in his room away from the family. On the other hand, when the child was behaving well, he received much affection and attention from the family. I decided to visit the child's classroom to observe him in the class setting. I had been warned by the teacher that her classroom was full of unruly and misbehaving students. After just a few minutes, it was obvious that most of the teacher's attention was being given to the "unruly" and "misbehaving" students, with constant comments such as, *Get busy, Joey!, Sit down, Johnny!, Stop talking, Sarah!,* and on and on. The few well-behaved children sitting quietly doing their work were barely even addressed by the teacher. The only attention available in this classroom was focused on disturbing behavior, thus, disturbing behavior was the means by which one acquired attention and a sense of belonging within this particular social group.

THE NEED TO BELONG

Dreikurs (1964) and Albert (1989) are in agreement that most misbehavior occurs as children attempt unsuccessfully to meet the universal psychological need to belong. Every person has this need to belong and children desire this very strongly by the groups in which they are members. They want to feel secure, valued by the group, and most kids can acquire this sense of belonging through acceptable behavior. They do what the situation requires and get a sense of belonging through feelings of usefulness and participation, or as Albert puts it, by "contributing" and feeling "connected" to the group.

Dreikurs refers to the desire for undue attention as a *mistaken goal* used by discouraged children as a means for feeling that they belong to the group.

Influenced by *mistaken assumptions* that they have significance only when they are the center of attention, these children develop great skill at attention-getting mechanisms. When they are unable, for whatever reason, to experience this sense of belonging to the group, children will turn to either *active* or *passive* attention-seeking behaviors.

Active attention-seeking behaviors include such behaviors as pencil tapping, calling out in class, asking unrelated and sometimes inappropriate questions, and doing or saying things to either make other students laugh or feel bad. Passive attention-seeking behavior is evident in students who lag behind, waste time, or refuse to do their work.

Attention-seeking behaviors, both active and passive, are reinforced by such responses as scolding the child in front of his classmates, moving him to a "special place" in the classroom, or arranging for the child to have a nice cozy lunch with the teacher (a.k.a. lunch detention).

The bottom line is—if appropriate, positive means of getting attention fail, a child will switch to disturbing methods, even if they elicit negative responses from others in the group (Dinkmeyer & Dreikurs, 1963), including the teacher. A child would rather receive negative, reprimanding attention, than no attention at all, for no attention at all would mean exclusion from the group and the consequent feelings of discouragement, inadequacy, and neglect. Kids just want and need to feel secure and valued by the class group.

STRATEGIES AND ACTIVITIES FOR ATTENTION-SEEKING BEHAVIOR

1. More attention must be given to students exhibiting appropriate, socially acceptable behavior in the class setting than to those students demonstrating disturbing attention-seeking behavior. When dealing with a student who often displays disturbing behaviors, "catch" him doing a task which is socially acceptable and give him the appropriate positive feedback.
2. Beware of displaying negative reactions to a student who is exhibiting disturbing behaviors, for he will be quite aware of the power he has over you—to manipulate your emotions. This sense of power is a positive reinforcer of negative behaviors for this type of child.
3. Implement an individualized program and chart the progress. Reinforce the child for displaying desired behaviors by providing the child with the following:
    - *Tangible* rewards (such as classroom privileges, "class bucks," class coupons for ten minutes of free reading time, responsibilities such as passing out materials, line leading, to name a couple)

- *Intangible* rewards (such as words of praise and encouragement, a smile, a pat on the back, a handshake).
4. Position attention-seeking students so that you can stand close to them, giving them frequent eye contact while giving directions to the class. Your proximity and direct eye contact often serve to give them the personal attention they seek.
5. When confronted with disruptive behavior, move close to the child in question and quietly use (perhaps even whisper) "*I Messages*," such as. *I find it difficult to teach the class when someone is talking* (tapping his pencil, refusing to participate). The following format may also be useful: *I feel _____ when you _____ because _____, and I need you to _____. Would you be willing? Would you prefer to go to "time-out? To Mrs. Jones class?* When choices are provided, the child feels empowered to make decisions for his own life and will "own" the choices he makes. This teaches him to be responsible for his own behavior.
6. Make a stack of pre-written index cards announcing various changes in activities throughout the day. Give ample opportunity for attention-seeking students to be *The Announcer* in front of the group. The following are a couple of examples of announcements:
    - *May I have your attention, please? Now it is time to put your math books away and get out your spelling books. Make sure you have a pencil and paper. The first thing we are going to do is write down the spelling words from page 25 so we can take them home and study them for Friday's spelling test. Thank you for your attention.* Have the class repeat, *Thank you, (child's name)*.
    - *Now it is time for a restroom break. Please clear off your desks. We will show respect for our group by walking quietly through the hall. After we have quietly used the restroom, we will wash our hands well, then return to the class line. Thank you for your attention.* Again, have the class repeat, *Thank you, (child's name)*.
7. *Team Disciplining* is often effective. When confronting kids with disruptive, attention-seeking behavior and *I messages* were ineffective, you might offer them the additional option to go to another classroom, which you have prearranged with your *team discipline teacher*. They undoubtedly will not want to go, but if all else fails, you can state to the child that you see by his behavior that he has "chosen" to be removed from this class group. Teachers are often amazed that kids usually stop the disruptive behavior when placed in another classroom. This makes perfect sense, for his previous behavior was an attempt to meet his *need to belong* to the social group of his class (perhaps as "the class clown," or "the class troublemaker"). When he is moved to another classroom in which he does not belong, to a social group of which he is not a member,

there is no *need* for the disturbing behavior. Thus, the disruptive behavior ceases.

8. *Attention for Positive Behavior*: One strategy which is prevalent among teachers is to write the names of kids who display disruptive behavior on the chalk or white board for all to see. For the attention-seeker, what a reward that is! A strategy you might try instead is to laminate a list of the youngsters in the class group. As you see them focusing on their various tasks, put a check, star, or a happy face next to their names. In some cases, you may have to "catch" an attention-seeking child focusing on his work. This is the time to provide the child with approving attention—such as, put a happy face next to his name, let him put the happy face on the poster himself, have the class repeat something like, *We're proud of you, Sam!* Now the child with attention-seeking needs is receiving notice for appropriate behavior.

9. Discuss with the child his option of placing a *Behavior Form* on his desk. When the child displays disturbing behavior, make a "/" (slash) mark in one of the boxes. Always allow the child to "make up" for the inappropriate behavior, so when you see him behaving appropriately, go to his desk and change the "/" into an "X." By the end of the day or week, or whatever timeframe you and the child have agreed upon, if all of the /s have been turned into Xs, he qualifies to join the group who will be doing a "special" activity at the end of the day or week (*Trash Can Basketball* and *Fun Friday* activities are examples).

10. *Calls Home/Written Reports:* Depending on the accommodations of telephones in your school (many schools have telephones in the classrooms now) or use the teacher's cell phone, and make a call home to say, *"I'm having a great day at school today!"* is often an effective, attention-getting reinforcement of appropriate behavior. If the child has been exhibiting disruptive behavior that day, have him write a brief report about it and call home and read it to a parent. Arrangements with the parents must be made ahead of time, and the child must agree to this consequence of negative behavior before implementing this strategy.

11. Discuss with the child his option of formulating a *Behavior Agreement*, perhaps as an alternative to talking to the principal or having a parent-teacher-student conference. Help him fill out the Agreement in a way that is acceptable to you both. Including input from the child, define the positive consequences if the agreement is fulfilled, as well as the negative ones if it is not. An example of positive consequences might be a *Something Good Happened at School Today* form sent home to the parents or receiving *The Announcer* privilege. (See #6 above.) Negative consequences might include losing classroom privileges, such as participating in *Fun Friday* activities.

REFERENCES & RESOURCES

Albert, L. (1989). *Cooperative discipline: How to manage your classroom and promote self-esteem.* Circle Pines, MN: American Guidance Services.

Dinkmeyer, D. & Dreikurs, R. (1963). *Encouraging children to learn.* New York: Hawthorn Books, Inc.

Dreikurs, R. (1964). *Children: The challenge.* New York: Hawthorn/Dutton.

Dreikurs, R., Grunwald, B., & Pepper, E. (1982). *Maintaining sanity in the classroom.* New York: Harper & Row.

Glasser, W. (1986). *Control theory in the classroom.* New York: Harper & Row.

Chapter 6

Bullying and Hate Crimes

Sure it is important to learn to read, write, think, and do math, but if kids do not learn to love themselves and each other, what difference does the rest really make for a successful future?

—C. M. Charles

DISCUSSION

Bullying is, without a doubt, a major problem in today's schools. Surveys indicate that as many as half of all children are bullied at some time during their school years (American Academy of Child and Adolescent Psychiatry, 2017). According to the U.S. Department of Justice, *one out of every four children will be bullied by a peer in school this month.* The American Association of School Psychologists reports that *over 160,000 children miss school every day for fear of being bullied.* Those are astounding statistics.

Bullying is defined as intentionally and repeatedly committing hurtful acts against others. It is abusive treatment and it occurs when children are teased, threatened, hit, punched, frightened, even terrorized and tortured into doing things they do not want to do. Oftentimes they are forced into giving up money or other personal belongings. It may involve verbal harassment, emotional abuse, physical assault or coercion, and sexual harassment and abuse.

Cyberbullying, which is any bullying done through technology, is becoming more and more prevalent. It includes abuse through email, instant messaging, text messaging, and social networking sites, such as Facebook, Twitter, Instagram, and others.

Hate crimes are similar to bullying but are related to an aversion to groups of people. They may be based on race, ethnic background, religion, physical disabilities, or sexual orientation. Gay bashing is a form of bullying. This is a form of hate crimes based on sexual orientation which remains a pervasive problem in American schools today. A rash of recent teen suicides as a result of bullying and hate crimes has brought a great deal of attention to the problem, and the need for schools to appropriately and effectively address it.

THE VICTIM OR "TARGET"

Some children may be frequent victims of bullies—before, during, after, and at school, on weekends, in their neighborhoods, or in their homes. Because of the frequency of such harassment, victims often become withdrawn, unhappy, and lonely and may suffer from anxiety, depression, and suicidal thoughts.

A child who suffers from the extreme fright of being under the powerful threat of a bully experiences the loss of personal dignity, a lowered self-esteem, and a compromised sense of personal safety. It is important that the child be aware that his feelings of inadequacy, fear for his safety, and general feelings of unhappiness are normal reactions to being abused by a bully.

One of the child's most important social groups, his school class, under the democratic guidance of a caring teacher, has a great opportunity to show concern and provide support. Within a warm and caring social climate of the classroom, the child is able to receive the encouragement necessary to rebuild his confidence, his self-worth, self-esteem, and his sense of security and safety. We must teach children to care for and protect each other during times of stress, turmoil, and threats from outside forces. That is the democratic way.

THE BYSTANDER: ANOTHER VICTIM

Even though most kids do not agree with bullying practices, there are very few who will intervene on behalf of the victim. These individuals are called "bystanders" and, unfortunately, they usually take the side of the bully. In 85 percent of bullying incidents, bystanders are involved in teasing the victim or egging on the bully (Leipe-Levinson & Levinson, 2005). This is an alarming statistic. If the bully faces no obstruction from people around, it gives permission to continue behaving in a threatening and harassing manner.

There are many reasons why kids choose not to intervene, but mainly it is because they worry that they will either make the situation worse, risk being the bully's next target, or they just do not want to get involved. We must raise awareness concerning the effects of bullying and give kids the tools to respond responsibly.

THE BULLY

Now let us consider the child doing the bullying, because the truth of the matter is, we have three victims here—the bullied, the bystander, *and* the bully. The bully is always a child who has mistakenly assumed he is important only when he can exert his power and dominance over people, often including his parents, his teachers, and other authority figures.

The bully often behaves in an unfriendly, hateful way because he lacks confidence in his ability to get appropriate, positive attention from his peers. He doubts his place in the social group except when he makes a bossy nuisance of himself. In an attempt to understand the kid who exhibits aggressive, bullying behavior, it may be helpful to consider the following scenarios (Note: These scenarios are similar to those suggested in chapter 2, "Anger and Aggression versus Self-Control," for young people who exhibit aggressive behavior.):

- The child's parents and/or siblings may use aggressive behavior to resolve conflicts at home, often ending in angry, abusive, even violent disputes. These are the youngster's role models. He may have grown up believing that aggressive acts are the only options available to him.
- The child experiences a sense of powerlessness in the home environment but discovers that there is power in angry, aggressive behavior toward less powerful kids at school and in the community.
- The child's home environment is chaotic and family members are abusive toward each other and toward the child. The child carries his emotional pain to school. His way of coping with this emotional pain may be to create havoc at school by exhibiting aggressive behavior toward other students and/or the teacher, thus taking the focus in his mind off of the emotional, and maybe even physical, pain inflicted upon him at home.
- The child receives more attention (albeit negative attention) when he displays aggressive, deviant, bullying behavior than when he is well behaved and compliant; thus, he chooses the behaviors which award him the most attention.
- The child has a reputation for being mean and aggressive—a bully. The child internalizes these views others have of him and is simply living up to their expectations as well as his own self-perceptions.
- All behavior has meaning and is purposeful within the child's social context (Dreikurs, 1964). If the child lacks a *sense of belonging* within the school social group, he may lack confidence in himself to succeed by useful and positive means. The feelings that result from this sense of exclusion from the group are discouragement, inadequacy, and neglect.

According to Dinkmeyer and Dreikurs (1963), the bully is always *discouraged*, which, by definition, means "deprived of courage." A child desperately wants to belong. If all goes well and the child maintains his courage, he presents few problems. He gets a sense of belonging through usefulness, cooperation, participation, and contribution. No child would switch to the socially unacceptable side of life if he were not discouraged in his belief that he has a place in the group and can succeed through useful means.

On the other hand, if the child has become *discouraged*, he no longer seeks to belong through useful means. His sense of belonging has become restricted, and his discouragement turns to useless and provocative behavior, such as bullying. It is better to be thought of as "the big, bad bully" than to be ignored, and as such, these kids often find their "place" hanging out with other discouraged, maladapted children.

Since every child has the universal psychological need to belong, he may look outside of the school to join a gang, or gang-like group, in which there is a powerful sense of belonging. Younger kids in this category are often referred to as "gang wannabees" using gang names and gang signs to proclaim their group membership, but not officially affiliated with any gang.

It is significant to recognize that bullying behavior can actually be the flip side of good leadership qualities, such as having a powerful influence on peers (albeit it *negative*, for the bully). Consider the following list of good leadership qualities (White, 2011) and compare them to effective bullying qualities:

- A good leader "walks the talk." (A bully certainly does that!)
- A good leader is enthusiastic about the cause. (A bully surely is enthusiastic about threatening and harassing others!)
- A good leader is confident in his leadership role. (I have never seen a bully who wasn't confident in his ability to frighten, even terrorize, others.)
- A leader needs to function in an orderly and purposeful manner. (The bully functions in what is orderly and purposeful for him, to get what he wants.)
- Storms, emotions, and crises come and go and a good leader takes these in stride. (An effective bully deals with these situations on a daily basis.)
- A good leader keeps the main goal in focus and is able to break it down into manageable steps to achieve it. (The effective bully knows what he wants and knows what steps to take to get it.)

The point is, a bully can actually have outstanding leadership qualities if his behavior can be turned into positive attributes. He can become a positive leader with a potentially powerful, positive influence on his peers.

A CASE STORY

A third-grade counselee of mine had recently enrolled in our school and had quickly gained the reputation of being a "big bad bully." He was large for his age and everyone was afraid of him. However, he had a teacher who was determined to make a difference in this bully's life, and she came to me for suggestions.

We discussed several options, and she began by appointing him to the position of Class Announcer and part of his job was to read the slips put in the box labeled "Random Acts of Kindness." Students would write down kind acts they observed during the day by their peers and the so-called bully would read them at the end of each day. The kids would applaud the acts.

Before long, the bully was doing acts of kindness himself, and the kids were entering them into the Kindness Box. The teacher continued throughout the year to find ways to meet the child's need to belong to the class group.

By the end of the school year, this young man was a different person. Kids liked him and wanted him as their friend. He was getting positive attention for positive behaviors and he bloomed as a natural leader. By the fourth grade he was elected president of the class and also served as a peer mediator on the playground. During his fifth-grade year, he was elected president of the student counsel and part of his job was to work with the principal in counseling younger students who exhibited bullying behavior.

This success story shows not only what a powerful influence dedicated and sensitive teachers can have on the lives of their students, but how, given the proper environment, kids not only grow and develop in healthy ways but flourish and thrive in becoming responsible, productive, and self-determining human beings, an advantage that can last a lifetime.

DEALING WITH BULLYING AND HATE CRIMES

The incidence and effects of bullying and hate crimes are grossly underreported in American schools and communities. We must raise awareness and adopt a zero-tolerance policy against bullying and hate crimes and their connection to other violent behaviors. Some suggestions for dealing with bullying and hate crimes include the following:

1. Schedule regular class meetings for teachers and students to engage in discussions, role-playing, and other activities to reduce bullying behavior and hate crimes.
2. Involve parents, guardians, and other family members of bullies and victims of bullying and hate crimes.

3. Listen receptively to those who report bullying and establish procedures whereby such reports are investigated and resolved expeditiously.
4. Form support groups for students who are being victimized by bullying or hate crimes.
5. Closely supervise students on the grounds and in classrooms, hallways, restrooms, cafeterias, and other areas where bullying can occur. Intervene if bullying is even suspected.
6. Post and publicize clear behavior standards, including rules against bullying. Involve students in establishing classroom rules against bullying.
7. Establish a confidential reporting system that allows students to report incidents of victimization by bullies.
8. Develop a plan of action so students will know what to do if they are victimized by a bully, as well as what to do if they observe an episode of others being bullied.
9. Don't try to mediate a bullying situation. The disparity in power between victims and bullies may cause victims to feel further victimized by the process.

SCHOOL BULLYING/HARASSMENT SURVEYS

Conducting periodic school bullying/harassment surveys should be part of a bullying prevention plan to reduce incidents and change attitudes about bullying. A positive school climate makes negative behaviors, such as bullying and harassment, unacceptable and empowers students to contribute to eliminating these kinds of behaviors.

A school bullying/harassment survey is one tool that can help schools identify the nature and extent of bullying and harassment problems. The initial assessment provides a baseline for the prevalence of bullying and harassment. Ongoing assessments help to determine whether programs are effective at reducing the bullying behavior and improving the school climate. See the section "Strategies and Activities for Bullies and Bullying" for age-appropriate bullying/harassment surveys.

SUMMARY

Bullying and harassment are underestimated and pervasive problems in our schools. They are often precursors to other violent behavior in our schools and communities. In schools where equity and inclusive education are important, all students have the right to feel safe, comfortable, and accepted. School staff and students value the differences among people and show respect for each other.

When students behave in a way that is not respectful toward other students—in a way that is meant to hurt them or put them down—they are often reacting to differences that they do not understand. This way of behaving includes bullying and harassment. These students do not realize that diversity—what makes people different from one another—is one of the best things about our schools. When people respect and accept one another and their many differences, there can be no bullying or harassment behavior.

In order for children to feel useful and valued by the group, they must feel important to themselves. As has been stated previously and worth repeating, "Sure it is important to learn to read, write, think, and do math, but if kids do not learn to love themselves and each other, what difference does the rest really make for a successful future?"

Self-esteem and the capacity for loving are the most basic qualities every child has the need and right to develop. Once you see a child's self-image begin to improve, you will see significant gains in areas of personal and social development, as well as in academic achievement (Baumeister & Leary, 1995). If all behavior has social meaning, as Dreikurs contends, then a sense of belonging is of primary importance to children's emotional, social, and intellectual development.

The school and home must be partners in taking responsibility for the development of attitudes—how children feel about themselves, about others, about school, and the world around them. Children must feel important, worthwhile, and valued. These attitudes are what motivate children to be responsible, achieving, self-enhancing human beings. The development of these positive attributes is our best hope for eliminating the negative social consequences associated with bullying, harassment, hate crimes, and racism.

STRATEGIES AND ACTIVITIES FOR BULLIES AND BULLYING

1. *A Bully/Harassment Survey* should be conducted periodically throughout the school year. Children are not required to sign their names to the survey and the information is confidential. If there are any questions they prefer not answering, tell them to leave it blank. Stress that this survey has no bearing on their grade in class. The surveys can be formatted for students to indicate a choice that includes always, often, sometimes, and hardly ever.

For younger children:
What grade are you in? _____ Are you a girl or boy? _____
   1) Has anyone ever called you a name?
   2) Has anyone ever told you that you can't be friends?

3) Has anyone ever hit, kicked, or pushed you?
4) Has anyone ever threatened you?
5) Was someone mean to you because of how you look?
6) Did you tell anyone about any of these incidents? Why or why not?
7) Have you ever seen someone else being bullied?
8) Have you ever called someone else a name, hit, kicked, pushed, threatened, or been mean to someone?

For older children:

What grade are you in? _____ Are you a male or female? _____

1) Do you feel safe at school? Why, or why not?
2) Have you ever stayed home from school because you were afraid of being bullied?
3) Do you feel safe on your way to school and going back home? Why or why not?
4) Do you feel safe in your neighborhood?
5) Have you ever been bullied?
6) Is someone bullying you while you are on your way to school, at school, or on your way home? Who is it? (Your answer will be private.)
7) Have you seen someone else being bullied? Who was it? Who was doing the bullying?
8) Have you seen groups of kids making fun of, seriously teasing, or harassing someone? If so, who was the person being harassed?
9) Who were the students doing the harassing? (Remember, this is a private survey.)
10) During the past four weeks, have you been bullied or harassed by other students in any of the following ways?
    a) Physically?
    b) Verbally?
    c) Socially?
    d) Cyberbullying? (texts, email, Facebook, and so on)
11) During the past four weeks, have you experienced bullying or harassment in any of the following areas?
    a) Race, ethnic group, culture?
    b) Sexual?
    c) Gender? (male or female issues)
    d) Religion?
    e) Disability?
    f) Homophobic, or life-style preference (such as gay bashing)?
    g) Economic status or income-based?

2. Educators must help children become aware of the presence of bullying. With adult guidance, the class needs to devise a plan of action designed to avoid becoming victims of a bully. Included in the plan might be the following:

1) Try to ignore the bully. If that doesn't work, tell the bully in a firm voice, *Stop bothering me.*
2) Walk away from the bully and seek a safe place close to an adult or other kids.
3) Socialize and make friends.
4) Participate in activities in which you excel.
5) If you see someone being bullied, seek the help of an adult or report the situation to the proper authorities.
6) If someone does bully you, find someone you trust and discuss the situation.
3. Build confidence by *role-playing* ways to deal with a bully. Practice ignoring the bully, walking away from the situation, and being assertive (like firmly telling the bully, *Stop bothering me*).
4. Inform students of their *rights* regarding bullying.
    1) You have the right to be treated with respect.
    2) You have the right to not be teased.
    3) You have the right to tell others to stop bothering you and have the request respected.
    4) You have the right to complain and be taken seriously.
    5) You have the right to make a report regarding the complaint and have it investigated.
    6) You have the right to expect support from school authorities.
5. Have kids develop a plan of action for what to do if they observe an episode of bullying.
6. Help kids develop a *sense of belonging*. This will help both the bully and the bullied. The following strategies are suggested:
    - Each student is given regular personal attention.
    - Students are involved in making *joint decisions* about a classroom code of conduct (class rules) and the consequences for misbehavior.
    - The teacher seeks student input in areas concerning procedures, policies, and problem-resolution.
    - The teacher makes sure that each student experiences success in learning.
    - Each student receives recognition for accomplishments.
    - Each student has a position of responsibility to the class group. The following are some examples of class positions (some may require students working in pairs):
        - Classroom monitor (e.g., checking to see if everyone has the materials they will need for a project)
        - Hall monitor
        - Cafeteria monitor
        - Boys'/girls' restroom monitor

- Class announcer (e.g., making announcements such as time for lunch)
- Class pet caretaker
- Class pencil pusher (sharpens pencils)

7. All students must be *encouraged*. Encouragement is conveying respect for students and believing in their abilities. Albert contends, "Perhaps no factor that influences how students choose to behave is as important as the amount of encouragement students receive from teachers" (1996, p. 15). The following are examples of providing encouragement:
   - Use *social reinforcers*, which consist of words and behaviors such as comments, gestures, and facial expressions. They may be verbal or nonverbal:
     - Verbal: *Wow! I knew you could do that. Excellent work. I like the way you did that. You are really working hard!*
     - Nonverbal: A smile, a pat on the arm or back, a handshake, a wink, eye contact, nods, thumbs up.
   - The *classroom climate* refers to the feeling or tone that prevails in the classroom and includes attitudes, emotions, values, and relationships. A good classroom climate is warm, friendly, supportive, and filled with good nature and acceptance. Such a climate encourages productive work and promotes a sense of self-worth and accomplishment.
   - *Social interest* is an objective which can be developed within the class group. The most effective teachers are those who sense the need each child has to find an acceptable place within the group. There are many opportunities to develop social interest—to show concern for others, and to participate in the give and take of personal relationships.

REFERENCES & RESOURCES

Albert, L. (1989). *Cooperative discipline: How to manage your classroom and promote self-esteem.* Circle Pines, MN: American Guidance Services.

Albert, L. (1996). *Cooperative discipline.* Circle Pines, MN: American Guidance Service.

American Academy of Child and Adolescent Psychiatry (AACAP). (2017, March). *Bullying.* No. 80. http://www.aacap.org/cs/root/facts_for_families/bully.

Baumeister, R. & Leary, M. (1995). The need to belong: Desire for interpersonal attachments as a fundamental human motivation. *Psychological Bulletin, 117,* 497–529.

Bolton, J. & Graeve, S. (2005). No room for bullies: From the classroom to cyberspace. *Boys Town.* Boys Town, NE: Boys Town.

Coloroso, B. (2003). *The bully, the bullied, and the bystander: From preschool to high school—How parents and teachers can break the cycle of violence.* New York: Harper Resource.

Dinkmeyer, D. & Dreikurs, R. (1963). *Encouraging children to learn.* New York: Hawthorn Books, Inc.

Dreikurs, R. (1964). *Children: The challenge.* New York: Hawthorn/Dutton.

Liepe-Levinson, K. & Levinson, M. (2005). A general semantics approach to bullying. *A Review of General Semantics*, 62(2), 127–43.

White, B. (2011). *Seven qualities of a good leader.* Greenstein, Rogoff, Olsen & Co., LLP, CPA's. Retrieved August 2011. www.GROCO.com.

Chapter 7

Child Abuse Indicators
Emotional, Physical, Sexual

It is estimated that at least two out of every ten girls and one out of every ten boys are sexually abused by the end of their 13th year.

—Child Molestation Research & Prevention Institute, Inc., 2019

EMOTIONAL ABUSE

Emotional abuse is a "systematic attempt to destroy a person's self-worth through words or actions" (Blum, 1998, p. 238). It is an attack on one's person and character. Continual harassment, whether it is by the child's parents, older siblings, inept teachers, or bullying peers, constitutes emotional abuse and has negative consequences for the child's personal, social, and academic development and well-being.

Emotional abuse is all about exerting control over the life of another, in this case a child. It can take many shapes and forms and is often paired with physical abuse. When children are continually being put down and belittled by parents, teachers, or peers, they are being emotionally abused by them.

When a parent or educator is constantly ridiculing a child for things he says or does, that child is being emotionally abused. When children repeatedly feel rejected or ignored by their school or family social groups, they are being abused by that group. Verbal attacks from the emotional abuser are insulting, threatening, controlling, devaluing, mocking, critical, and undermining of self-esteem and self-worth.

The signs of emotional abuse can sometimes be difficult to spot. The most obvious is if you see or hear a person being openly verbally abusive to the child in question. Look for the more subtle signs, too. The child is often frightened of the abuser or fearful of angering or displeasing the abuser. The victim of emotional abuse judges everything according to how the abuser will react to it—whether it is with approval, disapproval, or rage. The victim may also withdraw from friends without warning, often at the request of the abuser.

Since emotional abuse can occur in so many different ways, it is often difficult to recognize the signs. Making things worse, victims of emotional abuse may be "brainwashed" into believing they deserve to be mistreated for "being bad" and they feel guilty and ashamed. They are reluctant to talk about the abuse or trust others with the information because they fear angering their abuser.

Keep in mind that you may never witness the actual abuse, but you may notice the effects of emotional abuse. For example, you may observe the victim's loss of self-confidence, depression, or behavioral disorders. The following indicators might be symptoms of emotional abuse (Blum, 1998; May, 2011; Kraizer, 2911):

1. *Physical Indicators*:
   - Speech disorders, such as stuttering
   - Delayed physical development
   - Poor appetite, extremely underweight or overweight
   - Sleep disorders
2. *Behavior Indicators:*
   - Habit disorders, such as biting, rocking, sucking thumb
   - Antisocial behaviors, such as being a loner or bullying
   - Destructive disorders, such as damaging others' or own property
   - Behavioral extremes, such as passive-aggressive, submissive-demanding, compliant-defiant
   - Neurotic traits, such as chronic lying, cheating, stealing
   - Excessively withdrawn, fearful, anxious about doing something wrong

It is also important to point out that emotionally abused children are more likely to go on to become involved in emotionally abusive relationships as teenagers and adults. This is why it is critical that parents, educators, and other school staff be on the lookout for possible indications of emotional abuse to insure the child is not being emotionally damaged in his delicate years of growth and development which could lead to serious long-term emotional problems and behavior disorders. If emotional abuse is even *suspected*, contact an appropriate school specialist or Child Protective Services (CPS) agency to conduct further investigations into the situation.

PHYSICAL ABUSE

Physical abuse is any act or behavior that inflicts or intends to inflict bodily harm. There are about an equal number of male and female victims in this category. Non-accidental physical injury may include severe beatings, burns, biting, strangulation and scalding with resulting bruises, welts, broken bones, scars, or serious internal injuries (National Committee for the Prevention of Child Abuse, from Wang & Daro, 1997).

An *abused child*, under the law, means "a child less than 18 years of age whose parent or other person legally responsible for the child's care inflicts or allows to be inflicted upon the child physical injury by other than accidental means which causes or creates substantial risk of death or serious disfigurement, or impairment of physical health, or loss or impairment of the function of any bodily organ" (National Committee for the Prevention of Child Abuse, from Wang & Daro, 1997).

One of the most common indications of possible physical abuse in children is an inconsistency about how an injury occurred. If a child has been coached to lie, often the details will change when questioned more than once about the injury. There should also be suspicion of physical abuse if a child refuses to relay information about how an injury occurred.

Other indications of possible physical abuse to be on the lookout for are patterned bruises, such as those made by a belt buckle, a wire, a coat hanger, or a stick, and patterned burns, such as those made by a cigarette, an electric iron, a spattering of a hot liquid, or immersion. The following lists of indicators are provided as a guide for possible child abuse situations (Blum, 1998; May, 2011; Saisan, Smith & Segal, 2011):

1. *Physical Indicators*:
    - Frequent injuries, unexplained bruises, black eyes
    - Bite marks
    - Burns
    - Lacerations, abrasions, welts
    - Fractures in unusual places
    - Injuries and swellings to face and extremities
    - Bald spots
2. *Behavioral Indicators:*
    - Avoids physical contact with others
    - Behavioral extremes of aggressiveness and withdrawal
    - Arrives at school early and seems reluctant to go home afterward
    - Pulls back when approached by adults/shies away from touch
    - Flinches at sudden movements

- Wears inappropriate clothing to cover up injuries, such as long-sleeved shirts, sweaters, or winter coats on hot days
- Gives inconsistent versions of the occurrence of injuries, burns, and so forth
- Seems frightened when parents or older siblings are around
- Plays aggressively and often hurts peers
- Complains of pain upon movement or contact
- Sudden change in behavior and/or grades
- Exhibits unexplained rage
- Shows signs of depression

If physical abuse is even *suspected*, contact an appropriate community agency, such as Child Protective Services (CPS) or consult with a school specialist to conduct further investigations into the circumstances.

SEXUAL ABUSE

It is estimated that at least two out of every ten girls and one out of every ten boys are sexually abused by the end of their thirteenth year (Child Molestation Research & Prevention Institute, Inc., 2019). While news stories of sexual predators are scary, what is even more disturbing is that sexual abuse usually occurs at the hands of someone the child knows and should be able to trust—most often close relatives and friends.

The shame and guilt of sexual abuse makes it difficult for kids to come forward. They may worry that others will not believe them, that they will get in trouble if they tell, or they may have been threatened by the abuser that something bad will happen to them or a loved one if they tell. When talking to abused children, the best thing you can provide is calm reassurance that it was not their fault, and unconditional support.

It is important to understand that sexual abuse does not always involve body contact. Exposing a child to sexual situations, or to sexual materials, such as adult magazines of a sexual nature, pornography, or obscene language, is sexually abusive, whether or not touching is involved. However, these situations often lead to touching—fondling, molesting, oral sex, and intercourse. The following list of indicators has been compiled for you to use as a guide for the possible occurrence of child sexual abuse (Blum, 1998; May, 2011; Saisan, Smith & Segal, 2011):

1. *Physical Indicators:*
   - Trouble walking or sitting
   - Torn, stained, or bloody underclothing

- Pain, swelling, or itching in genital area
- Frequent urinary or yeast infections
2. *Behavioral Indicators:*
   - Excessive seductiveness
   - Overly concerned for siblings
   - Extreme weight loss or gain
   - Threats or attempts of suicide
   - Inappropriate sex play/unusual interest in sex
   - Premature understanding of sex
   - Threatened by physical contact and/or closeness
   - Makes strong attempts to avoid a specific person, without any obvious reason
   - Unusual fears and anxieties

HELPING CHILDREN WHO HAVE BEEN ABUSED

When talking to children who have been emotionally, physically, and/or sexually abused, the first thing to provide is calm assurance and unconditional caring and support. You can make an enormous difference in an abused child's life. The following are some suggestions to consider when providing unconditional caring and support:

- Try to convince the children that the abuse was not their fault.
- Build self-esteem by exploring the areas in which the children excel, such as artistic talent, athletic ability, math skills, being a good friend, and so forth.
- Build the children's optimistic attitude by reinforcing the good experiences they have had and make plans for fun activities.
- Let the children know with whom they can talk when they have problems or concerns.
- Give the children responsibilities so they feel they are contributing to their class or family group, thus enhancing their sense of belonging.
- Let the children know they are important and valued by the class or family group.
- Engage the children in activities they are good at to build self-esteem and self-confidence.
- Read amusing and funny stories or antidotes to help the children develop a sense of humor.
- Help the children make friends and form relationships with children their own age.
- Listen to the children and let them know they are respected.
- Reinforce the good experiences the children have had.

WHAT YOU SHOULD DO IF YOU SUSPECT CHILD ABUSE

Just remember, you can make a tremendous difference in the life of an abused child, especially when you take steps to stop the abuse early. Child abuse is not always obvious. By learning some of the common warning signs of child abuse, you can catch the problem as early as possible and get the help that both the child and the abuser need. Although not every school has all of these specialists on hand full time, most at least have access to these professionals who could be of assistance in assessing your concern for the child: school counselor, school psychologist, school nurse, school social worker, or home-school liaison. The following resources are also available:

- Call your local Child Protective Services (CPS).
- Call 1-888-PREVENT or go to *Stop It Now* at http://www.stopitnow.org/.
- Call 1-800-656-HOPE, *Rape, Abuse & Incest National Network* (RAINN) or go to their website at http://www.rainn.org/.

REFERENCES & RESOURCES

Blum, D. (1998). *The school counselor's book of lists.* San Francisco: Jossey-Bass.

Child Molestation Research & Prevention Institute, Inc. (2019). *Child molestation prevention.* http://childmolestationprevention.org/.

Kraizer, S. (2011). Emotional abuse. *Coalition for children.* Retrieved May 2011. http://www.safechild.org/childabuse3.htm.

May, G. (2011). Child discipline: Guidelines for parents. *National Children's Advocacy Center.* Retrieved June 2011. http://www.nationalcac.org/families/forworkers/abuse_indicators.html.

Saisan, J., Smith, M., & Segal, J. (2011). *Child abuse and neglect: Recognizing and preventing child abuse.* Helpguide.org. Updated June 2011. Retrieved July 2011. http://helpguide.org/mental/child_abuse.

Wang, C. & Daro, D. (1997). *Current trends in child abuse reporting and fatalities: The results of the 1996 annual fifty state survey.* Chicago: National Center on Child Abuse Prevention Research, National Committee to Prevent Child Abuse.

Chapter 8

Cooperation versus Defiance

Children will do whatever it takes—whether it is exhibiting socially acceptable or socially unacceptable behavior—to satisfy their basic need of belonging to the group.

DISCUSSION

Children choose their behavior; how they behave is not beyond their control (Albert, 1996). Every action has a purpose, the goal being to find one's place within the group, whether in the school setting or in the home. A well-behaved and well-adjusted child finds his way toward social acceptance by cooperating and conforming to the rules of the group and by making useful contributions. The child who misbehaves is convinced that the only way he can achieve recognition and social status within the group is either by attempting to prove his power, to seek revenge, to exhibit inadequacy, or to display outright defiance to the rules which govern the group.

NEGATIVE WAYS TO GET RECOGNITION

The following is a description of the negative methods used to gain recognition and social status when acceptable means appear unavailable to the child:

- *Power:* If the adult gets into a power struggle with the child and wins, the child is only convinced of the value of power and is more determined to win next time.

- *Revenge*: Revenge is the result of antagonism and animosity. The child finds his place in the group by making himself disliked.
- *Inadequacy*: The child "expects" failure and uses inability and helplessness to escape positive participation.
- *Defiance*: Defiance is the refusal to abide by the rules that govern the group. A child would rather be punished than ignored.

These are attempts to foster the basic need that every child has—to belong to the group. In the school setting this youngster may take on the role as *The Class Clown, The Class Bully, or The Class Jerk*, but at least he feels like he *belongs* to "The Class" group. In the home environment, a child might achieve his recognition, attention, and social status within the family by taking on the role as The Clown of the Family, The Baby of the Family, The Family Troublemaker, and so forth, in order to attain his sense of belonging to "The Family" group.

A RESPECTFUL LEARNING ENVIRONMENT

As Glasser (1998) points out, all children have the basic psychological need to *belong* to his or her various social groups and they develop this sense of belonging when they are involved in class matters, receive attention from the teacher and peers, and are brought into discussions of matters that concern the class. Children sense *power* when the teacher asks for their help in making decisions about topics to be studied and procedures to be followed and this promotes student cooperation.

Nelson, Lott, and Glenn (2000) focus on developing a joy for learning through *teacher acceptance* and *dignified regard.* A positive, respectful learning environment invites student cooperation. Ginott (1971) asserts that cooperation is encouraged when there is *congruent communication* between teachers and students. In other words, kids are more likely to cooperate when they can communicate with their teachers on the same level. Effective teachers invite cooperation of their students by describing the situation to the class and indicating what needs to be done. They do not dictate to students, boss them around, or demand compliance, all of which provoke resistance.

Teachers should decide *with the class* before an activity, what kinds of behavior will be needed during the activity. Teachers need to send their students the message that they believe in their ability to determine for themselves what needs to be done. Instead of giving lengthy explanations and directions about how an activity is to be done, simply say, *It is math time. The assignment is on page 125. If you should need help, I am available.* This sends the message that you believe in your students' ability to be self-managing and self-determining individuals, which invites them to cooperate in the activity and challenges them to use critical thinking and problem-solving skills.

DEVELOPING SOCIAL INTEREST

Developing social interest is an important aspect of promoting cooperation. Social interest is more than a feeling of belonging. It is having compassion, empathy, and concern for others; it is the capacity to give and take. Kids with sufficient social interest accept responsibility not only for themselves but also for and to the groups to which they belong (Dreikurs, 1964). It is within these social settings that a child's character develops. Thus, cooperation is an essential skill for kids to learn if they are to be successful in their academic, social, and personal lives.

STRATEGIES AND ACTIVITIES FOR COOPERATION VERSUS DEFIANCE

1. Activity: *Cooperation Cards* (can be adapted for grades 1 +)
   Materials: Eleven sheets of construction paper with the letters C-O-O-P-E-R-A-T-I-O-N, one letter per card, written on them. On the reverse side, numbers 1 through 11, with number 1 corresponding to C; blank sheets of construction paper cut in half or blank 5" x 7" index cards; pencils and crayons.
   Examples of words that can be used on cards for this activity, depending on age:

CARING	COOPERATION
SHARING	RESPONSIBILITY
FRIENDLY	REGULATIONS
ACCEPTING	ACCEPTANCE
APPRECIATE	COMPASSION
RESPECT	RESPECTFUL
DETERMINATION	COMMITMENT
HELPFUL	SUPPORTIVE

Instructions: The word "cooperation," has been chosen as an example for this activity.
   1) Begin by asking for eleven volunteers, corresponding to the number of letters in the word, and have them line up in front of the class.
   2) Hand each volunteer a random number and tell them to hold the "letter side" close to their stomachs, making sure their numbers are right side up.

3) Ask them to turn their cards around so the class can see the letters.
4) Say to the class, *Try to read the word which is formed here.*
5) Then say, *Wow, it sure is hard to read the word with all of its letters doing their own thing. There's no way to read it as long as those letters are not getting along.*
6) Then say to the volunteers, *You can help the letters to cooperate by using the numbers on the back of your cards. Number one, go to the far left of the line and number eleven, to the far right. The rest of you quietly find your number place in the line.*
7) When the word spells C-O-O-P-E-R-A-T-I-O-N, read it, define it, and talk about what it means.
8) Then say, *Now that we know what cooperation looks like, and we know what it means, we can practice it.*
9) Arrange the students in groups of five or six. Give each group member a blank paper or index card.
10) Say, *Each group is going to show how to grow a flower garden. Number your cards on the back 1 through 5* (or 6, depending how many members are in the group).
11) Then tell them, *Number one will be buying the packet of flower seeds at the store. Number 5 will be when the garden is full of flowers. You will need to decide what steps numbers 2, 3 and 4 are. Each of you will write your step on the back of your card next to your number.*
12) Have the students draw a picture on the front of their card which shows the step they are responsible for in the process of growing a flower garden, and then color it.
13) Using masking tape, connect the cards in order and display on a bulletin board.
14) Have each group relate in what ways they had to cooperate in order to produce their picture story of growing a flower garden.

2. Activity: *Teamwork Mural*

   Materials: Large sheets of construction or butcher paper, pencils, and crayons

   Instructions:
   1) Have the children sit around a small table or with desks situated front-to-front (three on each side to make a group of six is a good number). Tape the sheets of paper, which will become the mural, onto the tables or desks.
   2) Explain that this is an exercise in "cooperation." Define it and discuss it.
   3) Provide several age-appropriate topics from which the children may choose. If they don't all agree on a specific topic, then have them vote on it. "A Day at the Zoo" is a favorite for children of all ages.

4) The activity is based on the concept of "Musical Chairs." Upon your cue, each child will begin to draw something you would see on a day at the zoo. Using a timer, stopwatch with verbal cues, or soft music, after a five- or ten-minute period or whatever time frame is appropriate for the group, have the children move one seat to the left.
5) Each child is now sitting in front of a drawing their neighbor started. Upon the cue to begin, the children start drawing on the new picture in front of them. This continues until all of the children have had an opportunity to add their contribution to every picture.
6) This activity can be done in one session, or the pictures can be stored, and the project can continue over several sessions. Once the pictures are finished, tape the pictures together to make a mural, or put them on a bulletin board and display as a collage.
7) It is important to point out that no one child could have created any of these pictures alone. They all cooperated as a team to make these creations.

3. Activity: *Paper Wad Scramble*

   Materials: Everyone takes two sheets of used notebook paper (be responsible to the environment and recycle!); two trashcans or boxes.
   Instructions:
   1) Divide the class into two groups and have them come up with a name for their group (e.g., the tigers and the lions).
   2) Kids take their two sheets of paper and wad each up separately, forming a wadded-up paper ball. Place them in a row along a center line between the two teams.
   3) Have the teams form a straight line across opposite ends of the classroom or gym.
   4) Place a trashcan or box in the middle of each team as their goal.
   5) Upon the signal, "go," the first team member runs to the center, grabs a paper wad (only one at a time is allowed), and takes it back to put in the team's "goal box." He "high-fives" the next team member in the line, and she then runs up to the center line and grabs a paper wad and runs back to deposit the paper wad and high-five the next student in the line.
   6) Once all the paper wads are in the goal boxes, the children count how many they have. The team with the most paper wads wins.
   7) Whichever team wins three out of five games are the paper wad scramble champs!
   8) Discuss how they used cooperation to play this game.

4. Activity: *The Lap Sit*
   Instructions:
   1) Say, *We can do many things as a group that we cannot do as individuals, and this game, called "The Lap Sit" is one of them.*

2) *Everyone form a circle, turn to your right and take one side step toward the center.*
3) *Put your hands on the waist of the person in front of you. When I say "sit," everyone is going to sit on the knees of the person behind you, keeping your own knees together as you do.*
4) *Guide the person in front of you to sit comfortably on your knees, and trust the person behind you will guide you, too.*
5) *First, we will have a trial run. On the count of three we are going to bend down, touch your back side to the knees and come right back up to make sure we are all standing closely enough together.* (Have them readjust their positions, if necessary.)
6) *Now you are going to sit down and then clap our hands. One, two, three, sit! Clap your hands!* This activity usually amazes young people by what they can do in solidarity. The game was originally called Empress Eugenie's Circle, because the soldiers of that Austrian empress did this to keep dry while resting in a wet field waiting for a royal visit.

5. Activity: *Untying the Human Knot*

This is a very simple (but fun) activity, and although it is not particularly physical, it encourages kids to work together to solve the problem that they have been set.
1) Arrange the children into groups (an even number of children—between eight and twelve—in each group)
2) Tell the children to stand in a tight circle, facing the center. Everyone should put their left hand in the circle and hold someone else's left hand.
3) Then everyone puts in their right hand and holds someone else's right hand.
4) Without letting go of each other's hands, the children should untangle themselves. It is possible, if they work as a team to solve the problem.

Variations: For younger kids, you might have them join hands in a circle first, and then tie themselves up in a knot. Then they untie themselves. Another variation is to have 12" pieces of rope with knots on the ends. This prevents some hand and wrist twisting and gives kids a little slack when untangling their human knot.

REFERENCES & RESOURCES

Albert, L. (1996). *Cooperative discipline.* Circle Pines, MN: American Guidance Services.

Dreikurs, R. (1964). *Children: The challenge.* New York: Hawthorn/Dutton.

Ginott, H. (1971). *Teacher and child.* New York: Macmillan.
Glasser, W. (1998). *The quality school: Managing students without coercion.* New York: Harper & Row.
Nelson, J., Lott, L., & Glenn, H. (2000). *Positive discipline in the classroom: Developing mutual respect, cooperation, and responsibility in the classroom* (3rd ed.). Roseville, CA: Prima.

Chapter 9

Decision-Making Difficulties

It can be difficult for you, as parents or teachers, to step out of the decision-maker shoes and into more of a coaching or guiding role.

—Barbara Colorosa

DISCUSSION

Traditionally, we tell children what is expected of them, we tell them what to do and when to do it, we watch what they do, and we judge their performance, both at home and in the school setting. And when they turn eighteen and graduate from high school, we expect them to suddenly and miraculously turn into good adult decision-makers in their personal, social, and academic worlds. But the development of good decision-making skills is like that of any other skill, it takes trials, errors, and practice to become proficient at making astute choices for one's life. The ability to make wise decisions is a combination of the following:

- A youngster's developmental stage;
- An inner sense of right and wrong;
- Receiving accurate information;
- A knowledge of a decision-making process;
- Trials, errors, and practice, practice, practice!

GLASSER'S CHOICE THEORY

Glasser (1999) contends that behavior is never caused by a response to an outside stimulus, but rather is inspired by what an individual wants most at any given point in time. Originally called the control theory, but more commonly known today as the choice theory, Glasser asserts that *all* behavior is intended to satisfy one of the following five basic internal needs: (1) to survive—food. shelter, safety; (2) to belong and be loved by others; (3) to have power and importance; (4) to have freedom and independence; and (5) to have fun—having a good time emotionally and intellectually.

Glasser alleges that teacher education courses do not teach prospective teachers how to relate to students so that students feel that teachers care about them and respect them. Without pay, no human being will work up to their ability if they do not feel cared for and respected. Glasser asserts that prospective teachers must be taught to use choice theory in their classrooms to replace the external control theory that is used in most schools today. Teachers must rely on cooperative, active learning techniques that enhance the power of the learners and meet their basic internal needs.

Charles (2013) observes that there is a trend toward the teaching of values, ethical behavior and decision-making. Black (1994) also notes that teachers are being asked to design lessons that include ethical judgments and decisions. This current trend toward encouraging teachers to give up part of their traditional control in favor of student decision-making is gaining more and more support from today's educators.

TEACHING KIDS TO MAKE WISE DECISIONS

So how do we teach kids to make wise decisions? Making simple choices is the first step in learning decision-making skills. From the first day of school on, you can provide simple choice-making opportunities, both of which are acceptable to you, thus allowing the child to exert control over his life from a young age without running the risk of getting a "No" for an answer. These choices are often based on simple preferences. In the kindergarten class children might choose which crayon to use or whether to look through a picture book or draw a picture.

As children get older, decision-making becomes more complex than simply choosing between two clear options. Their ability to reason critically, think hypothetically, understand logical consequences of decisions, and apply others' experiences to their own life increases.

There are many opportunities in which kids can actually be the decision-makers. It can be hard for you, as teachers, to step out of the decision-maker shoes and into more of a coaching or guiding role. Coloroso (1994) says let kids experience the results of their decisions, in order to produce rapid growth in problem solving. Mistakes and poor choices then become the kids' responsibility. If they experience discomfort, they have the power to make better choices in the future.

Take advantage of opportunities to coach children by asking them questions, such as, *And if you did it this way, how would your friend feel?* Or, *If you did it this other way, how might your teacher respond?* And, *How do you think* [trusted friend] *might handle it?* The more you open the process of making decisions to children, the more ownership they will have over the consequences of their decisions. On the other hand, the more you exert unnecessary control, the more children will resent the domination and rebel, so use every opportunity to allow children to make choices and decisions about matters that affect their lives.

A DECISION-MAKING PROCESS

In order to learn how to make good choices, children need to learn a decision-making process. Most decision-making processes involve the following steps:

1. Identify the *need* to make a decision. *Why do you need to make a decision?*
2. Identify the *decision* to be made. *What is the decision you have to make?*
3. State the *goal* in simple terms. *What do you want the results to be?*
4. Gather *information* and brainstorm possible solutions. *What are some ways you could deal with the problem? Which ones might be a good move? Which ones might be a bad move?*
5. Narrow down to a few possible *choices/solutions*.
6. Evaluate each choice/solution by its *consequences*:
   - *Will it help meet the specified goal?*
   - *What are the advantages?*
   - *What are the disadvantages?*
   - *What are the risks?*
   - *How will it affect others?*
   - *How will I feel about this choice/solution?*
7. *Rank choices* by priority. *Which one do you think is best? Second best?* and so forth.
8. Make a decision by choosing *one choice/solution*. Choose the decision you think might work best to resolve the problem.
9. *Make a plan* to put the choice into effect. *What are the steps you will need to take to make this solution happen?*
10. *Follow through* with the plan.
11. *Evaluate* the decision. *Did your plan solve your problem?*
12. *Repeat* the decision-making process as needed.

Remember that until you try something at least a few times you cannot really know how well it works. You might say, *Well, this seems like the choice you want to make. Why don't you try it, and then we'll discuss how it's going. If you like it, you keep doing it. If not, you can try something else.*

Let your children know that it's okay to change course if a decision they made is not working or they feel they made the wrong choice. This way you keep the door open for continual reevaluation. Since this happens in life situations all the time, building flexibility into the process is very important.

As we teach kids to be good decision-makers, they learn to think for themselves, find out what works best for them, begin to trust themselves, become responsible for their lives, and gain confidence in their ability to make wise choices. They will be on their way to becoming self-directing and self-managing individuals.

STRATEGIES AND ACTIVITIES FOR DECISION-MAKING DIFFICULTIES

1. Activity: *SODAS*

    One decision-making process you can teach kids, which is similar to the one cited in the discussion above, uses the acronym SODAS, which stands for situation, options, disadvantages, advantages, and solution. The purpose of this activity is to teach children to reason out a situation and evaluate the advantages and disadvantages of choices before making a decision.

    Instructions for the five-step decision-making process:

    1) Identify the *situation*. What exactly is the decision to be made? Be specific about the issue to be decided. Answer the *who, what, where, when,* and *why* questions. Try to avoid being emotional, because emotion tends to cloud judgment.
    2) List all of the *options*. What are the possible choices at hand? List both the good and bad options.
    3) List the *disadvantages* of each option given above. The idea is to get the child to see the negative consequences of an option. For example, will the decision hurt someone's feelings?
    4) List the *advantages* of each option given above. By exploring both the advantages and disadvantages of an option, the child will be better prepared to see why an option might work or fail.
    5) Choose a *solution*. Give the child some time to think about the solutions, then allow him/her to make the choice as to which option might be the best. It may not be the choice you want, but this is part of the learning process. As long as the choice is not immoral or illegal, let them make the choice and deal with the consequences. Be supportive and empathetic if your child does not succeed, then go back to SODAS to make another choice.

2. Activity: *Don't Get on My Nerves!*
   This activity identifies annoying behaviors of others and helps kids to learn to make positive choices when dealing with them.
   Instructions:
   1) Have the class brainstorm behaviors that annoy them and write them on the board (this may also be done with an individual child or with a small group). The following is a list of some annoying behaviors:
      - A classmate has told a lie about you to your best friend and now your best friend is mad at you.
      - Your group has finished an art project and now it is time to clean up. One of the group members is not helping, but rather is just sitting there talking.
      - A classmate spilled glitter on the floor and said it was you who did it.
      - Your friend always wants to decide what to play at recess and gets mad when you suggest something else.
      - A classmate throws a wad of paper at you when the teacher isn't looking, then laughs at you when you get upset.
   2) Divide the class into small groups and assign two or three annoying behaviors to each group.
   3) Have the group members answer the following questions on paper about each of their situations:
      - How would you feel?
      - How do you think you would respond?
   4) Ask the group members to share their responses and then answer the following questions as a group:
      - What are some positive ways to respond?
      - Which choice would have the best consequences?
   5) Have the groups share their annoying situations and their best solutions with the rest of the class.
   6) Summarize the lesson by discussing how making good choices, such as learning to respond to annoying situations in positive ways, will not only prevent others from bothering them but also help them to make and keep friends.
3. Activity: *Playing Checkers and Chess*
   These "thinking games" and others help kids to look at their options, and decide when a move is a good one or bad one. The following steps may be used for teaching decision-making skills while playing the game:
   1) Think of three good moves you could make. Pick the best move.
   2) Once you have made the move, ask yourself, is this a good move or bad move? If I do this, what will happen next? If I move here, where will the other player move?

3) If you look ahead and don't like the consequences of your move, go ahead and change your move. Think ahead.
4) When you are satisfied with your move decision, say, "I'm done" and let the other player make a move decision.

REFERENCES & RESOURCES

Black, S. (1994). Throw away the hickory stick. *Executive Educator, 16*(4), 44–47.
Blum, D. (1998). *The school counselor's book of lists.* San Francisco: Jossey-Bass.
Charles, C. (2013). *Building classroom discipline* (11th ed.). New York: Pearson.
Coloroso, B. (1994). *Kids are worth it! Giving your child the gift of inner discipline.* New York: William Morrow.
Glasser, W. (1999). *Choice theory: A new psychology of personal freedom.* New York: Harper Collins.
Kohn, A. (1996). *Beyond discipline: From compliance to community.* Alexandria, VA: Association for Supervision and Curriculum Development.

Chapter 10

Depression and Sadness

Since kids live in a world controlled by adults, they often feel powerless over what is happening to them.

DISCUSSION

Sadness is a common, natural emotion that everyone experiences from time to time. Children who have high levels of sadness are more withdrawn from family, friends, and activities. This withdrawal may lead to feelings of isolation and loneliness, which in turn promotes more feelings of sadness. If the child has recently experienced a significant disappointment, the end of an important relationship, or the death of a loved one, temporary feelings of sadness are normal and appropriate.

Concerned teachers often wonder when sadness in children is a normal reaction, and when it may be a sign of serious depression. Luby's research results (2010) show that childhood depression is widely under-recognized and the younger the child, the greater number of cases go unrecognized and unreported. About 5 percent of children in the general population suffer from depression at any given point in time. Children under stress, who experience loss, or who have attention, learning, conduct or anxiety disorders are at a higher risk for depression (Academy of Child and Adolescent Psychiatry, 2008).

DEPRESSION DEFINED

Persistent sadness is a classic symptom of depression, and according to the DSM-5 (Diagnostic and Statistical Manual of Mental Disorders), when a depressed mood lasts at least two weeks, it is a symptom of major depressive disorder (MDD). However, for our purposes, if you observe any of the following signs, it is important to have the child evaluated by a professional, as they may be signs of serious depression:

- Feelings of sadness and/or emptiness that last more than two weeks
- Sadness along with other symptoms of depression (see "warning signs")
- Tearfulness and/or frequent crying spells
- Inability to experience joy in things formerly pleasurable

The symptoms of depression in children vary. Medical studies used to focus on "masked" depression, where a child's depressed mood was exhibited by "acting out" or angry behavior. Although this does occur, especially in younger kids, youngsters usually display sadness or low moods similar to adults who are depressed.

In order to recognize depression in children, it is important to become aware of the symptoms and signs to look for. Because children are not as articulate as adults in expressing their emotions, it is unlikely that they will come to us and say, "I'm depressed," as an adult might do. They might not even realize that something is wrong or out of the ordinary.

Since kids live in a world controlled by adults, they often feel powerless over what is happening to them. This puts the responsibility on significant adults to look for signs of trouble so you can help kids become aware of what is happening to them, teach them skills to cope with their problem, or, if appropriate, refer them for further evaluation by the school counselor or a mental health specialist.

WARNING SIGNS OF DEPRESSION

The warning signs of depression in kids fall into four basic categories: emotional indicators, cognitive signs, physical complaints, and behavior changes. The following summary of the warning signs of depression has been compiled from various sources (Schimelpfening, 2008; Sarafolean, 2009; DiMaria, 2011; MedicineNet, 2011) to assist teachers and parents in recognizing and understanding childhood depression:

1. *Emotional Indicators.* Typical emotions experienced by children suffering from depress include the following:
    - *Sadness*: The child may feel hopeless and unhappy. He or she may cry easily.
    - *Loss of pleasure and interest*: A child who has always enjoyed a certain activity in the past may no longer show interest in participating in it.

- *Anxiety*: The child may become anxious, tense, or even panicky. Investigating the source of the anxiety might give a clue as to what is causing the depression.
- *Turmoil*: The child may feel irritable, worried, and confused. They may fret, mope, or lash out in anger as a result of the distress they are experiencing.

2. *Cognitive Signs.* A depressive state of mind can bring on negative, self-defeating thoughts. This can make the child resistant to words of advice or encouragement. The signs to look for include the following:
   - *Difficulty concentrating*: Kids with depression often have problems with organizing thoughts and remembering information, as exhibited by problems in school or inability to complete tasks.
   - *Feelings of worthlessness or guilt*: Depressed kids often obsess over what they perceive as faults or failures and think of themselves as worthless and feel a tremendous guilt as a result.
   - *Negative view of self*: Depressed kids may perceive themselves, their life, and their world in a very negative and pessimistic manner.
   - *Feelings of helplessness and hopelessness*: Kids with depression often believe there is nothing they can do to relieve their feelings of distress and sadness.
   - *Feelings of isolation*: Depressed kids often feel left out, like they do not belong to their social groups, and are often very sensitive to any negative comments or rejection from peers.
   - *Suicidal thoughts*: Depressed kids may have thoughts of ending their life and wishing they were dead and may express these thoughts.

3. *Physical Signs.* Depression is not just an illness that affects the mind; it causes physical changes as well.
   - *Changes in appetite and weight*: Kids with depression often experience significant changes in their appetite. Kids who had healthy appetites may suddenly lose interest in eating, or the opposite may occur, and they may begin eating too much in an attempt to relieve the distress.
   - *Sleep disturbances*: Depressed kids may have difficulty falling asleep or staying asleep. They may wake up several times throughout the night or they may wake up too early or too late. Others may want to sleep more than is appropriate for someone their age or more than they had previously.
   - *Listlessness*: Kids with depression are often lethargic and talk, react, and walk slowly. They may be less active than usual and complain of fatigue.
   - *Physical complaints*: These kids may have physical complaints, such as stomachaches or headaches, that do not respond to treatment.

4. *Behavioral Signs.* Changes in behavior are the most obvious signs to detect.
   - *Withdrawal*: Depressed kids may withdraw from friends and family and may avoid responsibilities and everyday activities once enjoyed.
   - *Agitation*: These kids may exhibit agitation by fidgeting and not being able to sit still. They may act up in class, exhibit irritability, or display reckless behavior.
   - *Clinging and demanding*: These kids may become more clingy and dependent on some relationships, and they may behave with an exaggerated sense of insecurity.
   - *Excessive activities*: Depressed kids may appear to be out of control when it comes to certain activities, such as spending long hours playing video games or watching television, or excessive eating.
   - *Self-harm*: Depressed children may cause themselves physical pain or take excessive risks. Self-injury is an example of such behavior.

Not all children will have all of these symptoms. In fact, most will display different symptoms at different times and in different settings. Although some kids may continue to function reasonably well, most kids with significant depression will exhibit a noticeable change in social activities, loss of interest in school activities and family life, poor academic performance, or a change in appearance.

If you suspect that a child is depressed, the next step is seeking professional help in obtaining an evaluation, diagnosis, and treatment. If you are not sure where to seek help, the child's school counselor or family physician can help with a referral.

STRATEGIES AND ACTIVITIES FOR DEPRESSION AND SADNESS

1. The following tips may help kids deal with mild depression and sadness:
   - *Reassure the child that depression and sadness are not something to be ashamed of.* All of us feel sad in response to sad situations. Some people have an illness that makes it harder to recover from sadness.
   - *Give the child the right to have these feelings.* Kids can easily get the idea that it is not okay to feel sad or depressed and may start hiding their feelings rather than dealing with them in healthy ways.
   - *Be honest with the child and tell the truth.* We want to protect our kids from pain, but they are quick to pick up on when something is not right. By being honest, we allow them to work through the pain.
   - *Give the child a chance to grieve.* Losing a pet turtle may seem like a small thing, but it may be a big deal to a child who has never experienced loss before.

- *Teach children that it is okay to ask for help when they need it.* You might role-play asking for help. Helping the child get a referral to see the school counselor might be appropriate.
2. Encourage the child to use *problem-solving skills* to deal with problems:
   1) Identify the problem. *What is the problem you want to solve?*
   2) Determine the goal. *What do you want to happen?*
   3) Develop strategies. *What are some ways you could deal with the problem? Which ones might be a good move? Which ones might be a bad move?*
   4) Choose one solution. *Choose the solution you think would best deal with your problem.*
   5) Make a plan of action and do it. *What are the steps you will need to take in order to make that solution happen? Try it and see how it goes.*
   6) Evaluate how well the plan worked. *Did your plan solve your problem?* (If not, go back to #3 and choose another solution.)
3. Increase the child's *sense of belonging* by giving him a specific task with a title which provides a service to the class group. Some examples are as follows:
   - *The Class Attendance Clerk* (e.g., make an unofficial classroom attendance card and have the student mark the students who are present each morning)
   - *The Chief Boys Restroom Monitor*
   - *The Class Cafeteria Captain*
   - *The Class Distributor* (passes out papers, supplies, and other tasks)

   *Frequently let children know how important their task is to the group.

REFERENCES & RESOURCES

American Academy of Child and Adolescent Psychiatry (AACAP). (2008). *Facts for families: The depressed child*, No. 4., pdf file. Updated May, 2008.

Depression and Suicide in Children and Adolescents. (2011, February 10). *A report of the surgeon general.* http://www.surgeongeneral.gov/mentalhealth/chapter3/sec5.html.

Diagnostic and Statistical Manual of Mental Disorders (5th Ed-Text Rev.). (2013). Washington, DC: American Psychiatric Press.

DiMaria, L. (2011, March 1). *Sadness in children: How to know if your child's sadness is depression.* 2011. Retrieved April, 2011. http://depression.about.com/od/symptoms/a/Sadness-In-Children.htm.

Luby, J. (2010, August). The importance of identification of depression early in development. *Current Trends in Psychological Science, 19*(4), 525–37.

MedicineNet.com. (2011). Depression in children. Retrieved April, 2011. http://www.medicinenet.com/depression_in_children/article.

Sarafolean, M. (2000, July/August). Depression in school-age children and adolescents: Characteristics, assessment and prevention. *A Pediatric Perspective, 4*(9), 1–5.

Chapter 11

Divorce and Separation Issues

Every dart you throw at the other parent hits the child first.

DISCUSSION

Kids experiencing divorce and/or separation frequently feel torn apart, uncertain about their present and future, and sometimes feel abandoned by the parting parent. Children often feel at fault for the separation, responsible for their parents' turmoil and unhappiness, and fearful of losing both parents.

They may feel disillusioned, betrayed, or rejected by one or both parents, and may lose trust in their parents or in relationships in general, including those at school (Branch & Shelton, 2011). Vulnerability to both physical and mental illnesses can originate in the traumatic loss of one or both parents through divorce (American Academy of Child and Adolescent Psychiatry, 2011).

COMMON REACTIONS

Children of all ages can have a variety of reactions, and the age at which the divorce or separation occurs is not related to whether or not the child will adjust well to the situation (Dufour & Mishara, 2011). School-age children who are dealing with divorce often experience grief, embarrassment, resentment, divided loyalty, and intense anger. They are old enough to understand that they are in pain because of their parents' separation, but too young to understand or control their reactions to this pain.

Wipfler (2011) contends that there are three basic sources of hurt for children when their parents separate: (1) The *loss of the family configuration* that has anchored them—who is at home changes, parents' work schedules change, and their own school situation may change; (2) The *awareness of intense unhappy feelings between parents* rocks a child's world; and (3) The *end of a living arrangement they trusted and depended on*—a breach in their ability to feel the world is a safe and welcoming place for them.

BEHAVIORAL CHANGES AT SCHOOL

Kids spend a substantial portion of their lives in school; therefore, it is not surprising that many of the behavioral consequences of divorce, separation, and family dysfunction are first seen in the school environment. These kids usually have increased behavioral problems that interfere with learning.

Parents who are going through separation and/or divorce are often emotionally distracted, upset with their present personal difficulties, fatigued, and, as parents, are not functioning very well. Teachers, counselors, childhood specialists, and other school staff are frequently called upon to fill in this parenting gap by maintaining a supportive role.

"RED FLAGS" TO LOOK FOR

There are various behaviors frequently displayed by kids of separating or divorcing parents to be on the lookout for. For example, they may direct anger outward into misbehavior or inward into shame, or develop physical symptoms. The main question is to know whether these behaviors are "red flags" which require intervention. The following are some of the behaviors that should be evaluated in the context of the divorce:

1. *No Changes in Behavior.* This is perhaps the biggest "red flag" of all, since separation or divorce creates such profound changes in a child's life. However, it is not unusual to hear of children whose grades remain good, their conduct excellent, and peer relations unchanged, initially. For some kids, the separation actually offers a respite from tensions, hostility, or even abuse and violence within the family setting. But the odds are, the child who shows no change in the face of the stress brought on by divorce or separation is likely repressing feelings or using school as a focus to avoid his or her feelings about the rest of life. Beneath the surface there are problems waiting to happen. Although they appear to be coping well initially, many of them start having considerable difficulty down the road. These kids are easy to overlook but they deserve as much or more attention than the child who is acting out.

2. *Changes in Compliance.* If a child who is going through divorce or separation becomes increasingly defiant, uncooperative, and nonconforming, this may reflect a new-found distrust and anger toward adults. It may be an attempt to be more in control of his or her life, or it may be a general rebellion against authority. It may also be the result of moving from one household to another with different rules and expectations regarding appropriate behavior, and the child feels unsettled, confused, and lost.
3. *Changes in Compliance.* These changes may be the result of chaos at home, perhaps having to assume additional responsibilities for home chores, taking on increased duties in caring for siblings, and even having to attend to needs of the remaining parent. Being tardy may be an early sign of school phobia or separation anxiety, which reflects fear and guilt for leaving the remaining parent alone, especially if that parent is experiencing emotional turmoil. The inability to meet normal time deadlines may also be a sign of depression.
4. *Changes in Class Participation.* These changes may reflect a lowered self-esteem and/or depression. These kids may appear sad, become quiet, and exhibit decreased activity. However, it may be more a product of a disrupted week involving two homes or not having access to the parent who is most helpful in helping with homework assignments.
5. *Changes in Peer Relationships.* Some kids may attempt to be in control of some part of their lives by displaying behaviors such as bullying or attempting to be a gang member. Others may seek attention by being the class clown or being disruptive and obnoxious in class. These kids often join groups, even gangs, in an effort to feel that they "belong" and are cared for in a way no longer available at home. On the other hand, they may be introverted and withdrawn from their peers in an effort to isolate themselves, or out of distrust of getting too close or caring too much about anyone who might leave them like the parent did. A final scenario for how divorce and/or separation may affect peer relationships is the child may focus all attention on one relationship, perhaps a girlfriend/boyfriend or a "best friend." The child will often become excessively protective of that one relationship.
6. *Negative Changes in Achievement.* There may be numerous causes for grades to suffer during this chaotic time in a child's life. They may reflect an inability to cope with sadness or anxiety about the uncertainty of the present and future. There may be inadequate time and space to do homework, a sudden absence of the person who formerly helped with homework completion, fatigue that limits performance, or distractions and anxiety due to the ongoing parent conflict.
7. *Obsession with Super-Achievement.* This often occurs as an effort to compensate for feelings of guilt that it was the child's fault that the

parents separated. It may be an attempt to make the parents happy, and maybe even to convince them to get back together again. On the other hand, the child may just be seeking relief from painful turmoil through concentration and focusing on schoolwork.

NORMAL FEELINGS AND CONCERNS

In summary, even though every case is unique, some normal, common feelings and concerns often experienced by kids going through divorce and/or separation frequently include the following:

- Feeling torn apart and in turmoil
- Feeling confused, bewildered, or shocked by the separation
- Feeling abandoned by either one or both parents
- Worrying about their current and future circumstances
- Feeling uncertain and insecure with the series of life-altering changes
- Feeling upset, worried, fearful, or anxious over the tension between the parents
- Feeling responsible or guilty for the relationship problems between the parents
- Feeling responsible for either one or both parents' happiness
- Fear of losing both parents and others close to them
- No longer feel like they belong to a family
- Anger and hostility toward the parent who is perceived to be responsible for the breakup

Understanding that all these reactions are normal is the first step in helping children adapt. It is important to realize that, even if the immediate reactions seem extreme, most children eventually adapt well to their new situation.

STRATEGIES AND ACTIVITIES FOR DIVORCE AND SEPARATION ISSUES

Tips for Teachers

Teachers and other school staff should maintain a supportive role to the child dealing with divorce and separation issues at home. The following are ways in which the teacher might be of assistance:

1) *Maintain consistency and adhere to the code of conduct.* When divorce disrupts a child's world, and most parents are changing rules and routines to accommodate new family circumstances, teachers can help by maintaining

well-defined expectations for performance and behavior. Educators are often tempted to bend the rules for children experiencing such confusion, turbulence, and instability in their lives, but by keeping the school environment stable and consistent in its expectations, educators increase the child's sense of security and well-being. When everything around him at home seems to be in a constant turmoil and transition, it is comforting to have the school environment remain the same with its rules and expectations.

2) *Preserve a positive self-image and feeling of competence.* Teachers utilize many strategies to help kids feel needed, important, and valued. They assign specific, achievable tasks and responsibilities—such as caring for the class pet, watering the plants, or cleaning the whiteboard—which increase kids' sense of belonging, enhance their value as contributing members of the group, and boost their self-image and self-esteem in general. It is important that teachers focus on competencies and strengths and provide appropriate positive feedback to kids for tasks well done.

3) *Listen to the child's point of view.* The teacher may be the only adult who actively encourages a child to express how he sees and feels about a situation. Frequently, asking questions is more productive than making statements. For example, *Why do you think you are feeling angry with Billy today?* rather than, *Do your work and leave Billy alone?* This allows the child to think about and express his feelings and actions, even if he cannot make a connection to the hostile environment at home, or other events which might be the cause of his anger. By offering a safe, nonjudgmental atmosphere, teachers reassure the child that at least one adult cares enough to notice how he is feeling.

4) *Be an advocate for the child.* Frequently, the teacher is the only adult aware of what is going on with the child and how the child is reacting to the confusion and turbulence of personal relationships at home and is willing to act as an advocate for the child. The teacher can alert parents, as well as other school staff, to areas of concern in the child's life. If the concerns interfere too drastically with learning, the teacher may refer the child to the school counselor or school psychologist.

Tips for Counselors

When children go through divorce and separation, they often have issues so severe they interfere with the learning process and are referred to the school counselor for assistance. The following are some guidelines for the school counselor to follow when providing the child with assistance:

1) *Establish rapport and listen to the child.* The counselor builds a trusting relationship by actively listening to the child, thus creating a warm,

comfortable, and safe environment in which feelings about the divorce or separation can be freely expressed. Avoid interrogating and probing for details. Instead, encourage the child to express what he or she is willing to share, especially feelings. Respect the personal nature of each child's reaction to the situation.

2) *Be accessible to the child.* Children need to voice their concerns as they arise. Provide a means where students can leave a note with their name and room number and a brief description of the current concern. Depending upon the gravity of their current situation, take them to your office at your earliest convenience, or at least make contact with them to evaluate the urgency of their concerns. It is important that children experiencing the trauma of divorce and/or separation feel the security of having someone who is *there* for them when they have the need to share their feelings and thoughts. In other words, be available as much as possible for nurturing, caring, and supporting when the child desires and needs it.

3) *Refer the child to a small group of kids going through divorce/separation.* Belonging to a small group of students who have similar concerns provides children with the opportunity to support and learn from each other. These groups usually include children at different stages of separation, divorce, and remarriage of parents. Among the topics usually discussed are (a) how to relate well to both parents, (b) how to live in two homes with different rules, (c) how to prepare for the holidays, and (d) understanding the separation is not your fault, and other related topics.

Guidelines for Parents

The following are some guidelines that you, as counselors and teachers, might share with parents to assist them in helping their children make healthy adjustments to a situation involving divorce and/or separation:

1) Kids need to verbalize their concerns. Being told not to worry, or "someone will always take care of you," may stifle their willingness to share their feelings and leave them feeling vulnerable and powerless over their lives.

2) Kids know when parents are worried, so model discussing your concerns so they will be more comfortable discussing theirs. You do not have to share all of the intimate details with your kids. Just let them know your general feelings of concern as they relate to the child and his or her reactions to the separation or divorce.

3) Listen to your children's anxieties and fears, and encourage them to discuss them with you.

4) Make sure your words of assurance, and any promises you make, can be matched by your actions. Fabrication, no matter how well intentioned, always leads to distrust, doubts, and skepticism.
5) Kids need their parents to be able to attend school functions without exuding all the hostility and anger between them. If there are unsettled issues, consider getting professional help to resolve them. Your kids' school success depends on it (Albert, 1984).
6) Whenever possible, include the kids in the process of building a new life. Letting them have a voice in decisions involving the new life will give them a renewed sense of belonging to a new family unit.
7) Don't underestimate the degree to which children worry about the consequences of what is happening. They worry about their own future as well as the future of each parent, and how they all will manage.
8) Don't force children to choose between parents.
9) Avoid criticizing your ex-spouse in front of the children. Every dart you throw at the other parent hits the child first. The old adage "if you can't say something nice, don't say anything at all" applies here.
10) Do not ask children to serve as messengers between you and your ex-spouse.
11) Set clear rules for the household, generated and agreed upon by all family members.
12) Insist upon respect, consideration, and cooperation among all family members.
13) Respect and be considerate of children's feelings but maintain the right to make the decision about relationships and remarriage.

Children who can both talk to a sympathetic parent and participate in a school counseling group hold the best chances of adjusting to divorce or separation in a healthy way.

REFERENCES & RESOURCES

Albert, L. (1984). *Coping with kids and school: A guide for parents.* New York: E.P. Dutton.

American Academy of Child and Adolescent Psychiatry (AACAP). (2011, March). *Children of divorce.* http://www.aacap.org/cs/root/facts_for_families/children_and_divorce.

Branch, J. & Shelton, L. (2011). *What children need to hear.* University of Vermont Extension. Separation & Divorce: A Parenting Seminar, pdf file.

Dufour, S. & Mishara, B. (2011). *Children's reaction to divorce and separation.* Partnership for Children.org. Retrieved August 2011. http://www.partnershipforchildren.org.uk/resources/my-child-is-worried-about/divorce-separation/children-s-reactions-to-divorce-and-separation.html.

Lewis, J. & Sammons, W. (2000, September). What schools are doing to help children of divorce. *The Journal of the National Association for the Education of Young Children, 55*(5), 64–65.

Wipfler, P. (2011). *Helping children with separation and divorce.* Retrieved January 2011. http://www.handinhandparenting.org/news/47/64/HelpingChildren-with-Separation-and-Divorce.

Chapter 12

Empathy and Compassion Development

Empathy is the foundation for the ability to love, and thus is at the core of good character.

—Dr. Liane Leedom, Psychiatrist

DISCUSSION

Empathy is an aspect of social and emotional learning that involves the ability to identify with other people's perceptions in order to understand and be sensitive to their feelings, thoughts, and experiences, and involves accurately conveying that understanding through an accepting response (Haynes & Avery, 1979). For youngsters, acquiring empathy and compassion is a crucial developmental step that enhances their social skills as well as their capacity for caring about what happens to others. Empathy is the foundation for the ability to love, and thus is at the core of good character (Leedom, 2009).

Empathy and compassion are basically learned skills, like any other skill kids can develop. They require constant practice and reinforcement through empathetic and compassionate behavior modeled by parents, teachers, and other significant persons in a child's life throughout childhood and adolescence.

Hoffman (2000) asserts that "empathy is an emotional, cognitive and motivational force for moral action, which encourages moral development" and begins in the preschool period before children are capable of appropriate understanding of moral rules. According to Hoffman, it is a basic "personal tool" which promotes children's pro-social behavior and sense of justice.

SHOULD EMPATHY AND COMPASSION BE TAUGHT IN SCHOOLS?

There are many who argue against including character education activities in schools because they feel that such activities would take time away from basic learning and higher-order thinking. However, Oswalt (2008) asserts that research shows taking the time to help children develop socially and emotionally can improve children's academic performance.

Researchers Bonner and Aspy (1984) have identified significant correlations between students' scores on measures of empathetic understanding and their grade point averages. Program evaluations have shown that schools where students are involved in programs to develop empathy and create "caring communities" have higher scores on reading comprehension than comparison schools on measures of higher-order reading comprehension (Kohn, 1991).

Another review of research related to empathy training and instruction indicates that training in empathy enhances both critical thinking skills and creative thinking (Gallo, 1989). Children who have received empathy training not only tend to show higher levels of creativity, reading comprehension, and critical thinking skills, but they also problem-solve on a deeper level and are less prone to make rash judgments (Cotton, 2008).

In general, children who have received training and instruction in empathy development do better in school. Schools are slowly beginning to recognize the importance of teaching social and emotional learning skills, including empathy.

IMPLICATIONS FOR DEVELOPING EMPATHY AND COMPASSION

Children with antisocial disorders, such as bullying and harassing, lack empathy (Carney, 2007). Kids who are under stress from a traumatic experience or have difficult home environments are not in a position to practice empathy and compassion. Similarly, youngsters who are focused on competition and social dominance do not practice empathy (Leedom, 2009).

Television programs, movies, and video games that involve violence and aggression give kids practice ignoring empathetic and compassionate feelings (*American Psychological Association*, 2008). Empathy and compassion are necessary for warm, caring behavior, and not teaching empathy and compassion robs kids of their ability to love. While children learn empathy and compassion largely through interactions with responsive parents, there are strategies and activities that can provide additional training in these areas of character development.

STRATEGIES AND ACTIVITIES FOR EMPATHY AND COMPASSION DEVELOPMENT

1. *Activity*: Feelings Flashcards to *"Name That Feeling"*
    This activity helps kids identify various emotions by observing facial expressions and body language
    Materials: Flashcards with pictures that show people experiencing various feelings, such as happy, sad, angry, surprised, and scared. For older kids, emotions such as, nervous, embarrassed, intimidated, and such, might be added.
    Instructions:
    1) Create a set of flashcards with pictures cut from magazines which show various emotions in different situations. (This could be used as a project for your kids prior to this activity.)
    2) Children are asked to *name that feeling* by guessing what a person is feeling.
    3) Ask *why* they think they feel that way, by observing and describing facial expressions and body language.
2. Activity: *You End the Story*
    This activity will help to stimulate empathy through the use of imagination.
    Materials: The Feelings Flashcards from activity 1.
    Instructions:
    1) Make up a simple little story about what was happening prior to the picture shown. An example for a little girl crying might be: *Mary walked home from school with her best friend, Linda. She invited Mary to come into her house and play for a while. Then . . .*
    2) Have the children write an ending to the story based on how the little girl looks in the picture.
    3) Ask the children to read their endings and discuss them with the class, emphasizing the feelings.
3. Activity: *"I Message" Partners*
    This activity will help kids to learn to express and reflect feelings with a partner.
    Instructions:
    Pair off students so everyone has a partner. Give each child a 3 x 5 index card with the following *I message* and *reflection* written on it:
    Student A: I feel/felt _____ when _____ because _____.
    Student B: So you feel/felt _____ when _____ because _____?
    Student A: Yes.
    Have students use the basic emotions: sad, happy, angry, scared, excited, and surprised to fill in the first blank. For older students

add emotions such as relieved, nervous, embarrassed, intimidated, and frustrated. Then have students change roles.
4. *Allow children to experience remorse.* When kids say or do hurtful things to others, they need to know it, and they need to understand the impact that their actions have on others. Remorse and guilt, while not pleasant, can serve as reminders to do things differently next time. You might ask questions such as, *How do you think she feels now? How would you feel if someone said that to you? What can you do to make her feel better? What can you do differently next time?*
5. *Label personal feelings.* Educators can model their own feelings by using *I Statements* when interacting with children. For example, *I felt disappointed when you didn't do your homework,* or *I feel frustrated because I can't get the computer to work properly.* This type of modeling helps to give children the language for expressing themselves.
6. *Model empathetic caring.* For example, *Alicia seems a little sad today. What can we do to make her feel better?* Statements like this help children to recognize opportunities for caring for other's needs and to think of ways to help. Be sure to verbalize how good it feels to help someone out.
7. *Provide opportunities for helping.* Give children the chance to help those less fortunate. A teacher might plan a field trip to a nursing home to sing a few songs and enact a short play for the group. The giving of one's time and talent to others helps children to develop compassion and feel competent and important in the world.

REFERENCES & RESOURCES

American Psychological Association (APA) Online. (2008, May 22). *What makes kids care? Teaching gentleness in a violent world.* http://www.apa.org/helpcenter/kids-care.aspx.

Bonner, T. & Aspy, D. (1984). A study of the relationship between student empathy and GPA. *Humanistic Education and Development, 22*(4), 149–54.

Cotton, K. (2008). *Developing empathy in children and youth.* Northwest Regional Educational Laboratory, August 31, 2001, Update May 2008. http://www.nwrel.org.

Gallo, D. (1989). Educating for empathy, reason and imagination. *The Journal of Creative Behavior, 23*(2), 98–115.

Haynes, L. & Avery, A. (1979). Training adolescents in self-disclosure and empathy skills. *Journal of Community Psychology, 26*(6), 526–30.

Hoffman, M. (2000). *Empathy and moral development.* Cambridge, UK: Cambridge University Press.

Kohn, A. (1991). Caring kids: The role of the schools. *Phi Delta Kappan, 72*(7), 496–506.

Leedom, L. (2009). Empathy—The cornerstone of ability to love. *Parenting the At-Risk Child,* August 1, 2009. http://www.parentingtheatriskchild.com/Empathy.html.

Oswalt, A. (2008, January 16). *Early childhood emotional and social development: Reflective empathy.* Mental Health Care, Inc. http://www.mhcinc.org.

Chapter 13

Following Directions

Praise is saying, "Good job!" Encouragement is adding, "I knew you could do it—you're that kind of person!"

DISCUSSION

One of the most common complaints from teachers is that so many children do not know how to follow directions, especially upon the first request. Following directions is a learned behavior. If a parent or teacher has the tendency to repeat directions over and over, the child will learn that it is not important to follow directions upon first request.

It is important for kids to acquire the learned behavior of following directions and instructions, not only to please adults or avoid negative consequences, but to make their own lives easier and safer as well. Kids' health and safety depend on their ability to follow instructions, and they function better in school, in sports, and in other group activities when they know how to carry out instructions.

Kids' ability to follow directions also affects their learning and performance in school. This "real world" skill will support children's learning throughout their lives. Activities involving crafts, cooking, and building things are just a few of the meaningful ways that children can learn to follow directions successfully.

MISTAKES TO AVOID

Before discussing what might work to teach kids how to follow directions, let's discuss what to avoid. According to Christopherson (1998) and other experts (Windell, 1997; Cool, 1996; Poole, Miller & Church, 2000), some methods used by parents and teachers not only are often ineffective but actually encourage noncompliance. Some common errors to avoid are as follows:

- *Don't make empty threats.* Making threats such as *You better get busy or you're going to get lunch detention!* or *If you don't clean your room right now I'm going to ground you* is a common mistake teachers and parents make. Kids resent being given ultimatums or being forced to give in, just like adults do, so they often end up focusing on the anger they feel, rather than the task at hand. The adults in these cases are left with either following through with the threats, thus increasing the tension even more, or giving in.
- *Don't say "Don't."* A negative instruction such as *Don't make me tell you again to get busy on your math paper*, or *Don't let me come back from the store and find that you haven't cleaned your room* is much more likely to be ignored.
- *The more you nag the less kids listen.* It is very easy to slip into the "nagging and shouting syndrome." When children do not respond the first time they are told to do something, teachers often continue repeating the request over and over until they finally reach their limit and start shouting the request. In this scenario, children are being conditioned to tune the teacher out until he or she is shouting.
- *Don't assume that your directions, or those contained in textbooks, are clear.* Take steps to ensure that every child understands what is expected of them. You may want them to read the directions out loud to you or have them write them down on a separate sheet of paper before they begin. When giving verbal instructions, it is often useful to have the child repeat them back to you.
- *Avoid phrasing directions as questions.* For example, do not say, *Bobby, would you like to get busy on your math now?* It is too tempting for the child to give a negative response.
- *Don't be vague.* Avoid vague phrases, such as: *Do your best. Get busy. Be good. Be careful.*

GIVING EFFECTIVE DIRECTIONS

The following suggestions are effective ways to give directions (Christopherson, 1998; Windell, 1997; Cool, 1996):

- *Get the child's attention.* Always get children's attention before giving directions. Make sure every child in the classroom is focusing on what you are about to say before beginning.
- *Discuss the importance of following directions.* Ask for situations when following directions might be important, such as, playing games, sports, cooking, assembling model cars, finding a friend's house, performing CPR, and so on.

- *Be clear and concise.* Always state directions and instructions clearly and precisely, being specific about what you expect the child to do. For example, instead of just telling a child to go clean up his room, a better procedure would be to say: *Go to your room, put all of your toys in the toy box, empty your trashcan into the big one in the kitchen, put all of your dirty clothes into the hamper, and make your bed.* Write the directions down for the child or give him two or three steps at a time.
- *Rehearse and role-play.* Rehearsing and role-playing new or unfamiliar directions give kids practice at following a new set of directions in order to make sure they understand what is expected of them.
- *Be prepared to enforce.* Teachers should avoid giving their kids a direction unless they are prepared to enforce it. There should be clear consequences, established by the group. If they do not enforce their directions, then kids learn that their teachers do not mean what they say.
- *Establish a clear system of positive and negative consequences.* Including children in formulating a clear system of positive and negative consequences for making good and poor choices helps to motivate kids to be more conscientious.
- *Praise and encourage.* Teachers should praise and encourage their children as soon as they have begun to follow the direction. You don't need to wait until the task is completed to offer words of praise and encouragement. Praise is saying, "Good job!" Encouragement is adding "I knew you could do it, you're that kind of person!" or "I bet you feel good about doing such a good job!"
- *Show appreciation.* When directions are followed, teachers should show appreciation for compliance. "I really like how you followed the directions when doing that math assignment."
- *Post reminders.* Posting reminders in the classroom for everyday tasks can provide additional help for following directions. An example would be "What to Put at the Top of Your Seatwork Paper," and then list Name, Date, Subject, Teacher, and so forth. When children are provided with real, authentic opportunities to follow directions, they understand the purpose, the importance, and the process of following directions, and the natural and logical consequences of not following them correctly.

STRATEGIES AND ACTIVITIES FOR FOLLOWING DIRECTIONS

1. Activity: *Coloring Sheet*

    A blank picture coloring sheet creates the basis of an activity for following directions. The activity works well in a group but can also be used with one child.

Instructions:
1) Each child needs the same picture and a set of crayons.
2) Color a copy of the picture ahead of time to serve as a reference.
3) Give directions for coloring each section of the picture. For example, you might instruct the kids to color the flower red, the sun yellow, the grass green, and the sky blue.
4) Display your picture so the children can compare their finished product with yours. If they followed the directions, each picture should look similar.

A variation for older children might be to post a set of instructions for drawing a picture (e.g., one of the instructions might be to draw an apple tree next to the house), then have the children compare their pictures. How are they alike and how are they different?

2. Activity: *Treasure Hunt*

A treasure hunt is a list of directions to follow to find a reward.

Instructions:
1) Create a set of step-by-step directions or clues that lead the kids to the end of the treasure hunt.
2) The kids follow each step to find the next clue.
3) Another option is to draw a map with specific directions. This might include directing your kids to take a set number of steps or go to specific landmarks.
4) If the kids follow the directions correctly, they are rewarded with the treasure at the end of the hunt.

3. Activity: *Block/Lego® Structures*

Blocks and Legos® are popular with children, but they also work well to teach kids about following directions. This helps kids break down a task and learn the importance of including all the steps.

Instructions:
1) Create a block structure ahead of time. The complexity of the structure depends on the age of the children.
2) Give step-by-step directions to reconstruct the block building.
3) A variation would be to have a building contest. The winner gives the other kids directions how to reconstruct his building project.

4. Activity: *Gardening Project*

Whether potting seeds or planting flowers, children can have individual responsibilities such as digging holes, counting seeds, putting seeds in the holes, patting dirt over the seeds, and watering. Gardening provides the fun opportunity for following directions. Assign children days of the week to water their plants or weed the garden.

5. Activity: *A fun "Following Directions" activity*

Hand out a worksheet with the following directions: *Read all the questions on the page and then go back to number 1 and begin answering them.*
1) Write your full name. _____
2) What is your address? _____
3) When was the last time you ate a hot dog? _____
4) What is the color of eyes of the person on your right? _____
5) Say, "I am a silly rabbit" out loud three times.
6) Stand up, clap your hands three times, and say "I am a silly goose."
7) Write down the name of your favorite color. _____
8) Sing, "Twinkle, Twinkle, Little Star" real fast.
9) Cover your eyes and count to twenty as fast as you can.
10) Ignore all of the above directions. Sign your name on the first line and be quiet so no one else catches on.

If they followed the directions and read all the questions before starting, they will sign their names on the first line and be sitting quietly. If they did not follow directions, they will be doing all kinds of silly things.

6. Projects which teach the skills of following directions can be taught in the various academic areas:
   - *Language Arts*: Make puppets, masks, and/or costumes to act out stories that the children have read or written.
   - *Mathematics*: Perform measurement activities, do origami, make paper airplanes.
   - *Social Studies*: Make crafts, musical instruments, food, and so on from other countries.
   - *Science*: Conduct science experiments, build models of the human anatomy, plants, insects, space shuttle, airplanes, and so on.
   - *Art*: Make finger paints, flour dough, watercolors, and follow instructions in order to draw people, animals, landscapes, and so on.
   - *Health and Physical Education*: Play games, practice health and safety procedures, such as "Stop, Drop and Roll."

REFERENCES & RESOURCES

Christophersen, E. (1998). *Beyond discipline: Parenting that lasts a lifetime.* Shawnee Mission, KA: Overland Press.

Cool, L. (1996, June). How kids learn to follow directions. *Working Mother.*

Poole, P., Miller, S., & Church, E. (2000, January). Ages & stages: Learning to follow directions. *Early Childhood Today.* The article is also online: http://www2.scholastic.com/browse/article.jsp?id=3745711.

Windell, J. (1997). *Children who say no when you want them to say yes.* New York: Macmillan.

Chapter 14

Following the Rules

The Code of Conduct stipulates how everyone is supposed to behave and interact, including the teacher.

—Dr. Linda Albert, *Cooperative Discipline*

DISCUSSION

Fair and reasonable rules give children a sense of security, a feeling they belong to the group, and they let kids know what kind of behavior is expected of them. Kids are far more likely to follow the rules and abide by the consequences of breaking the rules if they have played an active role in creating them. In a democratic society, we have a voice in making the laws by which we are expected to live, and so should kids have a voice in making the rules that guide them in the home and school settings.

MODEL THE BEHAVIOR YOU WANT TO SEE

Kids are able, even eager, to rise to high standards of behavior. Model the behavior you want to see. Lay the foundation by modeling the routines, thus creating a sense of order, predictability, and trust. When teachers and students respect each other, work together, and listen to each other, behavior problems seem to diminish.

CREATE A CARING AND RESPECTFUL CLIMATE

Coloroso (1994) asserts that discipline works best when students have developed an inner sense of self-control. She contends that classrooms are an ideal place for students to learn to make responsible decisions. Classrooms should be places where students feel cared for and are encouraged to care about others. This sends the message that respect, kindness, and learning will prevail. Students will begin feeling connected to each other and a sense of community will develop. Most students will act responsibly if taught the procedures to do so. Procedures provide students with a structure that lets them know what is expected of them.

DEVELOPING A CLASS CODE OF CONDUCT

Since for many kids the term "rules" has the connotation of being teacher-imposed policies that kids better obey or be punished, Albert (1996) strongly recommends that teachers work together with their students to establish a *Code of Conduct*. A brief summary is provided here for educators to consider as a tool for when *following the rules* is a problem. The Code of Conduct stipulates how everyone is supposed to behave and interact, *including the teacher*. Every individual is held accountable for his or her own behavior at all times.

The following teacher-generated Code of Conduct is used as the basis from which students will create their class Code of Conduct (Albert, 1989):

1. I am respectful.
2. I am responsible.
3. I am safe.
4. I am prepared.

Because "Excellence in Education" is our motto:

5. I will do nothing to prevent the teacher from teaching or prevent anyone, myself included, from participating in educational activities.
6. I will cooperate with all members of the school community.
7. I will treat everyone with respect and courtesy.

Students are involved in interpreting the above principles by following these steps as follows:

1. *Identify appropriate and inappropriate behaviors* for each of the principles. Have students brainstorm the behaviors and write them on the board.

2. *Clarify the appropriate and inappropriate behaviors.* It is not enough to just list the behaviors. They must be clarified so everyone knows exactly what they mean. This is done through explanations, modeling, and role-playing.
3. *Involve parents.* Students might write a letter to their parents to explain the Code of Conduct by listing the appropriate and inappropriate behaviors they have identified.

CONSEQUENCES FOR VIOLATING THE CODE

Involve students in generating the consequences for serious and/or repeated violations of the Code of Conduct. As Albert (1996) points out, they should be related, reasonable, respectful, and reliably enforced. There are four categories of consequences for teachers to discuss with their students:

1. *Loss or delay of privileges*, such as a favorite activity;
2. *Loss of freedom of interaction,* such as talking with other students;
3. *Restitution* (such as return, repair, or replacement of objects), *doing school service,* or *helping other students one has offended*;
4. *Reteaching appropriate behavior*, such as practicing correct behavior and writing about how one should behave in a given situation

Letting children suffer the consequences is a "hassle-free" way to discipline young people. Children learn from experiences, just like adults. Children learn that every act has a consequence, and they learn to be responsible.

SENSE OF BELONGING ENCOURAGES COMPLIANCE

It is essential to instill in your kids a sense of belonging to the group. Give them responsibilities they can complete successfully, so they can become productive, competent, contributing members of "the group." When they sense belonging, and when they find success, students show relatively little misbehavior and are more willing to follow the rules. The emphasis is on teaching and reinforcing appropriate, socially acceptable behavior, rather than on punishing improper behavior.

STRATEGIES AND ACTIVITIES FOR FOLLOWING THE RULES

Present the class or individual student with the following example of a Code of Conduct to consider:

1) I am respectful.
2) I am responsible.
3) I am safe.
4) I am prepared.

Because "Excellence in Education" is our motto:

5) I will do nothing to prevent the teacher from teaching or prevent anyone, myself included, from participating in educational activities.
6) I will cooperate with all members of the school community.
7) I will treat everyone with respect and courtesy.

1. Brainstorm appropriate and inappropriate behaviors for each of the seven principles above. The longer the list, the better to help kids develop an understanding necessary for evaluating their own behavior choices. For example, when discussing what one does when you "treat everyone with respect and courtesy" kids might suggest the following *appropriate* behaviors:
   - Listen when others are speaking.
   - Use a pleasant tone of voice.
   - Use proper language.
   - Respond politely to requests from teachers and classmates.

   Behaviors that students might list as *inappropriate* could be as follows:
   - Putting others down.
   - Pushing and shoving.
   - Interrupting when others are speaking.
   - Making fun of others.

2. Clarify each behavior and have students model and role-play both the appropriate and inappropriate behaviors.

3. Many misbehaviors are the result of kids lacking the skills to solve problems. Teach kids the skills they need to become good problem-solvers. Encourage kids to use a problem-solving process:
   1) Identify the problem. *What is the problem you want to solve?*
   2) Determine the goal. *What do you want to happen?*
   3) Develop strategies. *What are some ways you could deal with the problem? Which ones might be a good move? Which ones might be a bad move?*
   4) Choose one solution. *Choose the solution you think would best deal with your problem.*
   5) Make a plan of action and do it. *What are the steps you will need to take in order to make that solution happen? Try it and see how it goes.*

6) Evaluate how well the plan worked. *Did your plan solve your problem?* (If not, have the child go back to #3 and choose another solution.)

REFERENCES & RESOURCES

Albert, L. (1996). *Cooperative discipline.* Circle Pines, MN: American Guidance Services.

Coloroso, B. (1994). *Kids are worth it! Giving your child the gift of inner discipline.* New York: William Morrow.

Kohn, A. (1996). *Beyond discipline: From compliance to community.* Alexandria, VA: Association for Supervision and Curriculum Development.

National Network for Child Care (NNCC). (1994). *Getting children to follow rules.* Pennsylvania State University Cooperative Extension. http://www.nncc.org/Guidance/better.rules.html.

Wood, C., Porter, D., Brady, K., & Forton, M. (2003). *Everyday rules that really work!* Scholastic. http://www2.scholastic.com/browse/article.jsp?id=3608.

Chapter 15

Goal Setting

Kids who succeed have goals, and kids who have goals succeed!
—Gary Ryan Blair, "The Goals Guy"

DISCUSSION

Teaching children to set and achieve goals is an important responsibility of parents, teachers, and other significant adults in children's lives. The ability to be able to determine one's goals is a necessity for living a fulfilling, successful life, and the earlier you encourage your children to think about what they want to accomplish, short term *and* long term, the better.

Knowing how to set reasonable goals and striving for them is an important life skill. Working toward a goal and receiving the reward of achieving it helps kids understand how life works. The following quote about goal setting is from Gary Ryan Blair (2011), known as "The Goals Guy" and recognized throughout the world as the authority on goal setting and personal strategic planning:

> Learning how to set and achieve a goal is perhaps the single most important thing your child can learn to prepare for school, adulthood, and for future employment. The more adept your child is at understanding this important life skill, the more options he or she will have throughout their life.

Teachers and parents set educational and personal goals for their children. Kids have a better chance of experiencing success when they clearly understand the goals for which they are striving. As Charles (2013) points out, children must see the goals as worthwhile, desirable, and attainable, and they are more likely to do so if brought into cooperative discussions about them. Timelines and checkpoints can be established to monitor progress toward goals, for continual progress encourages children to keep trying.

BENEFITS OF SETTING GOALS

When we teach our kids how to set and achieve goals, and how to apply these principles to their schoolwork, they learn to be more in control of their own education, which increases their chances for success. Simply telling kids they need to set goals is not enough. In order for goal setting to be relevant to them, you will have to help them determine *why* it is important and teach them *how* to do it. Goal setting works best when kids set realistic goals that require them to work toward achieving them without it seeming overwhelming. Most importantly, they need to see how it will make their lives better.

By learning how to set and achieve goals, how to overcome challenges or roadblocks, the importance of being positive, and how to measure their own progress, our children learn how to increase their chances for success now and throughout their lives. Teaching your kids how to effectively set and achieve goals is a gift that will last a lifetime.

TEACHING THE VALUE OF SETTING GOALS

Understanding the value of setting goals is an abstract concept for children, so you should try and make it as concrete as possible with a hands-on activity. Put the children in groups of four or five and ask them to plan what they are going to take with them on a family vacation. Give them a few minutes to think about it. Inevitably, they will come to the conclusion that they need to know where they are going and how long they will be gone before they can plan what to take with them. Will they need warm or light clothes? Many clothes or just a few? Will they need to pack food? The answer to all of these questions lies in where they are going and how long they will be gone. Without knowing this information, they cannot make proper plans. They need to know the destination of the trip, before they can set a course of action.

Then give each group a destination, such as a week in a mountain cabin, a day at the beach, a three-day camping trip at the lake, a day at Disneyland, and so forth. Then have the groups each make a plan for the things they need to take. Have each group read their plan. They will see that every goal has its own, unique plan of action.

HOW TO SET GOALS

The best way to teach kids how to set goals is to have them first observe you setting goals, making plans of action, and carrying out the plans. For example, a teacher might announce that she has the goal of changing a bulletin board display. She writes the steps she will follow on the whiteboard:

GOAL: Change the bulletin board display
PLAN OF ACTION:
  1. Take down the current display
  2. Arrange the new items on the table to see how I want to display them
  3. Staple the new items onto the bulletin board
EVALUATION: Am I pleased with how the new display looks? Are there any changes to be made? How would I do it differently next time? Did I achieve my goal satisfactorily?

Involve your children as much as possible in setting goals with you and carrying out the plans of action so they can gain experience in the process. Explain that plans of action are not written in stone—sometimes changes have to be made. In the above example, perhaps the stapler could not be located, so thumbtacks were used instead to put up the display.

In order for children to learn how to set goals, they need a process to follow. The steps involved in setting goals are as follows:

1. *Determine the Goal.* The goal should always be age appropriate and something the child really wants to achieve. We can encourage children to explore various ideas, but if the goal is not something your child really wants, the chances are she will give up before she even starts. Let's use as an example, a 4th grade student, Sarah, who just received her report card and is not happy with her grade in math. She has determined she wants to set a goal: to earn a better grade in math.
2. *Set up a Plan of Action.* As with the goal, the plan of action must also be age appropriate. The younger the child the more simple the goal, the shorter the time frame, and the fewer the steps to achieve it. Sarah tells her teacher she wants to earn a better grade in math, and her teacher helps her set up a plan of action to achieve her goal:
   1) Complete all seat work assignments.
   2) Complete all homework assignments.
   3) Study for tests and quizzes.
   4) Participate in class.
   5) Show attentive behavior in class.
   6) Ask questions when confused.

7) Work well with others.
   8) Work well independently.
3. *Measuring Success:* How to measure success is different for everyone, and different for every goal. In Sarah's case, her goal may be to raise her grade in math from a D to a C, or from a C to a B, or from a B to an A, depending on what grade she had received previously on her report card. The teacher could help her monitor her success by providing her with a weekly progress report on which the eight steps of her plan of action above are listed. Sarah could keep a checklist of the steps on her desk to remind her of what needs to be done. Her teacher could check the steps of the plan that were completed successfully, as well as give her a grade for the week. At the end of the grading period, if Sarah has indeed achieved her goal and raised her grade in math, her teacher and parents should celebrate her success with her!

Most youngsters are interested in improving their social skills, and this is an excellent area in which to work cooperatively with kids to practice setting and achieving goals. Once the need for a goal is established, such as making new friends, for example, and various options for the plan of action have been devised by the class to achieve that goal, it is helpful to have students role-play and model the various options to see what might work best for them.

IMPORTANT AREAS FOR SETTING GOALS

In an article "Teaching Children Goal Setting" (Blair, 2011), it is suggested that if we want our children to have successful, satisfying, and happy lives, they must learn to set goals in the following areas:

- *To be healthy.* (Set good health goals, such as eating healthy foods, getting exercise, and so on.)
- *To achieve.* (Set goals for academic improvement.)
- *How to manage themselves.* (Set goals to motivate and to improve their attitudes.)
- *To work well with other people.* (Set goals to improve teamwork, cooperation, and so on.)
- *To be more organized.* (Set goals for completing homework, to organize their notebooks, and so forth.)
- *To manage their money.* (Set goals to save part of their allowance, for example.)

It is important to teach kids to set goals in all of the above critical life skills areas. Kids who succeed have goals, and kids who have goals succeed!

In summary, teaching children how to set goals and develop plans for reaching them is one of the most important responsibilities that parents, teachers, and other significant adults in a child's life have. As they grow, their ability to set goals and determine how to achieve them will grow as well. You will be providing your kids with the tools they need to be successful in the present as well as in the future.

STRATEGIES AND ACTIVITIES FOR GOAL SETTING

1. Activity: *My Personal Improvement Plan*
   This activity will help students understand things they like about themselves and things that they could improve on.
   "My Personal Improvement Plan" worksheet:
   A. Three things I really like about myself:
       1. _____
       2. _____
       3. _____
   B. Three things I would like to improve on:
       1. _____
       2. _____
       3. _____
   C. My short-term plan for improving myself (three things):
       1. What? _____
          How? (The Plan) _____
          When? _____
       2. What? _____
          How? (The Plan) _____
          When? _____
       3. What? _____
          How? (The Plan) _____
          When? _____
2. Activity: *The Goal Setting Process*
   Teach children the steps involved in the process of setting and achieving goals. Make sure the goal is something the child really wants to do.
   1) State the Goal—*what do you want to happen?*
   2) The Plan of Action—*what are the steps you will need to take in order to reach your goal?*
   3) Evaluation—*how well did your plan work? Did you reach your goal? What changes might you make for next time?*

4) Celebrate the Success—*good job in reaching your goal!* (praise) *I knew you could do that—you're that kind of person!* (encouragement)
3. Activity: *Goal Setting Games.*

    Playing goal setting games teaches children the process of setting and achieving goals. It isn't what the goal is that matters so much as learning to achieve them. Simple games such as ring toss, horseshoes, and trash can basketball can be used. Using trash can basketball as an example, place the trash can in the corner of the room. Make a ball out of used papers wadded up, wrapped in masking tape. Make a series of lines with masking tape (chalk might be used if playing outdoors). Let each child decide where they want to begin. Some will opt to begin on the first line where it is easy and others will choose to begin on the farthest line, may fail, but can always begin again on a closer line. The goal is to be able to make a basket from the line they chose.
4. Activity: *If I can dream it, I can achieve it.*

    Give every child a sheet of paper and access to pencils, crayons, and/or markers. Have them write this quote at the top and draw a picture of themselves as adults in the center. Then have them draw little pictures around their self-portrait of things they hope to have (e.g., maybe their car, house, big-screen TV, something that represents their profession, and so forth). Allow them to color their pictures, decorate them however they want. Encourage them to keep their pictures in a special place, maybe on their bedroom wall.
5. Activity: *Checkers and Chess.*

    Playing games such as checkers and chess teach children to stop and think before they act. Remind them to look at all of their options and consider whether it is a good move or a bad move for reaching their goal. Emphasize the importance of thinking ahead and asking themselves, *If I do this, what will happen next?*
6. Activity: *Arts and Crafts Projects*

    Arts and crafts can be used to teach goal setting skills. Give children various scraps of material and pieces of yarn and string, as well as construction paper, scissors, and glue and ask them to set a goal of making a picture of something they plan to do or a place they would like to go. They can use their scissors to cut out shapes and pieces and glue them on a large construction paper to make their pictures. They will have to think about and plan their pictures to make them turn out how they want them. They will give their project a title, such as "A Day at the Lake with My Family." The goal would be to create a picture to represent the title by cutting out shapes and forms, using pieces of yarn, string, and so forth.

REFERENCES & RESOURCES

Blair, G. (2011). Teaching children goal setting. *Achieve Goal Setting Success.com.* http://www.achieve-goal-setting-success.com/teaching-children-goal-setting.html.

Charles, C. (2013). *Building classroom discipline* (11th ed.). New York: Pearson.

Cohen, J. (2003). *Teach school children to set and achieve goals.* http://www.solveyourproblem.com/setting-goals/.

Chapter 16

Honesty Issues

Learning the value of honesty is part of the development of moral and emotional strength which helps to develop character and positive self-esteem.

DISCUSSION

Teaching kids the virtues of honesty can be a real challenge, given the examples of dishonesty they will encounter every day in the world around them. Learning the value of honesty is part of the development of moral and emotional strength which helps to develop character and positive self-esteem. It is the backbone for establishing trusting relationships in all facets of life.

Lying, cheating, and stealing often go together. They cause mistrust and suspicion among those affected by the child's actions. Lying is almost always found in situations where there is physical, emotional, or sexual abuse. Kids are often encouraged to lie in situations where there is separation or divorce. Some other possible reasons why kids exhibit dishonest behavior are peer pressure, to get attention, lack of discipline in the home, to protect friends or family members, to get revenge, to avoid obligations, or it may be a hidden cry for help.

INFLUENCES ON HONEST BEHAVIOR

The parents' example as well as the teachers' can be powerful influences on children's behavior. Frequent positive feedback about children's honest behavior can also have a heavy influence on how youngsters behave. Kids need to believe that the long-term positive consequences of honesty are always better than the negative consequences of dishonest behaviors such as lying, cheating, and stealing.

TEACHING THE VIRTUES OF HONESTY

You teach honesty by encouraging kids to tell the truth and that it is okay to let you know what is on their minds. Maintain open communication with your children and give them plenty of opportunities to express their feelings. It should not be a frightening experience for kids to say what is on their minds. They need to feel comfortable telling what events actually happened and that keeping their promises is important.

Teach children that in order to be trusted and to trust others, they need to be honest. Discuss the virtues of honesty and demonstrate, model, and expect those virtues. The following are some points to consider, when teaching children the virtues of honesty:

1. *Discuss what honesty means.* Sometimes children, and even teens, do not understand the fine lines between the truth, lies, "little white lies," telling stories and the world of make-believe. A good way to show the importance of honesty is to read stories where honesty plays a role, such as in *The Little Boy Who Cried Wolf.* You want children to be honest, yet not so honest that they hurt people's feelings. For example, "Linda, your hair looks really terrible today." In this case it is better not to say anything. Other times you might look for something positive to say. Instead of saying, "Grandma, this is a dumb present. I'm too old for teddy bears" you might say, "Thank you for the birthday present, Grandma."
2. *Set a good example.* The best way to teach honesty is to *be* honest. In other words, practice what you preach. If you lie to kids, or they see you lie to someone else, they will think that lying is acceptable. If children ask you questions that you cannot answer for whatever reasons, then rationally explain why. You may have to point out that certain adult issues are inappropriate to discuss with children. You want to avoid the perception that you are evading the truth since that is exactly what you do not want them to do.
3. *Create a safe and secure atmosphere.* Kids are often motivated to lie as a way to avoid getting in trouble. They may give the answer they know the adult wants to hear, rather than the truth of how it really was, out of fear of angering the adult. Kids need to feel it is safe to tell the truth, which is not to say there will not be consequences for not doing the right thing. Be compassionate and caring, but talk to them about why they lied,

what they could have done differently, and what they need to do to make things right. Kids who feel safe and secure are less likely to feel the need to lie in the first place.
4. *Teach children to think before they speak or act.* Some kids are more impulsive than others by nature, and many times lying, stealing, and other acts of dishonesty are the result of not stopping and thinking about the consequences (McCarney, Wunderlich & Bauer. 1993)
5. *Do not overreact if a child is dishonest.* Giving too much attention to negative behavior may actually reinforce it, and they may be more apt to repeat it. On the one hand, kids must not think that dishonest conduct is acceptable, but on the other hand, they should not be so frightened they are afraid to admit the truth. Discuss the misbehavior when you are calm, and the child feels unthreatened.
6. *Praise and encourage the truth.* When you see children being honest about an action or event that seemed particularly difficult for them to share, verbally recognize the courage it took to tell the truth. Thank them for being honest.
7. *Don't ask questions when you know the answer.* If you are quite sure a child has not finished his homework, for example, resist the urge to ask, *Did you finish your homework?* You may be setting the child up to lie to avoid punishment. Instead say, *I see you didn't finish your homework. Was there a problem doing it?* This way, you are able to deal with one problem at a time—the issue of the incomplete homework.
8. *Invoke logical consequences for poor choices.* When children repeatedly violate the code of conduct in regard to honesty which has been agreed upon by the class, logical consequences, established by the group as well, are invoked. This tool is designed to help children make better choices in the future.

ALBERT'S FOUR R'S OF LOGICAL CONSEQUENCES

Albert (1996) stresses that consequences are used to teach proper behavior, not to punish. She emphasizes the four Rs of logical consequences:

1. *RELATED to the issue or event:* The consequence involves an act directly related to the misbehavior. For example, if the child lied about finishing his homework, the consequence might be to have the child call his parents to inform them the homework was not completed.
2. *REASONABLE but not too harsh:* The consequence is proportional to the misbehavior. It is meant to teach students proper behavior, not to punish them.

3. *RESPECTFUL of the student's dignity:* The consequence is administered in a friendly but firm manner without blaming or shaming. For example, *Jack, I see you have chosen not to complete the homework assignment. You may call your mother and let her know.*
4. *RELIABLY ENFORCED:* The educator consistently follows through and invokes the consequence for the misbehavior.

When we allow children to experience the consequences of their actions, we provide honest and real learning situations for them. If logical consequences are used as a threat or are invoked in anger, they cease being consequences and become punishment. Kids are quick to discern the difference. They learn from and respond to consequences; they fight back and rebel when punished. Make a conscious effort to be consistent and persistent.

STRATEGIES AND ACTIVITIES FOR HONESTY ISSUES

1. Activity: *Read stories about honesty.*

    There are many age-appropriate stories that will help you talk about the good reasons to tell the truth and why lying does not work. The following are some examples of books about honesty you can read with your kids:
    1) *The Boy Who Cried Wolf*

        This classic story tells of the young shepherd who cried "wolf" to see if the villagers would come help protect his sheep. The villagers all came running to the field, but there was no wolf. The boy cried "wolf" twice more, the villagers came running, and still there was no wolf. Everyone went back to the village grumbling. Then, the shepherd saw the wolf coming over the hill and began to shout, "Wolf! Wolf! Wolf!" But, no one came to help. They knew the boy had lied several times before. They could no longer believe or trust the boy. So, the wolf ran away with all the sheep.
    2) *The Empty Pot* by Demi

        In this Chinese tale, a young boy named Ping is an excellent gardener. His flowers and vegetables are always the most wonderful. Imagine how excited he was when the old emperor called all the young people together and said, "Whoever grows the most beautiful flower from the seed I give you will become emperor." Each young person got a pot and a seed from the emperor and went home to make the flower grow. Ping watered the seed, gave it fresh soil, fertilized it, but still no flower grew. When it was time to bring the pots and flowers back to the emperor, Ping's seed had not grown at all. But all

the other pots were filled with beautiful flowers. The emperor looks at each flower. Then, he stops at Ping's empty pot and smiles, "You will be the next emperor. The seeds I gave everyone were fake and would not grow. You are the only one who was honest and brought back the pot with the seed you had received."
3) *The Berenstain Bears and the Truth* by Stan and Jan Berenstain
Brother and Sister Bear lie to Mama when they accidentally break a lamp, and the lie grows bigger and bigger.
4) *Edwurd Fudwupper Fibbed Big* by Berke Breathed
Edwurd loves to tell lies. His sister wishes he would notice her, and when she saves him from getting in trouble, he learns to appreciate her. Of course, he still gets a time-out.
5) *Too Many Tamales* by Gary Soto
Maria tries on her mother's wedding ring while helping to make tamales for a Christmas family get-together. Panic ensues when hours later, she realizes the ring is missing.
6) *The Adventures of Pinocchio* by C. Collodi
The adventures of a talking wooden marionette whose nose grows whenever he tells a lie.

2. Activity: *The "Tale of Truth" Trophy*.
This is a motivational way to get children to evaluate their personal honesty. During the "Weekly Class Meeting," ask who had a situation during the past week where it was a challenge to be honest. For older kids, you can have a weekly contest of written honesty reports, with an award with a trophy on it as a prize and perhaps some additional treat. Kids will begin thinking about times when it was particularly difficult to be honest, and it is this kind of thinking and recognition that strongly reinforces honesty.

3. Activity: *Honesty Posters*
Using words that kids can understand, explain what honesty means. Putting up little posters around the classroom or school reinforces the messages. It could also be a project to have kids make them:
- "We are the _____ (mascot) and we tell the truth!"
- "If we have done something dishonest, we own up to it!"
- "We tell the truth even when it is hard to do!"
- "We are honest. That's just how it is in this classroom!"
- "When you tell the truth, people will respect you."
- "Tell the truth and feel better about yourself!"
- "Put brain in gear before putting mouth in motion."
- "Stop! Think! Speak!"

4. Activity: *Multimedia Art Activities* to explore the theme of *honesty:*
1) Use brainstorming to explore ideas related to honesty.
2) Draw a cartoon with conversation bubbles to show a situation of honesty.

3) Create a collage that expresses honesty.
4) Write a poem about honesty.
5) Write a short story about honesty.
6) Write a song about honesty.
7) Keep an *Honesty Journal* and write about the times you were honest or dishonest.

5. Activity: The Dilemma Game (Goh, 2011)

Present various age-appropriate scenarios that describe a moral dilemma involving honesty and ask children to respond. The following are some examples:
- You are in a grocery store and you see a young girl put a lollypop in her pocket. What should you do?
- Bill was at his friend's house and he found a dollar on the floor. What should he do?
- Jane was playing with her friend's toy and accidentally broke it. What should she do?
- John saw some boys teasing a younger child. What should he do?
- Carol's dad ordered two sandwiches but was charged for only one. What should he do?
- Danny found a toy car on the ground in front of his neighbor's house. What should he do?

REFERENCES & RESOURCES

Albert, L. (1996). *Cooperative discipline.* Circle Pines, MN: American Guidance Service.

Begun, R. (Ed.). (1996). *Social skills lessons & activities for grades 4-6.* West Nyack, NY: The Center for Applied Research in Education.

Goh, K. (2011). *Teaching honesty to our children.* Retrieved March 2011. http://ezinearticles.com/?Teaching-Honesty-to-Our-Children&id=1651126.

Chapter 17

Listening Skills

In one of the Family Circus cartoons, the little girl looks up at her father, who is reading the newspaper, and says: "Daddy, you have to listen to me with your eyes as well as your ears.""

DISCUSSION

The passive nature of *hearing* is very different from the active nature of *listening*. Hearing is the *physical* ability in which the ears receive sound and transmit those waves to the brain. Listening is a *skill* that is learned and allows for comprehension of those sounds. It is an important skill for academic and social development and requires focusing and concentration. It is essential for success in school and helps us understand the world around us.

Basically, listening skills are fundamental to learning, since they enable us to acquire insights, information, and knowledge, and to achieve success in communicating with others. Poor listening skills can lead to unnecessary arguments and problems and decreased academic performance.

THE PROCESS OF LISTENING

The process of listening can be summed up in the following three steps:

1) The most basic step of listening is *hearing* whatever the speaker has just said. Hearing the information correctly is important in order to retain it and recall it at a later date.

2) The next part of listening is to *understand.* This means that you have not only heard the information, but you have taken the knowledge you have acquired and comprehend it in your own unique way.
3) The final step of listening is making a *judgment.* You have heard the information, you have understood it in your own way, and then you make a decision as to whether the information makes sense to you. Do you believe what you have just heard or not?

IMPORTANCE OF LISTENING SKILLS

The value of learning listening skills cannot be underestimated. It is estimated that between 50 percent and 75 percent of students' classroom time is spent listening to the teacher, to other students, or to audio media (Smith, 1992). Listening skills are essential for learning since they enable students to acquire information and insights, and to achieve success in communicating with others. Learning to listen is fundamental in learning to read since listening and oral language are integral parts of the reading process.

Kids who listen well are more likely to understand and follow directions and less likely to make unnecessary mistakes. This means they spend more time on task and use their time more wisely and efficiently. Students with good active listening skills are generally more successful than their peers who are passive listeners. They do not have to spend much time asking questions, clarifying information, or correcting mistakes.

In one of the Family Circus cartoons, the little girl looks up at her father, who is reading the newspaper, and says: "Daddy, you have to listen to me with your eyes as well as your ears." That statement says almost all there is to say about listening, whether in our personal conversations or in learning in school.

TEACHING LISTENING SKILLS

Significant adults should model good active listening skills to kids. If educators half-listen to kids, they learn to half-listen back. Listening skills are an important part of communication and are essential for success in school, as well as later on in the work force. Consider the following tips when teaching children to be good listeners:

1. Explain the importance of listening, as well as your expectations for the child to listen and follow directions.
2. Make sure you have your youngster's attention when you speak. Kids can be easily distracted, so if they are engrossed in a game or in a

conversation with classmates, they may not hear you. To overcome this issue, you might ask them to respond in a particular way, so you know they are listening. It might be, *Yes, Mrs. Smith*, or some agreed-upon phrase such as *Escucho* (which means "I'm listening" in Spanish). It is always fun to have a secret code.
3. Reduce distracting stimuli in the immediate environment. This may mean sitting the child in the front row or going to a special carrel or "office space" away from distractions. Include the child in deciding where he or she feels more comfortable working. Be sure this is a strategy for reducing distractions and not a form of punishment.
4. Reinforce good listening skills. You could keep a star chart on the wall and kids earn stars that could lead to treats or special privileges for listening well, such as listening to a story on tape at a learning center. The more motivated kids are to listen, the more likely they will develop the skill quickly.

In summary, listening skills are essential to children's overall development. They are important to social development and the ability to interact and communicate with others. They are fundamental to academic success.

STRATEGIES AND ACTIVITIES FOR DEVELOPING LISTENING SKILLS

1. Activity: *"Active Listening" Exercise*
   Kids can be taught to be good active listeners, but they need to have the opportunity to practice. Have students find a partner and give topics to relate, such as "Something Good That Happened at School This Week." After the first student has related his story, have them switch roles. The following list of active listening skills should be provided for kids to follow:
   1) Maintain eye contact when someone is speaking to you.
   2) Do not interrupt the speaker.
   3) Stand or sit still while the speaker is talking.
   4) Nod your head to show that you are understanding and interested in what the speaker is saying.
   5) Lean slightly toward the speaker when he or she is talking to you.
   6) After the speaker is finished talking, ask questions for clarification or respond appropriately to what the speaker has related to you.
2. Activity: Provide *Practice in Listening*
   Parents and teachers of preschoolers should begin teaching their kids listening skills at an early age. The following are some activities that teach listening skills which may be adapted for older kids as well:

1) Read stories as often as possible to your children, pausing from time to time to ask age-appropriate questions to check for comprehension.
2) Reading "chapter books" to older children after they come in from lunch/recess is a fun, positive, and calming exercise which enhances listening skills.
3) Even preteens and adolescents can hone their listening skills by being read to. Popular teen magazines might be a source, with stories about rock stars, music, movie and television celebrities, racecar champions, and so forth.
4) Watch an age-appropriate video with your students, followed by questions about the presentation.

3. Activity: *Taking Notes*

Students' listening skills may be enhanced and tested by asking them questions about what they have heard. By the third grade, students may be given practice in taking notes and can be asked questions about important facts in the presentation. They can be taught to recognize the difference between the main points and less relevant ideas and information. Taking notes during a cartoon video is a fun activity which gives kids practice in picking out the main points of the story.

4. Activity: *Active Listening Games*

Play games that require active listening to be successful, such as *Simon Says, Red Light, Green Light* or *Mother/Father May I*. The following are some other ideas for games:

1) *Cooperative Learning Games*: Divide the class into groups of four students and give each team a card with a scenario on it that they have to act out without directly stating where they are. The other groups put their heads down or cover their eyes and listen to the skit. They have to determine where the skit takes place by what they hear. For example, a card says, "camping out." The team members talk to each other about camping-related topics such as setting up a tent, building a fire, and roasting hotdogs. After five minutes, stop the dialogue and allow a couple of minutes for the other groups to discuss what they heard, and then guess what the scenario is. The scenarios should increase in complexity depending on the age of the students. Some examples of other scenarios might be *At the Lake, At an Amusement Park, At the Zoo, At the Park.*
2) Use "Time-Filler" listening games for when there are a few minutes before the bell rings or time to go to lunch:

- *Who Is It?* Start describing a student, such as the color of eyes and hair, type of shirt or blouse, and so on, until someone guesses who it is.
- *What Is It?* Start describing the physical properties, uses, and so forth, of an object in the classroom until someone guesses what it is.

5. Listen to a story on a CD or a short, high-interest news broadcast on the internet. Then set a timer for ten minutes and have the children write a summary about what they heard. After the timer sounds, have the children share what they remembered about the story.
6. Use math and reading games that require active listening skills. Memory activities are fun to play and reinforce the skill of remembering what has been said when having to recall verbalized information.

REFERENCES & RESOURCES

Rose, D. & Dalton, B. (2007). *Learning through listening in the digital world.* Wakefield, MA: Center for Applied Science Technology, Inc., No. 40.

Smith, C. (1992, Fall). *Do listening skills affect learning?* ERIC Clearinghouse on Reading and Communication Skills. http://www.proteacher.com/redirect.php?goto=2419.

Wallace, T., Stariba, W., & Walberg, H. (2004). *Teaching speaking, listening and writing. Educational Practices Series-14.* Geneva, Switzerland: International Education Academy. http://www.ibe.unesco.org.

Chapter 18

Motivation Concerns

Education is not the filling of a pail, but the lighting of a fire.

—William Butler Yeats, Irish Poet
and Playwright (1865–1939)

DISCUSSION

Young kids are naturally curious, and they learn from exploring and discovering. If their explorations bring pleasure and success, they will want to learn more. During the early years, youngsters form attitudes about learning from significant others that will last a lifetime. Children are born with an innate curiosity to learn, but by the time they reach school, their motivation has often been lost or replaced by extrinsically motivated learning strategies (Carlton & Winsler, 1998).

If parents, teachers, and other significant adults nurture a child's self-confidence and curiosity and provide resources that invite exploration, they instill the message that learning is useful, fun, and exciting. Kids who receive this kind of support and encouragement will be creative, adventurous learners throughout their lives.

Kids who do not receive this kind of support and encouragement are likely to have a much different attitude about learning, not only as young children, but as students in school and as adults later in life, unless someone comes along and sparks their desire to learn. As the Irish poet and playwright William Butler Yeats (1865–1939) so eloquently stated, "Education is not the filling of a pail, but the lighting of a fire."

INTRINSIC AND EXTRINSIC MOTIVATION

Youngsters engage in activities either to please themselves or to please others. When they do things simply because they want to do them, we say they are "intrinsically motivated." The motivation comes from within. Other activities they do either because they have been told by someone to do them, or in an effort to please others, then we say they are "extrinsically motivated," or motivated by some outside force.

Intrinsically motivated activity is more gratifying, and children learn more and retain the learning better. These kids are more creative and more involved in their own learning and development. Unstructured play is an essential component of children's motivation, learning, and development (Carlton, 2003).

It is more difficult for a child to maintain extrinsically motivated activities because the motivation has to be continually provided for the child to maintain interest in the activity. Extrinsically motivated children have a more difficult time learning because they are continually reliant upon some outside force.

Praise for accomplishments is appropriate, but be sure kids do tasks because they want to, because they are interested, not because they think it will bring praise or rewards from you. It is better to praise specific abilities, such as persistence, hard work, or concentration, rather than completion of the task.

Difficulties arise when kids are provided with too many external rewards such as candy, class bucks, or excessive praise. Kids then begin to feel successful only if someone rewards them for their accomplishments. This can severely interfere with youngsters' motivational development.

If children lose their intrinsic motivation, they may feel successful only if someone else judges them as successful. This will interfere with their sense of self-worth and they will judge their own value by someone else's standards. "Striking the spark that motivates a child produces an internally fueled quest for success that no amount of external rewards, threats or pleas can equal" (Goldstein, 2010).

GLASSER'S CHOICE THEORY

According to Glasser (1999), behavior is not caused by an outside stimulus at all, but by what an individual wants most at any given time. More commonly known as Choice Theory, Glasser contends that *all* behavior is intended to satisfy one of the following five basic internal needs:

1. To survive and be protected from harm.
2. To belong and be loved by others.

3. To have power and importance.
4. To have freedom and independence.
5. To have fun—emotionally and intellectually.

This theory bridges the diversity gap because it focuses on how all individuals are alike, rather than how they are different. By understanding the drives and needs for survival, belonging, love, power, significance, freedom, independence, and fun, we become more aware of the need for our world to be a quality world of our choosing and of our making.

HOW MOTIVATION AFFECTS KIDS' ATTITUDES

Motivated kids are more likely to choose tasks that are challenging, begin tasks without having to be urged, and show effort and concentration. They tend to be persistent until successful completion when working on tasks and have a positive attitude toward schoolwork and learning in general. Motivated kids maintain a joy for learning for its own sake, even in the face of their struggles and frustrations.

Unmotivated kids, on the other hand, choose work that is inappropriately easy, need lots of prodding to get started on a task, and put forth minimal effort. They give up easily, leave tasks unfinished, and have a negative or apathetic attitude toward schoolwork and learning. Based on these characteristics, it is not difficult to see why motivated youngsters are more successful in school.

NURTURING INTRINSIC MOTIVATION

Parents and teachers play a large role in whether kids are motivated or not to do their best in school. In the end it is up to the youngsters, but you can create an encouraging environment conducive to the development of motivation in children. Consider the following strategies to encourage intrinsic motivation in children (adapted from *The Parent Institute*, 2005):

1. *Set appropriate expectations.* When you *expect* children to succeed, their chances for success improve greatly; *expect* them not to do well and the odds are they won't. Children are usually aware how parents and teachers view them, and they often adapt their actions to fit those views. This is why it is important to have appropriately high expectations, based on children's strengths and weaknesses, and to communicate them to your youngsters.

2. *Help your children set goals.* First, children need to know what they are expected to do, and then they need a plan how to do it. Goals turn ideas into actions, into reality. Teach kids the steps involved in the process of setting and achieving goals (see Chapter 15, "Goal Setting," for more information). Make sure the goal is something the child really wants to do, then teach him the process to set and achieve goals:
   1) *State the Goal.* The goal should always be age appropriate and, as mentioned before, something the child really wants to achieve.
   2) *The Plan of Action.* As with the goal, the plan of action must also be age appropriate. The younger the child, the more simple the goal, the shorter the time frame, and the fewer the steps to achieve it.
   3) *Evaluation.* A measurable goal allows you and the child to chart the progress. How to measure success is different for everyone, and different for every goal. If the goal is not measurable, change it.
   4) *Celebrate the Success.* Rather than providing excessive praise for completing tasks successfully, which promotes *extrinsic* motivation, praise, encourage, and reward such qualities as persistence, perseverance, focusing, and concentrating.
3. *Provide messages of encouragement more often than praise.* Even though parents and teachers enjoy praising children with phrases such as, *Good job! That looks great! Way to go!* research shows that messages of encouragement has a greater effect than praise on children's motivation. So, what is the difference between praise and encouragement? Praise is saying, *Way to go!* while encouragement is adding, *I knew you could do it, you're that kind of person.* Some characteristics of encouraging messages are as follows:
   1) They notice effort and progress. *You really worked hard on that project! I can tell you spent a lot of time on that assignment! Your focusing skills have really improved!*
   2) They use descriptive words. *Look at that neat handwriting! I like the way you took your time and did the assignment carefully. You really followed the directions well.*
   3) Encouragement can be given regardless of the child's performance. *I can see you're disappointed, but I know you will keep trying. That didn't work out the way you wanted, so what do you think you might do differently next time? You have really worked hard on that project. I'm impressed with your perseverance.*

The big difference between praise and encouragement is that praise leads children to rely on your evaluation of their accomplishments, whereas words of encouragement lead them to form their own positive assessment of themselves. Encouragement makes motivation soar!

TIPS TO ENCOURAGE MOTIVATION

Given the choice between ability and hard work as the most important key to success in school and in life, hard work is by far the most important (Goldstein, 2010), or as Albert Einstein put it, "It's not that I'm so smart, it's just that I stay with problems longer." By finding ways to motivate children to work hard and make the most of educational opportunities, educators can help their children use whatever strengths and abilities they have now in order to experience success and encourage future learning. The following are suggestions to encourage motivation among children:

1. Create a warm, supportive, and caring environment where kids feel respected, valued, and appreciated.
2. Enhance children's sense of belonging by giving them responsibilities from which the class group would benefit. When kids are provided with opportunities to contribute to the group, they develop responsibility, compassion, and a social conscience (Goldstein, 2010).
3. Involve kids in formulating class rules (a.k.a. code of conduct) and the consequences for failure to comply. When kids are involved in the process, they learn to "own" their behavior.
4. Emphasize children's strengths, their "islands of competence" (Goldstein, 2011), and support them as they work on their weaknesses. Find out what children are interested in and encourage their passions.
5. Use consistent discipline, a system generated by the group, and maintain an organized, calm classroom conducive to focusing and concentrating. This type of discipline promotes self-discipline and self-worth.
6. Vary your teaching methods and make the lessons interesting and enjoyable. For example, play "Trash Can Basketball" to review for a unit test (see the section "Strategies and Activities for Motivation Concerns," #3), or play a form of "Bingo" to learn new words. This meets every child's basic need to have fun—having a good time intellectually and emotionally.
7. Emphasize cooperation rather than competition and provide opportunities for kids to help one another. This develops compassion and empathy, essential character qualities for successful kids.
8. Let children know you have faith in them, *as they are*, not as they could be. Like them so they can like themselves. Send the message, *"You are the kind who can do it."*

Motivation is truly the secret to help children develop to their full potential. Motivated children develop resilience, and resilient kids are ready for whatever challenges life throws at them.

STRATEGIES AND ACTIVITIES FOR MOTIVATION CONCERNS

1. Educators *determine and support your students' learning styles*. Children are more likely to want to learn if they use the learning style they feel most natural and comfortable using. Help them figure out, and use, their best learning style. The following are descriptions of the various learning styles:
    1) *Auditory Learners*. These kids feel motivated and engaged when they can integrate more *listening* into schoolwork. Here are some ways to motivate auditory learners:
        - Have the child record himself reading, reviewing spelling words, practicing math facts, and so forth.
        - Use rhymes, songs, jingles, and associative words (letters or words that make you think of other words) to remember facts.
        - Have your youngster ask friends and family members to give him an oral quiz, such as spelling words, math facts, history facts, and so on.
        - Suggest that he talk himself through a problem, such as *"i before e except after c"* when learning to spell certain words, or *"multiply and divide before you add and subtract"* when doing order of operations in math.
        - Audio books, or books on tape, are found in most public libraries as well as in schools, and these kids love listening to stories being read to them.
    2) *Visual Learners*. These kids feel more motivated when they can integrate *seeing* into their schoolwork. Here are some ways to motivate visual learners:
        - Have the child use color whenever possible. Taking notes using different colored pens, writing spelling words "rainbow style," highlighting key concepts, and so forth.
        - When reading a book, suggest they go through and look at all the pictures, charts, and diagrams first and see if they can figure out what they are illustrating from the text.
        - Help the child make a visual chart of drawings to depict what he needs to get accomplished.
        - Flashcards work well for visual learners. They may be used for spelling words, math facts, vocabulary words, or anything he needs to memorize.
    3) *Kinesthetic Learners*. These kids feel more motivated and engaged when they can integrate more *doing* into their schoolwork. These ideas can be used to motivate kinesthetic learners:

- Encourage these youngsters to look for ways to make learning "hands-on." For small children, counters can be used to learn addition and subtraction; for older children they can be used to divide into halves, thirds, and fourths to learn fractions. Spelling words can be learned by using Scrabble® tiles.
- Try to help these students combine focused study with physical activity whenever possible. For example, after thirty minutes of focused study, they can do an activity with manipulatives for ten minutes.
- Reading comprehension can be taught by having these learners act out passages from the book they are reading.
- Encourage these kids to do "hands-on" projects. They love to create things and they shine at science fairs and art shows. Participation in these types of projects boosts their self-esteem, which in turn boosts their level of motivation.

2. Make learning interesting and fun by varying activities.
   1) *Trash Can Basketball* might be used to study for a unit test.

   Divide the class into teams of about five members each. Place a trash can in the corner of the room with masking tape strips on the floor at various intervals where students can choose to shoot from—first line = one point, second line = two points, and so on. Ask a student a unit question, if he answers it correctly, he gets to shoot from the line of his choice. The team with the most points is the winner and they get a treat. Use either a Nerf® ball or make a ball out of discarded papers wadded and wrapped in masking tape.
   2) A variation of Bingo can be used for teaching vocabulary, history facts, geographical locations, and the like.
   3) Math games can be used to stimulate and encourage learning math facts and other principles.

REFERENCES & RESOURCES

Albert, L. (1996). *Cooperative discipline.* Circle Pines, MN: American Guidance Services.

Carlton, M. & Winsler, A. (1998, Spring). Fostering intrinsic motivation in early childhood classrooms. *Early Childhood Education Journal, 25*(3), 159–66.

Davies, L. (2004, February). *Motivating children.* http://www.kellybear.com/TeacherArticles/TeacherTip42.html.

Dinkmeyer, D. & Dreikurs, R. (1963). *Encouraging children to learn.* New York: Hawthorn Books, Inc.

Fanning, R. (2008, October). *Fostering motivation in kids with learning and attention problems.* http://www.greatschools.org/special-education/support/816-motivating-kids-learning-attention-poblems.gs.

Goldstein, S. (2010). Questions and answers about resilience. *SamGoldstein.com.* Retrieved November 2010. www.samgoldstein.com/articles/articles29.pdf.

The Parent Institute. (2005). *Seven proven ways to motivate children to do better in school.* Fairfax, Station, VA: The Parent Institute.

Stipek, D. (1993). *Motivation to learn: From theory to practice.* Needham Heights, MA: Allyn & Bacon.

Chapter 19

Organizational Skills

The more organized kids are, the more empowered they are to have control over their own educational pursuits, as well as personal lives.

DISCUSSION

Teaching your kids organizational skills is an important responsibility shared by parents and educators. They are essential skills for school-age children as they meet increasing educational demands. Many capable kids of all grade levels experience frustration and sometimes even failure in school, not because they lack ability, but because they do not have adequate organizational skills (National Association of School Psychologists, 1998). These skills are crucial for success in school, as they foster competence, persistence, and positive attitudes about learning. Developing good organizational skills is a key ingredient to ensure success in school and in life.

THE BENEFITS

All kids, regardless of their age, can learn strategies and techniques to become more organized. Kids need to see how setting goals will make their lives better. Motivate your kids to learn organizational skills, such as setting goals, by pointing out the benefits:

1. You spend less time on homework assignments, because you have a plan of action to complete them.

2. You get less frustrated and overwhelmed, because you know what tasks needs to be done, and you know the steps you need to take to do them.
3. You will have a sense of ownership of your tasks.
4. You will feel more pride in your work and have a feeling of satisfaction when the work is completed.
5. They will help you be more successful in your future, such as when you go to college or get a job. You are already in training to be whatever it is you will become someday.

The more organized kids are, the more empowered they are to have control over their own educational pursuits and personal lives. They are able to manage daily responsibilities, have the ability to plan ahead, and will be more likely to experience success and productivity that will have lifelong effects.

SETTING AND ACHIEVING GOALS

Setting and achieving goals is one of the most important aspects of acquiring organizational skills. By learning how to set and achieve goals, how to overcome challenges, and how to measure their own progress, children learn how to increase their chances for success now and throughout their lives.

Blum (1998) suggests using the following criteria for formulating a goal: (1) set a specific time frame to complete it, (2) make it concrete enough to plan and take action, (3) make it specific enough to observe and check progress, (4) make it realistic and achievable, given past experience, and (5) make it independent of another person's actions. Make sure the goal is something the child really wants to do. Once the goal has been established, provide kids the following steps for the process of setting and achieving goals:

1. State the Goal—*what do you want to happen?*
2. The Plan of Action—*what are the steps you will need to take in order to reach your goal?*
3. Evaluation—*how well did your plan work? Did you reach your goal? What changes might you make for next time?*

Suggest making a "My Goals Journal" to your young people. Take a few pages of typing paper, fold the pages in half, staple down one side, and decorate the cover. Using the steps above, have them set goals that will help make their lives more organized.

STRATEGIES AND ACTIVITIES FOR ORGANIZATIONAL SKILLS

Appropriately, assigned seatwork and homework is vital for learning and development, as new skills require a great deal of practice to achieve mastery. Kids need the independent practice to reinforce learning so they can become proficient. The following suggestions will help them to manage their time, to work independently, and to complete multistep projects:

1. *Have students keep a Daily Planner or Agenda Book.* All students need to have a daily planner or agenda book large enough to write instructions and other reminders, such as what supplies will be needed. Check the planner at the end of the day to make sure all assignments have been written down accurately.
2. *Teach students to take notes.* Communicate instructions clearly, have students repeat them if necessary, and teach them to take notes in their planners concerning the instructions. Write assignments and complex directions on the board in addition to saying them, and have kids write them into their planners. Teach students how to highlight important information.
3. *Have students monitor and chart their work completion.* Give kids a weekly chart where they can enter their assignments and indicate when they are completed and turned in.
4. *Break down large assignments into manageable tasks.* For example, when a book report is assigned, make a checklist of the tasks to be completed:
    1) ___ Choose a book
    2) ___ Make time to read each day
    3) ___ Take notes about what you read each day
    4) ___ Using your notes, write a rough draft of the report
    5) ___ Write the final report
    6) ___ Turn in the report.
5. *Provide children with an "Oranizational Think Sheet"* (Bos & Vaughn, 1994). This is especially helpful for lengthy assignments, such as book reports and science projects, as well as new, difficult information being taught. You might include the following information on the "Think Sheet":
    1) What is being explained?
    2) Materials and supplies you will need
    3) Class notes
    4) Steps to complete the project
    5) Date for completing the project

6. *Use Checklists.* As students master new skills, they can check them off their list. Checklists can also be used to ensure all steps or procedures are followed, such as in the book report checklist above. It gives them a sense of accomplishment and a feeling of competence, which enhance self-esteem and self-confidence, as they become more self-managing individuals.
7. *Assist students in keeping organized notebooks.* They can be organized in various ways. They might use dividers for the various academic subjects with sections for "Work to Do," "Work Done," "Notices," "For Parents," and the like.
8. *Encourage students to conduct a weekly clean-up.* Urge students to go through their backpacks, notebooks, desks, lockers, and so forth, to sort out their books and supplies, clean out trash, and put completed papers in their "Take Home" folder or "Class Portfolio"

REFERENCES & RESOURCES

Bos, C. & Vaughn, S. (1994). *Strategies for teaching students with learning and behavior problems* (3rd ed.). Boston: Allyn & Bacon.

National Association of School Psychologists (NASP). (1998). Teaching study skills: A guide for parents. Adapted from a handout by Virginia Smith Harvey (University of Massachusetts, Boston), published in *Helping children at home and school: Handouts from your school psychologist.* http://www.teachersandfamilies.com/open/parent/homework1.cfm.

White, H. (2011). *How to teach children organizational skills.* Live Strong. http://www.livestrong.com/article/78655-teach-children-organization-skills/.

Chapter 20

Personal-Social Issues

Having faith in your kids allows them to develop faith in themselves.

DISCUSSION

One of the major components in children's personal-social adjustment is the development of the self-concept—their personal perceptions of themselves and the world around them. An important factor in the development of the self-concept is the primary need to *belong*. Children must feel that they are valued by the group, that they contribute to the general welfare of the group, in order to feel a sense of belonging to the group. Children who exhibit fear, anxiety, sadness, isolation, and other antisocial behaviors at school often lack a sense of belonging to their various social groups.

Most misbehavior is the result of children trying unsuccessfully to meet the psychological need of belonging to their social group. They want to feel secure, wanted, and valued, and fortunately, most students are able to achieve this sense of belonging through acceptable behavior.

As mentioned previously, when students are unable, for whatever reason, to achieve a sense of belonging by acceptable means, they often turn to the *mistaken goal*, that through misbehavior they can somehow fulfill this need to belong, such as the "Class Clown" or the "Class Troublemaker."

MEETING KIDS' BASIC NEEDS

The need to belong is a fundamental psychological need of every child. Research conducted by Baumeister and Leary (1995) shows that all human beings, children included, need a certain minimum amount of regular, satisfying, social interaction. The inability to meet this need results in feelings of loneliness, mental distress, and a strong desire to form relationships of any kind.

FOSTERING POSITIVE PERSONAL-SOCIAL DEVELOPMENT

The following are suggestions for fostering positive personal-social development in kids:

1. Create a warm, supportive, and caring atmosphere where kids feel respected and valued.
2. Boost kids' sense of belonging by giving them responsibilities that would benefit the class.
3. Involve kids in making the class code of conduct and consequences for violations to enhance a sense of ownership and responsibility for their own behavior.
4. Emphasize children's strengths. Do not dwell on their weaknesses but be supportive and encouraging as they work on self-improvements.
5. Define tasks in specific, short-term goals that can help kids associate effort with success.
6. Make expectations clear and provide positive feedback and credit for putting forth effort.
7. Emphasize cooperation rather than competition and provide opportunities for kids to help one another. This develops compassion and empathy—valuable character traits.
8. Provide kids with as many social and academic successes as possible.

Teachers can actually bring about a change in personal-social adjustment through their relationship with the child. As they act in an encouraging manner, the child's *mistaken attitudes* may be reshaped. As the personality of the child develops, certain beliefs about life begin to emerge. These beliefs are about himself, his values and goals, and about others and how they feel toward him. The teacher who is concerned about the individual is usually able to recruit the support of the class.

DIFFERENT STROKES FOR DIFFERENT FOLKS

It is important to acknowledge, however, that not all children are, by nature, outgoing. Some children like to hang around with a crowd, while others prefer to hang out with one or two close friends. Some children like to play outside games with friends, or group games, such as sports. Others prefer to play jump rope or hop-scotch with one or two friends.

Albert (1996) warns against labeling these children as "shy," a "loner," or "antisocial" in their presence, because children tend to live up to their labels. It is also important not to pressure the child into changing, for the more the pressure, the more the resistance in most cases. Contrary to popular opinion, introverted children are not asocial, nor are they friendless loners who lack social skills. They simply have different social needs and preferences (Bainbridge, 2010).

YOUR ATTITUDE MAKES A DIFFERENCE

It is paramount, then, that you, as educators, provide positive, social learning experiences for the child experiencing personal-social difficulties. You must show faith in the child's value as a person. Having faith in your kids allows them to develop faith in themselves. Your relationship with the child becomes a model for other class members to follow. As kids are guided in becoming responsible for their own actions and recognized for their contributions to and participation in their social groups, their social skills, self-esteem and self-concepts are nurtured and enhanced. They are becoming self-determining and self-managing individuals.

STRATEGIES AND ACTIVITIES FOR PERSONAL-SOCIAL ISSUES

1. Enhance kids' sense of belonging by giving them responsibilities from which the class would benefit. The following is a list of examples that might be adapted:
   - Classroom Monitor (such as checking for names and dates on student seatwork, making sure everyone has a pencil, checking to see if everyone is on the correct page)
   - Hall Monitor
   - Cafeteria Monitor
   - Restroom Monitor
   - Class Announcer (e.g., making announcements such as time for lunch, time to get spelling books out, get ready to go home)
   - Sergeant-in-Charge of Whiteboards (erasing/cleaning)
   - Sergeant-in-Charge of the Pencil Sharpener (emptying, sharpening pencils for the teacher, and so on)
   - Sergeant-in-Charge of Handing Out Materials
   - Sergeant-in-Charge of Holding the Door
   - Sergeant-in-Charge of Classroom Litter

- Sergeant-in-Charge of School Ground Litter (several students take turns picking up litter on the playground during recess and receive some type of acknowledgment or reward for their "school service")
- Class Clerk (laminate an unofficial attendance card and have the student put a star beside all students present that day)
2. Initiate a Peer Tutoring Program. Give the child the responsibility of tutoring another student. It may involve tutoring a student from the same class who is having difficulty with a particular activity or partnering with another class and sharing peer tutors. Another option is having lower-functioning kids tutor students from a lower grade level.
3. Invite the child to be a leader of a small group activity for which he possesses mastery of the skills or in which he shows an interest in that area.
4. Be certain to recognize the child as often as possible for appropriate social interactions.
5. Teach the child appropriate positive ways to make requests (such as, "Please pass the paper." "Will you please help me?" "May I sharpen my pencil?"). This can be accomplished through modeling and role-playing.
6. Invite the student to act as the Teacher's Assistant for an activity (e.g., holding up visuals, writing on the whiteboard, demonstrating an activity).
7. Communicate with kids on an individual basis as often as possible, in order to determine their needs and give positive feedback for appropriate social behavior.
8. Communicate with parents or appropriate parties to inform them of a problem in order to determine the causes. Be sure to include the child in finding solutions to the problem.
9. Encourage children to use problem-solving skills when dealing with personal-social problems:
   1) Identify the problem.
   2) Determine the goal.
   3) Develop strategies.
   4) Form a plan of action.
   5) Carry out the plan.
   6) Evaluate how successful the plan was.

REFERENCES & RESOURCES

Albert, L. (1996). *Cooperative discipline.* Circle Pines, MN: American Guidance Service.

Baumeister, R. & Leary, M. (1995). The need to belong: Desire for interpersonal attachments as a fundamental human motivation. *Psychological Bulletin, 117,* 497–529.

Dreikurs, R., Grunwald, B., & Pepper, E. (1982). *Maintaining sanity in the classroom.* New York: Harper & Row.

Chapter 21

Problem-Solving Skills

When you share some creative problem-solving techniques, you have given a lifelong gift.

DISCUSSION

Problem solving in children is a critical survival skill. It is also one of the most important skills for personal and academic success (Loh, 2009). Learning how to solve problems provides the following benefits for children:

1. Development of confidence and courage;
2. Stimulation of learning and comprehension;
3. Enhancement of self-image and self-esteem;
4. Ability to face challenges and confront difficulties.

In our everyday lives, at school, at play, at work, we are constantly being challenged with problems to solve. Some people rise to the challenge and see them as opportunities for growth and development. They have a clear and systematic way of approaching problems which works in most cases.

Others fear the challenge and have no set process for tackling their problems. Once children have developed problem-solving skills, the ability will serve them throughout the rest of their lives. When you share some creative problem-solving techniques, you have given a lifelong gift.

A PROBLEM-SOLVING PROCESS

As adults, we solve problems every day without even thinking about the process we use to do it. But children have not had the experience or practice and they need guidance in learning the process of problem solving. Always stress how important it is to first identify the problem accurately. Unless you are completely clear on the details of the problem, solving it becomes difficult, if not impossible. Understanding the exact nature of the problem can be one of the biggest roadblocks when it comes to teaching problem-solving skills. The following are some suggested questions to ask when identifying the problem (Terry, 1993):

1. What should happen or not happen if this problem is solved?
2. When did the problem start?
3. How often does the problem occur?
4. When does the problem not occur?

Identifying when a problem is *not* happening can be as enlightening as identifying when it *is* happening. Problem solving is basically a process of identifying a problem, determining what you want to happen, forming a plan of action, carrying out the plan, and then evaluating how well the plan worked to solve the initial problem.

Admitting to and owning a problem, making a plan, and following through with it are not always an easy thing to do, even for adults. It means excuses are not acceptable, and it means one must accept responsibility for one's own actions, including mistakes, and deal with the consequences.

THE "THINK BEFORE YOU ACT" PRINCIPLE

Begun (1996) encourages significant adults to teach children to resolve problems through communication and to "think before you act." In other words, do some detective work and investigate the problematic situation to get a better understanding of what the problem truly is. Ask questions and get all the facts before establishing the need to resolve the problem.

Once the need is firmly established, then list your options to satisfy that need. List the negative and positive consequences for the options, and based on those consequences, make an *informed decision* on a plan of action to resolve the problem. After the plan has been carried out, evaluate the actions and ask if the problem was resolved satisfactorily.

USING PROBLEM SOLVING TO SETTLE DISPUTES

When teaching kids the problem-solving process to settle disputes, Nelson, Lott, and Glenn (1997) suggest using the following steps:

Step 1 might be to leave the area of conflict for a cooling-off period.
Step 2 is an opportunity for students to tell each other how they feel, to listen to each other, to figure out what they might have done to contribute to the problem, and to tell the other person what they are willing to do differently.
Step 3 involves brainstorming possible solutions or simply apologizing.
Step 4 lets kids know it is okay to ask for help, and they may choose to put it on the "class meeting agenda." If the problem is too serious to wait for a class meeting, they may need immediate assistance from peer mediators, the teacher, or the school counselor.

In everyday lives, children are constantly being challenged with problems to solve and disputes to resolve. Competence in effective problem solving is critical for resiliency. When children have developed the skills necessary to solve problems, they have a clearer and more systematic way of tackling life's challenges. This gives them a greater degree of self-confidence and contributes to an enhanced self-esteem and sense of well-being.

STRATEGIES AND ACTIVITIES FOR PROBLEM-SOLVING DIFFICULTIES

1. Encourage children to use problem-solving skills. The following brief outline might be used as a guide:
   1) Identify the problem. *What is the problem you want to solve?*
   2) Determine the goal. *What do you want to happen?*
   3) Develop strategies. *What are some ways you could deal with the problem? Which ones might be a good move? Which ones might be a bad move?*
   4) Choose one solution. *Choose the solution you think would best deal with your problem.*
   5) Make a plan of action and do it. *What are the steps you will need to take in order to make that solution happen? Try it and see how it goes.*
   6) Evaluate how well the plan worked. *Did your plan solve your problem?* (If not, have the child go back to #3 and choose another solution.)

2. Model the problem-solving process for children by talking through your thought process as you deal with everyday problematic situations.
3. Discuss problem-solving approaches to hypothetical situations. Use news events, storybook plots, or invent situations and have the children discuss what strategies could be used to resolve the problematic situation.
4. Playing games such as Checkers and Chess teach children to stop and think before they act. Remind them to look at all of their options and consider whether it is a good move or a bad move. Emphasize the importance of thinking ahead and asking themselves, *If I do this, what will happen next?*
5. Activity: *Problem solving through arts and crafts*

    Arts and crafts can be used to teach problem-solving skills. Give children various scraps of material and pieces of yarn and string, as well as construction paper, scissors, and glue, and ask them to make a picture of something they like to do or a place they would like to go. They can use their scissors to cut out shapes and pieces and glue them on a large construction paper to make their pictures. They will have to think about and plan their pictures to make them turn out how they want them. Have them write their goal, or what they want their pictures to depict. Then have them write down the steps they think will be needed to reach their goal. Tell them to evaluate if their plan led to achieving their goal.
6. Activity: *Glued Shoes*

    This is an initiative test of the group's ability to cooperate and solve the problem of moving together. This is surprisingly difficult, but very inspiring when the group together figures out how to solve the problem. It can be done!

    Instructions: Divide the class into two teams. Give them the following steps:
    1) *Stand together side by side in a line. Your feet should be comfortably spaced about equal distance as your shoulder width. Every foot must be touching the foot of the person on each side of you.*
    2) *The problem is to move together, as if your shoe were glued together to the shoe of the person on each side of you.*
    3) *As a group, you have to walk to the finish line (about twenty feet away) without separating your feet from your partner's. You have to keep your shoes "glued" together.*
    4) *If your shoe separates from the shoe of your partner, the group has to stop and walk back (separately) to the starting line and start over.*
    5) *The first team to solve the problem of keeping your shoes together and cross the finish line wins.*

REFERENCES & RESOURCES

Begun, R. (Ed.). (1996). *Social skills lessons & activities for grades 4-6.* West Nyack, NY: The Center for Applied Research in Education.

Coloroso, B. (1994). *Kids are worth it! Giving your child the gift of inner discipline.* New York: William Morrow.

Loh, A. (2009). *Teaching problem solving skills to children—Why are they so important?* http://www.brainy-child.com/articles/teach-problem-solving-skills.shtml.

Nelsen, J., Lott, L., & Glenn, H. (1997). *Positive discipline in the classroom.* Rocklin, CA: Prima.

Chapter 22

Respect for Authority

Children who have been taught to be respectful toward authority figures, and toward each other, have a greater advantage to succeed in life.

DISCUSSION

Respect is one of the most important values we can teach our children. *Respect for authority* means that a person possesses and shows a high positive regard for the worth of those individuals who make important decisions concerning his or her life and who provide directives to live by.

It is an attitude that will have a huge impact on children's sense of wellbeing at home and their ability to succeed at school. Respect is not the same as obedience. Children might obey out of fear of punishment. If they respect you as parents and educators, they follow your directives because they know you want what is best for them.

We should do all we can do to make sure our children have the best opportunity possible to live successful and contented lives. Children who have been taught to be respectful toward authority figures, and toward each other, have a greater advantage to succeed in life. Ultimately, a healthy respect for authority will positively impact their futures by becoming productive and well-adjusted individuals in their work worlds, in their communities, and in the larger society.

KIDS LEARN FROM ADULT MODELING

Respect is an abstract concept and there is no step-by-step model to use for teaching kids respect for authority. Ideally, they learn to respect authority from the time they are very young, but unfortunately this does not always happen. Just as the best way to teach a child how to love is to show love, the best way to teach a child respect is to show respect.

Children imitate the behavior of the significant adults in their lives, and as kids experience being respected, they begin understanding the importance of it. Respect for self, for peers, and for authority are all part of the process of learning about respect. The following are some ways adults model and encourage respect in children (Bell, 2009; McChesney, 2009; Faerber, 2011):

1. *Be honest.* Honesty means saying and doing what is true. It is a straightforwardness of conduct. When dealing with children and others, always be as honest as possible. If you say or do something wrong, admit it and apologize.
2. *Be positive.* Do not embarrass, insult, or make fun of children. Encourage them to do the right thing and compliment them when a task is completed successfully.
3. *Keep promises.* Make promises that you can keep and keep the promises that you make. Adults who fail to keep their word teach kids that it is okay to break promises. If you expect kids to keep their word and follow through with what they say they will do, then you must do the same. This teaches children to be reliable and trustworthy.
4. *Be trusting.* Allow children to make choices whenever possible and trust that they will make good decisions for themselves. *Expect* kids to take responsibility for their actions and make good choices.
5. *Show compassion.* This means having a sympathetic awareness of others' distress. When adults show that they care about the feelings and needs of their young people, they are teaching them about compassion.
6. *Be forgiving.* When you show forgiveness, you give up feelings of resentment for something someone has said or done. When you forgive kids, you teach them how to let go of bad feelings for someone, and they feel they have another chance to do good. When kids make mistakes, let them know they are still loved. Let them know you may not have liked something they *did*, but you still like *them* as a person.
7. *Be generous.* Showing generosity means sharing what you have. By modeling kindness through acts of sharing with your children, they learn to be generous and share with others. Sharing is caring!
8. *Show loyalty.* Loyalty means being faithful to the friendship or relationship you have with someone. By being loyal to your children, you are teaching them to hold your mutual relationship in high regard.
9. *Be fair.* Kids are more likely to show respect for adults who make fair rules. Involve your kids in making classroom and family codes of conduct, as well as the consequences for violations. Kids are more apt to

follow the rules and abide by the consequences when they have had a voice in making them. Encourage children to tell their side of the story and listen carefully to what they have to say before making conclusions.

In order for children to develop a healthy respect for their authority figures, the authority figures must show respect to *each other*. It is not uncommon for parents to put each other down, or for parents to bad-mouth teachers.

The expectation of success is a complex relationship involving teachers, parents, and children. It assumes an atmosphere of respect and trust. Snide, angry, or distrustful remarks undermine respect and trust. The way significant adults respect themselves, respect others, and respect authority figures in their own lives will set the stage for how their kids will show respect for themselves and others. Kids follow the principle "do as I do" not "do as I say."

TIPS FOR ENCOURAGING COMPLIANCE

One of the principal complaints that teachers and parents have in regard to respect for authority is noncompliance with adult requests. A teacher gives an assignment and the child just sits there or is busy doing something else. A mother tells her child to go pick up her toys in her room, and she continues watching TV. Here are some strategies you might try to encourage compliance with requests (Albert, 1989; Bell, 2009; Faerber, 2011):

1. "Catch" a child doing something right, then make a positive request where compliance is practically guaranteed. For example, the class has been given a math sheet to do, and Jimmy is just sitting in his seat staring into space. You walk up to him and say, *Even though you aren't working on your math sheet, I like the way you are sitting quietly and not bothering anyone, Jimmy. Here's a star for you to put at the top of your math sheet.* Once he has put the star on his sheet, say something like, *Thank you, Jimmy, for following directions and putting the star at the top of your math sheet. Now please get busy on your assignment. I will come back in a few minutes to see if you have earned another star.*
2. Defiance of authority is usually grounded in the need for control, so go ahead and give the child some control by offering fixed choices. For very young children, it might just be a matter of offering two different pencils with which to do the work. *Susan, would you like to use the yellow pencil or the red pencil to write your spelling words?* For older children you might offer a choice such as, *David, you have a choice. You can begin working on your math sheet, or you can read silently for ten minutes. You*

decide. If the student still doesn't get busy, you might say, *Do you need me to make a choice for you?* That will usually trigger a response.
3. A variation of the fixed choice strategy is to make one of the choices totally undesirable so the child will choose to respond in the way you want. *You may choose to do your math sheet now, or you may choose to go to detention after lunch and do it.* If he chooses to do his math sheet now, thank him for complying with your request, that you appreciate his cooperation. Tell him you are proud of how he is taking responsibility for completing his work. This will give him the attention he is most likely seeking.
4. Sometimes noncompliance is the result of not understanding the directions, rather than a deliberate attempt to defy authority. The child may be embarrassed to ask questions in front of his peers, so have the child repeat the directions to you quietly, in his or her own words, to make sure they are correctly understood.
5. Even though you may get exasperated with noncompliant children, do not lose your cool. Keep your composure and use a normal tone of voice. Since kids tend to model the adult's behavior, remain calm so things do not escalate.

As children learn to behave in a respectful manner, there will be times when you may have to confront inappropriate behavior. If a child says or does something which shows disrespect, take time to talk to the child privately, in a quiet, nonthreatening manner. Point out the behavior that was disrespectful, explain why it was disrespectful, and have the child help you come up with a response that would have been more appropriate for the situation. Point out that you agree to be respectful to him, and you are asking for the same in return.

CREATING A MUTUALLY RESPECTFUL CLIMATE

Educators and parents promote a climate of mutual respect when they use encouragement strategies. Albert (1989) provides the Three C's of belonging, which are as follows:

1. Help kids feel *CAPABLE*.
    - Make mistakes okay. It is not a crime to make errors.
    - Build confidence.
    - Focus on past success.
    - Recognize achievement.
2. Help kids *CONNECT*. Give your kids the five A's:
    - *Acceptance*. Accept kids just as they are, regardless of culture, abilities, disabilities, and personal style, so they will learn to accept others just as they are.

- *Attention.* Give kids your attention when they are speaking, so they will learn to give you attention when you are speaking.
- *Appreciation.* Give positive acknowledgment of kids' accomplishments and good deeds.
- *Affirmation.* Recognize and appreciate acts of respect, courage, cheerfulness, persistence, and so forth.
- *Affection.* This means developing a closeness to your kids, showing them that you care about them. Nothing is required in return to receive your affection.
3. Help kids *CONTRIBUTE.*
    - Encourage kids to contribute to the class.
    - Encourage kids to help each other. This develops compassion and empathy.

Borda (2001) is concerned that lack of respect is rampant in most segments of society, manifested in the decline of civility, rise of vulgarity, fall of the golden rule, disrespect for authority, and low respect for children (from Charles, 2013). She makes the following suggestions for dealing with disrespect:

1. Discuss, model, and teach the differences between respect and disrespect.
2. Encourage respect for authority and stifle rudeness. This is accomplished by teaching respectful "replacer" behaviors by using signals to call attention to sassiness, back talk, vulgarity, and other types of disrespect.
3. Emphasize and expect good manners and courtesy. Help kids to learn the basic manners that will enable them to function productively in society.
4. Involve peers in creating a respectful learning environment and reinforcing each other's pro-social, respectful behavior (Borba, 2001, p. 131).

As children's primary role models, parents and educators have the greatest influence on them as they learn respectful ways of relating to others. Children learn to have respect for themselves and for others by first experiencing respect from significant adults in their lives.

REFERENCES & RESOURCES

Albert, L. (1989). *Cooperative discipline: How to manage your classroom and promote self-esteem.* Circle Pines, MN: American Guidance Services.

Bell, R. (2009). 5 tips for teaching students to respect authority. *The Apple: Where Teachers Meet and Learn.* Retrieved October 2009. http://theapple.monster.com/benefits/articles/7576-5-tips-for-teaching-students-to- respect-authority.

Borba, M. (2001). *Building moral intelligence: How to raise kids with solid minds and caring hearts.* San Francisco: Jossey-Bass.
Charles, C. (2013). *Building classroom discipline* (11th ed.). New York: Pearson.
Faerber, Y. (2011, May 8). *Teaching our children respect.* The Parent Institute. http://beepdf.com/doc/129347/teaching our_children_respect.html.
McChesney, S. (2009). Respect–How to teach it and how to show it. *Teachnology.* Retrieved October 2009). http://www.teach-nology.com/tutorials/teaching/respect/.
Nelsen, J., Lott, L., & Glenn, H. (1997). *Positive discipline in the classroom.* Rocklin, CA: Prima.

Chapter 23

Respect for Self and Others

Practice what you preach, because kids will do as you do, not do as you say.

DISCUSSION

Respect is one of the most important character traits we can develop in our kids. *Respect for others* means that a person possesses and shows a high positive regard for other individuals around him or her. It is an attitude that will have a huge impact on children's ability to get along with others at home, in the school setting, and in their neighborhoods.

Ultimately, a healthy respect for others will positively impact their futures by increasing their chances of becoming well-adjusted coworkers in their work worlds, respected members of their communities, and contributing citizens in the larger society. As you will note, there are many similarities in teaching children respect for authority and respect for themselves, peers, and other significant individuals in children's lives, so some of the information will be repetitive.

MODELING RESPECT

"Respect" is an abstract term, and as such, there is no step-by-step process for teaching an attitude of respect. It has been pointed out that the best way to teach children how to love is to show them love, and it holds true, the best way to teach children how to respect is to show them respect. Kids imitate the behavior of significant adults in their lives and as they experience being respected, they begin comprehending how important it is. The way significant adults model respect for themselves and others in their lives will determine how their kids will respect themselves and others as well.

RESPECTFUL WAYS OF RELATING

Vassar (2011) provides a list of suggestions for some basic ways we can show respect when relating to others. These are also characteristic of reflective and active listening skills. They can be modeled by adults and role-played by children:

1. Face the person who is talking to you when possible.
2. Make appropriate eye contact for the situation.
3. Use facial expressions that are friendly and match what the person is expressing.
4. Use body language that is open and accepting, such as nodding, smiling, and connecting emotionally with others.
5. Stand or sit straight. Slouching gives a message of disinterest.
6. Give the other person time to express thoughts, feelings, needs, concerns, beliefs, or perspectives.
7. Use *I Messages* to share your feelings or opinions. Do not state opinions as facts. (I feel/felt___ when you ___ because ___.)
8. When there are disagreements, maintain your cool and speak with a calm voice.
9. Speak slowly and clearly when you want to be understood.
10. Do not interrupt the speaker.
11. Be polite and courteous when speaking to others.
12. Be caring about other's feelings and concerns.

When having kids role-play the above ways to show respect, provide a variety of scenarios for them to act out. For example, "face the person who is talking to you when possible," have the child begin talking to you and turn away or turn your back to the child. Ask the child how it made him/her feel when you turned away. Then have the child begin talking to you again and give him/her your full attention. Discuss how both scenarios would make them feel.

TEACHING RESPECT TO KIDS

Silverman (2008) points out that children will take their cues from you, the important adults in their lives. If you show respectful behavior, they will learn it. If you show disrespectful behavior, they will learn that as well. He provides ten tips on teaching respect to children:

1. *Model it*: If you want them to do it, you have to do it, too.
2. *Expect it*: When your expectations are reasonably high, children will rise to the occasion.
3. *Teach it*: Give kids the tools they need to show respect by providing various situations for them to respond to.
4. *Praise it*: When you see or hear your kids using respectful language and making respectful choices, recognize it and praise them for making positive, respectful decisions.
5. *Discuss it*: Be on the lookout for times when you see other kids using respectful or disrespectful language or behavior and discuss it with your kids.
6. *Correct it*: Be strong, firm, and direct when teaching respect. Be sure you are being respectful yourself when correcting the behavior.
7. *Acknowledge it*: Be sure to notice when respectful behavior is being exhibited as well as calling them on disrespectful behavior.
8. *Understand it*: Your kids are growing, learning, and changing. Sometimes word choices and behavioral decisions are made because they do not have the appropriate words or behavior to express how they are feeling, such as *I'm tired*, *I'm frustrated*, or *I'm angry*.
9. *Reinforce it*: Remind kids of their good decisions so they remember how they felt, the praise they received, and the overall experience of being respectful.
10. *Reward it*: Respectful behavior should be something kids want to do without overindulgent rewards. However, it is appropriate to associate respectful behavior with positive consequences, such as praise, encouragement, recognition, extra privileges, and an occasional tangible reward.

As children's primary role models, parents and educators have the greatest influence on the learning of respectful ways to relate to others. Youngsters learn to have respect for themselves and for others by first experiencing respect from the most important adults in their lives—their parents and teachers.

We should do all we can do to make sure our kids have the best opportunity possible to live successful and self-determining lives. Kids who have been taught to be respectful toward themselves and others have a greater advantage to succeed. Teaching respect to children takes patience, time, and a willingness to do what you preach, as kids will take their cues from you, the important adults in their life.

REFERENCES & RESOURCES

Charles, C. (2013). *Building classroom discipline* (11th ed.). New York: Pearson.

Faerber, Y. (2011, May 8). *Teaching our children respect*. The Parent Institute. http://beepdf.com/doc/129347/teaching_our_children_respect.html.

McChesney, S. (2009). Respect–How to teach it and how to show it. *Teachnology*. Retrieved October 2009. http://www.teach-nology.com/tutorials/teaching/respect/.

Silverman, R. (2008, April 12). *10 tips on teaching respect to children: You can't get it if you don't give it!*. http://www.drrobynsilverman.com/parenting-tips/10-tips-on-teaching-respect-to-children-you-cant-get-it-if-you-dont-give-it/.

Vassar, G. (2011, April 28). Respect: One antidote for shame. *Educational Network*. http://lakesideconnect.com/anger-and-violence/respect-one-antidote-for-shame/?gclid=CLeh7Yy2oKkCFQUGbAodblJAvQ.

Chapter 24

Self-Discipline

We need to talk self-discipline, walk self-discipline, and live self-discipline, because everything we say and do and don't say and do is a lesson for kids.

—Debbie Roswell, "Guide to Self-Discipline"

DISCUSSION

Self-discipline is an essential attribute we must help our young people develop. It means taking ownership, accountability, and responsibility for one's own behavior. It gives young people the ability to think before they act, improves their relationship with others, enables them to perform better at school, and to become good problem-solvers and decision-makers.

Teaching kids self-discipline will help them to get along with others, to control their impulses, to make good choices, to organize their lives, and to stay safe. Gordon (1989) contends that the only truly effective discipline is self-discipline that occurs internally in each child. We must guide young people in making positive decisions, becoming more self-reliant, and controlling their own behavior.

Self-discipline and self-control are learned skills, but changes in our culture have created a generation of kids used to getting what they want, when they want it—whether it be the latest hi-tech cell phone, current fad in athletic shoes, or even a new car when they reach driving age. Their lives are saturated with instant gratification from technology that delivers information and entertainment results faster than ever.

The difficulty lies in how this instant gratification has affected our kids' values and character, especially in the area of self-discipline and self-control. It has affected their ability to wait, to think before they act, and to foresee potential consequences of their actions (Whitehead, 2011).

As troubling as today's culture may be, teaching kids self-discipline has always been part of a parent's job, with teachers sharing the responsibility during school hours. Parenting and teaching may be more challenging in today's world, but it does not mean we give up on our kids. It means we make even more of a concerted effort to guide our kids in ways that promote the development of self-discipline.

In today's competitive, fast-moving world, children and teens can make big mistakes that have serious, even lifelong, consequences. That is why self-discipline and self-control are so important, and this is why parents need to help guide their kids to find and listen to that small voice inside—the one that reflects values, knowing what is right and wrong, and leads to sound reasoning (Fay & Cline, 2000). We are their role models and as their guides, we need to *talk* self-discipline, *walk* self-discipline, and *live* self-discipline, because *everything we say and do and don't say and do is a lesson for kids* (Roswell, 1999).

Dr. Stephen Covey, recognized as one of *Time Magazine*'s 25 most influential Americans and internationally respected family expert, puts it well, "You have to put your ladder of success up to the right wall, or you will never find success, no matter how hard you climb" (Roswell, 1999). To do the best job we can at guiding children's development, we have to know where we are headed—what it is we want our kids to learn.

DEVELOPING SELF-DISCIPLINE IN KIDS

Self-discipline is an essential quality for all kids, as they learn how to manage their time, to work independently, and to complete multistep projects. If students do not acquire the self-discipline needed to complete homework assignments on time, for example, they will struggle in their adult lives. It is important that expectations and goals for self-discipline be age appropriate for each stage of development, thus it is essential for educators to be familiar with what is normal and what is not when it comes to their children's lack of impulse control. Some other suggestions for developing self-discipline include the following:

1. Keep a Daily Planner or Agenda Notebook to track homework and other activities.
2. Have the child come up with a system to ensure that homework is not only completed but turned in.

3. Focus on feelings to help kids build an internal reward system and not rely on external rewards. You want them to eventually be motivated by the good feeling of a job well done.
4. Put your attention on positive behaviors and if they mess up, do not make a big deal out of it. Do not lecture, shame, or embarrass them—let them experience the natural consequences of their actions. The more attention you give to poor choices, the more you reinforce them, and the less self-discipline they will exhibit.
5. Have kids monitor and chart their own completion of tasks. "To-do" checklists are valuable in teaching kids to be independent. This will help kids to be more self-managing.
6. Allocate kids ample time when working on difficult tasks to allow for persistence. When kids are deeply involved in an activity, try to make sure they can finish without interruption.
7. Be cautious about using praise. They tend to undermine kids' ability to value themselves. They should be based on specific skills and behaviors, such as effort, hard work, and persistence, rather than on the actual completion of the task.
8. Encourage kids to take on extra activities that require self-discipline. Sports is an example.

Responsibility is *doing the right thing even when no one is watching*. The rewards for being responsible are called *privileges*. Remember to always include kids when formulating logical consequences for compliance and non-compliance to the rules or code of conduct. They have a right to be involved in decisions which affect their lives.

STRATEGIES AND ACTIVITIES FOR DEVELOPING SELF-DISCIPLINE

1. Activity: *My Situations Journal* (grades 3 +)
    Allow the children to choose a name for their journal, such as *My Self-Control Journal*, *My Personal Journal*, *My Annoyance Journal*, or *My Feelings Journal*. When problems arise, suggest that they write the following information in their journals:
    1) What was happening *before* the incident?
    2) What happened *during* the incident?
    3) What happened *after* the incident? (Include the consequences of the actions.)
    4) What could you have *chosen* to do differently? Why?

(Younger children might keep a picture journal of times when they showed self-control and times when they lost control. Then have them circle the times when they showed proper self-control.)
2. Activity: *We've Got a Problem*

   Give children a variety of problematic scenarios, and using the problem-solving format below, have them practice resolving the issues.

   Instructions:
   1) Identify the problem. *In your own words, what is the problem?*
   2) Determine the goal. *What do you want to happen?*
   4) List the options. *What are some ways you could choose to deal with the problem?*
   5) Choose one option. *Choose the way you think would be best.*
   6) Carry out the plan. *Follow through with the best option.*
   7) Evaluate how successful the plan was in solving the problem.
3. Activity: *SODAS*

   Use SODAS, a decision-making process to teach kids self-control. *SODAS* stands for Situation, Options, Disadvantages, Advantages and Solution. Provide various scenarios and allow the children to practice resolving the issue using this model. The purpose is to teach kids to reason out a situation and evaluate the advantages and disadvantages of choices before making a decision.

   Instructions for the five-step SODAS decision-making process:
   1) Identify the *Situation*. What exactly is the decision to be made? Be specific about the issue to be decided. Answer the *who, what, where, when,* and *why* questions. Try to avoid being emotional, because emotion tends to hamper judgment.
   2) List all of the *Options*. What are the possible choices at hand? List both the good and bad options, even those that show out-of-control behavior.
   3) List the *Disadvantages* of each option given above.
   4) List the *Advantages* of each option given above.
   5) Choose a *Solution*. Take time to think about the solutions, then choose which option might be the best one.
4. Activity: Play "thinking" games, such as Checkers and Chess.

   Playing games such as checkers and chess teach children to stop and think before they act. Remind them to look at all of their options and consider whether it is a good move or a bad move for reaching their goal. Emphasize the importance of thinking ahead and asking themselves, *If I do this, what will happen next? If I make this move, what move will my opponent make?*

REFERENCES & RESOURCES

Brooks, R. & Goldstein, S. (2001). *Raising resilient children.* New York: McGraw-Hill.

Coloroso, B. (1994). *Kids are worth it! Giving your child the gift of inner discipline.* New York: William Morrow.

Fay, J., Cline, F., & Sornson, B. (2000). *Meeting the challenge: Using love and logic to help children develop attention and behavior skills.* Golden, CO: The Love and Logic Press, Inc.

Roswell, D. (1999). Guiding self-discipline. *Today's Child.* http://www.angelfire.com/on3/todayschild/discipline.htm.

Whitehead, S. (2011). How to teach kids self-discipline. *Parenthood.* http://www.parenthood.com/article-topics/how_to_teach_kids_selfdiscipline.html/full-view.

Chapter 25

Self-Esteem

> *With unconditional support early on, children internalize positive regard so that when they are older, they can approve of themselves, pat themselves on the back, give themselves psychological hugs.*
>
> —Dr. Susan Harter, Psychologist

DISCUSSION

Most parents want their children to have a healthy sense of self-esteem, and this desire can also be seen in education, with schools around the country including self-esteem among their goals. Self-esteem refers to the extent to which young people expect to be accepted, cared for, and valued by the adults and peers who are important to them. Simply put, when we talk about the need to have a healthy self-esteem, we usually mean that children should have "good feelings" about themselves.

Kids with a healthy level of self-esteem feel that the significant adults and peers in their lives accept them, care about them, and would go out of their way to make certain they are safe and well. Kids with low self-esteem, on the other hand, feel that the important adults and peers in their lives do not accept them the way they are, do not care much about them, and probably would not go out of their way to ensure their safety and well-being.

FACTORS THAT CONTRIBUTE TO POSITIVE SELF-ESTEEM

The extent to which kids *believe* they have the characteristics valued by the significant adults and peers in their lives, the greater are the chances they will develop a positive self-esteem. Take, for example, families, communities, and even schools that put a high value on athletic ability. The children who excel in athletics are much more likely to have high levels of self-esteem, whereas those who are judged as less athletic, physically inadequate, or clumsy tend to suffer from low self-esteem.

In Harter's Self-Perception Profile for Children (1985), she divides self-esteem into the following domains: (1) scholastic competence, (2) athletic competence, (3) physical appearance, (4) peer acceptance, (5) behavioral conduct, and (6) general feelings of self-worth. She goes on to say that "general feelings of self-worth" are related to two independent factors: (1) one's feelings of competence in the domains one *believes* are important and (2) emotional and social support from important adults, family members, and peers.

It is important to understand that families, communities, and various ethnic and cultural groups differ in the criteria on which self-esteem is based. For example, some cultural groups may emphasize physical appearance, and some may judge boys and girls differently. Stereotyping, prejudices, and discrimination of certain groups are factors that may contribute to low self-esteem among children (Katz, 1993). The four key aspects of improving children's self-esteem, according to Santrock, (1997) are as follows:

1. *Identifying the causes of low self-esteem and the domains important to the child.* Children have the highest self-esteem when they perform competently in the domains important to the self.
2. *Emotional support and social approval.* Both adults and peer support are important influences on a child's self-esteem.
3. *Achievement.* In Erik Erikson's 4th stage of development, "Industry vs. Inferiority," children develop a higher self-esteem when they are able to achieve goals they make.
4. *Coping.* Self-esteem increases when a child faces a problem and tries to deal with it rather than avoiding it.

FOSTERING KIDS' SELF-ESTEEM

As parents and educators, our kids are our life's work. We want our children to have all the self-confidence, self-worth, and self-esteem they need to be successful and happy in life. Helping children to have optimum levels of self-esteem is one of the most important goals of parents and educators. As Harter (1996) points out,

> With unconditional support early on, children internalize positive regard so that when they are older, they can approve of themselves, pat themselves on

the back, give themselves psychological hugs—all of which contribute to high self-esteem. Another major part of self-esteem, beginning at age eight, is feeling competent and adequate across various domains of life. One does not have to feel competent in every domain in order to experience high self-esteem. Rather one needs to feel competent in every domain that he or she judges to be important. (Harter 1996, p. 38)

The foundations of self-esteem are laid early in life and as youngsters learn to trust their parents and others who care for them to satisfy their basic needs, they begin to feel wanted, valued, and loved. According to Maslow's Hierarchy of Needs (1943), the basic needs that must be satisfied are (1) esteem, (2) friendship and love, (3) security, and (4) physical needs. If these fundamental needs are not met, the child will feel anxious and tense, negative conditions for the development of positive self-esteem.

As children grow, their self-esteem is related to their feelings of belonging to, and adequately functioning in, their various social groups, such as the family, the school class, and their circle of close friends. Albert (1996) devised *the three Cs* to help children feel they belong, thus increasing self-esteem: capable, connect, and contribute. The following summarizes the main points of this strategy:

CAPABLE or *I-Can Level:*

1. *Make mistakes okay.* The fear of failure and making mistakes often undermine a child's sense of feeling capable, and when feeling fearful, many will not try. Let kids know that mistakes are a natural part of learning something new. Teach kids to learn from their mistakes and move on.
2. *Build confidence.* In order for kids to feel capable, they must have confidence that success is possible. Think of learning as a process of improvement, and when improvement occurs, acknowledge it.
3. *Focus on past successes.* Very few people are motivated by having their mistakes pointed out. On the other hand, when they experience success, they will continue moving forward.
4. *Make learning tangible.* Provide children with tangible evidence of their progress. Grades such as "B" and "satisfactory" are not effective because they tell little about specific accomplishments. Albert suggests using I-Can cans, accomplishment albums and portfolios, checklists of skills, and flowcharts of concepts. (I-Can cans are coffee cans that have been decorated and are used by younger children, in which kids place strips of paper indicating skills they have mastered, books they have read, and so on.)
5. *Recognize achievement.* By giving attention to kids for accomplishments, you increase kids' sense of feeling capable and their level of self-esteem.

Have students acknowledge each other's accomplishments in class, recognize students at award ceremonies, set up exhibits, and make presentations for other classes and for parents.

CONNECT: Help students connect, which means they initiate and maintain positive relationships with peers and teachers. Albert accomplishes this by using *The Five A's:*

1. *Acceptance* means communicating to kids that it is okay to be as you are, in regard to culture, race, abilities, disabilities, and personal style.
2. *Attention* means making yourself available to kids by sharing time and energy with them.
3. *Appreciation* requires showing kids that you are proud of their efforts and accomplishments or pleased by their behavior.
4. *Affirmation* refers to making positive statements about kids, statements that recognize desirable traits, such as cheerfulness, bravery, enthusiasm, kindness, thoughtfulness, persistence, and helpfulness, to name a few.
5. *Affection* refers to displays of kindness and caring freely given and not dependent on desirable behaviors, such as rewards are.

CONTRIBUTE: Help students contribute by making them feel *needed* and *valued* by the group. Some of the ways you can do this are as follows:

1. *Encourage students to contribute to the class.* This is done by asking for opinions and preferences about such matters as class requirements, routines, the class code of conduct, and the consequences for violations of the code.
2. *Encourage students to contribute to the school.* Assign school service time in which students perform such tasks as dusting shelves, beautifying the classroom, and cleaning the school grounds, all of which instill a sense of pride in the school.
3. *Encourage students to contribute to the community.* An example would be to adopt a health-care center or nursing home and provide services such as reading, singing, and writing letters for the residents. Promote volunteerism by suggesting students volunteer their services to local institutions. Encourage random acts of kindness, such as opening doors for people and helping them with their packages. You might keep a box labeled "Random Acts of Kindness" in which kids can drop notes about acts of kindness they have either observed a peer perform or that they themselves have done. They can be read at the end of the day or in "class meetings."

4. *Encourage students to work to protect the environment.* One suggestion is to adopt a street or section of the community and keep it litter free. Another suggestion is to recycle paper, glass, and plastic.
5. *Encourage students to help other students by*
   - establishing a *circle of friends* who make sure everyone has someone to talk with, to sit with during lunch, and to play with at recess;
   - doing *peer tutoring*, to help students who are having difficulties with an activity;
   - providing *peer mediating* where students mediate disputes between other students;
   - giving *peer recognition*, where students recognize efforts and contributions of fellow students.

Educators, parents, and caregivers give emotional and social support to kids as they grow and mature. They play an important role in strengthening self-esteem by treating children respectfully, taking their views and opinions seriously, and expressing appreciation to them. Helping children learn to feel secure about themselves and helping them learn how to make everyday decisions that affect their lives will serve as solid footing for lifelong learning.

Doing well in school, being able to manage feelings, and making friends and keeping them are all areas that kids must learn. Children who learn these skills adequately, who feel capable of success, and who feel connected as contributing members of their social groups will feel positive about themselves and this will serve them well into adulthood. The following is a quote from a teacher, Haim Ginott (1972). Think about how this could hold true for your role as an educator:

> I've come to the frightening conclusion that I am the decisive element in the classroom. It's my personal approach that creates the climate. It's my daily mood that makes the weather. As a teacher, I possess a tremendous power to make a child's life miserable or joyous. I can be a tool of torture or an instrument of inspiration. I can humiliate or humor, hurt or heal. In all situations, it is MY response that decides whether a crisis will be escalated or de-escalated and a child humanized or dehumanized.

STRATEGIES AND ACTIVITIES FOR ENHANCING SELF-ESTEEM

1. Activity: *Tangible Evidence of Progress*

   Teachers should provide tangible evidence of student progress to increase feelings of capability and thus, self-esteem:

1) *I-Can Cans.* These work well for younger kids. Take empty coffee cans, have students decorate them, and then place strips of paper indicating skills they have mastered, books they have read, and any other accomplishments they have had. This strategy gives kids a sense of accomplishment, which enhances self-esteem. The cans are also useful for sharing in parent-teacher conferences.
2) *Accomplishment Albums and Portfolios.* These are appropriate for older students. Students place evidence of personal accomplishments in albums or portfolios. These accomplishments might include papers written, book reviews for books they have read, projects completed, and evidence of skills attained.
3) *Checklists.* Some classes might use lists of specific skills as objectives. As students attain the skills, they check off the objective. Graphs and charts can also be used to indicate progress. Most academic programs contain flowcharts which can be duplicated and kept with students' records, which show where the student began, where he is now, and how much progress has been made.
4) *Recognize Achievement.* Have students recognize each other's accomplishments, recognize students at award ceremonies, set up bulletin boards to display improved work, and make presentations of student accomplishments for parents and other classes.

2. Activity: *Goal Setting*

Setting goals and achieving them gives kids a sense of accomplishment, which leads to feelings of capability, which enhances positive self-esteem. Make sure the goal is something the child really wants to do. (See chapter 15, "Goal Setting," for more ideas.) The steps in setting and achieving a goal are as follows:
1) State the Goal—*What do you want to happen?*
2) The Plan of Action—*What are the steps you will need to take in order to reach your goal?*
3) Evaluation—*How well did your plan work? Did you reach your goal? What changes might you make for next time?*
4) Celebrate the Success—*Good job in reaching your goal!* (praise) *I knew you could do that!* (encouragement)

3. Activity: *My Personal Improvement Plan*

This activity will help kids understand things they like about themselves and things that they could improve on.

"My Personal Improvement Plan" worksheet:

A. Three things I really like about myself at school:
    1. _____
    2. _____
    3. _____

B. Three things I would like to improve on at school:
   1. _____
   2. _____
   3. _____
C. My short-term plan for improving myself:
   1. What? _____
      How? (The Plan) _____
      When? _____
   2. What? _____
      How? (The Plan) _____
      When? _____
   3. What? _____
      How? (The Plan) _____
      When? _____

4. Activity: *My Self-Improvement Journal*

   As a class or home project have children keep a journal in which they enter goals for self-improvement, including the date set, the goal, the plan of action, measuring success, and the date achieved. The goals will not all be major life decisions. Have them enter as many little goals they can think of that would improve their life. Students might want to divide their journals into three sections: at home, at school, and with my friends. The "My Personal Improvement Plan" worksheet may also be used as a guide for writing up goals in the journal.

5. Activity: *"If I can dream it, I can achieve it"* picture.

   Give every child a sheet of paper and access to pencils, crayons, and/or markers. Have them write this quote at the top and draw a picture of themselves as adults in the center. Then have them draw little pictures around their self-portrait of things they hope to have and achieve (e.g., their car, house, big-screen TV, something that represents their profession, some sport they might excel in, and so forth). Allow them to color their pictures, decorate them however they want. Mount them on construction paper and laminate them. Encourage them to keep their pictures in a special place, maybe on their bedroom wall.

REFERENCES & RESOURCES

Albert, L. (1996). *Cooperative discipline.* Circle Pines, MN: American Guidance Service.

Erikson, E. (1963). *Childhood and society* (2nd ed.). New York: Norton.

Ginott, H. (1972). I am angry! I am appalled! I am furious! *Today's Education,* 61, 20–25.

Harter, S. (1985). *Manual for the self-perception profile for children.* Denver: University of Denver.

Katz, L. G. (1993). *Distinctions between self-esteem and narcissism: Implications for practice.* Urbana, IL: ERIC Clearinghouse on Elementary and Early Childhood Education. ED 363 452.

Maslow, A. (1943). A theory of human motivation. *Psychological Review, 50*(4), 370–96.

Santrock, J. (1997). *Life-span development* (7th ed.). New York: McGraw-Hill.

Chapter 26

Separation Anxiety

Without treatment, as many as 40–50% of these youths are at risk for not graduating from high school due to the intensity and chronic nature of their anxiety.

—Christopher A. Kearney, Clinical Child Psychologist

DISCUSSION

Although it can be difficult, separation anxiety is a normal stage in development. From approximately eight months of age through the preschool years, healthy youngsters may show intense distress and anxiety at times of separation from their parents or other persons with whom they are close, and it is actually an indication of developing a healthy attachment to loved ones.

In some kids, however, fears about separation seem to only intensify as time passes or resurface out of the blue. If anxieties are persistent and excessive enough to get in the way of school or other activities, it is possible that your child has separation anxiety disorder, which may lead to school refusal behavior. The following definition of separation anxiety is provided by the Diagnostic and Statistical Manual of Mental Disorders (DSM-V):

> Separation anxiety is a fairly common anxiety disorder—occurring in children younger than 18 years and lasting for at least 4 weeks—that consists of excessive anxiety beyond that expected for the child's developmental level related to separation or impending separation from the attachment figure (such as primary caretaker, close family member).

Prompt treatment of school refusal is key to shorten the course of the disorder. Without treatment, as many as 40 percent to 50 percent of these youths are at risk for not graduating from high school due to the intensity and chronic nature of their anxiety (Kearney, 2008).

SYMPTOMS OF SEPARATION ANXIETY

Bernstein (2011) points out the typical symptoms of separation anxiety and they include the following:

1. *Fear that something terrible will happen to a loved one.* Children with separation anxiety have constant thoughts and intense fears about the safety of parents and caretakers. For example, the child may constantly worry about a parent becoming sick or getting hurt during their absence.
2. *Worry that something will happen to make the separation permanent.* Some youngsters have the fear that an unpredicted event, for example, being kidnapped or getting lost, would happen to keep the child permanently separated from the parent.
3. *Display reluctance to go to sleep.* Children with separation anxiety often have nightmares about their fears and are reluctant to go to sleep without being near to the primary attachment figure. They also may fear being alone in their room and their anxiety makes them insomniacs.
4. *Refuse to go to school.* Separation anxiety may cause the child to have an unreasonable fear of school and will do almost anything to stay home. Once the parent has insisted that the child go to school, he will do almost anything to be sent home, such as crying, throwing temper tantrums, even getting sick, and vomiting.
5. *Complain of physical illness.* Before, during, and/or after the separation from a parent or caregiver, the child may frequently complain of headaches, stomachaches, and other physical complaints.
6. *Be overly clingy.* Children with separation issues may follow the parent around the house, cling to the parent's leg or arm, shadow the teacher whenever possible, find an adult to stand next to at recess, and so on.

According to Watkins (2004), the following factors may contribute to separation anxiety:

- Tiredness
- Minor or major illness
- Changes in the household routine
- Changes within the family, such as birth of a sibling, divorce, or death
- Change in caregiver or routine

Separation anxiety and refusal to go to school often begin or resurface following a period at home in which children have become closer to the parent, such as a summer vacation, a holiday break, or a brief or extended illness, during which they experienced more attention than usual.

Separation anxiety is also more common for children ages five to seven and eleven to fourteen, as they deal with the new challenges of elementary and middle school. These children may suffer from a paralyzing fear of leaving the safety of their parents' home, but these fears and behaviors can be treated successfully with professional help (American Academy of Child and Adolescent Psychiatrists, 2011).

As mentioned before, normal childhood fears usually change with age. If anxious feelings persist beyond the appropriate developmental stage, they can take a toll on a child's sense of well-being, and school refusal behavior may become a serious problem. Intervention by a mental health professional may be warranted.

HELPING KIDS DEAL WITH SEPARATION ANXIETY

For children with *normal* separation anxiety, there are steps that can be taken to make the process of separation easier.

1. *Schedule check-ins for arrival.* This will reduce the child's initial anxiety and facilitate transition into school.
2. *Identify a safe place where the child may go.* This will reduce anxiety during stressful periods. Guidelines should be developed for appropriate use of the safe place.
3. *Develop relaxation techniques.* This will reduce anxiety at school.
4. *Ask the parent to send short notes for the child.* These can be read as a reward for staying at school and coping with separation. For example, let's say the school day is from 8:00 a.m. to 3:00 p.m. The parent provides a little note (or a little drawn picture for younger children) for every hour from 9:00 a.m. on. In most cases, these same notes or pictures can be used each day. They not only give the child a sense of security to receive a note from the parent, but it also helps them to keep track of how long it will be until it is time to go home. It helps them cope with separation one hour at a time.
5. *Encourage the child to help develop interventions.* The more the child is involved in determining ways for him to cope with the separation, the more likely they will work for him.
6. *Reward and encourage the child's efforts.* Every good effort or step in the right direction deserves words of praise (*Way to go!*) and encouragement (*I knew you could do it, you're that kind of kid.*)

Flexibility and a supportive environment, where children experience a sense of belonging and at least some control over their lives, are essential for kids with separation anxiety to achieve success in school. Educators and parents must work together, as well as include the child, in developing remedies that reduce the child's challenges.

REFERENCES & RESOURCES

American Academy of Child and Adolescent Psychiatrists (AACAP). (2011). *Children who won't go to school (Separation)*. No. 7. Updated March 2011. http://aacap.org.

American Psychiatric Association. (2013). *Diagnostic & statistical manual of mental disorders: DSM-V* (6th ed.). Washington, DC: American Psychiatric Press.

Bernstein, B. (2011, March). Separation and school refusal. *Medscape*. http://emedicinemedscape.com/article/916737-overview.

Kearney, C. (2008, March). School absenteeism and school refusal behavior in youth: A contemporary review. *Clinical Psychology Review, 28*(3), 451–71.

The Parent Institute. (2005). *Seven proven ways to motivate children to do better in school*. Fairfax Station, VA: The Parent Institute.

Stickney, M. & Miltenberger, R. (1998). School refusal behavior: Prevalence, characteristics, and schools' response. *Education & Treatment of Children, 21*(2), 160–70.

Watkins, C. (2004). *Separation anxiety*. Northern County Psychiatric Associates. http://www.baltimorepsych.com/separation_anxiety.

Chapter 27

Sexual Harassment

Sexual harassment is not about love or healthy relationships, it is about the bullying power of one person over another and it is a form of violence.

—American Academy of Child and Adolescent Psychiatry

DISCUSSION

It is important to remember that sexuality is a part of life and an integral part of being human. Avoiding or ignoring sexual issues with your kids can be as harmful as teaching them incorrect information. Integrate age-appropriate sexual topics, including sexual harassment, into everyday conversations with your children. It is important to give kids the facts, beginning in early childhood and continuing through the teenage years.

Let kids know that you expect and want them to come to you if anyone ever says or does anything to make them feel uncomfortable in a sexual way. This opens the door for kids to feel comfortable confiding in you if something of this nature happens to them.

Discuss what parts of the body are considered "private" and that no one has a right to touch, or even talk about, that part of their body without their permission. For younger girls and boys, and for educators talking to children about sexual harassment, you might refer to the "private parts" as "that part of the body a swimsuit covers."

Why is it vitally important to talk to kids about sexual harassment? The Office for Civil Rights, a part of the Department of Education, states the alarming statistic that *four out of five students will become the victims of sexual harassment.* That is 80 % of our boys and girls will be sexually harassed this year. They report that just as many boys as girls will be involved as both victims and perpetrators.

Sexual harassment may be happening in school halls, in the classroom, in the cafeteria, in the restrooms, on the playground, and in all the places that students assemble and also even *where adults are present.* Incidents of sexual harassment and bullying are extremely commonplace, yet student incidents are underreported to school officials.

According to a recent study conducted by the American Association of University Women (AAUA), peer-to-peer sexual harassment is one of the most widespread forms of violence in schools today. School officials often dismiss instances of sexual harassment and bullying as part of normal adolescent development and they fail to provide meaningful or effective intervention.

Sexual harassment goes well beyond our school borders into our communities, neighborhoods, youth groups, and other childhood hangouts. Young harassers learn their behaviors from adults, peers, and the media. We must teach children to respect their rights, their bodies, and the property of others, and to reject gender stereotypes that say boys are expected to be dominant and aggressive, while girls are expected to be passive and submissive. These cultural values set boys up to be harassers and girls to be victims.

TEACHING OUR KIDS ABOUT SEXUAL HARASSMENT

The good news is that sexual harassment can be prevented. The first step is educating parents, school staff, and most importantly children, about what sexual harassment encompasses. So, what do our kids need to know about sexual harassment? Here are five key elements we need to teach our kids, both male and female:

1. *Sexual harassment* is defined by the Department of Education as *any* unwanted behavior that is sexual in nature. This includes, but is not limited to, obscene jokes, name-calling, picture-drawing, obscene notes, clothing with sexual innuendoes or messages, degrading graffiti, sexual gestures, talk of sexual acts in the presence of others, spreading rumors of a sexual nature about others, and, of course, unwanted touches or inappropriate touches by the perpetrator on his or her person, such as groping, grabbing, pinching, and patting.

2. Kids need to know that these types of inappropriate advances can come from members of the opposite sex *and* members of the same sex. With the growing acceptance of homosexuality in our culture, same sex harassment is on the rise.
3. We need to emphasize to our boys that they are as susceptible to sexual harassment as girls and that there is no shame in reporting sexual advances toward them. If the behavior is making them feel uncomfortable, then it is unwanted, and therefore harassment.
4. Sexual harassment is not about love or healthy relationships, it is about the bullying power of one person over another and it is a form of violence. A child who has suffered from the fright of being under the powerful threat of a bully experiences the loss of personal dignity, a lowered self-esteem, and a compromised sense of personal safety. Children who have a high level of self-esteem are less likely to allow sexual advances toward them, and bullies are less likely to pursue them.
5. Sexual harassment is both illegal and immoral behavior. Kids need to know that not only should they disallow such behavior toward themselves, but they must not participate in any such behavior toward another. We need to teach kids the concept of "guilty by association." If someone they are with is exhibiting sexual harassment behavior, even if they are not themselves participating, they are just as guilty in the eyes of the law.

Sexual harassment is a problem that occurs in schools throughout the nation, whether they are urban or rural, poor or affluent, private or public, elementary or secondary.

We can no longer ignore it, deny it, and not hold ourselves accountable for its impact on students and their opportunity to receive an education in a safe environment. The fact remains, sexual harassment is illegal both in the educational and home environments, as it is in the workplace. Kids who are subjected to sexual harassment in school are being denied equal educational opportunity based on Title IX of the Educational Amendments (Penny-Velázquez, 1994).

PREVENTING SEXUAL HARASSMENT

School districts must get serious about implementing and reinforcing policies and procedures for dealing with sexual harassment. Parents and school staff need to be clear about what the policies and procedures are for their school district regarding sexual harassment and what to do if their children are being sexually harassed. School districts must take a stand and not tolerate harassment in any form. The district should provide awareness training to students, school staff, and parents about the following:

- What is sexual harassment?
- What are the prohibitions of sexual harassment? What does the law say about it? What can students do if they are being sexually harassed?
- How can students be empowered to stand up for themselves and protect themselves from unwanted, unwelcome sexual advances?

The following guidelines are provided by the Office for Civil Rights, U.S. Department of Education (2008):

- "Sexual harassment of students is illegal. A federal law, *Title IX of the Education Amendments of 1972*, prohibits discrimination on the basis of sex, including sexual harassment, in education programs and activities. All public and private education institutions that receive any federal funds *must* comply with *Title IX*."
- "*Title IX* protects students from harassment connected to any of the academic, educational, extracurricular, athletic, and other programs or activities of schools, regardless of the location."
- "*Title IX* protects both male and female students from sexual harassment by any school employee, another student, or a non-employee third party."
- "*Title IX* prohibits harassing conduct that is of a sexual nature if it is unwelcome and denies or limits a student's ability to participate in or benefit from a school's program, regardless of whether the harassment is aimed at gay or lesbian students or is perpetrated by individuals of the same or opposite sex." (For more information on sexual harassment, go to the Office for Civil Rights website, see "References.")

By teaching children to respect one another and by encouraging healthy relationships between the sexes and within the sexes, they can become more sensitive to one another and realize that harassment of any kind is demoralizing and degrading. By educating kids about sexual harassment and teaching them how to protect themselves from unwanted, unwelcome sexual advances, they become key players in creating a safe, nonhostile learning environment.

STRATEGIES AND ACTIVITIES FOR SEXUAL HARASSMENT

1. Inform kids what sexual harassment encompasses:
   It is *any unwanted behavior that is sexual in nature*. Discuss examples of sexual harassment, such as obscene jokes, name-calling,

picture-drawing, obscene notes, clothing with sexual innuendoes or messages, degrading graffiti, sexual gestures, talk of sexual acts in the presence of others, spreading rumors of a sexual nature about others, and unwanted touches or inappropriate touches of the perpetrator on his person, such as groping, grabbing, pinching, and patting. Emphasize that boys are victims of sexual harassment as often as girls.
2. Teach kids what they should do in case of sexual harassment. The following are some tips to teach kids how to deal with harassment situations:
   1) Report it to a caring adult. If that adult doesn't resolve the issue, find another one who will listen.
   2) Avoid locations and situations where harassment has taken place.
   3) Do not maintain eye contact with the harasser.
   4) Be with friends when possible instead of alone.
   5) If hurt, get to a well-lit, safe place immediately.
   6) Do not respond to a threat.
   7) Depending on the offense, tell the harasser to, *Please stop! I don't want to!* or *Don't touch me like that!*
3. Tell kids to try not to personalize the harassing offense, knowing that it is a reflection of the harasser and not of them personally.
4. Find out what the policy and procedures are for your school district and make it clear what the consequences are for kids who sexually harass other students.
5. Inform students of their rights:
   1) You have the right to be treated with respect.
   2) You have the right to not be teased about your body.
   3) You have the right to tell others to stop bothering you and have the request respected.
   4) You have the right to complain and be taken seriously.
   5) You have the right to make a report regarding the complaint and have it investigated.
   6) You have the right to expect support from school authorities.
6. Teach kids how to cope with sexual harassment (Blum, 1998):
   1) Maintain self-confidence and self-respect, knowing the person who is harassing is wrong.
   2) Try not to personalize the harassment, knowing that it is a reflection of the harasser, not of you.
   3) Develop friendships with kids who share your values.
   4) Avoid locations and situations where harassment has taken place.
7. Teach kids *assertiveness skills*. Assertiveness is expressing one's thoughts, feelings, opinions, perceptions, and beliefs in direct, honest, and appropriate ways, and standing up for one's own rights without

violating the rights of others (Blum, 1998). The following is a guide for teaching kids assertiveness skills:
1) Give examples of assertive behavior.
   - Make eye contact, stand comfortably on two feet, hands loosely at side, talking in a strong, steady tone of voice.
   - Use "I Messages," such as *I feel ___, I want ___, I like it when ___.*
   - Elicit other's ideas: *How can we resolve this? What do you think? What do you see as the problem?*
2) Teach specific techniques for assertive behavior.
   - Be as specific and clear as possible about what you want, think, and feel.
   - Explain exactly what you mean and what you don't mean.
   - Do not demand that others agree with you.
   - Talk about a problem directly with the person involved, not a third party.
   - Acknowledge that your statements are your beliefs, opinions, perceptions, and feelings and invite others to express theirs as well.
   - Show anger appropriately and when warranted.
   - Stand up for yourself: Say "No" to participating in undesirable behaviors and respond appropriately to others' criticism and put downs.
3) Provide opportunities for students to practice assertive responses.
   - Elicit situations when assertiveness is desirable.
   - Role-play assertiveness in realistic situations.
     - Responding to peer pressure
     - Responding to aggressive behavior
     - Standing up for one's rights and dignity
     - Standing up for the rights of a friend
     - Responding to criticism
     - Expressing a complaint
     - Requesting a change
     - Making and refusing requests
   - Coach students to continually improve assertive responses.
   - Encourage students to transfer assertiveness skills to realistic situations outside of the group or class.
   - Encourage students to continually help each other improve assertiveness skills.

REFERENCES & RESOURCES

American Academy of Child and Adolescent Psychiatry (AACAP). (2011). *Talking to your kids about sex.* http://aacap.org/cs/root/facts_for_families/talking_to_your_kids_about_sex.

American Association of University Women (AAUA). (2001). *Hostile hallways: Bullying, teasing, and sexual harassment in schools.* AAUA Educational Foundation.

Child Molestation Research & Prevention Institute, Inc. (2011). http://childmolestationprevention.org/.

Diamond, L. (2003). *Talking to your kids about sexual topics.* Family TLC. http://familytlc.net/sexual_topics_pre.html.

Fineran, S. & Bennett, L. (1999). Gender and power: Issues of peer sexual harassment among teenagers. *Journal of Interpersonal Violence, 14*(6), 626–41.

Office for Civil Rights. (2008). *Sexual harassment: It's not academic.* U.S. Department of Education. Revised September 2008. http://www2.ed.gov/about/offices/list/ocr/docs/ocrshpam.html#_t1a.

Penny-Velázquez, M. (1994, March). Combating students' peer-to-peer sexual harassment: Creating gender equity in schools. *IDRA Newsletter.* San Antonio, TX: Intercultural Development Research Association, 10–12.

Penny-Velázquez, M. (1995, March). Preventing sexual harassment in schools: A pro-active agenda. *IDRA Newsletter.* San Antonio, TX: Intercultural Development Research Association.

Stein, N. (1998). Sexual harassment in school: The public performance of gendered violence. In C. Woyshner, & H. Gelfond (Eds.), *Minding women: Reshaping the educational realm* (pp. 227–45). Cambridge, MA: Harvard Educational Review.

Chapter 28

Social Anxiety and Shyness

Fear of failure among children in America today is at epidemic proportions.

—Dr. Jim Taylor, Psychologist and Parenting Expert

DISCUSSION

Social anxiety disorder (SAD) is actually quite common. According to Hauser (2006), the lifetime prevalence for social phobia in the United States is 5 percent to 10 percent, meaning that about 20 million Americans will have this condition during their lifetime. Many students get nervous or self-conscious when they have to speak in front of the class or talk to the teacher one-on-one, but true social anxiety is more than shyness or occasional nervousness.

If a youngster has social anxiety, his fear of embarrassing himself is so intense that he may go to great lengths to avoid any situation that would evoke those feelings. This is particularly true of situations in which he will be watched, judged, or evaluated by others. The following situations are often stressful for children with social anxiety, due to the intense fear of being embarrassed in front of others:

- Being called on in class
- Speaking in front of the class
- Being the center of attention
- Being watched while performing a task or activity

- Speaking up in class
- Performing on stage
- Being teased or criticized
- Talking with "important" people or authority figures
- Meeting new people
- Using public restrooms
- Eating in public
- Taking exams

Just because there is occasional nervousness in social situations does not mean a youngster has social anxiety disorder, or social phobia. Many people are shy or self-conscious, at least from time to time and under certain circumstances, yet it does not interfere in their everyday functioning.

AVOIDANCE BEHAVIORS

Avoidance behaviors of kids who have shyness issues include the following:

- Canceling social events at the last moment
- Avoiding situations that provide positive social interactions
- Few or no friends
- Avoidance of activities that are otherwise pleasurable
- Passivity, pessimism, and low self-esteem
- Excessive computer use that is not social in nature

Kids who have shyness issues are intensely sensitive to any types of shaming experiences. They have a difficult time adjusting to new situations, such as moving from one school or city to another. Children who are shy tend to react strongly to disruptions and/or abrupt changes in family life, such as the birth of a sibling, death, or divorce.

Although shyness causes discomfort and stress, it does not interfere with daily functioning. Social anxiety disorder, on the other hand, *does* interfere with the child's normal routine and causes tremendous distress. For example, it is perfectly normal to get the jitters or even be quite nervous before speaking in front of the class or performing in front of an audience. Frequently the added alertness enhances one's performance. But youngsters who have severe social anxiety might worry for days, even weeks, ahead of time, fake an illness the day of the speech or performance to get out of it, or start trembling so bad during the event that they can hardly speak or move.

According to Montgomery (1995), approximately 40% of social phobias start before the age of 10 and approximately 95% before the age of 20.

The early onset of social phobia can have serious consequences for children's social and academic development. If left untreated, social anxiety can lead to increased risk of alcoholism, drug abuse, developing further psychological problems, and even suicide.

Therefore, it is important not to dismiss a child's anxiety by saying they will grow out of their excessive shyness or self-consciousness, as many will not without (1) appropriate assistance from other people such as parents, other family members, and teachers or (2) treatment by a mental health professional.

SYMPTOMS OF SOCIAL ANXIETY

Social anxiety, also known as *social phobia*, involves intense fear of certain social situations, especially situations that are unfamiliar and where one is watched or evaluated by others. The following symptoms may be found in youngsters with social anxiety (Hauser, 2006):

1. *Psychological Symptoms*
   - Intense worry for days, even weeks, before an upcoming social situation
   - Extreme fear of being watched or judged by others
   - Fear of acting in ways that will be embarrassing or humiliating
   - Excessive self-consciousness and anxiety in everyday social situations
   - Fear that others will notice their nervousness
   - Avoidance of social situations to the point that activities are limited, and life is disrupted
2. *Physical Symptoms*
   - Pounding heartbeat
   - Trembling or shaking
   - Shaky or trembling voice
   - Rapid breathing
   - Shortness of breath
   - Blushing
   - Dry mouth
   - Upset stomach, nausea
   - Dizziness, feeling faint
   - Clammy hands
   - Body perspiration or hot flashes
   - Tight muscles
   - Muscle twitches, as in the upper lip or corner of the eye

There is nothing abnormal about a youngster being shy, but kids with severe social anxiety experience intense distress over everyday activities and social situations. Often these children are so paralyzed by their social anxiety they do not want to go to school. Social anxiety can severely interfere with normal development and quality of life (Children's Anxiety Institute, 2009).

FEAR OF FAILURE

A common manifestation of social anxiety is the fear of failure. According to Taylor (2003), fear of failure among children in America today is at epidemic proportions. It causes kids to experience debilitating anxiety before taking a test, competing in a sport, or performing in a music recital. It causes kids to give less than their best effort, not take risks, and consequently, never achieve complete success.

Taylor says kids get this destructive perspective on failure from American popular culture. American popular culture, through television and movies, defines failure as being poor, powerless, unpopular, or physically unattractive. These "losers" are teased, bullied, and rejected. With this definition of failure, popular culture has created a culture of fear and avoidance of failure.

OVERCOMING SOCIAL ANXIETY AND SHYNESS

There are various strategies that can be used to help kids overcome social fears and shyness in order to learn to control their fear of certain social situations. Some may be more effective with certain kids than others, and some kids may benefit significantly from regular application of a few strategies. Malouff (2002) provides an extensive list of strategies for helping children overcome shyness, among which are the following:

1. *Explain the benefits of acting outgoing.* The benefits include making more friends, having more fun, and enjoying school and other social activities more. Kids who expect to benefit from a behavior tend to engage in that behavior.
2. *Show empathy when children feel afraid to interact.* For example, if a child refuses, out of fear, to go out on the field for soccer practice, you might say, "I sense you are feeling worried about going out there. I feel worried sometimes too, when I'm not sure what to do and other people are watching me."
3. *Avoid labeling children as "shy."* When talking with others, parents and teachers sometimes comment how shy the child is, when the child is present. Children who are told they are shy begin to think of themselves as shy, and then they fulfill the role without making the effort to change.

Whenever you see a shy child do anything the least bit outgoing, tell him how bold, brave, or courageous he is.
4. *Set goals for more outgoing behavior and measure progress.* For many shy children, a realistic goal might be to say at least one word to someone new every day. Other possible goals might be to join in playing with another child, asking the teacher a question, or talking in front of the whole class. Keep a chart and have the child place a star or sticker on it every time he achieves a goal.
5. *Model outgoing behavior.* Children learn a great deal from observing the behavior of adults and significant others. Model friendly, outgoing behavior in front of the child whenever possible. Even more importantly, model outgoing behavior with other children the age of the child in question, even joining in games. You are showing the child how to interact with others, and he will see how other children respond to outgoing behavior.
6. *Teach children to identify their feelings and express their emotions.* The first step in teaching children to control their feelings of embarrassment and humiliation is for them to be able to identify and talk about their feelings and emotions in various situations.

DEVELOPING A SENSE OF BELONGING

If all behavior has social meaning, as Dreikurs (1964) contends, and a sense of belonging is of primary importance to children's emotional and social development, then developing a sense of belonging is especially critical for youngsters who suffer from social anxiety and/or shyness. Parents and educators must share the responsibility for the development of attitudes—how children feel about themselves, about others, about school, and the world around them. Children must feel important, worthwhile, and valued in order to overcome many of the challenges they encounter in life.

STRATEGIES AND ACTIVITIES FOR SOCIAL ANXIETY AND SHYNESS

1. The following strategies will help to develop a *sense of belonging*, which is essential in helping children overcome social anxiety and shyness.
   1) Each student is given regular *personal attention.*
   2) Students are involved in making *joint decisions* about a class code of conduct and the consequences for misbehavior (violations of the code).

3) The teacher seeks *student input* in areas concerning procedures, policies, and problem and group resolution.
4) The teacher makes sure that each student experiences *success in learning*.
5) Each student receives *recognition for accomplishments*. This boosts self-confidence and enhances self-esteem.
6) Each student has a *position of responsibility* to the class group. The following are a few examples of class positions that can foster self-confidence in social situations:
   - Classroom Monitor (e.g., checking to see if everyone has a pencil)
   - Hall Monitor
   - Cafeteria Monitor
   - Restroom Monitor
   - Class Pet Caretaker

2. All students must be *encouraged*, but it is especially true of children who are shy. Encouragement is conveying respect for students and believing in their abilities. The following are examples of providing encouragement which is extremely beneficial to the child who is shy.
   1) Use *social reinforcers*, which consist of words and behaviors such as comments, gestures, and facial expressions. They may be verbal or nonverbal:
      - Verbal: *I knew you could do that. I really like the way you were so friendly toward Susan. You really showed courage when you spoke in front of the class.*
      - Nonverbal: A smile, a pat on the arm or back, a handshake, winks, eye contact, nods, thumbs up, and so forth.
   2) Provide an "encouraging classroom climate" that is warm, friendly, supportive, respectful, and filled with good nature and acceptance. Such a climate promotes a sense of self-worth and accomplishment.
   3) *Social interest* is an objective which can be developed within the class group. The most effective teachers are those who sense the need each child has to find an acceptable and comfortable place within the group. There are many opportunities to develop social interest, to show concern for others and to participate in the give and take of human relations.

3. Teach children to express their feelings using "I Messages":
   - I *feel/felt* ____ when ____ because ____.
   - Give children a variety of scenarios to fill in *"when ____"* and have them express how they would feel and why (*"because ____"*).
   - Role-play the various social situations so children who are shy can practice new ways of responding.

4. Read and discuss books about children who overcome shyness or fears. The following books were taken from a list Malouff (2002) compiled:
   - *The Brave Little Grork*. An easily frightened creature overcomes fears by thinking brave thoughts (Cave, K., and Maland, N., London: Hadder Headline, 2002)
   - *Let's Talk about Being Shy*. Explains shyness and encourages children to try to act more outgoing (Johnson, M., New York: Rosen, 1996)
   - *Cat's Got Your Tongue?* A story for children afraid to speak out (Schaefer, C., Milwaukee: Gareth Stevens, 1992)
   - *The Playground*. A timid boy stays near the teacher and refuses to join other children on the playground until children pull him out and involve him in their games (Wilmer, D., London: Collins, 1986)
   - *Buster the Very Shy Dog*. Buster becomes less shy when he befriends a crying girl, realizes that he has a special talent of listening, and teams up with another dog to achieve a common goal (Bechtold, L., Boston: Houghton Mifflin, 1999)
   - *I Don't Know Why . . . I Guess I'm Shy*. A story about a boy who finds new ways to respond to situations that trigger shyness, with an addendum for parents who want to help their child overcome shyness (Cain, B., Washington, D.C.: Magination Press, 2000)

REFERENCES & RESOURCES

Albert, L. (1996). *Cooperative discipline*. Circle Pines, MN: American Guidance Services.

Children's Anxiety Institute. (2009). *Social phobias in children*. http://childrenwithanxiety.com/articles-resources/social-phobias-in-children.

Dreikurs, R. (1964). *Children: The challenge*. New York: Hawthorn/Dutton.

Hauser, J. (2006). *Shyness and social phobia in children*. Retrieved August 31, 2011. http://psychcentral.com/lib/2006/shyness-and-social-phobia-in-children/.

Malouff, J. (2002). *Helping young children overcome shyness*. Retrieved December 31, 2007, from University of New England, http://www.une.edu.au/psychology/staff/malouffshyness.php

Montgomery, S. (1995). *Pocket reference to social phobia*. London: Science Press Ltd.

Pincus, D. & Otis, J. (2001). Social phobia. *The Child Anxiety Network*. http://www.childanxiety.net/Social_Phobia.htm.

Taylor, J. (2005, April). *Fear of failure: A childhood epidemic*. http://www.keepkidshealthy.com/parenting_tips/fear_of_failure.html.

Chapter 29

Underachievement

These low perceptions and beliefs about their abilities to achieve become firmer and more inflexible as they grow older.

—William Glasser

DISCUSSION

Underachievement at school can be one of the most frustrating challenges for teachers and concerned parents. Underachieving students can be identified because there is a considerable gap between their ability and their achievement levels in school. Their academic performance is significantly below what you know they are capable of doing.

It is important to point out that there is no typical profile for an underachiever. Some kids scrape by with passing grades, and others get an A on one exam and fail on another. According to Goldstein (2011), there are four foundational blocks that must be strong enough to provide support for further learning to occur:

1. The ability to *pay attention* and *control impulses* in order to focus on a task;
2. *Healthy emotions* and *self-esteem*, which contribute to how children feel about themselves;
3. A *positive attitude about learning*, which determines how well children will stay with a task until completed successfully;
4. A *safe, supportive, respectful environment for learning*, both at home and in school, which is caring and consistent.

Strengths in these areas will help children to compensate for lesser abilities and to persist when challenged with difficult tasks.

All of us, adults and children alike, make an effort to succeed in areas where the outcome of our efforts is important to us. If we do not value or desire an outcome, we simply will not work to achieve it. Kids who do not believe that academic success is important will not work to achieve it. Furthermore, kids who do not believe they can be successful in school, even if they believe success in school is important, will not make a consistent effort to do well in school.

If we want our kids to be successful in school, we must instill in them the value and importance of academic achievement *and* we must encourage and inspire them into believing they can be successful students.

CONTRIBUTING FACTORS

Although underachievement is a complex problem, the following factors might be considered:

1. Late bloomers, so they mature more slowly than others
2. Depression
3. High levels of school anxiety
4. Low levels of healthy self-esteem
5. Family stresses such as parents fighting, separation, or divorce
6. Personal problems such as abuse or being bullied
7. Parents with excessively high or extremely low expectations for school achievement
8. Some have other behavioral problems such as being defiant, resistant, and oppositional, which interfere with achievement
9. Need for tutoring and extra attention to feel confident in certain areas
10. Parental disinterest and apathetic attitudes about education and lack of involvement with school-related events—these attitudes carry over to the child
11. Overly indulgent and protective parents who have done almost everything for the child, so he has not learned to be responsible, self-reliant, or self-sufficient

Kids begin developing opinions, perceptions, and beliefs about themselves at an early age in regard to their strengths and weaknesses in many areas, including their abilities as students. If parents and educators do not help underachievers develop to their potential academic levels, these low perceptions and beliefs about their abilities to achieve become firmer and more inflexible as they grow older.

CHARACTERISTICS OF UNDERACHIEVERS

Most academic underachievers find it challenging to do what they perceive as difficult or boring tasks. They are usually unable to do things they do not "feel" like doing, thus many times they are seen as lazy and irresponsible. Other underachievers have an intense fear of failure, of looking "dumb" in the eyes of their peers.

As Taylor (2003) points out, fear of failure among children in America is at epidemic proportions. The following characteristics of many underachievers are provided to assist in understanding the underachiever better:

1. Reluctant to accept challenges, being excessively afraid of failure
2. Tend to be disorganized and inefficient in their work
3. Excessively dependent upon attention of their parents and teachers
4. Some use achievement to control and manipulate significant adults to get what they want
5. Tend to have poor study skills and produce poor quality of work
6. Lack self-confidence
7. Lack self-discipline
8. Failure in being able to set and carry out goals
9. Some have other behavioral problems such as being defiant, resistant, and oppositional, which interfere with achievement

TIPS FOR HELPING UNDERACHIEVERS

The reasons for underachievement are diverse and complex, and there is no step-by-step process to follow to help these children overcome their difficulties. Many of the suggestions provided are things most teachers and parents already do with all of their kids; they are just more critical for underachievers. The following are suggestions to keep in mind as you work with underachievers:

1. Provide the child with opportunities for social and academic successes and give frequent, positive feedback which indicates he or she is important and respected.
2. Express your confidence in your kids' abilities to achieve and let them know you *expect* them to be successful in those activities.
3. Focus on your kids' strengths and support and encourage them as they work on their weaknesses.
4. Help underachievers to set obtainable goals (always making sure it is something they *want* to achieve) and guide them in making an appropriate plan of action to successfully achieve their goal.

5. Instill in your kids a sense of belonging to the group. Give them responsibilities they can complete successfully.
6. Maintain a positive relationship with underachieving kids. They can be frustrating and annoying, and it is easy to become impatient and dismissive with them, especially if they are acting defiant, resistant, or oppositional. It is important to remain calm, use a friendly tone of voice and strive to be supportive and encouraging as you guide the child into more productive behaviors. It is difficult, if not impossible, to help underachieving kids if they perceive you as an adversary, rather than an ally.
7. Emphasize to underachievers that they are not in competition with anyone but themselves. Some kids underachieve because they feel intimidated by competition and will avoid any direct contests with others. Then there are those who believe they will be ostracized by their peers if they perform at a level higher than theirs. Either way, underachievers must see their academic improvements and successes as relative only to their own past performance.
8. Be cautious and judicious with criticism. Underachievers are often sensitive and easily embarrassed. Never criticize them in front of their peers or other significant adults. A better tactic is to "catch" them doing something right and give words of praise and encouragement. Avoid sarcasm and never use labels such as "lazy" or "dumb." If a child is refusing to get busy on his seat work, instead of yelling or using put downs, try asking him, *What can I do to help you get busy on your work?*
9. Assess that the difficulty of a given task is within the child's ability to perform successfully, given the allotted amount of time for completion.
10. Provide the child with as many high-interest and "fun" activities within the academic setting, thus increasing his level of happiness and sense of well-being.
11. Provide a quiet place for the child to work independently, away from peer interactions. Include his opinion in determining where he might feel most comfortable.
12. Reinforce appropriate behavior and making good choices by providing tangible rewards, such as a "Class Buck," a coupon for 10 minutes of free time to draw a picture about a story he read, a coupon to work on a seek and find puzzle of spelling words, and so forth. We all like bonuses for a job well done.

All kids go through basic developmental stages on their way to maturity and they are relatively brief and of limited intensity. They enter a stage, react, learn, integrate, and move on.

Underachievers often become "stuck" in a stage, or even regress from a later one. This is confusing and provokes anxiety for everyone involved, but especially for the underachievers. Even more confounding is the tendency for these kids to be in different stages regarding different aspects of their personality. For example, their intellectual level may be below their emotional level, and both may be below their chronological level.

It is also not uncommon for kids who underachieve academically to be performing well in other areas. For example, they may perform well physically, as in sports, and be well-adjusted socially, but yet underachieve academically. The problem of underachievement is a highly complex one and every child has to be dealt with on an individual basis to ensure they experience academic success.

STRATEGIES AND ACTIVITIES FOR UNDERACHIEVEMENT

1. Activity: *My Personal Improvement Plan*
   This activity helps kids understand things they like about themselves and things that they could improve on. This may be used both at school and in the home.
   "My Personal Improvement Plan" worksheet:
   A. Three things I really like about myself at school (home):
      1) _____
      2) _____
      3) _____
   B. Three things I would like to improve on at school (home):
      1) _____
      2) _____
      3) _____
   C. My short-term plan for improving myself:
      1) What? _____
         How? (The Plan) _____
         When? _____
      2) What? _____
         How? (The Plan) _____
         When? _____
      3) What? _____
         How? (The Plan) _____
         When? _____
2. Activity: *Goal Setting Games*
   Playing goal setting games teaches children the process of setting and achieving goals. It isn't what the goal is that matters so much as learning to achieve them. Simple games such as Ring Toss, Horseshoes, and Trash

Can Basketball can be used. Using Trash Can Basketball as an example, place the trash can in the corner of the room. Use a soft sponge ball or make a ball out of used papers wadded up, wrapped in masking tape. Make a series of lines with masking tape (chalk might be used if playing outdoors). Let each child decide where they want to begin. Some will opt to begin on the first line where it is easy and others will choose to begin on the farthest line, may fail, but can always begin again on a closer line. The goal is to be able to make a basket from the line they chose before beginning the game.

3. Activity: *Developing a Sense of Belonging*

Increase the child's sense of belonging by giving him a specific task with a title which provides a service to the class or home group. Some examples are as follows:

- *The Class Attendance Clerk* (for example, make an unofficial classroom attendance card and have the student mark the absences each morning),
- *The Chief Boys Restroom Monitor*
- *The Class Cafeteria Captain*
- *The Class Distributor* (passes out papers, supplies, and so on)

  **Frequently let children know how important their task is to the group.*

REFERENCES & RESOURCES

Billings, D. (2010, October 8). 9 reasons children underachieve. *The Heart Link Network*. http://www.theheartlinknetwork.com.

Goldstein, S. (2011). *Overcoming underachieving: Understanding children's school problems*. Retrieved September 2011. http://www.addwarehouse.com/.

Taylor, J. (2005, April). *Fear of failure: A childhood epidemic*. http://www.keepkidshealthy.com/parenting_tips/fear_of_failure.html

Varvil-Weld, D. (2011). *Your child's underachievement and what to do about it*. The Pauquette Center of Psychological Services. Updated July 2011. http://www.pauquette.com.

Chapter 30

Work Completion

Home study time should be a family commitment—if you don't commit to it, don't expect your kids to.

—M. L. McCormick

DISCUSSION

One of the most common complaints from teachers is how to get kids to do homework, and it has become a national issue in the United States. Homework is supposed to facilitate mastery of new information and skills, giving kids opportunities for practicing the new skills they are learning. However, all too often it has become a focal point for power struggles at home and at school.

Parents and teachers have argued, nagged, and struggled to get kids to do their homework, and even bribing, threatening, and punishing them have not produced consistent, positive results. Many teachers have given up assigning much, if any, homework, convinced that few of their students will actually follow through.

Many parents, pressed for finding any quality time to spend with their kids, let alone helping them with homework issues, also support having homework reduced or eliminated. The general attitude of many parents is kids don't *like* it, you can't *make* them do it, and it's *their* problem anyway. So why do we even bother giving kids homework?

WHY ASSIGN HOMEWORK?

When homework is appropriately assigned, it is *vital* for learning and development. Dobkin (2007) lists some reasons why assigning appropriate homework is beneficial:

1. *Skill Mastery.* New skills, especially in math and critical thinking, require practice to achieve mastery. There is normally not enough time during the school day for students to obtain all the practice they need. Once they "get it" in the classroom, they need independent practice to cement the learning.
2. *Supplementary Skill Development.* Some skills are vital for real life but may not be part of the official curriculum. For example, internet research and practicing a speech without peers around are valuable skills that are not always practical or possible during the school day.
3. *Self-Discipline.* This is an essential skill for all students. They must learn how to manage their time, to work independently, and to complete multistep projects. If students do not acquire the self-discipline needed to complete homework assignments on time, they will not only have difficulties at school, but will struggle in their adult lives.

MOTIVATORS FOR DOING HOMEWORK

So, what can we do to motivate our kids to do homework without all the drama of arguing and fighting? Every child is motivated differently, so here is a smorgasbord of suggestions you might try (adapted from Moorman & Haller, 2005):

1. *Change the name!* Consult with your child and give homework another name, such as "school studies," "home studies," "after-school studies," or some other name such as "tarea" (Spanish for "homework" and pronounced tah-ray-ah).
2. Involve kids in making a *plan* for completing their home studies. A plan might include having the child come up with a system to ensure that home studies are not only completed but turned in. A separate clear folder marked "Completed Home Studies" and always placed in the front of the backpack where it is most visible might be helpful as a reminder.
3. Focus on feelings if you want kids to build an internal reward system and not rely on external rewards such as Class Bucks or coupons. You want them to eventually be motivated by the good feeling of a job well done. Rewards may be used in the beginning, then becoming less and less,

until they are ultimately replaced by intrinsic motivators. You help your child develop this kind of inner motivation when you emphasize feelings: *Great job finishing that project and I am so proud of you! I bet you are proud of yourself, too! Doesn't it feel good to have that finished? Aren't you glad you started your project early?*
4. Put your attention on positive behaviors and if they mess up, do *not* make a big deal out of it. Do not lecture, shame, or embarrass them—let them experience the natural consequences of their actions. The more attention you give to poor choices, the more you reinforce them, in the long run.

TIPS FOR TEACHERS

Teachers must accommodate a wide range of student abilities in their classrooms, and appropriate homework assignments must be given accordingly. The following are some tips for teachers in assisting kids to complete homework assignments:

1. Communicate instructions clearly. When necessary, have students repeat the instructions back.
2. Keep instructions brief. Break lengthy, multistep directions into smaller subsets. Have students complete one subset before moving on to another.
3. Write assignments and complex directions on the board in addition to saying them.
4. Match students' ability level with the assignment to insure a high rate of success.
5. Have students monitor and chart their own homework completion.
6. Help students prioritize assignments by importance and deadlines.
7. Have students write their homework assignments into a daily planner.
8. Check the daily planner at the end of the day to ensure all assignments have been written down accurately.
9. Make sure students have all the necessary textbooks, materials, and so forth. If necessary, discuss with parents the need to have an organized study area at home, as well as the benefits of having a fixed after-school schedule for completing homework.

Being responsible for doing homework develops self-discipline, an essential skill for all students. They must learn to manage their time, work independently, and to complete multistep projects. Developing good self-discipline skills will give kids a considerable advantage in their adult lives.

STRATEGIES AND ACTIVITIES FOR WORK COMPLETION

1. Use cooperative learning activities to teach course content. Cooperative learning, or small groups, allows kids to learn while getting motivating social reinforcement through interaction with peers. Have students help each other to write down all homework assignments.
2. Weave high-interest topics into homework assignments to capture and hold student attention.
3. Offer kids choices in how they structure their learning experience. For example, consider allowing students to choose where they want to sit in the classroom, or what books they want to use for an assignment, what order they think is best to do their homework assignments.
4. Give students a voice in structuring the lesson. For example, you might have the class vote on whether to work in pairs, groups, or independently.
5. Allocate kids ample time when working on difficult tasks to allow for persistence. When kids are deeply involved in an activity, try to make sure they can finish without interruption.
6. Provide learning situations that give children an adequate challenge. Activities that are slightly difficult will be more motivating and will provide stronger feelings of success when completed.
7. Be cautious about using praise and rewards. They tend to undermine kids' ability to value themselves. They should be based on behaviors, such as kids' effort, persistence, or self-discipline, rather than on the actual completion of the task.
8. *Fun Friday at the Movies*: Students and teachers need to decide on the time frame, but let's use the last Friday of every month for our example. A good inspirational movie with a positive message is shown on the last Friday of the month for students who meet the following criteria:
   - Perfect Attendance (meaning no "unexcused" absences);
   - Perfect Behavior (meaning no major "misbehavior reports");
   - Perfect Work Completion (meaning all seat work and homework assignments turned in).

All students look forward to *Fun Friday at the Movies*, which is shown in the school gym or cafeteria the last two hours of the day. This activity may be provided the last Friday of the month, the last Friday of the grading period, or whatever time frame is agreed upon. A parent group might serve popcorn and some type of juice to the attending students. Each student is given a ticket as they enter and during intermission there is a drawing for prizes. Those students who choose not to meet the above criteria are sent to designated classrooms for study hall during this time. This is a great motivator for kids to be in school every day, to behave in an acceptable manner, and to make sure all schoolwork assignments are completed and turned in. Emphasis should be placed on kids "earning" the right to attend the movie due to the good choices they have made.

REFERENCES & RESOURCES

Albert, L. (1989). *Cooperative discipline: How to manage your classroom and promote self-esteem.* Circle Pines, MN: American Guidance Services.

Dobkin, A. (2007, May 14). *Train your kids to do homework without arguing!.* http://sparksofgenius.wordpress.com/2007/05/14/train-your-kids-to-do-homework-without-arguing/.

Moorman, C. & Haller, T. (2005). *How to motivate your kids to do homework.* http://www.newsforparents.org/expert_motivate_kids_homework.

Bibliography

Adler, A. (2009). *Social interest: Adler's key to the meaning of life* (Reprint ed.). Oxford: OneWorld.
Albert, L. (1984). *Coping with kids and school: A guide for parents*. New York: E. P. Dutton.
Albert, L. (1989). *Cooperative discipline: How to manage your classroom and promote self-esteem*. Circle Pines, MN: American Guidance Services.
Albert, L. (1996a). *A teacher's guide to cooperative discipline* (Rev. ed.). Circle Pines, MN: American Guidance Service.
Albert, L. (1996b). *Cooperative discipline*. Circle Pines, MN: American Guidance Services.
American Academy of Child and Adolescent Psychiatry (AACAP). (2008). *Facts for families: The depressed child*, No. 4. Updated May, 2008. http://aacap.org.
American Academy of Child and Adolescent Psychiatry (AACAP). (2011). *Children who won't go to school (Separation)*. No. 7. Updated March, 2011. http://aacap.org/.
American Academy of Child and Adolescent Psychiatry (AACAP). (2011, March). *Bullying*. No. 80. http://www.aacap.org/cs/root/facts_for_families/bully.
American Academy of Child and Adolescent Psychiatry (AACAP). (2011, March). *Children of divorce*. http://www.aacap.org/cs/root/facts_for_families/children_and_divorce.
American Association of University Women (AAUW). (2001). *Hostile hallways: Bullying, teasing, and sexual harassment in schools*. Washington, DC: AAUW Educational Foundation.
American Psychiatric Association (APA). (2013). *Diagnostic and statistical manual of mental disorders* (5th Ed-Text Revision). Washington, DC: American Psychiatric Association.
American Psychological Association (APA) Online. (2008, May 22). *What makes kids care? Teaching gentleness in a violent world*. http://www.apa.org/helpcenter/kids-care.aspx.

Anxious child, No. 47. Updated November (2004). http://aacap.org.
Baumeister, R. & Leary, M. (1995). The need to belong: Desire for interpersonal attachments as a fundamental human motivation. *Psychological Bulletin, 117,* 497–529.
Bear, G., Cavalier, A., & Manning, M. (2005). *Developing self-discipline and preventing and correcting misbehaviour.* Boston: Allyn & Bacon.
Begun, R. (Ed.). (1996). *Social skills lessons & activities for grades 4-6.* West Nyack, NY: The Center for Applied Research in Education.
Bell, R. (2009). 5 tips for teaching students to respect authority. *The Apple.* Retrieved October 2009. http://theapple.monster.com/benefits/articles/7576-5-tips-for-teaching-students-to-respect-authority.
Bernstein, B. (2011, March). *Separation and school refusal.* http://emedicine.medscape.com/article/916737-overview.
Billings, D. (2010, October 8). 9 reasons children underachieve. *The Heart Link Network.* http://www.theheartlinknetwork.com.
Black, S. (1994). Throw away the hickory stick. *Executive Educator, 16*(4), 44–47.
Blair, G. (2011). Teaching children goal setting. *Achieve Goal Setting Success.com.* http://www.achieve-goal-setting-success.com/teaching-children-goal-setting.html.
Blum, D. (1998). *The school counselor's book of lists.* San Francisco: Jossey-Bass.
Bolton, J. & Graeve, S. (2005). *No room for bullies: From the classroom to cyberspace.* Boys Town. Boys Town, NE: Boys Town.
Bonner, T. & Aspy, D. (1984). A study of the relationship between student empathy and GPA. *Humanistic Education and Development, 22*(4), 149–54.
Borba, M. (2001). *Building moral intelligence: How to raise kids with solid minds and caring hearts.* San Francisco: Jossey-Bass.
Bos, C. & Vaughn, S. (1994). *Strategies for teaching students with learning and behavior problems.* Boston: Allyn & Bacon.
Branch, J. & Shelton, L. (2011). *What children need to hear.* University of Vermont Extension. Separation & Divorce: A Parenting Seminar, pdf file.
Brooks, R. & Goldstein, S. (2001). *Raising resilient children.* New York: McGraw-Hill.
Carlton, M. (2003). *Early childhood motivation.* National Association of School Psychologists (NASP). http://www.nasponline.org/resources/home_school/earlychildmotiv/.
Carlton, M. & Winsler, A. (1998, Spring). Fostering intrinsic motivation in early childhood classrooms. *Early Childhood Education Journal, 25*(3), 159–66.
Charles, C. (1983). *Elementary classroom management.* New York: Longman.
Charles, C. (2008). *Building classroom discipline* (9th ed.). Boston: Allyn & Bacon.
Charles, C. (2013). *Building classroom discipline* (11th ed.). New York: Pearson.
Child Molestation Research & Prevention Institute, Inc. (2011). *Child molestation prevention.* http://childmolestationprevention.org/.
Christophersen, E. (1998). *Beyond discipline: Parenting that lasts a lifetime.* Shawnee Mission, KA: Overland Press
Cohen, J. (2003). *Teach school children to set and achieve goals.* http://www.solveyourproblem.com/setting-goals/.
Coloroso, B. (1994). *Kids are worth it! Giving your child the gift of inner discipline.* New York: William Morrow.

Coloroso, B. (2003). *The bully, the bullied, and the bystander: From preschool to high school—How parents and teachers can break the cycle of violence.* New York: HarperResource.

Conner, M. (2008). Anxiety in children. *Crisis Counseling.* http://crisiscounseling.com/Articles/AnxietyinChildren.

Cool, L. (1996, June). How kids learn to follow directions. *Working Mother.*

Cotton, K. (2008). *Developing empathy in children and youth.* Northwest Regional Educational Laboratory. August 31, 2001, Update May 2008. HYPERLINK "http://www.nwrel.org" http://www.nwrel.org.

Dacey, J. & Fiore, B. (2001). *Your anxious child: How parents and teachers can relieve anxiety in children.* San Francisco: Jossey-Bass.

Davies, L. (2004, February). *Motivating children.* http://www.kellybear.com/TeacherArticles/TeacherTip42.html.

Depression and Suicide in Children and Adolescents. (2011). *A Report of the Surgeon General.* http://www.surgeongeneral.gov/mentalhealth/chapter3/sec5.html.

Diagnostic and statistical manual of mental disorders: DSM-IV (5th ed.). (2013). Washington, DC: American Psychiatric Press.

Diamond, L. (2003). *Talking to your kids about sexual topics.* Family TLC. http://familytlc.net/sexual_topics_pre.html.

DiMaria, L. (2011, March 1). *Sadness in children: How to know if your child's sadness is depression.* Retrieved April, 2011.http://depression.about.com/od/symptoms/a/Sadness-In-Children.htm.

Dinkmeyer, D. & Dreikurs, R. (1963). *Encouraging children to learn.* New York: Hawthorn Books, Inc.

Dobkin, A. (2007, May 14). *Train your kids to do homework without arguing!.* http://sparksofgenius.wordpress.com/2007/05/14/train-your-kids-to-do-homework-without-arguing/.

Dreikurs, R. (1964). *Children: The challenge.* New York: Hawthorn/Dutton.

Dreikurs, R. (1968). *Psychology in the classroom.* New York: Harper & Row.

Dreikurs, R. (2009). *Child guidance and education: Collected papers of Rudolf Dreikurs.* New York: The Alfred Adler Institute.

Dreikurs, R., Grunwald, B., & Pepper, E. (1982). *Maintaining sanity in the classroom.* New York: Harper & Row.

Dufour, S. & Mishara, B. (2011). *Children's reaction to divorce and separation.* Partnership for Children.org. Retrieved August 2011. http://www.partnershipforchildren.org.uk/resources/my-child-is-worried-about/divorce-separation/children-s-reactions-to-divorce-and-separation.html.

Erikson, E. (1963). *Childhood and society.* New York: Norton.

Faerber, Y. (2011, May 8). *Teaching our children respect.* The Parent Institute. http://beepdf.com/doc/129347/teaching_our_children_respect.html.

Fanning, R. (2008, October). *Fostering motivation in kids with learning and attention problems.* http://www.greatschools.org/special-education/support/816-motivating-kids-learning-attention-problems.gs.

Fay, J. & Cline, F. (2000). *Pearls of love and logic for parents and teachers.* Golden, CO: The Love and Logic Press, Inc.

Fay, J., Cline, F., & Sornson, B. (2000). *Meeting the challenge: Using love and logic to help children develop attention and behavior skills*. Golden, CO: The Love and Logic Press, Inc.

Fineran, S. & Bennett, L. (1999). Gender and power: Issues of peer sexual harassment among teenagers. *Journal of Interpersonal Violence, 14*(6), 626–41.

Gallo, D. (1989). Educating for empathy, reason and imagination. *The Journal of Creative Behavior, 23*(2), 98–115.

Ginott, H. (1971). *Teacher and child.* New York: Macmillan.

Ginott, H. (1972). I am angry! I am appalled! I am furious! *Today's Education,* 61, 20–25.

Glasser, W. (1986). *Control theory in the classroom.* New York: Harper & Row.

Glasser, W. (1998a). *Choice theory in the classroom.* New York: HarperCollins.

Glasser, W. (1998b). *The quality school: Managing students without coercion.* New York: HarperCollins.

Glasser, W. (1998c). *The quality school teacher.* New York: HarperCollins.

Glasser, W. (1999). *Choice theory: A new psychology of personal freedom.* New York: Harper Collins.

Glasser, W. (2001). *Every student can succeed.* Chatsworth, CA: William Glasser, Inc.

Goh, K. (2011). *Teaching honesty to our children.* Retrieved March 2011. http://ezinearticles.com/?Teaching-Honesty-to-Our-Children&id=1651126.

Goldman, W. (2001). *Childhood and adolescent anxiety disorders.* Updated June 2001. Retrieved August 2011. http://www.keepkidshealthy.com/anxiety_disorders.html.

Goldstein, S. (2010). *Questions and answers about resilience.* Retrieved November 2010. www.samgoldstein.com/articles/articles29.pdf.

Goldstein, S. (2011). *Overcoming underachieving: Understanding children's school problems.* Retrieved September 2011. http://www.addwarehouse.com/.

Gordon, T. (1989). *Discipline that works: Promoting self-discipline in children.* New York: Random House.

Greenspan, S. (1995). *Challenging child: How to understand, raise, and enjoy your "difficult child".* Cambridge, MA: Perseus Books.

Harter, S. (1985). *Manual for the self-perception profile for children.* Denver: University of Denver.

Hauser, J. (2006). *Shyness and social phobia in children.* Retrieved August 2011. http://psychcentral.com/lib/2006/shyness-and-social-phobia-in-children/.

Haynes, L. & Avery, A. (1979). Training adolescents in self-disclosure and empathy skills. *Journal of Community Psychology, 26*(6), 526–30.

Henderson, L, Zimbardo, P., & Rodino. E. (2001). *Painful shyness in children and adults.* American Psychological Association. http://www.apa.org/helpcenter/shyness.aspx.

Hoffman, M. (2000). *Empathy and moral development.* Cambridge, UK: Cambridge University Press.

Kearney, C. (2008, March). School absenteeism and school refusal behavior in youth: A contemporary review. *Clinical Psychology Review, 28*(3), 451–71.

Kraizer, S. (2011). Emotional abuse. *Coalition for children.* Retrieved May 2011. http://www.safechild.org/childabuse3.htm.

Katz, L. (1993). *Distinctions between self-esteem and narcissism: Implications for practice*. Urbana, IL: ERIC Clearinghouse on Elementary and Early Childhood Education. ED 363 452.

Kohn, A. (1991). Caring kids: The role of the schools. *Phi Delta Kappan, 72*(7), 496–506.

Kohn, A. (1996). *Beyond discipline: From compliance to community*. Alexandria, VA: Association for Supervision and Curriculum Development.

Leedom, L. (2009, August). Empathy—The cornerstone of ability to love. *Parenting the At-Risk Child*. http://www.parentingtheatriskchild.com/Empathy.html.

Lewis, J. & Sammons, W. (2000, September). What schools are doing to help children of divorce. *The Journal of the National Association for the Education of Young Children, 55*(5), 64–65.

Lewis, O. (1998, January). The culture of poverty. *Society, 35*(2), 7.

Liepe-Levinson, K. & Levinson, M. (2005). A general semantics approach to bullying. *A Review of General Semantics, 62*(2), 127–43.

Loh, A. (2009). *Teaching problem solving skills to children—Why are they so important?* http://www.brainy-child.com/articles/teach-problem-solving-skills.shtml.

Luby, J. (2010, August). The importance of identification of depression early in development. *Current Trends in Psychological Science, 19*(4), 525–37.

Malouff, J. (2002). *Helping young children overcome shyness*. Retrieved December 31, 2007, from University of New England. http://www.une.edu.au/psychology/staff/malouffshyness.php.

Maslow, A. (1943). A theory of human motivation. *Psychological Review, 50*(4), 370–96.

May, G. (2011). *Child discipline: Guidelines for parents*. National Children's Advocacy Center. Retrieved June 2011. http://www.nationalcac.org/families/forworkers/abuse_indicators.html.

Mayo Clinic. (2011, May 14). *Children and divorce: Helping kids after a breakup*. http://www.mayoclinic.com/health/divorce/HO00055.

McChesney, S. (2009). Respect–How to teach it and how to show it. *Teachnology*. Retrieved October 2009. http://www.teach-nology.com/tutorials/teaching/respect/.

McFadden, A. & Cooper, K. (2004). *Leave no ANGRY child behind: The ABC's of anger management for grades K-12*. Chapin, SC: YouthLight, Inc.

MedicineNet.com. (2011). Depression in children. Retrieved April 2011. http://www.medicinenet.com/depression_in_children/article

Miller, J. (2008). *Getting played: African American girls, urban inequality, and gendered violence*. New York: New York University Press.

Montgomery, S. (1995). *Pocket reference to social phobia*. London: Science Press Ltd.

Moorman, C. & Haller, T. (2005). *How to motivate your kids to do homework*. http://www.newsforparents.org/expert_motivate_kids_homework.html.

National Association of School Psychologists (NASP). (1998). Teaching study skills: A guide for parents. Adapted from a handout by V. H. Harvey (University of Massachusetts-Boston), published in *Helping children at home and school: Handouts from your school psychologist*. http://www.teachersandfamilies.com/open/parent/homework1.cfm.

National Network for Child Care (NNCC). (1994). *Getting children to follow rules.* Pennsylvania State University Cooperative Extension. http://www.nncc.org/Guidance/better.rules.html.

Nelsen, J., Lott, L., & Glenn, H. (1997). *Positive discipline in the classroom.* Rocklin, CA: Prima.

Nelson, J., Lott, L., & Glenn, H. (2000). *Positive discipline in the classroom: Developing mutual respect, cooperation, and responsibility in the classroom.* Roseville, CA: Prima.

Office for Civil Rights. (2008). *Sexual harassment: It's not academic.* U.S. Department of Education. Revised September. http://www2.ed.gov/about/offices/list/ocr/docs/ocrshpam.html#_t1a.

Oswalt, A. (2008, January 16). *Early childhood emotional and social development: Reflective empathy.* Mental Health Care, Inc. http://www.mhcinc.org.

Paxton, J. (2006, August). Fun ways to increase your child's attention span. *Garden & Hearth Magazine.*

Penny-Velázquez, M. (1994, March). Combating students' peer-to-peer sexual harassment: Creating gender equity in schools. *IDRA Newsletter.* San Antonio, TX: Intercultural Development Research Association, 10–12.

Penny-Velazquez, M. (1995, March). Preventing sexual harassment in schools: A pro-active agenda. *IDRA Newsletter.* San Antonio, TX: Intercultural Development Research Association.

Pincus, D. & Otis, J. (2001). Social phobia. *The Child Anxiety Network.* http://www.childanxiety.net/Social_Phobia.htm.

Poole, P., Miller, S., & Church, E. (2000, January). Ages & stages: Learning to follow directions. *Early Childhood Today.* Also online at: http://www2.scholastic.com/browse/article.jsp?id=3745711

Rogers, T. (2010, December 10). *Explaining American schools' gay bullying epidemic.* http://www.salon.com/life/lgbt.

Rose, D. & Dalton, B. (2007). *Learning through listening in the digital world.* Wakefield, MA: Center for Applied Science Technology, Inc., No. 40.

Roswell, D. (1999). Guiding self-discipline. *Today's Child.* http://www.angelfire.com/on3/todayschild/discipline.htm.

Saisan, J., Smith, M., & Segal, J. (2011). *Child abuse and neglect: Recognizing and preventing child abuse.* Helpguide.org. Updated June 2011. Retrieved July, 2011. http://helpguide.org/mental/child_abuse.

Santrock, J. (1997). *Life-span development* (7th ed.). New York: McGraw-Hill.

Sarafolean, M. (2000, July/August). Depression in school-age children and adolescents: Characteristics, assessment and prevention. *A Pediatric Perspective, 9*(4), 1–5.

Schimelpfening, N. (2010, April 2). *Childhood depression: Signs and symptoms of depression in children.* http://depression.about.com/od/childhood/a/signssymptom.htm.

Schneier, F. & Welkowitz, L. (1996). *The hidden face of shyness.* New York: Avon Books.

Silverman, R. (2008, April 12). *10 tips on teaching respect to children: You can't get it if you don't give it!.* http://www.drrobynsilverman.com/parenting-tips/10-tips-on-teaching- respect-to-children-you-cant-get-it-if-you-dont-give-it/.

Stein, N. (1998). Sexual harassment in school: The public performance of gendered violence. In C. Woyshner, & H. Gelfond (Eds.), *Minding women: Reshaping the educational realm* (pp. 227–45). Cambridge, MA: Harvard Educational Review.

Stickney, M. & Miltenberger, R. (1998). School refusal behavior: Prevalence, characteristics, and schools' response. *Education & Treatment of Children, 21*(2), 160–70.

Stipek, D. (1993). *Motivation to learn: From theory to practice.* Needham Heights, MA: Allyn & Bacon.

Substance Abuse and Mental Health Services Administration (SAMHSA). (2011). *Teaching honesty.* U.S. Department of Health and Human Services. Updated January 19, 2011. http://www.bblocks.samhsa.gov/family/activities/family_activities/TTeachHonesty.aspx.

Taylor, J. (2005, April). *Fear of failure: A childhood epidemic.* http://www.keepkidshealthy.com/parenting_tips/fear_of_failure.html

Teaching Children Goal Setting. (2011). *Achieve Goal Setting Success.com.* http://www.achieve-goal-setting-success.com/teaching-children-goal-setting.html.

Temke, M. & Carman, R. (2006). *The effects of divorce on children.* University of New Hampshire Extension. Family and Consumer Resources, pdf file. Updated May 2006.

Terry, R. (1993). *Courage in action.* San Francisco: Jossey-Bass.

The Parent Institute. (2005). *Seven proven ways to motivate children to do better in school.* Fairfax Station, VA: The Parent Institute.

Vanderwalker, M. (2003). *Study skills fun!* Warminster, PA: Mar*co Products, Inc.

Varvil-Weld, D. (2011). *Your child's underachievement and what to do about it.* The Pauquette Center of Family Services. Updated July. http://www.pauquette.com.

Vassar, G. (2011, April 28). Respect: One antidote for shame. *Educational Network.* http://lakesideconnect.com/anger-and-violence/respect-one-antidote-for-hame/?gclid=CLeh7Yy2oKkCFQUGbAodblJAvQ.

Wang, C. & Daro, D. (1997). *Current trends in child abuse reporting and fatalities: The results of the 1996 annual fifty state survey.* Chicago: National Center on Child Abuse Prevention Research, National Committee to Prevent Child Abuse.

Watkins, C. (2004). *Separation anxiety.* Northern County Psychiatric Associates. http://www.baltimorepsych.com/separation_anxiety.

White, B. (2011). *Seven qualities of a good leader.* Greenstein, Rogoff, Olsen & Co., LLP, CPA's. Retrieved August 2011. www.GROCO.com.

White, H. (2011). *How to teach children organizational skills.* http://www.livestrong.com/article/78655-teach-children-organization-skills/.

Whitehead, S. (2010). How to teach kids self-discipline. *Parenthood.* Retrieved August 2010. http://www.parenthood.com/article-topics/how_to_teach_kids_selfdiscipline.html/full-view.

Williams, K., Forgas, D., & von Hippel, W. (Eds.). (2005). *The social outcast: Ostracism, social exclusion, rejection, & bullying.* New York: Psychology Press.

Windell, J. (1997). *Children who say no when you want them to say yes.* New York: Macmillan.

Wipfler. P. (2011). *Helping children with separation and divorce*. Retrieved January 2011. http://www.handinhandparenting.org/news/47/64/Helping-Children-with-Separation-and-Divorce.

Wittner, J., Thompson, D., & Loesch, L. (1997). *Classroom guidance activities: A sourcebook for elementary counselors*. Minneapolis: Educational Media Corporation.

About the Author

Mary Lou McCormick is a licensed professional guidance counselor who has made it her life-long career working with young people in "at-risk" schools in Texas, New Mexico, and Nevada. Along with her regular duties as a school guidance counselor in Las Vegas, she served as a Clark County School District crisis counselor for all grade levels for many years. She earned a master's degree in Education from West Texas A&M and pursued graduate studies in psychological and educational counseling at Texas Tech University. As a former elementary and secondary school teacher, she first realized many of today's youth are in serious trouble. As she relays, "Without new methods and strategies compatible with democratic principles for raising and training today's kids, in place of punishment, intimidation and threats, the incidence of maladjustment, deficiency, and outright rebellion and violence found among many of today's kids will most likely continue to rise."

www.ingramcontent.com/pod-product-compliance
Lightning Source LLC
Chambersburg PA
CBHW051810230426
43672CB00012B/2681

prochait son ordination précipitée et son élévation irrégulière ; son prédécesseur Ignace, qu'on avait forcé d'abdiquer, avait encore pour lui la compassion publique et l'opiniâtreté de ses adhérens. Ils en appelèrent à Nicolas 1ᵉʳ, l'un des plus orgueilleux et des plus ambitieux pontifes romains, qui saisit avidement l'occasion de juger et de condamner son rival. Leur querelle fut encore aigrie par un conflit de juridiction ; les deux prélats se disputaient le roi et la nation des Bulgares, dont la récente conversion au christianisme paraissait de peu d'importance à l'un et à l'autre, s'il ne comptait pas ces nouveaux prosélytes au nombre de ses sujets spirituels. Avec l'aide de sa cour, le patriarche grec remporta la victoire ; mais, dans la violence de la contestation, il déposa à son tour le successeur de saint Pierre, et enveloppa toute l'Église latine dans le reproche de schisme et d'hérésie ; Photius sacrifia la paix du monde à un règne court et précaire. Le César Bardas, son patron, l'entraîna dans sa chute ; et Basile le Macédonien fit un acte de justice en replaçant Ignace, dont on n'avait pas assez considéré l'âge et la dignité. Du fond de son couvent ou de sa prison, Photius sollicita la faveur du nouveau souverain par des plaintes pathétiques et d'adroites flatteries ; et à peine son rival eut-il fermé les yeux, qu'il remonta sur le siége patriarchal de Constantinople. Après la mort de Basile, Photius éprouva les vicissitudes des cours et l'ingratitude d'un élève monté sur le trône. Le patriarche fut déposé pour la seconde fois, et, dans la solitude de ses derniers momens, regretta peut-être d'avoir sacrifié à l'ambition les douceurs de l'étude et la liberté de la vie séculière. A chaque révolution, le clergé docile cédait, sans hésiter, au souffle de la cour et au signe du souverain ; un synode composé de trois cents évêques était toujours également préparé à célébrer le triomphe du saint, ou à anathématiser la chute de l'exécrable Photius (1); et, les papes, séduits par des promesses trompeuses de secours ou de récompenses, se laissèrent entraîner à approuver ces opérations diverses, et ratifièrent, par leurs lettres ou par leurs légats, les synodes de Constantinople : mais la cour et le peuple, Ignace et Photius, rejetaient également les prétentions des papes; on insulta, on emprisonna leurs ministres ; la procession du Saint-Esprit fut oubliée, la Bulgarie annexée pour toujours au trône de Byzance, et le schisme prolongé par leur censure rigoureuse des ordinations multipliées qu'avait faites un patriarche irrégulier. L'ignorance et la corruption du dixième siècle suspendirent les rapports des deux nations sans adoucir leur inimitié; mais lorsque l'épée des Normands eut fait rentrer les églises de la Pouille sous la juridiction de Rome, le patriar-

---

(1) Le synode de Constantinople, tenu en l'an 869, est le huitième des conciles généraux, la dernière assemblée de l'Orient qui ait été reconnue par l'Église romaine. Elle rejette les synodes de Constantinople des années 867 et 872, qui furent cependant également nombreux et bruyans; mais ils furent favorables à Photius.

che, en faisant les derniers adieux à son troupeau, l'avertit, par une lettre violente, d'éviter et d'abhorrer les erreurs des Latins. La naissante majesté du pontife romain ne put souffrir l'insolence d'un rebelle; et Michel Cerularius fut publiquement excommunié par ses légats au milieu de Constantinople. Secouant la poussière de leurs pieds, ils déposèrent sur l'autel de Sainte-Sophie un anathême (1) terrible qui détaillait les sept mortelles hérésies des Grecs, et dévouait leurs coupables prédicateurs et leurs infortunés sectaires à l'éternelle société du démon et de ses anges de ténèbres. La concorde parut quelquefois se rétablir : selon que l'exigeaient les besoins de l'Église et de l'État, on affecta de part et d'autre le langage de la douceur et de la charité; mais les Grecs n'ont jamais abjuré leurs erreurs, les papes n'ont point révoqué leur sentence; et l'on peut dater de cette époque la consommation du schisme de l'Orient. Il s'augmenta de chacune des entreprises audacieuses des pontifes romains. Les malheurs et l'humiliation des souverains de l'Allemagne firent rougir et trembler les empereurs de Constantinople, et le peuple se scandalisa de la puissance temporelle et de la vie militaire du clergé latin (2).

Les papes excommunient le patriarche de Constantinople et les Grecs. A. D. 1054, 16 juillet.

---

(1) *Voyez* cet anathême dans les *Conciles*, t. XI, p. 1457-1460.

(2) Anne Comnène (*Alexiad.*, l. I, p. 31-33) peint l'horreur, non-seulement de l'Église, mais de la cour, pour

L'antipathie des Grecs et des Latins se nourrit et se manifesta dans les trois premières expéditions de la Palestine. Alexis Comnène employa tous ses artifices, au moins à éloigner ces redoutables pèlerins. Ses successeurs, Manuel et Isaac l'Ange, conspirèrent avec les musulmans la ruine des plus illustres chefs des Francs, et leur politique insidieuse et perfide fut toujours secondée par l'obéissance volontaire de leurs sujets de toutes les classes. On peut sans doute attribuer en partie cette aversion à la différence du langage, de l'habillement et des manières, qui divise et aliène les unes des autres presque toutes les nations du globe. L'orgueil et la prudence du souverain s'indignaient également de ces invasions d'armées étrangères qui réclamaient impérieusement le droit de traverser ses États et de passer sous les murs de sa capitale. Ses sujets étaient pillés et insultés par les grossiers habitans de l'Occident, et la haine de ces Grecs pusillanimes était envenimée par la secrète jalousie que leur inspiraient les pieuses et courageuses entreprises des Francs ; mais le zèle aveugle de la religion ajoutait encore aux motifs profanes de l'aversion nationale : au lieu de se voir amicalement reçus par leurs frères, les chrétiens de l'Orient, les chrétiens d'Occident entendaient retentir autour d'eux les noms de

---

Grégoire VII, les papes et la communion romaine. Le style de Cinnamus et de Nicétas est encore plus véhément. Combien cependant la voix de l'histoire est calme et modérée en comparaison de celle des théologiens !

schismatiques et d'hérétiques, plus offensans pour les oreilles orthodoxes que ceux de païens ou d'infidèles. Au lieu d'inspirer de la confiance par la conformité du culte et de la foi, les Francs étaient abhorrés des Grecs pour quelques règles de discipline ou quelques questions de théologie, dans lesquelles ils différaient, eux ou leur clergé, de l'Église orientale. Dans la croisade de Louis VII, les prêtres grecs lavèrent et purifièrent un autel souillé par le sacrifice qu'y avait offert un prêtre français. Les compagnons de Frédéric Barberousse déplorent les insultes et les mauvais traitemens qu'ils ont éprouvés, particulièrement des évêques et des moines. Ceux-ci, dans leurs prières et leurs sermons, animaient le peuple contre des Barbares impies; et le patriarche est accusé d'avoir déclaré que les fidèles pouvaient obtenir la rémission de tous leurs péchés en exterminant les schismatiques (1). Un enthousiaste, nommé Dorothée, alarma

---

(1) Son historien anonyme (*de Expedit. Asiat. Fred.* 1, *in Canisii Lection. antiq.*, t. III, part. II, p. 511, édit. de Basnage) cite les sermons du patriarche grec : *Quomodo Græcis injunxerat in remissionem peccatorum peregrinos occidere et delere de terrâ.* Taginon observe (*in Scriptores Freher*, t. I, p. 409, édit. de Struv.): *Græci hæreticos nos appellant: clerici et monachi dictis et factis persequuntur.* Nous pouvons ajouter la déclaration de l'empereur Baudouin, quinze ans après : *Hæc est (gens) quæ Latinos omnes non hominum nomine, sed canum dignabatur, quorum sanguinem effundere penè inter merita reputabant.* (*Gesta Innocent.* III, c. 92, *in* Muratori, *Script. rerum italicar.*, t. III, part. I, p. 536.) Il peut y avoir quelque exagération, mais elle n'en

l'empereur et le tranquillisa en même temps en lui prédisant que les hérétiques allemands attaqueraient la porte de Blachernes, mais que leur punition offrirait un exemple effrayant de la vengeance divine. Les passages de ces grandes armées étaient des événemens rares et dangereux; mais les croisades firent naître entre les deux nations une correspondance qui étendit leurs lumières sans affaiblir leurs préjugés. Le luxe et les richesses de Constantinople attiraient les productions de tous les climats. Le travail et l'industrie de ses nombreux habitans balançaient cette importation. Sa position invite le commerce de toutes les parties du monde; et son commerce fut dans tous les temps entre les mains des étrangers. Lorsque Amalfi eut perdu son importance, les Vénitiens, les Pisans et les Génois, établirent des factoreries dans la capitale de l'empire; on récompensa leurs services par des honneurs et des priviléges; ils acquirent des terres et des maisons; leurs familles se multiplièrent par des mariages avec les nationaux; et lorsqu'on eut toléré une mosquée mahométane, il fut impossible d'interdire les églises du rit romain (1). Les deux femmes de Manuel Comnène (2) étaient de

<small>Les Latins à Constantinople.</small>

---

contribua pas moins efficacement à l'action et à la réaction de la haine, qui était réelle.

(1) *Voyez* Anne Comnène (*Alexiad.*, l. VI, p. 161, 162), et un passage remarquable de Nicétas dans Manuel, (l. v, c. 9), qui observe sur les Vénitiens, κατα βμηνη και φρατριας την Κωνσταντινου πολιν της οικειας ηλλαξαντο, etc.

(2) Ducange, *Fam. Byzant.*, 186, 187.

la race des Francs; la première, belle-sœur de l'empereur Conrad, et l'autre, fille du prince d'Antioche. Il obtint pour son fils Alexis une fille de Philippe-Auguste, roi de France, et il donna sa fille à un marquis de Montferrat, qui avait été élevé dans le palais de Constantinople et revêtu des dignités de la cour. Ce prince grec aspirait à la conquête de l'Occident, dont il avait combattu les armées; il estimait la valeur des Francs, se fiait à leur fidélité (1), et récompensait assez singulièrement leurs talens militaires par des offices lucratifs de juges et de trésoriers. La politique de Manuel lui suggéra de solliciter l'alliance du pape, et la voix publique l'accusa de partialité pour la nation et la religion des Latins (2). Sous son règne et sous celui de son successeur Alexis, on les désignait également sous les noms odieux d'étrangers, d'hérétiques, ou de favoris. Ce triple crime fut sévèrement expié dans le tumulte qui an-

---

(1) Nicétas, *in* Manuel, l. VII, c. 2. *Regnante enim (Manuele).... apud eum tantam latinus populus reperarat gratiam, ut neglectis Græculis suis tanquam viris mollibus effœminatis.... solis Latinis grandia committeret negotia.... erga eos profusâ liberalitate abundabat.... ex omni orbe ad eum tanquam ad benefactorem nobiles et ignobiles concurrebant.* Guillaume de Tyr, XXII, c. 10.

(2) Les soupçons des Grecs auraient été confirmés s'ils eussent vu les lettres politiques de Manuel au pape Alexandre III, l'ennemi de son ennemi Frédéric Ier, dans lesquelles l'empereur déclare le désir de réunir les Grecs et les Latins en un seul troupeau sous un seul berger, etc. *Voy.* Fleury, *Hist. ecclés.*, t. XV, p. 187, 213-243.

nonça le retour et l'élévation d'Andronic (1). Le peuple courut aux armes ; des côtes de l'Asie le tyran envoya ses troupes et ses galères seconder la vengeance nationale; et la résistance impuissante des étrangers ne servit qu'à motiver et redoubler la fureur de leurs assassins. Ni l'âge, ni le sexe, ni les liens de l'amitié ou de la parenté, ne purent sauver les victimes dévouées de la haine, de l'avarice et du fanatisme. Les Latins furent massacrés dans les rues et dans leurs maisons ; leur quartier fut réduit en cendres ; on brûla les ecclésiastiques dans leurs églises, et les malades dans leurs hôpitaux. On peut se faire une idée du carnage par l'acte de clémence qui le termina : on vendit aux Turcs quatre mille chrétiens qui survivaient à la proscription générale. Les prêtres et les moines se montraient les plus actifs et les plus acharnés à la destruction des schismatiques ; ils chantèrent pieusement un *Te Deum* lorsque la tête d'un cardinal romain, légat du pape, eut été séparée de son corps, attachée à la queue d'un chien, et traînée, avec des railleries féroces, à travers les rues de la ville. Les plus prudens des Latins s'étaient, dès la première alarme, retirés sur leurs vaisseaux; ils échappèrent à travers l'Hellespont à cette scène de carnage. Dans leur fuite, ils portèrent le ravage

---

(1) *Voyez* les relations des Grecs et des Latins dans Nicétas, dans Alexis Comnène (c. 10), et Guillaume de Tyr (l. XXII, c. 10, 11, 12, 13); la première, modérée et concise; la seconde, verbeuse, véhémente et tragique.

et l'incendie sur une côte de deux cents milles d'étendue, exercèrent une cruelle vengeance sur les innocens sujets de l'empire, firent particulièrement sentir leurs fureurs aux prêtres et aux moines, et se dédommagèrent, par le butin qu'ils enlevèrent, de la perte de leurs richesses et de celles de leurs amis. A leur retour, ils firent connaître à l'Italie et à l'Europe la faiblesse, l'opulence, la perfidie et la haine des Grecs, dont les vices furent représentés comme les suites naturelles du schisme et de l'hérésie. Les pélerins de la première croisade avaient négligé, par un scrupule de conscience, les plus belles occasions de s'ouvrir pour toujours le chemin de Jérusalem en s'assurant la possession de Constantinople; mais une révolution domestique invita et força presque les Français et les Vénitiens à la conquête de l'empire d'Orient.

Dans le cours de l'histoire de Byzance, j'ai déjà raconté l'hypocrisie, l'ambition, la tyrannie et la chute d'Andronic, le dernier rejeton mâle de la famille des Comnènes qui ait régné à Constantinople. La révolution qui le précipita du trône sauva la vie et produisit l'élévation d'Isaac l'Ange, qui descendait, par les femmes, de la même dynastie (1). Le succes-

Règne et caractère d'Isaac l'Ange. A. D. 1185-1195, septembre 12.

---

(1) Le sénateur Nicétas a composé en trois livres l'histoire du règne d'Isaac l'Ange (p. 228-290), et les charges de logothète ou principal secrétaire, et de juge du voile ou du palais, ne donnent pas lieu d'attendre de sa part une grande impartialité. Il est vrai qu'il n'écrivit qu'après la chute et la mort de son bienfaiteur.

seur d'un second Néron aurait facilement obtenu l'estime et l'affection de ses sujets ; mais ils furent forcés quelquefois de regretter l'administration d'Andronic. Doué d'un esprit solide et d'une tête forte, ce tyran avait su apercevoir les rapports qui liaient son intérêt personnel avec celui du public ; et tandis qu'il faisait trembler ceux qui pouvaient lui donner de l'inquiétude, les particuliers obscurs et les provinces éloignées bénissaient la justice rigoureuse de leur souverain. Son successeur, vain et jaloux du pouvoir suprême, manquait à la fois du courage et des talens nécessaires pour l'exercer ; ses vices devinrent funestes à ses sujets, et ses vertus (si toutefois il en eut) leur furent inutiles. Les Grecs, qui imputaient toutes leurs calamités à sa négligence, lui refusèrent le mérite des avantages passagers ou accidentels dont ils purent jouir sous son règne. Isaac sommeillait sur son trône et ne se réveillait qu'à la voix du plaisir. Ses heures de loisir étaient consacrées à des comédiens et à des bouffons, et même pour ces bouffons Isaac était un objet de mépris. Le luxe de ses fêtes et de ses bâtimens surpassa tout ce qu'en avaient jamais étalé les cours ; le nombre de ses eunuques ou de ses domestiques montait à vingt mille, et la dépense de sa table et de sa maison à quatre mille livres d'argent par jour, ou environ quatre millions sterling par an. L'oppression était le seul moyen de fournir à ses besoins, et le peuple s'indignait également et des abus commis dans la levée des revenus publics et de celui qui s'en faisait à la cour. Tandis que les Grecs comptaient les jours de leur esclavage ; un prophète, auquel Isaac accorda pour récompense la dignité de patriarche, lui annonça que, durant un règne heureux de trente-deux ans, il étendrait son empire jusqu'au mont Liban et ses conquêtes au-delà de l'Euphrate. Mais sa seule démarche à l'appui de cette prédiction, fut de réclamer de Saladin (1), par une ambassade scandaleuse autant que fastueuse, la restitution du saint-sépulcre, et de proposer à l'ennemi du nom chrétien une alliance défensive et offensive. Entre les indignes mains d'Isaac et de son frère, les débris de l'empire grec furent abaissés jusque dans la poussière. L'île de Chypre, dont le nom réveille les idées de l'élégance et du plaisir, fut envahie par un prince de la maison des Comnènes ; et, par un singulier enchaînement de circonstances, la valeur de Richard d'Angleterre fit passer ce royaume à la maison de Lusignan, pour qui il compensa richement la perte de Jérusalem.

La révolte des Valaques et des Bulgares fut également honteuse pour la monarchie et inquiétante pour la capitale. Depuis la victoire de Basile II, ils avaient conservé durant plus de cent soixante-dix ans aux princes de Byzance une soumission très-peu

Révolte des Bulgares.
A. D. 1186.

---

(1) *Voyez* Bohadin (*Vit. Saladin.*, p. 129-131, 226, vers. Schultens). L'ambassadeur d'Isaac parlait également le français, le grec et l'arabe, et c'est un phénomène pour ce siècle. On reçut honorablement ses ambassades ; mais elles ne produisirent d'autre effet que beaucoup de scandale dans l'Occident.

gênante; mais on n'avait point essayé, par quelque moyen efficace de soumettre ces tribus sauvages au joug des mœurs et des lois. Par l'ordre d'Isaac, on les priva de leur unique moyen de subsistance en leur enlevant leurs troupeaux pour servir à la pompe des fêtes nuptiales du souverain, et le refus d'une égalité de paye et de rang dans le service militaire, acheva d'aliéner ces guerriers indociles. Pierre et Asan, deux chefs puissans de la race des anciens rois (1), défendirent leurs droits et la liberté nationale : les énergumènes qui leur servaient de prédicateurs annoncèrent au peuple que le glorieux saint Démétrius, leur patron, avait abandonné pour toujours le parti des Grecs; et la rebellion s'étendit des bords du Danube aux montagnes de la Thrace et de la Macédoine. Après quelques efforts impuissans, Isaac l'Ange et son frère reconnurent leur indépendance, et les troupes impériales furent bientôt découragées par la vue des ossemens de leurs camarades, dispersés le long des passages du mont Hémus. La valeur et la politique de Jean ou Joannice établirent solidement le second royaume des Bulgares. Ce rusé Barbare envoya une ambassade à Innocent III. Il se reconnut enfant de Rome par la naissance et la religion (2), et reçut humblement du

---

(1) Ducange, *Fam. dalmat.*, pag. 318, 319, 320. La correspondance du pontife romain avec le roi des Bulgares se trouve dans les *Gesta Innocent. III*, chap. 66-82, p. 513-525.

(2) Le pape reconnaît son origine, *à nobili urbis Romæ*

pontife la permission de battre monnaie, le titre de roi et un archevêque ou patriarche latin. Le Vatican triompha de cette conquête spirituelle, première cause du schisme; et si les Grecs eussent conservé leur suprématie sur l'Église de Bulgarie, ils auraient abandonné sans regret toute prétention sur la monarchie.

Les Bulgares haïssaient assez l'empire grec pour demander au ciel, dans leurs prières, la durée du règne d'Isaac l'Ange, le plus sûr garant de leur indépendance et de leur prospérité ; cependant leurs chefs enveloppaient dans le même mépris toute la nation et toute la famille de l'empereur. « Chez tous les Grecs, dit Asan à ses soldats, le climat, le caractère et l'éducation, sont toujours les mêmes et produiront toujours les mêmes effets : regardez au bout de cette lance les longues banderoles qui flottent au gré du vent; elles ne diffèrent que par la couleur : composées de la même soie, ouvrées par les mêmes mains, celles qui sont teintes en pourpre n'ont ni plus de prix ni plus de valeur que les autres (1). » Le règne d'Isaac vit s'élever et tomber

Usurpation et caractère d'Alexis l'Ange. A. D. 1195-1203, 8 avril.

---

prosapiâ genitores tui originem traxerunt. M. d'Anville (*États de l'Europe*, p. 258-262) explique cette tradition et la forte ressemblance de la langue latine avec l'idiome de Valachie. Le torrent des émigrations avait entraîné les colonies placées par Trajan dans la Dacie, des bords du Danube sur ceux du Wolga ; et une seconde vague les avait ramenées du Wolga au Danube. Cela est possible, mais fort extraordinaire.

(1) Cette parabole est bien dans le style sauvage; mais

plusieurs prétendans à l'empire. Un général qui avait repoussé les flottes de Sicile, fut entraîné à la révolte et à sa perte par l'ingratitude de son souverain; et le voluptueux repos du prince fut souvent troublé par des émeutes et de secrètes conjurations. Sauvé plusieurs fois par hasard ou par le zèle de ses domestiques, il succomba enfin sous les trames d'un frère ambitieux, qui, pour acquérir la possession précaire d'un trône chancelant, oublia les sentimens de la fidélité, de la nature et de l'affection (1). Tandis qu'Isaac chassait presque seul dans les vallées de la Thrace, Alexis, dans le camp, se revêtit de la pourpre aux acclamations de toute l'armée. La capitale et le clergé souscrivirent à ce choix ; et la vanité du nouveau souverain rejeta le nom de ses pères pour le nom pompeux de la race royale des Comnènes. J'ai épuisé toutes les expressions du mépris en parlant de son frère Isaac ; et j'ajouterai seulement que l'indigne Alexis (2) ne se soutint, durant un règne de huit ans, que par les vices plus mâles de son

---

je voudrais que le Valaque n'y eût pas fait entrer le nom classique des Mysiens, les expériences de la pierre d'aimant, et le passage d'un ancien poëte comique. Nicétas, *in Alex. Comneno*, l. 1, p. 299-300.

(1) Les Latins aggravent l'ingratitude d'Alexis, en supposant que son frère Isaac l'avait délivré des mains des Turcs qui le tenaient en captivité. On a sans doute affirmé ce conte pathétique à Venise et à Zara, mais je n'en trouve aucune trace dans les historiens grecs.

(2) *Voyez* le règne d'Alexis l'Ange ou Comnène dans les trois livres de Nicétas, p. 291-352.

épouse Euphrosyne. Isaac n'apprit sa chute qu'en se voyant poursuivi en ennemi par ses gardes infidèles. Il courut en fuyant devant eux jusqu'à Stagyre en Macédoine, éloignée d'environ cinquante milles; mais seul, sans projet et sans ressource, le malheureux Isaac ne put éviter son sort; il fut arrêté, conduit à Constantinople, privé de la vue et jeté dans une tour solitaire, où il fut réduit au pain et à l'eau pour toute subsistance. Au moment de la révolution, son fils Alexis, élevé dans l'espérance de l'empire, n'avait encore que douze ans. L'usurpateur épargna son enfance, et le destina, soit durant la paix, soit durant la guerre, à faire partie de la pompe de sa cour. L'armée étant campée sur les bords de la mer, un vaisseau italien favorisa la fuite du jeune prince; sous l'habit d'un matelot, il échappa aux recherches de ses ennemis, passa l'Hellespont, et se trouva bientôt en Sicile à l'abri du danger. Après avoir salué la demeure des saints apôtres et imploré la protection du pape Innocent III, Alexis se rendit à l'invitation de sa sœur Irène, épouse de Philippe de Souabe, roi des Romains. Mais, en traversant l'Italie, il apprit que la fleur des chevaliers d'Occident, assemblés à Venise, se préparaient à passer dans la Terre-Sainte; et il s'éleva dans son cœur un rayon d'espoir d'obtenir de leurs invincibles armes le rétablissement de son père.

Environ dix ou douze ans après la perte de Jérusalem, la noblesse de France fut appelée de nouveau au service de la guerre sainte par la voix d'un

Quatrième croisade, A. D. 1198.

troisième prophète, moins extravagant peut-être que Pierre l'Ermite, mais fort au-dessous de saint Bernard, comme politique et comme orateur. Un prêtre ignorant, des environs de Paris, Foulques (1) de Neuilly, abandonna le service de sa paroisse pour le rôle plus flatteur de missionnaire ambulant et de prédicateur du peuple. La réputation de sa sainteté et de ses miracles se répandit au loin ; il déclamait avec véhémence contre les vices du siècle, et les sermons qu'il prêchait à Paris, en pleine rue, convertirent des voleurs, des usuriers, des filles publiques et jusqu'à des docteurs et des écoliers de l'université. A peine Innocent III avait pris possession de la chaire de saint Pierre, qu'il fit proclamer en Italie, en Allemagne et en France, la nécessité ou l'obligation d'une nouvelle croisade (2). L'éloquent pontife déplorait pathétiquement la ruine de Jérusalem, le triomphe des païens et la honte de la chrétienté : sa libéralité proposait la rémission des péchés et une indulgence plénière à tous ceux qui serviraient dans la Palestine une année en personne

---

(1) *Voyez* Fleury (*Hist. ecclés.*, t. XVI, p. 26, etc.), et Villehardouin, n° 1, avec les *Observations* de Ducange, que je suis toujours censé citer avec le texte original.

(2) La *Vie contemporaine du pape Innocent III*, publiée par Baluze et Muratori (*Script. rerum ital.*, t. III, part. I, p. 486-568), est très-précieuse par l'importance des instructions insérées dans le texte ; on peut y lire la bulle de la croisade, c. 84, 85.

ou deux ans par un substitut (1). Parmi les légats et les orateurs qui entonnèrent la trompette sacrée, Foulques de Neuilly tint le premier rang par l'éclat de son zèle et par ses succès. La situation des principaux monarques de l'Europe n'était pas favorable aux vœux du saint père. L'empereur Frédéric II, encore enfant, voyait déchirer ses États d'Allemagne par la rivalité des maisons de Souabe et de Brunswick et les factions mémorables des Guelfes et des Gibelins. Philippe-Auguste de France avait accompli ce vœu dangereux et n'était point disposé à le renouveler ; mais comme ce monarque n'était pas moins avide de louanges que de puissance, il assigna volontiers un fonds perpétuel pour le service de la Terre-Sainte. Richard d'Angleterre, rassasié de gloire et dégoûté par les accidens de sa première expédition, osa répondre par une plaisanterie aux exhortations de Foulques de Neuilly, qui réprimandait avec la même assurance les peuples et les rois. « Vous me conseillez, lui dit Plantagenet, de me défaire de mes trois filles ; l'orgueil, l'avarice et l'incontinence : pour les remettre à ceux à qui elles conviennent le mieux, je lègue mon orgueil aux templiers, mon avarice aux moines de Cîteaux, et

---

(1) « Porce cil pardon fut issi gran, se s'en esmeurent mult li cuers des genz, et mult s'en croisierent, porce que li pardons ere si gran. » (Villehardouin, n° 1.) Nos philosophes peuvent raffiner sur les causes des croisades ; mais tels étaient les véritables sentimens d'un chevalier français.

mon incontinence aux évêques. ». Mais les grands vassaux et les princes du second ordre obéirent docilement au prédicateur. Le jeune Thibaut, comte de Champagne, âgé de vingt-deux ans, s'élança le premier dans cette sainte carrière, animé par l'exemple de son père et de son frère aîné, dont le premier avait marché à la tête de la seconde croisade, et l'autre était mort en Palestine avec le titre de roi de Jérusalem. Deux mille deux cents chevaliers lui devaient l'hommage (1) et le service militaire ; la noblesse de Champagne excellait dans l'exercice des armes (2), et par son mariage avec l'héritière de Navarre, Thibaut pouvait ajouter à ses troupes une bande courageuse de Gascons tirés des deux côtés des Pyrénées. Il eut pour compagnon d'armes Louis, comte de Blois et de Chartres, qui tirait comme lui son origine du sang royal ; ces deux princes étaient l'un et l'autre neveux en même temps du roi de France et de celui d'Angleterre. Dans la foule des barons et des prélats qui imitèrent leur zèle, je distingue la naissance et le mérite de Matthieu de Montmorency, le fameux Simon de Montfort, le fléau

Les barons français se croisent.

---

(1) Ce nombre de fiefs, dont dix-huit cents devaient hommage lige, était enregistré dans l'église de Saint-Étienne de Troyes, et fut attesté en 1213 par le maréchal de la Champagne (Ducange, *Observ.*, p. 254).

(2) *Campania.... militiæ privilegio singularis excellit.... in tyrociniis... prolusione armorum*; etc. Ducange, p. 249, tiré de l'ancienne Chronique de Jérusalem, A. D. 1177-1199.

des Albigeois, et le vaillant Geoffroi de Villehardouin (1), maréchal de Champagne (2), qui a daigné écrire ou dicter dans l'idiome (3) barbare de son siècle et de son pays (4), la relation des conseils et des expéditions dans lesquelles il joua lui-même un des principaux rôles. A la même époque, Baudouin, comte de Flandre, qui avait épousé la sœur de Thibaut, prit la croix à Bruges, ainsi que son frère Henri et les principaux chevaliers et citoyens de cette

---

(1) Le nom de Villehardouin tire son origine d'un village ou château du diocèse de Troyes, entre Bar et Arcis. La famille était noble et ancienne. La branche aînée de notre historien subsista jusqu'en 1400; la cadette, qui acquit la principauté de l'Achaïe, se fondit dans la maison de Savoie (Ducange, p. 235-245).

(2) Son père et ses descendans possédèrent cet office; mais Ducange n'en a pas suivi la trace avec son activité ordinaire. Je trouve qu'en 1356 cet office passa dans la maison de Conflans; mais ces maréchaux de province sont éclipsés depuis long-temps par les maréchaux de France.

(3) Ce langage, dont je donnerai quelques échantillons, a été expliqué par Vigenère et Ducange dans une version et un glossaire. Le président de Brosses (*Mécanisme des langues*, t. II, p. 83) le donne comme un modèle du langage qui a cessé d'être français, et qui ne peut être compris que par les grammairiens.

(4) Son âge et son expression, « moi qui *ceste œuvre dicta* » (n° 62, etc.), peuvent faire naître le soupçon (plus fondé que celui de M. Wood relativement à Homère) qu'il ne savait ni lire ni écrire. Cependant la Champagne peut se vanter d'avoir produit les deux premiers historiens, les nobles pères de la prose française, Villehardouin et Joinville.

riche et industrieuse province (1). Les chefs prononcèrent solennellement leur vœu dans l'église et le ratifièrent dans des tournois. Après avoir débattu les opérations de l'entreprise dans plusieurs assemblées générales, on résolut, pour délivrer la Palestine, de porter la guerre en Égypte, contrée ruinée, depuis la mort de Saladin, par la famine et les guerres civiles. Mais le sort de tant d'armées conduites par des souverains démontrait le danger d'entreprendre par terre cette longue expédition; et quoique les Flamands habitassent les côtes de l'Océan, les barons français manquaient de vaisseaux et n'avaient pas la moindre connaissance de l'art de la navigation. Ils nommèrent sagement six députés ou représentans, du nombre desquels était Villehardouin, et leur donnèrent le pouvoir de traiter pour la confédération et de diriger tous ses mouvemens. Les États maritimes de l'Italie pouvaient seuls transporter les pèlerins, leurs armes et leurs chevaux; et les six députés se rendirent à Venise pour solliciter, par des motifs de dévotion et d'intérêt, le secours de cette puissante république.

Etat des Vénitiens. A. D. 697-1200.

Dans l'invasion d'Attila en Italie, j'ai raconté (2)

---

(1) La croisade, les règnes du comte de Flandre, de Baudouin et de son frère Henri, font le sujet particulier d'une Histoire composée par Doutremens, jésuite (*Constantinopolis Belgica*, Tournai, 1638, in-4º), que je ne connais que d'après ce qu'en a dit Ducange.

(2) *Hist.*, etc., t. VI, p. 340.

que les Vénitiens, échappés des villes détruites du continent, avaient cherché une obscure retraite dans la chaîne des petites îles qui bordent l'extrémité du golfe Adriatique. Environnés de la mer, libres, indigens, laborieux et inaccessibles, ils se réunirent insensiblement en république : les premiers fondemens de Venise furent jetés dans l'île de Rialto, et l'élection annuelle de douze tribuns fut remplacée par l'office à vie d'un duc ou doge perpétuel. Placés entre les deux empires, les Vénitiens s'enorgueillissent de l'opinion qu'ils ont toujours conservé leur indépendance primitive (1); ils ont soutenu par les armes leur liberté contre les Latins, et pourraient facilement établir leurs droits par des écrits. Charlemagne lui-même abandonna toute prétention de souveraineté sur les îles du golfe Adriatique; son fils Pépin échoua dans l'attaque des lagunes ou canaux, trop profonds pour sa cavalerie et trop peu pour l'approche de ses vaisseaux; et sous le règne de tous les empereurs d'Allemagne, les terres de la république ont été clairement distinguées du royaume d'Italie. Mais les habitans de Venise adoptaient eux-mêmes l'opinion générale des nations étrangères et des Grecs leurs souverains, qui

---

(1) Pagi (*Critica*, t. III, A. D. 810, n° 4, etc.) discute la fondation, l'indépendance de Venise, et l'invasion de Pepin. (*Voyez* la *Dissert.* de Beretti, *Chor. Ital. medii ævi*; *in* Muratori, *Script.*, t. x, p. 153.) Les deux critiques montrent un peu de partialité, le Français contre, et l'Italien pour la république.

les considéraient comme une portion inaliénable de l'empire d'Orient (1). Les neuvième et dixième siècles offrent des preuves nombreuses et incontestables de leur dépendance ; et les vains titres, les serviles honneurs de la cour de Byzance, si recherchés de leurs ducs, auraient avili les magistrats d'un peuple libre. Mais l'ambition de Venise et la faiblesse de Constantinople relâchèrent insensiblement les liens de cette dépendance, qui n'avait jamais été ni bien sévère ni bien absolue. L'obéissance se convertit en respect, les priviléges devinrent des prérogatives, et l'indépendance du gouvernement politique affermit la liberté du gouvernement civil. Les villes maritimes de l'Istrie et de la Dalmatie obéissaient aux souverains de la mer Adriatique ; et lorsque les Vénitiens armèrent contre les Normands en faveur d'Alexis, l'empereur ne réclama point leurs secours comme un devoir de sujets, mais comme un bienfait d'alliés reconnaissans et fidèles. La mer était leur patrimoine (2) : les Génois et

---

(1). Lorsque le fils de Charlemagne réclama ses droits de souveraineté, les fidèles Vénitiens lui répondirent : Ότι ημεις δουλοι θελομεν ειναι του Ρομαιων βασιλεως (Constant. Porphyrogénète, *de Admin. Imper.*, part. II, c. 28, p. 85) ; et la tradition du neuvième siècle établit le fait du dixième, confirmé par l'ambassade de Luitprand de Crémone. Le tribut annuel que l'empereur leur permit de payer au roi d'Italie double leur servitude en l'allégeant ; mais le mot odieux de δουλοι doit se traduire, comme dans la chartre de 827 (Laugier, *Hist. de Venise*, t. I, p. 67, etc.), par le terme plus doux de *subditi fideles*.

(2) *Voyez* les vingt-cinquième et trentième Dissertations.

les Pisans, leurs rivaux, occupaient, à la vérité, la partie occidentale de la Méditerranée, depuis la Toscane jusqu'à Gibraltar; mais Venise acquit de bonne heure une forte part dans le commerce lucratif de la Grèce et de l'Égypte; ses richesses s'augmentaient en proportion des demandes de l'Europe; ses manufactures de glaces et de soies, et peut-être l'institution de sa banque, sont de la plus haute antiquité, et les fruits de l'industrie brillaient dans la magnificence de la république et des particuliers. Lorsqu'il s'agissait de maintenir l'honneur de son pavillon, de venger ses injures ou de protéger la liberté de la navigation, la république pouvait lancer et armer en peu de temps une flotte de cent galères, qu'elle employa successivement contre les Grecs, contre les Sarrasins et contre les Normands; elle fut d'un grand secours aux Francs dans leur expédition sur les côtes de la Syrie. Mais le zèle des Vénitiens n'était ni aveugle ni désintéressé; après la conquête de Tyr, ils partagèrent la souveraineté de cette ville, le premier entrepôt d'un commerce universel. On apercevait dans la politique de cette république l'avarice d'un peuple commerçant et l'insolence d'une puissance maritime. La

---

des antiquités du moyen âge par Muratori. L'histoire du commerce par Anderson ne date le commerce des Vénitiens avec l'Angleterre que de l'année 1323. L'abbé Dubos (*Hist. de la Ligue de Cambrai*, t. II, p. 443-480.) donne une description intéressante de l'état florissant de leur commerce et de leurs richesses au commencement du quinzième siècle.

prudence guida cependant toujours son ambition, et elle oublia rarement que si l'abondance de ses galères armées était la suite et la sauvegarde de sa grandeur, ses vaisseaux marchands en étaient la cause et le soutien. Venise évita le schisme des Grecs, mais elle n'eut jamais pour le pontife romain une obéissance servile; et sa fréquente correspondance avec les infidèles de tous les climats paraît avoir tempéré de bonne heure, pour elle l'influence de la superstition. Son gouvernement primitif était un mélange informe de démocratie et de monarchie; l'élection du doge se faisait par les suffrages d'une assemblée générale : tant que son administration plaisait au peuple, il régnait avec le faste et l'autorité d'un souverain; mais dans les fréquentes révolutions, ces magistrats furent déposés, bannis, et quelquefois massacrés par une multitude toujours violente et souvent injuste. Le douzième siècle vit naître les commencemens de l'habile et vigilante aristocratie qui réduit aujourd'hui le doge à n'être qu'un fantôme, et le peuple un zéro (1).

---

(1) Les Vénitiens n'ont écrit et publié leur histoire que fort tard. Leurs plus anciens monumens sont 1° la sèche Chronique (peut-être) de Jean Sagornin (Venise, 1765, in-8°), qui représente l'état et les mœurs de Venise dans l'année 1028; 2° l'histoire plus volumineuse du doge (1342-1354) André Dandolo, publiée pour la première fois dans le douzième tome de Muratori, A. D. 1728. L'histoire de Venise, par l'abbé Laugier (*Paris*, 1728), est un ouvrage de quelque mérite, dont je me suis servi principalement pour la partie de la constitution de cette république.

Lorsque les six ambassadeurs des Français arri- Alliance des Français et des Vé-
vèrent à Venise, ils furent amicalement reçus dans nitiens.
le palais de Saint-Marc par le doge, Henri Dandolo, A. D. 1201.
qui, au dernier période de la vie humaine, brillait
parmi les hommes les plus illustres de son siècle (1).
Chargé du poids des ans et privé de la vue (2), Dandolo conservait toute la vigueur de son courage et
de son jugement, l'ardeur d'un héros ambitieux de
signaler son règne par quelques exploits mémorables,
et la sagesse d'un patriote plein du désir d'établir sa
renommée sur la gloire et la puissance de sa patrie.
La valeur et la confiance des barons et de leurs députés obtinrent son approbation et ses louanges; s'il
n'eût été qu'un particulier, c'était, leur dit-il, en

---

(1) Henri Dandolo avait quatre-vingt-quatre ans quand il fut élu doge (A. D. 1192), et quatre-vingt-dix-sept quand il mourut (A. D. 1205). *Voyez* les *Observations* de Ducange sur Villehardouin, n° 204. Mais les écrivains originaux ne font aucune réflexion sur cette extraordinaire longévité. Il n'existe pas, je crois, un second exemple d'un héros presque centenaire. Théophraste pourrait servir d'exemple d'un écrivain de près de quatre-vingt-dix ans : mais au lieu de εννενηκοντα (*Proœm. ad Character.*), je me sens aussi disposé à lire εϐδομηκοντα, comme l'a jugé son dernier éditeur Fischer, et comme l'a pensé d'abord Casaubon. Il est presque impossible que le corps et l'imagination conservent leur vigueur dans un âge si avancé.

(2) Les Vénitiens modernes (Laugier, t. II, p. 119) accusent l'empereur Manuel ; mais cette calomnie est réfutée par Villehardouin et les anciens écrivains, qui supposent que Dandolo perdit la vue à la suite d'une blessure (n° 34 et Ducange).

soutenant une semblable cause et dans une pareille société qu'il eût désiré de finir ses jours; mais, comme magistrat de la république, il leur demanda quelque temps pour consulter ses collègues sur cette affaire importante. La proposition des Français fut d'abord discutée par les six *sages* récemment nommés pour surveiller l'administration du doge ; on en fit part ensuite aux quarante membres du conseil d'État, et elle fut enfin communiquée à l'assemblée législative, composée de quatre cent cinquante membres élus annuellement dans les six quartiers de la ville. Soit en paix, soit en guerre, le doge était toujours le chef de la république, et la réputation personnelle de Dandolo ajoutait du poids à son autorité légale : on examina et on approuva ses raisons en faveur de l'alliance, et il fut autorisé à informer les ambassadeurs des conditions du traité (1). On proposait aux croisés de s'assembler, vers la fête de Saint-Jean de l'année suivante, à Venise; ils devaient y trouver des bâtimens à fond plat pour embarquer quatre mille cinq cents chevaux et neuf mille écuyers, avec un nombre de vaisseaux suffisant pour transporter quatre mille cinq cents chevaliers et vingt mille hommes de pied. Les Vénitiens devaient, durant neuf mois, fournir la flotte de toutes les provisions nécessaires, et la conduire partout où le service de Dieu ou de la chrétienté pourrait l'exiger, et la ré-

---

(1) *Voyez* le traité original dans la *Chronique* d'André Dandolo, p. 323-326.

publique devait y joindre une escadre de cinquante galères armées. Les pélerins devaient payer, avant le départ, la somme de quatre-vingt-cinq mille marcs d'argent; toutes les conquêtes devaient se partager également entre les confédérés. Ces conditions étaient un peu dures; mais la circonstance était pressante, et les barons français ne savaient épargner ni leur sang ni leurs richesses. On convoqua une assemblée générale pour la ratification du traité. Dix mille citoyens remplirent la grande chapelle et la place de Saint-Marc, et les nobles français furent réduits à la nécessité, nouvelle pour eux, de s'abaisser devant la majesté du peuple. « Illustres Vénitiens, dit le maréchal de Champagne, nous sommes députés par les plus grands et les plus puissans barons de la France, pour supplier les souverains de la mer de nous aider à délivrer Jérusalem. Ils nous ont recommandé de nous prosterner à vos pieds, et nous ne nous relèverons pas que vous n'ayez promis de venger avec nous les injures du Christ. » Ce discours accompagné de leurs larmes (1), leur air martial et leur attitude suppliante, arrachèrent un cri universel

---

(1) En lisant Villehardouin, on ne peut s'empêcher de remarquer que le maréchal et ses confrères les chevaliers répandaient fréquemment des larmes. « Sachiez que la ot mainte lerme plorée de pitié (n° 17); mult plorant (*ibid.*); mainte lerme plorée (n° 34); si orent mult pitié et plorèrent mult durement (n° 60); i ot maint lerme plorée de pitié (n° 202). » Ils pleuraient dans toutes les occasions, tantôt de douleur, tantôt de joie, et tantôt de dévotion.

d'applaudissement, dont le bruit, dit Geoffroi, fut semblable à celui d'un tremblement de terre. Le vénérable doge monta sur son tribunal pour alléguer en faveur de la requête les motifs honorables et vertueux qui peuvent seuls déterminer l'assemblée de tout un peuple. Le traité fut transcrit sur un parchemin, scellé, attesté par des sermens, accepté mutuellement avec des larmes de joie par les représentans de France et de Venise, et envoyé sur-le-champ à Rome pour obtenir l'approbation du pape Innocent III. Les marchands prêtèrent deux mille marcs pour les premières dépenses de l'armement; et des six députés, deux repassèrent les Alpes pour annoncer le succès de la négociation, tandis que les quatre autres firent inutilement un voyage à Gênes et à Pise, pour engager ces deux républiques à entrer dans la sainte confédération.

Assemblée de la croisade et départ de Venise. A. D. 1202, octobre 8.

Des délais et des obstacles imprévus retardèrent l'exécution de ce traité. Le maréchal, de retour à Troyes, fut affectueusement reçu et avoué de tout par Thibaut, comte de Champagne, que les pélerins avaient unanimement choisi pour leur général; mais la santé de ce valeureux jeune homme commençait à s'altérer; on perdit bientôt tout espoir de le sauver: il déplora la destinée qui le condamnait à périr avant le temps, non sur le champ de bataille, mais sur un lit de douleur. Il distribua en mourant ses trésors à ses braves et nombreux vassaux, et leur fit jurer en sa présence d'accomplir son vœu et le leur. Mais, dit le maréchal, tous ceux qui acceptèrent ses dons ne lui tinrent pas leur parole. Les plus déterminés champions de la croix s'assemblèrent à Soissons pour choisir un nouveau général ; mais, soit incapacité, jalousie ou répugnance, parmi les princes français il ne s'en trouva aucun qui joignît aux talens nécessaires pour conduire l'expédition, la volonté de l'entreprendre. Les suffrages se réunirent en faveur d'un étranger, et l'on résolut d'offrir le commandement à Boniface, marquis de Montferrat, rejeton d'une race de héros, et personnellement distingué par ses talens politiques et militaires (1). Ni la piété ni l'ambition ne permettaient au marquis de se refuser à cette honorable invitation. Après avoir passé quelques jours à la cour de France, où il fut reçu comme un ami et un parent, il accepta solennellement, dans l'église de Soissons, la croix de pélerin et le bâton de général, puis repassa aussitôt les Alpes pour se préparer à cette longue expédition. Vers la fête de la Pentecôte, il déploya sa bannière et se mit en route pour Venise, à la tête de ses Italiens ; il y fut précédé ou suivi des comtes de Flandre et de Blois, et des plus illustres barons de France, auxquels se joignit un corps nombreux de pélerins allemands conduits par des motifs semblables à ceux qui les

---

(1) Par une victoire contre les citoyens d'Asti (A. D. 1191), par une croisade dans la Palestine et par une ambassade du pape chez les princes allemands (Muratori, *Annali d'Italia*, t. x, p. 163-202).

animaient (1). Les Vénitiens avaient rempli et même passé leurs engagemens ; ils avaient construit des écuries pour les chevaux et des baraques pour les soldats. Les magasins étaient abondamment pourvus de fourrages et de provisions ; les bâtimens de transport, les vaisseaux et les galères, n'attendaient pour mettre à la voile que le paiement stipulé par le traité pour le fret et l'armement; mais cette somme excédait de beaucoup les richesses réunies de tous les pélerins assemblés à Venise. Les Flamands, dont l'obéissance pour leur comte était volontaire et précaire, avaient entrepris sur leurs propres vaisseaux la longue navigation de l'Océan et de la Méditerranée; et un grand nombre de Français et d'Italiens avaient préféré les moyens de passage moins chers et plus commodes que leur offraient Marseille et la Pouille. Ceux qui s'étaient rendus à Venise pouvaient se plaindre de ce qu'après avoir fourni leur contribution personnelle, ils se trouvaient responsables de celle des absens. Tous les chefs livrèrent volontairement au trésor de Saint-Marc leur vaisselle d'or et d'argent; mais ce sacrifice généreux ne pouvait pas suffire, et, après tous leurs efforts, il manquait trente-quatre mille marcs pour compléter la somme convenue. La poli-

---

(1) *Voyez* la croisade des Allemands dans l'*Historia C. P.* de Gunther (*Can. antiq. Lect.*, t. IV, p. v-viij), qui célèbre le pélerinage de Martin, son abbé, un des prédicateurs rivaux de Foulques de Neuilly. Son monastère, de l'ordre de Cîteaux, était situé dans le diocèse de Bâle.

tique et le patriotisme du doge levèrent cet obstacle. Il proposa aux barons de se joindre à ses compatriotes pour réduire quelques villes révoltées de la Dalmatie, et promit, à cette condition, d'aller combattre en personne dans la Palestine, et d'obtenir en outre de la république qu'elle attendît, pour le surplus de leur dette, que quelque riche conquête les mît en état d'y satisfaire. Après beaucoup de scrupules et d'hésitation, ils acceptèrent cette offre plutôt que de renoncer à leur entreprise ; et les premières hostilités de la flotte et de l'armée furent dirigées contre Zara (1), ville forte, sur la côte de la Sclavonie, qui avait abandonné les Vénitiens et s'était mise sous la protection du roi de Hongrie (2). Les croisés rompirent la chaîne ou barre qui défendait le port, débarquèrent leurs chevaux, leurs troupes et leurs machines

Siége de Zara. nov. 10.

---

(1) Jadera, aujourd'hui Zara, était une colonie romaine qui reconnaissait Auguste pour son fondateur. Elle a environ, dans l'état présent, deux milles de tour, et contient cinq à six mille habitans ; mais elle est très-bien fortifiée, et tient à la terre ferme par un pont. *Voy.* les *Voyages* de Spon et de Wheeler, *Voyages de Dalmatie, de Grèce*, etc., t. 1, p. 64-70 ; *Voyage en Grèce*, p. 8-14. Ce dernier, confondant *sestertia* et *sestertii*, évalue un arc de triomphe décoré de colonnes et de statues, à douze livres st. Si de son temps il n'y avait point d'arbres dans les environs de Zara, c'est qu'on n'y avait pas encore planté apparemment les cerisiers qui nous fournissent de si excellent marasquin.

(2) Katona (*Hist. crit. reg. Hungar. Stirpis Arpad.*, t. IV, p. 536-558) rassemble les faits et les témoignages les plus défavorables aux conquérans de Zara.

de guerre, et, le cinquième jour, forcèrent la ville de se rendre à discrétion. On épargna la vie des habitans, mais, en punition de leur révolte, on pilla leurs maisons, et les murs de la ville furent démolis. La saison étant fort avancée, les confédérés résolurent de choisir un port sûr dans un pays fertile, pour y passer tranquillement l'hiver ; mais leur repos y fut troublé par les animosités nationales des soldats et des mariniers, et les fréquentes querelles qui en étaient la suite. La conquête de Zara avait été une source de discorde et de scandale. La première expédition des alliés avait teint leurs armes, non pas du sang des infidèles, mais de celui des chrétiens ; le roi de Hongrie et ses nouveaux sujets étaient eux-mêmes au nombre des champions de la croix, et la crainte ou l'inconstance augmentait les scrupules des dévots. Le pape avait excommunié des croisés parjures qui pillaient et massacraient leurs frères (1) : l'anathême du pontife n'épargna que le marquis Boniface et Simon de Montfort; l'un, parce qu'il ne s'était point trouvé au siége, et l'autre, parce qu'il abandonna tout-à-fait la confédération. Innocent aurait pardonné volontiers aux simples et dociles pénitens français; mais il s'indignait contre l'opiniâtre raison des Vénitiens qui refusaient d'avouer leur faute, d'accepter le pardon et de reconnaître l'autorité d'un prêtre; relativement à leurs affaires temporelles.

---

(1) *Voyez* toute la transaction et les sentimens du pape dans les *Épîtres d'Innocent* III. *Gesta*, c. 86, 87, 88.

La réunion d'une flotte et d'une armée si puissantes avait ranimé l'espoir du jeune Alexis (1). A Venise et à Zara, il pressa vivement les croisés d'entreprendre son rétablissement et la délivrance de son père (2). La recommandation de Philippe, roi d'Allemagne, la présence et les prières du jeune Grec, excitèrent la compassion des pélerins : le marquis de Montferrat et le doge de Venise embrassèrent et plaidèrent sa cause. Une double alliance et la dignité de César avaient lié les deux frères aînés de Boniface (3) avec la famille impériale. Il espérait que l'importance de ce service lui vaudrait l'acquisition d'un royaume, et l'ambition plus généreuse de Dandolo lui donnait un ardent

Alliance des croisés avec le jeune Alexis.

---

(1) Un lecteur moderne est surpris d'entendre nommer le jeune Alexis le valet de Constantinople, à raison de son âge, comme on dit les *infants* d'Espagne et le *nobilissimus puer* des Romains : les pages ou valets des chevaliers étaient aussi nobles que leurs maîtres (Villehardouin et Duc., n° 36).

(2) Villehardouin (n° 38) nomme l'empereur Isaac *sursac*, mot dérivé probablement du mot français *sire* ou du grec Κυρ (κυριος), avec la terminaison du nom propre ; les noms corrompus de Tursac et de Conserac, que nous trouverons par la suite, nous donneront une idée de la licence que prenaient à cet égard les anciennes dynasties d'Assyrie et d'Égypte.

(3) Reinier et Conrad : l'un épousa Marie, fille de l'empereur Manuel Comnène ; l'autre était marié à Théodora Angela, sœur des empereurs Isaac et Alexis. Conrad abandonna la cour de Byzance et la princesse pour aller défendre la ville de Tyr contre Saladin (Ducange, *Fam. Byzant.*, p. 187-203).

désir d'assurer à son pays les avantages inestimables qui devaient en résulter pour son commerce et sa puissance (1). Leur influence obtint aux ambassadeurs d'Alexis une réception favorable ; et si la grandeur de ses offres excita quelque défiance, les motifs et les récompenses qu'il présentait purent justifier le retard apporté à la délivrance de Jérusalem, et l'emploi des forces qui y avaient été consacrées. Il promit, pour lui et pour son père, qu'aussitôt qu'ils auraient recouvré le trône de Constantinople, ils termineraient le long schisme des Grecs, et se soumettraient, eux et leurs sujets, à la suprématie de l'Église romaine. Il s'engagea à récompenser les travaux et les services des croisés, par le paiement immédiat de deux cent mille marcs d'argent, à suivre les pélerins en Égypte, ou, si on le jugeait plus avantageux, à entretenir, durant une année, dix mille hommes, et durant toute sa vie, cinq cents chevaliers pour le service de la Terre-Sainte. La république de Venise accepta ces conditions séduisantes ; et l'éloquence du doge et du marquis persuadèrent aux comtes de Blois, de Flandre et de Saint-Pol, ainsi qu'à huit barons de France, de prendre part à cette glorieuse entreprise. On scella, par les sermens ordinaires, un traité d'alliance offensive et

---

(1) Nicétas (*in Alex. Comn.*, l. III, c. 9) accuse le doge et les Vénitiens d'avoir été les auteurs de la guerre contre Constantinople, et ne considère que comme κυμα υπερ κυματι l'arrivée et les offres honteuses du prince exilé.

défensive ; chaque individu fut séduit, selon sa situation ou son caractère, par les motifs de l'avantage général ou ceux de l'intérêt personnel; par l'honneur de replacer un souverain sur son trône, ou par l'opinion assez raisonnable que tous les efforts des croisés pour délivrer la Palestine seraient impuissans, à moins que l'acquisition de Constantinople ne précédât et ne facilitât la conquête de Jérusalem. Mais ils commandaient une troupe de guerriers libres et de volontaires, quelquefois leurs égaux, qui raisonnaient et agissaient d'après eux-mêmes ; quoiqu'une forte majorité acceptât l'alliance, le nombre et les argumens de ceux qui la rejetaient étaient dignes de considération (1). Les cœurs les plus intrépides se troublaient au tableau qui leur était fait des forces navales de Constantinople et de ses fortifications inaccessibles. Ils déguisaient en public leurs craintes, et se les dissimulaient peut-être à eux-mêmes par des objections plus honorables de devoir et de religion. Les dissidens alléguaient la sainteté du vœu qui les avait éloignés de leur famille et de leur maison pour courir à la délivrance du saint-sépulcre, et ne pensaient pas que les motifs obscurs et incertains de la politique dussent les détourner d'une sainte entreprise dont l'événement était entre les mains de la

---

(1) Villehardouin et Gunther expliquent les sentimens des deux partis. L'abbé Martin quitta l'armée à Zara, passa dans la Palestine, fut envoyé comme ambassadeur à Constantinople, et devint malgré lui le témoin du second siége.

Providence. Les censures du pape et les reproches de leur conscience avaient assez sévèrement puni l'attaque de Zara, leur première faute, pour qu'ils évitassent de souiller à l'avenir leurs armes en répandant le sang des chrétiens ; l'apôtre romain avait prononcé, et il ne leur appartenait pas de punir le schisme des Grecs, ou de venger les droits suspects des empereurs de Byzance. D'après ces principes ou ces prétextes, un grand nombre de pélerins, les plus distingués par leur valeur et leur piété, se retirèrent du camp, et leur départ fut moins funeste que l'opposition ouverte ou secrète d'un parti de mécontens qui saisirent toutes les occasions de désunir l'armée, et de nuire au succès de l'entreprise.

Départ de Zara pour Constantinople. A. D. 1203, avril 7. Arrivée. juin 24.

Malgré cette défection, les Vénitiens pressèrent vivement le départ, et cachèrent probablement, sous l'extérieur d'un zèle généreux pour Alexis, leurs ressentimens contre sa nation et contre sa famille. La préférence accordée récemment à la république de Pise, leur rivale dans le commerce, blessait leur cupidité; et ils avaient de longs et terribles comptes à régler avec la cour de Byzance. Dandolo ne démentait peut-être pas le conte populaire qui accusait l'empereur Manuel d'avoir violé, dans la personne du doge, les droits des nations et de l'humanité, en le privant de la vue tandis qu'il était revêtu du caractère sacré d'ambassadeur. On n'avait point vu, depuis plusieurs siècles, un pareil armement sur la mer Adriatique : cent vingt bateaux plats, ou *palandres*, pour les chevaux ; deux cent quarante vaisseaux chargés de soldats et d'armes; et soixante-dix de provisions, soutenus par cinquante fortes galères, bien préparées pour le combat, composaient cette flotte formidable (1). Le vent était favorable, la mer tranquille et le ciel serein ; tous les regards se fixaient avec admiration sur cette scène martiale et brillante. Les boucliers des chevaliers et des écuyers, servant à la fois d'ornement et de défense, étaient rangés sur les deux bords des vaisseaux ; les diverses bannières des nations et des familles, flottant à la proue, formaient un spectacle magnifique et imposant. Des catapultes et des machines propres à lancer des pierres et à ébranler des murs, tenaient lieu de notre artillerie moderne : une musique militaire charmait la fatigue et l'ennui de la navigation, et les guerriers s'encourageaient mutuellement dans la confiance que quarante mille héros chrétiens suffisaient pour faire la conquête de l'univers (2). La flotte fut heureusement conduite de Venise à Zara

(1) La naissance et la dignité d'André Dandolo lui donnaient des motifs et des moyens pour rechercher dans les archives de Venise l'histoire de son illustre ancêtre. Le laconisme de son récit rend un peu suspectes les relations modernes et verbeuses de Sanudo (*in* Muratori, *Scriptores rerum italicarum*, t. XXII), Blondus, Sabellicus et Rhamnusius.

(2) Villehardouin, n° 62. Ses sentimens sont aussi originaux que sa manière de les exprimer; il est sujet à pleurer, mais ne se réjouit pas moins de la gloire et du danger des combats avec un enthousiasme auquel un écrivain sédentaire ne peut atteindre.

par l'habileté et l'expérience des pilotes vénitiens; elle arriva sans accident à Durazzo, située sur le territoire de l'empereur grec. L'île de Corfou lui servit de relâche et de repos. Après avoir doublé sans accident le dangereux cap Malée, qui forme la pointe méridionale de l'Hellespont ou de la Morée, les confédérés firent une descente dans les îles de Négrepont et d'Andros (1), et jetèrent l'ancre à Abydos, sur la rive asiatique de l'Hellespont. Les préludes de la conquête ne furent ni difficiles ni sanglans. Les provinciaux grecs, sans patriotisme et sans courage, n'entreprirent point de résister. La présence de l'héritier légitime pouvait justifier leur obéissance, dont ils furent récompensés par la modération et la discipline sévère des confédérés. En traversant l'Hellespont, leur flotte se trouva resserrée dans un canal étroit, et leurs voiles innombrables obscurcirent la surface des eaux. Ils reprirent leur distance dans le vaste bassin de la Propontide, et voguèrent sur cette mer tranquille jusqu'aux attérages de la côte d'Europe, à l'abbaye de Saint-Étienne, environ à trois lieues à l'ouest de Constantinople. Le doge les dissuada sagement de se séparer sur une côte ennemie et peuplée; et comme les provisions tiraient à leur

---

(1) Dans ce Voyage, presque tous les noms géographiques se trouvent défigurés par les Latins: le nom moderne de Chalcis et de toute l'Eubée est dérivé du nom de l'*Euripus*, d'où *Evripo*, *Negripo*, *Négrepont*, qui déshonore nos cartes. D'Anville, *Géogr. ancienne*, t. 1, p. 263.

fin, on résolut de les renouveler, durant le temps des moissons, dans les îles fertiles de la Propontide. Les confédérés dirigèrent leur course conformément à cette intention ; mais un coup de vent et leur impatience les poussèrent à l'est, et si près de la terre et de la ville, que les remparts et les vaisseaux se saluèrent mutuellement de quelques volées de pierres et de dards. L'armée, en passant, contempla avec admiration, la capitale de l'Orient, qui semblait plutôt être celle du monde, s'élevant sur les cimes de ses sept collines, et dominant le continent de l'Europe et de l'Asie. Les rayons du soleil doraient les dômes des palais et des églises, et les réfléchissaient sur la surface des eaux ; les murs fourmillaient de soldats et de spectateurs, dont le nombre frappait leurs regards, et dont ils ignoraient la lâcheté ; tous les cœurs furent frappés de crainte lorsqu'on songea que jamais, depuis la naissance du monde, un si petit nombre de guerriers n'avait osé tenter une entreprise si périlleuse. Mais la valeur et l'espérance dissipèrent bientôt cette émotion passagère ; et chacun, dit le maréchal de Champagne, jeta les yeux sur l'épée ou sur la lance dont il devait bientôt se servir glorieusement (1). Les Latins jetèrent l'ancre devant le faubourg de Chalcédoine. Les matelots restèrent seuls

---

(1) *Et sachiez que il ne ot si hardi cui le cuer ne fremist* (c. 67)...... *Chascuns regardoit ses armes.... que par tems en aront mestier* (c. 68). Telle est la franchise du vrai courage.

sur les vaisseaux ; les soldats, les chevaux et les armes, furent débarqués sans obstacles ; et le pillage d'un des palais de l'empereur fit goûter aux barons les premières jouissances du succès. Le troisième jour, la flotte et l'armée tournèrent vers Scutari, le faubourg asiatique de Constantinople ; quatre-vingts chevaliers français surprirent et mirent en fuite un corps de cinq cents hommes de cavalerie grecque, et une halte de neuf jours suffit pour fournir abondamment le camp de fourrages et de provisions.

<small>L'empereur tente inutilement une négociation.</small>

Il pourra paraître extraordinaire qu'en racontant l'invasion d'un grand empire, je n'aie point parlé des obstacles qui devaient s'opposer au succès des conquérans. Les Grecs manquaient, à la vérité, de courage ; mais ils étaient riches et industrieux, et ils obéissaient à un prince absolu. Mais il aurait fallu que ce prince pût être capable de prévoyance tandis que ses ennemis furent éloignés, et de courage dès qu'il les vit approcher. Il reçut avec dédain les premières nouvelles de l'alliance de son neveu avec les Français et les Vénitiens ; ses courtisans lui persuadèrent que ce mépris était sincère et l'effet de son courage. Chaque soir, sur la fin d'un banquet, il mettait trois fois en déroute les Barbares de l'Occident. Ces Barbares redoutaient avec raison ses forces navales ; et les seize cents bateaux pêcheurs de Constantinople (1) auraient fourni des matelots pour ar-

---

(1) *Eandem urbem plus in solis navibus piscatorum abun-*

mer une flotte capable d'ensevelir les galères vénitiennes dans la mer Adriatique, ou de leur fermer le passage de l'Hellespont. Mais toutes les ressources peuvent devenir impuissantes par la négligence du prince et la corruption de ses ministres. Le grand-duc ou amiral faisait un trafic scandaleux, et presque public, des voiles, des mâts et des cordages. On réservait les forêts royales pour la chasse, objet bien plus important ; et les eunuques, dit Nicétas, gardaient les arbres comme s'ils eussent été consacrés au culte religieux. Le siége de Zara, et l'approche rapide des Latins, réveillèrent Alexis de son rêve d'orgueil ; dès que le danger lui parut réel, il le crut inévitable. La présomption disparut et fit place au lâche découragement et au désespoir. Ces Barbares méprisables campèrent impunément à la vue de son palais, et le monarque tremblant eut recours à une ambassade, dont la pompe et le ton menaçant déguisèrent mal aux Français l'effroi qu'avait répandu leur arrivée. Les ambassadeurs demandèrent, au nom de l'empereur des Romains, dans quelle intention l'armée des Latins campait sous les murs de sa capitale ; ils déclarèrent que si les croisés avaient sincèrement pour objet l'accomplissement de leur vœu et la délivrance de Jérusalem, Alexis applaudissait à

---

dare, quàm illos in toto navigio. Habebat enim mille et sexcentas piscatorias naves.... Bellicas autem sive mercatorias habebant infinitæ multitudinis, et portum tutissimum. Gunther, *Hist. C. P.*, c. 8, p. 10.

leur pieux dessein, et était prêt à le seconder de ses trésors; mais que s'ils osaient pénétrer dans le sanctuaire de l'empire, leur nombre, fût-il dix fois plus considérable, ne les sauverait pas de son juste ressentiment. La réponse du doge et des barons fut simple et noble. « Engagés, dirent-ils, dans la cause de la justice et de l'honneur, nous méprisons l'usurpateur de la Grèce, ses offres et ses menaces. Nous devons notre amitié, il doit obéissance à l'héritier légitime, au jeune prince qui siége ici parmi nous, et à son père, l'empereur Isaac, privé de son trône, de sa liberté et de la vue, par un frère ingrat; qu'il confesse son crime, qu'il implore la clémence de celui qu'il a persécuté, et nous intercèderons pour qu'il lui soit permis de vivre dans la paix et dans l'abondance. Mais nous regarderons une seconde ambassade comme une insulte, et nous n'y répondrons que le fer à la main dans le palais de Constantinople (1). »

Passage du Bosphore.
6 juillet.

Dix jours après leur arrivée à Scutari, les croisés se préparèrent, comme soldats et comme catholiques, au passage du Bosphore. L'entreprise était dangereuse : le canal était large et rapide; dans un calme, le courant de l'Euxin pouvait descendre au milieu de la flotte les feux formidables connus sous le nom de feux grégeois; et soixante-dix mille hom-

---

(1) Καθαπερ ιερων αλσεων, ειπειν δε και θεοφυτευτων παραδεισων εφειδοντο τουτωνι. Nicétas, *in Alex. Comneno*, l. III, c. 9, p. 348.

mes, rangés en bataille, défendaient la rive opposée. Dans cette journée mémorable, où le hasard voulut que le temps fût doux et le ciel serein, les Latins distribuèrent leur ordre de bataille en six divisions. La première, ou avant-garde, était conduite par le comte de Flandre, un des plus puissans parmi les princes chrétiens par le nombre et l'habileté de ses arbalétriers; les quatre qui suivaient étaient commandées par son frère Henri, par les comtes de Saint-Pol et de Blois, et par Matthieu de Montmorency; c'était sous les ordres de ce dernier que marchaient volontairement le maréchal et les nobles de la Champagne. Le marquis de Montferrat, à la tête des Allemands et des Lombards, conduisait la sixième division, l'arrière-garde et la réserve de l'armée. Les chevaux de bataille, sellés et couverts de leurs longs caparaçons pendans jusqu'à terre, furent embarqués sur les palandres (1). Les chevaliers se tenaient debout auprès de leurs chevaux, le casque en tête, la lance à la main et complétement armés. Les sergens et les archers passèrent sur les bâtimens de

---

(1) D'après la traduction de Vigenère, j'adopte le nom sonore de palandre, dont on se sert, je crois, encore dans les parages de la Méditerranée. Cependant, si j'écrivais en français, j'emploierais le mot primitif et expressif de *vessiers* ou *huissiers*, tiré de *huis*, vieux mot qui signifiait une porte que l'on baissait comme un pont-levis, mais qui à la mer se relevait en dedans du bâtiment. Voyez Ducange au Villehardouin, n° 14; et Joinville, p. 27, 28, édition du Louvre.

transport, et chacun de ces bâtimens fut toué par une galère forte et rapide. Les six divisions traversèrent le Bosphore sans rencontrer ni ennemis ni obstacle. Le vœu de chaque corps et de chaque soldat était de débarquer le premier ; sa résolution, de vaincre ou de mourir. Les chevaliers, jaloux du droit d'affronter les plus grands dangers, sautèrent tout armés dans la mer, et gagnèrent le rivage ayant de l'eau jusqu'à la ceinture. Les sergens (1) et les archers imitèrent leur exemple ; les écuyers baissèrent les ponts des palandres et débarquèrent les chevaux. A peine les chevaliers en selle commençaient à former leurs escadrons et à baisser leurs lances, que les soixante-dix mille Grecs disparurent. Le timide Alexis donna l'exemple à ses soldats, et ne laissa d'autres traces de sa présence qu'un riche pavillon, dont le pillage apprit aux Latins qu'ils avaient combattu contre un empereur. On résolut de profiter de la première terreur de l'ennemi pour forcer, par une double attaque, l'entrée du port. Les Français emportèrent d'assaut la tour de Galata (2),

---

(1) Pour éviter l'expression vague de suite ou suivans, etc., je me sers, d'après Villehardouin, du nom de sergens, pour indiquer tous les cavaliers qui n'étaient point chevaliers. Il y avait des sergens d'armes et des sergens de lois, et on peut, à la parade et dans la salle de Westminster, observer l'étrange résultat de cette distinction. Ducange, *Gloss. lat.*, *Servientes*, etc., t. VI, p. 226-231.

(2) Il est inutile d'observer qu'au sujet de Galata, de la chaîne, etc., le récit de Ducange est complet et circons-

située dans le faubourg de Péra, tandis que les Vénitiens entreprenaient la tâche plus difficile de rompre la barre ou chaîne tendue de cette tour au rivage de Byzance. Après quelques efforts inutiles, ils en vinrent à bout par leur intrépide persévérance : vingt vaisseaux de guerre, restes de la marine des Grecs, furent pris ou coulés bas. Les éperons, où le poids des galères (1), coupèrent ou brisèrent les énormes chaînons ; et la flotte des Vénitiens, victorieuse et tranquille, jeta l'ancre dans le port de Constantinople. Tels furent les exploits par lesquels les Latins achetèrent les moyens d'approcher pour l'assiéger, avec environ vingt mille hommes qui leur restaient encore, une ville qui renfermait plus de quatre cent mille hommes (2) ; auxquels il ne manquait que du

---

tancié. Consultez aussi les chapitres particuliers du *C. P. Christiana* du même auteur. Les habitans de Galata étaient si vains et si ignorans, qu'ils s'appliquèrent l'Épître de saint Paul aux Galatiens.

(1) Le vaisseau qui rompit la chaîne portait le nom d'*Aquila*, l'Aigle (Dandolo, *Chron.*, p. 322), que Blondus (*de Gestis Venet.*) a transformé en *Aquilo*, vent du nord. Ducange (dans ses *Observations*, n° 83) adopte ce dernier; mais il ne connaissait pas le texte irrécusable de Dandolo, et il négligea d'observer la topographie du port ; le vent du sud-est aurait été infiniment plus favorable à l'expédition que le vent du nord.

(2) *Quatre cent mille hommes* ou *plus* (Villehardouin, n° 134), doit s'entendre d'hommes en état de porter les armes. Le Beau (*Hist. du Bas-Empire*, t. xx, p. 417) accorde à Constantinople un million d'habitans, soixante mille

courage pour la défendre. Ce calcul suppose, à la vérité, une population d'environ deux millions d'habitans; mais en admettant que les Grecs ne fussent point en si grand nombre, il n'est pas moins vrai que les Français croyaient à cette multitude, et que cette opinion est une preuve évidente de leur intrépidité.

Premier siège et conquête de Constantinople par les Latins. Juillet 7-18. Dans le choix de l'attaque, les Français et les Vénitiens différèrent d'opinion; chacun d'eux préférait le genre de combat dans lequel il avait plus d'expérience : les derniers soutenaient, avec raison, que Constantinople était plus accessible du côté de la mer et du port; mais les premiers purent déclarer sans honte qu'ils avaient suffisamment hasardé leur vie et leur fortune dans une barque et sur un élément perfide, et demandèrent à haute voix des épreuves dignes de la chevalerie, un terrain solide et un combat corps à corps, soit à pied, soit à cheval. On s'accorda prudemment à employer les deux nations au service qui leur convenait le mieux. L'armée pénétra, sous la protection de la flotte, jusqu'au fond du port; on répara diligemment le pont de pierre placé sur le

---

hommes de cavalerie, et une multitude innombrable de soldats. Dans son état de dégradation, la capitale de l'empire ottoman contient aujourd'hui quatre cent mille âmes (*Voyages de Bell*, vol. II, p. 401, 402); mais comme les Turcs ne tiennent aucun registre des morts ni des naissances, et que tous les rapports sont suspects, il est impossible de constater leur population réelle. Niebuhr, *Voyag. en Arab.*, t. I, p. 18, 19.

fleuve; et les six divisions des Français formèrent leur camp en face de la capitale, sur la base du triangle qui s'étend à quatre milles depuis le port jusqu'à la Propontide (1). Placés au bord d'un fossé large et profond, et au pied d'un rempart élevé, ils eurent tout le loisir de considérer la difficulté de leur entreprise. Des portes de la ville, il sortait continuellement, à la droite et à la gauche de leur petit camp, des partis de cavalerie et d'infanterie légère, qui massacraient les traîneurs, dépouillaient la campagne de tout moyen de subsistance, et faisaient prendre les armes cinq ou six fois par jour. Les Français furent contraints, pour leur sûreté, de planter une palissade et de creuser un fossé. Soit que les Vénitiens eussent fourni trop peu de provisions ou que les Francs les eussent prodiguées, ceux-ci commencèrent, comme à l'ordinaire, à se plaindre de la disette, et peut-être à l'éprouver réellement : il ne restait de la farine que pour trois semaines, et les soldats, dégoûtés de viande salée, commençaient à manger des chevaux. Le lâche usurpateur était défendu par son gendre, Théodore Lascaris, jeune homme plein de valeur, qui aspirait à devenir le libérateur et le maître de son pays. Les Grecs, indifférens pour leur patrie, avaient été ré-

---

(1) D'après les plans les plus corrects de Constantinople, je ne puis admettre qu'une étendue de quatre mille pas. Cependant Villehardouin fixe l'espace à trois lieues (n° 86). Si ses yeux ne l'ont pas trompé, il faut croire qu'il comptait par lieues gauloises, qui n'étaient que de quinze cents pas, et dont peut-être on se sert encore en Champagne.

veillés par le danger où se trouvait leur religion ; mais ils fondaient leur principal espoir dans le courage des gardes varangiennes, composées, au rapport des historiens, de Danois et d'Anglais (1). Après dix jours d'un travail sans relâche, le fossé fut rempli, les assiégeans formèrent régulièrement leur attaque ; et deux cent cinquante machines élevées contre le rempart travaillèrent continuellement à en chasser les défenseurs, à battre les murs et à saper les fondemens. A la première apparence d'une brèche, les Français plantèrent leurs échelles ; mais le nombre et l'avantage du terrain l'emportèrent sur l'audace. Les Latins furent repoussés ; mais les Grecs ne purent refuser leur admiration à l'intrépidité de quinze chevaliers ou sergens, qui, montés sur la muraille, se maintinrent dans ce poste périlleux jusqu'au moment où ils furent précipités ou faits prisonniers par les gardes impériales. Du côté du port, les Vénitiens conduisirent plus heureusement leur attaque. Ces marins industrieux employèrent toutes les ressources connues avant l'invention de la poudre. Les galères et les vaisseaux formèrent une double ligne dont le front s'étendait environ à trois jets de trait. Les galères étaient soutenues dans leurs évolutions rapides par la force et la pesanteur des vaisseaux, dont les ponts, les

---

(1) Villehardouin (n°s 89-95) désigne les gardes ou Varangi par les noms d'*Anglois* et de *Danois* avec leurs haches. Quelle que fût leur origine, un pèlerin français ne pouvait se tromper sur les nations dont ils étaient alors composés.

poupes et les tours, servaient de plate-forme à des machines qui lançaient des pierres par-dessus la première ligne. Les soldats qui sautaient des galères sur le rivage, plantaient aussitôt leurs échelles et les montaient, tandis que les gros vaisseaux s'avançaient plus lentement dans les intervalles, et, baissant un pont-levis, offraient aux soldats un chemin dans les airs de leur mât sur le rempart. Dans le fort du combat, le doge vénérable et majestueux se tenait, armé de toutes pièces, debout sur le pont de sa galère ; le grand étendard de saint Marc flottait devant lui ; il employait les menaces, les instances et les promesses, pour animer l'activité de ses rameurs ; son vaisseau aborda le premier, et Dandolo précéda tous les guerriers sur le rivage. Les peuples admirèrent la magnanimité d'un vieillard aveugle, sans réfléchir que son âge et ses infirmités diminuaient autant pour lui le prix de la vie, qu'ils augmentaient celui de la gloire qui ne meurt jamais. Tout à coup une main invisible (le porte-étendard ayant probablement été tué) planta sur le rempart l'étendard de la république. Les Vénitiens s'emparèrent rapidement de vingt-cinq tours, et le cruel expédient de l'incendie chassa les Grecs du quartier environnant. Le doge avait fait annoncer ses succès à ses alliés, lorsque la nouvelle de leur danger vint l'arrêter au milieu de sa course ; il déclara noblement qu'il aimait mieux se perdre avec eux que de remporter la victoire en les laissant périr. Abandonnant ses avantages, il rappela ses troupes et courut à leur secours. Il trouva les restes harassés des six divisions françaises environnés par soixante escadrons de cavalerie grecque, dont un seul surpassait en nombre la plus forte division des Français. La honte et le désespoir avaient déterminé enfin Alexis à tenter le dernier effort d'une sortie générale; mais la contenance ferme des Latins anéantit son espérance et sa résolution. Après avoir escarmouché de loin, il disparut avec ses troupes sur la fin du jour. Le silence ou le tumulte de la nuit augmenta sa terreur: l'usurpateur épouvanté fit transporter dans une barque dix mille livres d'or, et, abandonnant lâchement son trône, son épouse et ses sujets, il traversa le Bosphore à la faveur de l'obscurité, et trouva un honteux refuge dans un petit port de la Thrace. Ses courtisans, dès qu'ils apprirent sa fuite, coururent implorer leur pardon et la paix au cachot où l'empereur aveugle attendait à chaque instant les exécuteurs qui devaient trancher ses jours. Redevable aux vicissitudes de la fortune de son salut et du retour de sa puissance, Isaac, revêtu de sa robe impériale, remonta sur son trône environné d'esclaves prosternés, dont il ne pouvait discerner ni la terreur réelle ni la joie affectée. Au point du jour, on suspendit les hostilités, et les Latins reçurent avec étonnement un message de l'empereur légitime, qui, rétabli dans ses droits, était impatient d'embrasser son fils et de récompenser ses généreux libérateurs (1).

---

(1) Pour le premier siége et la conquête de Constantinople, on peut lire la lettre originale des croisés à Inno-

Mais ces libérateurs généreux n'étaient point disposés à relâcher leur ôtage avant d'avoir obtenu de son père le paiement ou au moins la promesse de leur récompense. Ils choisirent quatre ambassadeurs, Matthieu de Montmorency, notre historien le maréchal de Champagne, et deux Vénitiens, pour féliciter l'empereur. Les portes de la ville s'ouvrirent à leur approche; une double file des gardes anglaises et danoises, la hache de bataille à la main, garnissait les deux côtés des rues; les yeux étaient éblouis dans la chambre du trône, de l'éclat de l'or et des diamans, substituts trompeurs de la puissance et de la vertu. L'épouse d'Isaac, fille du roi de Hongrie, siégeait à côté de son mari, et son retour avait attiré toutes les nobles matrones de la Grèce, qui se trouvaient confondues avec un cercle de sénateurs et de soldats. Les Français, par l'organe du maréchal, parlèrent en hommes qui sentaient ce qu'on devait à leurs services, mais qui respectaient l'œuvre de leurs mains; et Isaac comprit clairement qu'il fallait remplir, sans hésiter et sans délai, les engagemens qu'avait pris son fils avec Venise et avec les pèlerins. Après avoir fait passer les quatre ambassadeurs dans une chambre in-

<small>Rétablissement de l'empereur Isaac l'Ange et de son fils Alexis. 19 juillet.</small>

---

cent III, Villehardouin (n°⁵ 75-99), Nicétas (*in Alexio Comneno,* l. III, c. 10, p. 349-352), Dandolo (*in Chron.*, p. 322). Gunther et l'abbé Martin n'étaient point encore de retour de leur premier pélerinage à Jérusalem ou à Saint-Jean-d'Acre, où ils demeuraient obstinément, quoique la plus grande partie de leurs compagnons y fussent morts de la peste.

térieure où il se rendit accompagné de l'impératrice, d'un chambellan et d'un interprète, le père du jeune Alexis demanda avec inquiétude en quoi consistaient les conventions de son fils. Le maréchal de Champagne lui ayant déclaré qu'il devait faire cesser le schisme en se soumettant, lui et ses peuples, à la suprématie du pape; contribuer par un secours à la délivrance de la Terre-Sainte, et payer comptant une contribution de deux cent mille marcs d'argent : « Ces engagemens sont pésans, répondit prudemment le monarque ; ils sont durs à accepter et difficiles à remplir ; mais rien ne peut surpasser vos mérites et vos services. » Satisfaits de cette assurance, les barons montèrent à cheval et accompagnèrent l'héritier du trône jusque dans son palais. Sa jeunesse et ses aventures lui gagnaient tous les cœurs; il fut couronné avec son père dans l'église de Sainte-Sophie. Dans les premiers jours de son règne, le peuple, enchanté du retour de la paix et de l'abondance, jouissait avec transport du dénouement de cette tragédie, et les nobles cachaient leurs regrets, leurs craintes et leur ressentiment, sous le masque de la joie et de la fidélité. Pour éviter le désordre qui aurait pu résulter dans la ville du mélange des deux nations, on assigna pour quartiers aux Vénitiens et aux Français les faubourgs de Péra et de Galata, en leur laissant cependant toute liberté de se promener et de commercer dans la ville. La dévotion et la curiosité attiraient tous les jours un grand nombre de pèlerins dans les églises et dans les palais de Constantinople.

Insensibles peut-être à la perfection des arts qu'on voyait s'y déployer, nos grossiers ancêtres étaient du moins frappés de leur magnificence. La pauvreté de leurs villes natales rehaussait à leurs yeux l'éclat et la population de la première métropole de la chrétienté (1). Entraîné par le sentiment de la justice et de sa reconnaissance, le jeune Alexis oubliait souvent sa dignité pour rendre des visites familières à ses bienfaiteurs; et, dans la liberté du repas, la vivacité légère des Français leur faisait oublier l'empereur d'Orient (2). On convint, dans des conférences plus sérieuses, que le temps pouvait seul opérer la réunion des deux Églises, et qu'il fallait l'attendre avec patience. Mais l'avarice fut moins traitable que le zèle, et il fallut payer comptant une somme très-forte, pour apaiser les besoins et les clameurs des croisés (3).

---

(1) Comparez, dans la grossière énergie de Villehardouin (n°⁸ 66-100) l'intérieur de Constantinople, ses environs, et l'impression que ce spectacle fit aux croisés : *Ceste ville*, dit-il, *que de toutes les autres ere souveraine*. *Voyez* les passages de cette description dans Foulcher de Chartres (*Hist. Hieros.*, tom. 1, chap. 4) et Guillaume de Tyr (II, 3; XX, 26).

(2) En jouant aux dés, les Latins lui ôtèrent son diadème; et le coiffèrent d'un bonnet de laine ou de poil. Το μεγαλοπρεπες και παγκλειστον κατερρυπαιγεν ονομα. (Nicétas, p. 358.) Si cette plaisanterie lui fut faite par des Vénitiens, c'était une suite de l'insolence naturelle aux négocians et aux républicains.

(3) Villehardouin, n° 181; Dandolo, p. 322. Le doge affirme que les Vénitiens furent payés plus lentement que

Alexis voyait avec inquiétude arriver le moment de leur départ. L'absence des confédérés l'aurait dispensé d'un engagement auquel il n'était point encore en état de satisfaire; mais elle l'aurait en même temps exposé sans secours aux caprices d'une nation perfide. Alexis offrit de défrayer leur dépense et d'acquitter en leur nom le fret des vaisseaux vénitiens, s'ils voulaient prolonger leur séjour durant une année. Cette offre fut agitée dans le conseil des barons : après de nouveaux débats et de nouveaux scrupules, les chefs des Français cédèrent une seconde fois à l'opinion du doge et aux prières du jeune empereur. Le marquis de Montferrat consentit, pour le prix de seize cents livres d'or, à conduire le fils d'Isaac avec une armée dans toutes les provinces d'Europe, pour y établir son autorité et poursuivre son oncle, tandis que la présence de Baudouin et des autres confédérés en imposerait aux habitans de Constantinople. L'expédition réussit; et les flatteurs qui environnaient le trône prédisaient à leur monarque aveugle, que la Providence qui l'avait tiré d'un cachot le guérirait de la goutte, lui rendrait la vue, et veillerait, durant de longues années, sur la prospérité de son empire. Le père d'Alexis, fier du succès de ses armes, les écou-

---

les Français; mais il observe que l'histoire des deux nations n'est point d'accord sur cet objet. Avait-il lu Villehardouin? Les Grecs se plaignirent, *quòd totius Græciæ opes transtulisset* (Gunther; *Hist. C. P.*, c. 13). *Voyez* les lamentations et les invectives de Nicétas, p. 355.

tait avec confiance ; mais la gloire toujours croissante de son fils commença bientôt à tourmenter l'âme soupçonneuse d'un vieillard ; et tout l'orgueil de ce père envieux ne pouvait lui dissimuler que tandis qu'on ne lui accordait qu'à regret quelques faibles acclamations (1), Alexis était le sujet des louanges les plus universelles et les plus sincères.

L'invasion des Français dissipa l'illusion qui durait depuis plus de neuf siècles. Les Grecs aperçurent avec étonnement que la capitale de l'empire romain n'était point inaccessible à une armée ennemie. Les Occidentaux avaient forcé la ville et disposé du trône de Constantin ; et les souverains qui l'occupaient sous leur protection furent bientôt aussi odieux au peuple que ceux qui les y avaient placés. Les infirmités d'Isaac ajoutaient au mépris qu'inspiraient ses vices, et la nation ne considéra plus le jeune Alexis que comme un apostat qui renonçait aux mœurs et à la religion de ses ancêtres : on connaissait ou du moins on soupçonnait ses conventions avec les Latins. Le peuple, et surtout le clergé, étaient inviolablement attachés à leur foi et à leurs superstitions. Les couvens, les maisons et jusqu'aux boutiques des marchands, retentissaient de la tyrannie du pape et du danger de l'Église (2). Un trésor épuisé fournissait

Querelles entre les Grecs et les Latins.

---

(1) Le règne d'Alexis Comnène contient dans Nicétas trois livres entiers ; et il expédie en cinq chapitres la courte restauration d'Isaac et de son fils (p. 352-362).

(2) Nicétas, en reprochant à Alexis son alliance impie,

difficilement au faste de la cour et aux exactions des confédérés. Les Grecs refusaient d'éviter, par une contribution générale, le danger menaçant du pillage et de la servitude ; on craignait, en opprimant les riches, d'exciter des ressentimens plus dangereux et plus personnels ; et, en fondant l'argenterie des églises, de s'attirer le reproche d'hérésie ou de sacrilége. En l'absence de Boniface et du jeune empereur, une calamité funeste affligea la ville de Constantinople, et on put en accuser justement le zèle indiscret des pélerins flamands (1). En parcourant un jour la capitale, ils furent scandalisés à la vue d'une mosquée ou d'une synagogue où l'on adorait un seul Dieu sans lui adjoindre un fils ou un associé ; leur manière ordinaire d'argumenter avec les infidèles était de les poursuivre le fer à la main, et de réduire en cendres leurs habitations ; mais ces infidèles et quelques chrétiens du voisinage entreprirent de défendre leur vie et leurs propriétés, et les flammes

---

insulte dans les termes les plus offensans à la religion du pape de Rome, μειζον και ατοπωτατον... παρεκτροπην πιστεως... των του Παπα προνομιων καινισμον.... μεταθεσιν τε και μεταποιησιν των παλαιων Ρωμαιοις εθων (p. 348). Telles furent les expressions de tous les Grecs jusqu'à la subdivision totale de leur empire.

(1) Nicétas (p. 355) est positif dans ses accusations, et charge particulièrement les Flamands (Φλαμιονες) ; mais il regarde mal à propos leur nom comme ancien. Villehardouin (n° 107) disculpe les barons, et ignore ou affecte d'ignorer le nom des coupables.

allumées par le fanatisme consumèrent indistinctement les édifices les plus orthodoxes. L'incendie dura huit jours et huit nuits, et consuma une surface d'environ une lieue depuis le port jusqu'à la Propontide, composant la partie la plus peuplée de Constantinople. Il ne serait pas facile de calculer le nombre d'églises et de palais réduits en cendres, la valeur des marchandises consumées ou pillées, et la multitude de familles réduites à l'indigence. Cet outrage, qu'en vain le doge et les barons affectèrent de désavouer, rendit le nom des Latins encore plus odieux au peuple; et une colonie d'Occidentaux, établie dans la ville, composée de plus de quinze mille personnes, crut devoir, pour sa sûreté, se retirer précipitamment dans le faubourg de Péra, à l'abri des drapeaux des confédérés. Le jeune empereur revint victorieux; mais la politique la plus ferme et la plus sage aurait échoué dans la tempête qui entraîna sa ruine et celle de son gouvernement. Son inclination et les conseils de son père l'attachaient à ses bienfaiteurs; mais Alexis hésitait entre la reconnaissance et le patriotisme, entre la crainte de ses sujets et celle de ses alliés (1). Sa conduite faible et irrésolue lui enleva l'estime et la confiance des deux

---

(1) Comparez les plaintes et les soupçons de Nicétas (p. 359-362) avec les accusations positives de Baudouin de Flandre (*Gesta Innocent. III*, chap. 92, pag. 534), *cùm patriarchá et mole nobilium, nobis promissis perjurus et mendax.*

partis. Tandis qu'à sa sollicitation le marquis de Montferrat occupait le palais, il souffrait que les nobles conspirassent et que le peuple prît les armes pour chasser les étrangers. Insensibles à l'embarras de sa situation, les chefs des Latins le pressèrent de remplir les conditions du traité, s'irritèrent des délais, soupçonnèrent ses intentions, et exigèrent que, par une réponse décisive, il déclarât la paix ou la guerre. Ce message orgueilleux lui fut porté par trois chevaliers français et trois vénitiens: ils traversèrent sur leurs chevaux, et l'épée au côté, la foule menaçante, et arrivèrent d'un air assuré jusque devant l'empereur. Là, récapitulant d'un ton péremptoire leurs services et ses engagemens, ils déclarèrent fièrement que si l'on ne satisfaisait sur-le-champ et pleinement à leurs justes demandes, ils ne reconnaissaient plus Alexis ni pour ami ni pour souverain. Après cette déclaration, la première de ce genre dont eût jamais été blessée l'oreille d'un empereur, ils s'éloignèrent sans laisser apercevoir le moindre symptôme de crainte, mais étonnés d'avoir pu sortir du palais d'un despote et d'une ville en fureur. Le retour au camp fut des deux côtés le signal de la guerre.

La guerre recommence. A. D. 1204.

Parmi les Grecs, la prudence et l'autorité étaient forcées de céder à l'impétuosité d'un peuple qui prenait sa rage pour de la valeur, sa multitude pour de la force, et l'impulsion du fanatisme pour une inspiration du ciel. Les deux nations méprisaient Alexis et l'accusaient également de parjure. Le peuple, qui exprimait hautement son mépris pour cette race vile et bâtarde, environna le sénat, lui demandant, par ses clameurs, un plus digne souverain. La pourpre fut successivement offerte à tous les sénateurs distingués par leur naissance ou par leur dignité, sans qu'aucun d'eux voulût accepter ce mortel honneur. Les sollicitations durèrent trois jours, et l'historien Nicétas, membre de cette assemblée, apprend que la crainte et la faiblesse soutinrent la fidélité des sénateurs. La populace proclama de force un fantôme qui fut bientôt abandonné (1). Mais Alexis, prince de la maison de Ducas, était le véritable auteur du tumulte, et le moteur de la guerre. Les historiens le distinguent par le surnom de Mourzoufle (2), qui, dans la langue vulgaire, désignait ses sourcils noirs, épais et rapprochés sans intervalle. A la fois patriote et courtisan, le perfide Mourzoufle, qui né manquait ni d'art ni de courage, opposa aux Latins son éloquence et son épée, s'insinua dans la confiance d'Alexis, et en obtint l'office de chambellan et les marques de la royauté. Dans le silence de la nuit, il courut précipitamment à la

---

(1) Il se nommait Nicolas Canabus. Nicétas en fait l'éloge, et Mourzoufle le sacrifia à sa vengeance (p. 362).

(2) Villehardouin (n° 116) en parle comme d'un favori, et semble ignorer qu'il était prince du sang impérial et de la maison de Ducas. Ducange, qui furète partout, soupçonne qu'il était le fils d'Isaac Ducas Sébastocrator, et cousin issu de germain du jeune empereur Alexis.

chambre du jeune empereur, et, d'un air effrayé, lui persuada que les ennemis avaient séduit ses gardes et forcé le palais. L'infortuné Alexis se livra sans défiance au traître qui méditait sa perte. Il descendit avec lui par un escalier dérobé ; mais cet escalier aboutissait à un cachot : on se saisit du prince, on le dépouilla, on le chargea de chaînes, et après lui avoir laissé savourer plusieurs jours toute l'amertume de la mort, le barbare Mourzoufle le fit empoisonner, étrangler ou assommer en sa présence. L'empereur Isaac suivit bientôt son fils au tombeau ; et la fortune épargna peut-être à Mourzoufle le crime inutile de hâter la mort d'un vieillard aveugle et sans moyens de se faire craindre.

<small>Alexis et son père sont déposés par Mourzoufle, le 8 février.</small>

<small>Second siège de Constantinople. Janv.-avril.</small>

La mort des empereurs et l'usurpation de Mourzoufle avaient changé la nature de la querelle. Il ne s'agissait plus d'une dispute entre alliés, dont les uns exagéraient leurs services, et les autres manquaient à leurs engagemens. Les Français et les Vénitiens oublièrent leurs griefs contre Alexis, versèrent quelques larmes sur le sort funeste de leur compagnon, et jurèrent de le venger d'une nation perfide qui avait couronné son assassin. Le sage Dandolo inclinait cependant encore à négocier; il exigeait, soit comme subside, comme dette ou comme amende, une somme de cinquante mille livres d'or, environ deux millions sterling; et la conférence n'aurait pas été si brusquement rompue, si, par zèle ou par politique, Mourzoufle n'eût pas refusé de sacrifier l'Église grecque au salut de l'État (1). A travers les invectives de ses ennemis étrangers ou domestiques, on aperçoit qu'il n'était pas indigne du rôle de défenseur de son pays. Le second siége de Constantinople offrit plus de difficultés que le premier. Par un examen sévère des abus du règne précédent, l'usurpateur avait rempli le trésor et ramené l'ordre. Mourzoufle, une masse de fer à la main, visitant les postes et affectant la démarche et le maintien d'un guerrier, se faisait redouter du moins de ses soldats et de ses compatriotes. Avant et après la mort d'Alexis, les Grecs avaient deux fois, par des entreprises vigoureuses et bien concertées, essayé de brûler la flotte dans le port; mais l'intelligence et la valeur des Vénitiens éloignèrent les brûlots, et ils se consumèrent au milieu de la mer sans causer aucun dommage (2). Henri, frère du comte de Flandre, repoussa l'empereur grec dans une sortie nocturne; l'avantage du nombre et de la surprise augmentèrent la honte de sa défaite. On trouva son bouclier sur le champ de bataille, et l'étendard impérial, sur lequel était une image miraculeuse de la Vierge, fut donné,

---

(1) Nicétas atteste cette négociation, qui paraît assez probable (p. 365); mais Villehardouin et Dandolo la regardent comme honteuse, et la passent sous silence.

(2) Baudouin parle de ces deux tentatives contre la flotte, (*Gesta*, c. 92, p. 534, 535); Villehardouin (n°^{s} 113-115) ne parle que de la première. Il est à remarquer qu'aucun de ces guerriers n'observe aucune propriété particulière aux feux grégeois.

comme un trophée et comme une relique, aux moines de Cîteaux, disciples de saint Bernard (1). Environ trois mois se passèrent en préparatifs et en escarmouches, sans en excepter le saint temps du carême, et sans que les Latins entreprissent de donner un assaut général. La ville avait été reconnue imprenable du côté de la terre; les pilotes vénitiens représentaient que l'ancrage n'étant pas sûr vers les bords de la Propontide, le courant pourrait entraîner les vaisseaux jusqu'au détroit de l'Hellespont, et ces difficultés plaisaient infiniment à une partie des pèlerins, qui désiraient trouver un prétexte pour abandonner l'armée. On résolut cependant de former une attaque du côté du port. Les assiégés s'y attendaient, et l'empereur avait placé son pavillon écarlate sur une hauteur voisine, d'où il dirigeait et animait les efforts de ses soldats. Un spectateur intrépide, et capable de jouir en ce moment d'un beau et magnifique spectacle, aurait admiré le vaste déploiement de ces deux armées rangées en bataille, et présentant chacune un front d'environ une demi-lieue, l'une sur les vaisseaux et les galères, l'autre sur les remparts et sur les tours dont l'élévation était encore augmentée par d'autres tours en bois à plu-

---

(1) Ducange (n° 119) nous inonde d'un torrent d'érudition relativement au *gonfanon impérial*. On montre encore cette bannière de la Vierge à Venise comme un trophée et une relique. Si c'est la véritable, le pieux Dandolo a trompé les moines de Cîteaux.

sieurs étages. L'attaque commença par une décharge réciproque de feux, de pierres et de dards ; mais les eaux étaient profondes, les Français audacieux, les Vénitiens habiles ; ils approchèrent des murs, et sur les ponts tremblans qui joignaient les batteries flottantes des Français aux batteries solides des Grecs, il se livra un combat terrible à l'épée, à la hache et à la lance. Ils formèrent au même instant plus de cent attaques différentes, soutenues avec une égale vigueur jusqu'au moment où l'avantage du terrain et la supériorité du nombre, décidant la victoire, forcèrent les Latins à songer à la retraite. Le lendemain ils renouvelèrent l'assaut avec la même valeur et aussi peu de succès. Pendant la nuit, le doge et les barons tinrent conseil ; ils n'étaient effrayés que du danger public, et pas une seule voix ne prononça le mot de traité ou de retraite. Chaque guerrier, selon son caractère, s'attacha à l'espérance de vaincre ou de mourir glorieusement (1). L'expérience du premier siége avait instruit les Grecs ; mais elle animait les Latins ; et la certitude que Constantinople pouvait être prise, était pour eux d'un bien plus grand avantage que ne le pouvait être pour leurs

---

(1) Villehardouin (n° 126) avoue que *mult erp grant péril;* et Gunther (*Hist. C. P.*, c. 13) affirme que *nulla spes victoriæ arridere poterat.* Cependant le chevalier parle avec mépris de ceux qui pensaient à la retraite, et le moine donne des louanges à ceux de ses compatriotes qui étaient résolus de mourir les armes à la main.

ennemis la connaissance de quelques précautions locales à prendre pour sa défense. Au troisième assaut, on enchaîna deux vaisseaux ensemble pour en doubler la force ; un vent du nord les chassait vers le rivage : les évêques de Troyes et de Soissons conduisaient l'avant-garde, et les noms de ces deux vaisseaux, *le Pélerin* et *le Paradis*, retentissaient le long de la ligne (1) comme un favorable augure. Les bannières épiscopales furent plantées sur les murs ; on avait promis cent marcs d'argent aux premiers qui les escaladeraient ; et si la mort les priva de leur récompense, la gloire a immortalisé leurs noms. On escalada quatre tours, on enfonça les portes, et les chevaliers français, qui n'étaient peut-être pas fort rassurés sur l'Océan, se crurent invincibles dès qu'ils se sentirent portés sur leurs chevaux et sur la terre ferme. Dois-je raconter que des milliers de soldats qui environnaient l'empereur, prirent la fuite à l'approche d'un seul guerrier ? Cette fuite ignominieuse est attestée par Nicétas, leur compatriote ; une armée de fantômes accompagnait le héros français, et il parut un géant aux yeux des Grecs (2). Tandis que

---

(1) Baudouin et tous les écrivains honorent les noms de ces deux galères de *felici auspicio*.

(2) En faisant allusion à Homère, Nicétas l'appelle εννεα οργυιας, haut de neuf *orgyæ* ou dix-huit verges anglaises, environ cinquante pieds. Une pareille taille aurait en effet rendu la terreur des Grecs fort excusable. L'auteur paraît dans cette occasion plus attaché aux merveilles qu'à son pays, ou peut-être à la vérité. Baudouin s'écrie, dans les

les vaincus abandonnaient leurs postes et jetaient leurs armes, les Latins entrèrent dans la ville sous les étendards de leurs chefs. Tous les obstacles disparurent à leur approche ; et, soit à dessein ou par accident, un troisième incendie consuma en peu d'heures une partie de la ville égale en étendue à trois des plus grandes villes de la France (1). Sur le soir, les barons rappelèrent leurs troupes et fortifièrent leurs postes. Ils étaient effrayés de l'étendue et de la population de cette capitale, dont les églises et les palais, si on en eût senti la force, pouvaient leur coûter encore plus d'un mois à réduire. Mais dès le grand matin une procession de supplians, portant des croix et des images, annonça la soumission des Grecs, et implora la clémence des vainqueurs. L'usurpateur prit la fuite par la porte d'or; le marquis de Montferrat et le comte de Flandre occupèrent les palais de Blachernes et de Boucoléon ; et les armes des pèlerins latins renversèrent un empire qui portait encore le titre de Romain et le nom de Constantin (2).

---

termes du psalmiste : *Persequitur unus ex nobis centum alienos.*

(1) Villehardouin (n° 130) ignore encore les auteurs de cet incendie, moins condamnable que le premier, et dont Gunther accuse *quidam comes Teutonicus* (c. 14). Ils semblent rougir, les incendiaires !

(2) Pour le second siége et la conquête de Constantinople, *voyez* Villehardouin (n°ˢ 113-132), la deuxième lettre de Baudouin à Innocent III (*Gesta*, c. 92, p. 534-537), et le

Pillage de Constantinople.

Constantinople avait été prise d'assaut : les lois de la guerre n'imposaient rien aux vainqueurs que ce que pourraient leur inspirer la religion et l'humanité. Ils reconnaissaient encore le marquis de Montferrat pour général ; et les Grecs, qui le considéraient déjà comme leur futur souverain, s'écriaient d'un ton lamentable : « Saint marquis roi, ayez pitié de nous ! » Sa prudence ou sa compassion fit ouvrir aux fugitifs les portes de la ville, et il exhorta les soldats de la croix à épargner le sang des chrétiens. Les flots de sang que fait couler Nicétas peuvent être réduits au massacre de deux mille de ses compatriotes égorgés sans résistance (1), et on ne peut pas même en accuser entièrement les conquérans : le plus grand nombre fut immolé par la colonie latine que les Grecs avaient chassée de la ville, et qui se livrait aux ressentimens d'une faction triomphante. Quelques-uns de ces exilés se montrèrent

règne entier de Mourzoufle dans Nicétas (p. 363-375). *Voy.* aussi quelques passages de Dandolo (*in Chron. Venet.*, p. 323-330), et Gunther (*Hist. C. P.*, c. 14-18), qui ajoutent le merveilleux des visions et des prophéties. Le premier cite un oracle de la sibylle Erythrée, qui annonce un grand armement sur la mer Adriatique, sous la conduite d'un général aveugle, et destiné contre Byzance, etc. ; prédiction fort surprenante, si elle n'était pas postérieure à l'événement.

(1) *Ceciderunt tamen eâ die civium quasi duo millia*, etc. (Gunther, c. 18.) L'arithmétique est une pierre de touche pour évaluer l'exagération de la passion et des figures de rhétorique.

cependant plus sensibles aux bienfaits qu'aux outrages, et Nicétas lui-même dut la conservation de sa vie à la générosité d'un marchand vénitien. Le pape Innocent accuse les pélerins de n'avoir respecté, dans leur emportement de débauche, ni le sexe, ni l'âge, ni la profession religieuse; il déplore amèrement que des œuvres de ténèbres, des viols, des adultères et des incestes, aient été commis en plein jour; et se plaint de ce que de nobles matrones et de saintes religieuses furent déshonorées par les valets et les paysans qui remplissaient l'armée catholique (1). Il est assez probable que la licence de la victoire servit d'occasion et d'excuse à une multitude de péchés; mais la capitale de l'Orient contenait sans doute un nombre de beautés vénales ou complaisantes, suffisant pour satisfaire les désirs de vingt mille pélerins, et le droit ou l'abus de l'esclavage ne s'étendait plus sur les femmes. Le marquis de Montferrat était le modèle de la discipline et de la décence, et l'on regardait le comte de Flandre comme le miroir de la chasteté. Ils défendirent sous peine de mort le viol des femmes mariées, des vierges et des religieuses; quelques-uns des vaincus

---

(1). *Quidam* (dit Innocent III, *Gesta*, c. 94, p. 538) *nec religioni, nec ætati, nec sexui peperceront: sed fornicationes, adulteria et incestus in oculis omnium exercentes, non solùm maritatas et viduas, sed et matronas et virgines Deoque dicatas exposuerunt spurcitiis garcionum.* Villehardouin ne parle point de ces accidens communs à la guerre.

invoquèrent cette proclamation (1), et les vainqueurs la respectèrent quelquefois. La débauche et la cruauté furent contenues par l'autorité des chefs et les sentimens naturels des soldats. Ce n'étaient plus des sauvages du Nord; et quelque féroces que pussent encore paraître les Européens à cette époque, le temps, la politique et la religion, avaient adouci les mœurs des Français, et surtout des Italiens : mais leur avarice eut la liberté de se satisfaire par le pillage de Constantinople, sans égard pour la semaine sainte. Toutes les richesses publiques et celles des particuliers appartenaient aux Latins par le droit de la guerre, que n'avait modifié aucune promesse ni aucun traité, et toutes les mains, selon leur pouvoir et leur force, étaient également propres à exécuter la sentence et à saisir les objets confisqués. L'or et l'argent monnayés ou non monnayés fournissaient des objets d'échange universels et portatifs, que chacun pouvait, ou sur le lieu même, ou ailleurs, convertir de la manière qui convenait le mieux à son caractère et à sa situation. Des richesses que le luxe et le commerce avaient accumulées dans la capitale, les étoffes de soie, les velours, les fourrures et les épices, étaient les plus précieuses, parce que, dans les parties moins civilisées de l'Europe, on ne pou-

---

(1) Nicétas sauva et épousa dans la suite une vierge noble qu'un soldat, επι μαρτυσι πολλοις ὁμηδον επιβρωμωμενος, avait presque violée, sans égard pour εντολαι, ενταλματα ευ γεγονοτων.

vait pas se les procurer pour de l'argent. On établit *Partage du butin.* un ordre dans le pillage, et l'on ne s'en remit pas au hasard ou à l'adresse particulière des vainqueurs du soin de régler la part de chacun ; trois églises furent choisies pour le dépôt général, et les pélerins reçurent l'ordre d'y porter tout leur butin, sans en rien distraire, sous les peines terribles réservées au parjure, la mort et l'excommunication. Un simple soldat recevait une part, le sergent à cheval deux parts, le chevalier quatre, et on augmentait ensuite en proportion du rang et du mérite des barons et des princes. On pendit, avec sa cotte d'armes et son bouclier à son cou, un chevalier du comte de Saint-Pol, convaincu d'avoir violé cet engagement sacré. Un exemple si sévère dut rendre les autres plus habiles et plus prudens ; mais l'avidité l'emporta sur la crainte, et l'opinion générale évalue le pillage secret fort au-dessus de celui qui fut publiquement distribué. Ce dernier surpassait cependant tout ce qu'on avait jamais vu et tout ce qu'on pouvait espérer (1). Après un partage égal entre les Français et les Vénitiens, les premiers prélevèrent une somme de cinquante mille marcs pour satisfaire à la dette contrac-

---

(1) En parlant de la masse générale des richesses, Gunther observe, *ut de pauperibus et advenis cives ditissimi redderentur* (*Hist. C. P.*, c. 18) ; Villehardouin (n° 132), que depuis la création *ne fut tant gaaignié dans une ville ;* Baudouin (*Gesta*, c. 92), *ut tantum tota non videatur possidere Latinitas*.

tée avec la république, et il leur restait encore quatre cent mille marcs d'argent (1), environ huit cent mille livres sterling : je ne puis pas mieux indiquer la valeur relative d'une pareille somme dans ce siècle, qu'en la représentant comme égale à sept années du revenu du royaume d'Angleterre (2).

Misère des Grecs.

Dans cette grande révolution, nous avons l'avantage de pouvoir comparer les relations de Villehardouin et de Nicétas, les sentimens opposés du maréchal de Champagne et du sénateur de Byzance (3). Il semblerait au premier coup d'œil que les richesses de Constantinople ne firent que passer d'une nation chez l'autre, et que la perte et la douleur des Grecs

---

(1) Villehardouin, n°⁵ 133-135. Il y a une variante dans le texte; et l'on peut lire cinq cent mille au lieu de quatre cent mille. Les Vénitiens avaient offert de prendre la masse entière des dépouilles, et de donner quatre cents marcs à chaque chevalier, deux cents à chaque prêtre ou cavalier, et cent à chaque soldat. Ce marché n'aurait pas été avantageux pour la république (Le Beau, *Hist. du Bas-Empire*, t. xx, p. 506; je ne sais d'où il a pris cela).

(2) Au concile de Lyon (A. D. 1245), les ambassadeurs d'Angleterre évaluèrent le revenu de la couronne comme inférieur à celui du clergé étranger, qui montait à soixante mille marcs chaque année (Matthieu Paris, p. 451; *Hist. d'Angleterre*, par Hume, vol. II, p. 170).

(3) Nicétas décrit d'une manière pathétique le sac de Constantinople et ses malheurs personnels (p. 367-369, et dans le *Status urbis C. P.*, p. 375-384); Innocent III (*Gesta*, c. 92) confirme la réalité même des sacriléges que déplorait Nicétas; mais Villehardouin ne laisse apercevoir ni pitié ni remords.

furent exactement compensées par la joie et l'avantage des Latins ; mais dans le jeu funeste de la guerre, le gain n'égale jamais la perte, et les jouissances sont faibles en comparaison des calamités. Les Latins n'obtinrent qu'un plaisir illusoire et passager, les Grecs pleurèrent sur la ruine irréparable de leur patrie ; le sacrilége et la raillerie aggravaient leur misère. Que revint-il aux vainqueurs des trois incendies qui détruisirent une si grande partie des richesses et des édifices de Constantinople ? Quel profit tirèrent-ils des objets qu'ils brisèrent ou mutilèrent parce qu'ils ne pouvaient pas les transporter, de l'or qu'ils prodiguèrent au jeu ou en débauches ? Combien d'objets précieux les soldats ne donnèrent-ils pas à vil prix par ignorance ou par impatience, dépouillés ainsi du prix de leur victoire par l'adresse des plus vils d'entre les Grecs ! Parmi ces derniers, ceux qui n'avaient rien à perdre purent seuls tirer quelque avantage de la révolution, mais tous les autres furent réduits à l'état le plus déplorable ; nous pouvons en juger par les aventures de Nicétas. Son magnifique palais avait été réduit en cendres dans le second incendie, et cet infortuné sénateur, suivi de sa famille et de ses amis, se réfugia dans une petite maison qui lui restait encore auprès de l'église de Sainte-Sophie. Ce fut à la porte de cette maison que le marchand vénitien monta la garde sous l'habit d'un soldat, jusqu'au moment où Nicétas put sauver, par une fuite précipitée, la chasteté de sa fille et les débris de sa fortune. Ces malheureux fugitifs, nourris dans le sein de la prospérité, partirent à pied au cœur de l'hiver. Son épouse était enceinte, et la désertion de ses esclaves les força de porter eux-mêmes leur bagage sur leurs épaules. Ils exhortèrent leurs femmes, placées au centre, au lieu de peindre et d'orner leur visage, à le couvrir de boue pour en déguiser la beauté; chaque pas les exposait à des insultes et à des dangers; et les menaces des étrangers leur paraissaient moins insupportables que l'insolence des plébéiens au niveau desquels ils se trouvaient maintenant réduits. Ils ne respirèrent en sûreté qu'à Sélymbrie, ville située à quarante milles de Constantinople, terme de leur douloureux pélerinage. Ils rencontrèrent sur la route le patriarche seul, à peine vêtu, monté sur un âne et réduit à l'indigence apostolique qui, si elle avait été volontaire, aurait pu être méritoire.

Sacriléges et railleries. Pendant ce temps, les Latins, entraînés par la licence et l'esprit de parti, pillaient et profanaient ses églises. Après avoir arraché des calices les perles et les pierres précieuses dont ils étaient ornés, les pélerins s'en servirent en guise de coupes. Ils jouaient et buvaient sur des tables où étaient représentées les figures du Christ et de ses apôtres, et foulaient aux pieds les objets les plus vénérables du culte des chrétiens. Dans l'église de Sainte-Sophie, les soldats déchirèrent en lambeaux le voile du sanctuaire pour en arracher la frange d'or; ils mirent en pièces et se partagèrent le maître-autel, monument de l'art et de la richesse des Grecs; on chargeait, au milieu des églises, sur des mulets et des chevaux, les ornemens d'or et d'argent qu'on arrachait des portes et de la chaire ; et lorsqu'ils pliaient sous le fardeau, leurs impatiens conducteurs les poignardaient, et leur sang inondait le pavé du sanctuaire. Une prostituée s'assit sur le siége du patriarche, et cette fille de Bélial, dit l'historien, chanta et dansa dans l'église pour ridiculiser les hymnes et les processions des Orientaux. L'avidité ne respecta pas même les tombeaux des souverains placés dans l'église des Apôtres ; et l'on prétend que le corps de Justinien, inhumé depuis six siècles, fut trouvé tout entier, et sans aucun signe de putréfaction. Les Français et les Flamands couraient les rues de la ville, coiffés de voiles flottans, et enveloppés de longues robes peintes dont ils caparaçonnaient jusqu'à leurs chevaux : l'intempérance grossière de leurs orgies (1) insultait à la sobriété fastueuse des Orientaux, et, en dérision des armes propres à un peuple de scribes et d'étudians, ils portaient à la main une plume, du papier et une écritoire, sans s'apercevoir que les instrumens de la science étaient entre les mains des Grecs modernes aussi faibles et aussi inutiles que ceux de la valeur.

Destruction des statues.

Leur langue et leur réputation semblaient cepen-

---

(1) Si j'ai bien compris le texte grec de Nicétas, leurs mets favoris étaient des culottes de bœuf bouillies, du porc salé avec des pois, et de la soupe avec de l'ail et des herbes âcres ou acides (p. 382).

dant les autoriser à mépriser l'ignorance des Latins et leurs faibles progrès (1). Dans l'amour ou le respect des arts, la différence des deux nations était encore plus sensible. Les Grecs conservaient avec vénération les monumens de leurs ancêtres qu'ils ne pouvaient pas imiter, et nous ne pouvons nous empêcher de partager la douleur et le ressentiment de Nicétas, lorsqu'il rapporte la destruction des statues de Constantinople (2). Nous avons vu le despotisme et l'orgueil de son fondateur constamment occupés d'embellir sa cité naissante. Des dieux et des héros avaient échappé à la destruction du paganisme; les restes d'un siècle plus florissant ornaient encore le Forum et l'Hippodrome. Nicétas (3) en

---

(1) Nicétas emploie des expressions très-dures : Παρ' αγραμματοις Βαρβαροις, και τελεον αναλφαβητοις (*Fragm.* apud Fabricius, *Bibl. græc.*, t. VI, p. 414). Il est vrai que ce reproche s'applique particulièrement à leur ignorance de la langue grecque et des sublimes ouvrages d'Homère. Les Latins des douzième et treizième siècles ne manquaient point d'ouvrages de littérature dans leur propre langue. *Voyez* les *Recherches philologiques* de Harris, p. 111, c. 9, 10, 11.

(2) Nicétas était né à Chonæ en Phrygie (l'ancienne Colosses de saint Paul). Il s'était élevé au rang de sénateur, de juge du Voile et de grand logothète. Après la ruine de l'empire, dont il fut témoin et victime, il se retira à Nicée, et composa une histoire complète et soignée depuis la mort d'Alexis Comnène jusqu'au règne de Henri.

(3) Un manuscrit de Nicétas (dans la *Biblioth. Bodléienne*) contient ce fragment curieux sur les statues de Constantinople, que la fraude ou la honte, ou plutôt la négligence, a

décrit plusieurs dans un style pompeux et rempli d'affectation. Je tirerai de cette description quelques détails sur les plus intéressans. 1º Les conducteurs des chars, qui avaient remporté le prix, étaient jetés en bronze, à leurs frais ou à ceux du public, et placés dans l'Hippodrome. On les voyait debout sur leur char, qui semblait courir dans la lice; et, en admirant l'attitude, les spectateurs pouvaient juger de la ressemblance. Les plus précieuses de ces statues pouvaient avoir été transportées du stade olympique. 2° Le sphynx, le cheval marin et le crocodile, indiquent l'ouvrage et les dépouilles de l'Égypte. 3º La louve, qui allaite Romulus et Remus, sujet également agréable aux Romains anciens et modernes, mais qui ne pouvait guère avoir été traité avant le déclin de la sculpture chez les Grecs. 4º Un aigle qui tient et déchire un serpent dans ses serres, monument particulier à la ville de Byzance, et attribué par les Grecs à la puissance magique du philosophe Apollonius, dont ce talisman passait pour avoir délivré Byzance des reptiles venimeux. 5º Un âne et son conducteur, qu'Auguste plaça dans sa colonie de Nicopolis, en commémoration d'un présage qui lui avait annoncé la victoire d'Actium. 6° Une statue équestre qui, dans l'opinion du peuple, représentait Josué, conquérant juif, étendant

---

omis dans les autres éditions. Il a été publié par Fabricius (*Bibl. græc.*, t. VI, p. 405-416), et loué excessivement par l'ingénieux M. Harris de Salisbury (*Rech. philologiques*, part. III, c. 5, p. 301-312).

le bras pour arrêter le cours du soleil. Une tradition plus classique aidait à reconnaître Bellérophon et Pégase; la libre attitude du coursier semblait indiquer qu'il marchait dans les airs plutôt que sur la terre. 7° Un obélisque de forme carrée, dont les faces, travaillées en bosse, présentaient une variété de scènes pittoresques et champêtres : des oiseaux qui chantaient, des gens de la campagne occupés de leurs travaux ou jouant de la musette ; des moutons bêlans, des agneaux bondissans, la mer, un paysage, une pêche et une quantité de différens poissons ; de petits amours nus, riant, folâtrant, et se jetant mutuellement des pommes; et sur la cime de l'obélisque, une figure de femme, que le moindre souffle de vent faisait tourner, et qu'on nommait *la suivante du vent*. 8° Le berger de Phrygie, qui présentait à Vénus le prix de la beauté, ou la pomme de discorde. 9° L'incomparable statue d'Hélène. Nicétas décrit du ton de l'admiration et de l'amour la délicatesse de ses pieds, ses bras d'albâtre, ses lèvres de rose, son sourire enchanteur, la langueur de ses yeux, la beauté de ses sourcils arqués, et la parfaite harmonie de ses formes, la légèreté de sa draperie, et sa chevelure qui semblait flotter au gré du vent. Tant de beautés auraient dû faire naître la pitié ou le remords dans le cœur de ses barbares destructeurs. 10° La figure virile ou plutôt divine d'Hercule (1), ranimée par la main savante

---

(1) Pour nous donner l'idée de la statue d'Hercule,

de Lysippe ; il était d'une telle dimension que son pouce était de la grosseur, et sa jambe de la hauteur d'un homme ordinaire (1). Il avait la poitrine et les épaules larges, les membres nerveux, les cheveux crépus et l'aspect impérieux ; sans massue, sans arc ou carquois, sa peau de lion négligemment jetée sur les épaules, il était assis sur un panier d'osier ; sa jambe et son bras droits étaient étendus de toute leur longueur ; son genou gauche plié soutenait son coude et sa tête appuyée sur sa main gauche ; ses regards pensifs annonçaient l'indignation. 11° Une autre statue colossale de Junon, l'ancien ornement de son temple de Samos ; quatre paires de bœufs transportèrent avec peine son énorme tête jusqu'au palais. 12° Un troisième colosse de Pallas ou Minerve, de trente pieds de hauteur, et qui représentait avec une admirable énergie le caractère et les attributs de cette vierge martiale. Il est juste d'observer que les Grecs détruisirent eux-mêmes cette Pallas, après le premier siége, par un motif de crainte et de superstition (2). Les croisés, dans leur cupidité incapable

---

M. Harris a cité une épigramme et donné la figure d'une superbe pierre, qui cependant ne copie point l'attitude de la statue, qui représentait Hercule sans massue, la jambe et le bras droits étendus.

(1) Je transcris littéralement les proportions données par Nicétas, qui me paraissent très-ridicules, et feront peut-être juger que le bon goût prétendu de ce sénateur se réduisait à de l'affectation et de la vanité.

(2) Nicétas, *in Isaaco Ang. et Alex.*, c. 3, p. 359. L'é-

de sentiment, brisèrent ou fondirent les autres statues de cuivre dont je viens de donner le détail ; le prix et le travail de ces ouvrages disparurent en un moment. Le génie des artistes s'évapora en fumée, et le métal grossier, converti en monnaie, servit à payer les soldats. Les monumens de bronze ne sont pas les plus durables : les Latins purent détourner avec un mépris stupide leurs regards des marbres animés par les Phidias et les Praxitèle (1); mais, à moins de quelque accident, ces blocs inutiles demeuraient en sûreté sur leurs piédestaux (2). Les plus éclairés d'entre les pélerins, ceux qui ne partageaient pas les goûts grossiers et sensuels de leurs compatriotes, exercèrent pieusement leur droit de conquête sur les reliques des saints (3). Cette révolution procura aux

---

diteur latin observe très-judicieusement que l'historien fait dans son style emphatique *ex pulice elephantem*.

(1) Nicétas, dans deux passages (édition de *Paris*, p. 360 ; Fabricius, p. 408) couvre les Latins du reproche piquant de οι του καλου, ανεραστοι Βαρβαροι ; et il s'explique clairement sur leur avidité pour le cuivre. Cependant les Vénitiens eurent le mérite de transporter quatre chevaux de bronze de Constantinople à la place de Saint-Marc (Sanuto, *Vite dei Dogi*, in Muratori, *Script. rerum italicar.*, tom. XXII, p. 534).

(2) Winckelmann, *Hist. de l'Art*, t. III, p. 269-270.

(3) *Voyez* le vol pieux de l'abbé Martin, qui transporta une riche cargaison dans son couvent de Paris, diocèse de Bâle (Gunther, *Hist. C. P.*, c. 19-23, 24). Cependant, en dérobant ces saintes dépouilles, le saint encourut la peine d'excommunication, et fut peut-être infidèle à un serment.

églises d'Europe une immensité de têtes, d'os, de croix et d'images, et augmenta tellement par ce moyen les pélerinages et les offrandes, que ces reliques devinrent peut-être la partie la plus lucrative du butin rapporté de l'Orient (1). Une grande partie des écrits de l'antiquité, perdus aujourd'hui, existaient encore au douzième siècle; mais les pélerins n'étaient empressés ni de conserver ni de transporter des volumes d'une langue étrangère. La multiplicité des copies peut seule perpétuer des papiers ou des parchemins que le moindre accident peut détruire; la littérature des Grecs était concentrée presque en totalité dans la capitale (2), et sans connaître toute l'étendue de notre perte, nous devons vivement re-

---

(1) Fleury, *Hist. ecclés.*, t. XVI, p. 139-145.

(2) Je terminerai ce chapitre par quelques mots sur une histoire moderne, qui donne les détails de la prise de Constantinople par les Latins, mais qui n'est tombée qu'un peu tard entre mes mains. Paolo Ramusio, le fils du compilateur de Voyages, fut nommé par le sénat de Venise pour écrire l'histoire de la conquête. Il reçut cet ordre dans sa jeunesse, et l'exécuta quelques années après. Il composa en latin un ouvrage élégamment écrit, intitulé : *de Bello Constantinopolitano et imperatoribus Comnenis per Gallos et Venetos restitutis* (Venise, 1635, in-folio). Ramusio ou Rhamnusus transcrit et traduit, *sequitur ad unguem*, un manuscrit de Villehardouin qu'il possédait; mais il a enrichi son récit de matériaux grecs et latins, et nous lui devons la description correcte de la flotte, les noms des cinquante nobles Vénitiens qui commandaient les galères de la république, et la connaissance de l'opposition patrio-

gretter les riches bibliothèques consumées dans les trois incendies de Constantinople.

---

tique de Pantaléon Barbi au choix du doge pour empereur.

CHAPITRE LXI.

Partage de l'empire entre les Français et les Vénitiens. Cinq empereurs latins des maisons de Flandre et de Courtenai. Leurs guerres contre les Bulgares et contre les Grecs. Faiblesse et pauvreté de l'empire latin. Les Grecs reprennent Constantinople. Conséquences générales des croisades.

Après la mort des princes légitimes, les Français et les Vénitiens se crurent suffisamment assurés de la justice de leur cause et de son succès, pour se partager d'avance les provinces de l'empire (1) : ils convinrent, par un traité, de nommer douze électeurs, six de chaque nation, et de reconnaître pour empereur de l'Orient celui qui obtiendrait la majorité de leurs suffrages. Les confédérés stipulèrent qu'en cas que les voix fussent également partagées, le sort déciderait entre les deux candidats. Ils lui accordèrent d'avance les titres et les prérogatives des empereurs précédens, les deux palais de Blachernes et de Boucoléon, et le quart de toutes les possessions qui composaient la monarchie des Grecs ; les trois

Élection de l'empereur Baudouin 1er. A. D. 1204, mai 9-16.

---

(1) *Voyez* l'original du traité de partage dans la *Chronique* d'André Dandolo (p. 326-336), et l'élection qui en fut la suite, dans Villehardouin (nos 136-140), les *Observations* de Ducange et le premier livre de l'*Histoire de Constantinople sous l'empire des Français*.

autres parts, divisées en deux portions égales, furent destinées à être partagées entre les Vénitiens et les barons français. On convint que tous les feudataires, dont, par une honorable distinction, le doge fut seul excepté, prêteraient au nouveau souverain foi, hommage et serment de service militaire, comme au chef suprême de l'empire; que celle des deux nations qui donnerait l'empereur, céderait à l'autre la nomination du patriarche; et que tous les pélerins, quelle que fût leur impatience de visiter la Terre-Sainte, consacreraient encore une année à la conquête et à la défense des provinces de l'empire grec. Lorsque les Latins furent les maîtres de Constantinople, ils confirmèrent le traité et l'exécutèrent. Le premier et le plus important de leurs soins fut l'élection d'un empereur. Les six électeurs français étaient tous ecclésiastiques : l'abbé de Loches, l'archevêque élu d'Acre en Palestine, et les évêques de Soissons, de Troyes, d'Halberstadt et de Bethléem : ce dernier remplissait dans le camp l'office de légat du pape. Respectables par leurs lumières et leur caractère sacré, ils étaient d'autant plus propres à faire un choix, qu'ils ne pouvaient pas en être l'objet. On choisit les six Vénitiens parmi les principaux ministres de l'État, et les illustres familles des Querini et des Contarini s'enorgueillissent encore d'y trouver leurs ancêtres. Les douze électeurs s'assemblèrent dans la chapelle du palais, et procédèrent à l'élection après avoir solennellement invoqué le Saint-Esprit. Le respect et la reconnaissance réunirent d'abord tous les suffrages en faveur du doge. Il était l'auteur de l'entreprise, et, malgré son âge et son état de cécité, ses exploits auraient pu mériter les éloges et l'envie des plus jeunes chevaliers; mais le patriote Dandolo dédaignait toute ambition personnelle, et se contenta de l'honneur des suffrages qui le déclaraient digne de régner. Les Vénitiens, ses compatriotes, et peut-être ses amis, s'opposèrent eux-mêmes à sa nomination (1) : ils représentèrent avec l'éloquence de la vérité les inconvéniens qui pouvaient résulter, pour la liberté nationale et pour la cause commune, de l'union incompatible de la première magistrature d'une république et de la souveraineté de l'Orient. L'exclusion du doge laissa le champ libre aux mérites plus balancés de Boniface et de Baudouin, et tous les candidats moins illustres abandonnèrent respectueusement leurs prétentions. La maturité de l'âge, une réputation brillante, le choix des aventuriers et le vœu des Grecs, recommandaient le marquis de Montferrat; et j'ai peine à croire que ses petites possessions au pied des Alpes (2)

(1) Après avoir rapporté la nomination du doge par un électeur français, son parent André Dandolo approuve son exclusion, *quidam Venetorum fidelis et nobilis senex, usus oratione satis probabili*, etc., que les écrivains modernes, depuis Blondus jusqu'à Le Beau, ont brodée chacun à leur fantaisie.

(2) Nicétas (p. 384), vain et ignorant comme un Grec, désigne le marquis de Montferrat comme le chef d'une puissance maritime, Λαμπάρδιαν δε οικεισθαι παράλιον ; peut-être

aient pu donner de l'inquiétude à la république de
Venise, maîtresse de la mer. Mais le comte de Flandre, âgé de trente-deux ans, vaillant, pieux et
chaste, était chef d'un peuple riche et belliqueux,
descendant de Charlemagne, cousin du roi de France,
et pair des barons et des prélats qui auraient consenti avec répugnance à se soumettre à l'empire d'un
étranger. Ces barons, le doge et le marquis à leur
tête, attendaient à la porte de la chapelle la décision
des électeurs. L'évêque de Soissons vint l'annoncer
au nom de ses collègues. « Vous avez juré, dit-il,
d'obéir au prince que nous choisirions : par nos suffrages unanimes, Baudouin, comte de Flandre et de
Hainaut, est votre souverain et empereur d'Orient. »
Le comte fut salué par de bruyantes acclamations,
que répétèrent bientôt, dans toute la ville, la joie
des Latins et la tremblante adulation des Grecs.
Boniface s'empressa le premier de baiser la main de
son rival et de l'élever sur un bouclier. Baudouin fut
transporté dans la cathédrale, où on lui chaussa solennellement les brodequins de pourpre. Trois semaines après l'élection, il fut couronné par le légat
du pape, faisant les fonctions de patriarche; mais
le clergé vénitien remplit bientôt le chapitre de
Sainte-Sophie, plaça Thomas Morosini sur le trône
ecclésiastique, et ne négligea aucun moyen pour
conserver à sa nation les honneurs et les bénéfices

---

a-t-il été induit en erreur par le thème byzantin de Lombardie, situé sur les côtes de la Calabre.

de l'Église grecque (1). Le successeur de Constantin ne tarda pas à envoyer dans la Palestine, en France et à Rome, la nouvelle de cette révolution mémorable; il fit transporter dans la Palestine, comme un trophée, les portes de Constantinople et les chaînes du port (2), et prit des Assises de Jérusalem, les lois et les usages qui convenaient le mieux à une colonie française et à une conquête d'Orient. Baudouin, par ses lettres, invite tous les Français à venir augmenter cette colonie, peupler une vaste et superbe capitale, et cultiver des terres fertiles préparées à récompenser amplement les travaux du prêtre et ceux du soldat. Il félicite le pontife de Rome sur le rétablissement de son autorité dans l'Orient, l'engage à éteindre le schisme des Grecs par sa présence dans un concile général, et sollicite son indulgence et sa bénédiction pour des pélerins qui avaient contrevenu à ses ordres (3). Innocent répondit avec autant de

---

(1) Ils exigèrent de Morosini qu'il fît serment de ne recevoir dans le chapitre de Sainte-Sophie, chargé de droit des élections, que des Vénitiens qui auraient habité Venise au moins pendant dix ans; mais le clergé fut jaloux de la prérogative qu'ils s'arrogeaient, le pape la désapprouva, et des six patriarches latins de Constantinople, le premier et le dernier furent seuls Vénitiens.

(2) Nicétas, p. 383.

(3) Les lettres d'Innocent III fournissent de riches matériaux pour l'histoire des institutions civiles et ecclésiastiques de l'empire latin de Constantinople. Les plus importantes de ces lettres (dont Étienne Baluze a publié la

dignité que de prudence : il attribue aux vices des hommes la subversion de l'empire d'Orient, et adore les décrets de la Providence ; les conquérans seront, dit-il, ou absous ou condamnés par leur conduite future, et la validité de leur traité dépend du jugement de saint Pierre; mais Innocent leur prescrit, comme leur devoir le plus sacré, d'établir une juste subordination d'obéissance et de tribut, des Grecs aux Latins, des magistrats au clergé et du clergé au pape.

<small>Partage de l'empire grec.</small>

Dans le partage des provinces de l'empire (1), la part des Vénitiens se trouvait plus considérable que celle de l'empereur latin. Il n'en possédait qu'un quart ; Venise se réserva la bonne moitié du reste, et l'autre moitié fut distribuée entre les aventuriers de France et de Lombardie. Le vénérable Dandolo fut proclamé despote de la Romanie, et, selon l'usage des Grecs, chaussé des brodequins de pourpre. Il termina sa longue et glorieuse carrière à Constantinople; et si sa prérogative ne passa point à ses successeurs, ils en conservèrent du moins le titre jusqu'au milieu du quatorzième siècle, en y joignant

---

collection en deux volumes *in-folio*) sont insérées dans ses *Gesta*, dans Muratori ; *Script. rerum italic.*, t. III, part. 1, c. 94-105.

(1) Dans le traité de partage les copistes ont défiguré presque tous les noms. On pourrait les rectifier, et une bonne carte adaptée au dernier siècle de l'empire de Byzance serait d'un grand secours à la géographie ; mais malheureusement d'Anville n'existe plus.

le titre réel, mais singulier, de seigneurs d'un quart et demi de l'empire romain (1). Le doge, esclave de l'État, avait rarement la permission de s'éloigner du timon de la république; mais il se faisait représenter en Grèce par un bailli ou régent revêtu d'une juridiction en dernier ressort sur la colonie des Vénitiens. Ceux-ci possédaient trois des huit quartiers de Constantinople; et leur tribunal indépendant était composé de six juges, quatre conseillers, deux chambellans, deux avocats fiscaux et un connétable. Une longue expérience du commerce d'Orient les avait mis à portée de choisir leur part avec discernement; ils firent cependant une imprudence en acceptant le gouvernement et la défense d'Andrinople; mais leur sage politique s'occupa de former une chaîne de villes, d'îles et de factoreries, le long de la côte maritime, qui s'étend depuis les environs de Raguse jusqu'à l'Hellespont et au Bosphore. Les travaux dispendieux de ces conquêtes épuisaient leur trésor; ils renoncèrent aux anciennes maximes de leur gouvernement, adoptèrent un système féodal, et se contentèrent de l'hommage des nobles (2) pour

---

(1) Leur style était *dominus quartæ partis et dimidiæ imperii Romani;* et ils le conservèrent jusqu'à l'année 1356, où Giovanni Dolfino fut nommé doge (Sanut, pag. 430-641). Pour le gouvernement de Constantinople, *voyez* Ducange, *Hist. C. P.,* 1, 37.

(2) Ducange (*Hist. C. P.,* II, 6) a rapporté la conquête que firent la république ou les nobles Vénitiens, des îles

les possessions que ceux-ci entreprenaient de conquérir et de défendre. Ce fut ainsi que la famille de Sanut acquit le duché de Naxos, qui comprenait la plus grande partie de l'Archipel. La république acheta du marquis de Montferrat, pour la somme de dix mille marcs, l'île fertile de Crète ou Candie, et les débris de cent villes (1). Mais les vues étroites d'une orgueilleuse aristocratie (2) ne permirent pas d'en tirer un grand parti, et les plus sages des sénateurs déclarèrent que ce n'était pas la possession des terres, mais l'empire de la mer, qui formait le trésor de Saint-Marc. Sur la moitié échue aux aventuriers, le marquis de Montferrat était sans contredit celui qui méritait la plus forte récompense. Outre l'île de Crète, on compensa son exclusion du trône par le titre de roi et les provinces au-delà de l'Hellespont; mais il échangea sagement cette conquête

---

de Candie, de Corfou, Céphalonie, Zanthe, Naxos, Paros, Mélos, Andros, Mycone, Scyros, Céos et Lemnos.

(1) Boniface vendit l'île de Candie le 12 du mois d'août de l'année 1204. *Voyez* la transaction dans Sanut, p. 534; mais j'ai peine à concevoir comment cette île était le patrimoine de sa mère, ou comment sa mère pouvait être la fille d'un empereur du nom d'Alexis.

(2) En 1212, le doge Pierre Zani envoya dans l'île de Candie une colonie tirée des différens quartiers de Venise; mais les natifs de cette île, par leurs mœurs sauvages et leurs fréquentes révoltes, pouvaient être comparés aux Corses sous le joug des Génois; et lorsque je rapproche le récit de Belon de celui de Tournefort, je ne vois pas grande différence entre la Candie des Vénitiens et celle des Turcs.

difficile et éloignée, pour le royaume de Thessalonique ou de Macédoine, à douze journées de la capitale, et assez près des États du roi de Hongrie, son beau-frère, pour en recevoir au besoin des secours. Sa marche à travers ces provinces fut accompagnée des acclamations sincères ou simulées des Grecs; et l'ancienne et véritable Grèce reçut encore un conquérant latin (1), qui foula cette terre classique d'un pied indifférent. Les beautés de la vallée de Tempé attirèrent à peine ses regards; il traversa avec précaution le passage étroit des Thermopyles, occupa Thèbes, Athènes et Argos, villes inconnues pour lui, et prit d'assaut Corinthe et Napoli (2), qui avaient essayé de lui résister. Les lots des pélerins latins furent réglés par le sort, ou le choix, et des échanges successifs. Dans la joie de leur triomphe,

---

(1) Villehardouin (n°ˢ 159, 160, 173-177) et Nicétas (p. 387-394) racontent l'expédition du marquis Boniface dans la Grèce. Le citoyen de Chones a pu tenir ces détails de son frère Michel, archevêque d'Athènes, qu'il représente comme un orateur éloquent, un homme d'État habile, et par-dessus tout comme un saint. On aurait pu tirer des manuscrits de Nicétas qui se trouvent à la Bibliothèque Bodléienne, son éloge d'Athènes et sa description de Tempé (Fabricius, *Bibl. græc.*, t. VI, p. 405), et elles auraient mérité d'occuper les recherches de M. Harris.

(2) Napoli de Romanie ou Nauplia, l'ancien port de mer d'Argos, est encore une place fort considérable; elle est assise sur une péninsule environnée de rochers, et a un bon port. *Voyez les Voyages de Chandler dans la Grèce,* p. 227.

ils abusèrent sans modération de leur pouvoir sur la vie et la fortune d'un grand nombre d'hommes. Après un examen exact des provinces, ils pesèrent dans la balance de l'avarice le revenu de chaque district, la situation plus ou moins avantageuse, et les ressources plus ou moins abondantes pour la subsistance des hommes et des chevaux. Leurs prétentions s'étendirent jusque sur les anciens démembremens de l'empire romain ; le Nil et l'Euphrate se trouvaient compris dans leurs partages imaginaires, et heureux était le guerrier qui se trouvait avoir dans son lot le palais du sultan d'Iconium (1). Je n'entreprendrai point de donner ici leur généalogie ni le détail de leurs possessions ; il me suffit de dire que les comtes de Blois et de Saint-Pol obtinrent le duché de Nicée et la seigneurie de Demotica (2) ; les principaux fiefs furent tenus à la charge du service de connétable, de chambellan, d'échanson, de sommelier et de maître-d'hôtel. Notre historien, Geoffroi de Villehardouin, acquit un riche établissement sur les bords de l'Hèbre, et

---

(1) J'ai adouci l'expression de Nicétas, qui s'efforce de faire ressortir la présomption des Francs. Voyez *de Rebus post C. P. expugnatam*, p. 375-384.

(2) Cette ville, environnée par la rivière de l'Hèbre, à six lieues d'Andrinople, reçut des Grecs, à raison de son double mur, le nom de Didymoteichos, qui fut insensiblement changé en celui de Demotica ou Dimot. J'ai préféré le nom moderne de Demotica. Ce fut le dernier lieu qu'habita Charles XII durant son séjour en Turquie.

réunit les offices de maréchal de Champagne et de Romanie. Chaque baron partit à la tête de ses chevaliers et de ses archers, pour s'emparer de son lot, et la plupart éprouvèrent d'abord peu de résistance; mais il résulta de cette dispersion une faiblesse générale, et l'on sent combien de querelles devaient s'élever dans un état de choses et parmi des hommes dont la force était l'unique loi. Trois mois après la conquête de Constantinople, l'empereur et le roi de Thessalonique marchèrent l'un contre l'autre : l'autorité du doge, les conseils du maréchal et la courageuse fermeté des pairs, parvinrent à les réconcilier (1).

Deux fugitifs qui avaient occupé le trône de Constantinople prenaient encore le titre d'empereurs, et les sujets de ces princes détrônés pouvaient céder à un mouvement de compassion pour l'ancien Alexis ou être excités à la vengeance par l'ambitieux Mourzoufle. Une alliance de famille, un intérêt commun, les mêmes crimes et le mérite d'avoir ôté la vie aux ennemis de son rival, engagèrent le second usurpateur à se réunir avec le premier. Mourzoufle se rendit dans le camp d'Alexis ; il y fut reçu avec des

Révolte des Grecs. A. D. 1204, etc.

---

(1) Villehardouin rend compte de leur querelle (n°ˢ 146-158) avec le ton de la franchise et de la liberté. L'historien grec (p. 387) rend hommage au mérite et à la réputation du maréchal, μεγα παρα τοις Λατινων δυναμενου στρατευμασι : il ne ressemble point à certains héros modernes, dont les exploits ne sont connus que par leurs mémoires.

caresses et des honneurs ; mais les scélérats sont incapables d'amitié, et doivent se méfier de ceux qui leur ressemblent. On le saisit dans le bain, et après l'avoir privé de la vue, Alexis s'assura de ses troupes, s'empara de ses trésors, et le fit chasser du camp, loin duquel Mourzoufle fut réduit à errer, objet de mépris et d'horreur pour ceux qui avaient, plus qu'Alexis, le droit de haïr et de punir l'assassin de l'empereur Isaac et de son fils. Poursuivi par la crainte et le remords, il cherchait à passer en Asie, lorsque les Latins de Constantinople le surprirent, et, par un jugement public, le condamnèrent à une mort ignominieuse. Après avoir balancé pour son supplice entre la hache, la roue et le pal, les juges firent placer (1) Mourzoufle sur le sommet d'un pilier de marbre blanc élevé de cent quarante-sept pieds, que l'on nommait la colonne de Théodose (2). Du haut de cette colonne, il fut précipité en bas la

---

(1) *Voyez* la mort de Mourzoufle dans Nicétas (p. 393), Villehardouin (nos 141, 145, 163) et Gunther (c. 20, 21). Ni le maréchal ni le moine n'annoncent le moindre mouvement de pitié pour un usurpateur ou un rebelle, dont le supplice était cependant d'un genre plus nouveau que ses crimes.

(2) La colonne d'Arcadius, dont les bas-reliefs représentent ses victoires ou celles de son père Théodose, existe encore à Constantinople ; on en trouve la description et la mesure dans les ouvrages de Gyllius (*Topograph.*, IV, 7), Banduri (*ad. l. i., Antiquit. C. P.*, p. 507, etc.) et Tournefort (*Voyage du Levant*, t. II, lett. 12, p. 231).

tête la première, et se brisa sur le pavé, en présence d'une multitude de spectateurs rassemblés dans le Forum de Taurus, et qui voyaient avec étonnement, dans ce singulier spectacle, l'explication et l'accomplissement d'une ancienne prédiction (1). Le sort d'Alexis est moins tragique : le marquis en fit présent au roi des Romains, et le lui envoya en Italie. Condamné à une prison perpétuelle, l'usurpateur fut transféré d'une forteresse des Alpes dans un monastère de l'Asie, et ne gagna pas beaucoup au change. Mais avant la révolution, Alexis avait donné sa fille en mariage à un jeune héros qui rétablit et occupa le trône des princes grecs (2). Théodore Lascaris avait signalé sa valeur dans les deux siéges de Constantinople. Après la fuite de Mourzoufle, les Latins étant déjà dans la ville, il s'offrit au peuple et aux soldats pour leur empereur; cette offre pouvait être un acte de vertu et était bien certainement une preuve de courage. S'il eût pu donner

Théodore Lascaris, empereur de Nicée. 1204-1222.

---

(1) Le conte ridicule de Gunther relativement à cette *columna fatidica* ne mérite aucune attention ; mais il est assez extraordinaire que cinquante ans avant la conquête des Latins, le poète Tzetzès (*Chiliad.*, IX, 277) ait raconté le songe d'une matrone qui avait vu une armée dans le Forum, et un homme assis sur la colonne, frappant ses mains l'une contre l'autre, et jetant un grand cri.

(2) Ducange (*Fam. byzant.*) a examiné soigneusement et représenté avec clarté les dynasties de Nicée, de Trébisonde et d'Épire, dont Nicétas vit les commencemens sans en concevoir de grandes espérances.

une âme à cette multitude, elle aurait écrasé sous ses pieds les étrangers qui la menaçaient ; mais le lâche désespoir des Grecs refusa son secours, et Théodore se retira dans l'Anatolie, pour y respirer l'air de la liberté, hors de la vue et de l'atteinte des conquérans. Sous le titre de despote et ensuite d'empereur, il attira sous ses drapeaux le petit nombre d'hommes courageux que le mépris de la vie soutenait contre l'esclavage ; et, regardant comme légitime tout ce qui pouvait contribuer au salut public, il implora sans scrupule l'alliance du sultan des Turcs. Nicée, où Théodore fixa sa résidence, Pruse, Philadelphie, Smyrne et Éphèse, ouvrirent leurs portes à leur libérateur. Ses victoires et même ses défaites augmentèrent ses forces et sa réputation, et le successeur de Constantin conserva cette portion de l'empire qui s'étendait depuis les bords du Méandre jusqu'aux faubourgs de Nicomédie, et dans la suite, jusqu'à ceux de Constantinople. L'héritier légitime des Comnènes, fils du vertueux Manuel et petit-fils du féroce Andronic, en possédait aussi une faible portion dans une province éloignée : on le nommait Alexis, et le surnom de Grand s'appliquait probablement plus à sa taille qu'à ses exploits. Les l'Ange, sans craindre son origine, l'avaient nommé gouverneur ou duc de Trébisonde (1) ; sa naissance lui

---

(1) Si l'on excepte quelques faits contenus dans Pachymère et Nicéphore Grégoras, et que nous citerons dans la suite, les historiens de Byzance ne daignent point parler

donnait de l'ambition, et la révolution lui valut l'indépendance. Sans changer de titre, il régna paisiblement sur la côte de la mer Noire, depuis Sinope jusqu'au Phase. Le fils qui lui succéda, et dont on ignore le nom, n'est connu que comme le vassal du sultan, qu'il suivait à la guerre avec deux cents lances. Ce prince Comnène n'était que duc de Trébisonde; ce fut le petit-fils d'Alexis qui, déterminé par l'orgueil et la jalousie, prit le titre d'empereur. Dans la partie occidentale de l'empire, Michel, bâtard de la maison des l'Ange, et connu avant la révolution comme ôtage, soldat et rebelle, sauva un troisième fragment du naufrage. Après s'être évadé du camp de Boniface, il obtint, par son mariage avec la fille du gouverneur de Durazzo, la possession de cette ville importante; il prit le titre de despote, et fonda une principauté puissante dans l'Épire, l'Étolie et la Thessalie, qui ont toujours été peuplées d'une race belliqueuse. Ceux des Grecs qui avaient offert leurs services aux Latins, leurs nouveaux souverains, furent refusés par ces souverains orgueilleux, et exclus (1) de tous les honneurs civils

de l'empire de Trébisonde ou de la principauté des Lazi. Les Latins n'en font guère mention que dans les romans des quatorzième et quinzième siècles. Cependant l'infatigable Ducange a découvert (*Fam. byzant.*, p. 192) deux passages authentiques dans Vincent de Beauvais (l. XXXI, c. 144) et le protonotaire Ogier (*ap.* Wadding, A. D. 1279, n° 4).

(1) Nicétas fait un portrait des Français-Latins, où l'on

et militaires, comme des hommes nés pour obéir et tremhler. Leur ressentiment les excita à prouver, en devenant des ennemis dangereux, qu'on aurait pu trouver en eux des amis utiles. L'adversité avait endurci leur courage, et tous les citoyens distingués par leur savoir ou leur vertu, leur valeur ou leur naissance, abandonnèrent Constantinople, et se retirèrent sous les gouvernemens indépendans de Trébisonde, d'Épire ou de Nicée. On ne cite qu'un seul patricien qui ait mérité le douteux éloge d'attachement et de fidélité aux Francs. Le peuple des villes et des campagnes se serait soumis sans peine à une servitude régulière et modérée; quelques années de paix et d'industrie auraient bientôt fait oublier la guerre et ses désordres passagers; mais la tyrannie du système féodal éloignait les douceurs de la paix et anéantissait les fruits de l'industrie. Une administration simple et des lois sages donnaient aux empereurs *romains* de Constantinople, s'ils avaient eu les talens nécessaires pour en faire usage, les moyens de protéger leurs sujets. Mais le trône des Latins était occupé par un prince titulaire, chef et souvent esclave de ses indociles confédérés. L'épée des barons disposait de tous les fiefs de l'empire, depuis

---

reconnaît partout la touche du ressentiment et des préjugés : Ουδεν των αλλων εθνων εις Αρεος εργα παρασυμβεβλησθαι ηνειχοντο, αλλ' ουδε τις των χαριτων η των μουσων παρα τοις βαρβαροις, τουτοις επεξενιζετο, και παρα τουτο οιμαι την φυσιν ησαν ανημεροι, και τον χολον ειχον του λογου προτρεχοντα.

le royaume jusqu'au plus mince château. Leur ignorance, leurs discordes et leur pauvreté, étendaient la tyrannie jusque dans les villages les plus éloignés. Les Grecs, également opprimés par le pouvoir temporel des prêtres et par la haine fanatique des soldats, se trouvaient séparés pour toujours de leurs conquérans par la barrière insurmontable du langage et de la religion. Tant que les croisés restèrent réunis dans la capitale, le souvenir de leur victoire et la terreur de leurs armes imposèrent silence à un pays subjugué. Leur séparation découvrit la faiblesse de leur nombre et les défauts de leur discipline ; quelques échecs causés par leur imprudence apprirent qu'ils n'étaient pas invincibles. La crainte des Grecs diminuait, et leur haine augmentait en proportion. Ils passèrent bientôt des murmures aux conspirations ; et avant la fin d'une année d'esclavage, le peuple vaincu implora ou accepta avec confiance le secours d'un Barbare dont il avait éprouvé la puissance, et à la reconnaissance duquel il se fiait (1).

Calo-Jean ou Joannice, chef révolté des Valaques et des Bulgares, s'était empressé de complimenter les Latins par une ambassade. Le titre de roi, et la

Guerre des Bulgares.
A. D. 1205.

---

(1) Je commence à me servir ici avec confiance et liberté des huit livres de l'*Hist. C. P. sous l'empire des Français*, que Ducange a donnés pour supplément à l'histoire de Villehardouin, et qui, bien qu'écrite d'un style barbare, a cependant le mérite d'être un ouvrage classique et original.

sainte bannière qu'il avait reçue du pontife romain, semblaient l'autoriser à se regarder comme leur frère, et en qualité de leur complice dans le renversement de l'empire grec, il croyait pouvoir aspirer au titre de leur ami. Joannice apprit avec étonnement que le comte de Flandre, imitant l'orgueil fastueux des successeurs de Constantin, avait renvoyé ses ambassadeurs en déclarant avec hauteur qu'il fallait que le rebelle vînt mériter son pardon en touchant de son front le marche pied du trône. S'il eût écouté son ressentiment, cet outrage aurait été lavé dans le sang ; mais, par une politique plus prudente (1), le roi des Bulgares, épiant avec soin les progrès du mécontentement des Grecs, se montra sensible à leurs malheurs, et promit de soutenir de sa personne et de toutes les forces de son royaume, les premiers efforts qu'ils tenteraient pour recouvrer leur liberté. La haine nationale étendit la conjuration et assura en même temps le secret et la fidélité. Les Grecs désiraient avec impatience le moment de plonger un poignard dans le sein de leurs ennemis victorieux ; mais ils attendirent prudemment que Henri, frère de l'empereur, eût emmené la fleur des troupes au-delà de l'Hellespont. La plupart des villes et des villages de la Thrace se montrèrent exacts au moment et au si-

---

(1) On peut voir dans la réponse de Joannice au pape, ses réclamations et ses plaintes (*Gesta Innocent. III*, chap. 108, 109) ; on le chérissait à Rome comme l'enfant prodigue.

gnal convenus; et les Latins, sans armes et sans soupçons, se trouvèrent en proie à l'impitoyable et lâche vengeance de leurs esclaves. De Demotica, où commença cette scène de massacres, quelques vassaux du comté de Saint-Pôl cherchèrent un asile à Andrinople; mais la populace furieuse avait ou chassé ou immolé les Français et les Vénitiens. Celles des garnisons qui parvinrent à faire leur retraite, se rencontrèrent sur la route de la capitale; et les forteresses isolées, qui résistaient aux rebelles, ignoraient mutuellement leur sort et celui de leur souverain. La renommée et la terreur annoncèrent au loin la révolte des Grecs et l'approche rapide du roi des Bulgares; Joannice avait ajouté à ses troupes nationales un corps de quatorze mille Comans, tirés des déserts de la Scythie, qui buvaient, dit-on, le sang de leurs captifs, et sacrifiaient les chrétiens sur les autels de leurs divinités (1).

Alarmé de cette révolte, l'empereur dépêcha un courrier pour rappeler son frère Henri; et si Baudouin eût attendu le retour de ce valeureux prince, qui devait lui ramener un secours de vingt mille Arméniens, il aurait pu attaquer le roi des Bulgares avec l'égalité du nombre et la supériorité décisive

---

(1) Les Comans étaient une horde de Tartares ou de Turcomans, qui campaient, dans les douzième et treizième siècles, sur les frontières de la Moldavie. Il y avait parmi eux un grand nombre de païens et quelques mahométans. Toute la horde fut convertie au christianisme (A. D. 1370) par Louis, roi de Hongrie.

des armes et de la discipline. Mais l'esprit de la chevalerie ne savait point distinguer la prudence de la lâcheté. L'empereur parut dans la plaine avec cent quarante chevaliers et leur suite ordinaire de sergens et d'archers. Après d'inutiles représentations, le maréchal obéit et conduisit l'avant-garde sur la route d'Andrinople ; le comte de Blois commandait le corps de bataille, le vieux doge suivait à l'arrière-garde. Les Latins fugitifs accoururent de toutes parts sous les drapeaux de cette petite armée : ils entreprirent le siége d'Andrinople ; et telles étaient les pieuses dispositions des croisés, qu'ils s'occupèrent, durant la semaine sainte, à piller la campagne pour leur subsistance, et à construire des machines destinées à la destruction d'un peuple chrétien. Mais ils furent bientôt troublés dans cette occupation par la cavalerie légère des Comans, qui vint audacieusement escarmoucher presque sur le bord de leurs lignes en désordre. Le maréchal fit publier une proclamation qui avertissait la cavalerie de se trouver prête, au premier son de la trompette, à monter à cheval et à se former en bataille, et défendait, sous peine de mort, qu'aucun se détachât à la poursuite de l'ennemi. Le comte de Blois désobéit le premier à cette sage proclamation, et son imprudence entraîna la perte de l'empereur. Les Comans, à la manière des Parthes ou des Tartares, prirent la fuite dès la première charge ; mais, après une course de deux lieues, ils firent volte-face, se rallièrent et enveloppèrent les pesans escadrons français au moment où les chevaliers et leurs chevaux, également essoufflés, étaient presque hors d'état de se défendre. Le comte fut tué sur le champ de bataille, l'empereur fut fait prisonnier; et si ce fut pour avoir, l'un dédaigné de fuir, l'autre refusé de céder, leur valeur personnelle compensa faiblement l'ignorance ou la négligence qu'ils montrèrent des devoirs imposés à un général (1).

Fier de la victoire et de son illustre captif, le Bulgare s'avança pour secourir Andrinople et achever la défaite des Latins; leur destruction eût été inévitable, si le maréchal de Romanie n'avait déployé ce courage calme et ces talens militaires rares dans tous les siècles, mais plus extraordinaires encore dans un temps où la guerre était moins une science qu'une passion. Villehardouin versa ses craintes et sa douleur dans le sein de son courageux et fidèle ami le doge; mais il répandit dans le camp une confiance qui était l'unique moyen de salut. Après avoir conservé durant tout un jour son poste dangereux entre la ville et l'armée ennemie, le maréchal décampa sans bruit dans la nuit, et sa savante retraite de trois jours consécutifs aurait été admirée de Xénophon et des dix mille : courant sans cesse de l'arrière à l'avant-garde, là il soutenait le poids de la poursuite des

Défaite et captivité de Baudouin.
A. D. 1205,
15 avril.

(1) Nicétas, par haine ou par ignorance, impute la défaite à la lâcheté de Dandolo (p. 383); mais Villehardouin partage sa propre gloire avec son vénérable ami, *qui viels home ere et gote ne veoit, mais mult ere sages et preus et vigueros* (n° 193).

uns, ici il retenait la précipitation des fugitifs. Partout où les Comans se présentaient, ils trouvaient une ligne de lances inébranlables. Le troisième jour, les troupes harassées aperçurent la mer, la ville solitaire de Rhodosto (1); et leurs compagnons arrivant des côtes de l'Asie; ils s'embrassèrent, versèrent des larmes, et réunirent leurs armes et leurs conseils. Le comte Henri prit, au nom de son frère, le gouvernement d'un empire encore dans l'enfance et déjà dans la caducité (2). Les Comans se retirèrent durant les chaleurs de l'été; mais au moment du danger, sept mille Latins, infidèles à leur serment et à leurs compatriotes, désertèrent la capitale, et de faibles succès compensèrent mal la perte de cent vingt chevaliers qui périrent dans la plaine de Rusium. Il ne restait plus à l'empereur que Constantinople et deux ou trois forteresses sur les côtes d'Europe et d'Asie. Le roi des Bulgares, irrésistible et inexorable, éluda respectueusement les instances du pape, qui conjurait son nouveau prosélyte de rendre aux La-

---

(1) La géographie exacte et le texte original de Villehardouin (n° 194) placent Rhodosto à trois journées de chemin (*trois jornées*) d'Andrinople; mais Vigenère, dans sa version, a ridiculement substitué trois heures; et cette erreur, que Ducange n'a point corrigée, a fourvoyé plusieurs modernes dont je tairai les noms.

(2) Villehardouin et Nicétas (p. 386-416) racontent le règne et la mort de Baudouin; et Ducange supplée à leurs omissions dans ses *Observations* et à la fin de son premier livre.

tins affligés la paix et leur empereur. « La délivrance de Baudouin, répondit Joannice, n'est plus au pouvoir des mortels. » Ce prince était mort en prison; l'ignorance et la crédulité ont produit sur le genre de sa mort plusieurs versions différentes. Ceux qui aiment les histoires tragiques, croiront volontiers que le chaste captif résista aux désirs amoureux de la reine des Bulgares, que son refus l'exposa aux calomnies d'une femme et à la jalousie d'un sauvage; qu'on lui coupa les pieds et les mains, que le reste du corps fut jeté tout sanglant parmi les carcasses des chiens et des chevaux, et qu'il respirait encore au bout de trois jours, lorsque les oiseaux de proie vinrent le dévorer (1). Vingt ans après, dans une forêt des Pays-Bas, un ermite s'annonça comme le comte Baudouin, empereur de Constantinople et légitime souverain de la Flandre ; il raconta les circonstances extraordinaires de sa fuite, ses aventures et sa pénitence, chez un peuple également disposé à la révolte et à la crédulité. Dans un premier transport, la Flandre reconnut le souverain qu'elle avait si long-temps pleuré. Mais la cour de France, après un court examen, démasqua l'imposteur, et il subit une mort

---

(1). Après avoir écarté toutes les circonstances suspectes et improbables, nous pouvons prouver la mort de Baudouin, 1° par l'opinion des barons qui n'en doutaient pas (Villehardouin, n° 230); 2° par la déclaration de Joannice ou Calo-Jean, qui s'excuse de n'avoir pas donné la liberté à l'empereur, *quià debitum carnis exsolverat cùm carcere teneretur* (*Gesta Innocent. III*, c. 109).

ignominieuse. Les Flamands n'abandonnèrent pas cependant une illusion qu'ils chérissaient, et les plus graves historiens accusent la comtesse Jeanne d'avoir sacrifié à l'ambition la vie de son malheureux père (1).

<small>Règne et caractère de Henri.
A. D. 1206, août 20.
A. D. 1216, juin 11.</small>

Toutes les nations civilisées établissent durant la guerre un cartel pour l'échange ou la rançon des prisonniers. Si leur captivité est prolongée, leur sort n'est point un mystère, et ils sont traités, selon leur rang, avec honneur ou avec humanité; mais les lois de la guerre étaient inconnues au sauvage prince des Bulgares; il était difficile d'éclairer la silencieuse obscurité de ses prisons, et une année entière s'écoula avant que les Latins acquissent la certitude de la mort de Baudouin, et que son frère Henri consentît à prendre le titre d'empereur. Les Grecs applaudirent à sa modération comme à l'exemple d'une rare et inimitable vertu; ambitieux, inconstans et perfides, ils étaient toujours prêts à saisir ou à anticiper l'occasion d'une vacance, dans le temps où presque toutes les monarchies de l'Europe avaient peu à peu reconnu et confirmé les lois de succession, qui font également la sûreté des peuples et des souverains. Les héros de la croisade moururent ou se retirèrent successivement, et Henri se trouva presque seul chargé de la guerre

---

(1) *Voyez* l'histoire de cet imposteur, d'après les écrivains français et flamands, dans Ducange (*Hist. de C. P.*, III, 9) et les fables ridicules adoptées par les moines de Saint-Alban, dans Matthieu Paris (*Hist. maj.*, p. 271, 272).

et de la défense de l'empire. Le vénérable Dandolo, chargé d'ans et de gloire, était descendu dans la tombe; le marquis de Montferrat revint lentement de la guerre qu'il faisait dans le Péloponèse, pour venger Baudouin et défendre Thessalonique. Dans son entrevue avec l'empereur, ils réglèrent quelques vaines contestations sur l'hommage et le service féodaux; une estime mutuelle et le danger commun les réunirent solidement, et ces deux princes scellèrent leur alliance par le mariage de Henri avec la fille de Boniface; mais Henri eut bientôt à pleurer la mort de son beau-père et de son ami. Par le conseil de quelques Grecs restés fidèles, le marquis de Montferrat fit avec succès une irruption hardie dans les montagnes de Rhodope. Les Bulgares prirent la fuite à son approche; mais ils se rallièrent pour harceler sa retraite. L'intrépide chevalier, ayant appris qu'ils attaquaient son arrière-garde, sauta sur son cheval, baissa sa lance et courut aux ennemis sans daigner se couvrir de son armure; mais, dans sa poursuite imprudente, il fut percé d'un trait mortel, et les Barbares fugitifs présentèrent sa tête à Calo-Jean, comme un trophée d'une victoire dont il n'avait point eu le mérite. C'est alors, c'est à cet accident funeste que tombe la plume de Villehardouin et que sa voix expire (1); et s'il

---

(1) Villehardouin., n° 257. Je cite avec regret cette triste conclusion. Nous perdons à la fois l'original de l'histoire et les *Commentaires* précieux de Ducange. Les deux lettres de

continua d'exercer l'office de maréchal de la Romanie, la suite de ses exploits n'est point connue de la postérité (1). Henri n'était point au-dessous de la situation difficile où il se trouvait alors. Au siége de Constantinople, et au-delà de l'Hellespont, il avait acquis la réputation d'un vaillant chevalier et d'un habile général. À l'intrépidité de son frère, Henri joignait la prudence et la douceur, vertus peu connues de l'impétueux Baudouin. Dans la double guerre contre les Grecs de l'Asie et les Bulgares de l'Europe, il fut toujours le premier à cheval ou sur les vaisseaux, et sans jamais négliger les précautions qui pouvaient assurer la victoire, il excita souvent, par son exemple, les Latins découragés à sauver et à seconder leur intrépide empereur; mais ses efforts et quelques secours d'hommes et d'argent de France contribuèrent moins à leurs succès que les fautes, la cruauté et la mort du plus formidable de leurs adversaires. En invitant Calo-Jean à les tirer d'esclavage, les Grecs avaient espéré qu'il protégerait leurs lois et leur liberté; mais ils eurent bientôt la triste occasion de

---

Henri au pape Innocent III jettent quelque clarté sur les dernières pages de notre auteur (*Gesta*, c. 106, 107).

(1) Le maréchal vivait encore en 1212; mais il est probable qu'il mourut peu de temps après cette époque, et qu'il ne retourna point en France (Ducange, *Observations sur Villehardouin*, p. 238). Son fief de Messinople, qu'il tenait de Boniface, était l'ancienne Maximianopolis, qui florissait du temps d'Ammien-Marcellin parmi les villes de la Thrace (n° 141).

comparer les degrés de férocité nationale et d'abhorrer le conquérant sauvage qui ne dissimulait plus l'intention de dépeupler la Thrace, de démolir les villes et de transplanter les habitans au-delà du Danube. Plusieurs villes et villages de la Thrace étaient déjà évacués; on ne voyait plus à la place de Philippopolis qu'un monceau de ruines, et les habitans d'Andrinople et de Demotica, premiers auteurs de la révolte, redoutaient le même sort. Un cri de douleur et de repentir s'éleva jusqu'au trône de Henri, et l'empereur eut la grandeur d'âme d'ajouter la confiance au pardon. Il ne put rassembler sous ses drapeaux que quatre cents chevaliers avec leur suite d'archers et de sergens; à la tête de ce petit corps d'armée, il chercha et repoussa le Bulgare, qui, outre son infanterie, commandait quarante mille hommes de cavalerie. Dans cette expédition, Henri eut occasion de sentir la différence d'avoir ou pour ou contre soi le vœu des habitans. Il sauva les villes qui subsistaient encore; le sauvage Joannice, battu et couvert de honte, fut forcé d'abandonner sa proie, et le siège de Thessalonique fut la dernière des calamités qu'il causa ou éprouva. Durant l'obscurité de la nuit, il fut assassiné dans sa tente, et le général, ou peut-être le meurtrier qui le trouva baigné dans son sang, attribua ce coup à la lance de saint Démétrius et fut généralement cru (1).

---

(1) L'église de ce patron de Thessalonique était desservie par les chanoines du saint-sépulcre; elle contenait une huile sainte qui distillait continuellement, et il s'y faisait

Après avoir remporté plusieurs victoires, Henri conclut sagement un traité de paix honorable avec le successeur de Joannice et les princes d'Épire et de Nicée. L'abandon de quelques limites incertaines valut à l'empereur et à ses feudataires la possession tranquille d'un vaste royaume; et son règne, qui ne dura que dix ans, procura à l'empire un court intervalle de paix et de prospérité. Supérieur à la politique étroite de Baudouin et de Boniface, il confiait sans crainte aux Grecs les emplois civils et militaires, et cette conduite généreuse devenait d'autant plus nécessaire, que les princes d'Épire et de Nicée avaient appris à séduire et à employer la valeur mercenaire des Latins. Henri s'attachait à unir tous ses sujets et à récompenser leur mérite, quels que fussent leur pays et leur langage; mais il parut moins empressé de travailler à l'impraticable réunion des deux Églises. Pélage, légat du pape, qui affectait à Constantinople l'autorité d'un souverain, avait interdit le culte grec, et exigeait à la rigueur le paiement des dîmes, la profession de foi relative à la procession du Saint-Esprit, et l'obéissance aveugle au pontife romain. Dans tous les temps, le parti le plus faible a réclamé les devoirs de la conscience et les droits de la tolérance. « Nos corps, disaient les Grecs, sont à César, mais nos âmes sont à Dieu. » La fermeté de l'empe-

---

d'étonnans miracles. Ducange, *Hist. de Constantinople*, II, 4.

reur arrêta la persécution (1); et s'il est vrai qu'il mourut empoisonné par les Grecs, cette preuve de folie et d'ingratitude doit nous donner une triste opinion du genre humain. Sa valeur n'était qu'une vertu commune qu'il partageait avec dix mille chevaliers; mais, dans un siècle de superstition, Henri eut le courage bien plus extraordinaire de s'opposer à l'orgueil et à l'avarice du clergé. Il osa placer, dans la cathédrale de Sainte-Sophie, son trône à la droite du patriarche, et cette présomption lui attira les plus aigres censures de la part du pape Innocent III. Par un édit salutaire, un des premiers exemples des lois de mainmorte, l'empereur défendit l'aliénation des fiefs. Un grand nombre de Latins, empressés de retourner en Europe, abandonnaient leurs terres à l'Église, qui les payait en argent comptant ou avec des indulgences. Ces terres sacrées étaient immédiatement déchargées du service militaire, et une colonie de soldats aurait été bientôt convertie en une communauté de prêtres (2).

Pierre de Courtenai, empereur d'Orient. A. D. 1217 9 avril.

Le vertueux Henri mourut à Thessalonique, où il

---

(1) Acropolita (c. 17) rapporte la persécution du légat et la tolérance de Henri (Ερη comme il l'appelle), κλυδωνα κατεστορεσε.

(2) *Voyez* le règne de Henri dans Ducange (*Hist. de C. P.*, l. I, c. 35-41; l. II, c. 1-12), à qui les lettres des papes ont été d'une grande ressource. Le Beau (*Hist. du Bas-Empire*, t. XXI, p. 120-122) a trouvé, peut-être dans Doutremens, quelques lois de Henri qui établissent le service des fiefs et les prérogatives de l'empereur.

était allé défendre le royaume et le fils, encore enfant, de son ami Boniface. La mort des deux premiers empereurs de Constantinople avait éteint la ligne mâle des comtes de Flandre; mais leur sœur Yolande était l'épouse d'un prince français, et la mère d'une nombreuse postérité. Une de ses filles avait épousé André, roi de Hongrie, brave et pieux champion de la croix. En le plaçant sur le trône, les barons de la Romanie se seraient assuré le secours d'un royaume puissant et voisin; mais le sage André respectait les lois de la succession, et les Latins invitèrent la princesse Yolande et son mari, Pierre de Courtenai, comte d'Auxerre, à venir ceindre le diadême de l'empire d'Orient. L'origine illustre de son père, la maison royale de sa mère, le faisaient respecter des barons français comme le plus proche parent de leur roi. Il jouissait d'une réputation brillante et dominait sur de vastes possessions; dans la sanglante croisade contre les Albigeois, les prêtres et les soldats avaient été pleinement satisfaits de son zèle et de sa valeur. La vanité pouvait s'applaudir de voir un Français sur le trône de Constantinople, mais la prudence devait inspirer moins d'envie que de compassion pour cette grandeur dangereuse et illusoire. Pour soutenir dignement ce titre, Courtenai fut contraint de vendre ou d'engager la plus riche partie de son patrimoine. A l'aide de ces expédiens, de la libéralité de son parent Philippe-Auguste, et de l'esprit de chevalerie qui régnait dans toute la nation, il fut en état de passer les Alpes à la tête de cent quarante chevaliers et de cinq mille cinq cents sergens ou archers. Après avoir hésité, le pape Honorius III consentit à couronner le successeur de Constantin; mais il fit cette cérémonie dans une église hors de l'enceinte de la ville, de peur qu'elle ne semblât supposer conférer quelque droit de souveraineté sur l'ancienne capitale. Les Vénitiens s'étaient engagés à transporter Pierre avec ses troupes au-delà de la mer Adriatique, et l'impératrice avec ses quatre enfans, dans le palais de Byzance; mais ils exigèrent pour prix de ce service qu'il reprît Durazzo, occupé par le despote de l'Épire. Michel l'Ange ou Comnène, le premier de sa dynastie, avait légué sa puissance et son ambition à son frère Théodore, qui menaçait et attaquait déjà les établissemens des Latins. Après avoir acquitté sa dette par un assaut inutile, l'empereur leva le siége, et continua par terre son dangereux voyage jusqu'à Thessalonique. Il se perdit dans les montagnes de l'Épire; les passages se trouvèrent fortifiés, les provisions manquèrent: on le retarda par de perfides apparences de négociation; Pierre de Courtenai et le légat romain furent arrêtés à l'issue d'un banquet; et les troupes françaises, sans chef et sans ressource, mirent bas les armes, sous la promesse trompeuse d'être nourries et traitées avec humanité. Le Vatican lança ses foudres sur l'impie Théodore, et le menaça de la vengeance de la terre et du ciel. Mais les clameurs du pape n'avaient pour objet que son légat; il oublia l'empereur captif et ses soldats, et pardonna au despote d'Épire ou plutôt le protégea dès qu'il eut délivré le légat, et promis l'o-

Sa captivité et sa mort. A. D. 1217-1219.

béissance spirituelle au pontife romain. Des ordres absolus d'Honorius réprimèrent l'ardeur des Vénitiens et celle du roi de Hongrie ; et une mort (1), soit naturelle, soit violente, termina seule la captivité de l'infortuné Pierre de Courtenai (2).

Robert, empereur de Constantinople.
A. D.
1221-1228.

La longue incertitude de son sort, la présence de la souveraine légitime Yolande, son épouse ou sa veuve, firent différer l'élévation d'un nouvel empereur. Avant de mourir, et au milieu de la douleur, cette princesse mit au monde un fils qui reçut le nom de Baudouin, et fut le dernier et le plus infortuné des princes latins de Constantinople : sa naissance était un titre à l'attachement des barons de la Romanie ; mais son enfance aurait long-temps exposé l'État aux troubles d'une minorité, et les droits de ses frères prévalurent. L'aîné, Philippe de Courtenai, qui, par sa mère, avait hérité de Namur, eut la sagesse de préférer la réalité d'un marquisat à l'ombre d'un empire. A son refus, Robert, le second des fils de Pierre et d'Yolande, fut appelé au trône de Constan-

---

(1) Acropolita (c. 14) affirme que Pierre de Courtenai périt par l'épée (εργον μαχαιρας γενεσθαι); mais ses expressions obscures me font présumer qu'il avait auparavant été en captivité ; ως παντας αρδην δεσμωτας ποιησαι συν πασι σκευεσι. La Chronique d'Auxerre diffère la mort de l'empereur jusqu'en 1219, et Auxerre est dans les environs de Courtenai.

(2) *Voyez* le règne et la mort de Pierre de Courtenai dans Ducange (*Hist. de C. P.*, l. 11, c. 22-28), qui fait de faibles efforts pour excuser Honorius III de son indifférence sur le sort de l'empereur.

tinople. Averti par le malheur de son père, il poursuivit lentement sa route à travers l'Allemagne et le long du Danube. Le mariage de sa sœur avec le roi de Hongrie lui ouvrit un passage, et le patriarche couronna Robert dans la cathédrale de Sainte-Sophie ; mais il n'éprouva, durant tout son règne, qu'humiliations et calamités, et la colonie de la Nouvelle-France, comme on l'appelait alors, céda de tous côtés aux efforts des Grecs de l'Épire et de Nicée. Après une victoire qu'il dut plus à sa perfidie qu'à sa valeur, Théodore l'Ange entra dans le royaume de Thessalonique, expulsa le faible Démétrius, fils du marquis Boniface, planta ses étendards sur les murs d'Andrinople, et ajouta orgueilleusement son nom à la liste des trois ou quatre empereurs rivaux. Jean Vatacès, gendre et successeur de Théodore Lascaris, envahit les restes de la province d'Asie, et déploya, dans un règne de trente-trois ans, toutes les vertus du conquérant et du législateur. Sous sa discipline, la valeur des Français mercenaires devint le plus sûr instrument de ses victoires, et leur désertion du service de leur pays fut en même temps l'annonce et la cause de la supériorité renaissante des Grecs. Vatacès construisit une flotte, fit la loi sur l'Hellespont, réduisit les îles de Lesbos et de Rhodes, attaqua les Vénitiens de Candie, et intercepta les secours lents et faibles qui arrivaient de l'Occident. L'empereur latin fit enfin l'effort d'opposer une armée à Vatacès, et, dans la défaite de cette armée, le reste des chevaliers et des premiers conquérans périt sur le champ de bataille. Mais le pusillanime Robert était moins sensible aux succès de son ennemi qu'à l'insolence de ses sujets latins, qui abusaient également de la faiblesse de l'empereur et de celle de l'empire. Ses malheurs personnels attestent la férocité du siècle et l'anarchie de son gouvernement. Séduit par la beauté d'une fille noble de la province d'Artois, Robert, oubliant ses engagemens avec la fille de Vatacès, introduisit sa maîtresse dans son palais, et la mère de cette jeune fille, éblouie par l'éclat de la pourpre, consentit à la lui donner, quoiqu'elle l'eût promise en mariage à un gentilhomme de Bourgogne. L'amour de celui-ci se convertit en fureur : il assembla ses amis, força les portes du palais, précipita dans l'Océan la mère de sa maîtresse, et coupa inhumainement le nez et les lèvres de la femme ou concubine de l'empereur. Loin de vouloir punir le coupable, les barons applaudirent à une action féroce (1) que Robert, comme prince ou comme homme, ne pouvait pas pardonner. Il s'échappa de sa coupable capitale, et courut implorer la justice ou la compassion des pontifes romains : le pape l'exhorta froidement à retourner dans son royaume ; mais, avant de pouvoir se rendre à ce conseil, il succomba sous le

---

(1) Marin Sanut (*Secreta fidelium crucis*, l. II, part. IV, c. 18, p. 83) est si enchanté de cette scène sanglante, qu'il la transcrit en marge comme *bonum exemplum*. Cependant il reconnaît la demoiselle pour femme légitime de Robert.

poids de la douleur, de la honte et d'un ressentiment impuissant (1).

<small>Baudouin II et Jean de Brienne, empereurs de Constantinople.
A. D.
1228-1237.</small>

Le siècle de la chevalerie est le seul dans lequel la valeur ait pu élever de simples particuliers sur les trônes de Jérusalem et de Constantinople. La souveraineté titulaire de Jérusalem appartenait à Marie, fille d'Isabelle et de Conrad de Montferrat, et petite-fille d'Alméric ou d'Amaury. La voix publique et le jugement de Philippe-Auguste lui avaient donné pour époux Jean de Brienne, d'une famille noble de la Champagne, désigné comme le plus brave défenseur de la Terre-Sainte (2). Dans la cinquième croisade, il conduisit cent mille Latins à la conquête de l'Égypte, et acheva la prise de Damiette : on attribua unanimement le revers dont elle fut suivie à l'avarice et à l'orgueil du légat. Après le mariage de sa fille avec Frédéric II (3), l'ingratitude de l'empereur lui fit accepter le commandement des troupes de l'Église ; quoique âgé et privé de sa couronne, le brave

---

(1) *Voyez* le règne de Robert dans Ducange, *Hist. de C. P.*, l. III, c. 1-12.

(2) *Rex igitur Franciæ, deliberatione habitâ, respondit nuntiis se daturum hominem Syriæ partibus aptum; in armis probum* (preux), *in bellis securum, in agendis providum, Johannem comitem Brennensem.* Sanut, *Secret. fidel.*, l. III, part. XI, c. 4, p. 205; Matthieu Paris, p. 159.

(3) Giannone (*Istoria civile*, t. II, l. XVI, p. 380-385) discute le mariage de Frédéric II avec la fille de Jean de Brienne, et la double union des couronnes de Naples et de Jérusalem.

et généreux Jean de Brienne était toujours prêt à tirer son épée pour le service de la chrétienté. Durant les sept années du règne de son frère, Baudouin de Courtenai n'était point encore sorti de l'enfance, et les barons de la Romanie sentaient la nécessité de placer le sceptre entre les mains d'un homme et d'un héros. Le vénérable roi de Jérusalem aurait dédaigné le nom et l'office de régent ; ils convinrent de l'investir pour sa vie du titre et des prérogatives d'empereur, sous la seule condition qu'il donnerait à Baudouin sa seconde fille pour épouse, et que, dans la maturité de son âge, ce jeune prince succèderait au trône de Constantinople. Le choix de Jean de Brienne, sa réputation et sa présence, ranimèrent l'espérance des Grecs et des Latins. Ils admirèrent l'air martial, la vigueur (1) d'un vieillard âgé de plus de quatre-vingts ans, et sa taille au-dessus des proportions ordinaires ; mais l'avarice et l'amour du repos avaient, à ce qu'il parut, refroidi en lui l'ardeur des entreprises ; ses troupes se débandèrent, et deux années s'écoulèrent dans une honteuse inaction. Il fut réveillé de cet assoupissement par l'alliance menaçante de Vatacès, empereur de Nicée, et d'Azan, roi des Bulgares. Ils assiégèrent Constantinople avec

---

(1) Acropolita, c. 27. L'historien était alors un enfant, et il fut élevé à Constantinople. En 1223, il avait onze ans, lorsque son père, pour échapper au joug des Latins, abandonna une fortune brillante et s'enfuit à la cour de Nicée, où son fils fut élevé aux premiers honneurs.

une armée de cent mille hommes et une flotte de trois cents vaisseaux de guerre, tandis que les forces de l'empereur latin ne consistaient qu'en cent soixante chevaliers et un petit nombre de sergens et d'archers. J'hésite à raconter qu'au lieu de défendre la ville, le héros fit une sortie à la tête de sa cavalerie, et que de quarante-huit escadrons ennemis, trois seulement échappèrent à son invincible épée. Enflammés par son exemple, l'infanterie et les citoyens s'élancèrent sur les vaisseaux qui étaient à l'ancre au pied des murs, et en amenèrent vingt-cinq en triomphe dans le port de Constantinople. A la voix de l'empereur, les vassaux et les alliés prirent les armes pour sa défense, renversèrent tous les obstacles qui s'opposaient à leur passage, et remportèrent, l'année suivante, une seconde victoire sur les mêmes ennemis. Les poëtes de ce siècle grossier ont comparé Jean de Brienne à Hector, Roland et Judas Machabée (1), mais le silence des Grecs affaiblit un peu la gloire du prince et l'autorité de ses panégyristes. L'empire perdit bientôt son dernier défenseur, et le monarque

---

(1) Philippe Mouskes, évêque de Tournai (A. D. 1274-1282), a composé une espèce de poëme, ou plutôt de chronique en vers, en vieux patois flamand, sur les empereurs de Constantinople; et Ducange l'a publié à la fin de l'histoire de Villehardouin; *voyez* (p. 224) les prouesses de Jean de Brienne.

N'Aie., Ector, Roll' ne Ogiers
Ne Judas Machabeus li fiers
Tant ne fit d'armes en estors

expirant eut l'ambition d'entrer en paradis vêtu de la robe d'un cordelier (1).

{Baudouin II.
A. D. 1237, mars 23.
A. D. 1261, juillet 25.}

Dans la double victoire de Jean de Brienne, je ne trouve point de traces du nom ou des exploits de Baudouin, son pupille, qui avait atteint l'âge du service militaire, et succéda au trône de son père adoptif (2). Ce jeune prince s'occupa de commissions plus convenables à son caractère; on l'envoya visiter les cours de l'Occident, et principalement celles du pape et du roi de France, pour exciter leur compassion par la vue de son innocence et de son malheur, et solliciter des secours d'hommes et d'argent. Il répéta trois fois ces humiliantes tournées, dans lesquelles il semble avoir toujours tâché de prolonger son absence et de différer son retour. Des vingt-cinq années de son règne, le plus grand nombre fut passé hors de son royaume, et il ne se crut jamais moins libre et moins en sûreté que dans sa patrie et dans sa capitale. Sa vanité put, dans quelques occasions, jouir avec complaisance des honneurs de la pourpre et du titre d'Auguste. Au concile général

---

Com fist li rois Jehans cel jors
Et il defors et il dedans
La paru sa force et ses sens
Et li hardiment qu'il avoit.

(1) *Voyez* le règne de Jean de Brienne dans Ducange, *Hist. de C. P.*, l. III, c. 13–26.

(2) *Voyez* le règne de Baudouin II, jusqu'à son expulsion de Constantinople, dans Ducange, *Hist. de C. P.*, l. IV, c. 1–34; la fin l. v, c. 1–33.

de Lyon, tandis que Frédéric II était excommunié et déposé, son collègue d'Orient siégeait sur son trône à la droite du pontife romain. Mais combien de fois cet empereur mendiant et exilé ne fut-il pas dégradé à ses propres yeux et à ceux de toutes les nations, par des mépris ou par une pitié insultante! Lorsqu'il passa pour la première fois en Angleterre, on l'arrêta à Douvres avec une sévère réprimande d'avoir osé entrer sans permission dans un royaume indépendant. Cependant, après quelques délais, il obtint la liberté de continuer sa route, fut reçu avec une politesse froide, et partit reconnaissant d'un présent de sept cents marcs d'argent (1). Baudouin ne tira de l'avarice de Rome que la proclamation d'une croisade et un trésor d'indulgences, monnaie dont on avait fait baisser la valeur par un usage trop fréquent et trop peu réfléchi. La naissance et les malheurs du prince grec intéressèrent l'âme généreuse de son cousin Louis IX; mais le zèle guerrier du saint roi se portait vers l'Égypte et la Palestine. Baudouin soulagea pour un moment sa pauvreté et celle de son empire par la vente du marquisat de Namur et de la seigneurie de Courtenai, seuls restes de ses États héréditaires (2). Au moyen de ces expédiens honteux

---

(1) Matthieu Paris raconte les deux visites de Baudouin II à la cour d'Angleterre (p. 396, 637), son retour en Grèce, *armatá manu* (p. 407), ses lettres de son *nomen formidabile*, etc. (p. 481). Ce dernier passage a échappé à Ducange; voyez l'expulsion de Baudouin, p. 850.

(2) Louis désapprouva l'aliénation de Courtenai et s'y

ou ruineux, il conduisit en Romanie une armée de trente mille hommes, dont la terreur doubla le nombre aux yeux des Grecs. Ses premières dépêches aux cours de France et d'Angleterre annoncèrent des succès et des espérances. Il avait soumis tous les alentours de la capitale jusqu'à la distance de trois jours de marche, et la conquête d'une ville importante, mais qu'il ne nomme pas, et que je présume être Chiorli, devait assurer la facilité du passage et la tranquillité de la frontière. Mais toutes ces espérances (supposé que Baudouin ait dit la vérité) s'évanouirent comme un songe; les troupes et les trésors de France se dissipèrent dans ses mains inhabiles, et l'empereur latin ne trouva d'appui pour son trône que dans une alliance honteuse avec les Turcs et les Comans. Pour sceller son traité, il donna sa nièce en mariage à l'infidèle sultan de Cogni, et pour plaire aux Comans, Baudouin se soumit aux cérémonies de leur religion. On immola un chien entre les deux armées, et les princes contractans goûtèrent du sang l'un de l'autre, comme un gage de fidélité (1). Le

---

opposa (Ducange, l. IV, c. 23). Cette seigneurie fait aujourd'hui partie des domaines de la couronne; mais on l'a *engagée* pour un terme à la famille de Boulainvilliers. Courtenai, élection de Nemours, dans l'Ile-de-France, est une ville qui contient environ neuf cents habitans; on y voit encore les restes d'un château (*Mélanges tirés d'une grande Bibliothèque*, t. x, l. v, p. 74-97).

(1) Joinville, p. 104, édit. du Louvre. Un prince coman qui mourut sans baptême, fut enterré aux portes de Cons-

successeur d'Auguste démolit les maisons vacantes de son palais ou de sa prison de Constantinople, pour en tirer du bois de chauffage, et il s'empara des plombs qui couvraient les églises pour fournir à la dépense de sa maison. Des marchands d'Italie lui firent quelques prêts à grosse usure; et Philippe, son fils et son successeur, servit, durant quelque temps, de gage pour une dette que l'empereur avait contractée à Venise (1). La faim, la soif et la nudité sont des maux réels, mais l'opulence n'est que relative; un prince qui serait riche comme particulier, peut être exposé, s'il étend ses besoins, à toutes les amertumes et les angoisses de l'indigence.

Dans cette humiliante détresse, il restait encore à l'empereur ou à l'empire un trésor qui tirait sa valeur imaginaire de la dévotion du monde chrétien. Le bois de la vraie croix avait un peu perdu par les partages qui en avaient été faits, et son long séjour entre les mains des infidèles jetait quelques soupçons sur la quantité de parcelles qu'on en avait répandues dans l'Orient et dans l'Occident; mais on conservait dans la chapelle impériale de Constantinople une autre relique de la passion : la couronne d'épines de Jésus-Christ était également précieuse et authentique. Dans l'absence de l'empereur, à l'exemple des anciens Égyptiens qui déposaient pour sûreté de leurs

La sainte couronne d'épines.

---

tantinople avec un certain nombre d'esclaves et de chevaux vivans.

(1) Sanut, *Secret. fidel. crucis*, l. IV, c. 18, p. 73.

dettes les momies de leurs pères, et engageaient ainsi leur honneur et leur religion au paiement de la somme, les barons de la Romanie empruntèrent treize mille cent trente-quatre pièces d'or, et donnèrent la sainte couronne pour gage (1) : à l'échéance ils se trouvèrent hors d'état de payer. Nicolas Querini, riche commerçant vénitien, consentit à rembourser les prêteurs, à condition que la couronne serait déposée à Venise, et qu'elle deviendrait sa propriété personnelle, si on ne la rachetait pas avant un terme court et convenu. Les barons informèrent leur souverain de cette fâcheuse convention et du danger qui le menaçait ; et comme l'État ne pouvait pas fournir une somme d'environ sept mille livres sterling, Baudouin mettait un grand prix à retirer une telle pièce des mains des Vénitiens et à la faire passer dans celles du roi très-chrétien (2), ce qui lui devenait à la fois plus honorable et plus avantageux : cependant la négociation éprouva quelque difficulté. Le pieux Louis IX aurait regardé l'achat d'une relique comme un crime de simonie ; mais en changeant seulement

---

(1) Ducange explique vaguement les mots *perparus, perpera, hyperperum*, par *monetæ genus*. D'après un passage de Gunther (*Hist. C. P.*, c. 8, p. 10), je soupçonne que le *perpera* était le *nummus aureus* ou la quatrième partie d'un marc d'argent, ou environ dix schellings sterling : en plomb, c'eût été trop peu de chose.

(2) Pour la translation de la sainte couronne, de Constantinople à Paris, *voyez* Ducange (*Hist. de C. P.*, l. IV, c. 11-14, 24-35), et Fleury (*Hist. eccl.*, t. XVII, p. 201-204).

le style de la convention, il pouvait rembourser la dette sans scrupule, recevoir le présent et en témoigner sa reconnaissance. Deux dominicains furent envoyés à Venise comme ambassadeurs, pour racheter et recevoir la sainte couronne qui avait échappé aux dangers de la mer et aux galères de Vatacès. A l'ouverture de la caisse, ils vérifièrent le sceau du doge et des barons qu'on avait apposé sur un reliquaire d'argent, dans lequel était renfermée la boîte d'or qui contenait le monument de la passion. Les Vénitiens cédèrent à regret à la justice et à la puissance, et l'empereur Frédéric accorda respectueusement le passage. La cour de France s'avança jusqu'à Troyes en Champagne au devant de cette précieuse relique: Le roi, nu-pieds et vêtu d'une simple chemise, la porta lui-même en triomphe dans les rues de Paris, et le don de dix mille marcs d'argent consola Baudouin de son sacrifice. Le succès de cette négociation engagea l'empereur latin à offrir avec la même générosité les autres ornemens de sa chapelle (1) : un reste considérable du bois de la vraie croix, le lange de Jésus-Christ, la lance, l'éponge et la chaîne de sa passion, la verge de Moïse et une partie du crâne de saint Jean-Baptiste. Saint Louis employa une somme de vingt mille marcs à fonder, pour y recevoir toutes

---

(1) *Mélanges tirés d'une grande bibliothèque*, t. XLIII, p. 201-205. Le *Lutrin* de Boileau représente l'intérieur, l'esprit et les habitudes de la Sainte-Chapelle; et ses commentateurs, Brossette et Saint-Marc, ont rassemblé et expliqué beaucoup de faits relatifs à son institution.

ces richesses spirituelles, la Sainte-Chapelle plaisamment immortalisée par la muse de Boileau. L'authenticité de ces reliques, si anciennes et tirées de pays si éloignés, ne peut plus se prouver par les témoignages des hommes; mais elle doit être admise par ceux qui croient aux miracles qu'elles ont opérés. Dans le milieu du dernier siècle, la sainte piqûre d'une des épines de la couronne guérit radicalement un ulcère invétéré (1) : ce prodige est attesté par les chrétiens les plus dévots et les plus éclairés de la France, et n'est pas aisé à démentir, excepté pour ceux qui se trouvent prémunis d'un antidote général contre toute crédulité religieuse (2).

Succès des Grecs. A. D. 1237-1261.

Les Latins de Constantinople (3) se trouvaient

---

(1) Cette cure fut accomplie, A. D. 1656, le 24 du mois de mars, sur la nièce du célèbre Pascal. Ce génie supérieur, Arnauld et Nicole, étaient présens pour croire et attester un miracle qui confondit les jésuites et sauva Port-Royal. *OEuvres de Racine*, t. VI, p. 176-187, dans l'éloquente Histoire de Port-Royal.

(2) Voltaire (*Siècle de Louis XIV*, c. 37, *OEuvres*, t. IX, p. 178, 179) s'efforce d'invalider le fait; mais Hume (*Essais*, vol. II, p. 483, 484) s'empare de la batterie avec plus d'habileté et de succès, et tourne le canon contre ses ennemis.

(3) On peut suivre dans les troisième, quatrième et cinquième livres de la compilation de Ducange, les pertes successives des Latins; mais il a laissé échapper beaucoup de circonstances relatives aux conquêtes des Grecs, qu'on peut retrouver dans l'histoire plus complète de George Acropolita, et dans les trois premiers livres de Nicéphore Grégoras, deux historiens de l'histoire byzantine, qui ont eu le bon-

environnés et pressés de toutes parts. La discorde et la division des Grecs et des Bulgares pouvaient seules différer leur destruction ; la politique et la supériorité des armes de Vatacès, empereur de Nicée, leur enlevèrent ce dernier espoir. Depuis la Propontide jusqu'aux rochers de la Pamphylie, l'Asie jouissait, sous son règne, de la paix et de la prospérité, et les succès de chaque campagne augmentaient son influence dans l'Europe. Il chassa les Bulgares des forteresses situées dans les montagnes de la Macédoine et de la Thrace, et resserra leur royaume, le long des bords du Danube, dans les limites qui le renferment aujourd'hui. L'empereur des Romains ne put souffrir plus long-temps qu'un duc d'Épire, un prince Comnène de l'Occident, prétendît lui disputer ou partager avec lui les honneurs de la pourpre ; Démétrius changea humblement la couleur de ses brodequins, et accepta avec reconnaissance le titre de despote. Sa bassesse et son incapacité révoltèrent ses sujets, et ils implorèrent la protection du prince grec, son seigneur suzerain. Après quelque résistance, il réunit le royaume de Thessalonique à celui de Nicée ; et Vatacès régna sans compétiteur depuis les frontières de la Turquie jusqu'au golfe Adriatique. Les princes d'Europe respectaient son mérite et sa puissance ; s'il eût voulu souscrire à la foi ortho-

---

heur d'être publiés par de savans éditeurs, Léon Allatius, à Rome, et Jean Boivin, de l'Académie des Inscriptions de Paris.

doxe, il est probable que le pape aurait abandonné sans regret l'empereur latin de Constantinople ; mais la mort de Vatacès, le règne court et troublé de son fils Théodore, et la minorité de Jean son petit-fils, suspendirent le rétablissement des Grecs. Dans le chapitre suivant, je rendrai compte de leurs révolutions intérieures ; il suffira d'observer ici que le jeune prince succomba sous l'ambition de son tuteur et de son collègue, Michel Paléologue, qui déploya le mélange de vices et de vertus ordinaire aux fondateurs d'une nouvelle dynastie. L'empereur Baudouin s'était flatté qu'une négociation que ne soutenait aucune force lui ferait recouvrer quelques provinces ou quelques villes. Ses ambassadeurs furent renvoyés de Nicée avec mépris et avec d'insultantes railleries : à chaque province qu'ils nommaient, Paléologue alléguait un prétexte qui l'obligeait à la conserver ; il était né dans l'une, il avait été élevé dans une autre au commandement militaire, il avait joui et se proposait de jouir long-temps, dans la troisième, des plaisirs de la chasse. « Et que vous proposez-vous donc de nous rendre ? lui demandèrent les ambassadeurs étonnés. — Rien, leur répondit le prince grec, pas un pouce de terre. Si votre maître désire la paix, qu'il me paie pour tribut annuel le produit des douanes de Constantinople ; à ce prix je puis lui permettre de régner : son refus sera le signal de la guerre. Je ne manque point d'expérience militaire, et je me fie de l'événement à Dieu et à mon épée (1). » Il fit le premier essai de ses armes contre le despote d'Épire. Sa victoire fut suivie d'une défaite; et si dans les montagnes d'Épire le pouvoir des l'Ange ou Comnène résista à ses efforts et survécut à son règne, la captivité de Villehardouin, prince d'Achaïe, priva les Latins du plus actif et du plus puissant vassal de leur monarchie expirante. Les républiques de Gênes et de Venise, engagées dans leur première guerre navale, se disputaient l'empire de la mer et le commerce de l'Orient. L'orgueil et l'intérêt attachaient les Vénitiens à la défense de Constantinople : leurs rivaux offrirent leurs secours à ses ennemis, et l'alliance des Génois avec le conquérant schismatique provoqua l'indignation de l'Église latine (2).

Occupé de son grand projet, Michel visita lui-même toutes les forteresses de la Thrace et augmenta les garnisons. Après avoir chassé les restes des Latins de leurs dernières possessions, il donna sans succès l'assaut au faubourg de Galata : un baron perfide, avec lequel il entretenait une correspondance,

<small>Les Grecs reprennent Constantinople.
A. D. 1261, juillet 25.</small>

---

(1) George Acropolita., c. 78, p. 89, 90, édit. de Paris.
(2) Les Grecs, honteux d'un secours étranger, dissimulèrent l'alliance des Génois et les secours qu'ils en reçurent; mais le fait est prouvé par le témoignage de Jean Villani (*Chron.*, l. VI, c. 71, dans Muratori, *Script. rer. ital.*, t. XIII, p. 202, 203), et Guillaume de Nangis (*Annales de saint Louis*, p. 248, dans le Joinville du Louvre), deux étrangers désintéressés; Urbain IV menaça de priver Gênes de son archevêque.

ne put ou ne voulut pas lui ouvrir les portes de la capitale. Au printemps suivant, Alexis Strategopolus, son général favori, qu'il avait décoré du titre de César, passa l'Hellespont à la tête de huit cents chevaux et de quelque infanterie (1), pour exécuter une expédition secrète. Ses instructions lui enjoignaient de s'approcher de Constantinople, de tout examiner avec attention, d'épier les occasions qui pourraient se présenter, mais de ne hasarder contre la ville aucune entreprise douteuse ou dangereuse. Le territoire des environs, entre la Propontide et la mer Noire, était habité par une race hardie de paysans et de malfaiteurs exercés aux armes, et d'une fidélité fort incertaine, mais attachés préférablement, par leur langage, leur religion et leur avantage présent, au parti des Grecs. On les appelait les Volontaires (2), et ils offrirent, en cette qualité, leurs services au général de Michel, dont l'armée, augmentée des Comans auxiliaires, se trouva composée de vingt-cinq mille hommes (3). L'ardeur de ces volontaires,

---

(1) Il faut quelque soin pour concilier les différences de nombre; les huit cents soldats de Nicétas, les vingt-cinq mille de Spandugino (apud Duc., l. v, c. 24), les Scythes et les Grecs d'Acropolita, et la nombreuse armée de Michel, dans les lettres du pape Urbain iv (1-129).

(2) Θεληματαριοι. Pachymère les nomme et en donne la description (l. ii, c. 14).

(3) Il est inutile d'aller chercher ces Comans dans les déserts de la Tartarie ou même de la Moldavie; une partie de la horde s'était soumise à Jean Vatacès, et avait proba-

et sa propre ambition, excitèrent le César à désobéir aux ordres précis de son maître, dans la juste confiance que le succès le justifierait de sa désobéissance. Les volontaires connaissaient l'état de faiblesse, de détresse et de terreur où se trouvaient les Latins, qu'ils étaient continuellement à portée d'observer, et ils présentèrent le moment comme très-favorable pour surprendre et envahir Byzance. Un jeune imprudent, qui gouvernait depuis peu la colonie de Venise, était parti avec trente galères et les plus braves chevaliers français pour une folle expédition contre la ville de Daphnusia, située sur les bords de la mer Noire, à quarante lieues de Constantinople. Le reste des Latins était sans force et sans soupçons. Ils apprirent qu'Alexis avait passé l'Hellespont; mais le faible nombre des troupes qu'il avait amenées dissipa leur inquiétude, et ils ne pensèrent point à s'informer de leur augmentation. En laissant son corps d'armée à une certaine distance, pour seconder au besoin ses opérations, il pouvait s'avancer, à la faveur de l'obscurité, avec un détachement choisi : tandis que quelques-uns devaient attacher des échelles à la partie la plus basse des murailles ; un vieux Grec avait promis d'introduire une partie de ses compatriotes, par un souterrain, jusque dans sa maison, d'où ils pourraient passer dans la ville et rompre en dedans la porte d'or qu'on n'ouvrait plus depuis long-temps,

---

blement établi une pépinière de soldats dans quelques terres désertes de la Thrace (Cantacuzène, l. 1, c. 2).

et le conquérant devait être maître de Byzance avant que les Latins fussent avertis du danger. Après avoir hésité quelque temps, Alexis s'en fia au zèle des volontaires : ils étaient hardis et confians, ils réussirent; et ce que j'ai dit du plan de l'entreprise apprend quels en furent l'exécution et le succès (1). Alexis n'eut pas plus tôt passé le seuil de la porte d'or, qu'il trembla de sa témérité ; il s'arrêta, il délibéra ; mais ses volontaires désespérés le déterminèrent à avancer, en lui peignant la retraite comme difficile et plus dangereuse que l'attaque. Tandis qu'Alexis tenait ses troupes régulières en ordre de bataille, les Comans se dispersèrent de tous côtés. On sonna l'alarme; et les menaces de pillage et d'incendie forcèrent les habitans à prendre un parti décisif. Les Grecs de Constantinople conservaient de l'attachement pour leurs anciens souverains. Les marchands génois considéraient l'alliance récente de leur république avec le prince grec, et la rivalité des Vénitiens. Tous les quartiers prirent les armes, et l'air retentit d'une acclamation générale : « Victoire et longue vie à Michel et à Jean, les augustes empereurs des Romains! » Baudouin fut réveillé par les cris, mais le plus pressant danger ne put l'obliger à tirer l'épée pour dé-

---

(1) Les Latins racontent brièvement la perte de Constantinople ; la conquête est détaillée avec plus de satisfaction par les Grecs ; savoir, par Acropolita (c. 85), Pachymère (l. II, c. 26, 27), Nicéphore Grégoras (l. IV, c. 1, 2). *Voyez* Ducange, *Hist. de C. P.* l. v, c. 19-27.

fendre une ville qu'il abandonnait, peut-être avec plus de plaisir que de regret. Il courut au rivage, et aperçut heureusement les voiles de la flotte qui revenait de sa vaine expédition contre Daphnusia. Constantinople était irrévocablement perdue ; mais l'empereur latin et les principales familles s'embarquèrent sur les galères de Venise, qui cinglèrent vers l'île d'Eubée, d'où elles conduisirent en Italie l'auguste fugitif, que le pape reçut avec un mélange de mépris et de compassion. Depuis la perte de sa capitale jusqu'à sa mort, Baudouin passa treize ans à solliciter les puissances catholiques de se réunir pour le replacer sur son trône. Cette supplique lui était familière; et il ne se montra pas, dans son dernier exil, plus indigent et plus avili qu'il ne l'avait été lors de ses trois premiers voyages dans les cours de l'Europe. Son fils Philippe hérita de son vain titre, et sa fille Catherine porta en mariage ses prétentions à Charles de Valois, frère de Philippe le Bel, roi de France. La ligne femelle de la maison de Courtenai fut successivement représentée par différentes alliances, jusqu'à ce que le titre d'empereur de Constantinople, trop pompeux et trop sonore pour se joindre au nom d'un particulier, s'éteignit modestement dans le silence et dans l'oubli (1).

---

(1) *Voyez* les trois derniers livres (l. v–viii) et les *Tables généalogiques* de Ducange. Dans l'année 1382, l'empereur titulaire de Constantinople était Jacques de Baux, duc d'Andria dans le royaume de Naples, fils de Marguerite, qui

Conséquences générales des croisades.

Après avoir raconté les expéditions des Latins dans la Palestine et à Constantinople, je ne puis quitter ce sujet sans considérer quelle fut l'influence des croisades dans les pays qui en furent les théâtres (1). L'impression que les Francs avaient faite dans les royaumes mahométans d'Égypte et de Syrie, s'effaça dès qu'ils en disparurent, quoiqu'on n'en perdît pas le souvenir. Les fidèles disciples de Mahomet n'éprouvèrent jamais le profane désir d'étudier les lois ou le langage des idolâtres ; et leurs rapports, soit d'alliance ou d'inimitié, avec les étrangers de l'Occident, n'apportèrent pas la moindre altération à la simplicité primitive de leurs mœurs. Les Grecs, qui se croyaient fiers parce qu'ils étaient vains, se montrèrent un peu moins inflexibles. Dans les efforts qu'ils firent pour recouvrer leur empire, ils s'attachèrent à égaler la valeur, la discipline et la tactique de leurs adversaires. Ils pouvaient à juste titre mépriser la littérature moderne de l'Occident ; mais l'esprit de liberté qui y régnait leur révéla une partie des droits communs à tous les hommes, et ils adoptèrent quelques-

---

avait eu pour mère Catherine de Valois, fille de Catherine, dont le père était Philippe, fils de Baudouin II (Ducange, l. VIII, c. 37, 38). On ne sait point s'il a laissé quelque postérité.

(1) Abulféda, qui vit la fin des croisades, parle des royaumes des Francs et de ceux des Nègres comme également inconnus (*Proleg. ad Geogr.*). S'il n'eût pas dédaigné la langue latine, le prince syrien aurait trouvé facilement des livres et des interprètes.

unes des institutions publiques et privées des Français. La correspondance de Constantinople avec l'Italie répandit l'usage de l'idiome latin, et l'on fit ensuite à quelques-uns des pères et des auteurs classiques l'honneur de les traduire en grec (1). Mais la persécution enflamma le zèle religieux et les préjugés nationaux des chrétiens de l'Orient, et le règne des Latins confirma la séparation des deux Églises.

Si nous comparons, dans le siècle des croisades, les Latins de l'Europe aux Grecs et aux Arabes, si nous considérons chez ces différens peuples les divers degrés des lumières, des arts et de l'industrie, nous n'accorderons sans doute à nos grossiers ancêtres que le troisième rang parmi les nations civilisées : on peut attribuer leurs progrès successifs et la supériorité dont ils jouissent aujourd'hui, à une énergie particulière de leur caractère, à un esprit d'imitation et d'activité inconnu à leurs rivaux plus avancés, mais chez lesquels tout alors se trouvait dans un état de stagnation ou dans un mouvement rétrograde. Avec ces dispositions, les Latins devaient naturellement tirer des avantages immédiats et essentiels d'une suite d'événemens qui déployaient à

---

(1) Huet (*de Interpretatione et de claris interpretibus*, p. 131-135) rend un compte abrégé et superficiel de ces traductions de latin en grec. Maxime Planudes, moine de Constantinople (A. D. 1327-1353), a traduit les Commentaires de César, le Songe de Scipion, les Métamorphoses et les Héroïdes d'Ovide; etc. Fabricius, *Bibl. græc.*, t. x, p. 533.

leurs yeux le tableau du monde, et leur ouvraient de longues et fréquentes communications avec les peuples les plus cultivés de l'Orient. Les progrès les plus précoces et les plus sensibles se manifestèrent dans le commerce, dans les manufactures et dans les arts que font naître la soif des richesses, la nécessité, le goût des plaisirs ou la vanité. Parmi la foule des fanatiques, il se pouvait trouver un captif ou un pélerin capable de remarquer une invention ingénieuse du Caire ou de Constantinople : celui qui rapporta celle des moulins à vent (1) fut le bienfaiteur des nations : l'histoire n'a pas daigné lui payer un tribut de reconnaissance ; mais les jouissances du luxe, le sucre et les étoffes de soie, tirés originairement de la Grèce et de l'Égypte, y tiennent une place honorable. Les Latins sentirent plus tard les besoins intellectuels, et s'occupèrent plus lentement de les satisfaire. Des causes différentes et des événemens plus récens, éveillèrent en Europe la curiosité, mère de l'étude ; et dans le siècle des croisades, la littérature des Grecs et des Arabes ne leur inspirait que de l'indifférence. Ils avaient peut-être fait passer dans leur pratique quelques principes de médecine et adopté quelques figures de mathémati-

---

(1) Les moulins à vent, originairement inventés dans l'Asie-Mineure, où les eaux sont rares, furent en usage en Normandie dès l'année 1105 (*Vie privée des Français*, t. 1, p. 42, 43 ; Ducange, *Gloss. lat.*, t. IV, p. 474). *Voy.* l'Angleterre, anc. trad. par Boulard, p. 282.

ques; la nécessité put former quelques interprètes d'un genre peu relevé, pour servir aux affaires des marchands et des soldats; mais le commerce des Orientaux n'avait point répandu dans les écoles d'Europe l'étude et la connaissance de leurs langues (1). Si un principe de religion, semblable à celui des mahométans, repoussait l'idiome du Koran, le désir de comprendre l'original de l'Évangile aurait dû exciter la patience et la curiosité des chrétiens, et la même grammaire leur eût découvert les beautés d'Homère et de Platon. Cependant, durant un règne de soixante ans, les Latins de Constantinople dédaignèrent le langage et l'érudition de leurs sujets; les manuscrits furent les seuls trésors qu'on ne leur envia point et qu'on ne chercha point à leur arracher. Les universités de l'Occident regardaient, à la vérité, Aristote comme leur oracle; mais c'était un Aristote barbare; et, au lieu de recourir à la source, elles se contentaient humblement d'une traduction fautive composée par des Juifs ou des Maures de l'Andalousie. Les croisades n'eurent pour principe qu'un fanatisme barbare, et leurs effets les plus importans furent analogues à leur cause. Chaque pélerin avait l'ambition de revenir chargé des

---

(1). *Voyez* les plaintes de Roger Bacon (*Biographia britannica*, vol. 1, p. 418, édit. de Kippis). Si Bacon ou Gerbert entendaient quelques auteurs grecs, ils étaient des prodiges dans leur siècle, et ne devaient point cet avantage au commerce de l'Orient.

dépouilles sacrées, des reliques de la Grèce et de la Palestine (1), et chacune de ces reliques était précédée et suivie d'une multitude de miracles et de visions; la foi des catholiques fut altérée par de nouvelles légendes, et leur pratique par de nouvelles superstitions. La guerre sainte fut la source funeste qui produisit l'établissement de l'inquisition, les moines mendians, les progrès définitifs de l'idolâtrie, et l'excès de l'abus des indulgences. L'esprit actif des Latins cherchait à se satisfaire aux dépens de leur raison et de leur religion; et si l'ignorance et l'obscurité régnèrent dans les neuvième et dixième siècles, on peut dire aussi que les treizième et quatorzième furent le temps des fables et des absurdités.

Les peuples du Nord qui conquirent l'empire romain, en adoptant le christianisme, en cultivant une terre fertile, se mêlèrent insensiblement avec les provinciaux, et réchauffèrent les cendres des arts de l'antiquité. Vers le siècle de Charlemagne, leurs établissemens avaient acquis un certain degré d'ordre et de stabilité, lorsque les invasions des Normands, des Sarrasins (2) et des Hongrois, nouveaux

---

(1) Telle était l'opinion du grand Leibnitz (*OEuvres de Fontenelle*, t. v, p. 458), un des maîtres de l'histoire du moyen âge. Je ne citerai que la généalogie des Carmélites et le miracle de la maison de Lorette, qui vinrent l'une et l'autre de Palestine.

(2) Si je place les Sarrasins au nombre des nations barbares, ce n'est que relativement à leurs guerres; ou plutôt

essaims de Barbares, replongèrent l'occident de l'Europe dans son premier état d'anarchie et de barbarie. Vers le onzième siècle, l'expulsion ou la conversion des ennemis du christianisme apaisèrent cette seconde tempête. La civilisation, qui depuis si longtemps semblait se retirer et se resserrer, recommença à s'étendre avec une constante rapidité, et ouvrit une nouvelle carrière aux épreuves et aux efforts de la génération naissante. Durant les deux siècles des croisades, les progrès des arts furent brillans et rapides; mais je ne suis point de l'avis de certains philosophes, qui ont applaudi à l'influence de ces guerres saintes (1). Il me semble qu'elles ont plutôt retardé qu'avancé la maturité de l'Europe (2). La vie et les travaux de plusieurs millions d'hommes ensevelis dans l'Orient, auraient été plus utilement employés à cultiver et à perfectionner leur pays natal; la masse toujours croissante des productions et de

à leurs incursions en Italie et en France, qui n'avaient d'autre but que le pillage et la dévastation.

(1) *Voyez* sur ce sujet l'ouvrage de M. Heeren, intitulé *Essai sur l'influence des Croisades* (*Paris*, 1808), où les résultats heureux, bien qu'éloignés, de ces guerres saintes, sont développés avec autant de sagacité philosophique que d'érudition. (*Note de l'Éditeur.*)

(2) Un rayon brillant de lumière philosophique est sorti de nos jours du fond de l'Écosse, et a enrichi la littérature sur le sujet intéressant des progrès de la société en Europe; et c'est avec autant de plaisir personnel que de justice, que je cite les noms respectables de Hume, Robertson et Adam Smith. *Voyez* deux ouvrages traduits de G. Stuart, par B.

l'industrie aurait encouragé le commerce et la navigation, et les Latins se seraient éclairés et enrichis par une correspondance amicale avec les peuples de l'Orient. Je n'aperçois qu'un seul point sur lequel les croisades aient produit un bien, ou du moins fait disparaître un mal. La portion la plus considérable des habitans de l'Europe languissait enchaînée sur sa terre natale, sans propriété, sans liberté et sans lumières; les nobles et les ecclésiastiques, qui ne composaient relativement qu'un très-petit nombre, semblaient seuls mériter le nom d'hommes et de citoyens. Les artifices du clergé et l'épée des barons maintenaient ce système tyrannique. L'autorité des prêtres avait été utile dans les siècles de barbarie; sans eux la lumière des sciences se serait tout-à-fait éteinte. Ils adoucirent la férocité de leurs contemporains; le faible et l'indigent trouvèrent chez eux un asile et des secours dans leurs besoins; enfin on leur dut la conservation ou le retour de l'ordre civil de la société. Mais l'indépendance, le brigandage et les discordes des nobles, ne produisirent jamais que des désordres et des calamités; la main de fer de l'aristocratie militaire détruisait tout espoir d'industrie et de perfectionnement. On doit considérer les croisades comme une des causes qui contribuèrent le plus efficacement à renverser l'édifice gothique du système féodal. Les barons vendirent leurs terres, et une partie de leur race disparut dans ces expéditions périlleuses et dispendieuses. Leur pauvreté força leur orgueil à accorder ces chartres de liberté qui relâchèrent les liens de l'esclave, affranchirent la ferme du paysan et la boutique de l'ouvrier, et rendirent par degrés une existence à la portion la plus nombreuse et la plus utile de la société. L'incendie qui détruisit les arbres élevés et stériles de la forêt, donna de l'air et de l'espace aux plantes humbles et nourrissantes dont se couvre la terre.

DIGRESSION SUR LA FAMILLE DES COURTENAI.

La pourpre des trois empereurs qui régnèrent à Constantinople légitimera ou excusera une digression sur l'origine de la maison de Courtenai, et sur les vicissitudes singulières de sa fortune (1), dans les trois principales branches, 1° d'Édesse, 2° de France, et 3° d'Angleterre; la dernière a survécu seule aux révolutions de huit cents ans.

C'est lorsque le commerce n'a pas encore répandu les richesses, quand les lumières n'ont pas encore dissipé les préjugés, que les prérogatives de la naissance se font sentir le plus fortement, et sont recon-

Origine de la famille de Courtenai.
A. D. 1020.

---

(1) Je me suis servi, sans m'y borner, d'une *histoire généalogique de la noble et illustre maison de Courtenai*, par Ezra Cleaveland, tuteur du chevalier Guill. de Courtenai, et recteur de Honiton, Oxford, 1735, in-fol. La première partie est tirée de Guillaume de Tyr; la seconde, de l'histoire de France de Bouchet; et la troisième, de différens Mémoires publics et particuliers des Courtenai du Devonshire. Le recteur de Honiton montre plus de reconnaissance que d'adresse, et plus d'adresse que de discernement.

nues avec le plus d'humilité. Dans tous les siècles, les lois et les usages des Germains ont distingué les divers rangs de la société. Les ducs et les comtes qui se partagèrent l'empire de Charlemagne, rendirent leurs offices héréditaires ; chaque baron léguait à ses enfans son honneur et son épée. Les familles les plus vaines de leurs prétentions se résignent à perdre dans l'obscurité du moyen âge la tige de leur arbre généalogique, dont les racines, quelque profondes qu'elles puissent être, aboutissent certainement à un plébéien ; et leurs généalogistes sont forcés de descendre à dix siècles après l'ère chrétienne, pour découvrir quelques renseignemens dans les surnoms, les armoiries et les archives. Les premiers rayons de lumière (1) nous font discerner Athon, chevalier français ; sa noblesse est prouvée par le rang de son père, dont on ne dit point le nom, et nous trouvons la preuve de son opulence dans la construction du château de Courtenai, à environ cinquante-six milles au sud de Paris, dans le district du Gâtinais. Depuis le règne de Robert, fils de Hugues Capet, les barons de Courtenai tiennent une place distinguée parmi les vassaux qui relevaient immédiatement de la couronne ; et Josselin, petit-fils d'Athon et d'une mère noble, est enregistré parmi

---

(1) Le premier renseignement sur sa famille est un passage du continuateur d'Aimoin, moine de Fleury, qui écrivit dans le douzième siècle. *Voyez* sa Chronique dans les *Historiens de France*, t. XI, p. 276.

les héros de la première croisade. Il s'attacha particulièrement aux étendards de Baudouin de Bruges, second comte d'Édesse, son parent; ils étaient fils de deux sœurs. Baudouin lui donna en fief une principauté dont il était digne, qu'il sut conserver, et dont le service prouve qu'il était suivi d'un grand nombre de guerriers. I. Après le départ de son cousin, Josselin fut investi du comté d'Édesse, et régna sur les deux rives de l'Euphrate. La sagesse de son gouvernement durant la paix lui attira un grand nombre de sujets de l'Europe et de la Syrie. Son économie remplit ses magasins de grains, d'huiles et de vins, et ses châteaux de chevaux, d'armes et d'argent. Dans le cours d'une sainte guerre de trente années, Josselin fut alternativement vainqueur et captif; mais il mourut en soldat, porté dans sa litière à la tête de ses troupes; et ses derniers regards virent la défaite des Turcs, qui s'étaient fiés sur son âge et ses infirmités. Son fils, successeur de son nom et de ses États, manquait moins de valeur que de vigilance; mais il oublia quelquefois qu'il faut autant de soins pour conserver un empire que pour en faire la conquête. Le prince d'Édesse défia les forces des Turcs sans s'assurer le secours du prince d'Antioche, et négligea, dans les plaisirs de Turbessel en Syrie (1), la défense de la frontière qui séparait

1° Les comtes d'Édesse.
A. D.
1101-1152.

---

(1). D'Anville place Turbessel, ou, comme on la nomme aujourd'hui, Telbesher, à vingt-quatre milles du grand passage sur l'Euphrate à Zeugma.

les chrétiens des Turcs au-delà de l'Euphrate. Tandis qu'il était absent, Zenghi, le premier des Atabeks, assiégea et emporta d'assaut Édesse sa capitale, faiblement défendue par une troupe de timides et perfides Orientaux. Les Francs entreprirent de rentrer dans Édesse ; ils furent vaincus, et Courtenai termina sa vie dans les prisons d'Alep. Il lui restait encore un ample patrimoine ; mais sa veuve et son fils encore enfant ne pouvaient résister aux efforts de leurs vainqueurs ; ils cédèrent à l'empereur de Constantinople, en échange d'une pension annuelle, le soin de défendre et la honte de perdre les dernières possessions des Latins. La comtesse douairière d'Édesse se retira dans la ville de Jérusalem avec ses deux enfans. Sa fille Agnès devint l'épouse et la mère d'un roi. Son fils, Josselin III, accepta l'office de sénéchal, le premier du royaume. Dans sa nouvelle seigneurie de la Palestine, il était tenu du service militaire de cinquante chevaliers, et son nom tient une place honorable dans toutes les transactions de la guerre et de la paix ; mais on le vit disparaître lors de la perte de Jérusalem, et le nom de Courtenai, de la branche d'Édesse, fut éteint par le mariage de ses deux filles avec deux barons allemand et français (1).

---

(1) Ses possessions sont enregistrées dans les *Assises de Jérusalem* (c. 326), parmi les mouvances de la couronne, qui doivent donc avoir été rassemblées entre les années 1153

II. Tandis que Josselin régnait au-delà de l'Eu- 2º Les Courtenai phrate, son frère aîné, Milon, fils de Josselin et de France. petit-fils d'Athon, jouissait en paix, sur les bords de la Seine, de ses biens et de son château héréditaire, qui passèrent, après sa mort, à son troisième fils Renaud ou Réginald. Dans les annales des anciennes familles, on trouve peu d'exemples de génie ou de vertu; mais l'orgueil de leurs descendans recueille avec soin les traits de rapines ou de violence, pourvu qu'ils annoncent une supériorité de valeur ou de puissance. Un descendant de Renaud de Courtenai devrait rougir du brigand qui dépouilla et emprisonna des marchands, quoiqu'ils eussent payé les droits du roi à Sens et à Orléans; mais il en tirera vanité, parce que le comte de Champagne, régent du royaume, fut obligé de lever une armée pour le forcer à la restitution (1). Renaud laissa ses domaines à sa fille aînée, et la donna en mariage au septième fils de Louis le Gros, qui en eut un grand nombre d'autres. Il serait naturel de supposer que ce nom Leur va s'élever à la dignité d'un nom royal, que les des- alliance cendans de Pierre de France et d'Élisabeth de Cour- famille tenai jouirent du titre et des honneurs de princes du A. D. 1150.

et 1187. On peut trouver sa généalogie dans les *Lignages d'outre-mer*, ç. 16.

(1) L'abbé Suger, ministre d'État, raconte d'une manière absurde la rapine et la réparation, dans ses Lettres 114 et 116, qui sont les meilleurs Mémoires du siècle (Duchesne, *Scriptor. Hist. Fr.*, t. IV, p. 530).

sang ; mais on négligea long-temps leurs réclamations, et on finit par les rejeter. Les motifs de cette disgrâce comprendront l'histoire de la seconde branche. 1° Dans les siècles des croisades, la maison royale de France était déjà révérée de l'Orient et de l'Occident. Mais on ne comptait que cinq règnes ou générations depuis Hugues Capet jusqu'à Pierre, et leur titre paraissait encore si précaire, que chaque monarque croyait nécessaire de faire couronner durant sa vie son fils aîné. Les pairs de France ont maintenu long-temps leur droit de préséance sur les branches cadettes de la maison régnante, et les princes du sang ne jouissaient pas, dans le douzième siècle, de cet éclat répandu aujourd'hui sur les princes les plus éloignés de la succession à la couronne. 2° Il fallait que les barons de Courtenai fissent grand cas de leur nom, et qu'il fût en grande vénération dans l'opinion publique, pour qu'ils imposassent au fils d'un monarque l'obligation d'adopter, en épousant leur fille, son nom et ses armes pour lui et pour toute sa postérité. Lorsqu'une héritière épouse son inférieur ou même son égal, on exige et on accorde souvent cet échange. Mais en s'éloignant de la tige royale, les descendans de Louis le Gros se trouvèrent insensiblement confondus avec les ancêtres de leur mère, et les nouveaux Courtenai méritaient peut-être de perdre les honneurs de leur naissance, auxquels un motif d'intérêt les avait fait renoncer. 3° La honte fut infiniment plus durable que la récompense, et leur grandeur passagère se termina par une longue obscurité. Le premier fruit de cette union, Pierre de Courtenai, avait épousé, comme je l'ai déjà dit., la sœur des comtes de Flandre, les deux premiers empereurs latins de Constantinople. Il se rendit imprudemment à l'invitation des barons de la Romanie; ses deux fils, Robert et Baudouin, occupèrent successivement le trône de Byzance, et perdirent les derniers restes de l'empire latin de l'Orient. La petite-fille de Baudouin II allia une seconde fois cette famille au sang de France et des Valois. Pour soutenir les frais d'un règne précaire et orageux, ils engagèrent ou vendirent toutes leurs anciennes possessions, et les derniers empereurs de Constantinople ne subsistèrent que des charités de Rome et de Naples.

Tandis que les aînés dissipaient leur fortune en courant les aventures romanesques, et que le château de Courtenai était profané par un plébéien, les branches cadettes de ce nom adoptif s'étendirent et se multiplièrent; mais le temps et le pauvreté obscurcirent l'éclat de leur naissance. Après la mort de Robert, grand-bouteiller de France, ils descendirent du rang de princes à celui de barons; les générations suivantes se confondirent avec les simples gentilshommes, et dans les seigneurs campagnards de Tanlai et de Champignelles on ne reconnaissait plus les descendans de Hugues Capet. Les plus aventureux embrassèrent sans déshonneur la profession de soldat; les autres, moins riches et moins actifs, descendirent, comme leurs cousins de la branche de Dreux, dans l'humble classe des paysans. Durant une période obscure de quatre cents ans, leur origine royale devint chaque jour plus douteuse, et leur généalogie, au lieu d'être enregistrée dans les annales du royaume, ne peut être vérifiée que par les recherches pénibles des généalogistes. Ce ne fut que vers la fin du seizième siècle, lorsqu'ils virent monter sur le trône une famille qui en était presque aussi éloignée, que les Courtenai sentirent se réveiller le souvenir de leur naissance. Des doutes élevés sur la légitimité de leur noblesse leur firent entreprendre de prouver qu'ils descendaient de la famille royale. Ils réclamèrent la justice et la compassion de Henri IV, obtinrent l'attestation de vingt jurisconsultes d'Italie et d'Allemagne, et se comparèrent modestement aux descendans de David, dont le laps des siècles et le métier de charpentier n'avaient point anéanti les prérogatives (1); mais toutes les circonstances leur furent contraires,

---

(1) De toutes les requêtes, apologies, etc., publiées par les *princes* de Courtenai, je n'ai vu que les trois suivantes, toutes *in-8°* : 1° *dé Stirpe et Origine Domûs* de Courtenai : *addita sunt responsa celeberrimorum Europæ jurisconsultorum;* Paris, 1607. 2° *Représentation du procédé tenu à l'instance faite devant le roi par M. de Courtenai, pour la conservation de l'honneur et dignité de leur maison, branche de la royale maison de France,* à Paris, 1613. 3° *Représentation du subject qui a porté messieurs de Salle et de Fraville, de la maison de Courtenai, à se retirer hors du royaume;* 1614. Ce fut un homicide, pour lequel les Courtenai demandaient qu'on leur fît ou grâce ou leur procès comme princes du sang.

toutes les oreilles furent sourdes à leurs justes réclamations. L'indifférence des Valois semblait justifier celle des Bourbons : les princes du sang, de la branche régnante, dédaignèrent l'alliance d'une parenté sans éclat : les parlemens ne rejetèrent point leurs preuves; mais, écartant un exemple dangereux par une distinction arbitraire, ils prétendirent que saint Louis était la véritable tige de la famille royale (1). Les Courtenai continuèrent en vain leurs plaintes et leurs réclamations, qui se sont terminées dans ce siècle par la mort du dernier mâle de la famille (2). Le sentiment de fierté qu'inspire la vertu adoucit la rigueur de leur situation ; ils rejetèrent toujours avec dédain les offres de faveurs et de fortune : un Courtenai, au lit de la mort, aurait sacrifié son fils unique,

---

(1) De Thou exprime ainsi l'opinion des parlemens : *Principis nomen nusquam in Galliá tributum nisi iis qui per mares è regibus nostris originem repetunt : qui nunc tantùm à Ludovico nono beatæ memoriæ numerantur : nam* Cortinæi *et* Drocenses, *à Ludovico Crasso genus ducentes, hodiè inter eos minimè recensentur.* Cette distinction est plus d'expédient que de justice. La sainteté de Louis IX ne pouvait lui donner aucune prérogative particulière, et tous les descendans de Hugues Capet doivent se trouver compris dans son pacte primitif avec la nation française.

(2) Le dernier mâle de la maison de Courtenai fut Charles Roger, qui mourut en 1730 sans laisser de fils; la dernière femelle fut Hélène de Courtenai, qui épousa Louis de Baufremont. Son titre de princesse du sang royal de France fut supprimé le 7 février 1737, par un arrêt du parlement de Paris.

s'il se fût montré capable de renoncer, pour le sort le plus brillant, au titre et aux droits de prince légitime du sang de France (1).

<small>3° Les Courtenai d'Angleterre.</small>

III. Selon les anciens registres de l'abbaye de Ford, les Courtenai de Devonshire descendent du prince Florus, second fils de Pierre et petit-fils de Louis le Gros (2). Cette fable, inventée par la reconnaissance ou la vénalité des moines, a été trop facilement adoptée par nos antiquaires Camden (3) et Dugdale (4); mais elle se rapporte si peu au temps et elle est si clairement contraire à la vérité, que la fierté judicieuse de la famille refuse d'adopter ce fondateur imaginaire. Les historiens les plus dignes de con-

---

(1) L'anecdote singulière à laquelle je fais allusion se trouve dans le *Recueil des Pièces intéressantes et peu connues* (Maestricht, 1786, en quatre vol. in-12); et l'éditeur inconnu cite son auteur, qui la tenait d'Hélène de Courtenai, marquise de Baufremont.

(2) Dugdale, *Monasticon anglicanum*, vol. 1, pag. 786. Cependant cette fable doit avoir été inventée avant le règne d'Édouard III. Les profusions pieuses des trois premières générations en faveur de l'abbaye de Ford furent suivies de tyrannie d'une part, et d'ingratitude de l'autre; et à la sixième génération, les moines cessèrent d'enregistrer la naissance, les actions et la mort de leur patron.

(3) Dans sa *Britannia* la liste des comtes de Devon indique cependant un doute par l'expression *è regio sanguine ortos credunt*.

(4) Dans son *Baronnage* (part. 1, p. 634) il renvoie à son propre Monasticon. N'aurait-il pas dû corriger les registres de l'abbaye de Ford, et effacer le fantôme de Florus par l'autorité irrécusable des historiens français?

fiance croient qu'après avoir donné sa fille en mariage au fils du roi, Renaud de Courtenai abandonna ses possessions de France, et obtint du monarque anglais une seconde femme et un nouvel établissement. Il est certain du moins que Henri II distingua dans ses camps et dans ses conseils un Réginald du même nom, portant les mêmes armes, et que l'on peut raisonnablement croire descendu de la race des Courtenai de France. Le droit de tutelle autorisait le seigneur suzerain à récompenser son vassal par le mariage d'une riche et noble héritière, et Courtenai acquit de belles possessions dans le Devonshire, où sa postérité réside depuis plus de six cents ans (1). Havise, l'épouse de Renaud, avait hérité de Baudouin de Briones, baron normand, investi par Guillaume le Conquérant, le bien honorifique de Okehampton, qui était tenu à la charge du service de quatre-vingt-treize chevaliers. Elle avait aussi le droit, quoique femme, de réclamer les charges masculines de vicomte héréditaire ou shérif, et de gouverneur du château royal d'Exeter. Robert, leur fils, épousa la sœur du comte de Devon. Environ un siècle après, à l'extinction de la famille des Rivers (2), Hugues II,

Les comtes de Devon.

---

(1) Outre le troisième et meilleur livre de l'histoire de Cleaveland, j'ai consulté Dugdale, le père de notre science généalogique (*Baronnage*, part. 1, p. 634-643).

(2) Cette grande famille de Ripuariis, Redvers ou Rivers, s'éteignit sous le règne d'Édouard Ier, dans la personne d'Isa-

son petit-fils, hérita du titre qu'on regardait encore comme une dignité territoriale ; et douze comtes de Devon, du nom de Courtenai, fleurirent successivement dans une période de deux cent vingt ans. On les comptait dans le nombre des plus puissans barons du royaume, et ce ne fut qu'après une opiniâtre contestation qu'ils cédèrent au fief d'Arundel la première place dans le parlement d'Angleterre. Les Courtenai contractèrent des alliances avec les plus illustres familles ; les Veres, les Despenser, les Saint-John, les Talbot, les Bohun, et même avec les Plantagenet. Dans une querelle avec Jean de Lancastre, un Courtenai, évêque de Londres, et depuis archevêque de Cantorbéry, montra une confiance profane dans le nombre et la puissance de sa famille et de ses alliés. En temps de paix, les comtes de Devon vivaient dans leurs nombreux châteaux et manoirs de l'Occident : ils employaient leur immense revenu à des actes de dévotion et d'hospitalité ; et l'épitaphe d'Édouard, qu'une infirmité a fait connaître sous le nom de *l'Aveugle*, et que ses vertus ont fait nommer *le Bon*, présente avec ingénuité une sentence de morale dont pourrait cependant abuser une imprudente générosité. Après une tendre commémoration de cinquante-cinq ans d'union et de

---

belle de Fortibus, fameuse et puissante douairière, qui survécut long-temps à son frère et à son mari (Dugdale, *Baronnage*, part. *1*, p. 254-257).

bonheur qu'il avait passés avec son épouse Mabel, le bon comte parle ainsi du fond de son tombeau :

> *What we gave, we have;*
> *What we spent, we had;*
> *What we left, we lost* (1).
>
> Ce qu'ai donné me semble avoir encor;
> J'ai eu ce que j'ai dépensé;
> J'ai perdu ce que j'ai laissé.

Mais leurs *pertes* dans ce sens furent fort supérieures à leurs dons et à leurs dépenses ; et leurs héritiers furent, aussi bien que les pauvres, l'objet de leurs soins paternels. Les sommes qu'ils payèrent pour droit de prise de possession et saisine attestent la grandeur de leurs biens, et plusieurs des domaines actuellement possédés par leur famille y sont depuis le quatorzième et même depuis le treizième siècle. Les Courtenai remplissaient à la guerre le devoir de chevaliers, et en méritèrent les honneurs ; on leur confia souvent la levée et le commandement des milices du Devonshire et de la Cornouailles ; ils suivirent quelquefois leur seigneur suzerain sur les frontières d'Écosse, et servirent quelquefois chez l'étranger, pour un prix convenu, avec une suite de quatre-vingts hommes d'armes et autant d'archers. Ils combattirent sur terre et sur mer avec les Édouard

---

(1) Cleaveland, p. 142. Quelques-uns l'attribuent à un Rivers, comte de Devon ; mais ce style anglais paraît plutôt appartenir au quinzième siècle qu'au treizième.

et les Henri. Leur nom paraît avec éclat dans les batailles, les tournois, et dans la première liste des chevaliers de la jarretière. Trois frères de cette famille contribuèrent à la victoire du prince Noir en Espagne. Au bout de six générations, les Courtenai d'Angleterre partageaient la méprisante aversion de leurs compatriotes pour la nation et le pays dont ils tiraient leur origine. Dans la querelle des deux roses, les comtes de Devon prirent le parti de la maison de Lancastre, et trois frères moururent successivement ou sur le champ de bataille ou sur l'échafaud. Henri VII les rétablit dans leurs biens et dans leurs titres ; une fille d'Édouard IV ne dédaigna pas d'épouser un Courtenai ; leur fils, créé marquis d'Exeter, jouit de la faveur de son cousin Henri VIII, et dans le camp du drap d'or il rompit une lance contre le monarque français. Mais la faveur de Henri était le prélude de la disgrâce, et la disgrâce annonçait la mort. Le marquis d'Exeter fut une des plus illustres et des plus innocentes victimes de la jalousie du tyran : son fils Édouard mourut en exil à Padoue, après avoir langui long-temps prisonnier dans la Tour. L'amour secret de Marie, qu'il négligea peut-être en faveur d'Élisabeth, répand un vernis romanesque sur l'histoire de ce jeune comte dont on vante la beauté. Les débris de son patrimoine passèrent dans différentes familles par les alliances de ses quatre tantes, et les princes qui succédèrent au trône d'Angleterre rétablirent ses honneurs personnels par des patentes, comme s'ils eussent été supprimés légalement ; mais il existait encore une branche qui descendait de Hugues 1ᵉʳ, comte de Devon, branche cadette de la maison de Courtenai, dont le château de Powderham a toujours été le siège depuis le règne d'Édouard III jusqu'à nos jours, c'est-à-dire depuis environ quatre cents ans. Des concessions et des défrichemens en Irlande ont considérablement augmenté leur patrimoine ; et ils viennent d'être récemment rétablis dans les honneurs de la pairie. Cependant les Courtenai conservent encore la devise plaintive qui déplore la chute de leur maison, et en affirme l'innocence (1). Le regret de leur grandeur passée ne les rend pas sans doute insensibles à leur prospérité présente. Dans les annales des Courtenai, l'époque la plus brillante est en même temps celle de leurs plus grandes calamités ; et un pair opulent de la Grande-Bretagne ne doit pas porter envie à des empereurs de Constantinople, qui parcouraient l'Europe en sollicitant des aumônes pour le soutien de leur dignité et la défense de leur capitale.

---

(1) *Ubi lapsus? quid feci?* Légende qui fut sans doute adoptée par la branche de Powderham après la perte du comté de Devon, etc. Les armes de Courtenai étaient primitivement d'or, trois tourteaux de gueules, qui semblent indiquer une affinité avec Godefroi de Bouillon et les anciens comtes de Boulogne.

CHAPITRE LXII.

Les empereurs grecs de Nicée et de Constantinople. Élévation et règne de Michel Paléologue. Sa fausse réunion avec le pape et l'Église latine. Projets hostiles du duc d'Anjou. Révolte de la Sicile. Guerre des Catalans dans l'Asie et dans la Grèce. Révolutions et situation présente d'Athènes.

<small>Rétablissement de l'empire grec.</small>

La perte de Constantinople rendit aux Grecs un instant de vigueur. Les princes et les nobles quittèrent le luxe de leurs palais pour courir aux armes, et les plus forts ou les plus habiles se saisirent des débris de la monarchie. On trouverait difficilement dans les longs et stériles volumes des annales de Byzance (1) deux princes comparables à Théodore Lascaris et à Jean Ducas Vatacès (2), qui replantèrent et maintin-

---

(1) Pour les règnes des empereurs de Nicée, et principalement de Vatacès et de son fils, nous n'avons point d'autre écrivain contemporain que George Acropolita leur ministre; mais George Pachymère revint à Constantinople avec les Grecs à l'âge de dix-neuf ans (Hanckius., *de Script. byzant.*, c. 33, 34, p. 564-578; Fabricius, *Bibl. græc.*, t. VI, p. 448-460). Cependant l'histoire de Nicéphore Grégoras, quoique du quatorzième siècle, est une excellente relation des événemens depuis la prise de Constantinople par les Latins.

(2) Nicéphore Grégoras (l. II, c. 1) distingue entre le οξεια ορμη de Lascaris et l'ευσταθεια de Vatacès. Les deux portraits sont également bien dessinés.

rent l'étendard romain sur les murs de Nicée en Bithynie. La différence de leur caractère se trouva parfaitement adaptée à leur situation. Durant ses premiers efforts, le fugitif Lascaris ne possédait que trois villes et ne commandait que deux mille soldats. Un généreux désespoir le soutint dans toutes les actions de son règne ; dans toutes ses opérations militaires, il mit au hasard sa vie et sa couronne. Son activité surprit ses ennemis de l'Hellespont et du Méandre, et son intrépidité parvint à les réduire. Dix-huit années de règne et de victoire donnèrent à la principauté de Nicée l'étendue d'un empire. Vatacès, gendre et successeur de Théodore Lascaris, trouva le trône fondé sur une base plus solide, et soutenu par de plus abondantes ressources. Le caractère du nouveau souverain ainsi que le genre de sa situation le portaient à calculer le danger, à épier l'occasion et à préparer le succès de ses desseins ambitieux. En racontant la chute de l'empire latin, j'ai brièvement rapporté les succès des Grecs, les démarches prudentes et les progrès successifs d'un conquérant qui, dans un règne de trente-trois années, délivra les provinces de la tyrannie des nationaux et des étrangers, et serra de toutes parts la capitale, tronc dépouillé et déraciné prêt à tomber au premier coup de la hache. Mais son économie intérieure et sa paisible administration sont encore plus dignes d'éloge et d'admiration (1). Les calamités de la guerre

Théodore Lascaris.
A. D.
1204-1222.

Jean Ducas Vatacès.
A. D.
1222-1225,
octobre 30.

―――――――――――――――――――――

(1) Pachymère, l. 1, c. 23, 24 ; Nicéphore Grégoras,

avaient diminué la population et détruit les moyens de subsistance : on n'avait plus ni moyens ni motifs pour s'occuper de l'agriculture ; les terres les plus fertiles demeuraient en friche et inhabitées. L'empereur en fit exploiter une partie à son bénéfice : elles profitèrent entre ses mains, sous ses yeux vigilans, plus qu'elles ne l'eussent pu faire par les soins minutieux d'un fermier. Les domaines royaux devinrent le jardin et le grenier de l'Asie, et, sans opprimer ses peuples, le souverain acquit un fonds de richesses fécondes et légitimes. Selon la nature du terrain, il faisait semer des grains ou planter des vignes, et couvrait de brebis ou de pourceaux ses vastes pâturages. En présentant à l'impératrice une couronne enrichie de perles et de diamans, l'empereur lui apprit en souriant que l'achat de cet ornement précieux avait été payé de la vente des œufs, produit de son immense basse-cour. Le revenu de ses domaines servait à la consommation de son palais et à celle des hôpitaux, à soutenir sa dignité et à satisfaire sa bienfaisance. L'influence de l'exemple fut encore plus avantageux que le revenu. La charrue reprit ses honneurs et sa sécurité. Renonçant à couvrir leur fastueuse indigence des dépouilles arrachées au peuple ou des faveurs mendiées à la cour, et que le peuple paie toujours, les nobles cherchèrent dans les productions de leurs domaines un revenu plus

---

¹ l. II, c. 6. Celui qui lira les historiens de Byzance observera combien il est rare d'y trouver des détails si précieux.

sûr et plus indépendant. Les Turcs s'empressèrent d'acheter le superflu des grains et des troupeaux ; Vatacès entretint soigneusement leur alliance ; mais il découragea l'importation des produits de l'industrie étrangère, des soieries du Levant et des manufactures de l'Italie. « Les besoins de la nature, disait Vatacès, sont indispensables à satisfaire, mais le caprice de la mode peut naître et périr en un jour. » Par ces préceptes et son exemple, le sage monarque encourageait la simplicité des mœurs, l'industrie nationale et l'économie domestique. L'éducation de la jeunesse et l'éclat des lettres furent principalement l'objet de ses soins ; et Vatacès disait avec vérité, sans prétendre décider de la préséance, qu'un prince et un philosophe sont les deux plus éminens caractères de la société humaine (1). Il eut pour première épouse Irène, fille de Théodore Lascaris, plus illustre par son mérite personnel et les vertus de son sexe, que par le sang des Comnènes qui coulait dans ses veines, et transmit à son mari ses droits à l'empire. Après la mort de cette princesse, il épousa Anne ou Constance, fille naturelle de l'empereur Frédéric II. Mais comme elle n'avait pas atteint l'âge de puberté, Vatacès reçut dans son lit une Italienne de sa suite. Les charmes ou les artifices de cette con-

---

(1) Μονοι γαρ απαντων ανθρωπων ονομαστοτατοι Βασιλευς και φιλοσοφος (Greg. Acropol.; c. 32). L'empereur examinait et encourageait, dans ses conversations familières, les études de son futur logothète.

cubine obtinrent de la faiblesse de son amant tous les honneurs d'une impératrice, dont il ne lui manqua que le titre. Les moines traitèrent cette faiblesse de crime énorme et damnable; mais la violence de leurs invectives ne servit qu'à faire éclater la patience de leur souverain. La philosophie de notre siècle pardonnera sans doute à ce prince un seul vice racheté par une foule de vertus; et les contemporains de Vatacès accordèrent à ses fautes, ainsi qu'aux passions plus impétueuses de Lascaris, une indulgence due aux restaurateurs de l'empire (1). Les Grecs qui gémissaient encore sous le joug des Latins, privés de lois et de tranquillité, vantaient le bonheur de ceux qui avaient recouvré la liberté nationale, et Vatacès, par une louable politique, eut soin de les convaincre qu'il était de leur intérêt de passer sous son gouvernement.

Théodore Lascaris II. A. D. 1255, octob. 30. A. D 1259, août.

La dégénération se fait fortement sentir entre Jean Vatacès et Théodore, son fils et son successeur, du fondateur de l'empire qui sut en soutenir le poids, à l'héritier qui ne fit que jouir de son éclat (2). Cepen-

---

(1) Comparez Acropolita (c. 18-52) avec les deux premiers livres de Nicéphore Grégoras.

(2) Un proverbe persan dit que Cyrus fut le père de ses sujets; et que Darius en fut le maître. On appliqua ce proverbe à Vatacès et à son fils; mais Pachymère a confondu Darius, prince humain, avec Cambyse, despote et tyran de son peuple. Le poids des taxes avait fait donner à Darius le nom moins odieux mais plus méprisable de Καπηλος, marchand ou courtier (Hérodote, III, 89).

dant le caractère de Théodore ne manquait pas d'énergie ; il avait été élevé à l'école de son père et dans l'exercice des armes et de la chasse. Constantinople ne tomba point encore ; mais, dans les trois années de son règne, il conduisit trois fois ses armées victorieuses jusque dans le cœur de la Bulgarie. La colère et la méfiance ternissaient ses vertus ; on peut attribuer la première peut-être au malheur de n'avoir jamais eu à supporter la contrariété, l'autre pouvait provenir de quelques aperçus obscurs et imparfaits sur la dépravation du genre humain. Dans une de ses marches en Bulgarie, il consulta ses principaux ministres sur une question de politique, et le grand logothète, George Acropolita, osa soutenir avec sincérité une opinion qui blessait l'empereur. Celui-ci porta la main sur son cimeterre ; mais, par un second mouvement, il réserva à Acropolita une punition plus ignominieuse. Cet officier, l'un des premiers de l'empire, reçut l'ordre de descendre de cheval ; il fut dépouillé de ses vêtemens en présence du prince et de l'armée, et après l'avoir étendu sur la terre, deux gardes ou exécuteurs le frappèrent si long-temps et si cruellement de leurs bâtons, qu'au moment où l'empereur leur ordonna de cesser, le grand logothète eut à peine la force de se relever et de se traîner dans sa tente. Après une retraite de quelques jours, les ordres absolus de Théodore le rappelèrent au conseil ; et les Grecs étaient si entièrement morts à tout sentiment d'honneur et de honte, que c'est l'offensé lui-même qui nous apprend son ignominie (1). Une maladie dangereuse, la perspective d'une mort prochaine et le soupçon du poison ou de la magie, irritèrent la cruauté de l'empereur; chacun de ses accès de colère coûtait la fortune ou la vie, la vue ou quelques membres à quelques-uns de ses parens et de ses principaux officiers; et sur la fin de sa vie, le fils de Vatacès mérita du peuple, où du moins de sa cour, le surnom de tyran. Offensé par le refus que fit une matrone de la famille des Paléologues, de donner sa fille, jeune personne d'une grande beauté, à un vil plébéien que l'empereur favorisait par caprice, il la fit mettre, sans égard pour son rang et son âge, jusqu'au cou dans un sac avec des chats dont on animait la fureur en les piquant avec des aiguilles. Dans ses derniers momens, Théodore exprima le désir d'obtenir le pardon de ses cruautés et de les effacer par la clémence; inquiet du sort d'un fils âgé de huit ans, que cet âge condamnait aux dangers d'une longue minorité, son dernier choix en confia la tutelle à la sainteté du patriarche Arsène et à la valeur de George Muzalon, grand-domestique, également chéri du prince et détesté du peuple. Les rapports des Grecs avec les Latins avaient

Minorité de Jean Lascaris. A. D. 1259, août.

───────────────────

(1) Acropolita (c. 63) semble s'applaudir de la fermeté avec laquelle il reçut la bastonnade, et son absence du conseil jusqu'au moment où il y fut rappelé. Il raconte les exploits de Théodore et ses propres services, depuis le chapitre 53 jusqu'au chapitre 74 de son histoire. *Voyez* le troisième livre de Nicéphore Grégoras.

introduit dans leur monarchie les titres et les priviléges héréditaires ; et les familles nobles (1) s'indignèrent de l'élévation d'un favori sans mérite, qu'elles croyaient coupable des erreurs du dernier empereur et des calamités de son règne. Dans le premier conseil, après la mort de Théodore, Muzalon prononça du haut du trône une apologie très-travaillée de sa conduite et de ses intentions ; on accabla sa modestie de protestations d'estime et de fidélité ; et ses plus implacables ennemis furent les plus empressés à lui donner le titre de gardien et de sauveur des Romains. Huit jours suffirent pour préparer le succès d'une conspiration. On célébra, le neuvième, les obsèques du monarque défunt dans la cathédrale de Magnésie (2), ville d'Asie, située sur les bords de l'Hermus, au pied du mont Sipylus, et dans laquelle il était mort. La cérémonie fut interrompue par une sédi-

---

(1) Pachymère (l. 1, c. 21) nomme et distingue quinze à vingt familles grecques ; και οσοι αλλοι, οις η μεγαλογενης σειρα και χρυση συγκεκροτητο. Entend-il par cette décoration une chaîne métaphorique ou réellement une chaîne d'or ? peut-être l'une et l'autre.

(2) Les anciens géographes, ainsi que Cellarius, d'Anville et nos voyageurs, particulièrement Pococke et Chandler, nous apprendront à distinguer les deux Magnésie de l'Asie-Mineure, celle du Méandre et celle du Sipylus. La dernière, celle dont nous avons parlé, est encore florissante pour une ville turque. Elle est située à huit heures de chemin ou huit lieues au nord-est de Smyrne. Tournefort, *Voyages du Levant*, t. III, lettre XXII, p. 365-370 ; *Voyages de Chandler dans l'Asie-Mineure*, p. 267.

tion des gardes; Muzalon, ses frères et tous leurs partisans, furent massacrés au pied de l'autel; et l'on donna pour nouveau collègue au patriarche absent, Michel Paléologue, le plus illustre des Grecs par son mérite et par sa naissance (1).

<small>Famille et caractère de Michel Paléologue.</small>

Parmi ceux qui sont fiers de leurs ancêtres, le plus grand nombre est réduit à se contenter d'une gloire locale ou domestique; il y en a peu qui osassent confier les mémoires particuliers de leur famille aux annales de leur nation. Dès le milieu du onzième siècle, la noble race des Paléologues (2) paraît avec éclat dans l'histoire de Byzance. Ce fut le vaillant George Paléologue qui plaça sur le trône le père des Comnènes; et ses parens ou ses descendans continuèrent, dans les générations suivantes, à commander les armées et à présider les conseils de l'État. La famille impériale ne dédaigna point leur alliance; et si l'ordre de succession par les femmes eût été strictement observé, la femme de Théodore Lascaris aurait cédé à sa sœur aînée, mère de Michel Paléologue, celui qui éleva depuis sa famille sur le trône. A l'illustration de la naissance; il joignait les plus bril-

---

(1) *Voyez* Acropolita (c. 75, 76, etc.), qui vivait trop près de cette époque; Pachymère (l. I; c. 12-25), Grégoras (l. III; c. 3, 4, 5).

(2) Ducange (*Famil. byzant.*, p. 230, etc.) éclaircit la généalogie de Paléologue. On trouve les événemens de sa vie privée dans Pachym. (l. I; c. 7-12) et Grégoras (l. II, 8; l. III, 2-4; l. IV, 1). Il favorise visiblement le fondateur de la dynastie régnante.

lantes qualités politiques et militaires. Paléologue avait été élevé, dès sa première jeunesse, à l'office de connétable ou commandant des Français mercenaires; sa dépense personnelle n'excédait jamais trois pièces d'or par jour, mais son ambition le rendait avide et prodigue, et ses dons tiraient un nouveau prix de l'affabilité de ses manières et de sa conversation. L'amour que lui portaient le peuple et les soldats excita les inquiétudes de la cour, et Michel échappa trois fois au danger qu'il courut par son imprudence ou par celle de ses partisans. 1° Sous le règne de Vatacès et de la justice, il s'éleva une dispute entre deux officiers (1), dont l'un accusait l'autre de soutenir le droit héréditaire des Paléologues. La contestation fut décidée d'après la jurisprudence nouvellement empruntée des Latins, par un combat singulier. L'accusé succomba, mais persista toujours à se déclarer seul coupable, et affirma que son patron n'avait point approuvé ses propos imprudens ou criminels, dont il n'était pas même instruit. Cependant des soupçons pesaient sur le connétable; les murmures de la malveillance le poursuivaient partout, et l'archevêque de Philadelphie, adroit courtisan, le pressa d'accepter le jugement de Dieu, et de se justifier par l'épreuve du feu (2). Trois jours avant l'épreuve, on envelop-

---

(1) Acropolita (c. 50) raconte les circonstances de cette curieuse aventure, qui semble avoir échappé aux historiens plus modernes.

(2) Pachym. (l. 1, c. 12), qui parle de cette épreuve bar-

pait le bras du patient dans un sac scellé du cachet royal, et il devait porter trois fois une boule de fer rougie au feu, depuis l'autel jusqu'à la balustrade du sanctuaire, sans employer d'artifice, et sans ressentir de mal. Paléologue éluda cette expérience dangereuse par une plaisanterie adroite. « Je suis soldat, dit-il, et prêt à combattre mes accusateurs les armes à la main; mais un profane, un pécheur n'a point le don des miracles; votre piété, très-saint prélat, mérite sans doute l'interposition du ciel, et je recevrai de vos mains la boule ardente qui doit être le garant de mon innocence. » L'archevêque fut déconcerté, l'empereur sourit; de nouveaux services et de nouveaux honneurs valurent à Michel son absolution ou son pardon. 2° Sous le règne suivant, tandis qu'il était gouverneur de Nicée, on l'informa, dans l'absence du prince, qu'il avait tout à craindre de sa méfiance, et que la mort ou au moins la perte des yeux finirait par être sa récompense. Au lieu d'attendre l'arrivée et la sentence de Théodore, le connétable, suivi de quelques serviteurs, s'échappa de la ville et de l'empire, fut pillé en route par les Turcomans du désert, mais trouva cependant un asile à la cour du sultan. Dans cette situation équivoque, l'illustre exilé

---

bare avec le mépris qu'elle mérite, affirme que dans sa jeunesse il a vu plusieurs personnes s'en tirer sans accident. Il était Grec, et par conséquent crédule; mais l'esprit ingénieux des Grecs leur avait peut-être fourni quelque remède ou quelque moyen d'adresse ou d'artifice à opposer à leur propre superstition ou à celle de leur tyran.

remplit également les devoirs de la reconnaissance et ceux du patriotisme, en repoussant les Tartares, en faisant passer des avis aux garnisons romaines de la frontière, et en parvenant à faire conclure un traité de paix dans lequel on stipula honorablement sa grâce et son rappel. 3° Tandis qu'il défendait l'Orient contre les entreprises du despote d'Épire, le prince le condamna sur de nouveaux soupçons; et, soit faiblesse ou fidélité, Michel se laissa charger de chaînes et conduire de Durazzo à Nicée, environ à six cents milles. Le respect du messager, chargé de le conduire, sut adoucir cette commission; la maladie de l'empereur fit cesser le danger; et Théodore, au moment d'expirer, en recommandant son fils à Paléologue, reconnut à la fois son innocence et son pouvoir.

Mais on avait trop outragé son innocence, et il connaissait trop bien son pouvoir pour qu'on dût espérer de l'arrêter dans la carrière ouverte à son ambition (1). Au conseil tenu après la mort de Théodore, il fut le premier à jurer fidélité à Muzalon; il fut ensuite le premier à violer ce serment, et sa conduite fut si adroite, qu'il tira tout l'avantage du massacre qui eut lieu peu de jours après, sans en partager le crime, ou du moins le reproche. Dans le

Son élévation au trône.

---

(1) Sans comparer Pachymère à Tacite ou à Thucydide, je dois louer l'éloquence, la clarté, et même à un certain point la liberté avec lesquelles il raconte l'élévation de Paléologue (l. 1, c. 13-32; l. ii, c. 1-9). Acropolita est plus circonspect, et Grégoras moins étendu.

choix d'un régent, il balança les intérêts et les passions des candidats, et, en les animant l'un contre l'autre, il disposa chacun d'eux à déclarer qu'après lui Paléologue méritait la préférence. Sous le titre de grand-duc, il accepta ou s'attribua dans l'État, durant une longue minorité, l'autorité exécutive. Le patriarche n'était qu'un fantôme respectable, et Paléologue séduisit ou dissipa les factions des nobles par l'ascendant de son génie. Vatacès avait déposé les fruits de son économie dans une forteresse située sur les bords de l'Hermus, sous la garde des fidèles Varangiens. Le connétable conserva son autorité ou son influence sur les troupes étrangères : il se servit des gardes pour envahir le trésor, et du trésor pour corrompre les gardes ; et quelque abus qu'il pût faire des richesses publiques, on ne le soupçonna jamais d'avarice ou d'avidité personnelle. Par ses discours et ceux de ses émissaires, Paléologue s'efforça de persuader aux sujets de toutes les classes que leur prospérité augmenterait en proportion de son pouvoir. Il suspendit la rigueur des taxes, objet des réclamations perpétuelles du peuple; et défendit les épreuves du feu et les combats judiciaires. Ces institutions barbares étaient déjà ou abolies ou décréditées en France (1) et en Angleterre (2), et le jugement

---

(1) Saint Louis abolit le combat judiciaire dans ses domaines, et à la longue, son exemple et son autorité prévalurent dans toute la France (*Esprit des lois*, l. XXVIII, c. 29).

(2) Dans les causes civiles, Henri II laissait le choix au

de l'épée était contraire à la raison d'un peuple civilisé (1), ainsi qu'aux dispositions d'un peuple pusillanime. Le régent s'affectionna les vétérans en assurant la subsistance de leurs veuves et de leurs enfans. Le prêtre et le philosophe applaudirent à son zèle pour le progrès des sciences et la pureté de la religion ; et tous les candidats s'appliquèrent personnellement ses promesses vagues de ne point laisser le mérite sans récompense. Connaissant l'influence du clergé, Michel travailla avec succès à s'assurer les suffrages de cet ordre puissant. Le voyage dispendieux de Nicée à Magnésie lui en fournit un prétexte honnête. Dans des visites nocturnes, le régent sé-

---

défendeur. Glanville préfère les preuves par témoins ; et le combat judiciaire est condamné dans le Fleta : cependant la loi anglaise n'a jamais abrogé l'épreuve par le combat, et les juges l'ordonnèrent encore au commencement du dernier siècle.

(1) Cependant un de mes amis, homme d'esprit, m'a fourni plusieurs motifs qui excusent cette pratique : 1° elle convenait peut-être à des peuples à peine sortis de la barbarie ; 2° elle modérait la licence de la guerre entre particuliers, et les fureurs des vengeances arbitraires ; 3° elle était moins absurde que les épreuves du feu, de l'eau bouillante ou de la croix, qu'elle contribua à abolir. Elle était au moins une preuve de valeur, qualité qui se réunit si rarement avec la bassesse des sentimens, que le danger de l'appel au combat pouvait contenir les poursuites de la malveillance, et devenir une barrière contre l'injustice soutenue du pouvoir. Le brave et malheureux comte de Surrey aurait probablement évité un sort qu'il ne méritait pas, si sa demande de combat n'eût pas été rejetée.

duisit les prélats par des libéralités, et flatta la vanité de l'incorruptible patriarche par l'hommage qu'il lui rendit, conduisant sa mule dans les rues de la ville, et écartant la foule à une distance respectueuse. Sans renoncer aux droits de sa naissance, Paléologue encouragea la libre discussion des avantages d'une monarchie élective, et ses partisans demandèrent d'un ton triomphant quel serait le malade qui voudrait confier le soin de sa santé, ou quel marchand voudrait hasarder la conduite de son vaisseau aux talens d'un médecin ou d'un pilote héréditaire. L'enfance de l'empereur, et les dangers d'une longue minorité, exigeaient la protection d'un régent qui eût de l'âge et de l'expérience ; d'un associé au-dessus de la jalousie de ses égaux, et revêtu du titre et des prérogatives de la royauté. Pour l'avantage du prince et des peuples, sans aucune vue d'intérêt pour lui-même ou pour sa famille, le grand-duc consentit à se charger de la tutelle et de l'éducation du fils de Théodore ; mais il attendait avec impatience l'heureux moment où les mains du jeune empereur seraient assez fermes pour débarrasser son tuteur des rênes de l'administration, et lui procurer la douceur de rentrer dans sa paisible obscurité. On lui donna d'abord le titre et les prérogatives de *despote*, qui faisaient jouir des honneurs de la pourpre et du second rang dans la monarchie romaine. Il fut ensuite convenu que Jean et Michel seraient proclamés empereurs collègues, et élevés l'un et l'autre sur un bouclier ; mais que le droit du premier à la succession lui conserverait la prééminence. Les augustes associés se jurèrent une amitié inviolable, et consentirent que les sujets s'obligeassent, par serment, à se déclarer contre l'agresseur; expression équivoque, propre à servir de prétexte à la discorde et à la guerre civile. Paléologue paraissait satisfait; mais, à la cérémonie du couronnement, dans la cathédrale de Nicée, ses partisans réclamèrent hautement la préséance due à son âge et à son mérite. On éluda cette contestation déplacée, en remettant le couronnement de Jean Lascaris à une circonstance plus favorable; et le jeune prince, décoré d'une légère couronne, parut à la suite de son tuteur, qui reçut seul le diadême impérial des mains du patriarche. Ce ne fut pas sans une extrême répugnance qu'Arsène abandonna les intérêts de son pupille; mais les Varangiens élevèrent leur hache de bataille, et arrachèrent à l'enfance timide du prince légitime un signe d'approbation. Quelques voix firent entendre que l'existence d'un enfant né devait plus mettre obstacle à la prospérité de la nation. Paléologue, reconnaissant, distribua libéralement à ses amis les emplois civils et militaires. Il créa dans sa propre famille un despote et deux sebastocrateurs; Alexis Strategopulus obtint le titre de César, et ce vieux général paya bientôt son élévation à l'empereur grec, en le remettant en possession de Constantinople.

Michel Paléologue, empereur. A. D. 1260, janv.

Ce fut dans la seconde année de son règne, tandis qu'il résidait dans le palais et les jardins de Nym-

Conquête de Constantinople. A. D. 1261, 25 juillet.

phée (1), près de Smyrne, que Michel reçut dans la nuit la première nouvelle de cet incroyable succès, que, par les tendres soins de sa sœur Eulogie, on ne lui annonça qu'après l'avoir fait éveiller avec précaution. Le messager, homme obscur et inconnu, ne produisait point de lettre du général victorieux; la défaite de Vatacès, et plus récemment l'entreprise inutile de Paléologue lui-même, ne lui permettaient point de penser que huit cents soldats eussent surpris la capitale. On arrêta le messager suspect, en lui promettant de grandes récompenses si sa nouvelle se réalisait, et la mort si elle se trouvait fausse. La cour demeura quelques heures dans les alternatives de la crainte et de l'espérance, jusqu'au moment où les messagers d'Alexis arrivèrent avec les trophées de la victoire, l'épée, le sceptre (2), les brodequins et le bonnet (3) de Baudouin l'usurpateur, qu'il avait

---

(1) Les géographies anciennes et modernes ne fixent pas précisément l'endroit où Nymphée était située; mais, d'après le récit des derniers momens de Vatacès, il est évident que le palais et les jardins qu'il se plaisait de préférence à habiter étaient dans le voisinage de Smyrne (Acropolita, c. 52). On peut vaguement placer Nymphée dans la Lydie (Grégoras, l. VI, 6).

(2) Ce sceptre, l'emblème de la justice et de la puissance, était un long bâton tel que ceux dont se servaient les héros d'Homère. Les Grecs modernes le nommèrent *dicanice*; et le sceptre impérial était distingué, comme le reste, par sa couleur rouge ou de pourpre.

(3) Acropolita affirme (c. 87) que ce bonnet était à la mode française; mais, à raison du rubis qui était sur la forme,

laissés tomber dans sa fuite précipitée. On convoqua sur-le-champ une assemblée des prélats, des nobles et des sénateurs; et jamais peut-être événement ne causa une joie plus vive et plus universelle. Le nouveau souverain de Constantinople se félicita, dans un discours étudié, de sa fortune et de celle de la nation. « Il fut un temps, dit-il, un temps bien éloigné, où l'empire des Romains s'étendait de la mer Adriatique au Tigre, et jusqu'aux confins de l'Éthiopie. Après la perte des provinces, la capitale elle-même, dans ces jours de calamité, a été envahie par les Barbares d'Occident. Du dernier degré du malheur, le flot de la prospérité nous a soulevés de nouveau; mais nous étions toujours exilés et fugitifs; et quand on nous demandait où était la patrie des Romains, nous indiquions en rougissant le climat du globe et la région du ciel. La Providence divine a favorisé nos armes: elle nous a rendu la ville de Constantin, le siége de l'empire et de la religion. Notre valeur et notre conduite peuvent faire de cette précieuse acquisition le présage et le garant de nouvelles victoires. » Telle était l'impatience du prince et du peuple, que vingt jours après l'expulsion des Latins, Michel entra triomphant dans Constantinople. A son approche on ouvrit la porte d'or; le pieux conquérant descendit de son cheval,

Retour de l'empereur grec.
A. D. 1261, 14 août.

Ducange (*Hist. de C. P.*, l. v, c. 28, 29) suppose que c'était un chapeau à haute forme, tel que les Grecs les portaient. Cependant Acropolita pouvait-il s'y tromper?

et fit porter devant lui une image miraculeuse de Marie la conductrice, afin que la Vierge semblât le conduire elle-même au temple de son fils, la cathédrale de Sainte-Sophie. Mais, après les premiers transports de dévotion et d'orgueil, il contempla en soupirant les ruines et la solitude que présentait sa capitale désolée. Le palais, souillé de fumée et de boue, portait partout les traces de la grossière intempérance des Français; des rues entières avaient été consumées par le feu, ou dégradées par les injures du temps; les édifices sacrés et profanes étaient dépouillés de leurs ornemens; et, comme si les Latins eussent prévu le moment de leur expulsion, ils avaient borné leur industrie au pillage et à la destruction. L'anarchie et la misère avaient anéanti le commerce, et la population avait disparu avec la richesse. Le premier soin du monarque grec fut de rétablir les nobles dans les palais de leurs pères; tous ceux qui purent présenter des titres rentrèrent en possession de leurs maisons ou du terrain qu'elles avaient occupé. Mais la plupart des propriétaires n'existaient plus, et le fisc en hérita. Michel repeupla Constantinople en y attirant les habitans des provinces, et les braves volontaires, ses libérateurs, y obtinrent un établissement. Les barons français et les principales familles s'étaient retirés avec l'empereur; mais la foule patiente des Latins obscurs chérissait le pays, et s'embarrassait peu du changement de maître. Au lieu de bannir les Pisans, les Génois et les Vénitiens de leurs factoreries, le sage conquérant reçut leur serment de fidélité, encouragea leur industrie, confirma leurs privilèges, et leur permit de conserver leur juridiction et leurs magistrats. Les Pisans et les Vénitiens continuèrent à occuper dans la ville leurs quartiers séparés; mais les Génois méritaient à la fois la reconnaissance des Grecs, et excitèrent leur jalousie. Leur colonie indépendante s'était d'abord fixée à Héraclée dans un port de la Thrace. On les rappela, et ils obtinrent la possession exclusive du faubourg de Galata, poste avantageux où ils ranimèrent leur commerce, et insultèrent à la majesté de l'empire de Byzance (1).

On célébra le retour à Constantinople comme l'époque d'un nouvel empire : le conquérant seul, et par le droit de son épée, renouvela la cérémonie de son couronnement dans la cathédrale de Sainte-Sophie ; Jean Lascaris, son pupille et son légitime souverain, vit insensiblement ses honneurs détruits et son nom effacé des actes du gouvernement ; mais ses droits subsistaient encore dans le souvenir des peuples, et le jeune monarque avançait vers l'âge de la virilité et de l'ambition. Soit crainte ou scrupule, Paléologue ne souilla point ses mains du sang d'un prince innocent ; mais, balancé entre les sentimens d'un usurpateur et ceux d'un parent, il s'assura la possession du trône par un de ces crimes imparfaits avec

Paléologue bannit le jeune empereur après lui avoir fait crever les yeux. A. D. 1261, 25 déc.

---

(1) *Voyez* Pachym. (l. II, 28-33), Acropolita (c. 88), Nicéphore Grégoras (l. IV, 7), et pour la manière dont furent traités les sujets latins, Ducange (l. V, c. 30, 31).

lesquels l'habitude avait familiarisé les Grecs modernes : la perte de la vue rendait un prince incapable de gouverner l'empire ; au lieu de lui arracher douloureusement les yeux, on en détruisit le nerf optique, en les exposant à la réverbération ardente d'un bassin rougi au feu (1), et Jean Lascaris fut relégué dans un château écarté, où il languit obscurément durant un grand nombre d'années. Ce crime réfléchi peut paraître incompatible avec les remords ; mais, en supposant que Michel comptât sur la miséricorde du ciel, il n'en demeurait pas moins exposé aux reproches et à la vengeance des hommes, qu'il avait mérités par sa barbare perfidie. Intimidés par sa cruauté, ses vils courtisans applaudissaient ou gardaient le silence ; mais le clergé pouvait parler au nom d'un maître invisible, et avait pour chef un prélat inaccessible aux tentations de la crainte et de l'espoir. Après une courte abdication de sa dignité, Arsène (2) avait consenti à occuper de nouveau le

---

(1) Cette manière moins barbare de priver de la vue fut essayée, dit-on, par Démocrite, qui en fit l'expérience sur lui-même lorsqu'il voulut se débarrasser de la vue du monde. Cette histoire est absurde. Le mot *abbacinare*, en latin et en italien, a fourni à Ducange (*Gloss. latin.*) l'occasion de passer en revue les différentes manières d'ôter la vue ou d'aveugler. Les plus violentes étaient d'arracher les yeux, de les brûler avec un fer rouge ou du vinaigre bouillant, ou de serrer la tête avec une corde si violemment que les yeux en sortissent. Que la tyrannie est ingénieuse !

(2) *Voyez* la première retraite et le rétablissement d'Arsène, dans Pachym. (l. II, c. 15 ; l. III, c. 1-2), et Nic.

trône ecclésiastique de Constantinople, et à présider
à la restauration de l'Église. Les artifices de Paléologue s'étaient joués long-temps de la pieuse simplicité
du prélat, qui se flattait, par sa patience et sa soumission, d'adoucir l'usurpateur et de protéger le jeune
empereur. Lorsque Arsène apprit le funeste sort de
Lascaris, il se résolut à employer les armes spirituelles, et cette fois la superstition combattit pour la
cause de la justice et de l'humanité. Dans un synode
d'évêques animés par son exemple, le patriarche prononça contre Michel une sentence d'excommunication ; mais il eut la prudence de continuer à le nommer dans les prières publiques. Les prélats d'Orient
n'avaient point adopté les dangereuses maximes de
l'ancienne Rome ; ils ne se croyaient point en droit,
pour appuyer leurs censures, de déposer les monarques et de délier leurs sujets du serment de fidélité ;
mais le criminel séparé de Dieu et de l'Église devenait un objet d'horreur, et dans une capitale habitée
par des fanatiques turbulens, cette horreur pouvait
armer le bras d'un assassin ou exciter une sédition.
Paléologue sentit le danger, confessa son crime, et
implora la clémence de son juge ; le mal était irréparable ; il en avait obtenu le prix, et la rigueur de
la pénitence qu'il sollicitait pouvait effacer la faute
et élever le pécheur à la réputation d'un saint ; mais

Paléologue est excommunié par le patriarche Arsène.
A. D. 1262-1268.

Grég. (l. III, c. 1 ; l. IV, c. 1). La postérité blâme avec justice dans Arsène l'αφελεια et la ραθυμια, vertus d'un ermite et
vices d'un ministre (l. XII, c. 2).

l'inflexible patriarche refusa d'indiquer un moyen d'expiation ou de donner aucun espoir de miséricorde. Il daigna seulement prononcer que pour un si grand crime la réparation devait être forte. « Faut-il, dit Michel, que j'abdique l'empire ? » et il offrait ou semblait offrir de remettre l'épée impériale. Arsène fit un mouvement pour saisir ce gage de la souveraineté ; mais lorsqu'il s'aperçut que l'empereur n'était point disposé à payer si cher son absolution (1), il se retira dans sa cellule avec indignation, et laissa le monarque suppliant, en larmes et à genoux devant la porte.

Schisme des arsénites. A. D. 1266-1312.

Le spectacle et le danger de cette excommunication subsistèrent durant plus de trois années. Le temps et le repentir de Michel firent cesser les clameurs du peuple, et les prélats condamnèrent la rigueur d'Arsène comme opposée à la douceur de l'Évangile. L'empereur fit adroitement pressentir que si on rejetait encore sa soumission, il pourrait trouver à Rome un juge plus indulgent ; mais il était plus simple et plus utile de placer à la tête de l'Église byzantine le juge que pouvait désirer l'empereur. On mêla le nom d'Arsène dans quelques bruits vagues de mécontentement et de conspiration ; quelques irrégularités de son ordination et de son gouverne-

---

(1) Le crime et l'excommunication de Michel sont racontés avec impartialité par Pachymère (l. III, c. 10, 14, 19, etc.) et par Grégoras (l. IV, c. 4) : sa confession et sa pénitence leur rendirent la liberté.

ment spirituel fournirent un prétexte ; un synode le déposa, et une garde de soldats le transporta dans une petite île de la Propontide. Avant de partir pour son exil, le patriarche exigea avec hauteur qu'on prît un état des trésors de l'Église, déclara qu'il ne possédait personnellement que trois pièces d'or, qu'il avait gagnées à copier des psaumes, conserva toute l'indépendance de son caractère, et refusa jusqu'au dernier soupir le pardon imploré par l'empereur (1). Quelque temps après son départ, Grégoire, évêque d'Andrinople, vint occuper le siége de Byzance ; mais il n'avait pas par lui-même assez d'autorité pour donner à l'absolution de l'empereur toute l'authenticité qu'on pouvait désirer : Joseph, vénérable moine, remplit cette importante fonction ; cette édifiante cérémonie eut lieu en présence du sénat et du peuple. Au bout de six ans, l'humble pénitent parvint à rentrer dans la communion des fidèles, et il est satisfaisant pour l'humanité de penser que la première condition imposée à l'usurpateur fut d'adoucir le sort de l'infortuné Lascaris ; mais l'esprit d'Arsène subsistait toujours dans une faction puissante qui s'était formée parmi les moines et le clergé, et qui entretint un schisme de plus de quarante-huit ans. Michel et son fils, respectant leurs scrupules, n'es-

---

(1) Pachymère raconte l'exil d'Arsène (l. IV, c. 1-16). Il fut un des commissaires qui le visitèrent dans son île déserte. Le dernier testament de l'inflexible patriarche existe encore. Dupin, *Biblioth. ecclés.*, t. x, p. 95.

sayèrent de les attaquer qu'avec délicatesse, et la réconciliation des arsénites occupa sérieusement l'État et l'Église. Pleins de la confiance qu'inspire le fanatisme, ils avaient proposé d'éprouver par un miracle la justice de leur cause : on jeta dans un brasier ardent deux papiers sur lesquels étaient inscrits leur sentiment et celui de leurs adversaires, et ils ne doutèrent pas que les flammes ne respectassent la vérité; mais hélas! les deux papiers furent également consumés, et cet accident imprévu, qui rétablit la paix durant un jour, prolongea la querelle pendant une génération (1). Le traité final donna la victoire aux arsénites : le clergé s'abstint, durant quarante jours, de toutes fonctions ecclésiastiques; une légère pénitence fut imposée aux laïques, on déposa le corps d'Arsène dans le sanctuaire; et, au nom du saint défunt, le prince et le peuple furent absous des péchés de leurs pères (2).

Règne de Michel Paléologue.
A. D. 1259, 1er déc.
A. D. 1282, 11 déc.

Le crime de Paléologue avait eu pour motif, ou

---

(1) Pachymère (l. vii, c. 22) raconte la cérémonie de cette épreuve miraculeuse en philosophe, et cite avec le même mépris un complot des arsénites, qui essayèrent de cacher une révélation dans le cercueil de quelque vieux saint (l. vii, c. 13); mais il compense cette incrédulité par une image qui pleure, une autre qui répand du sang (l. vii, c. 30), et la cure miraculeuse d'un homme sourd et muet de naissance (l. xi, c. 32).

(2) Pachymère a dispersé dans ses treize livres l'histoire des arsénites; mais il a laissé le récit de leur réunion et de leur triomphe à Nicéphore (l. vii, 9), qui ne les aime ni ne les estime.

du moins pour prétexte, l'établissement de sa famille ; il s'empressa d'assurer la succession en partageant les honneurs de la pourpre avec son fils aîné. Andronic, depuis surnommé *l'Ancien*, fut couronné et proclamé empereur des Romains dans la seizième année de son âge ; il porta ce titre auguste durant un règne long et peu glorieux, neuf ans comme le collègue de son père, et cinquante ans comme son successeur. Michel aurait été jugé lui-même plus digne du trône s'il n'y fût jamais monté : les assauts de ses ennemis spirituels et domestiques lui laissèrent rarement le temps de travailler à sa propre gloire ou au bonheur de ses sujets. Il enleva aux Francs plusieurs des îles les plus précieuses de l'Archipel, Lesbos, Chio et Rhodes : sous la conduite de son frère Constantin, qui commandait à Sparte et dans la Malvasie, les Grecs recouvrèrent toute la partie orientale de la Morée depuis Argos et Napoli jusqu'au cap de Ténare. Le patriarche censura sévèrement l'effusion du sang chrétien, et osa insolemment opposer aux armes des princes ses craintes et ses scrupules ; mais tandis qu'on s'occupait de ces conquêtes d'Occident, les Turcs ravageaient tous les pays au-delà de l'Hellespont, et leurs déprédations justifièrent le sentiment d'un sénateur, qui prédit, au moment de sa mort, que la reprise de Constantinople serait la perte de l'Asie. Les conquêtes de Michel furent faites par ses lieutenans ; son épée se rouilla dans le palais des empereurs, et ses négociations avec les papes et

Règne d'Andronic l'Ancien.
A. D. 1273, 8 novemb.
A. D. 1332, 13 février.

le roi de Naples présentent des traits d'une politique perfide et sanguinaire (1).

<small>Son union avec l'Église latine.
A. D.
1274-1277.</small>

I. Le Vatican était le refuge le plus naturel d'un empereur latin chassé de son trône; le pape Urbain IV, sensible aux malheurs du prince fugitif, sembla vouloir soutenir ses droits. Il fit prêcher contre les Grecs schismatiques une croisade avec indulgence plénière; il excommunia leurs alliés et leurs adhérens, sollicita les secours de Louis IX en faveur de son parent, et demanda un dixième des revenus ecclésiastiques de la France et de l'Angleterre pour le service de la guerre sainte (2). Le rusé Michel, qui épiait attentivement les progrès de la tempête naissante, essaya de suspendre les hostilités du pape et de calmer son zèle par des ambassades suppliantes et des lettres respectueuses; mais il insinuait qu'un établissement de paix solide devait être le premier pas vers la réunion des deux Églises. La cour de Rome ne pouvait s'en laisser imposer par un artifice si grossier; on répondit à Michel que le repentir du fils devait précéder le pardon du père,

---

(1) Des treize livres de Pachymère, les six premiers contiennent, ainsi que les quatrième et cinquième de Nicéphore Grégoras, le règne de Michel Paléologue. Lorsque ce prince mourut, Pachymère avait quarante ans. Au lieu de diviser son histoire en deux parties, comme le père Poussin, son éditeur, je suis Ducange et Cousin, qui ne font des treize livres qu'une seule série.

(2) Ducange, *Hist. de C. P.*, l. v, c. 33, etc., tirée des lettres d'Urbain IV.

et que la foi, condition équivoque, pouvait seule préparer une base d'alliance et d'amitié. Après beaucoup de délais et de détours, l'approche du danger et les importunités de Grégoire x obligèrent Paléologue d'entamer une négociation plus sérieuse : il allégua l'exemple du grand Vatacès, et le clergé grec, qui pénétrait les intentions du prince, ne s'alarma point des premières démarches de respect et de réconciliation. Mais lorsqu'il voulut presser la conclusion du traité, les prélats déclarèrent positivement que les Latins étaient, non-seulement de nom, mais de fait, des hérétiques, et qu'ils les méprisaient comme la plus vile portion de l'espèce humaine (1). L'empereur tâcha de persuader, d'intimider ou de corrompre les ecclésiastiques les plus estimés du peuple, et d'obtenir individuellement leurs suffrages. Il se servit alternativement des motifs de la sûreté publique et des argumens de la charité chrétienne. On pesa le texte des pères et les armes des Français dans la balance de la politique et de la théologie ; et, sans approuver le supplément ajouté au symbole de Nicée, les plus modérés furent amenés à avouer qu'ils croyaient possible de conci-

---

(1) A raison de leurs relations mercantiles avec les Génois et les Vénitiens, les Grecs appelaient avec insulte les Latins κάπηλοι et βάναυσοι (Pachymère., l. v, c. 10). « Les uns sont hérétiques de nom, et les autres de fait, » comme les Latins, dit le savant Veccus (l. v, c. 12); qui se convertit peu de temps après (c. 15) et fut fait patriarche (c. 24).

lier les deux propositions qui occasionaient le schisme, et de réduire la procession du Saint-Esprit, du père *par* le fils, ou du père *et* du fils, à un sens catholique et orthodoxe (1). La suprématie du pape paraissait plus facile à concevoir, mais plus pénible à confesser. Cependant Michel représentait aux moines et aux prélats qu'ils pouvaient consentir à considérer l'évêque de Rome comme le premier des patriarches; et que, dans un pareil éloignement, leur prudence saurait bien garantir les libertés de l'Église d'Orient des fâcheuses conséquences du droit d'appel. Paléologue protesta qu'il sacrifierait son empire et sa vie plutôt que de céder le moindre article de foi orthodoxe ou d'indépendance nationale, et cette déclaration fut scellée et ratifiée par une bulle d'or. Le patriarche Joseph se retira dans un monastère, pour se décider, selon l'événement du traité, soit à abandonner son siége, soit à y remonter; l'empereur, son fils Andronic, trente-cinq archevêques et évêques métropolitains, et leurs synodes, signèrent les lettres d'union et d'obéissance, et on grossit la liste du nom de plusieurs des diocèses anéantis par l'invasion des infidèles. Une ambassade, composée de ministres et de prélats de confiance, dont les ordres secrets autorisaient et recommandaient une complai-

---

(1) Dans cette classe, nous pouvons placer Pachymère lui-même, dont le récit complet et impartial occupe les livres v et vi de son histoire. Cependant il ne parle point du concile de Lyon, et semble croire que les papes résidaient toujours à Rome ou dans l'Italie (l. v, c. 17-21).

sance sans bornes, s'embarqua pour l'Italie, portant des parfums et des ornemens précieux pour l'autel de Saint-Pierre. Le pape Grégoire x les reçut dans le concile de Lyon, à la tête de cinq cents évêques (1). Il versa des larmes de joie sur ses enfans si long-temps égarés mais enfin repentans, reçut le serment des ambassadeurs qui abjurèrent le schisme au nom des deux empereurs, décora les prélats de l'anneau et de la mitre, chanta en grec et en latin le symbole de Nicée, avec l'addition du *filioque*, et se félicita de ce qu'il lui avait été réservé de réunir les deux Églises. Les nonces du pape suivirent bientôt après les députés de Byzance, pour terminer cette pieuse opération, et leurs instructions attestent que la politique du Vatican ne se contentait point d'un vain titre de suprématie. Ils reçurent ordre d'examiner les dispositions du monarque et du peuple, d'absoudre les membres du clergé schismatique qui feraient les sermens d'abjuration et d'obéissance, d'établir dans toutes les églises l'usage du symbole orthodoxe, de préparer la réception d'un cardinal légat avec les pleins pouvoirs de sa dignité et de son office, et de faire sentir à l'empereur les avantages qu'il pourrait tirer de la protection temporelle du pontife romain (2).

---

(1) *Voyez* les Actes du concile de Lyon dans l'année 1274; Fleury, *Hist. ecclés.*, t. xviii, p. 181-199; Dupin, *Biblioth. ecclés.*, t. x, p. 135.

(2) Cette instruction curieuse, tirée avec plus ou moins

Il persécute les Grecs.
A. D. 1277-1282.

Mais ils ne trouvèrent pas un seul partisan chez une nation qui prononçait avec horreur les noms de Rome et de l'union. A la vérité, Joseph n'occupait plus le siége de patriarche; on lui avait substitué Veccus, ecclésiastique rempli de lumières et de modération, et les mêmes motifs obligeaient encore l'empereur à persévérer dans ses protestations publiques. Mais en particulier il affectait de blâmer l'orgueil des Latins et de déplorer leurs innovations, et Paléologue, avilissant son caractère par cette double hypocrisie, encourageait et punissait en même temps l'opposition de ses sujets. Du consentement des deux Églises, on prononça une sentence d'excommunication contre les schismatiques obstinés; Michel se fit l'exécuteur des censures ecclésiastiques; et lorsque les moyens de persuasion ne réussissaient pas, il employait les menaces, la prison, l'exil, le fouet et les mutilations, pierres de touche, dit un historien, du courage et de la lâcheté. Deux princes grecs qui régnaient encore avec le titre de despotes sur l'Étolie, l'Épire et la Thessalie, s'étaient soumis au souverain de Constantinople; mais ils rejetèrent les chaînes du pontife romain, et soutinrent avec succès leur refus par les armes. Sous leur protection, les évêques et les moines fugitifs assemblèrent des synodes d'opposition, rétorquèrent le nom d'hé-

---

d'exactitude, par Wading et Leo Allatius, des archives du Vatican, est donnée en extrait ou en traduction par Fleury, t. XVIII, p. 252-258.

rétique et y ajoutèrent le nom injurieux d'apostat. Le prince de Trébisonde prit le titre d'empereur que Michel n'était plus digne de porter, et même les Latins de Négrepont, de Thèbes, d'Athènes et de la Morée, oubliant le mérite de la conversion, se joignirent, soit ouvertement ou secrètement, aux ennemis de Paléologue. Ses généraux favoris, qui faisaient partie de sa famille, désertèrent ou trahirent successivement une cause sacrilége. Sa sœur Eulogie, sa nièce et deux de ses cousines, conspirèrent contre lui ; une autre de ses nièces, Marie, reine des Bulgares, négocia la ruine de son oncle avec le sultan d'Égypte ; et leur perfidie passa dans l'opinion publique pour l'effet de la plus haute vertu (1). Lorsque les nonces du pape le pressèrent de consommer le saint ouvrage, Paléologue leur exposa dans un récit sincère tout ce qu'il avait fait et ce qu'il avait souffert pour eux. Ils ne pouvaient douter que les sectaires des deux sexes et de tous les rangs n'eussent été privés de leurs honneurs, de leur fortune et de leur liberté. La liste des confiscations et des châtimens contenait les noms des personnes les plus chéries de l'empereur, et de celles qui méritaient le

---

(1) Cette confession franche et authentique de la détresse de Michel est écrite en latin barbare par Ogier, qui s'intitule protonotaire des interprètes, et transcrite par Wading, d'après les manuscrits du Vatican (A. D. 1278, n° 3). J'ai trouvé par hasard ses Annales de l'ordre franciscain; *Fratres minores*, en dix-sept volumes *in-folio* (Rome, 1741), parmi les papiers de rebut chez un libraire.

mieux ses bienfaits. Ils furent conduits à la prison où ils virent quatre princes du sang impérial, enchaînés aux quatre coins et agitant leurs fers dans un accès de rage. Deux d'entre eux sortirent de captivité, l'un par sa soumission, et l'autre par la mort; les deux autres furent punis de leur obstination par la perte des yeux, et les Grecs les moins opposés à l'union déplorèrent cette cruelle et funeste tragédie (1). Les persécuteurs doivent s'attendre à la haine de leurs victimes; mais ils tirent ordinairement quelque consolation du témoignage de leur conscience, des applaudissemens de leur parti, et peut-être du succès de leur entreprise. Michel, dont l'hypocrisie n'était animée que par des motifs de politique, devait se haïr lui-même, mépriser ses partisans, estimer et envier les rebelles courageux auxquels il s'était rendu également odieux et méprisable. Tandis qu'à Constantinople on abhorrait sa violence, on se plaignait à Rome de sa lenteur; on y révoquait en doute sa sincérité; enfin, le pape Martin exclut de la communion des fidèles celui qui travaillait à y faire rentrer une Église schismatique.

L'union dissoute. A. D. 1283. Dès que le tyran eut expiré, les Grecs, d'un consentement unanime, abjurèrent l'union; on purifia les églises, on réconcilia les pénitens, et Andronic,

---

(1) *Voyez* le sixième livre de Pachymère, et particulièrement les chapitres 1-11-16-18-24-27; il inspire d'autant plus de confiance, qu'il parle de cette persécution avec plus de douleur que d'aigreur.

versant des larmes sur les erreurs de sa jeunesse, refusa pieusement aux restes de son père les obsèques d'un prince et même d'un chrétien (1).

II. Les Latins, durant leurs calamités, avaient laissé tomber en ruine les tours de Constantinople ; Paléologue les fit rétablir, fortifier et garnir abondamment de grains et de provisions salées, dans la crainte d'un siége qu'il s'attendait à soutenir bientôt contre les puissances de l'Occident. Le monarque des Deux-Siciles était le plus formidable de ses voisins ; mais tant que Mainfroi, bâtard de Frédéric II, occupait ce trône, ses États étaient pour l'empire d'Orient un rempart plutôt qu'un sujet d'inquiétude. Quoique actif et brave, l'usurpateur Mainfroi, séparé de la cause des Latins et proscrit par les sentences successives de plusieurs papes, était assez occupé à se défendre ; et la croisade dirigée contre l'ennemi personnel de Rome, occupait les armées qui auraient pu assiéger Constantinople. Le frère de saint Louis, Charles, comte d'Anjou et de Provence, conduisait la chevalerie de France à cette sainte (2)

<small>Charles d'Anjou s'empare de Naples et de la Sicile. A. D. 1266, fév. 26.</small>

---

(1) Pachymère, l. VII, c. 1-11-17. Le discours d'Andronic l'Ancien (l. XII, c. 2) est un monument curieux qui prouve que si les Grecs étaient esclaves de l'empereur, l'empereur n'était pas moins esclave de la superstition et du clergé.

(2) Les meilleures relations de la conquête de Naples par Charles d'Anjou, les plus contemporaines et en même temps les plus complètes et les plus intéressantes, se trouvent dans les Chroniques florentines de Ricordano Malaspina (c. 175-

expédition ; le vengeur de Rome obtint pour prix la couronne des Deux-Siciles. L'aversion de ses sujets chrétiens obligea Mainfroi d'enrôler une colonie de Sarrasins, que son père avait établie dans la Pouille ; et cette ressource odieuse peut expliquer la méfiance du héros catholique, qui rejeta toutes les propositions d'accommodement. « Portez, dit Charles, ce message au sultan de Nocera ; dites-lui que Dieu et nos épées décideront entre nous, et que s'il ne m'envoie pas en paradis, je l'enverrai sûrement en enfer. » Les armées se joignirent : j'ignore dans quel endroit de l'autre monde alla Mainfroi ; mais dans celui-ci il perdit, près de Bénévent, la bataille, ses amis, la couronne et la vie. Naples et la Sicile se peuplèrent d'une race belliqueuse de noblesse française ; et leur chef ambitieux se promit la conquête de l'Afrique, de la Grèce et de la Palestine. Des motifs spécieux pouvaient le déterminer à essayer d'abord ses armes contre Constantinople, et Paléologue, qui ne comptait point sur ses propres forces, en appela plusieurs fois de l'ambition de Charles à l'humanité de saint Louis, qui conservait un juste ascendant sur l'esprit féroce de son frère. Charles fut retenu quelque temps dans ses États par

___

193) et de Jean Villani (l. VII, c. 1-10, 25-30), publiées par Muratori dans les huitième et treizième volumes des *Historiens de l'Italie*. Il a abrégé dans ses *Annales* (t. XI, p. 56-72) ces grands événemens dont on trouve aussi le récit dans l'*Istoria civile* de Giannone (t. II, l. XIX ; t. III, liv. XX).

l'invasion de Conradin, dernier héritier de la maison impériale de Souabe; mais ce jeune prince succomba dans une entreprise au-dessus de ses forces, et sa tête, publiquement abattue sur un échafaud, apprit aux rivaux de Charles à craindre pour leur vie autant que pour leurs États. La dernière croisade de saint Louis sur la côte d'Afrique donna encore un répit au souverain de Byzance. Le devoir et l'intérêt obligeaient également le roi de Naples à seconder cette sainte entreprise de ses troupes et de sa personne. La mort de saint Louis le débarrassa du joug importun d'un censeur vertueux. Le roi de Tunis se reconnut vassal et tributaire de la couronne de Sicile; et les plus intrépides des chevaliers français eurent la liberté de marcher sous sa bannière contre l'empire grec. Un mariage et un traité réunirent ses intérêts à ceux de la maison de Courtenai: il promit sa fille Béatrix à Philippe, fils et héritier de l'empereur Baudouin; on accorda à celui-ci une pension de six cents onces d'or pour soutenir sa dignité; son père distribua généreusement à ses alliés les royaumes et les provinces de l'Orient, ne réservant pour lui que la ville de Constantinople et ses environs, jusqu'à la distance d'une journée de marche(1). Dans ce danger menaçant, Paléologue s'empressa de souscrire le symbole et d'implorer la protection du

Il menace l'empire grec.
A. D. 1270, etc.

---

(1) Ducange, *Hist. C. P.*; l. v, c. 49-56; l. vi, c. 1-13. *Voy.* Pachymère, l. iv, c. 29; l. v, c. 7-10-25; l. vi, c. 30-32-33, et Nicéphore Grégoras, l. iv, 5; l. v, 1, 6.

pape, qui se montra alors véritablement un ange de paix et le père commun des chrétiens. Sa voix enchaîna la valeur et l'épée de Charles d'Anjou, et les ambassadeurs grecs l'aperçurent qui, profondément blessé du refus qui lui avait été fait de permettre son entreprise et de consacrer ses armes, mordait de fureur son sceptre d'ivoire dans l'antichambre du pontife romain. Il paraît que ce prince respecta la médiation désintéressée de Grégoire x ; mais l'orgueil et la partialité de Nicolas III l'éloignèrent insensiblement, et l'attachement de ce pontife pour sa maison, la famille des Ursins, aliéna du service de l'Église le plus fidèle de ses champions. La ligue contre les Grecs, composée de Philippe, l'empereur latin, du roi des Deux-Siciles et de la république de Venise, allait avoir son exécution, et l'élection de Martin IV, Français de nation, au trône pontifical, donna une sanction à l'entreprise. Philippe fournissait son nom, Martin une bulle d'excommunication, les Vénitiens une escadre de quarante galères, et les redoutables forces de Charles consistaient en quarante comtes, dix mille hommes d'armes, un corps nombreux d'infanterie, et une flotte de plus de trois cents vaisseaux de transport. On fixa un jour éloigné pour le rassemblement de cette nombreuse armée dans le port de Brindes, et trois cents chevaliers s'étant d'avance emparés de l'Albanie, essayèrent d'emporter la forteresse de Belgrade. Leur défaite put flatter un instant la vanité de la cour de Constantinople ; mais Paléologue, trop éclairé pour ne pas désespérer de ses forces, se fia de sa sûreté aux effets d'une conspiration, et, s'il est permis de le dire, aux travaux secrets du *rat* qui rongeait la corde de l'arc du tyran de Sicile (1).

On comptait parmi les adhérens fugitifs de la maison de Souabe, Jean de Procida, qui avait été chassé d'une petite île de ce nom, qu'il possédait dans la baie de Naples. Il descendait d'une famille noble ; mais comme son éducation avait été soignée dans son exil, Jean se tira de l'indigence en pratiquant la médecine, qu'il avait étudiée dans l'école de Salerne. Il ne lui restait plus rien à perdre que la vie ; et la première qualité d'un rebelle est de la mépriser. Procida possédait l'art de négocier, de faire valoir ses raisons et de déguiser ses motifs. Dans ses diverses transactions, soit avec des nations, soit avec des particuliers, il savait persuader à tous les partis qu'il ne s'occupait que de leurs intérêts. Les nouveaux États de Charles étaient accablés de toutes espèces de vexations, soit fiscales ou militaires (2). Il sacrifiait

Paléologue excite les Siciliens à se révolter.
A. D. 1280.

---

(1) Le lecteur d'Hérodote se rappellera de quelle manière miraculeuse l'armée assyrienne de Sennachérib fut désarmée et détruite (l. II, c. 141).

(2) Selon un guelfe zélé, Sabas Malaspina (*Hist. de Sicile*, l. III, c. 16 ; dans Muratori, t. VIII, p. 832), les sujets de Charles, qui avaient poursuivi Mainfroi comme un loup, le regrettèrent comme un agneau ; et il justifie leur mécontentement par la tyrannie du gouvernement des Français (l. VI, c. 2-7). Voyez le *Manifeste sicilien* dans Nicolas Specialis (l. 1, c. 11, dans Muratori, t. x, p. 930).

la fortune et la vie de ses sujets italiens à sa propre grandeur et à la licence de ses courtisans ; sa présence contenait la haine des Napolitains ; mais l'administration faible et vicieuse des lieutenans ou des gouverneurs excitait le mépris et l'indignation des Siciliens. Procida ranima par son éloquence le sentiment de la liberté, et fit trouver à chaque baron son intérêt personnel à soutenir la cause commune. Dans l'espérance d'un secours étranger, Jean visita successivement la cour de l'empereur grec et celle de Pierre, roi d'Aragon (1), qui possédait les pays maritimes de Valence et de Catalogne. On offrit à l'ambitieux Pierre une couronne qu'il pouvait justement réclamer en faisant valoir les droits de son mariage avec la sœur de Mainfroi, et le dernier vœu de Conradin qui, de l'échafaud où il perdit la vie, avait jeté son anneau à son héritier et à son vengeur. Paléologue se décida facilement à distraire son ennemi d'une guerre étrangère, en l'occupant chez lui d'une révolte ; il fournit vingt-cinq mille onces d'or, dont on se servit utilement pour armer une flotte de Catalans qui mirent à la voile sous un pavillon sacré, et sous le prétexte d'attaquer les Sarrasins de l'Afrique. Déguisé en moine ou en mendiant, l'infatigable agent de la révolte vola de Constantinople à Rome,

---

(1) *Voyez* le caractère et les conseils de Pierre, roi d'Aragon, dans Mariana (*Hist. Hispan.*, l. xiv, c. 6, t. ii, p. 133). Le lecteur pardonnera les défauts du jésuite en faveur de son style, et souvent en faveur de son discernement.

et de Sicile à Saragosse. Le pape Nicolas, ennemi personnel de Charles, signa lui-même le traité; et son acte de donation transporta les fiefs de saint Pierre, de la maison d'Anjou dans celle d'Aragon. Le secret, quoique répandu dans tant de différens pays, et librement communiqué à un si grand nombre de personnes, fut gardé, durant plus de deux années, avec une discrétion impénétrable ; chacun des nombreux conspirateurs s'était pénétré de la maxime de Procida, qui déclarait qu'il se couperait la main gauche s'il soupçonnait qu'elle pût connaître l'intention de sa main droite. La mine se préparait avec un artifice profond et dangereux ; mais on ne peut assurer si le tumulte de Palerme, qui amena l'explosion, fut accidentel ou prémédité.

La veille de Pâques, tandis qu'une procession de citoyens sans armes visitait une église hors de la ville, la fille d'une maison noble fut grossièrement insultée par un soldat français (1). La mort suivit aussitôt son insolence. Les soldats qui survinrent dispersèrent pour un instant la multitude ; mais à la fin le nombre et la fureur l'emportèrent : les conspirateurs saisirent cette occasion ; l'incendie se répandit sur toute

---

(1) Après avoir détaillé les griefs de ses compatriotes, Nicolas Specialis ajoute dans le véritable esprit de la jalousie italienne : *Quæ omnia et graviora quidem, ut arbitror, patienti animo Siculi tolerassent, nisi, quod primum cunctis dominantibus cavendum est, alienas feminas invasissent* (l. 1, c. 2, p. 924).

l'île, et huit mille Français furent indistinctement égorgés dans cette révolution, à laquelle on a donné le nom de Vêpres siciliennes (1). On déploya dans toutes les villes la bannière de l'Église et de la liberté. La présence ou l'esprit de Procida animait partout la révolte; et Pierre d'Aragon, qui cingla de la côte d'Afrique à Palerme, entra dans la ville aux acclamations des habitans, qui le nommèrent le monarque et le libérateur de la Sicile. Charles apprit avec autant de consternation que d'étonnement la révolte d'un peuple qu'il avait si long-temps foulé aux pieds avec impunité; et on l'entendit s'écrier, dans le premier accès de douleur et de dévotion : « Grand Dieu, si tu as résolu de m'humilier, fais-moi du moins descendre plus doucement du faîte de la grandeur! » Il rappela précipitamment, de la guerre contre les Grecs, la flotte et l'armée qui remplissaient déjà les ports de l'Italie; et Messine se trouva exposée, par sa situation, aux premiers efforts de sa vengeance. Sans confiance en leurs propres forces, et sans espoir de secours étrangers, les citoyens auraient ouvert leurs portes, si le monarque eût voulu assurer le pardon et la conservation des anciens priviléges; mais il avait déjà repris tout son orgueil.

---

(1) On rappela long-temps aux Français cette sanglante leçon. « Si on me pousse à bout, disait Henri IV, j'irai déjeûner à Milan et dîner à Naples. — Votre majesté, lui répondit l'ambassadeur d'Espagne, pourrait arriver en Sicile pour les vêpres. »

Les plus vives instances du légat ne purent lui arracher que la promesse d'épargner la ville, à condition qu'on lui remettrait huit cents des rebelles dont il donnerait la liste, et dont le sort serait à sa discrétion. Le désespoir des Messinois ranima leur courage; Pierre d'Aragon vint à leur secours (1). Le manque de provisions et les dangers de l'équinoxe forcèrent son rival de se retirer sur les côtes de la Calabre. Au même instant l'amiral des Catalans, le célèbre Roger de Loria, balaya le canal avec son invincible escadre. La flotte française, moins nombreuse en galères qu'en bâtimens de transport, fut ou brûlée ou détruite, et le même événement assura l'indépendance de la Sicile et la sûreté de Paléologue. Peu de jours avant sa mort, il apprit avec joie la chute d'un ennemi qu'il estimait et haïssait également, et peut-être se laissa-t-il gagner à cette opinion populaire, que si Charles n'eût pas rencontré Paléologue pour adversaire, Constantinople et l'Italie n'auraient eu bientôt qu'un seul maître (2). Depuis

---

(1) Deux écrivains nationaux racontent les détails de cette révolte et de la victoire dont elle fut suivie, Barthélemy de Néocastro (*in* Muratori, t. XIII) et Nicolas Specialis (*in* Muratori, t. X); l'un était contemporain et l'autre vivait dans le siècle suivant. Le patriote Specialis rejette le nom de rebelle, et nie la correspondance préliminaire avec Pierre d'Aragon (*nullo communicato consilio*), qui se trouva *par hasard* avec une flotte et une armée sur la côte d'Afrique (l. I, c. 4-9).

(2) Nicéphore Grégoras (l. v, c. 6) admire la sagesse de

cette époque funeste, la vie de Charles ne fut plus qu'une suite continuelle d'infortunes. Les ennemis insultèrent sa capitale, et firent son fils prisonnier. Charles mourut sans avoir recouvré la Sicile, qui, après une guerre de vingt ans, fut définitivement séparée du royaume de Naples, et transférée, comme royaume indépendant, à une branche cadette de la maison d'Aragon (1).

<small>Service et guerres des Catalans dans l'empire grec.
A. D. 1303-1307.</small>

On ne me soupçonnera pas, j'espère, de superstition; mais je ne puis m'empêcher de remarquer que, même dans ce monde, l'ordre naturel des événemens offre quelquefois les plus fortes apparences d'une rétribution morale. Le premier Paléologue avait sauvé son empire en couvrant les royaumes de l'Occident de révoltes et de sang; ces germes de discorde produisirent une génération d'hommes terribles qui assaillirent et ébranlèrent le trône de son fils. Dans nos siècles modernes, les dettes et les taxes sont le poison secret qui nous ronge au sein de la paix; mais dans les gouvernemens faibles et irréguliers du moyen âge, elle était continuellement troublée par les calamités actuelles qui provenaient du licenciement des armées. Trop paresseux pour travailler, et trop fiers

---

la Providence dans cette balance égale des États et des princes. Pour l'honneur de Paléologue, j'aimerais mieux que cette balance eût été observée par un Italien.

(1) *Voyez* la *Chronique* de Villani, le onzième volume des *Annali d'Italia* par Muratori, et les vingtième et vingt-unième livres de l'*Istoria civile* de Giannone.

pour mendier leur subsistance; les mercenaires vivaient de brigandage; appuyés du nom de quelque chef dont ils déployaient la bannière, ils devenaient plus dangereux et semblaient un peu moins méprisables; le souverain, à qui leur service devenait inutile et que leur présence incommodait, tâchait de s'en débarrasser sur ses voisins. Après la paix de Sicile, des milliers de Génois, de *Catalans*, etc. (1), qui avaient combattu par terre ou par mer pour la maison d'Aragon ou d'Anjou, se rassemblèrent et formèrent un corps de nation réunie par des mœurs et des intérêts semblables. Ayant appris l'irruption des Turcs dans les provinces asiatiques de l'empire d'Orient, ils résolurent d'aller chercher, en combattant contre eux, une solde et du butin; et Frédéric, roi de Sicile, contribua libéralement à leur fournir les moyens de s'éloigner. Depuis vingt ans qu'ils faisaient la guerre, ils ne connaissaient plus d'autre patrie que les camps ou les vaisseaux. Ils ne savaient que se battre, n'avaient d'autre propriété que leurs armes, et ne concevaient d'autre vertu que la valeur. Les femmes qui suivaient la troupe étaient devenues aussi intrépides que leurs maris ou leurs amans : on prétendait que d'un seul coup de sabre les Catalans

---

(1) Les plus braves de cette multitude de Catalans et d'Espagnols étaient connus des Grecs sous le nom d'*Almugavares* qu'ils se donnaient eux-mêmes. Moncade les fait descendre des Goths, et Pachymère (l. xi, c. 22) des Arabes; en dépit de la vanité nationale et religieuse, je crois que le dernier a raison.

fendaient en deux un cavalier et son cheval ; et cette seule opinion était une arme puissante. Roger de Flor était de tous leurs chefs celui qui avait le plus de crédit ; et il effaçait par son mérite personnel les fiers Aragonais, ses rivaux. Issu du mariage d'un gentilhomme allemand de la cour de Frédéric II et d'une demoiselle noble de Brindes, Roger fut successivement templier, apostat, pirate, et enfin le plus riche et le plus puissant amiral de la Méditerranée (1). Il cingla de Messine vers Constantinople, suivi de dix-huit galères, quatre gros vaisseaux et huit mille aventuriers. Andronic l'Ancien exécuta fidèlement le traité préliminaire que le général avait dicté avant de quitter la Sicile, et reçut ce formidable secours avec un mélange de joie et de terreur. On logea Roger dans un palais ; et l'empereur donna sa nièce en mariage au vaillant étranger, qu'il décora aussitôt du titre de grand-duc ou d'amiral de la Romanie. Après quelque temps de repos, il transporta ses troupes au-delà de la Propontide, et attaqua hardiment les Turcs. Trente mille musulmans périrent dans deux batailles sanglantes ; Roger fit lever le siége de Philadelphie, et mérita d'être nommé le libérateur de l'Asie. Mais l'esclavage et la ruine de

---

(1) *Voyez*, sur Roger de Flor et ses compagnons, un fragment historique, détaillé et intéressant, intitulé *les Espagnols du quatorzième siècle*, et inséré dans *l'Espagne en* 1808, ouvrage traduit de l'allemand, t. II, p. 167. Cette relation fait apercevoir de légères erreurs qui se sont glissées dans celle de Gibbon.   (*Note de l'Éditeur.*)

cette malheureuse province furent bientôt la suite de cette courte prospérité. Les habitans, dit un historien, s'échappèrent de la fumée pour tomber dans les flammes : les hostilités des Turcs étaient moins funestes que l'amitié des Catalans. Ils considéraient comme leur propriété la vie et la fortune de ceux qu'ils avaient sauvés ; les jeunes filles n'avaient échappé à des amans circoncis que pour passer de gré ou de force dans les bras des soldats chrétiens ; la perception des amendes et des subsides était accompagnée de rapines sans frein et d'exécutions arbitraires, et le grand-duc assiégea Magnésie, ville de l'empire, pour la punir de la résistance qu'elle lui avait opposée (1). Il s'excusa de cette violence sur les ressentimens d'une armée victorieuse et irritée, qui aurait méconnu son autorité et peut-être attaqué sa vie, s'il eût prétendu châtier de fidèles soldats justement offensés du refus qu'on faisait de leur accorder le prix convenu de leur service. Les menaces et les plaintes d'Andronic découvraient la faiblesse et la misère de l'empire. Le monarque n'avait demandé, par sa bulle d'or, que cinq cents cavaliers et mille soldats d'infanterie ; il avait cependant généreusement enrôlé et nourri la foule de volontaires qui étaient accourus dans ses États. Tandis que ses

---

(1) On peut se former une idée de la population de ces villes par les trente-six mille habitans de Tralles, qui avait été rebâtie sous le règne précédent, et qui fut ruinée par les Turcs (Pachymère, l. VI; c. 20, 21).

plus braves alliés se contentaient d'une paye de trois byzans d'or par mois, les Catalans recevaient chaque mois une ou même deux onces d'or, et l'on peut évaluer ainsi la paye d'une année à cent livres sterling. Un de leurs chefs avait taxé modestement à trois cent mille écus le prix de ses services futurs, et il était déjà sorti plus d'un million du trésor royal pour l'entretien de ces dispendieux mercenaires. On avait imposé une taxe cruelle sur la récolte des laboureurs ; on avait retranché un tiers des appointemens aux officiers publics, et le titre de la monnaie avait été si honteusement altéré, qu'il ne se trouvait plus que cinq parties d'or pur sur vingt-quatre (1). Roger obéit volontiers à l'ordre que lui donna l'empereur d'évacuer une province où il ne restait plus rien à piller, mais il refusa de disperser ses troupes. Sa réponse fut respectueuse, mais sa conduite an-

---

(1) J'ai recueilli ces détails dans Pachymère (l. XI, c. 21 ; l. XII, c. 4, 5-8-14-19), qui fait connaître l'altération graduelle de la monnaie d'or. Même dans les temps les plus heureux du règne de Jean Ducas Vatacès, les byzans étaient composés de moitié or et moitié alliage. La pauvreté de Michel Paléologue le força de frapper de nouvelles monnaies, où il entrait neuf parties ou carats d'or et quinze de cuivre. Après sa mort, le titre monta à dix carats, jusqu'à ce que, dans l'excès des calamités publiques, on le réduisit à moitié. Le prince fut soulagé pour un moment ; mais cette ressource passagère anéantit irrévocablement le crédit et le commerce. En France, le titre est de vingt-deux carats et d'un douzième d'alliage, et le titre d'Angleterre et de Hollande est encore plus haut.

nonça l'indépendance et la révolte. Le grand-duc protesta que si l'empereur marchait contre lui, il s'avancerait de quarante pas pour baiser la terre devant lui, mais qu'en se relevant de cette humble posture, Roger n'oublierait point que sa vie et son épée étaient au service de ses compagnons. Il daigna accepter le titre de César et les marques de cette dignité, et rejeta la nouvelle proposition du gouvernement de l'Asie, avec un subside de blé et d'argent, à condition qu'il réduirait ses troupes au nombre peu dangereux de trois mille hommes. L'assassinat est la dernière ressource des lâches. La curiosité conduisit le nouveau César au palais d'Andrinople, où la cour faisait sa résidence ; les Alains de la garde le poignardèrent dans l'appartement et en présence de l'impératrice ; et quoiqu'on ait prétendu qu'ils l'avaient immolé à leur vengeance particulière, ses compatriotes, tranquilles à Constantinople sur la foi des traités, furent enveloppés dans une proscription prononcée par le prince et le peuple. La plus grande partie de ces aventuriers, intimidés par la perte de leur chef, se réfugièrent sur leurs vaisseaux, mirent à la voile et se répandirent sur les côtes de la Méditerranée. Mais une vieille bande, composée de quinze cents Catalans ou Français, se maintint dans la forteresse de Gallipoli sur l'Hellespont ; ils y déployèrent la bannière d'Aragon, et offrirent de justifier et de venger leur général par un combat de dix ou de cent guerriers contre un nombre égal de leurs ennemis. Au lieu d'accepter cet audacieux défi, l'empereur Michel, fils et collègue d'Andronic, résolut de les écraser sous le nombre. Il vint à bout, en épuisant toutes les ressources de l'empire, de rassembler une armée de treize mille chevaux et de trente mille hommes d'infanterie : les vaisseaux grecs et génois couvrirent la Propontide. Dans deux batailles consécutives, les Catalans, animés par le désespoir et dirigés par la discipline, triomphèrent sur mer et sur terre de ces forces imposantes. Le jeune empereur s'enfuit dans son palais, et laissa un corps de cavalerie légère, insuffisant pour la défense du pays. Ces victoires ranimèrent l'espoir des aventuriers et augmentèrent bientôt leur nombre. Des guerriers de toutes les nations se réunirent sous la bannière et le nom de la *grande compagnie*, et trois mille mahométans convertis désertèrent les étendards de l'empereur pour se joindre à cette association militaire. La possession de Gallipoli donnait aux Catalans la facilité d'intercepter le commerce de Constantinople et de la mer Noire, tandis que leurs compagnons ravageaient, des deux côtés de l'Hellespont, les frontières de l'Europe et de l'Asie. Pour prévenir leur approche, les Grecs dévastèrent eux-mêmes tous les environs de Byzance : les paysans se retirèrent dans la ville avec leurs troupeaux, et égorgèrent en un seul jour tous les animaux qu'ils ne pouvaient ni renfermer ni nourrir. Andronic renouvela quatre fois ses propositions de paix et fut toujours repoussé avec inflexibilité ; mais le manque de provisions et la discorde des chefs forcèrent les Catalans à s'éloigner des bords de l'Hellespont et des environs de la capitale. Après s'être séparés des Turcs, les restes de la grande compagnie continuèrent leur marche à travers la Macédoine et la Thessalie, et cherchèrent un nouvel établissement dans le cœur de la Grèce (1).

Après quelques siècles d'oubli, l'irruption des Latins réveilla la Grèce pour lui faire éprouver de nouveaux malheurs. Durant les deux cent cinquante années qui s'écoulèrent entre la première et la dernière conquête de Constantinople, une multitude de petits tyrans se disputèrent cette vénérable contrée. Ses villes antiques essuyaient encore tous les désordres des guerres civiles et étrangères, sans en être consolées par les dons du génie ou de la liberté; et si la servitude est préférable à l'anarchie, la Grèce doit se reposer avec joie sous le joug des Ottomans. Je n'entreprendrai point l'histoire obscure des différentes dynasties qui s'élevèrent et tombèrent successivement

<small>Révolutions d'Athènes.
A. D.
1204-1456.</small>

---

(1) Pachymère, dans ses onzième, douzième et treizième livres, fait le récit très-détaillé de la guerre des Catalans jusqu'à l'année 1308. Nicéphore est plus complet et moins diffus (l. VII, 3-6). Ducange, qui regarde ces aventuriers comme Français, a suivi leurs traces avec son exactitude ordinaire (*Hist. de C. P.*, l. VI, c. 22-46) : il cite une histoire d'Aragon que j'ai lue avec plaisir, et que les Espagnols préconisent comme un modèle de style et de composition (*Expedicion de los Catalanos y Aragones contra los Turcos y Griegos*; Barcelone, 1623, in-4°; Madrid, 1777, in-8°). Don Francisco de Moncada, comte d'Ossone, peut imiter César ou Salluste; il peut avoir traduit les contemporains grecs ou

sur le continent et dans les îles; mais un sentiment de reconnaissance pour le premier séjour des muses et de la philosophie, doit naturellement intéresser tout lecteur instruit à la destinée d'Athènes (1). Dans le partage de l'empire, la principauté d'Athènes et de Thèbes avait été la récompense d'Othon de La Roche, noble guerrier de la Bourgogne (2), avec le titre de grand-duc (3), auquel les Latins attribuaient un sens particulier, et dont les Grecs faisaient ridiculement remonter l'origine au siècle de Constantin (4). Othon

---

italiens; mais il ne cite jamais ses autorités, et je ne trouve aucun témoignage national des exploits de ses compatriotes (*).

(1) *Voyez* l'histoire du laborieux Ducange et sa table soignée des *Dynasties françaises*, dans laquelle il récapitule les trente-cinq passages où il cite les ducs d'Athènes.

(2) Villehardouin le cite honorablement en deux endroits (n°s 151-235); et dans le premier passage, Ducange ajoute tout ce qui a pu être connu de sa personne et de sa famille.

(3) C'est de ces princes latins du quatorzième siècle que Boccace, Chaucer et Shakspeare ont emprunté leur Thésée, duc d'Athènes. Un siècle ignorant applique ses mœurs et son langage aux temps les plus reculés.

(4) Le même Constantin donna un roi à la Sicile, à la Russie un *magnus dapifer* de l'empire, à Thèbes le *primicerius*. Ducange (*ad* Nicéph. Grégor., l. VII, c. 5.) traite

(*) Ramon Montaner, l'un des Catalans qui accompagnèrent Roger de Flor, et qui fut gouverneur de Gallipoli, a écrit en espagnol l'histoire de cette bande d'aventuriers à laquelle il avait appartenu, et dont il se sépara lorsqu'elle quitta la Chersonèse de Thrace pour pénétrer en Macédoine et en Grèce. (*Note de l'Éditeur.*)

suivait les étendards du marquis de Montferrat; son fils et ses deux petits-fils possédèrent paisiblement le vaste patrimoine qu'il avait acquis par un miracle de conduite ou de fortune (1), jusqu'au moment où l'héritière de cette famille contracta un mariage qui, sans le faire sortir des mains des Français, le fit passer à la branche aînée de la maison de Brienne. Gauthier de Brienne, issu de ce mariage, succéda au duché d'Athènes; et avec le secours de quelques Catalans mercenaires, qu'il investit de fiefs, le grand-duc se rendit maître de plus de trente châteaux appartenant à des seigneurs ses vassaux, ou seulement ses voisins. Mais ayant été informé de l'approche et des desseins de la grande compagnie, Gauthier rassembla sept cents chevaliers, six mille chevaux et environ huit mille hommes d'infanterie; et marcha hardiment à leur rencontre jusque sur les bords du Céphise en Béotie. Les forces des Catalans ne montaient qu'à trois mille cinq cents chevaux et quatre mille hommes d'infanterie; mais, suppléant au nombre par l'ordre et la ruse, ils environnèrent leur camp d'une inon-

---

ces fables absurdes avec le mépris qu'elles méritent. Les Latins appelaient par corruption le seigneur de Thèbes *megas kurios* ou *grand sire*.

(1) *Quodam miraculo*, dit Albéric. Il fut probablement reçu par Michel le Choniate, l'archevêque qui avait défendu Athènes contre le tyran Léon Sgurus (Nicétas, *in Balduino*). Michel était frère de l'historien Nicétas, et son éloge d'Athènes existe encore en manuscrit dans la Bibliothèque Bodléienne (Fabr., *Bibl. græc.*, t. VI, p. 405).

dation artificielle. Le duc, suivi des chevaliers, s'étant avancé sans crainte et sans précaution dans la prairie, leurs chevaux s'enfoncèrent dans la boue, et il fut taillé en pièces avec la plus grande partie de la cavalerie française. Sa famille et sa nation furent chassées de la Grèce, et son fils Gauthier de Brienne, duc titulaire d'Athènes, tyran de Florence et connétable de France, perdit la vie dans les champs de Poitiers. Les victorieux Catalans se partagèrent l'Attique et la Béotie; ils épousèrent les veuves et les filles des vaincus, et durant quatorze années, la grande compagnie fit trembler toute la Grèce. Des discordes les déterminèrent à reconnaître le chef de la maison d'Aragon pour leur souverain; et jusqu'à la fin du quatorzième siècle, les rois de Sicile disposèrent d'Athènes comme d'un gouvernement ou d'un apanage de leur empire. Après les Français et les Catalans, la famille des Acciajuoli, plébéienne à Florence, puissante à Naples, et souveraine en Grèce, forma la troisième dynastie. Athènes, qu'ils embellirent de nouveaux édifices, devint la capitale d'un royaume qui comprenait Thèbes, Argos, Corinthe, Delphes et une portion de la Thessalie. Leur empire fut détruit par le victorieux Mahomet II, qui fit étrangler le dernier grand-duc, et élever ses enfans dans la discipline et la religion du sérail.

Situation présente d'Athènes.

Quoiqu'il ne reste plus aujourd'hui que l'ombre d'Athènes (1), elle contient encore huit ou dix mille

---

(1) Cet état d'Athènes moderne est tiré de Spon (*Voyage*

habitans. Les trois quarts sont Grecs de langage et de religion ; le reste est composé de Turcs, dont les liaisons avec les citoyens ont un peu adouci l'orgueil et la gravité nationale. L'olivier, don de Minerve, fleurit toujours dans l'Attique, et le miel du mont Hymette n'a rien perdu de son parfum exquis (1). Mais le commerce languissant est entre les mains des étrangers, et la culture de cette terre stérile est abandonnée aux Valaques errans. Les Athéniens se distinguent toujours par la subtilité et la vivacité de leur esprit ; mais ces avantages, lorsqu'ils ne sont pas dirigés et éclairés par l'étude, et ennoblis par le sentiment de la liberté, dégénèrent en une vile disposition à la ruse. Les habitans des environs ont adopté pour proverbe, « Que Dieu nous garde des Juifs de Thessalonique, des Turcs de Négrepont, et des Grecs d'Athènes ! » Ce peuple artificieux a évité la tyrannie des bachas par un expédient qui adoucit son esclavage en aggravant sa honte. Vers le milieu du dernier

---

en Grèce, t. II, p. 79-190), et de Wheeler (*Voyage en Grèce*, p. 337-414), de Stuart (*Antiquités d'Athènes*, passim) et Chandler (*Voyage en Grèce*, p. 23-172). Le premier de ces voyageurs visita la Grèce dans l'année 1676, le dernier en 1765 ; et la révolution de près d'un siècle n'avait presque pas produit de changement sur ce théâtre tranquille.

(1) Les anciens, ou au moins les Athéniens, croyaient que toutes les abeilles du monde étaient originaires du mont Hymette, qu'en mangeant du miel et se frottant d'huile on pouvait conserver sa santé et prolonger sa vie. *Geoponica*, l. xv, c. 7, p. 1089-1094, édit. de Niclas.

siècle, les Athéniens choisirent pour leur protecteur le kislar aga, ou chef des eunuques noirs du sérail. Cet esclave d'Éthiopie, qui jouit de la confiance du sultan, daigne accepter un présent de trente mille écus; le waivode, son lieutenant, qu'il confirme à la fin de chaque année, peut en prendre cinq ou six mille de plus pour lui; et telle est la politique adroite des Athéniens, qu'ils parviennent presque toujours à faire punir ou déposer le gouverneur dont ils ont à se plaindre. Dans leurs différends particuliers, ils prennent pour juge leur archevêque. Ce prélat, le plus riche de l'Église grecque, jouit d'un revenu d'environ mille livres sterling. Ils ont en outre un tribunal composé de huit *geronti* ou vieillards choisis dans les huit quartiers de la ville. Les familles nobles ne peuvent pas remonter authentiquement à plus de trois siècles; mais leurs principaux membres se distinguent par l'affectation d'un maintien grave, un bonnet fourré et le nom pompeux d'*archonte*. Ceux qui aiment les contrastes, représentent le langage moderne d'Athènes comme le plus barbare des soixante-dix dialectes du grec corrompu (1). Ce reproche est exagéré; mais il ne serait pas aisé de trouver dans la patrie de Platon et de Démosthènes un lecteur ou une

---

(1) Ducange (*Gloss. græc.*, *Præf.*, p. viij) cite pour autorité Théodose Zygomalas, grammairien moderne. Cependant Spon (t. II, p. 194) et Wheeler (p. 355), qui peuvent passer pour juges compétens, ont une opinion plus favorable du dialecte de l'Attique.

copie de leurs admirables compositions. Les Athéniens foulent, avec une indifférence insultante, les ruines glorieuses de l'antiquité ; et tel est l'excès de leur dégradation, qu'ils sont hors d'état d'admirer le génie de leurs prédécesseurs (1).

---

(1) Nous ne pouvons cependant pas les accuser d'avoir corrompu le nom d'Athènes, qu'ils nomment encore Athini. D'après l'εις την Αθηνην, nous avons formé notre dénomination barbare de *Setines*.

CHAPITRE LXIII.

Guerres civiles et ruine de l'empire grec. Règnes d'Andronic l'Ancien ; d'Andronic le Jeune et de Jean Paléologue. Régence, révolte, règne et abdication de Jean Cantacuzène. Établissement d'une colonie génoise à Péra et Galata. Leurs guerres contre l'empire et contre la ville de Constantinople.

<small>Superstition d'Andronic et du siècle.
A. D.
1282-1320.</small>

Le long règne d'Andronic l'Ancien (1) n'est guère mémorable que par les querelles de l'Église grecque, l'invasion des Catalans et l'accroissement de la grandeur ottomane. On le célèbre comme le prince le plus savant et le plus vertueux de son siècle ; mais sa science et ses vertus ne contribuèrent ni à son propre perfectionnement ni au bonheur de la société. Esclave de la superstition la plus absurde, il était toujours environné d'ennemis réels ou imaginaires, et son imagination n'était pas moins frappée de la crainte des flammes de l'enfer que de celle des Turcs ou des Catalans. Sous le règne des Paléologues on considérait le choix d'un patriarche comme la plus sérieuse affaire de l'État. Les chefs

---

(1) Andronic justifie lui-même la liberté que nous prenons à son égard, par les invectives qu'il a prononcées (Nicéphore Grégoras, l. 1, c. 1) contre la partialité de l'histoire ; il est vrai que sa censure est plus particulièrement dirigée contre la calomnie que contre l'adulation.

de l'Église grecque étaient des moines ambitieux et fanatiques, dont les vices et les vertus, le savoir et l'ignorance, étaient également méprisables ou funestes. La discipline rigoureuse du patriarche Athanase (1) irrita le peuple et le clergé; on l'entendit déclarer que le pécheur boirait jusqu'à la lie le calice de pénitence, et l'on répandit le conte ridicule d'un âne sacrilége qu'il avait puni; disait-on, pour avoir mangé une laitue dans le jardin d'un couvent. Chassé de son siége par la clameur publique, Athanase, avant de se retirer, composa deux écrits d'une teneur tout-à-fait opposée. Son testament public était sur le ton de la résignation et de la charité; le codicile particulier lançait les plus terribles anathêmes sur les auteurs de sa disgrâce, et les excluait pour toujours de la communion de la sainte Trinité, des anges et des saints. Le prélat déposa ce dernier papier dans un pot de terre, qui fut placé par ses ordres sur le haut d'un pilier du dôme de Sainte-Sophie, dans l'espérance que la découverte de cet arrêt pourrait quelque jour le venger. Au bout de quatre ans, des enfans, grimpant sur des échelles pour chercher des nids de pigeons, découvrirent ce

---

(1) Pour l'anathême trouvé dans le nid de pigeons, *voy.* Pachymère (l. IX, c. 24). Il raconte toute l'histoire d'Athanase (l. VIII, c. 13-16-20-24; l. X, c. 27-29-31-36; l. XI, c. 1-3-5, 6; l. XIII, c. 8-10-23-35), et il est suivi par Nicéphore Grégoras (l. VI, 5-7; l. VII, c. 1-9), qui comprend dans son récit la seconde retraite de ce second Chrysostôme.

fatal secret, et Andronic, se trouvant compris dans l'excommunication, trembla sur le bord de l'abîme perfidement caché sous ses pas. Il fit immédiatement assembler un synode d'évêques pour discuter cette importante question : on condamna unanimement la précipitation qui avait dicté cet anathême clandestin; mais comme il ne pouvait être levé que par celui qui l'avait prononcé, et que ce prélat chassé de son siége n'en avait plus le pouvoir, on jugea qu'aucune puissance de la terre ne pouvait infirmer la sentence. On arracha à l'auteur du désordre quelques faibles témoignages de pardon et de repentir; mais la conscience de l'empereur était toujours alarmée, et ce prince ne désirait pas moins vivement qu'Athanase lui-même le rétablissement d'un patriarche qui pouvait seul le tranquilliser. Au milieu de la nuit, un moine, après avoir heurté rudement à la porte de la chambre où l'empereur reposait, lui annonça une révélation de peste, de famine, de tremblement de terre et d'inondation. Andronic épouvanté sauta de son lit, passa le reste de la nuit en prières, et sentit ou crut sentir la terre trembler. L'empereur, suivi d'un cortége d'évêques, se rendit à pied à la cellule d'Athanase; et après une résistance convenable, le saint, de qui venait ce message qui avait alarmé l'empereur, consentit à absoudre le prince et à gouverner l'Église de Constantinople. Mais loin que sa disgrâce l'eût adouci, la solitude avait encore aigri son caractère, et le pasteur s'attira de nouveau la haine de son troupeau. Ses ennemis se servirent avec succès d'un singulier moyen de vengeance. Ils enlevèrent durant la nuit le marchepied ou tapis de pied de son siége, et le replacèrent, sans être aperçus, orné d'une caricature des plus satiriques. L'empereur y paraissait avec une bride dans sa bouche; Athanase tenait les rênes, et conduisait aux pieds du Christ le docile animal. On découvrit et l'on punit les auteurs de cette insulte; mais le patriarche, indigné de ce qu'on avait épargné leur vie, se retira une seconde fois dans sa cellule, et les yeux d'Andronic, ouverts pour un instant, se refermèrent sous son successeur.

Si cette transaction est une des plus curieuses et des plus intéressantes d'un règne de cinquante ans, je ne puis du moins me plaindre de la rareté des matériaux, lorsque je réduis en un petit nombre de pages les énormes in-folio de Pachymère (1), de Cantacuzène (2) et de Nicéphore Grégoras (3), qui

---

(1) Pachymère, dans sept livres en 377 pages *in-folio*, donne l'histoire des trente-six premières années d'Andronic l'Ancien, et fait connaître la date de son ouvrage par les nouvelles ou mensonges courans du jour (A. D. 1308). La mort ou le dégoût l'empêchèrent de continuer.

(2) Après un intervalle de deux ans depuis le moment où finit l'ouvrage de Pachymère, Cantacuzène prend la plume, et son premier livre (chap. 6-59, pag. 9-150) renferme le récit des guerres civiles et des huit dernières années du règne d'Andronic l'Ancien. Le président Cousin, son traducteur, est l'auteur de la comparaison ingénieuse de Moïse et de César.

(3) Nicéphore Grégoras raconte en raccourci le règne et la vie entière d'Andronic l'Ancien (l. VI, c. 1; l. X, c. 1

ont composé la prolixe et languissante histoire de cette époque. Le nom et la situation de l'empereur Jean Cantacuzène doivent sans doute attirer une vive curiosité sur ses ouvrages. Ses Mémoires comprennent un espace de quarante années, depuis la révolte d'Andronic le Jeune, jusqu'au moment où il abdiqua lui-même l'empire; et l'on a remarqué qu'il était, comme Moïse et César, le principal acteur des scènes qu'il décrit. Mais dans son éloquent ouvrage on chercherait en vain la sincérité d'un héros ou d'un pénitent; retiré dans un cloître, loin des vices et des passions du monde, il présente moins une confession qu'une apologie de la vie d'un politique ambitieux. Au lieu de développer les caractères et les desseins des hommes, il ne présente que la surface spécieuse et adoucie des événemens, colorés des louanges qu'il se donne ainsi qu'à ses partisans. Leurs motifs sont toujours purs, et leur but légitime. Ils conspirent et se révoltent sans aucune vue d'intérêt, et les violences qu'ils exercent ou tolèrent sont toujours louées comme les effets naturels de la raison et de la vertu.

Premières querelles entre les deux Andronic. A. D. 1320.

A l'imitation du premier des Paléologues, Andronic l'Ancien associa son fils Michel aux honneurs de la pourpre; et depuis l'âge de dix-huit ans jusqu'à sa mort prématurée, ce prince fut considéré durant

---

p. 96-291). C'est de cette partie que Cantacuzène se plaint, comme d'une représentation fausse et malveillante de sa conduite.

plus de vingt-cinq ans comme le second empereur des Grecs (1). A la tête des armées il n'excita ni l'inquiétude des ennemis ni la jalousie de la cour : sa patiente modération ne calcula point les années de son père; et ce père n'eut jamais, ni dans les vices ni dans les vertus de son fils, aucun motif pour se repentir de la faveur qu'il lui avait accordée. Le fils de Michel portait le nom d'Andronic comme son grand-père, dont cette ressemblance avait de bonne heure déterminé la tendresse. L'esprit et la beauté d'Andronic augmentèrent l'affection du vieillard, qui se flattait que ses espérances trompées, dans sa première génération, se réaliseraient avec éclat dans la seconde. Son petit-fils fut élevé dans le palais comme l'héritier de l'empire et le favori de l'empereur; et dans les sermens comme dans les acclamations du peuple, les noms du père, du fils et du petit-fils, formaient une trinité auguste : mais cette grandeur précoce corrompit bientôt le jeune Andronic; il voyait avec une impatience puérile le double obstacle qui arrêtait et pouvait arrêter long-temps l'essor de son ambition. Elle n'avait pour mo-

---

(1) Il fut couronné le 21 mai 1295, et mourut le 12 octobre 1320 (Ducange, *Fam. byzant.*, p. 239). Son frère Théodore hérita, par un second mariage, du marquisat de Montferrat, embrassa la religion et les mœurs des Latins (οτι και γνωμη και πιστει και σχηματι, και γενειων κουρα και πασιν εθεσιν Λατινος ην ακραιφνης, Nicéph. Grég., l. IX, c. 1), et fonda une dynastie de princes italiens qui fut éteinte en 1353 (Ducange, *Fam. byzant.*, p. 249-253).

tif ni le désir de la gloire ni celui de travailler au bonheur de ses peuples ; l'opulence et l'impunité étaient à ses yeux les plus précieuses prérogatives d'un monarque, et il commença ses indiscrétions par la demande qu'il fit d'être investi de quelques îles riches et fertiles où il pût vivre dans les plaisirs et l'indépendance. L'empereur s'offensa des nombreux et bruyans désordres qui troublaient la tranquillité de sa capitale ; le jeune prince emprunta des usuriers génois de Péra les sommes que lui refusait la parcimonie de son grand-père ; et cette dette onéreuse, au moyen de laquelle il affermit l'intérêt de la faction qu'il s'était formée, fut telle bientôt qu'elle ne pouvait plus être payée qu'au moyen d'une révolution. Une femme belle et d'un rang distingué, mais dont les mœurs étaient celles d'une courtisane, avait donné au jeune Andronic les premières leçons de l'amour. Il eut lieu de soupçonner les visites nocturnes d'un rival, et ses gardes, placés en embuscade à la porte de sa maîtresse, percèrent de leurs flèches un étranger qui passait dans la rue. Cet étranger était le prince Manuel son frère, qui languit et mourut de sa blessure. L'empereur Michel, leur père, dont la santé déclinait, expira environ huit jours après, pleurant la perte de ses deux enfans (1). Quoique le jeune Andronic n'eût pas eu l'intention de commettre un pareil crime, il ne de-

---

(1) Nous devons à Nicéphore Grégoras (l. vIII, c. 1) la connaissance de cette aventure tragique. Cantacuzène cache

vait pas moins considérer la perte de son frère et de son père comme la suite de ses déréglemens; et ce fut avec une profonde douleur que les hommes capables de sentiment et de réflexion, aperçurent qu'au lieu d'éprouver de la tristesse et des remords, il dissimulait faiblement sa joie d'être débarrassé de deux odieux compétiteurs. Ces événemens funestes et de nouveaux désordres aliénèrent par degrés le chef de l'empire. Après avoir épuisé en vain les conseils et les reproches, il transporta sur un autre de ses petits-fils ses espérances et son affection (1). Ce changement fut annoncé par un nouveau serment de fidélité fait au souverain et à la personne qu'il voudrait choisir pour son successeur. L'héritier naturel du trône, après s'être porté à de nouvelles insultes et avoir essuyé de nouveaux reproches, se vit exposé à l'ignominie d'un procès public. Avant de prononcer la sentence qui l'aurait probablement condamné à passer sa vie dans un cachot ou dans la cellule d'un monastère, l'empereur apprit que les partisans armés de son petit-fils remplissaient les cours de son palais. Il consentit à changer son jugement en un traité de réconciliation; et cette

---

discrètement les vices du jeune Andronic, dont il fut le témoin et peut-être le complice (l. 1, c. 1, etc.).

(1) Il destinait sa succession à Michel Catharus, bâtard de Constantin, son second fils. Nicéphore Grégoras (l. VIII, c. 3) et Cantacuzène (l. 1, c. 1, 2) s'accordent sur le projet d'exclure son petit-fils Andronic.

victoire encouragea le jeune Andronic et sa faction. Cependant la capitale, le clergé et le sénat, tenaient à la personne du vieil empereur, ou du moins à son gouvernement; et les mécontens ne pouvaient espérer de faire triompher leur cause et de renverser son trône que par la fuite, la révolte et des secours étrangers. Le grand domestique, Jean Cantacuzène, était l'âme de l'entreprise. C'est de sa fuite de Constantinople que datent ses opérations et ses Mémoires; et si c'est lui-même qui a vanté son patriotisme, un historien du parti contraire a du moins loué le zèle et l'habileté qu'il déploya en faveur du jeune empereur. Le jeune prince s'échappa de la capitale sous le prétexte d'une partie de chasse, leva à Andrinople l'étendard de la rebellion, et eut en peu de temps une armée de cinquante mille hommes, que le devoir ni l'honneur n'auraient pu décider à prendre les armes contre les Barbares. Des forces si considérables étaient capables de sauver l'empire ou de lui imposer la loi; mais la discorde régnait dans les conseils des rebelles, leurs opérations étaient lentes et incertaines, et la cour de Constantinople retardait leurs progrès par des intrigues et des négociations. Les deux Andronic prolongèrent, suspendirent et renouvelèrent, durant sept années, leurs désastreuses contestations. Par un premier traité, ils partagèrent les restes de l'empire: Constantinople, Thessalonique et les îles, appartinrent au vieil Andronic; le jeune acquit la souveraineté indépendante de presque toute la Thrace, depuis Philippi jusqu'au district de Byzance. Par son second traité, le jeune Andronic stipula son couronnement immédiat, le paiement de son armée, et le partage égal des revenus et de la puissance. La surprise de Constantinople et la retraite définitive du vieil Andronic terminèrent la troisième guerre civile, et le jeune vainqueur régna seul sur l'empire. On peut découvrir les raisons de ces lenteurs dans le caractère des hommes et dans l'esprit du siècle. Lorsque l'héritier du trône exposa ses premiers griefs et annonça ses craintes, les peuples l'écoutèrent avec intérêt et lui prodiguèrent des applaudissemens. Ses émissaires répandirent de tous côtés qu'il augmenterait la paye des soldats et déchargerait ses sujets d'une partie des impôts; et on ne réfléchit point que ces deux promesses se détruisaient mutuellement. Toutes les fautes commises durant un règne de quarante ans servirent de prétexte à la révolte. La génération naissante voyait avec mécontentement se prolonger à l'infini le règne d'un prince dont les maximes et les favoris étaient de l'autre siècle; et la vieillesse d'Andronic n'inspirait point de respect, parce que sa jeunesse avait manqué d'énergie. Il tirait des taxes publiques un revenu de cinq cent mille livres pesant d'or, et ce monarque, le plus riche des princes chrétiens, ne pouvait entretenir trois mille hommes de cavalerie et trente galères pour arrêter les progrès et les ravages des Turcs (1).

<small>Couronnement d'Andronic le Jeune. A. D. 1325, 2 février.</small>

---

(1) *Voyez* Nicéph. Grég., l. viii, c. 6. Andronic le Jeune

« Que ma situation, disait le jeune Andronic, est différente de celle du fils de Philippe ! Alexandre se plaignait de ce que son père ne lui laisserait rien à conquérir ; hélas ! mon grand-père ne me laissera rien à perdre. » Mais les Grecs s'aperçurent bientôt qu'une guerre civile ne guérirait point les maux de l'État, et que leur jeune favori n'était pas destiné à devenir le sauveur d'un empire à son déclin. A la première défaite son parti se trouva rompu par la légèreté du chef, par les différends qui s'élevèrent entre ses partisans, et par les intrigues de l'ancienne cour, qui sut engager les mécontens à déserter ou à trahir la cause du rebelle. Andronic le Jeune se laissa toucher par le remords, fatiguer par les affaires ou tromper par les négociations. Il cherchait plus les plaisirs que la puissance ; et la liberté qu'il eut d'entretenir mille chiens de chasse, mille faucons et mille chasseurs, suffit pour ternir sa renommée et désarmer son ambition.

<small>Andronic l'Ancien abdique l'empire. A. D. 1328, 24 mai.</small>

Considérons à présent la catastrophe de cette intrigue compliquée, et la situation définitive des principaux acteurs (1). Andronic l'Ancien passa presque toute sa vieillesse dans la discorde civile ; les

---

se plaignait qu'il lui était dû depuis quatre ans et quatre mois une somme de trois cent cinquante mille byzans d'or pour les dépenses de sa maison (Cantacuzène, l. 1, c. 48). Cependant il aurait volontiers remis cette dette si on lui eût permis de rançonner les fermiers du revenu public.

(1) Je suis la chronologie de Nicéphore, qui est singulièrement exacte. Il est prouvé que Cantacuzène a fait des

différens événemens de la guerre où des traités diminuèrent successivement et sa réputation et sa puissance, jusqu'à la nuit fatale où le jeune Andronic s'empara de la ville et du palais sans éprouver de résistance. Le commandant en chef, dédaignant les avis qu'on lui donnait sur le danger, dormait paisiblement dans son lit, dans toute la sécurité de l'ignorance, tandis que le faible monarque, agité d'inquiétudes, était abandonné à une troupe de pages et d'ecclésiastiques. Ses terreurs ne tardèrent pas à se réaliser; des acclamations se firent entendre, et proclamèrent le nom et la victoire d'Andronic le Jeune. Prosterné au pied d'une image de la Vierge, il envoya humblement remettre le sceptre et demander la vie au conquérant. La réponse de celui-ci fut convenable et respectueuse. Il se chargeait, dit-il, du gouvernement pour satisfaire le vœu du peuple; mais son grand-père n'en conserverait pas moins son rang et sa supériorité. Le vainqueur lui laissait son palais, et lui assignait une pension de vingt-quatre mille pièces d'or, dont une moitié devait être fournie par le trésor royal, et l'autre par la pêche de Constantinople. Mais, dépouillé de sa puissance, Andronic tomba bientôt dans le mépris et dans l'oubli. Le silence de son palais n'était plus troublé que par les bestiaux et les volailles du voisinage, qui en parcouraient impunément les cours solitaires. Sa

---

erreurs dans les dates de ses propres opérations, ou que son texte a été défiguré par l'ignorance des copistes.

pension fut réduite à dix mille pièces d'or (1), dont il ne pouvait obtenir le paiement. L'affaiblissement de sa vue vint encore aggraver ses souffrances. On rendait chaque jour sa détention plus rigoureuse; et durant une absence et une maladie de son petit-fils, ses barbares gardiens l'obligèrent, en le menaçant de la mort, à quitter la pourpre pour l'habit et la profession monastique. Le moine Antoine (c'était le nom qu'il avait pris) avait renoncé aux vanités de ce monde; mais il se trouva avoir besoin d'une grossière robe fourrée pour l'hiver : comme le vin lui était défendu par son confesseur, et l'eau par son médecin, il se trouvait réduit, pour toute boisson, au sorbet d'Égypte. Ce ne fut pas sans peine que l'ancien empereur des Romains parvint à se procurer trois ou quatre pièces d'or pour pourvoir à ses modestes besoins; et s'il est vrai qu'il ait sacrifié cet or pour soulager les maux encore plus pressans d'un ami, ce sacrifice est de quelque mérite aux yeux de la religion et de l'humanité. Quatre ans après son abdication, Andronic ou Antoine expira dans sa cellule, âgé de soixante-quatorze ans; et tout ce que purent lui promettre les derniers discours de la flatterie, ce fut une couronne plus brillante que celle qu'il avait portée dans ce monde corrompu (2).

Sa mort.
A. D. 1332,
13 février.

---

(1) J'ai tâché de concilier les vingt-quatre mille pièces de Cantacuzène (l. II, c. 1) avec les dix mille de Nicéphore Grégoras (l. IX, c. 2). L'un voulait cacher, et l'autre cherchait à exagérer les calamités du vieil empereur.

(2) *Voyez* Nicéph. Grég., l. IX, 6, 7, 8-10-14; l. X,

DE L'EMPIRE ROMAIN. CHAP. LXIII.   229

Le règne d'Andronic le Jeune ne fut ni plus glo- Règne
d'Andronic
le Jeune.
rieux ni plus fortuné que celui de son grand-père (1).
Il ne jouit que momentanément et avec amertume A. D. 1328,
24 mai.
A. D. 1341,
juin 15.
des fruits de son ambition. Monté sur le trône, il
perdit les restes de son ancienne popularité; les défauts de son caractère furent alors plus en vue. Les
murmures du peuple le forcèrent à marcher en personne contre les Turcs. Andronic ne manqua pas de
courage au moment du danger; mais il ne remporta
qu'une blessure pour trophée de son expédition, et
la victoire des Ottomans consolida l'établissement de
leur monarchie. Les désordres du gouvernement civil
parvinrent à leur dernier période; sa négligence à
observer les usages et à conserver l'intégrité du costume national, a été déplorée par les Grecs comme
le funeste symptôme de la décadence de l'empire. Les
débauches de sa jeunesse avaient hâté pour lui l'âge
des infirmités, et le monarque, à peine sauvé par la
nature, ou les médecins, ou la Vierge, d'une maladie
très-dangereuse, fut enlevé presque subitement dans
la quarante-cinquième année de son âge. Il avait été Ses deux
épouses.

---

c. 1. L'historien avait partagé la prospérité de son bienfaiteur; il le suivit dans sa retraite. « Celui qui suit son
maître jusqu'à l'échafaud ou dans le monastère, ne devrait
pas être légèrement traité de mercenaire prostituant l'é-
loge. »

(1) Cantacuzène (l. II, c. 1-40, p. 191-339) et Nicéphore
Grégoras (l. IX, c. 7; l. XI, c. 11, p. 262-361) ont donné
l'histoire du règne d'Andronic le Jeune depuis la retraite
de son grand-père.

marié deux fois, et comme les progrès des Latins
dans les armes et dans les arts avaient adouci les préjugés de la cour de Byzance, ses deux épouses furent
prises parmi les princesses de l'Allemagne et de l'Italie; la première, connue dans son pays sous le nom
d'Agnès, et en Grèce sous celui d'Irène, était fille
du duc de Brunswick. Son père (1), petit souverain(2)
d'un pays indigent et sauvage dans le nord de l'Allemagne (3), tirait quelques revenus du produit de ses

---

(1) Agnès ou Irène était fille du duc Henri le Merveilleux, chef de la maison de Brunswick, et le quatrième descendant du fameux Henri le Lion, duc de Saxe et de Ba-
vière, et vainqueur des Slaves de la côte de la Baltique;
elle était sœur de Henri, que ses deux voyages en Orient
firent surnommer le Grec; mais ces deux voyages furent
postérieurs au mariage de sa sœur, et je ne sais ni comment
Andronic découvrit Agnès dans le fond de l'Allemagne, ni
les raisons qui contribuèrent à former cette alliance (Rimius, *Mémoires de la maison de Brunswick*, p. 126-137).

(2) Henri le Merveilleux fut le fondateur de la branche
de Grubenhagen, éteinte dans l'année 1596 (Rimius, p. 287).
Il habitait le château de Wolfenbuttel, et ne possédait qu'un
sixième des États allodiaux de Brunswick et de Lunebourg,
que la famille des Guelfes avait sauvés de la confiscation
des grands fiefs. Les fréquens partages entre frères avaient
presque anéanti les maisons des princes d'Allemagne, lorsque enfin les droits de primogéniture vinrent par degrés
écarter cette loi juste, mais pernicieuse. La principauté de
Grubenhagen, un des derniers débris de la forêt Hercy-
nienne, est un pays stérile, rempli de bois et de montagnes (*Géographie de Busching*, vol. VI, p. 270-286; tra-
duct. angl.)

(3) Le royal auteur des *Mémoires de Brandebourg* nous

mines d'argent (1), et les Grecs ont célébré sa famille comme la plus ancienne et la plus noble de la race teutonique (2). Irène mourut sans laisser d'enfans, et Andronic épousa Jeanne, sœur du comte de Savoie (3). On préféra l'empereur grec au roi de

---

apprend combien le nord de l'Allemagne méritait encore, dans des temps beaucoup plus modernes, l'épithète de pauvre et de barbare (*Essai sur les mœurs*, etc.). Dans l'année 1306, des hordes de race venède, qui habitaient les bois de Lunebourg, avaient pour usage d'enterrer tout vivans les vieillards et les infirmes (Rimius, p. 136).

(1) On ne doit adopter qu'avec quelques restrictions l'assertion de Tacite, même relativement à son siècle, lorsqu'il prétend que l'Allemagne était totalement dépourvue de métaux précieux (*Germania*, c. 5; *Annal.*, xi, 20). Selon Spener (*Hist. Germaniæ pragmatica*, t. 1, p. 351), *argentifodinæ in Hercyniis montibus imperante Othone magno* (A. D. 968) *primum apertæ, largam etiam opes augendi dederunt copiam.* Mais Rimius (p. 258, 259) diffère jusqu'à l'année 1016 la découverte des mines d'argent de Grubenhagen ou du Hartz supérieur, qu'on exploita dès le quatorzième siècle, et qui produisent encore des sommes considérables à la maison de Brunswick.

(2) Cantacuzène a rendu un témoignage très-honorable: Ἦν δ' ἐκ Γερμανῶν αὐτὴ θυγάτηρ δουκὸς ντὶ μπρούζουικ (les Grecs modernes se servent du ντ pour le *d*, et du μπ pour le *b*, et le tout fera en italien *di Brunzuic*), τοῦ παρ' αὐτοῖς ἐπιφανεστάτου, καὶ λαμπρότητι πάντας τοὺς ὁμοφύλους ὑπερβάλλοντος τοῦ γένους. Cet éloge est équitable, et ne peut qu'être flatteur pour un Anglais.

(3) Anne ou Jeanne était une des quatre filles d'Amédée le Grand par un second mariage, et sœur de père de son successeur Édouard, comte de Savoie (*Tables d'Anderson*, p. 650). *Voyez* Cantacuzène, l. 1, c. 40-42.

France (1) ; et le comte, honorant en sa sœur le titre d'impératrice, la fit accompagner d'une nombreuse suite de filles nobles et de chevaliers : elle fut régénérée et couronnée dans l'église de Sainte-Sophie, sous le nom plus orthodoxe d'Anne. A la suite de ses noces, les Grecs et les Italiens se disputèrent le prix de l'adresse et de la valeur dans des tournois et des exercices militaires.

Règne de Jean Paléologue.
A. D. 1341, 15 juin.
A. D. 1391.

Bonheur de Jean Cantacuzène.

L'impératrice Anne de Savoie survécut à son mari. Jean Paléologue, leur fils, hérita du trône dans la neuvième année de son âge ; et son enfance eut pour protecteur le plus illustre et le plus vertueux des Grecs. La sincère et tendre amitié que son père conserva toujours pour Cantacuzène, fait également honneur au prince et au ministre. La noblesse du dernier égalait presque (2) celle de son maître ; leur attachement s'était formé au milieu des plaisirs de leur jeunesse, et l'énergie résultante d'une éducation modeste compensait chez le sujet le lustre nouveau que la pourpre donnait au prince. Nous avons vu

---

(1) Ce roi, supposé que le fait soit vrai, doit être Charles le Bel, qui, dans l'espace de cinq ans, épousa trois femmes (1321-1326 : Anderson, p. 628). Anne de Savoie fut reçue dans la ville de Constantinople dans le mois de février de l'année 1326.

(2) La noble race des Cantacuzènes, illustre dans les annales de Byzance depuis le onzième siècle, tirait son origine des paladins de France, les héros de ces romans qui furent traduits et lus par les Grecs dans le treizième. Ducange, *Fam. byzant.*, p. 258.

Cantacuzène enlever le jeune empereur à la vengeance de son grand-père, et le ramener triomphant dans le palais de Constantinople, après six ans de guerre civile. Sous le règne d'Andronic le Jeune, le grand-domestique gouverna l'empereur et l'empire : ce fut lui qui recouvra l'île de Lesbos et la principauté d'Étolie ; ses ennemis avouent qu'au milieu des déprédateurs du bien public, Cantacuzène seul se montra modéré et retenu ; et l'état qu'il donne volontairement de sa fortune (1), laisse présumer qu'il l'avait reçue par héritage, et ne l'augmenta point par des rapines. Il ne spécifie pas à la vérité la valeur de son argent comptant, de sa vaisselle et de ses bijoux. Cependant, après le don volontaire de deux cents vases d'argent, après que ses amis en eurent mis un grand nombre en sûreté, et que ses ennemis en eurent beaucoup pillé, ses trésors confisqués suffirent pour équiper une flotte de soixante-dix galères. Cantacuzène ne donne point l'état de ses domaines, mais ses greniers renfermaient une quantité immense d'orge et de froment ; et d'après la pratique de l'antiquité, les mille paires de bœufs, employés à la culture de ses terres, indiquent environ soixante-deux mille cinq cents acres de labour (2).

---

(1) *Voyez* Cantacuzène (l. III, c. 24-30-36).

(2) Saserne en Gaule, et Columelle en Italie ou en Espagne, calculent à raison de deux paires de bœufs, deux conducteurs et six manouvriers, pour deux cents *jugera* (cent vingt-cinq acres d'Angleterre de terres labourables),

Ses pâturages renfermaient deux mille cinq jumens poulinières, deux cents chameaux, trois cents mulets, cinq cents ânes, cinq mille bêtes à cornes, cinquante mille cochons et soixante-dix mille moutons (1). Ce précieux détail d'opulence rurale a droit de nous paraître étonnant dans la décadence de l'empire, et principalement dans la Thrace, province successivement dévastée par tous les partis. La faveur dont son maître l'honorait était fort au-dessus de sa fortune. Dans quelques momens de familiarité et durant sa maladie, l'empereur désira détruire la distance demeurée entre eux, et pressa son ami d'accepter la pourpre et le diadême. Le grand-domestique eut assez de vertu pour résister à cette offre séduisante; il l'affirme du moins dans son histoire : le dernier testament d'Andronic le Jeune le nomma tuteur de son fils et régent de l'empire.

Il est nommé régent de l'empire.

Si, pour récompense de ses services, on eût accordé au régent un juste tribut de reconnaissance et de docilité, la pureté de son zèle pour les intérêts de son pupille ne se serait peut-être jamais démen-

Sa régence est attaquée.
A. D. 1341.

---

et ils ajoutent trois hommes de plus lorsqu'il s'y trouve du taillis (Columelle, *de Re rusticâ*, l. II, c. 13; p. 441, édit. de Gesner).

(1) En traduisant ce détail, le président Cousin a commis trois erreurs palpables et essentielles : 1º il omet les mille paires de bœufs de labour; 2º il traduit πεντακόσιαι προς δισχιλίαις, par le nombre de quinze cents; 3º il confond myriades avec chyliades, et ne donne à Cantacuzène que cinq mille porcs. Ne vous fiez pas aux traductions.

tie (1). Cinq cents soldats choisis gardaient le jeune empereur et son palais; on célébra avec décence les obsèques de son père; la tranquillité de la capitale annonçait sa soumission; et cinq cents lettres envoyées dans les provinces dès le premier mois qui suivit la mort du monarque, leur apprirent ses dernières volontés. L'ambition du grand-duc ou amiral Apocaucus fit disparaître l'heureuse perspective d'une minorité tranquille, et pour rendre sa perfidie plus odieuse, l'auguste historien confesse l'imprudence qu'il avait eue d'élever Apocaucus à la dignité de grand-duc, contre l'avis de son souverain plus pénétrant que lui. Audacieux et rusé, avide et prodigue, l'amiral faisait alternativement servir tous ses vices aux vues de son ambition, et ses talens à la ruine de sa patrie. Énorgueilli par le commandement d'une forteresse et celui des forces navales, Apocaucus conspirait contre son bienfaiteur; et lui prodiguait en même temps des assurances d'attachement et de fidélité. Toutes les femmes de la cour de l'impératrice lui étaient vendues et agissaient d'après ses plans. Il sut exciter Anne de Savoie à réclamer la tutelle de son fils; on déguisa le désir de commander sous le masque de la sollicitude maternelle, et l'exemple du premier des Paléologues ins-

Par Apocaucus.

Par l'impératrice Anne de Savoie.

---

(1) *Voyez* la régence et le règne de Jean Cantacuzène, et tout le cours de la guerre civile, dans sa propre histoire (l. III, c. 1-100, p. 348-700) et dans celle de Nicéphore Grégoras (l. XII, c. 1; l. XV, c. 9, p. 353-492).

truisait sa postérité à tout craindre d'un tuteur perfide. Le patriarche Jean d'Apri, vieillard vain, faible et environné d'une parenté nombreuse et indigente, produisit une ancienne lettre d'Andronic, par laquelle l'empereur léguait le prince et le peuple à ses soins pieux. Le sort de son prédécesseur Arsène l'engageait à prévenir le crime d'un usurpateur plutôt que d'avoir à le punir ; et Apocaucus ne put s'empêcher de sourire du succès de ses flatteries, lorsqu'il vit l'évêque de Byzance s'environner du même appareil que le pontife romain, et réclamer les mêmes droits temporels (1). Une ligue secrète se forma entre ces trois personnes si différentes de caractère et de situation : on rendit au sénat une ombre d'autorité, et l'on séduisit les peuples par le nom de liberté. Cette confédération puissante attaqua le grand-domestique, d'abord d'une manière détournée et ensuite à force ouverte. On disputa ses prérogatives, on rejeta ses conseils ; ses amis furent persécutés, et il courut souvent des risques pour sa vie au milieu de la capitale et à la tête des armées. Tandis qu'il s'occupait au loin du service de l'État, on l'accusa de trahison, on le déclara ennemi de l'empire et de l'Église, et on le dévoua lui et tous ses adhérens au

Par le patriarche.

---

(1) Il prit les souliers ou brodequins rouges, se coiffa d'une mitre d'or et de soie , signa ses lettres avec de l'encre verte, et réclama pour la nouvelle Rome tous les priviléges que Constantin avait accordés à l'ancienne. Cantacuzène, l. III, c. 36; Nicéph. Grég., l. XIV, c. 3.

glaive de la justice, à la vengeance du peuple et aux puissances de l'enfer. Sa fortune fut confisquée; on jeta dans une prison sa mère, déjà avancée en âge: tous ses services furent mis en oubli, et Cantacuzène se vit forcé, par la violence et l'injustice, à commettre le crime dont on l'avait accusé (1). Rien dans sa conduite précédente n'autorise à penser qu'il eût formé aucun dessein coupable; la seule chose du moins qui pût le faire soupçonner, serait la véhémence de ses protestations réitérées d'innocence, et les éloges qu'il donne à la sublime pureté de sa vertu. Tandis que l'impératrice et le patriarche conservaient encore avec lui les apparences de l'amitié, il sollicita, à plusieurs reprises, la permission d'abandonner la régence et de se retirer dans un monastère. Lorsqu'on l'eut déclaré ennemi public, Cantacuzène résolut d'aller se jeter aux pieds du prince, et de présenter sa tête à l'exécuteur sans murmure et sans résistance. Ce ne fut qu'avec répugnance qu'il prêta l'oreille à la voix de la raison, sentit qu'il était de son devoir de sauver sa famille et ses amis, et qu'il n'y pouvait réussir qu'en prenant les armes et le titre de souverain.

Cantacuzène prend la pourpre.
A. D. 1341
26 octob.

Ce fut dans la forteresse de Demotica, son patri-

---

(1) Nicéphore Grégoras (l. xii, c. 5) atteste l'innocence et les vertus de Cantacuzène, les vices honteux et le crime d'Apocaucus, et ne dissimule point ses motifs d'inimitié personnelle et religieuse pour le premier; νυν δε δια κακιαν αλλων, αιτιος ο πραοτατος της των ολων εδοξεν ειναι φθορας.

moine particulier, que l'empereur Jean Cantacuzène prit les brodequins pourpres. Sa jambe droite fut chaussée par ses nobles parens, et la gauche par les chefs latins auxquels il avait conféré l'ordre de la chevalerie. Mais, s'attachant à conserver encore dans sa révolte les formes de la fidélité, il fit proclamer les noms de Paléologue et d'Anne de Savoie avant le sien et celui d'Irène son épouse. Une vaine cérémonie déguise mal la rebellion, et aucune injure personnelle ne peut sans doute excuser un sujet qui prend les armes contre son souverain ; mais le manque de préparatifs et de succès peut confirmer ce que nous assure Cantacuzène, qu'il fut entraîné dans cette entreprise décisive moins par choix que par nécessité. Constantinople resta fidèle au jeune empereur. On sollicita le roi des Bulgares de secourir Andrinople. Les principales villes de la Thrace et de la Macédoine, après avoir hésité quelque temps, abandonnèrent le parti du grand-domestique ; et les chefs des troupes et des provinces pensèrent que leur intérêt particulier devait les engager à préférer le gouvernement sans vigueur d'une femme et d'un prêtre. L'armée de Cantacuzène, partagée en seize divisions, se cantonna sur les bords du Mélas, pour contenir ou intimider la capitale. La terreur ou la trahison dispersa ses troupes, et les officiers, particulièrement les Latins mercenaires, acceptèrent les présens de la cour de Byzance et passèrent à son service. Après cet événement, l'empereur rebelle (car sa fortune flottait entre ces deux titres) se retira vers

Thessalonique avec un reste de soldats choisis. Mais il échoua dans son entreprise sur cette place importante, et son ennemi Apocaucus le poursuivit par terre et par mer à la tête de forces très-supérieures. Chassé de la côte, Cantacuzène, en se retirant ou plutôt en fuyant les montagnes de Servie, assembla ses soldats dans le dessein de ne conserver que ceux qui offriraient volontairement de suivre sa fortune abattue. Un grand nombre l'abandonna bassement avec quelques protestations, et sa troupe fidèle se trouva réduite d'abord à deux mille, et enfin à cinq cents hommes. Le *cral* ou despote des Serviens (1) le reçut avec humanité; mais du rôle d'allié il descendit successivement à celui de suppliant, d'ôtage et de captif, réduit à attendre à la porte d'un Barbare qui pouvait disposer à son gré de la vie et de la liberté d'un empereur romain. Les offres les plus séduisantes ne purent cependant déterminer le cral à violer les lois de l'hospitalité; mais il se rangea bientôt du côté du plus fort, et renvoya, sans lui faire

---

(1) On nommait les princes de Servie (Ducange, *Fam. dalmat.*, etc., c. 2, 3, 4-9) *despotes* en langue grecque, et *crals* dans leur idiome national (Ducange, *Gloss. græc.*, p. 751). Ce titre, l'équivalent de roi, paraît tirer son origine de la Sclavonie, d'où il est passé chez les Hongrois, chez les Grecs et même chez les Turcs (Leunclavius, *Pandect. turc.*, p. 422); qui réservent le nom de *padishah* pour l'empereur. Obtenir le premier au lieu du dernier, est l'ambition des Français à Constantinople (*Avertissement à l'Histoire de Timur-Bec*, p. 39).

aucune insulte, son ami Cantacuzène s'exposer ailleurs à de nouvelles vicissitudes d'espérances et de dangers. Des succès variés alimentèrent durant près de six années les fureurs de la guerre civile. Les factions des Cantacuzains et des Paléologues, des nobles et des plébéiens, remplissaient les villes de leurs dissensions, et invitaient mutuellement les Bulgares, les Serviens et les Turcs, à consommer la ruine commune des deux partis. Le régent déplorait les calamités dont il était l'auteur et la victime; et sa propre expérience a pu lui dicter la juste et piquante observation qu'il fait sur la différence qui existe entre les guerres civiles et les guerres étrangères. « Les dernières, dit-il, ressemblent aux chaleurs extérieures de l'été, toujours tolérables et souvent utiles; mais les autres ne peuvent se comparer qu'à une fièvre mortelle, dont l'ardeur consume et détruit les principes de la vie (1). »

L'imprudence qu'ont eue les nations civilisées de mêler des peuples barbares ou sauvages dans leurs contestations, a toujours tourné à leur honte et à leur malheur; cette ressource, favorable quelquefois à l'intérêt du moment, répugne également aux principes de l'humanité et de la raison. Il est d'usage que les deux partis s'accusent réciproquement d'avoir

---

(1) Nicéphore Grégoras, l. xii, c. 14. Il est surprenant que Cantacuzène n'ait point inséré dans ses propres écrits cette comparaison juste et ingénieuse.

contracté les premiers cette indigne alliance ; et ceux qui ont échoué dans leur négociation, sont ceux qui témoignent le plus d'horreur pour un exemple qu'ils envient et qu'ils ont tâché inutilement d'imiter. Les Turcs de l'Asie étaient moins barbares peut-être que les pâtres de la Bulgarie et de la Servie; mais leur religion les rendait les plus implacables ennemis de Rome et des chrétiens. Les deux factions employèrent à l'envi les profusions et les bassesses pour gagner l'amitié des émirs. L'adresse de Cantacuzène lui obtint la préférence ; mais le mariage de sa fille avec un infidèle, et la captivité de plusieurs milliers de chrétiens, furent le prix odieux du secours et de la victoire, et le passage des Ottomans en Europe précipita la ruine des débris de l'empire romain. La mort d'Apocaucus, juste mais singulière récompense de ses crimes, fit pencher la balance en faveur de son ennemi. L'amiral avait fait saisir dans la capitale et dans les provinces une foule de nobles et de plébéiens, objets de sa haine ou de ses craintes : ils étaient enfermés dans le vieux palais de Constantinople, et leur persécuteur s'occupait avec activité de faire hausser les murs, resserrer les chambres, et de tout ce qui pouvait assurer leur détention et aggraver leur misère. Un jour qu'ayant laissé ses gardes à la porte, il veillait dans la cour intérieure au travail de ses architectes, deux courageux prisonniers de la famille des Paléologues, armés de bâtons et animés par le désespoir, s'élancèrent sur l'amiral et l'étendirent mort à leurs pieds (1). La prison retentit des cris de vengeance et de liberté ; tous les captifs rompirent leurs fers ; ils barricadèrent leur retraite, et exposèrent sur les créneaux la tête d'Apocaucus, dans l'espérance d'obtenir l'approbation du peuple et la clémence de l'impératrice. Anne de Savoie vit peut-être sans regret la chute d'un ministre ambitieux et arrogant ; mais tandis qu'elle hésitait à prendre un parti, la populace et particulièrement les mariniers, animés par la veuve de l'amiral, enfoncèrent la prison, firent main-basse sur tous ceux qui se présentèrent : les prisonniers la plupart innocens du meurtre d'Apocaucus, ou qui plutôt n'en avaient pas partagé la gloire et qui s'étaient réfugiés dans une église, furent égorgés au pied des autels ; et la mort du monstre fut aussi funeste et aussi sanglante que l'avait été sa vie. Cependant ses talens soutenaient seuls la cause du jeune empereur ; après sa mort, ses partisans, remplis de soupçons les uns contre les autres, abandonnèrent la conduite de la guerre et rejetèrent toutes les offres de réconciliation. Dès le commencement de la guerre civile l'impératrice avait senti et avoué que les ennemis de Cantacuzène la trompaient ; mais le patriarche prêcha

---

(1) Les deux prisonniers qui assommèrent Apocaucus, étaient l'un et l'autre des Paléologues, et pouvaient ressentir en prison la honte de leurs fers. Le fait de la mort d'Apocaucus mérite qu'on renvoie le lecteur à Cantacuzène (l. III ; c. 86) et à Nicéphore Grégoras (l. XIV, c. 10).

fortement contre le pardon des injures, et lia la princesse par un serment de haine éternelle qu'elle ne pouvait rompre sans s'exposer aux foudres redoutables de l'excommunication (1). La haine d'Anne de Savoie fut bientôt indépendante de cette crainte; elle contempla les calamités de l'empire avec l'indifférence d'une étrangère. La concurrence d'une impératrice enflamma sa jalousie, et elle menaça à son tour le patriarche, qui semblait incliner pour la paix, d'assembler un synode et de le dégrader de sa dignité. L'usurpateur aurait pu tirer un avantage décisif de la discorde et de l'incapacité de ses ennemis; mais la faiblesse des deux partis prolongea la guerre civile, et la modération de Cantacuzène n'a point échappé au reproche d'indolence et de timidité. Il s'empara successivement des villes et des provinces, et le royaume de son pupille se trouva bientôt réduit à l'enceinte de Constantinople; mais la capitale contre-balançait seule le reste de l'empire, et Cantacuzène, avant d'entreprendre cette importante conquête, voulait s'y assurer et la faveur publique et de secrètes intelligences. Un Italien nommé Facciolati (2) avait succédé à la dignité de grand-duc; il

Cantacuzène rentre dans Constantinople.
A. D. 1347,
8 janv.

―――

(1) Cantacuzène accuse le patriarche et épargne l'impératrice, mère de son souverain (l. III, 33, 34) contre laquelle Nicéphore exprime une animosité particulière (l. XIV, 10, 11; xv, 5.). Il est vrai qu'ils ne parlent pas exactement de la même époque.

(2) Nicéphore Grégoras révèle la trahison et le nom du traître (l. xv, c. 8); mais Cantacuzène (l. III, c. 99) sup-

commandait la flotte, les gardes et la porte d'or :
cependant son humble ambition ne dédaigna point
le prix de la perfidie; la révolution s'exécuta sans
danger et sans qu'il en coûtât une goutte de sang.
Dépourvue de tout moyen de résistance et de tout
espoir de secours, l'inflexible Anne de Savoie voulait
encore défendre le palais : plutôt que de livrer Byzance à sa rivale, elle aurait volontiers réduit la ville
en cendres; mais les deux partis s'opposèrent également à ses fureurs, et le vainqueur, en dictant son
traité, renouvela ses protestations de zèle et d'attachement pour le fils de son bienfaiteur. Le mariage
de sa fille avec Jean Paléologue s'accomplit, et l'on
stipula les droits héréditaires de son pupille; mais
toute l'administration fut confiée pour dix ans à
Cantacuzène. On vit deux empereurs et trois impé-
ratrices s'asseoir à la fois sur le trône de Constantinople, et une amnistie générale calma les craintes et
assura les propriétés des sujets les plus coupables.
On célébra les noces et le couronnement avec un
extérieur de concorde et de magnificence également
dépourvues de réalité. Durant les derniers troubles,
on avait dissipé les trésors de l'État, et dégradé ou
vendu jusqu'aux meubles du palais. La table impériale
fut servie en étain ou en poterie, et la vanité remplaça
l'or et les bijoux par du verre et du plomb doré (1).

prime discrètement le nom de celui qu'il avait daigné compter pour son complice.

(1) Nicéphore Grégoras, l. xv, 11. Il y avait cependant

Je me hâte de conclure l'histoire personnelle de Jean Cantacuzène (1) : sa victoire lui valut l'empire ; mais le mécontentement des deux partis troubla son règne et ternit son triomphe. Ses partisans purent regarder l'amnistie générale comme un acte de pardon pour ses ennemis et d'oubli de ses amis (2). Ils avaient vu pour sa cause leurs biens confisqués ou pillés, réduits à l'aumône dans les rues de Constantinople, ils maudissaient la générosité intéressée d'un chef qui, placé sur le trône de l'empire, avait pu aisément renoncer à son patrimoine. Les adhérens de l'impératrice rougissaient de devoir leur vie et leur fortune à la faveur précaire d'un usurpateur, et les désirs de vengeance se couvraient du masque d'une

Règne de Jean Cantacuzène.
A. D. 1347, 8 janv.
A. D. 1355, janvier.

---

encore quelques perles fines, mais bien clair-semées ; le reste des pierres n'avait que παντοδαπην χροιαν προς το διαυγες.

(1) Cantacuzène continue son histoire et celle de l'empire depuis son retour à Constantinople jusqu'à l'année qui suivit celle où son fils Matthieu abdiqua, A. D. 1357 (l. IV, c. 1-50, p. 705-911). Nicéphore Grégoras finit la sienne au synode de Constantinople, dans l'année 1351 (l. XXII, c. 3, p. 660 ; le reste, jusqu'à la fin du l. XXIV, p. 717, ne traite que de controverse), et ses quatorze derniers livres sont encore en manuscrit dans la Bibliothèque royale à Paris.

(2) L'empereur Cantacuzène (l. IV, c. 1.) parle de ses propres vertus, et Nicéphore Grégoras des plaintes des amis de ce prince, que ses vertus réduisaient à la misère. Je leur ai prêté les expressions de nos pauvres chevaliers ou partisans de Charles après la restauration.

tendre inquiétude pour les intérêts et même pour la vie du jeune empereur. Ils furent alarmés avec raison de la demande que firent les partisans de Cantacuzène d'être dégagés de leur serment de fidélité envers les Paléologues, et mis en possession de quelques places de sûreté. Ils plaidèrent leur cause avec éloquence et n'obtinrent, dit l'empereur Cantacuzène lui-même, « qu'un refus de ma vertu sublime et presque incroyable. » Des séditions et des complots troublèrent continuellement son gouvernement; il tremblait sans cesse que quelque ennemi étranger ou domestique n'enlevât le prince légitime pour faire de son nom et de ses injures le prétexte de la révolte. A mesure qu'il avançait en âge, le fils d'Andronic commençait à agir et à sentir par lui-même; les vices qu'il avait hérités de son père hâtèrent, plutôt qu'ils ne les retardèrent, les progrès de son ambition naissante, et Cantacuzène, si nous pouvons en croire ses protestations, travailla avec un zèle sincère à le retirer de la honte de ses inclinations sensuelles, et à élever son âme au niveau de sa fortune. Dans l'expédition de Servie, les deux empereurs, affectant l'un et l'autre un air de satisfaction et d'intelligence, se montrèrent ensemble aux troupes et aux provinces, et Cantacuzène initia son jeune collègue aux sciences de la guerre et du gouvernement. Après la conclusion de la paix, il laissa son rival à Thessalonique, résidence royale située sur la frontière, afin de le soustraire aux séductions d'une ville voluptueuse, et d'assurer par son absence la tranquillité de la capitale ; mais en s'éloignant il perdit de son pouvoir, et le fils d'Andronic, entouré de courtisans artificieux ou irréfléchis, apprit à haïr son tuteur, à déplorer son exil et à revendiquer ses droits. Il fit une alliance secrète avec le despote de Servie, et bientôt après déclara ouvertement sa révolte. Cantacuzène, placé sur le trône d'Andronic l'Ancien, défendit la cause de l'âge et de la prééminence qu'il avait si vigoureusement attaquée durant sa jeunesse. A sa sollicitation, l'impératrice mère consentit à employer sa médiation, et fit un voyage à Thessalonique, d'où elle revint sans succès ; mais, à moins que l'adversité n'eût produit chez Anne de Savoie une grande métamorphose, on peut douter du zèle et même de la sincérité qu'elle mit dans cette démarche. Tout en retenant le sceptre d'une main ferme et vigoureuse, le régent avait chargé Anne de représenter à son fils que les dix années de l'administration de son beau-père allaient bientôt expirer, et que ce prince, après avoir essayé des vains honneurs de ce monde, ne soupirait que pour le repos du cloître et ne désirait que la couronne du ciel. Si ces sentimens eussent été sincères, il pouvait en abdiquant rendre la paix à l'empire, et tranquilliser sa propre conscience par un acte de justice. Paléologue était à l'avenir seul responsable de son gouvernement ; et quels que fussent ses vices, on ne pouvait pas en craindre des suites plus funestes que les calamités d'une guerre civile, dans laquelle les deux partis se servirent encore des Barbares et des infidèles pour consommer récipro-

Jean Paléologue prend les armes contre Cantacuzène. A. D. 1353.

quement leur propre destruction. Le secours des Turcs, qui s'établirent alors en Europe d'une manière définitive, fit encore triompher Cantacuzène dans cette troisième querelle ; et Paléologue, battu sur mer et sur terre, fut contraint de chercher un asile parmi les Latins de l'île de Ténédos. Son insolence et son obstination engagèrent le vainqueur dans une démarche qui devait rendre la querelle irréconciliable. Il revêtit son fils Matthieu de la pourpre, l'associa à l'empire, et établit ainsi la succession dans la famille des Cantacuzènes ; mais Constantinople était encore attachée au sang de ses anciens maîtres, et cette dernière injure accéléra le retour de l'héritier légitime. Un noble Génois entreprit de rétablir Paléologue, obtint la promesse d'épouser sa sœur, et termina la révolution avec deux galères et deux mille cinq cents auxiliaires. Sous le prétexte de détresse, ces galères furent admises dans le petit port : on ouvrit une porte ; les soldats latins s'écrièrent tous ensemble : « Victoire et longue vie à l'empereur Jean Paléologue ! » et les habitans répondirent à leurs acclamations par un soulèvement en sa faveur. Il restait encore à Cantacuzène un parti nombreux et fidèle ; mais ce prince affirme dans son histoire (espère-t-il qu'on le croie?) que, sûr d'obtenir la victoire, il en fit le sacrifice à la délicatesse de sa conscience ; et que ce fut volontairement, et pour obéir à la voix de la religion et de la philosophie, qu'il descendit du trône pour s'enfermer avec joie dans la solitude d'un monastère(1). Dès qu'il eut renoncé à l'empire, son suc- cesseur le laissa jouir paisiblement de la réputation de sainteté ; il dévoua les restes de sa vie à l'étude et aux exercices de la piété monastique. Soit à Constantinople, où dans le monastère du mont Athos, le moine Josaphat fut toujours respecté comme le père temporel et spirituel de l'empereur, et il ne sortit de sa retraite que comme ministre de paix, pour vaincre l'obstination et obtenir le pardon de son fils rebelle (2).

Abdication de Cantacuzène, au mois de janvier. A. D. 1355.

Cependant Cantacuzène exerça dans le cloître son esprit à la guerre théologique. Il aiguisa contre les Juifs et contre les mahométans tous les traits de la controverse (3); et, dans toutes les situations de sa

Dispute concernant la lumière du mont Thabor. A. D. 1341-1351.

(1.) On peut suppléer à l'apologie ridicule de Cantacuzène, qui raconte (l. IV, c. 39-42) sa propre chute avec une confusion visible, par la relation moins complète, mais plus sincère, de Matthieu Villani (l. IV, c. 46, *in Script. rerum ital.*, t. XIV, p. 268) et par celle de Ducas (c. 10, 11).

(2) Cantacuzène reçut dans l'année 1375 une lettre du pape (Fleury, *Hist. ecclés.*, t. XX, p. 250); et des autorités respectables placent sa mort au 20 novembre 1411 (Duc., *Fam. byzant.*, p. 260). Mais s'il était de l'âge d'Andronic le Jeune, compagnon de sa jeunesse et de ses plaisirs, il faut qu'il ait vécu cent seize ans, et cette longue carrière d'un si illustre personnage aurait été généralement remarquée.

(3) Ses quatre discours ou livres furent imprimés à Bâle en 1543 (Fabricius, *Bibl. græc.*, t. VI, p. 473); il les composa pour tranquilliser un prosélyte que ses amis d'Ispahan persécutaient continuellement de leurs lettres. Cantacuzène avait lu le Koran; mais je vois, d'après Maracci, qu'il adop-

vie, défendit avec un zèle égal la lumière divine du mont Thabor, question mémorable, et chef-d'œuvre de la folie religieuse des Grecs. Les fakirs de l'Inde (1) et les moines de l'Église orientale étaient également persuadés que, dans l'abstraction totale des facultés du corps et de l'imagination, le pur esprit pouvait s'élever à la jouissance ou à la vision de la Divinité. Les expressions de l'abbé qui gouvernait les monastères du mont Athos (2) dans le onzième siècle, développeront d'une manière plus sensible l'opinion et les pratiques de ces religieux. « Quand vous serez seuls dans votre cellule, dit le docteur asiatique, fermez la porte et asseyez-vous dans un coin ; élevez votre imagination au-dessus de toutes les choses vaines et transitoires ; appuyez votre barbe et votre menton sur votre poitrine ; tournez vos regards et vos pensées vers le milieu de votre ventre, où est placé votre nombril, et cherchez l'endroit du cœur, siége de l'âme. Tout vous paraîtra d'abord triste et sombre ; mais si vous persévérez jour et nuit, vous éprouverez une joie ineffable. Dès que l'âme a découvert la place du cœur, elle se trouve enveloppée dans une lumière mystique et éthérée. » Cette

---

tait toutes les fables que l'on débitait contre Mahomet et sa religion.

(1) *Voyez* les *Voyages de Bernier*, t. 1, p. 127.

(2) Mosheim, *Instit. ecclés.*, p. 522, 523 ; Fleury, *Hist. ecclés.*, t. xx, p. 22-24-107-114, etc. Le premier développe philosophiquement les causes ; le second transcrit et traduit avec les préjugés d'un prêtre catholique.

lumière, production d'une imagination malade, d'un estomac et d'un cerveau vides, était adorée des quiétistes comme l'essence pure et parfaite de Dieu lui-même. Tant que cette folie se renferma dans les monastères du mont Athos, les solitaires, simples dans leur foi, ne pensèrent point à s'informer comment l'essence divine pouvait être une substance *matérielle*, ou comment une substance *immatérielle* pouvait se rendre sensible aux yeux du corps. Mais sous le règne d'Andronic le Jeune, ces couvens reçurent la visite de Barlaam, moine de la Calabre (1), également versé dans la philosophie et la théologie, dans la langue des Grecs et celle des Romains, et dont le génie souple pouvait, selon l'intérêt du moment, soutenir leurs opinions opposées ; un solitaire indiscret révéla au voyageur les mystères de l'oraison mentale ou contemplative. Barlaam ne laissa point échapper l'occasion de ridiculiser les quiétistes qui plaçaient l'âme dans le nombril, et d'accuser les moines du mont Athos d'hérésie et de blasphême. Ses argumens forcèrent les plus instruits à renoncer aux opinions peu approfondies de leurs frères ou du moins à les dissimuler, et Grégoire Palamas introduisit une distinction scolastique entre l'essence de Dieu et son

---

(1) Basnage (*in Canisii antiq. Lect.*, t. IV, p. 363-368) a examiné l'histoire et le caractère de Barlaam. La contradiction de ses opinions en différentes circonstances a fait naître des doutes sur l'identité de sa personne. *Voyez* aussi Fabricius, *Bibl. græc.*, t. x, p. 427-432.

opération. Son essence inaccessible réside, selon Grégoire, au milieu d'une lumière éternelle et incréée, et cette vision béatifique des saints s'était manifestée aux disciples du mont Thabor, dans la transfiguration de Jésus-Christ. Mais cette distinction ne put se soustraire au reproche de polythéisme; Barlaam nia avec violence l'éternité de la lumière du mont Thabor, et accusa les palamites de reconnaître deux substances éternelles ou deux divinités, l'une visible et l'autre invisible. Du mont Athos, où la fureur des moines menaçait sa vie, le moine calabrois s'enfuit à Constantinople, où ses manières agréables et polies lui gagnèrent la confiance du grand-domestique et celle de l'empereur. La cour et la ville prirent part à cette querelle théologique, suivie avec ardeur au milieu des désordres de la guerre civile. Mais Barlaam déshonora sa doctrine par sa fuite et son apostasie; les palamites triomphèrent, et le patriarche Jean d'Apri, leur adversaire, fut déposé par le consentement unanime des deux factions de l'État. Cantacuzène présida, en qualité d'empereur et de théologien, le synode de l'Église grecque qui établit comme article de foi la lumière incréée du mont Thabor; et après tant d'autres insultes, la raison humaine dut se regarder comme peu blessée par l'addition d'une seule absurdité. Un grand nombre de rouleaux de papier ou de parchemins furent salis de cette dispute; les sectaires impénitens qui refusèrent de souscrire à ce nouveau symbole, furent privés des honneurs de la sépulture chrétienne; mais dès le siècle suivant cette question tomba dans l'oubli, et je ne vois point que le glaive ou le feu aient été employés à extirper l'hérésie du moine Barlaam (1).

J'ai réservé pour la fin de ce chapitre la guerre des Génois, qui ébranla le trône de Cantacuzène et démontra la faiblesse de l'empire. Les Génois, qui occupaient le faubourg de Péra ou Galata depuis que les Latins avaient été chassés de Constantinople, recevaient cet honorable fief de la bonté du souverain; on leur permettait de conserver leurs lois et d'obéir à leurs magistrats particuliers, mais en se soumettant aux devoirs de vassaux et de sujets. On emprunta des Latins la dénomination expressive *d'hommes liges* (2), et leur podestat ou chef, avant de prendre possession de son office, prêtait à l'empereur le serment de fidélité. Gênes fit avec les Grecs une alliance solide, et s'engagea à fournir à l'empire, en cas de guerre défensive, une flotte de cent galères,

{Établissement des Génois à Péra ou Galata. A. D. 1291-1347.}

(1) *Voyez* Cantacuzène (l. II, c. 39, 40; l. IV, c. 3-23, 24, 25) et Nicéphore Grégoras (l. XI, c. 10; l. XV, 3-7) dont les derniers livres, depuis le dix-neuvième jusqu'au vingt-quatrième, ne traitent guère que de ce sujet, si intéressant pour les auteurs. Boivin (*in Vit.* Nicéph. Grég.), d'après les livres qui n'ont point été publiés, et Fabricius (*Biblioth. græc.*, t. x, p. 462-473), ou plutôt Montfaucon, d'après des manuscrits de la bibliothèque de Coislin, ont ajouté quelques faits et quelques documens.

(2) Pachymère (l. V, c. 10) traduit très-bien λιξιους (*ligios*) par ιδιους. Les Glossaires de Ducange enseignent amplement l'usage de ces mots en grec et en latin sous le règne féodal (*Græc.*, p. 811, 812; *Latin.*, t. IV; p. 109-111).

dont la moitié devait être armée et équipée aux frais de la république. Michel Paléologue s'attacha durant son règne à relever la marine nationale, afin de ne plus dépendre d'un secours étranger; et la vigueur de son gouvernement contint les Génois de Galata dans les bornes que l'insolence de la richesse et l'esprit républicain les disposaient souvent à franchir. Un de leurs matelots se vanta un jour que ses compatriotes seraient bientôt les maîtres de la capitale, et tua le Grec qui s'était offensé de cette menace. Un de leurs vaisseaux de guerre, en passant devant le palais, refusa le salut, et se permit ensuite quelques actes de piraterie sur la mer Noire. Les Génois se disposaient à défendre les coupables ; mais, environnés des troupes impériales dans le long village de Galata ouvert de toutes parts, prêts à se voir donner l'assaut, ils implorèrent humblement la clémence de leur souverain. La facilité de pénétrer dans leur résidence, en assurant leur soumission, les exposait aux attaques des Vénitiens, leurs rivaux, qui, sous le règne d'Andronic l'Ancien, osèrent insulter la majesté du trône. A l'approche de leurs flottes, les Génois se retirèrent dans la ville avec leurs familles et leurs effets. Le faubourg qu'ils habitaient fut réduit en cendres; et le prince pusillanime, témoin de cet incendie, en témoigna pacifiquement son ressentiment dans une ambassade. Les Génois tirèrent un avantage durable de cette calamité passagère, et abusèrent bientôt de la permission qu'ils obtinrent d'environner Galata d'un mur fortifié, d'introduire l'eau de la mer dans le fossé, et de garnir le rempart de tours et de machines propres à le défendre. Les limites étroites de leur habitation ne purent contenir long-temps l'accroissement de leur colonie : ils acquirent successivement de nouveaux terrains, et les montagnes voisines se couvrirent de leurs maisons de campagne et de leurs châteaux, qu'ils unirent et défendirent par de nouvelles fortifications (1). Les empereurs grecs, maîtres du passage étroit qui forme pour ainsi dire la porte de la mer intérieure, regardaient le commerce et la navigation du Pont-Euxin comme une partie de leur patrimoine. Sous le règne de Michel Paléologue, le sultan d'Égypte reconnut leur prérogative, en sollicitant et en obtenant la permission d'expédier tous les ans un vaisseau dans la Circassie et dans la Petite-Tartarie, pour l'achat des esclaves; permission dangereuse pour les chrétiens, puisque ces esclaves étaient ceux qu'on élevait pour recruter la redoutable troupe des mamelüks (2). La

---

(1) Ducange décrit l'établissement et les progrès des Génois à Péra ou Galata (*C. P. Christiana*, l. 1, p. 68, 69), d'après les historiens de Byzance; Pachymère (l. 11, c. 35; l. v, 10-30; l. ix, 15; l. xii, 6-9), Nicéphore Grégoras (l. v, c. 4; l. vi, c. 11; l. ix, c. 5; l. xi, c. 1; l. xv, c. 1-6), et Cantacuzène (l. 1, c. 12; l. 11, c. 29, etc.).

(2) Pachymère (l. 111, c. 3, 4, 5) et Nicéphore Grégoras (l. iv, c. 7) sentent et déplorent l'un et l'autre les effets de cette pernicieuse indulgence. Bibaras, sultan d'Égypte, et Tartare de nation mais zélé musulman, obtint des enfans de Gengis la permission de construire une mosquée dans

Commerce et insolence des Génois.

colonie génoise de Péra fit avec avantage le commerce lucratif de la mer Noire; ils fournirent les Grecs de grains et de poissons, deux articles presque également indispensables à un peuple superstitieux. Il semble que la nature prenne soin de faire croître elle-même les fertiles moissons de l'Ukraine, produits d'une culture grossière et sauvage; et les énormes esturgeons que l'on pêche vers l'embouchure du Don ou du Tanaïs, lorsqu'ils s'arrêtent dans le riche limon et les eaux profondes des Palus-Méotides, renouvellent sans cesse une exportation inépuisable de caviar et de poisson salé (1). Les eaux de l'Oxus, de la mer Caspienne, du Volga et du Don, ouvraient un passage pénible et hasardeux aux épiceries et aux pierres précieuses de l'Inde. Après une marche de trois mois, les caravanes de Carizme trouvaient les vaisseaux d'Italie dans les ports de la Crimée (2). Les Génois s'emparèrent de toutes ces

---

la capitale de la Crimée (de Guignes, *Hist. des Huns*, t. III, p. 343).

(1) On assura Chardin à Caffa (*Voyages en Perse*, t. 1, p. 48) que ces poissons avaient quelquefois jusqu'à vingt-six pieds de longueur, pesaient huit ou neuf cents livres, et donnaient trois ou quatre quintaux de caviar ou d'*œufs*. Du temps de Démosthènes, le Bosphore fournissait de grains la ville d'Athènes.

(2) De Guignes, *Hist. des Huns*, t. III, p. 343, 344; *Voyages de Ramusio*, t. 1, fol. 400. Mais ce transport par terre ou par eau n'était praticable que lorsque toutes les hordes de Tartares étaient réunies sous le gouvernement d'un prince sage et puissant.

branches de commerce, et forcèrent les Vénitiens et les Pisans d'y renoncer. Ils tenaient les nationaux en respect par les villes et les forteresses qui s'élevaient insensiblement sur les fondemens de leurs modestes factoreries; et les Tartares assiégèrent inutilement Caffa (1), leur principal établissement. Les Grecs, totalement dépourvus de vaisseaux, étaient à la merci de ces audacieux marchands, qui approvisionnaient ou affamaient Constantinople au gré de leur caprice ou de leur intérêt. Les Génois s'approprièrent la pêche, les douanes et jusqu'aux droits seigneuriaux du Bosphore, dont ils tiraient un revenu de deux cent mille pièces d'or; et c'était avec répugnance qu'ils en laissaient trente mille à l'empereur (2). La colonie de Péra ou Galata agissait soit en temps de paix, soit en temps de guerre, comme un État indépendant; et le podestat génois oubliait souvent, comme cela arrivera toujours dans les établissemens éloignés, qu'il dépendait de la république.

L'insolence des Génois fut encouragée par la faiblesse d'Andronic l'Ancien et par les guerres civiles qui affligèrent sa vieillesse et la minorité de son petit-fils. Les talens de Cantacuzène furent employés

Guerre des Génois contre l'empereur Cantacuzène.
A. D. 1348

---

(1) Nicéphore Grégoras (l. XIII, c. 12) se montre judicieux et bien instruit, en parlant du commerce et des colonies de la mer Noire. Chardin décrit les ruines de Caffa, où il vit en quarante jours plus de quatre cents voiles employées au commerce de grains et de poisson (*Voyages de Perse*, t. 1, p. 46-48).

(2) *Voyez* Nicéph. Grég., l. XVII, c. 1.

à ruiner l'empire plutôt qu'à le défendre ; et après avoir terminé victorieusement la guerre civile, il se trouva réduit à la honte de faire juger qui des Grecs ou des Génois devait régner à Constantinople. Le refus de quelques terres voisines, de quelques hauteurs où ils voulaient construire de nouvelles fortifications, offensa les marchands de Péra, et durant l'absence de l'empereur qu'une maladie retenait à Démotica, ils bravèrent le faible gouvernement de l'impératrice. Ces audacieux républicains attaquèrent et coulèrent bas un vaisseau de Constantinople, qui avait osé pêcher à l'entrée du port ; ils en massacrèrent l'équipage, et ensuite, au lieu de solliciter leur pardon, ils osèrent demander satisfaction. Ils prétendirent que les Grecs renonçassent à tout exercice de navigation, et repoussèrent avec des forces régulières les premiers mouvemens de l'indignation du peuple. Tous les Génois de la colonie, sans distinction de sexe ni d'âge, travaillèrent avec une diligence incroyable à occuper le terrain qu'on leur refusait, à élever un mur solide, et à l'environner d'un fossé profond. En même temps ils attaquèrent et brûlèrent deux galères byzantines. Trois autres, dans lesquelles consistaient les restes de la marine impériale, prirent la fuite pour éviter le même sort. Toutes les habitations situées hors du port ou le long du rivage furent pillées et détruites ; le régent et l'impératrice ne s'occupèrent que de défendre la capitale. Le retour de Cantacuzène calma l'alarme publique. L'empereur inclinait pour des mesures pacifiques ; mais ses ennemis refusèrent toutes les propositions raisonnables, et il céda à l'ardeur de ses sujets, qui menaçaient les Génois, dans le style de l'Écriture, de les briser comme un vase d'argile, et qui payèrent cependant avec répugnance les taxes imposées pour la construction des vaisseaux et les dépenses de la guerre. Les deux nations étant maîtresses, l'une de la terre et l'autre de la mer, Constantinople et Péra éprouvaient également tous les inconvéniens d'un siége. Les marchands de la colonie, qui s'étaient flattés de voir terminer la querelle en peu de jours, commençaient à murmurer de leurs pertes; la république de Gênes, déchirée par des factions, tardait à envoyer des secours; et les plus prudens profitèrent de l'occasion d'un vaisseau de Rhodes pour éloigner leur fortune et leur famille du théâtre de la guerre. Au commencement du printemps, la flotte de Byzance, composée de sept galères et de quelques petits vaisseaux, sortit du port, cingla, rangée sur une seule ligne, vers le rivage de Péra, et présenta maladroitement le flanc à la proue de ses adversaires. Les équipages étaient composés de paysans ou d'ouvriers qui n'avaient point, pour compenser leur ignorance, le courage naturel des Barbares. Le vent était fort, la mer haute : à peine aperçurent-ils de loin l'escadre ennemie encore immobile, qu'ils se précipitèrent dans la mer, se livrant à un danger certain pour éviter un danger douteux. Les troupes qui marchaient à l'attaque des lignes de Péra, furent au même instant saisies de la

Défaite de la flotte de Cantacuzène.

même terreur panique, et les Génois furent étonnés, presque honteux du peu que leur avait coûté cette double victoire : ayant couronné de fleurs leurs vaisseaux, ils amarinèrent les galères abandonnées, et les promenèrent plusieurs fois en triomphe devant les murs du palais. La seule vertu que pût en ce moment exercer l'empereur était la patience, et l'espoir de la vengeance sa seule consolation. Cependant la détresse où se trouvaient réduits les deux partis, les contraignit à un arrangement momentané, et l'on essaya de couvrir la honte de l'empire de quelques légères apparences de dignité et de puissance. Cantacuzène, ayant convoqué les chefs de la colonie, feignit de mépriser l'objet de la contestation, et, après quelques doux reproches, accorda généreusement aux Génois les terres dont ils s'étaient emparés, et que, pour la forme seulement, il avait voulu ou paru remettre sous la garde de ses officiers (1).

Victoire des Génois sur les Grecs et les Vénitiens. 13 février 1352.

Mais l'empereur fut bientôt sollicité de violer cet accord et de joindre ses armes à celles des Vénitiens, ennemis éternels des Génois et de leurs colonies. Tandis qu'il balançait entre la paix et la guerre, les habitans de Péra ranimèrent son juste ressentiment

---

(1) Cantacuzène (l. IV, c. 11) raconte les événemens de cette guerre, mais son récit est obscur et confus; celui de Nicéphore Grégoras (l. XVII, c. 1-7) est clair et fidèle; le prêtre était moins responsable que le prince, des fautes et de la défaite de la flotte.

en lançant de leur rempart un bloc de pierre qui tomba au milieu de Constantinople. Lorsqu'il en fit des plaintes, ils s'excusèrent froidement sur l'imprudence de leur ingénieur. Mais ils recommencèrent dès le lendemain, et se félicitèrent d'une épreuve qui leur apprenait que Constantinople n'était point hors de l'atteinte de leur artillerie. Cantacuzène signa aussitôt le traité proposé par les Vénitiens ; mais la puissance de l'empire romain influa bien peu dans la querelle de ces deux riches et puissantes républiques (1). Depuis le détroit de Gibraltar jusqu'à l'embouchure du Tanaïs, leurs flottes combattirent plusieurs fois sans avantages décisifs, et donnèrent enfin une bataille mémorable dans l'étroite mer qui baigne les murs de Constantinople. Il ne serait pas facile de concilier ensemble les relations des Grecs, des Vénitiens et des Génois (2). En suivant le récit d'un historien impartial (3), j'emprunterai de chaque na-

---

(1) Cantacuzène est encore obscur dans le récit de cette seconde guerre (l. IV, c. 18; p. 24, 25-28-32); il déguise ce qu'il n'ose nier. Je regrette cette partie de Nicéphore Grégoras, qui est encore en manuscrit à Paris.

(2) Muratori (*Annali d'Italia*, t. XII, p. 144) renvoie aux anciennes Chroniques de Venise (Caresinus, continuateur d'André Dandolo, t. XII, p. 421, 422) et de Gênes (George Stella, *Annales genuenses*, t. XVII, p. 1091, 1092). Je les ai consultées soigneusement l'une et l'autre dans la grande Collection des *Historiens de l'Italie*.

(3) Voyez la *Chronique* de Matthieu Villani de Florence, (l. II, c. 59, 60, p. 145-147; c. 74, 75, p. 156, 157, dans la Collection de Muratori, t. XIV).

tion les faits qui sont à son désavantage ou à l'honneur de ses ennemis. Les Vénitiens, soutenus de leurs alliés les Catalans, avaient l'avantage du nombre; et leur flotte, en y comprenant le faible secours de huit galères byzantines, était composée de soixante-quinze voiles. Les Génois n'en avaient pas plus de soixante-quatre; mais leurs vaisseaux de guerre surpassaient, dans ce siècle, en force et en grandeur, ceux de toutes les puissances maritimes. Les amiraux étaient Doria et Pisani, dont les familles et les noms tiennent une place honorable dans les annales de leur patrie; mais les talens et la réputation du premier éclipsaient le mérite personnel de son rival. Doria attaqua les ennemis dans un moment de tempête, et le combat tumultueux dura depuis l'aurore jusqu'à la fin du jour. Les ennemis des Génois font l'éloge de leur valeur, et la conduite des Vénitiens n'obtient pas même l'approbation de leurs amis; mais les deux partis admirent unanimement l'adresse et la valeur des Catalans, qui, couverts de blessures, soutinrent tout l'effort du combat. Lorsque les deux flottes se séparèrent, la victoire pouvait paraître incertaine. Cependant si les Génois perdirent treize galères prises ou coulées bas, ils en détruisirent vingt-six, deux des Grecs, dix des Catalans, et quatorze des Vénitiens. Le chagrin des vainqueurs fit connaître qu'ils étaient accoutumés à compter sur des victoires plus décisives; mais Pisani avoua sa défaite en se retirant dans un port fortifié, d'où ensuite, sous le prétexte d'exécuter les ordres du sénat, il fit voile avec les restes d'une flotte fugitive et en désordre pour l'île de Candie, laissant la mer libre à ses rivaux. Dans une lettre adressée publiquement au doge et au sénat, Pétrarque (1) emploie son éloquence à réconcilier les deux puissances maritimes, les deux flambeaux de l'Italie. L'orateur célèbre la valeur et la victoire des Génois, qu'il considère comme les plus habiles marins de l'univers, et déplore le malheur de leurs frères les Vénitiens. Il les engage à poursuivre avec la flamme et le fer les vils et perfides Grecs, et à purger la capitale de l'Orient de l'hérésie dont elle est infectée. Abandonnés de leurs alliés, les Grecs ne pouvaient plus espérer de faire résistance : trois mois après cette bataille navale, l'empereur Cantacuzène sollicita et signa un traité par lequel il bannissait pour toujours les Catalans et les Vénitiens, et accordait aux Génois tous les droits du commerce et presque de la souveraineté. L'empire romain (on ne peut s'empêcher de sourire en lui donnant encore ce nom) serait bientôt devenu une dépendance de Gênes, si l'ambition de cette république n'eût pas été arrêtée par la perte de sa liberté et la destruction de sa marine. Une longue

---

(1) L'abbé de Sade (*Mémoires sur la vie de Pétrarque*, t. III, p. 257-263) a traduit cette lettre, qu'il avait copiée dans un manuscrit de la Bibliothèque du roi de France. Quoique attaché au duc de Milan, Pétrarque ne cache ni sa surprise ni ses regrets de la défaite et du désespoir des Génois dans l'année suivante (p. 323-332).

rivalité de cent trente ans se termina par le triomphe de Venise ; et les factions des Génois forcèrent leur nation à chercher la paix domestique sous la domination d'un maître étranger, du duc de Milan ou du roi de France. Cependant, en renonçant aux conquêtes, les Génois conservèrent le génie du commerce ; la colonie de Péra continua de dominer la capitale, et resta maîtresse de la navigation de la mer Noire, jusqu'au moment où la conquête des Turcs l'enveloppa dans la ruine de Constantinople.

CHAPITRE LXIV.

Conquêtes de Gengis-khan et des Mongouls depuis la Chine jusqu'à la Pologne. Danger des Grecs et de Constantinople. Origine des Turcs ottomans en Bithynie. Règnes et victoires d'Othman, Orchan, Amurath 1er et Bajazet 1er. Fondation et progrès de la monarchie des Turcs en Asie et en Europe. Situation critique de Constantinople et de l'empire grec.

Des petites querelles d'une ville avec ses faubourgs, des discordes et de la lâcheté des Grecs dégénérés, je vais passer aux brillantes victoires des Turcs, dont l'esclavage civil était ennobli par la discipline militaire, l'enthousiasme religieux et l'énergie du caractère national. L'origine et les progrès des Ottomans, aujourd'hui souverains de Constantinople, se trouvent liés aux plus importantes scènes de l'histoire moderne; mais elles exigent la connaissance préliminaire de la grande irruption des Mongouls et des Tartares, dont on peut comparer les conquêtes rapides aux premières convulsions de la nature, qui agitèrent et changèrent la surface du globe. Je me suis déjà cru permis de faire entrer dans mon ouvrage les détails relatifs aux nations qui ont contribué de près ou de loin à la chute de l'empire romain, et je ne puis me déterminer à passer sous silence des événemens dont la grandeur peu commune peut intéresser le philosophe à l'histoire du carnage et de la destruction (1).

<small>Zingis-khan, ou Gengis-khan, premier empereur des Mongouls et des Tartares.
A. D.
1206-1227.</small>

Toutes ces émigrations sont sorties successivement des vastes montagnes situées entre la Chine, la Sibérie et la mer Caspienne. Les anciennes résidences des Huns et des Turcs étaient habitées, dans le douzième siècle, par des hordes ou tribus de pâtres, qui descendaient de la même origine et conservaient les mêmes mœurs. Le redoutable Gengiskhan les réunit et les conduisit à la victoire. Ce Barbare, connu primitivement sous le nom de Témugin, s'était élevé, en écrasant ses égaux, au faîte de la grandeur. Il descendait d'une race noble; mais ce fut dans l'orgueil de la victoire que le prince ou son peuple imaginèrent d'attribuer l'origine de la famille de Gengis à une vierge immaculée, mère de son septième ancêtre. Son père avait régné sur treize hordes formant environ trente ou quarante mille familles. Durant l'enfance de Témugin, plus des deux tiers lui refusèrent l'obéissance et le tribut. À l'âge de treize ans, Témugin livra bataille à ses sujets rebelles, et le futur conquérant de l'Asie fut obligé de céder et de prendre la fuite. Mais il se montra supérieur à la fortune; et à l'âge de qua-

---

(1) J'invite le lecteur à repasser ceux des chapitres de cette histoire qui traitent des mœurs des nations pastorales, des conquêtes d'Attila et des Huns, et que j'ai composés dans un temps où j'avais le désir plutôt que l'espérance de continuer mon ouvrage.

rante ans, Témugin faisait respecter son nom et son pouvoir à toutes les tribus environnantes. Dans un état de société où la politique est encore grossière et la valeur générale, l'ascendant d'un seul ne peut être fondé que sur le pouvoir et la volonté de punir ses ennemis et de récompenser ses partisans. Lorsque Témugin conclut sa première ligue militaire, les cérémonies se bornèrent au sacrifice d'un cheval, et à goûter réciproquement de l'eau d'un ruisseau. Il promit de partager avec ses compagnons les faveurs et les revers de la destinée, et leur distribua ses effets et ses chevaux, conservant pour fortune leur reconnaissance et son espoir. Après sa première victoire, il fit placer soixante-dix chaudières sur une fournaise, et soixante-dix rebelles des plus coupables furent jetés dans l'eau bouillante. Sa sphère d'attraction s'agrandit tous les jours par la ruine de ceux qui résistaient et la prudente soumission des autres ; les plus hardis tremblèrent en contemplant, enchâssé dans de l'argent, le crâne du khan des Kéraïtes (1), qui, sous le nom de Prêtre-Jean, avait entretenu une correspondance avec le pape et les

---

(1) Les khans des Kéraïtes n'auraient probablement pu même lire les éloquentes épîtres que composèrent en leur nom les missionnaires nestoriens ; qui enrichissaient leur royaume de toutes les fabuleuses merveilles attribuées aux royaumes indiens. Peut-être ces Tartares (nommés le Prêtre-Jean) s'étaient-ils soumis au baptême et à l'ordination. *Voyez* Assem., *Bibl. orient.*, t. III, part. II, p. 487-503.

princes de l'Europe. L'ambitieux Témugin ne négligea point l'influence de la superstition ; et ce fut d'un prophète de ces hordes sauvages, qui montait quelquefois au ciel sur un cheval blanc, qu'il reçut le titre de Gengis (1), *le plus grand*, et le droit divin à la conquête et à l'empire de l'univers. Dans un *couroultaï* ou diète générale, il s'assit sur un feutre, qu'on révéra long-temps comme une relique ; et on le proclama solennellement grand khan ou empereur des Mongouls (2) et des Tartares (3). De ces noms devenus rivaux, bien que sortis de la même source, le premier s'est perpétué dans la race impériale, et

---

(1) Depuis que Voltaire a publié son histoire et sa tragédie, le nom de Gengis paraît, au moins en français, avoir été généralement adopté. Cependant Abulghazi-khan devait savoir le véritable nom de son ancêtre : son étymologie paraît juste ; *zin*, en langue mongoule, signifie *grand*, et *gis* est la terminaison du superlatif (*Hist. généalog. des Tartares*, part. III, p. 194, 195). D'après les mêmes idées de grandeur, on a donné le surnom de Zingis à l'Océan.

(2) Le nom de Mongouls a prévalu parmi les Orientaux, et s'applique encore au souverain titulaire, au grand Mogol de l'Indoustan.

(3) Les Tartares (ou proprement les Tatars) descendaient de Tatar-khan, frère de Mogul-khan (*Voyez* Abulghazi, première et seconde parties). Ils formèrent une horde de soixante-dix mille familles sur les bords du Kitay (p. 103-112) ; dans la grande invasion d'Europe (A. D. 1238), il paraît qu'ils marchaient à la tête de l'avant-garde, et la ressemblance du nom de *Tartarei* rendit celui de Tartares plus familier aux Latins (M. Paris, p. 398).

l'autre, par erreur ou par hasard, s'est étendu à tous les habitans des vastes déserts du Nord.

Le code de lois dicté par Gengis à ses sujets protégeait la paix domestique et encourageait les guerres étrangères. Les crimes d'adultère, de meurtre, de parjure, le vol d'un cheval ou d'un bœuf, étaient punis de mort, et les plus féroces des hommes conservèrent entre eux de la modération et de l'équité. L'élection du grand khan fut réservée à l'avenir aux princes de sa famille et aux chefs de tribus. Il fit des réglemens pour la chasse, source des plaisirs et de la subsistance d'un camp de Tartares. La nation victorieuse ne pouvait être soumise à aucun travail servile : elle en chargeait les esclaves et les étrangers, et tous les travaux étaient serviles à ses yeux, excepté la profession des armes. L'exercice et la discipline des troupes indiquent l'expérience d'un ancien commandant. Elles étaient armées d'arcs, de cimeterres et de massues de fer, et divisées par cent, par mille et par dix mille. Chaque officier ou soldat répondait, sur sa propre vie, de la sûreté ou de l'honneur de ses compagnons ; et le génie de la victoire semble avoir dicté la loi qui défend de faire la paix avec l'ennemi, qu'il ne soit suppliant et vaincu. Mais c'est à la religion de Gengis que nous devons principalement nos éloges et notre admiration. Tandis que les inquisiteurs de la foi chrétienne défendaient l'absurdité par la cruauté, un Barbare, prévenant les leçons de la philosophie, établissait par ses lois un système de théisme pur et de parfaite to-

Lois de Gengiskhan.

lérance (1). Son premier et seul article de foi était l'existence d'un Dieu, l'auteur de tout bien, qui remplit de sa présence la terre et les cieux, créés par son pouvoir. Les Tartares et les Mongouls adoraient les idoles particulières de leur tribu; des missionnaires étrangers en avaient converti un grand nombre à la loi du Christ, à celle de Moïse ou de Mahomet. Ils professaient tous, librement et sans querelles, leur religion dans l'enceinte du même camp. Le bonze, l'iman, le rabbin, le nestorien et le prêtre catholique, jouissaient également de l'exemption honorable du service et du tribut. Dans la mosquée de Bochara, le fougueux conquérant put fouler le Koran aux pieds de ses chevaux; mais dans les momens de calme, le législateur respecta les prophètes et les pontifes de toutes les sectes. La raison de Gengis ne devait rien aux livres: le khan ne savait ni lire ni écrire; et, en exceptant la tribu des Igours, presque tous les Mongouls ou les Tartares étaient aussi ignorans que leur souverain. Le souvenir de leurs exploits s'est conservé par tradition. Soixante-huit ans après la mort de Gengis, on a recueilli et écrit ces traditions (2). On peut suppléer à

---

(1) On trouve une conformité singulière entre les lois religieuses de Gengis-khan et celles de M. Locke (*Constitut. de la Caroline*, dans ses *OEuv.*, vol. IV, p. 535, édit. in-4°, 1777).

(2) Dans l'année 1294, et par l'ordre de Cazan, khan de Perse, et le quatrième descendant de Gengis. D'après ces traditions, son visir Fadlallah composa l'*Histoire des Mongouls* en langue persane; Petis de La Croix s'en est servi

l'insuffisance de leurs annales par celles des Chinois (1), des Persans (2), des Arméniens (3), des Sy-

---

(*Hist. de Gengis-khan*, p. 537-539). *L'Histoire généalogique des Tartares* (à Leyde, 1726, *in-*12; 2 vol.) a été traduite par les Suédois prisonniers en Sibérie, sur le manuscrit mongoul d'Abulghazi-Bahadar-khan, descendant de Gengis, qui régnait sur les Usbeks de Charasme ou Charizme (A. D. 1644-1663). Il est fort précieux par l'exactitude des noms, des généalogies et des mœurs de sa nation. De ses neuf parties, la première descend depuis Adam jusqu'à Mogul-khan; la seconde, depuis Mogul jusqu'à Gengis; la troisième contient la vie de Gengis; les quatrième, cinquième, sixième et septième, racontent l'histoire générale de ses quatre fils et de leur postérité; les huitième et neuvième renferment l'histoire particulière des descendans de Sheibani-khan, qui régna dans le Maurenahar et le Charasme.

(1) *Histoire de Gengis-khan et de toute la dynastie des Mongouls ses successeurs, conquérans de la Chine, tirée de l'Histoire de la Chine*, par le R. P. Gaubil, de la Société de Jésus, missionnaire à Pékin, à Paris, 1739, *in-*4°. Cette traduction porte l'empreinte chinoise de l'exactitude scrupuleuse pour les faits domestiques, et de la plus parfaite ignorance pour tout ce qui est étranger.

(2) *Voyez l'Histoire du grand Gengis-khan, premier empereur des Mongouls et des Tartares*, par M. Petis de La Croix, à Paris, 1710; *in-*12. Cet ouvrage lui a coûté dix ans de travaux; il est tiré en grande partie des écrivains persans, entre autres de Nisavi. Ce secrétaire du sultan Gelaleddin a le mérite et les préjugés d'un contemporain. On peut reprocher au compilateur ou aux originaux un style un peu trop romanesque. *Voyez* aussi les articles de Gengis-khan, Mohammed, Gelaleddin, etc., dans la *Bibliothèque orientale* de d'Herbelot.

(3) Haithonus ou Aithonus, prince arménien, et depuis

riens (1), des Arabes (2), des Grecs (3), des Russes (4), des Polonais (5), des Hongrois (6) et des

---

moine prémontré (Fabricius, *Bibl. lat. med. ævi*, t. 1, p. 34), dicta en français son livre *de Tartaris*, ses anciens compagnons de guerre. Il fut immédiatement traduit en latin; et inséré dans le *Novus Orbis* de Simon Grynæus (*Bâle*, 1555, *in-folio*).

(1) Gengis-khan et ses premiers successeurs occupent la fin de la neuvième dynastie d'Abulpharage (*vers*. Pococke, *Oxford*, 1663, *in*-4°), et sa dixième dynastie est celle des Mongouls de Perse. Assemanni (*Bibl. orient.*, t. II) a extrait quelques faits de ses écrits syriaques, et de la Vie des maphriens jacobites ou primats de l'Orient.

(2) Parmi les Arabes de langage et de religion, nous pouvons distinguer Abulféda, sultan de Hamah en Syrie, qui combattit en personne contre les Mongouls, sous les drapeaux des Mamelucks.

(3) Nicéphore Grégoras (l. II, c. 5, 6) a senti la nécessité de lier l'histoire des Scythes à celle de Byzance. Il décrit avec élégance et exactitude l'établissement et les mœurs des Mongouls dans la Perse; mais il n'est point instruit de leur origine, et il défigure les noms de Gengis et de ses fils.

(4) M. Lévesque (*Hist. de Russie*, t. II) a raconté la conquête de la Russie par les Tartares, d'après le patriarche Nicon et les anciennes Chroniques.

(5) Pour la Pologne, je me contente de la *Sarmatia asiatica et europæa*, de Matthieu de Michou ou Michovia, médecin et chanoine de Cracovie (A. D. 1506), insérée dans le *Novus Orbis* de Grynæus (Fabricius, *Bibl. lat. mediæ et infimæ ætatis*, t. V, p. 56).

(6) Je citerais Thuroczius, le plus ancien écrivain de l'*Hist. générale* (part. II, c. 74, p. 150), dans le premier volume des *Scriptor. rerum hungaricarum*, si ce même vo-

Latins (1); et chacune de ces nations peut obtenir confiance lorsqu'elle raconte ses pertes et ses défaites (2).

Les armes de Gengis et de ses lieutenans soumirent successivement toutes les hordes du désert, qui campaient entre le mur de la Chine et le Volga. L'empereur mongoul devint le monarque du monde

Son invasion de la Chine.
A. D.
1210-1214.

---

lume ne contenait pas le récit original d'un contemporain qui fut témoin et victime (*M. Rogerii Hungari, varidiensis capituli canonici, carmen miserabile seu Historia super destructionem regni Hungariæ, temporibus Belæ* IV *regis per Tartaros facta*, p. 292-321). C'est un des meilleurs tableaux que je connaisse des circonstances qui accompagnent une invasion de Barbares.

(1) Matthieu Paris a représenté, d'après des renseignemens authentiques, les terreurs et le danger de l'Europe (*consultez* son volumineux Index au mot *Tartari*). Deux moines, Jean de Plano Carpini et Guillaume Rubruquis, et Marc-Paul, noble Vénitien, visitèrent, au treizième siècle, la cour du grand-khan, par des motifs de zèle ou de curiosité. Les relations latines des deux premiers sont insérées dans le premier volume de Hackluyt; l'original italien ou la traduction de la troisième (Fabricius, *Bibl. lat. medii ævi*, t. II, p. 198, t. V, p. 25) se trouve dans le second tome de Ramusio.

(2) Dans sa grande histoire des Huns, M. de Guignes a traité à fond de Gengis-khan et de ses successeurs: (*Voyez* t. III, l. XV-XIX, et dans les art. des Seljoucides de Roum, t. II, l. XI; des Carizmiens, l. XIV; et des Mamelucks, t. IV, l. XXI.) *Consultez* aussi les *Tables* du premier volume; il est très-instruit et très-exact. Cependant je n'ai pris de lui qu'une vue générale et quelques passages d'Abulféda, dont le texte n'est point encore traduit de l'arabe.

pastoral, de plusieurs millions de pâtres et de soldats fiers de leur réunion, et impatiens d'essayer leurs forces contre les riches et pacifiques habitans du Midi. Ses ancêtres avaient été tributaires des empereurs de la Chine, et Témugin lui-même s'était abaissé à recevoir un titre d'honneur et de servitude. La cour de Pékin reçut avec surprise une ambassade de son ancien vassal, qui, du ton d'un roi, prétendait lui imposer le tribut de subsides et d'obéissance qu'il avait précédemment payé lui-même, et affectait de traiter le *fils du ciel* avec le plus grand mépris. Les Chinois déguisèrent leurs craintes sous une réponse hautaine, et ces craintes furent bientôt justifiées par la marche d'une nombreuse armée, qui perça de tous côtés à travers la faible barrière de leur grand mur. Les Mongouls prirent quatre-vingt-dix villes d'assaut ou par famine. Les dix dernières se défendirent avec succès; et Gengis, qui connaissait la piété filiale des Chinois, couvrit son avant-garde de leurs parens captifs; indigne abus de la vertu de ses ennemis, qui insensiblement cessa de répondre au but qu'il se proposait. Cent mille Khitans, qui gardaient la frontière, se révoltèrent et se joignirent aux Tartares. Le vainqueur consentit cependant à traiter: une princesse de la Chine, trois mille chevaux, cinq cents jeunes hommes, autant de vierges, et un tribut d'or et d'étoffes de soie, furent le prix de sa retraite. Dans sa seconde expédition, il força l'empereur de la Chine à se retirer au-delà de la rivière Jaune, dans une résidence plus méridionale. Le siége de Pékin fut long et difficile (1); la famine réduisit les habitans à se décimer pour servir de pâture à leurs concitoyens : quand ils manquèrent de pierres, ils lancèrent des lingots d'or et d'argent. Mais les Mongouls firent jouer une mine au milieu de la ville, et l'incendie du palais dura trente jours. La Chine, ravagée par les Tartares, était encore intérieurement déchirée par des factions; et Gengis ajouta à son empire les cinq provinces septentrionales de ce royaume.

Vers l'occident, ses possessions touchaient aux frontières de Mohammed, sultan de Carizme, dont les vastes États s'étendaient depuis le golfe Persique jusqu'aux limites de l'Inde et du Turkestan, et qui, ambitieux d'imiter Alexandre le Grand, avait oublié la sujétion et l'ingratitude de ses ancêtres envers la maison de Seljouk. Gengis, dans l'intention d'entretenir une liaison de commerce et d'amitié avec le plus puissant des princes musulmans, rejeta les sollicitations secrètes du calife de Bagdad, qui voulait sacrifier l'État et sa religion à sa vengeance personnelle. Mais un acte de violence et d'inhuma- *De Carizme, de la Transoxiane et de la Perse. A. D. 1218-1224.*

---

(1) Plus proprement Yen-king, une ancienne ville dont les ruines sont encore visibles à quelque distance au sudest de la ville moderne de Pékin, qui fut bâtie par Cublaikhan (Gaubil, page 146). Pé-king et Nan-king sont des noms vagues, et désignent la cour du nord et celle du sud. On est continuellement embarrassé dans la géographie chinoise, tantôt par la ressemblance, et tantôt par le changement des noms (p. 177).

nité attira justement les armes des Tartares dans l'Asie méridionale. Mohammed fit arrêter et massacrer à Otrar une caravane composée de trois ambassadeurs et de cent cinquante marchands. Ce ne fut cependant qu'après la demande et le refus d'une satisfaction, après avoir prié et jeûné durant trois nuits sur une montagne, que l'empereur mongoul en appela au jugement de Dieu et de son épée. Nos batailles d'Europe, dit un écrivain philosophe (1), ne sont que de faibles escarmouches, si nous les comparons aux armées qui combattirent et périrent dans les plaines de l'Asie. Sept cent mille Mongouls ou Tartares marchèrent, dit-on, sous les ordres de Gengis et de ses quatre fils ; ils rencontrèrent dans les vastes plaines qui s'étendent au nord du Sihon ou Jaxartes, le sultan Mohammed à la tête de quatre cent mille guerriers ; et dans la première bataille qui dura jusqu'à la nuit, cent soixante mille Carizmiens perdirent la vie. Mohammed, surpris du nombre et de la valeur de ses ennemis, fit sa retraite et distribua ses troupes dans les villes de ses frontières, persuadé que ces Barbares, invincibles sur le champ de bataille, se laisseraient rebuter par la longueur et la difficulté d'un si grand nombre de siéges régu-

---

(1) M. de Voltaire, *Essai sur l'Histoire générale*, t. III, c. 60, p. 8. On trouve dans son histoire de Gengis et des Mongouls, comme dans tous ses ouvrages, beaucoup de réflexions judicieuses et de vérités générales mêlées de quelques erreurs particulières.

liers ; mais Gengis avait sagement formé un corps d'ingénieurs et de mécaniciens chinois, instruits peut-être du secret de la poudre, et capables d'attaquer sous sa discipline un pays étranger avec plus de vigueur et de succès qu'ils n'avaient défendu leur patrie. Les historiens persans racontent les siéges et la réduction d'Otrar, Cogende, Bochara, Samarcande, Carizme, Hérat, Merou, Nisabour, Balch et Candahar, et la conquête des riches et populeuses contrées de la Transoxiane, de Carizme et du Khorasan : les ravages de Gengis et des Mongouls nous ont déjà servi à donner une idée de ce qu'avaient pu être les invasions des Huns et d'Attila, et je me contenterai d'observer que depuis la mer Caspienne jusqu'à l'Indus, les conquérans convertirent en un désert une étendue de plusieurs centaines de milles, que la main des hommes avait cultivée et ornée de nombreuses habitations, et que cinq siècles n'ont pas suffi à réparer le ravage de quatre années. L'empereur mongoul encourageait ou tolérait les fureurs de ses soldats : emportés par l'ardeur du carnage et celle du pillage, ils oubliaient toute idée de jouissance future, et la cause de la guerre excitait encore leur férocité par les prétextes de la justice et de la vengeance. La chute et la mort du sultan Mohammed, qui, abandonné de tous et sans exciter de pitié, expira dans une île déserte de la mer Caspienne, sont une faible expiation des calamités dont il fut l'auteur. Son fils Gelaleddin arrêta souvent les Mongouls dans la carrière de la victoire; mais la valeur d'un seul héros ne suffisait pas pour sauver l'empire des Carizmiens : écrasé par le nombre dans une retraite qu'il faisait sur les bords de l'Indus, Gelaleddin poussa son cheval au milieu des flots ; et, traversant avec intrépidité le fleuve le plus rapide et le plus large de l'Asie, il excita chez son vainqueur un mouvement d'admiration. Ce fut après cette victoire que l'empereur mongoul, cédant à regret aux murmures de ses soldats enrichis et fatigués, consentit à les ramener dans leur terre natale. Chargé des dépouilles de l'Asie, il retourna lentement sur ses pas, laissa voir quelque pitié pour la misère des vaincus, et annonça l'intention de rebâtir les villes détruites par son invasion. Au-delà de l'Oxus et du Jaxartes, les deux généraux qu'il avait détachés avec trente mille hommes de cavalerie pour réduire les provinces méridionales de la Perse, joignirent son armée. Après avoir renversé tout ce qui s'opposait à leur passage, forcé le défilé de Derbend, traversé le Volga et le désert, et fait le tour entier de la mer Caspienne, ils revenaient triomphans d'une expédition dont l'antiquité n'offrait point d'exemples, et qu'on n'a jamais essayé de renouveler ; Gengis signala son retour par la défaite de tout ce qui restait de peuples tartares rebelles ou indépendans, et mourut plein d'années et de gloire, en exhortant ses fils à achever la conquête de la Chine.

<small>Sa mort.
A. D. 1227.</small>

Le harem de Gengis renfermait cinq cents femmes ou concubines, et parmi sa nombreuse postérité, il avait choisi quatre de ses fils, illustres par leur mérite autant que par leur naissance, qui exerçaient sous leur père les principaux emplois civils et militaires. Toushi était son grand veneur, Zagatai (1) son juge, Octaï son ministre, et Tuli son général. Leurs noms et leurs actions se font souvent remarquer dans l'histoire de ses conquêtes. Fermement unis par le sentiment de leur intérêt et de l'intérêt public, trois de ces frères ainsi que leurs familles se contentèrent de royaumes dépendans, et d'un consentement unanime Octaï fut proclamé grand-khan ou empereur des Mongouls ou des Tartares. Octaï eut pour successeur son fils Gayuk, dont la mort transmit le sceptre de l'empire à ses cousins Mangou et Cublaï, fils de Tuli et petits-fils de Gengis. Dans les soixante-huit années qui suivirent sa mort, ses quatre premiers successeurs soumirent presque toute l'Asie et une grande partie de l'Europe. Sans m'asservir à l'ordre des temps ou m'étendre sur les détails des événemens, je donnerai un tableau général du progrès de leurs armes, 1° à l'orient, 2° au sud, 3° à l'occident et au nord.

I. Avant l'invasion de Gengis, la Chine était par-

Conquêtes des Mongouls sous les successeurs de Gengis.
A. D. 1227-1295.

De l'empire septentrional de la Chine.
A. D. 1234.

---

(1) Zagatai donna son nom à ses États de Maurenahar ou Transoxiane, et les Persans donnent la dénomination de Zagataïs aux Mongouls qui émigrèrent de ce pays. Cette étymologie authentique et l'exemple des Usbeks, Nogais, etc., doivent nous apprendre à ne pas nier affirmativement que des nations aient adopté un nom personnel.

tagée en deux empires ou dynasties du nord et du midi (1), et la conformité des lois, du langage et des mœurs, adoucissait les inconvéniens de la différence d'origine et d'intérêt. La conquête de l'empire du nord démembré par Gengis fut totalement accomplie sept ans après sa mort. Forcé d'abandonner Pékin, l'empereur avait fixé sa résidence à Kaifiong, ville dont l'enceinte formait une circonférence de plusieurs lieues, et qui, si l'on peut en croire les annales chinoises, contenait quatorze cent mille familles d'habitans et de fugitifs. Il fallut encore avoir recours à la fuite : il s'échappa suivi de sept cavaliers, et se réfugia dans une troisième capitale, où, perdant tout espoir de sauver sa vie, il monta sur un bûcher en protestant de son innocence et accusant son malheur, et ordonna qu'on y mît le feu dès qu'il se serait poignardé. La dynastie des *Song*, les anciens souverains nationaux de tout l'empire, survécut environ quarante-cinq ans à la chute des usurpateurs du nord. La conquête totale ne s'exécuta que sous le règne de Cublaï; les Mongouls, durant cet intervalle, en furent souvent détournés par des guerres étrangères, et les Chinois, qui osaient rare-

---

(1) Marc-Paul et les géographes orientaux distinguent les empires du nord et du midi par les noms de Cathay et de Mangi; c'est ainsi que la Chine fut partagée entre le grand-khan et les Chinois, depuis l'an de grâce 1234 jusqu'en l'an 1279. Après qu'on eut trouvé la Chine, la recherche du Cathay égara nos navigateurs du seizième siècle dans leur recherche d'un passage au nord-est.

ment faire tête à leurs vainqueurs dans la plaine, leur offraient dans les villes, par leur résistance passive, une suite interminable d'assauts à livrer et des millions d'hommes à massacrer. On employait alternativement pour l'attaque et pour la défense les machines de guerre des anciens et le feu grégeois : il paraît qu'on était déjà familiarisé avec l'usage de la poudre, des bombes et des canons (1). Les siéges étaient dirigés par des mahométans et par des Francs, que les libéralités de Cublaï attiraient à son service. Après avoir passé la grande rivière, les troupes et l'artillerie furent transportées, sur une longue suite de différens canaux, jusqu'à la résidence royale de Hamcheu ou Quinsay, dans le pays où se fabrique la soie, et le plus délicieux climat de la Chine. L'empereur, prince jeune et timide, se rendit sans résis-

---

(1) Je me fie à l'érudition et à l'exactitude du père Gaubil, qui traduit le texte chinois des Annales mongoules ou d'Yuen (p. 71-93-153); mais j'ignore dans quel temps ces Annales furent composées et publiées. Les deux oncles de Marc-Paul, qui servaient comme ingénieurs au siége de Siengyangfou (l. II, c. 61, *in Ramusio*, t. II; *voyez* Gaubil, p. 155-157), devraient avoir connu et raconté les effets de cette poudre destructive, et leur silence est une objection qui paraît presque décisive. Je soupçonne que la découverte récente fut portée d'Europe en Chine par les caravanes du quinzième siècle, et adoptée faussement comme une ancienne découverte nationale antérieure à l'arrivée des Portugais et des jésuites. Cependant le père Gaubil affirme que l'usage de la poudre est connu en Chine depuis plus de seize cents ans.

tance, et avant de partir pour son exil, au fond de la Tartarie, frappa neuf fois la terre de son front, soit pour implorer la clémence du grand-khan ou pour lui rendre grâces. Cependant la guerre, désormais appelée révolte, se soutenait toujours dans les provinces méridionales, depuis Hamcheu jusqu'à Canton; et les restes obstinés du courage et de la liberté, chassés de la terre, se réfugièrent sur les vaisseaux; mais lorsque les Song se virent enveloppés et accablés par une flotte supérieure : « Il est plus glorieux pour un monarque, dit le plus brave de leurs champions, de mourir libre que de vivre esclave, » et il se précipita dans la mer tenant dans ses bras l'empereur encore enfant. Cent mille Chinois imitèrent cet exemple, et tout l'empire, depuis Tonkin jusqu'au grand mur, reconnut Cublai pour son souverain. Son ambition insatiable méditait la conquête du Japon ; la tempête détruisit deux fois sa flotte, et cette expédition malheureuse coûta inutilement la vie à cent mille Mongouls ou Chinois; mais la force ou la terreur de ses armes réduisit les royaumes circonvoisins de la Corée, du Tonkin, de la Cochinchine, de Pégu, du Bengale et du Thibet, à différens degrés de tribut et d'obéissance. Il parcourut l'océan Indien avec une flotte de mille vaisseaux ; une navigation de soixante-huit jours les conduisit, à ce qu'il paraît, à l'île de Borneo, située sous la ligne équinoxiale ; et quoiqu'ils n'en revinssent pas sans gloire et sans dépouilles, l'empereur fut mécontent d'avoir laissé échapper le sauvage souverain de cette contrée.

II. Les Mongouls firent plus tard la conquête de l'Indoustan sous la conduite des princes de la maison de Timour ; mais Holagou-khan, petit-fils de Gengis, frère et lieutenant des deux empereurs Mangou et Cublai, acheva celle de l'Iran ou de la Perse. Sans entrer dans le détail monotone d'une foule de sultans, d'émirs ou d'atabeks qu'il écrasa sous sa puissance, j'observerai seulement la défaite et la destruction des *Assassins* ou Ismaélites (1) de la Perse, destruction qu'on peut regarder comme un service rendu à l'humanité. Ces odieux sectaires avaient régné durant plus de cent soixante ans avec impunité dans les montagnes situées au sud de la mer Caspienne, et leur prince ou iman nommait un lieutenant pour conduire et gouverner la colonie du mont Liban, si formidable et si fameuse dans l'histoire des croisades (2). Au fanatisme du Koran, les Ismaélites joignaient les opinions indiennes de la transmigration des âmes, et les visions de leurs propres prophètes. Leur premier devoir était de dévouer aveuglément leur âme et leur corps aux ordres du vicaire de Dieu.

De la Perse et de l'empire des califes.
A. D. 1258.

---

(1) Tout ce qu'on peut savoir relativement aux *Assassins* de la Perse et de la Syrie, est dû à M. Falconet. *Voyez* ses deux *Mémoires* lus à l'Académie des Inscriptions, dans lesquels il a versé une érudition surabondante (t. XVII, p. 127-170).

(2) Les Ismaélites de Syrie ou *Assassins*, au nombre de quarante mille, avaient acquis ou élevé dix forteresses dans les montagnes au-dessus de Tortose. Ils furent exterminés par les Mamelucks vers l'an 1280.

Les poignards de ses missionnaires se firent sentir dans l'Orient et l'Occident. Les chrétiens et les musulmans comptent un grand nombre d'illustres victimes sacrifiées au zèle, à l'avarice ou au ressentiment du Vieux de la montagne, nom qu'on lui donnait par corruption. L'épée de Holagou brisa ses poignards, les seules armes dont il sût faire usage : il ne reste aujourd'hui d'autre vestige de ces ennemis de l'humanité que le mot d'*assassin*, que les langues de l'Europe ont adopté dans son sens le plus odieux. Le lecteur qui a suivi la grandeur et le déclin de la maison des Abbassides, ne verra point son extinction avec indifférence. Depuis la chute des descendans de l'usurpateur Seljouk, les califes avaient recouvré leurs États héréditaires de Bagdad et de l'Irak d'Arabie ; mais la ville était déchirée par des factions théologiques, et le commandeur des fidèles s'ensevelissait dans son harem, composé de sept cents concubines. A l'approche des Mongouls, il leur opposa de faibles armées et des ambassades hautaines. « C'est par l'ordre de Dieu, dit le calif Mostasem, que les fils d'Abbas commandent sur la terre. Il soutient leur trône, et leurs ennemis seront châtiés dans ce monde et dans l'autre. Qui est donc ce Holagou qui ose s'élever contre eux ? S'il veut la paix, qu'il se retire à l'instant de leur territoire sacré, et il obtiendra peut-être de notre clémence le pardon de sa faute. » Un visir perfide entretenait cette aveugle présomption, et assurait son maître que, les Barbares fussent-ils dans la ville, les femmes et les enfans suffiraient pour les écraser du haut de leurs terrasses. Mais à peine Holagou eut-il touché le fantôme, qu'il s'évanouit en fumée : après deux mois de siége, Bagdad fut emportée d'assaut et pillée par les Mongouls; leur féroce commandant prononça la sentence du calife Mostasem, dernier successeur temporel de Mahomet, et dont la famille, descendue d'Abbas, avait occupé durant plus de cinq siècles les trônes de l'Asie. Quels que fussent les desseins du conquérant, le désert de l'Arabie protégea contre son ambition les saintes cités de la Mecque et de Médine (1). Mais les Mongouls se répandirent au-delà du Tigre et de l'Euphrate, pillèrent Alep et Damas, et menacèrent de se joindre aux Francs pour délivrer Jérusalem. C'en était fait de l'Égypte, si elle n'eût été défendue que par ses faibles enfans ; mais les Mamelucks avaient respiré dans leur jeunesse l'air vivifiant de la Scythie; ils égalaient les Mongouls en valeur, et les surpassaient en discipline. Ils attaquèrent plusieurs fois l'ennemi dans des batailles rangées, et repoussèrent le cours de ce torrent à l'orient de l'Euphrate, sur les royaumes de l'Arménie et de l'Anatolie, qu'il envahit avec une violence irrésistible. Le premier appartenait aux chrétiens, et le second était occupé par les Turcs. Les sultans d'Iconium résis-

De l'Anatolie.
A. D.
1242-1272.

---

(1) Quelques historiens chinois étendent les conquêtes que Gengis fit durant sa vie jusqu'à Médine, la patrie de Mahomet (Gaubil, p. 42); et rien ne prouve mieux leur parfaite ignorance de tout ce qui est étranger à leur pays.

tèrent quelque temps aux Mongouls; mais enfin l'un d'entre eux, Azzadin, fut forcé de chercher un asile chez les Grecs de Constantinople, et les khans de Perse exterminèrent ses faibles successeurs, les derniers descendans de la race de Seljouk.

<small>Du Kipzak, de la Russie, de la Pologne, de la Hongrie, etc. A. D. 1235-1245.</small>

III. Octai avait à peine renversé l'empire du nord de la Chine, qu'il résolut de porter ses armes jusqu'aux pays les plus reculés de l'Occident. Quinze cent mille Mongouls ou Tartares inscrivirent leurs noms sur les registres militaires; le grand-khan choisit un tiers de cette multitude, dont il confia le commandement à son neveu Batou, fils de Tuli, qui régnait sur les conquêtes de son père au nord de la mer Caspienne. Après des réjouissances qui durèrent quarante jours, Batou partit pour cette grande expédition; et telle fut l'ardeur et la rapidité de ses innombrables escadrons, qu'ils parcoururent en moins de six années quatre-vingt-dix degrés de longitude; ou le quart de la circonférence du globe. Ils traversèrent les grands fleuves de l'Asie et de l'Europe, le Volga et le Kama, le Don et le Borysthène, la Vistule et le Danube, ou à la nage sur leurs chevaux, ou sur la glace durant l'hiver, ou dans des bateaux de cuir qui suivaient toujours l'armée et servaient à transporter les bagages et l'artillerie. Les premières victoires de Batou anéantirent les restes de la liberté nationale dans les plaines immenses du Kipzak (1)

---

(1) Le *Dashté-Kipzak*, ou plaine de Kipzak, s'étend des deux côtés du Volga dans un espace immense vers le Jaïk

et du Turkestan. Dans sa course rapide, il traversa les royaumes connus aujourd'hui sous les noms de Cazan et d'Astrakhan, et les troupes qu'il détacha vers le mont Caucase pénétrèrent dans le cœur de la Géorgie et de la Circassie. La discorde civile des grands-ducs ou princes de Russie livra leur pays aux Tartares. Ils se répandirent depuis la Livonie jusqu'à la mer Noire. Kiow et Moscou, les deux capitales ancienne et moderne, furent réduites en cendres ; calamité passagère, et moins fatale peut-être aux Russes que la tache profonde et peut-être indélébile qu'une servitude de deux cents ans a imprimée sur leur caractère. Les Tartares ravagèrent avec une égale fureur les pays qu'ils se proposaient de conserver et ceux dont ils s'empressaient de sortir. De la Russie, où ils s'étaient établis, ils firent une irruption passagère, mais destructive, dans la Pologne et jusqu'aux frontières de l'Allemagne. Les villes de Lublin et de Cracovie disparurent. Ils approchèrent des côtes de la mer Baltique, défirent dans la bataille de Lignitz les ducs de Silésie, les palatins polonais et le grand-maître de l'ordre Teutonique, et remplirent neuf sacs des oreilles droites de tous ceux qu'ils avaient tués. De Lignitz, qui fut du côté de l'Occident le terme de leur marche, ils se dirigèrent sur la Hongrie ; et cette armée de cinq cent mille hommes, excitée par la présence de Batou, sembla animée de son esprit. Leurs

---

et le Borysthène, et est supposé avoir donné naissance aux Cosaques et à leur nom.

colonnes, partagées en différentes divisions, franchirent les montagnes Carpathiennes, et l'on doutait encore de leur approche lorsqu'ils firent éprouver leurs premières fureurs. Le roi Bela IV assembla les forces militaires de ses comtes et de ses évêques; mais il avait aliéné la nation en recevant une horde errante de Comans, composée de quarante mille familles. Un soupçon de trahison et le meurtre de leur prince excitèrent ces hôtes sauvages à la révolte. Tout le pays au nord du Danube fut perdu en un jour, et dépeuplé dans un été; les ruines des villes et des églises furent parsemées des ossemens des citoyens qui expièrent les péchés des Turcs leurs ancêtres. Un ecclésiastique échappé du sac de Waradin a donné la description des calamités dont il avait été le témoin; et les fureurs sanguinaires des siéges et des batailles sont infiniment moins atroces que la perfidie qu'éprouvèrent les fugitifs. Après les avoir attirés hors des bois sous la promesse du pardon et de la paix, on les égorgea de sang-froid lorsqu'ils eurent achevé les travaux de la moisson et de la vendange. Durant l'hiver, les Tartares passèrent le Danube sur la glace, et s'avancèrent vers Gran ou Strigonium, colonie germaine et capitale du royaume. Ils dressèrent trente machines contre les murs, comblèrent les fossés avec des sacs de terre et des cadavres; et à la suite d'un massacre sans choix, le khan fit égorger en sa présence trois cents nobles matrones. De toutes les villes et forteresses de la Hongrie, il n'en demeura que trois sur pied après l'invasion; et l'infortuné Bela courut se cacher dans les îles de la mer Adriatique.

La terreur se répandit dans le monde latin : un Russe fugitif porta l'alarme en Suède; les nations des bords de la Baltique et de l'Océan tremblèrent à l'approche des Tartares (1), que la crainte et l'ignorance représentaient comme une espèce différente du genre humain. Depuis l'invasion des Arabes dans le huitième siècle, l'Europe n'avait point été exposée à une pareille calamité; et si les disciples de Mahomet opprimaient les consciences et la liberté, il y avait à craindre que les pâtres de la Scythie n'anéantissent les villes, les arts et toutes les institutions de la société civile. Le pontife de Rome essaya d'apaiser et de convertir les invincibles païens; il leur envoya des moines de l'ordre de Saint-Dominique et de Saint-François. Mais le grand-khan leur répondit que les fils de Dieu et de Gengis étaient revêtus d'un pouvoir divin pour soumettre ou exterminer les nations, et que le pape serait enveloppé dans la destruction gé-

---

(1) Dans l'année 1238, les habitans de la Gothie, aujourd'hui la Suède, et ceux de la Frise, n'osèrent point envoyer comme à l'ordinaire leurs vaisseaux à la pêche du hareng sur les côtes d'Angleterre, parce qu'ils redoutaient les Tartares; et comme il n'y eut point d'exportation, on vendait quarante ou cinquante de ces poissons pour un schelling (Matthieu Paris, p. 396). Il est assez plaisant que les ordres d'un khan des Mongouls qui régnait sur les confins de la Chine, aient fait baisser le prix des harengs dans les marchés de l'Angleterre.

nérale, s'il ne venait visiter lui-même, comme suppliant, la horde royale. L'empereur Frédéric II employa un moyen plus courageux de défense. Il écrivit aux princes d'Allemagne, aux rois de France et d'Angleterre; il leur peignit le danger commun, et les pressa d'armer leurs vassaux pour cette juste et sage croisade (1). La valeur et la réputation des Francs en imposèrent aux Tartares eux-mêmes; cinquante chevaliers et vingt arbalétriers défendirent avec succès le château de Newstadt en Autriche; et les Barbares levèrent le siége à l'approche d'une armée d'Allemands. Après avoir ravagé dans le voisinage les royaumes de Servie, de Bosnie et de Bulgarie, Batou se retira lentement du Danube au Volga, pour jouir des fruits de ses victoires, dans la ville où le palais de Serai, qui, à son ordre, s'éleva du milieu du désert.

De la Sibérie.
A. D. 1242.

IV. Il n'y eut pas jusqu'aux régions pauvres et glacées du septentrion qui n'attirassent les armes

---

(1) Je vais copier les épithètes caractéristiques ou flatteuses, par lesquelles il désigne les différentes nations de l'Europe. *Furens ac fervens ad arma Germania, strenuæ militiæ genitrix et alumna Francia, bellicosa et audax Hispania, virtuosa viris et classe munita fertilis Anglia, impetuosis bellatoribus referta Alemannia, navalis Dacia, indomita Italia, pacis ignara Burgundia, inquieta Apulia, cum maris Græci, Adriatici, et Thorrheni insulis piraticis et invictis Cretâ, Cypro, Siciliâ, cum Oceano conterminis insulis et regionibus, cruentâ Hiberniâ, cum agili Walliâ, palustris Scotia, glacialis Norwegia, suam electam militiam sub vexillo crucis destinabunt*, etc. Matthieu Paris, p. 498.

des Mongouls. Sheibani-khan, frère du grand Batou, conduisit une horde de quinze mille familles dans les déserts de la Sibérie; et ses descendans régnèrent à Tobolsk durant plus de trois siècles, jusqu'à la conquête des Russes. En suivant le cours de l'Oby et du Jenisey, l'esprit d'entreprise doit les avoir conduits à la découverte de la mer Glaciale; et après avoir écarté des monumens qui nous en restent, ces fables monstrueuses d'hommes avec des têtes de chiens et des pieds fourchus, nous trouverons que quinze ans après la mort de Gengis, les Mongouls connaissaient le nom et les mœurs des Samoïèdes, qui habitent aux environs du cercle polaire, dans des huttes souterraines, et ne connaissent d'autre occupation que la chasse, dont ils tirent leur nourriture et les fourrures qui leur servent de vêtemens (1).

Tandis que les Mongouls et les Tartares envahissaient à la fois la Chine, la Syrie et la Pologne, les auteurs de ces grands ravages se contentaient d'apprendre et de s'entendre dire que leur parole était le glaive de la mort. De même que les premiers califes, les premiers successeurs de Gengis parurent rarement en personne à la tête de leurs armées victorieuses. Sur les bords de l'Onon et du Selinga, *la horde dorée* ou royale présentait le contraste de la

<small>Les successeurs de Gengis.
A. D.
1227-1259.</small>

---

(1) *Voy.* dans Hackluyt la relation de Carpin, v. 1, p. 30. Abulghazi donne la généalogie des khans de Sibérie (part. VIII, p. 485-495). Les Russes n'ont-ils trouvé aucune chronique tartare à Tobolsk?

grandeur et de la simplicité, d'un repas de mouton rôti et de lait de jument, et de cinq cents chariots d'or et d'argent distribués dans un seul jour. Les princes de l'Europe et de l'Asie furent contraints d'envoyer des ambassadeurs ou d'entreprendre eux-mêmes ce long et pénible voyage. Le trône et la vie des grands-ducs de Russie, des rois de la Géorgie et de l'Arménie, des sultans d'Iconium et des émirs de la Perse, dépendaient d'un geste du grand-khan des Tartares. Les fils et les petits-fils de Gengis avaient été habitués à la vie pastorale; mais on vit s'agrandir par degrés le village de Caracorum (1), où se faisait l'élection des khans, et dans lequel ils fixèrent leur résidence. Octai et Mangou quittèrent leurs tentes pour habiter une maison, ce qui indique un changement dans les mœurs; et leur exemple fut imité par les princes de leur famille et par les grands officiers de l'empire. Au lieu des immenses forêts qui avaient été le théâtre de leurs chasses, l'enceinte d'un parc leur offrit un exercice moins fatigant : la peinture et la sculpture embellirent leurs nouvelles habitations; et les trésors superflus se convertirent en bassins, en fontaines et en statues d'argent massif.

---

(1). La carte de d'Anville et les itinéraires chinois de de Guignes (t. 1, part. 11, p. 57), semblent fixer la position de Holin ou Caracorum environ à six cents milles au nord-ouest de Pékin. La distance entre Selinginsky et Pékin est à peu près de deux mille verstes russes, ou treize à quatorze cents milles d'Angleterre (*Voyages de Bell*, vol. 11, pag. 67).

Les artistes de la Chine et de Paris exercèrent leur génie au service du grand-khan (1). Il avait à Caracorum deux rues occupées, l'une par des ouvriers chinois, et l'autre par des marchands mahométans : on y voyait une église nestorienne, deux mosquées et douze temples consacrés au culte des différentes idoles, d'où l'on peut se former à peu près une idée du nombre des habitans et des nations dont ils étaient composés. Cependant un missionnaire français affirme que la capitale des Tartares n'offrait pas une ville aussi considérable que celle de Saint-Denis, près Paris ; et que le palais de Mangou valait à peine le dixième de l'abbaye des bénédictins de cette ville. Les grands-khans pouvaient amuser leur vanité des conquêtes de la Syrie et de la Russie ; mais ils étaient fixés sur les frontières de la Chine. L'acquisition de cet empire était le principal objet de leur ambition, et l'habitude de l'économie pastorale leur avait appris sans doute que le berger trouve son avantage à protéger et à multiplier ses troupeaux. J'ai déjà célébré la sagesse et la vertu d'un mandarin, qui prévint la destruction de cinq provinces fertiles et peuplées. Durant une administration de trente ans, exempte de tout reproche, ce bienfaisant ami de son pays et

Ils adoptent les mœurs de la Chine.
A. D. 1259-1368.

―――――

(1) Rubruquis rencontra à Caracorum son compatriote *Guillaume Boucher, orfèvre de Paris*, qui avait exécuté pour le grand-khan un arbre d'argent soutenu par quatre lions qui lançaient quatre liqueurs différentes. Abulghazi (part. IV, p. 366) cite les peintres du Kitay ou la Chine.

de l'humanité travailla constamment à suspendre ou adoucir les calamités de la guerre, à ranimer le goût des sciences, à sauver les monumens, à mettre des bornes au despotisme des commandans militaires, en rétablissant les magistrats civils; enfin, à inspirer aux Mongouls des sentimens de paix et de justice. Il lutta courageusement contre la barbarie des premiers conquérans; et ses leçons salutaires furent payées, dès la seconde génération, par une abondante récolte. L'empire du nord, et insensiblement, celui du midi, se soumirent au gouvernement de Cublai, le lieutenant et ensuite le successeur de Mangou; et la nation fut fidèle à un prince élevé dans les mœurs de la Chine. Il lui rendit les anciennes formes de sa constitution; et les vainqueurs adoptèrent les lois, les usages, et jusqu'aux préjugés du peuple vaincu. On peut attribuer ce triomphe paisible, dont il y eut plus d'un exemple, à la multitude et en même temps à la servitude des Chinois. Les empereurs des Mongouls voyaient leur armée absorbée en quelque manière dans l'immense population d'un vaste royaume; ils adoptaient avec plaisir un système politique qui offrait aux princes les jouissances réelles du pouvoir despotique, et abandonnait aux sujets les vains noms de philosophie, de liberté et d'obéissance filiale. Sous le règne de Cublai, on vit fleurir les lettres et le commerce; les peuples jouirent des bienfaits de la justice et des douceurs de la paix. On ouvrit le grand canal de cinq cents milles, qui conduit de Nankin à la capitale. Le monarque fixa sa résidence à Pékin, et déploya dans sa cour la magnificence des plus riches souverains de l'Asie. Cependant ce savant prince s'écarta de la pureté et de la simplicité de la religion adoptée par son grand-père : il offrit des sacrifices à l'idole de Fo ; et sa soumission aveugle pour les lamas et les bonzes de la Chine, lui attira la censure (1) des disciples de Confucius. Ses successeurs souillèrent le palais d'une foule d'eunuques, d'empiriques et d'astrologues, tandis que dans les provinces treize millions de leurs sujets périssaient par la famine. Cent quarante ans après la mort de Gengis, les Chinois révoltés expulsèrent du trône la dynastie des Yuen, race dégénérée de ce fameux conquérant ; et les empereurs mongouls allèrent s'ensevelir dans l'obscurité du désert. Avant l'époque de cette révolution, ils avaient déjà perdu leur suprématie sur les différentes branches de leur maison : les khans du Kipzak ou de la Russie, du Zagathai ou de la Transoxiane, de l'Iran ou de la Perse, d'abord simples lieutenans du grand-khan, avaient trouvé dans leur pouvoir et dans leur éloignement les moyens de se dégager des devoirs de l'obéissance ; et après la mort de Cublai,

Division de l'empire des Mougouls. A. D. 1259-1300.

---

(1) L'attachement des khans et la haine des mandarins pour les bonzes et les lamas de la Chine (Duhalde, *Hist. de la Chine*, t. 1, pag. 502, 503) semblent indiquer qu'ils étaient les prêtres du même dieu, de Fo, divinité de l'Inde, dont le culte prévaut parmi les sectes de l'Indoustan, de Siam, du Thibet, de la Chine et du Japon. Mais ce sujet mystérieux est enveloppé d'un nuage que les recherches de notre société asiatique parviendront peut-être à dissiper.

ils dédaignèrent d'accepter un sceptre ou un titre de ses méprisables successeurs. Conformément à leur situation, les uns conservèrent la simplicité primitive des mœurs pastorales, et les autres adoptèrent le luxe des villes de l'Asie ; mais les princes et les peuples étaient également disposés à recevoir un nouveau culte. Après avoir hésité entre l'Évangile et le Koran, ils se décidèrent pour la religion de Mahomet, adoptèrent les Arabes et les Persans pour leurs frères, et renoncèrent à toute communication avec les Mongouls ou les idolâtres de la Chine.

<small>Danger de Constantinople et de l'empire grec.
A. D.
1240-1304.</small>

On peut s'étonner que dans le bouleversement général, l'empire romain, démembré par les Grecs et les Latins, ait échappé à l'invasion des Mongouls. Moins puissans qu'Alexandre, les Grecs se trouvaient, comme lui, pressés en Asie et en Europe par les pâtres de Scythie ; et Constantinople aurait inévitablement partagé le sort de Pékin, de Samarcande et de Bagdad, si les Tartares eussent entrepris de l'assiéger. Lorsque Batou, comblé de gloire, repassa volontairement le Danube, la vanité des Grecs et des Francs insulta sa retraite (1). Le conquérant se mit une seconde fois en marche, dans le dessein d'attaquer la capitale des Césars ; mais la mort le surprit et

---

(1) Quelques échecs que les Mongouls essuyèrent en Hongrie (Matthieu Paris, p. 545, 546) ont pu faire répandre le bruit de l'union et de la victoire des rois francs sur les frontières de la Bulgarie. Abulpharage (*Dynast.*, p. 310), quarante ans après, et au-delà du Tigre, peut avoir aisément été induit en erreur.

sauva Byzance. Son frère Borga conduisit les Tartares dans la Thrace et dans la Bulgarie; mais il fut détourné de la conquête de Constantinople par un voyage à Novogorod, située au cinquante-septième degré de latitude, où il fit le dénombrement des Russes et régla les tributs de la Russie. Le khan des Mongouls fit une alliance avec les Mamelucks contre ses compatriotes de la Perse. Trois cent mille hommes de cavalerie passèrent le défilé de Derbend; et les Grecs se félicitèrent de ce commencement de guerre civile. Après avoir recouvré Constantinople, Michel Paléologue (1), éloigné de sa cour et de son armée, fut surpris et environné par vingt mille Tartares, dans un château de la Thrace; mais leur expédition n'avait pour but que de délivrer le sultan turc Azzadin, et ils se contentèrent, en l'emmenant, d'emporter les trésors de l'empereur. Noga, leur général, dont le nom s'est perpétué dans les hordes d'Astrakhan, excita une révolte redoutable contre Mengo-Timour, le troisième khan du Kipzak; il obtint en mariage Marie, fille naturelle de Paléologue, et défendit les États de son beau-père et de son ami. Les irruptions suivantes ne furent composées que de brigands fugitifs, et quelques milliers d'Alains et de Comans chassés de leur patrie, renonçant à leur vie errante, s'enrôlèrent au service de l'empereur

---

(1) *Voyez* Pachymère (l. III, c. 25; et l. IX, c. 26, 27) et la fausse alarme de Nicée (l. III, c. 27; Nicéphore Grégoras, l. IV, c. 6).

grec. Tel fut en Europe l'effet de l'invasion des Mongouls : loin de troubler la paix de l'Asie romaine, la première terreur de leurs armes assura sa tranquillité. Le sultan d'Iconium sollicita une entrevue personnelle avec Jean Vatacès, dont la politique artificieuse encouragea les Turcs à défendre leur barrière contre l'ennemi commun (1). Cette barrière, à la vérité, ne résista pas long-temps ; la défaite et la captivité des Seljoucides mit à découvert le dénuement des Grecs. Le formidable Holagou menaça de marcher à Constantinople à la tête d'une armée de quatre cent mille hommes ; et la terreur panique qui s'empara des habitans de Nicée donnera une idée de l'effroi qu'il inspirait. La cérémonie accidentelle d'une procession et la répétition de la litanie lugubre : « Préservez-nous, mon Dieu, de la fureur des Tartares ! » firent répandre dans la ville la fausse nouvelle d'un assaut et d'un massacre. Les rues furent aussitôt remplies d'une multitude d'habitans des deux sexes, aveuglés par la frayeur et fuyant sans savoir où ni pourquoi : ce ne fut qu'au bout de plusieurs heures que la fermeté des officiers de la garnison parvint à délivrer la ville de ce malheur imaginaire. La conquête de Bagdad détourna heureusement l'ambition de Holagou et de ses successeurs; ils soutinrent dans la Syrie une longue guerre, où ils ne furent pas toujours victorieux ; leur querelle avec les musulmans les dis-

---

(1) G. Acropolita, p. 36, 37 ; Nicéphore Grégoras, l. II, c. 6 ; l. IV, c. 5.

posa à s'unir aux Grecs et aux Francs (1); et, par générosité ou par mépris, ils offrirent le royaume de l'Anatolie pour récompense à un de leurs vassaux arméniens. Les émirs qui occupaient des villes et des montagnes, se disputèrent les débris de la monarchie des Seljoucides; mais ils reconnurent tous la suprématie du khan de la Perse, et il interposa souvent son autorité, quelquefois même ses armes, pour arrêter leurs déprédations et maintenir la paix et l'équilibre de sa frontière turque. La mort de Cazan (2), un des plus illustres descendans de Gengis, anéantit cette salutaire suprématie; et le déclin des Mongouls laissa le champ libre à l'élévation et aux progrès de l'empire ottoman (3).

Déclin des empereurs ou khans mongouls de la Perse.
A. D. 1304,
mai 31.

---

(1) Abulpharage, qui écrivit en 1284, affirme que depuis la fabuleuse défaite de Batou, les Mongouls n'avaient attaqué ni les Grecs ni les Francs, et on peut le regarder comme un témoin irrécusable. Hayton, prince d'Arménie, s'applaudit aussi de leur amitié pour lui et pour sa nation.

(2) Pachymère nous représente sous les traits les plus brillans, Cazan-khan, le rival de Cyrus et d'Alexandre (l. XII, c. 1); dans la conclusion de son histoire (l. XIII, c. 36), il exprime l'espérance où il est de voir arriver trente mille Tochars ou Tartares, commandés par le successeur de Cazan, pour repousser les Turcs de Bithynie (A. D. 1308).

(3) L'origine de la dynastie ottomane est savamment éclaircie par l'érudition de MM. de Guignes (*Histoire des Huns*, t. IV, p. 329-337) et d'Anville (*Empire turc*, p. 14-22), deux habitans de Paris, de qui les Orientaux pourraient apprendre l'histoire et la géographie de leur propre pays.

Origine des Ottomans.
A. D. 1240, etc.

Après la retraite de Gengis, Gelaleddin, sultan de Carizme, était revenu de l'Inde gouverner et défendre ses États de Perse. Dans l'espace de onze années, ce héros donna en personne quatorze batailles rangées, et telle était son activité qu'il fit en soixante-dix jours, à la tête de sa cavalerie, une marche de mille milles, de Teflis à Kerman; mais la jalousie des princes musulmans et les armées innombrables des Mongouls le firent succomber. Après sa dernière défaite, le brave Gelaleddin périt sans gloire dans les montagnes du Curdistan. Sa mort dispersa sa vieille et courageuse armée, qui, sous le nom de Carizmiens ou Corasmins, comprenait un grand nombre de hordes turcomanes qui s'étaient attachées à la fortune du sultan. Les plus audacieux et les plus puissans de leurs chefs firent une invasion dans la Syrie, et pillèrent le saint-sépulcre de Jérusalem; les autres s'enrôlèrent au service d'Aladin, sultan d'Iconium; et c'est parmi ceux-ci que se trouvaient les obscurs ancêtres de la race ottomane. Ils avaient originairement campé sur la rive méridionale de l'Oxus, dans les plaines de Mahan et de Néza; et j'observerai, comme un fait assez extraordinaire, que de ce même endroit sont sortis les Parthes et les Turcs qui ont fondé deux puissans empires. Soliman-Shah, qui commandait l'avant ou l'arrière-garde de l'armée carizmienne, se noya au passage de l'Euphrate. Son fils Orthogrul devint le sujet et le soldat d'Aladin, et établit à Surgut, sur les bords du Sangarius, un camp de quatre cents tentes ou familles, dont il dirigea cinquante-deux ans le gouvernement civil et militaire. Il fut le père de Thaman ou Athman, dont le nom a été changé en celui de calife Othman; et si on se représente ce chef de horde comme un pâtre et un brigand, il faut séparer de ces dénominations toute idée de bassesse et d'ignominie. Othman, doué à un degré éminent de toutes les vertus d'un soldat, profita habilement des circonstances de temps et de lieu qui favorisaient son indépendance et ses succès. La race de Seljouk n'existait plus; la puissance expirante des khans mongouls et leur éloignement l'affranchissaient de toute subordination; il se trouvait placé sur les frontières de l'empire grec; le Koran recommandait *le gazi* ou guerre sainte contre les infidèles; leur fausse politique avait ouvert les passages du mont Olympe, et l'invitait à descendre dans les plaines de Bithynie. Jusqu'au règne de Paléologue, ces passages avaient été vaillamment défendus par la milice du pays, qui jouissait pour récompense de la sûreté de ses propriétés et de l'exemption de toutes les taxes. L'empereur abolit leur privilége et se chargea de la défense; on exigea rigoureusement le tribut; mais les passages furent oubliés, et les vigoureux montagnards devinrent des paysans timides, sans énergie et sans discipline. Ce fut le 27 juillet de l'année 1299 de l'ère chrétienne, qu'Othman entra pour la première fois dans le district de Nicomédie (1); et l'exac-

Règne d'Othman.
A. D.
1299-1326.

---

(1) *Voyez* Pachymère (l. x, c. 25, 26; l. xiii, c. 33,

titude singulière avec laquelle on a fixé la date de cet armement, semblerait indiquer qu'on avait entrevu quel devait être l'accroissement rapide et destructeur du monstre qui menaçait l'empire. Les annales des vingt-sept années que dura son règne, n'offriraient qu'une répétition des mêmes incursions. A chaque campagne il recrutait et augmentait son armée de captifs et de volontaires. Au lieu de se retirer dans les montagnes, Othman conservait tous les postes utiles et susceptibles de défense; après avoir pillé les villes et les châteaux, il en réparait les fortifications, et préférait à la vie errante des nations pastorales les bains et les palais des villes qu'il commençait à se former. Ce ne fut cependant que vers la fin de sa vie, lorsqu'il était accablé par l'âge et les infirmités, qu'Othman eut la joie d'apprendre la conquête de Pruse, dont la famine ou la perfidie avait ouvert les portes à son fils Orchan. La gloire d'Othman est principalement fondée sur celle de ses descendans; mais les Turcs ont conservé de lui, ou composé en son nom, un testament qui renferme des conseils remplis de justice et de modération (1).

34-36); et relativement à la défense des montagnes (l. 1, c. 3-6), Nicéphore Grégoras (l. vii, c. 1) et le premier livre de Laonicus Chalcocondyles l'Athénien.

(1) J'ignore si les Turcs ont des historiens plus anciens que Mahomet ii, et je n'ai pu remonter au-delà d'une assez maigre chronique (*Annales Turcici ad annum* 1550), traduite par Jean Gaudier et publiée par Leunclavius (*ad*

La conquête de Pruse peut servir de véritable date à l'établissement de l'empire ottoman. Les sujets chrétiens rachetèrent leur vie et leurs propriétés par un tribut ou une rançon de trente mille écus d'or; et la ville fut bientôt transformée, par les soins d'Orchan, en une capitale mahométane. Il la décora d'une mosquée, d'un collège et d'un hôpital; on refondit les monnaies des Seljoucides; les nouvelles pièces portèrent le nom et l'empreinte de la nouvelle dynastie, et les plus habiles professeurs des connaissances humaines et divines attirèrent les étudians persans et arabes des anciennes écoles de l'Orient. Aladin porta le premier le titre de visir, dont

Règne d'Orchan. A. D. 1326-1360.

---

calcem Laonic. Chalcocondyles, pag. 311–350), avec de copieux commentaires. L'histoire des progrès et du déclin de l'empire ottoman (A. D. 1300-1683) a été traduite en anglais du manuscrit de Démétrius Cantemir, prince de Moldavie (*Londres*, 1734, *in-folio*). L'auteur est sujet à de fortes méprises relativement à l'histoire orientale; mais il paraît instruit de l'idiome, des annales et des institutions des Turcs. Cantemir tire une partie de ses matériaux de la *Synopsis* de Saadi, effendi de Larisse, dédiée en 1696 au sultan Mustapha, qui est un abrégé précieux des écrivains originaux. Le docteur Johnson fait l'éloge de Knolles (*Hist. générale des Turcs* jusqu'à la présente année, *Londres*, 1603) comme du premier des historiens, mais qui a malheureusement choisi un sujet ingrat. Cependant je doute qu'une compilation volumineuse et partiale des écrivains latins, contenant treize cents pages *in-folio* de harangues et de batailles, puisse instruire, amuser ou éclairer la postérité, qui exige d'un historien un peu de saine critique et de philosophie.

son frère Orchan institua l'office en sa faveur; d'après ses lois, l'on put distinguer par l'habillement les habitans de la ville de ceux de la campagne, et les musulmans des infidèles. Les troupes d'Othman n'étaient composées que d'escadrons indociles de cavalerie turcomane, qui servaient sans paye et combattaient sans discipline ; mais son fils pensa prudemment devoir former et exercer un corps d'infanterie. Il enrôla un grand nombre de volontaires qui se contentaient d'une faible paye, avec la liberté de rester chez eux lorsqu'on n'avait pas besoin de leurs services. La rudesse de leurs mœurs et leur caractère séditieux déterminèrent Orchan à élever ses jeunes captifs de manière à en faire des soldats du prophète et une partie de ses troupes; mais les paysans turcs conservèrent le privilége de former à la suite de l'armée un corps de cavalerie sous le nom de *partisans*. Par ses soins et son intelligence, il parvint à se créer une armée de vingt-cinq mille musulmans ; il fit construire les machines nécessaires pour le siége ou l'attaque des villes, et en fit usage pour la première fois et avec succès contre Nicée et Nicomédie. Orchan accorda des sauf-conduits à tous ceux qui voulurent se retirer avec leurs familles et leurs effets; mais il disposa des veuves des vaincus en faveur des conquérans qui les épousèrent; les livres, les vases et les images, furent achetés ou rachetés par les habitans de Constantinople. L'empereur Andronic le Jeune fut vaincu et

Il fait la conquête de la Bithynie.
A. D.
1326-1339.

blessé par Orchan (1), qui soumit toute la province ou le royaume de Bithynie jusqu'aux rives du Bosphore ou de l'Hellespont, et les chrétiens ne purent méconnaître la justice et la clémence d'un prince qui avait su s'attacher volontairement les Turcs de l'Asie. Orchan se borna modestement au titre d'émir. Parmi les princes de Roum et de l'Anatolie (2), quelques-uns lui étaient supérieurs en forces militaires; les émirs de Ghermian et de Caramanie avaient l'un et l'autre à leurs ordres une armée de quarante mille hommes : placés au centre du royaume des Seljoucides, ils ont fait moins de bruit dans l'histoire que les saints guerriers qui, bien qu'inférieurs en puissance, se firent connaître en formant de nouvelles principautés dans l'empire grec. Les pays maritimes, depuis la Propontide jusqu'au Méandre et à l'île de Rhodes, si long-temps menacés et si souvent pillés, en furent démembrés irrévoca-

Division de l'Anatolie entre les émirs turcs. A. D. 1300, etc.

---

(1) Quoique Cantacuzène raconte les batailles et la fuite héroïque d'Andronic le Jeune (l. II, c. 6, 7, 8), il dissimule la perte de Pruse, de Nicée et de Nicomédie, que Nicéphore Grégoras avoue clairement (l. VIII, 15; IX, 9, 13; XI, 6). Il paraît qu'Orchan prit Nicée en 1330, et Nicomédie en 1339; ce qui ne se rapporte pas tout-à-fait aux dates turques.

(2) La division des émirs turcs est extraite de deux contemporains, du Grec Nicéphore Grégoras (l. VII, 1) et de l'Arabe Marakeschi (de Guignes, t. II, part. II, p. 76, 77). *Voyez* aussi le premier livre de Laonicus Chalcocondyles.

<small>Perte des provinces asiatiques. A. D. 1312, etc.</small>

blement sous le règne d'Andronic l'Ancien (1). Deux chefs turcs, Aidin et Sarukhan, donnèrent leur nom à leurs conquêtes, et ces conquêtes passèrent à leur postérité; ils asservirent ou ruinèrent les sept Églises de l'Asie, et ces maîtres barbares foulent encore en Lydie et en Ionie les antiques monumens du christianisme. En perdant Éphèse, les chrétiens déplorèrent la chute du premier ange et l'extinction du premier flambeau des révélations (2). La destruction est complète, et les traces du temple de Diane et de l'église de Sainte-Marie ont également disparu. Le cirque et les trois théâtres de Laodicée servent de repaire aux renards et aux loups; Sardes n'est plus qu'un misérable village. Le dieu de Mahomet, ce dieu qui n'a ni fils ni rival, est invoqué à Pergame et à Thyatire dans de nombreuses mosquées; et Smyrne ne doit sa population qu'au commerce étranger des Francs et des Arméniens. Philadelphie seule a été sauvée par une prophétie ou par son courage. Éloignés de la mer, oubliés des empereurs, environnés par les Turcs de toutes parts, ses intrépides

---

(1) Pachymère, l. xii, c. 13.

(2) *Voy.* les *Voyages* de Wheeler et de Spon, de Pococke et de Chandler, et principalement les *Recherches* de Smith sur les sept Églises de l'Asie, p. 205-276. Les antiquaires les plus dévots tâchent de concilier les promesses et les menaces du premier auteur des révélations, avec l'état présent des sept villes. Il serait peut-être plus prudent de borner ses prédictions aux événemens de son siècle.

citoyens défendirent leur religion et leur liberté durant plus de quatre-vingts ans, et obtinrent enfin du plus fier des Ottomans une capitulation honorable. Après la destruction des colonies grecques et des Églises d'Asie, on voit encore subsister Philadelphie, telle qu'une colonne au milieu des ruines ; et cet exemple satisfaisant peut servir à prouver que la voie la plus honorable est aussi quelquefois la plus sûre. Les chevaliers de Saint-Jean de Jérusalem (1) défendirent la liberté de Rhodes durant plus de deux siècles : cette île acquit, sous leur discipline, l'éclat de l'opulence et de la renommée ; ces nobles et braves religieux méritèrent une gloire égale sur mer et sur terre, et leur île, boulevard de la chrétienté, attira et repoussa souvent les nombreuses armées des Turcs et des Sarrasins.

Les chevaliers de Rhodes. A. D. 1310, 15 août. A. D. 1523, 1ᵉʳ janv.

Les discordes des Grecs furent la principale cause de leur destruction. Durant les guerres civiles du premier et du second Andronic, le fils d'Othman accomplit presque sans obstacle la conquête de la Bithynie ; les mêmes désordres encouragèrent les émirs turcomans de Lydie et d'Ionie à construire une flotte et à piller les îles voisines de la côte d'Europe. Réduit à défendre son honneur et sa vie, Cantacuzène, soit qu'il voulût prévenir ou imiter ses

Premier passage des Turcs en Europe. A. D. 1341-1347.

---

(1) Consultez le quatrième livre de l'*Histoire de Malte* par l'abbé de Vertot. Cet agréable écrivain décèle son ignorance, en supposant qu'Othman, un partisan des collines de la Bithynie, a pu assiéger Rhodes par terre et par mer.

adversaires, eut recours aux ennemis de son pays et de sa religion. Amir, fils d'Aidin, cachait sous la robe d'un mahométan la politesse et l'humanité d'un Grec; une estime mutuelle et des services réciproques l'attachaient au grand-domestique; et leur amitié a été comparée, dans le langage du temps, à celle d'Oreste et de Pylade (1). Lorsqu'il apprit le danger de son ami persécuté par une cour ingrate, le prince d'Ionie réunit à Smyrne une flotte de trois cents vaisseaux et une armée de vingt-neuf mille hommes; il mit à la voile au milieu de l'hiver; et jeta l'ancre à l'embouchure de l'Hèbre. Suivi d'une troupe choisie de deux mille Turcs, Amir avança sur les bords du fleuve, et délivra l'impératrice, que les sauvages Bulgares tenaient assiégée dans la ville de Démotica. A cette époque, son cher Cantacuzène, réfugié en Servie, laissait ignorer quel était son sort; Irène, impatiente de voir son libérateur, l'invita à entrer dans la ville, et accompagna cette invitation d'un présent de cent chevaux et de bijoux précieux.; mais, par un genre particulier de délicatesse, ce sensible Barbare refusa, en l'absence de son ami mal-

---

(1) Nicéphore Grégoras s'est étendu avec plaisir sur l'amabilité de son caractère (l. XII, 7; XIII, 4-10; XIV, 1-9; XVI, 6). Cantacuzène parle honorablement de son allié (l. III, c. 56, 57-63, 64-66, 67, 68-86, 89-96); mais il désavoue l'extrême penchant qu'on lui supposait pour les Turcs, et nie en quelque façon la possibilité d'une amitié si peu naturelle (l. IV, c. 40).

heureux, de voir son épouse et de jouir des agrémens de son palais. Il soutint dans sa tente l'inclémence de la saison, et rejeta toutes les faveurs de l'hospitalité pour partager les souffrances de ses deux mille compagnons, aussi dignes que lui de l'honneur qu'on voulait lui faire. Le désir de venger Cantacuzène et le besoin de subsistances peuvent servir d'excuse à ses excursions par terre et par mer : il laissa neuf mille cinq cents hommes pour garder sa flotte, et parcourut inutilement la province pour découvrir son ami. De fausses lettres, la rigueur de l'hiver, les clameurs de ses volontaires, la quantité de dépouilles et le nombre des captifs, le déterminèrent enfin à se rembarquer. Le prince d'Ionie revint deux fois en Europe dans le cours de la guerre civile; il joignit ses troupes à celles de l'empereur, assiégea Thessalonique et menaça Constantinople. La calomnie a pu tirer quelque parti de l'insuffisance de ses secours, de son départ précipité, et d'un présent de dix mille écus qu'il accepta de la cour de Byzance; mais son ami fut satisfait, et la conduite d'Amir était suffisamment justifiée par la nécessité de défendre contre les Latins ses États héréditaires. Le pape, le roi de Chypre, la république de Venise et l'ordre de Saint-Jean, s'étaient réunis dans une louable entreprise contre la puissance maritime des Turcs. Les galères des confédérés abordèrent sur la côte d'Ionie, et Amir fut tué d'une flèche à l'attaque de la citadelle de Smyrne, défendue par les chevaliers de

Rhodes (1). Avant de mourir, il procura généreusement à son ami un autre allié de sa nation, non pas plus sincère et plus ardent que lui, mais plus en état, par sa proximité de la Propontide et de Constantinople, de lui donner un prompt et puissant secours. La promesse d'un traité plus avantageux décida le prince de Bithynie à rompre ses engagemens avec Anne de Savoie. L'orgueil d'Orchan l'engagea à promettre, de la manière la plus solennelle, que si Cantacuzène consentaît à l'accepter pour son gendre, il remplirait envers lui, sans jamais s'en écarter, tous les devoirs d'un sujet et d'un fils. L'ambition l'emporta sur la tendresse paternelle; le clergé grec se prêta à l'alliance d'une princesse chrétienne avec un disciple de Mahomet; et le père de Théodora nous détaille lui-même, avec une honteuse satisfaction, le déshonneur de son diadême (2). Des ambassadeurs, suivis d'un corps de cavalerie turque, arrivèrent dans trente vaisseaux devant son camp de

Mariage d'Orchan avec une princesse grecque.
A. D. 1346.

---

(1) Après la conquête de Smyrne par les Latins, le pape chargea les chevaliers de Rhodes de défendre cette forteresse. *Voyez* Vertot, l. v.

(2) *Voyez* Cantacuzène, l. III, c. 95. Nicéphore Grégoras, qui, relativement à la lumière du Thabor, charge l'empereur des noms injurieux de tyran et d'Hérode, paraît disposé à excuser ce mariage plutôt qu'à le blâmer, et allègue la passion et la puissance d'Orchan, εγγυτατος και τη δυναμει τους κατ' αυτου ηδη Περσικους (*Turcs*). υπεραιρων Σατραπας (l. xv, 5). Il célèbre ensuite son gouvernement civil et militaire. *Voyez* son règne dans Cantemir, pages 24-30.

Selymbrie. On dressa un magnifique pavillon, sous lequel l'impératrice Irène passa la nuit avec ses filles. Dès le matin, Théodora se plaça sur un trône entouré de rideaux de soie brodés en or. Les troupes étaient sous les armes; mais l'empereur était à cheval. A un signal, les rideaux s'ouvrirent et présentèrent l'épouse ou la victime environnée de torches nuptiales et d'eunuques prosternés. L'air retentit du bruit des trompettes; et des poëtes tels que le siècle pouvait les fournir célébrèrent, dans leurs chants nuptiaux, le prétendu bonheur de Théodora. Elle fut livrée au Barbare qui devenait son maître, sans aucune des cérémonies du culte chrétien; mais on était convenu, par le traité, qu'elle continuerait à professer librement sa religion dans le harem de Bursa, et son père fait l'éloge de sa conduite pieuse et charitable dans cette situation équivoque. Lorsque l'empereur grec se vit paisiblement assis sur le trône de Constantinople, il rendit visite à son gendre, qui, accompagné de ses quatre fils de différentes épouses, vint l'attendre à Scutari, sur la côte asiatique. Les deux princes partagèrent, avec une apparente cordialité, les plaisirs de la chasse et d'un festin; et Théodora obtint la permission d'aller au-delà du Bosphore passer quelques jours dans la société de sa mère. Mais Orchan, dont l'amitié était subordonnée aux intérêts de sa politique et de sa religion, se joignit sans hésiter, dans la guerre des Génois, aux ennemis de Cantacuzène.

Dans son traité avec l'impératrice Anne, le prince

Établissement des Ottomans en Europe. A. D. 1353.

ottoman avait stipulé cette singulière condition, qu'il lui serait permis de vendre ses prisonniers à Constantinople ou de les transporter en Asie. Une foule de chrétiens des deux sexes, de tous les âges, de prêtres et de moines, de vierges et de matrones, furent exposés nus dans les marchés publics, et souvent maltraités à coups de fouet pour exciter la charité à les racheter plus promptement; mais l'indignation des Grecs ne leur permettait guère que de déplorer le sort de leurs concitoyens, qu'ils voyaient emmener au loin dans un esclavage qui assujettissait leur âme et leur corps (1). Cantacuzène fut forcé de se soumettre aux mêmes conditions, et leur exécution doit avoir été encore plus funeste à l'empire. L'impératrice Anne avait obtenu un secours de dix mille Turcs; mais Orchan employa toutes ses forces au service de son père. Ces calamités n'étaient cependant que passagères; dès que l'orage cessait, les fugitifs retournaient dans leurs anciennes habitations: à la fin de la guerre, les musulmans évacuaient totalement l'Europe et se retiraient en Asie. Ce fut à l'occasion de sa dernière querelle avec son pupille, que Cantacuzène fixa dans le sein de l'empire le germe de destruction que ses successeurs ne purent déraciner, et ses dialogues théologiques contre le prophète Mahomet n'ont point expié cette faute irré-

---

(1) On trouvera dans Ducas (c. 8) une peinture animée et concise de cette captivité, dont Cantacuzène convient avec la rougeur d'un coupable.

parable. Les Turcs modernes ignorent leur propre histoire, confondent leur premier passage de l'Hellespont (1) avec le dernier, et représentent le fils d'Orchan comme un brigand obscur qui, suivi de quatre-vingts aventuriers, passa par stratagême sur une terre ennemie et peu connue. Soliman, à la tête d'un corps de dix mille hommes de cavalerie turque, fut transporté sur les vaisseaux de l'empereur grec, et traité comme son allié. Les troupes mahométanes rendirent quelques services et commirent beaucoup de désordres dans les guerres civiles de la Romanie. Mais la Chersonèse se trouva insensiblement peuplée d'une colonie de Turcs, et la cour de Byzance sollicita en vain la restitution des forteresses de la Thrace. Après quelques délais artificieusement prolongés par le prince ottoman et son fils, on en fixa le rachat à la somme de soixante mille écus, et le premier paiement avait été acquitté, lorsque les murs et les fortifications de la plupart de ces villes furent renversés par un tremblement de terre : les Turcs occupèrent les places démantelées ; ils rebâtirent Gallipoli, et Soliman eut soin de repeupler de

---

(1) Cantemir, dans ce passage et relativement aux premières conquêtes d'Europe, donne fort mauvaise opinion de ses autorités turques, et je n'ai pas beaucoup plus de confiance en Chalcocondyles (l. 1, p. 12, etc.). Ils oublient de consulter le quatrième livre de Cantacuzène, qu'on peut regarder comme le monument le plus authentique. Je regrette aussi les derniers livres de Nicéphore Grégoras, qui sont encore en manuscrit.

mahométans cette ville, clef de l'Hellespont. L'abdication de Cantacuzène rompit les faibles liens de l'alliance domestique. Par ses derniers conseils, il engageait ses compatriotes à éviter une guerre imprudente, à comparer le nombre, la discipline et l'enthousiasme des Turcs à la faiblesse et à la pusillanimité des Grecs. Ces avis prudens furent méprisés par l'opiniâtre vanité d'un jeune homme, et justifiés par les victoires des mahométans. Au milieu de ses succès, Soliman tomba de cheval dans un exercice militaire du *Jerid*, et perdit la vie; le vieil Orchan succomba peu de temps après à sa douleur.

Mort d'Orchan et de son fils Soliman.

Mais les Grecs n'eurent pas le loisir de se réjouir de la mort de leurs ennemis; le glaive des Turcs se montra également redoutable entre les mains d'Amurath 1er, fils d'Orchan et frère de Soliman; on découvre à travers l'obscurité des annales byzantines (1), qu'il s'empara presque sans résistance de toute la Romanie et de la Thrace, depuis l'Hellespont jusqu'au mont Hémus, et que, presque aux portes de la capitale, il choisit Andrinople pour le siége de son gouvernement et de sa religion en Europe. Constantinople, dont la décadence date presque de l'époque de sa fondation, avait été successivement attaquée, durant le cours de dix siècles, par

Règne d'Amurath 1er, et ses conquêtes en Europe. A. D. 1360-1389, septemb.

―――――

(1) Depuis l'époque où Grégoras et Cantacuzène terminent leur histoire, on trouve une lacune de plus d'un siècle. George Phranza, Michel Ducas et Laonicus Chalcocondyles, n'écrivirent qu'après la prise de Constantinople.

les Barbares de l'Orient et de l'Occident. Mais jusqu'à cette époque fatale, les Grecs ne s'étaient point vus environnés du côté de l'Asie et de l'Europe par les forces d'une même puissance ennemie. Cependant Amurath, par prudence ou par générosité, suspendit encore pour quelque temps cette facile conquête; et son orgueil se contenta d'appeler fréquemment auprès de lui l'empereur Jean Paléologue et ses quatre fils, qui, dès qu'ils en recevaient l'ordre, se rendaient à la cour ou à l'armée du prince ottoman. Il marcha successivement contre les nations esclavonnes, qui habitaient entre le Danube et la mer Adriatique, contre les Bulgares, les Serviens, les Bosniens, les Albanais, et il écrasa à plusieurs reprises, par ses excursions, ces tribus belliqueuses qui avaient si souvent insulté l'empire romain. Leur pays n'abondait ni en or ni en argent; leurs rustiques hameaux n'étaient pas enrichis par le commerce, ni décorés par les arts de luxe ; mais les naturels de ces contrées avaient été de tout temps distingués par leur vigueur corporelle et l'énergie de leur courage : une institution sage en fit les plus fermes et les plus fidèles soutiens de la grandeur ottomane (1). Le visir d'Amurath rappela à son souverain que les lois de Mahomet lui accordaient la cinquième partie des dépouilles et de tous les captifs ; le ministre ajouta que des officiers vigilans, placés à Gallipoli, lèveraient

---

(1) *Voyez* Cantemir (pag. 37-41) et ses notes intéressantes.

facilement ce tribut au passage, et pourraient choisir les plus beaux et les plus vigoureux parmi les enfans des chrétiens. Le conseil fut adopté; on publia l'édit: des milliers de captifs européens furent élevés dans la religion de Mahomet et dans l'exercice des armes. Un dervis célèbre fit la cérémonie de consacrer cette nouvelle milice et de lui donner un nom. Placé à la tête de leurs rangs, il étendit la manche de sa robe sur la tête du soldat qui était le plus à sa portée, et leur donna sa bénédiction dans les termes suivans : « Qu'on les nomme janissaires (*yengi chéri* ou nouveaux soldats). Puisse leur valeur être toujours brillante, leur épée tranchante et leur bras victorieux ! Puisse leur lance être toujours suspendue sur la tête de leurs ennemis, et quelque part qu'ils aillent, puissent-ils en revenir avec un visage *blanc* (1) ! » Telle fut l'origine de cette troupe formidable, la terreur des nations et quelquefois des sultans. Ils sont aujourd'hui déchus de leur valeur; leur discipline s'est relâchée, et leurs rangs tumultueux ne peuvent résister à l'artillerie et à la tactique des nations modernes; mais au temps de leur institution ils jouissaient d'une supériorité décisive, parce qu'aucune des puissances de la chrétienté n'entretenait constamment sous les armes un corps régulier d'infanterie.

Les janissaires.

―――――――――

(1) *Visage blanc* et *visage noir*, sont en langage turc des expressions proverbiales de louange et de reproche; *Hic niger est, hunc tu Romane caveto*, était aussi un *apophthegme* latin.

Les janissaires combattaient contre leurs idolâtres compatriotes avec le zèle et l'impétuosité du fanatisme, et la bataille de Cossova anéantit la ligue et l'indépendance des tribus esclavonnes. En parcourant après sa victoire la scène du carnage, Amurath observait que la plupart des morts n'étaient que des adolescens, et son visir lui répondait, en courtisan, que des hommes d'un âge plus raisonnable n'auraient point entrepris de résister à ses invincibles armes. Mais l'épée de ses janissaires ne put le sauver du poignard du désespoir : un soldat servien s'élança du milieu des morts, et le blessa dans le ventre d'un coup mortel. Ce prince, petit-fils d'Othman, avait des mœurs simples et un caractère indulgent ; il aimait les sciences et la vertu, mais il scandalisa les musulmans par son peu d'attention à assister à leurs prières publiques ; et le mufti eut le courage de lui faire sentir sa faute, en refusant son témoignage dans une cause civile. On trouve assez fréquemment dans l'histoire orientale ce mélange de servitude et de liberté (1).

(1.) *Voyez* la vie et la mort de Morad ou Amurath 1er. dans Cantemir (p. 33-45), le premier livre de Chalcocondyles et les Annales turques de Leunclavius. Une autre histoire rapporte que le sultan fut poignardé dans sa tente par un Croate, et l'on allégua cet accident à Busbequius (*ep.* 1, p. 98) comme une excuse de la précaution insultante dont on usait avec les ambassadeurs, qui n'étaient admis en la présence du souverain qu'accompagnés de deux gardes, qui,

Règne de Bajazet 1er ou Ilderim. A. D. 1389-1403, 9 mars.

Le caractère de Bajazet, fils et successeur d'Amurath, se peint fortement dans le surnom qui lui fut donné d'*Ilderim* ou l'Éclair ; et il put s'enorgueillir d'une épithète qui exprimait l'ardente énergie de son âme et la rapidité de ses marches destructives. Durant les quatorze années de son règne (1), Bajazet courut sans cesse à la tête de ses armées, de Bursa à Andrinople, du Danube à l'Euphrate ; et, quoique très-zélé pour la propagation de sa religion, il attaqua indistinctement, en Europe et en Asie, les princes chrétiens et les mahométans, et réduisit sous son obéissance toute la partie septentrionale de l'Anatolie, depuis Angora jusqu'à Amasie et Erzeroum. Les émirs de Ghermian, de Caramanie, d'Aidin et de Sarukhan, furent dépouillés de leurs États héréditaires ; et après la conquête d'Iconium, la dynastie ottomane releva l'ancien royaume des Seljoucides. Les conquêtes de Bajazet en Europe ne furent ni moins rapides ni moins importantes. Dès qu'il eut assujetti les Serviens et les Bulgares à un joug régulier, il courut au-delà du Danube chercher de nouveaux ennemis et de nouveaux sujets dans le cœur

Ses conquêtes depuis l'Euphrate jusqu'au Danube.

---

placés à leur droite et à leur gauche, tenaient chacun un de leurs bras.

(1) L'histoire du règne de Bajazet 1er, ou Ilderim Bayazid, se trouve dans Cantemir (p. 46), dans le second livre de Chalcocondyles et les Annales turques. Le surnom d'Ilderim ou *Éclair* semble prouver que les conquérans et les poëtes ont dans tous les temps senti la vérité du système qui établit la terreur pour principe du sublime.

de la Moldavie (1). Tout ce qui reconnaissait encore l'empire grec dans la Thrace, la Macédoine et la Thessalie, passa sous celui du victorieux Ottoman. Un évêque complaisant le conduisit en Grèce à travers les Thermopyles; et nous remarquerons comme un fait singulier, que la veuve d'un chef espagnol, qui possédait le pays où se rendaient jadis les fameux oracles de Delphes, acheta la protection du sultan par le sacrifice d'une de ses filles remarquable par sa beauté. Pour assurer d'Asie en Europe la communication des Turcs, qui jusqu'alors avait été dangereuse et précaire, Bajazet établit à Gallipoli une flotte en croisière, qui commandait l'Hellespont et interceptait tous les secours que les Latins envoyaient à Constantinople. Tandis que ce prince sacrifiait sans scrupule à ses passions la justice et l'humanité, il forçait ses soldats à observer rigoureusement les règles de la décence et de la sobriété : les moissons se faisaient et se vendaient paisiblement au milieu de ses armées. Irrité de la négligence et de la corruption qui s'étaient introduites dans l'administration de la justice, il rassembla dans une maison tous les juges et gens de loi de ses États, qui ne redoutaient pas moins que d'y être brûlés vifs. Ses ministres trem-

---

(1) Cantemir, qui célèbre les victoires du grand Étienne sur les Turcs (p. 47), a composé une description de la principauté ancienne et moderne de Moldavie, que l'on promet depuis long-temps et qui n'a pas encore été publiée.

blaient en silence; mais un bouffon d'Éthiopie osa lui représenter la véritable cause de ce désordre; et le souverain ôta pour l'avenir toute excuse à la vénalité, en annexant à l'office de cadi un revenu convenable (1). Enorgueilli de ses succès, il dédaigna son ancien titre d'émir, et accepta la patente de sultan du calife, esclave en Égypte sous les ordres des Mamelucks (2). Entraînés par la force de l'opinion, les Turcs victorieux rendirent ce dernier et frivole hommage à la race d'Abbas et aux successeurs de Mahomet. Le nouveau sultan, jaloux de mériter son titre, porta la guerre en Hongrie, théâtre perpétuel des triomphes des Turcs et de leurs défaites. Sigismond, roi de Hongrie, était fils et frère des empereurs d'Occident. Sa cause était celle de l'Église et de l'Europe; au premier bruit de son danger, les plus braves chevaliers français et allemands s'empressèrent de se croiser sous ses drapeaux. Bajazet défit à la journée de Nicopolis une armée de

Bataille de Nicopolis.
A. D. 1396,
28 sept.

---

(1) Leunclav., *Annal. Turcici*, p. 318, 319. La vénalité des cadis est depuis long-temps un sujet de plainte et de scandale; et si nous ne voulons pas nous en rapporter à nos voyageurs, nous pouvons du moins en croire les Turcs eux-mêmes (d'Herbelot, *Bibl. orient.*, pag. 216, 217-229, 230).

(2) Ce fait, qui est attesté dans l'histoire arabe de Ben-Schounah, contemporain et Syrien (de Guignes, *Hist. des Huns*, t. IV, p. 336), détruit le témoignage de Saad Effendi et Cantemir (p. 14, 15), qui prétendent qu'Othman avait été élevé à la dignité de sultan.

cent mille chrétiens, qui s'étaient orgueilleusement vantés que si le ciel menaçait de tomber, ils le soutiendraient sur le bout de leurs lances. Le plus grand nombre périt dans la plaine ou se noya dans le Danube, et Sigismond, après s'être réfugié par la mer Noire à Constantinople, fit un long circuit pour retourner dans ses États épuisés (1). Dans l'orgueil de la victoire, Bajazet menaça d'assiéger Bude, d'envahir l'Allemagne et l'Italie, et de faire manger l'avoine à son cheval sur l'autel de Saint-Pierre à Rome. Ses projets furent arrêtés, non par la miraculeuse interposition de l'apôtre, non par une croisade des puissances chrétiennes, mais par un long et violent accès de goutte. Les désordres du monde physique ont quelquefois remédié à ceux du monde moral ; et un peu d'humeur âcre, en affectant une seule fibre d'un seul homme, peut suspendre les malheurs et la ruine des nations.

Tel est le tableau général de la guerre de Hongrie ; mais nous devons à la désastreuse aventure des Français quelques mémoires qui font connaître le caractère de Bajazet et les circonstances de sa victoire (2).

Croisade et captivité des princes français.
A. D.
1396-1398.

---

(1) *Voyez* les *Decades rerum hungaricarum* (*Dec.* III, l. II, p. 379) de Bonfinius, Italien, qui dans le quinzième siècle fut appelé en Hongrie pour y composer son éloquente histoire de ce royaume. Je donnerais la préférence à une chronique toute brute du temps et du pays, si je savais qu'elle existât et qu'on pût se la procurer.

(2) Je n'aurais point à me plaindre des peines et des soins qu'exige cet ouvrage, si je pouvais tirer tous mes

Le duc de Bourgogne, souverain de la Flandre et oncle de Charles VI, n'avait pu retenir l'ardeur intrépide de Jean son fils, comte de Nevers, qui partit accompagné de quatre princes ses cousins et ceux du monarque français. Le sire de Couci, un des meilleurs et des plus vieux capitaines de la chrétienté, guidait leur inexpérience (1); mais l'armée, commandée par un connétable, un amiral et un maréchal (2) de France, n'était composée que de mille

matériaux de livres semblables à la chronique de l'honnête Froissard (vol. IV, c. 67-69-72-74-79-83-85-87-89), qui lisait peu, faisait beaucoup de questions, et croyait tout. Les Mémoires du maréchal de Boucicault (part. 1, c. 22-28) ajoutent quelques faits; mais ils paraissent secs et incomplets, lorsqu'on les compare à l'agréable loquacité de Froissard.

(1) Le baron de Zurlauben (*Hist. de l'Acad. des Inscript.*, t. XXV) a donné des Mémoires complets de la vie d'Enguerrand VII, sire de Couci. Il jouissait également d'un rang distingué et de possessions considérables en France et en Angleterre. En 1375, il conduisit dans la Suisse un corps d'aventuriers pour recouvrer un vaste patrimoine qu'il prétendait lui appartenir comme héritier de sa grand'mère, fille de l'empereur Albert Ier d'Autriche (Sinner, *Voyage dans la Suisse occidentale*, t. I, p. 118-124).

(2) Cet office militaire, si respectable encore aujourd'hui, l'était encore davantage lorsqu'il n'était possédé que par deux personnes (Daniel, *Histoire de la Milice française*, t. II, p. 5). L'un de ces deux, le fameux Boucicault, était maréchal de la croisade. Il défendit depuis Constantinople, gouverna la république de Gênes, s'empara de toute la côte d'Asie, et fut tué à la bataille d'Azincourt.

chevaliers et de leurs écuyers : l'éclat de leurs noms était une source de présomption et un obstacle à la discipline. Chacun se croyait digne de commander, personne ne voulait obéir, et les Français méprisaient également leurs alliés et leurs ennemis. Persuadés que Bajazet devait inévitablement périr ou prendre la fuite, ils calculaient déjà ce qu'il leur faudrait de temps pour se rendre à Constantinople et délivrer le saint-sépulcre. Lorsque les cris des Turcs annoncèrent leur approche, les jeunes Français étaient à table, se livrant à la gaîté, à l'irréflexion; et, déjà échauffés par le vin, ils se couvrirent avec précipitation de leurs armes, s'élancèrent sur leurs chevaux, coururent à l'avant-garde, et prirent pour un affront l'avis de Sigismond, qui voulait les priver de l'honneur de la première attaque. Les chrétiens n'auraient pas perdu la bataille de Nicopolis, si les Français eussent voulu déférer à la prudence des Hongrois; mais ils auraient probablement obtenu une victoire glorieuse, si les Hongrois eussent imité la valeur des Français. Après avoir rapidement dispersé les troupes d'Asie qui formaient la première ligne, ils forcèrent les palissades établies pour arrêter la cavalerie, mirent en désordre, après un sanglant combat, les janissaires eux-mêmes, et furent enfin accablés par la multitude d'escadrons qui sortirent des bois et attaquèrent de tous côtés cette poignée de guerriers intrépides. Dans cette journée funeste, Bajazet se fit admirer de ses ennemis par le secret et la rapidité de sa marche, par son ordre de bataille et ses savantes évolutions ; mais ils l'accusent d'avoir inhumainement abusé de la victoire. Après avoir réservé le comte de Nevers et vingt-quatre princes ou seigneurs, dont ses interprètes lui attestèrent le rang et l'opulence, le sultan fit amener successivement devant lui le reste des Français captifs, et, sur leur refus d'abjurer leur religion, les fit successivement décapiter en sa présence. La perte de ses plus braves janissaires animait sa vengeance ; et s'il est vrai que, dans la journée qui précéda la bataille, les Français eussent massacré leurs prisonniers turcs (1), ils ne durent imputer qu'à eux les effets d'une juste représaille. Un des chevaliers dont il avait épargné la vie, obtint la permission d'aller à Paris raconter cette lamentable histoire et solliciter la rançon des princes captifs. En attendant, l'armée turque traîna le comte de Nevers et les barons français dans ses marches ; ils servirent de trophée aux musulmans en Europe et en Asie, et furent rigoureusement emprisonnés à Bursa, toutes les fois que le sultan résida dans cette capitale. On pressait chaque jour Bajazet d'expier par leur sang celui des martyrs musulmans ; mais il leur avait promis la vie, et, soit qu'il eût ou pardonné ou condamné, sa parole était irrévocable. Au retour du messager, les présens et l'intercession des rois de France et de Chypre ne laissèrent point de doutes au

---

(1) Relativement à ce fait odieux, l'abbé de Vertot cite l'histoire anonyme de Saint-Denis, l. XVI, c. 10-11; *Ordre de Malte*, t. II, p. 310.

vainqueur sur le rang et l'importance de ses prisonniers. Lusignan lui présenta une salière d'or d'un travail exquis, estimée dix mille ducats, et Charles vi envoya, par la voie de Hongrie, un vol d'oiseaux de fauconnerie tirés de la Norwége, six charges de chevaux du drap écarlate qu'on fabriquait alors à Reims, et de tapisseries d'Arras qui représentaient les batailles d'Alexandre. Après quelques délais occasionés par l'éloignement plutôt que par aucun projet, Bajazet accepta deux cent mille ducats pour la rançon du comte de Nevers et des barons encore existans. Le maréchal de Boucicault, fameux guerrier, était de ce petit nombre d'heureux ; mais l'amiral de France avait péri dans la bataille, et le connétable, ainsi que le sire de Couci, dans la prison de Bursa. Cette rançon, dont les frais accidentels avaient doublé la somme, tombait principalement sur le duc de Bourgogne ou plutôt sur ses sujets flamands, que les lois féodales obligeaient de contribuer lorsque le fils aîné de leur souverain était armé chevalier, et pour le délivrer de captivité. Quelques marchands génois se rendirent caution pour cinq fois la valeur de cette somme ; d'où ce siècle guerrier put comprendre que le commerce et le crédit sont les liens des nations et de la société. On avait stipulé dans le traité que les captifs français jureraient de ne jamais porter les armes contre leur vainqueur ; mais Bajazet lui-même les dispensa de cette condition peu généreuse. « Je méprise, dit-il à l'héritier de la Bourgogne, tes armes et tes sermens. Tu es jeune, et tu auras peut-être l'ambition d'effacer la honte ou le malheur de ta première entreprise. Rassemble tes forces militaires, annonce ton projet, et sois sûr que Bajazet se réjouira de te rencontrer une seconde fois sur le champ de bataille. » Avant leur départ, ils furent admis à la cour de Bursa; les princes français admirèrent la magnificence du sultan, dont l'équipage de chasse et de fauconnerie était composé de sept mille chasseurs et d'autant de fauconniers (1). Il fit devant eux ouvrir le ventre à un de ses chambellans, qu'une pauvre femme accusait d'avoir bu le lait de ses chèvres. Les étrangers furent étonnés de cet acte de justice; mais c'était la justice d'un sultan qui dédaigne d'examiner la valeur des preuves ou le degré de la faute.

L'empereur Jean Paléologue.
A. D. 1355, 8 janv.
A. D. 1391.

Après s'être délivré d'un tuteur impérieux, Jean Paléologue fut durant trente-six années le spectateur oisif et, à ce qu'il paraît, indifférent, de la ruine de son empire (2) : totalement livré à l'amour

---

(1) Sherefeddin-Ali (*Hist. de Timour-Bec*, l. v, c. 13) fixe à douze mille les officiers et les valets appartenant à l'équipage de chasse de Bajazet. Timour exposa une partie des dépouilles du prince turc dans une partie de chasse : 1° des chiens courans avec des housses de satin; 2° des léopards avec des colliers enrichis de pierres précieuses; 3° des levriers grecs; et 4° des dogues d'Europe, qui égalaient pour la force les lions d'Afrique (*idem.*, l. vi, c. 15). Bajazet se plaisait particulièrement à faire prendre des grues par ses faucons (Chalcocond., l. ii, p. 35).

(2) Pour les règnes de Jean Paléologue et de son fils Ma-

ou plutôt à la débauche, sa seule passion forte, l'esclave des Turcs oubliait la honte de l'empereur romain dans les bras des filles et des femmes de Constantinople. Andronic, son fils aîné, avait formé durant son séjour à Andrinople une liaison d'amitié et de crime avec Sauzes, le fils d'Amurath, et ils firent de concert le projet d'arracher à leurs pères le sceptre et la vie. Amurath, passé en Europe, découvrit et dissipa bientôt cette conjuration; après avoir privé Sauzes de la vue, il menaça son vassal de le traiter comme le complice de son fils, s'il ne lui infligeait pas le même châtiment. Paléologue obéit, et, par une précaution barbare, il enveloppa dans son arrêt l'enfance innocente du prince Jean, fils du criminel Andronic; mais on exécuta l'opération avec tant de douceur ou si peu d'habileté, que l'un conserva l'usage d'un œil, et que l'autre n'éprouva d'autre infirmité que de loucher. Ainsi exclus de la succession, les deux princes furent renfermés dans la tour d'Anéma, et l'empereur récompensa la fidélité de Manuel, son second fils, en partageant avec lui la pourpre impériale; mais, au bout de deux ans, les factions des Latins et l'inconstance des Grecs produisirent une révolution : les princes prisonniers montèrent sur le trône, et les deux empereurs pri-

Discorde des Grecs.

nuel, depuis 1354 jusqu'en 1402, consultez Ducas (c. 9-15), Phranza (l. 1, c. 16-21) et les premier et second livres de Chalcocondyles, qui a enseveli son sujet dans un amas d'épisodes.

rent leur place dans la tour. Avant l'expiration des deux années suivantes, Paléologue et Manuel parvinrent à s'échapper par le secours d'un moine accusé de magie, alternativement désigné par les noms d'ange ou de diable. Ils se réfugièrent à Scutari; leurs partisans prirent les armes, et les Grecs des deux partis déployèrent l'ambitieuse animosité de César et de Pompée, lorsqu'ils se disputaient l'empire de l'univers. Le monde romain ne consistait plus que dans un coin de la Thrace, entre la Propontide et la mer Noire, dont l'étendue, de cinquante milles en longueur sur une largeur d'environ trente milles, aurait été comparable à une des plus petites principautés d'Allemagne ou d'Italie, si les restes de Constantinople n'avaient pas encore présenté la richesse et la population de la capitale d'un royaume. Pour rétablir la paix, il fallut partager ce fragment d'empire. Paléologue et Manuel conservèrent la capitale; Andronic et son fils fixèrent leur résidence à Rhodosto et Sélymbrie, et gouvernèrent presque tout ce qui n'était pas renfermé dans l'enceinte de Byzance. Dans le tranquille sommeil de la royauté, les passions de Jean Paléologue survivaient à sa raison et à ses forces. Il priva son fils bien-aimé, son collègue et son successeur, d'une jeune et belle princesse de Trébisonde; et tandis que le vieillard épuisé s'efforçait de consommer son mariage, le jeune Manuel se rendait aux ordres de la Porte ottomane, suivi de cent Grecs des plus illustres maisons. Ils servirent avec honneur dans les armées de Bajazet;

mais l'entreprise de rétablir les fortifications de Constantinople irrita le prince ottoman. Il menaça leur vie ; on démolit aussitôt les nouveaux ouvrages ; et c'est peut-être faire trop d'honneur à la mémoire de Jean Paléologue que d'attribuer sa mort à cette dernière humiliation.

Manuel, promptement averti de cet événement, s'échappa secrètement et en diligence du palais de Bursa et prit possession du trône de Constantinople. Bajazet, affectant de mépriser la perte de ce précieux ôtage, poursuivit ses conquêtes en Asie et en Europe, tandis que le nouvel empereur de Byzance faisait la guerre à son neveu, Jean de Sélymbrie, qui défendit durant huit années ses droits légitimes à la succession des restes de l'empire. Le victorieux sultan voulut enfin terminer ses exploits par la conquête de Constantinople ; mais il se rendit aux représentations de son visir, qui lui fit craindre que cette entreprise n'attirât sur lui une seconde et plus redoutable croisade de tous les princes de la chrétienté. Bajazet écrivit à l'empereur grec une lettre conçue dans ces termes : « Par la faveur divine notre invincible cimeterre a réduit sous notre obéissance presque toute l'Asie, et une portion considérable de l'Europe, à laquelle il ne manque que la ville de Constantinople, car il ne te reste plus rien hors de son enceinte ; sors de cette ville, remets-la dans nos mains, stipule ta récompense, ou tremble pour toi et ton malheureux peuple des suites d'un imprudent refus. » Mais les

<small>L'empereur Manuel.
A. D.
1391-1425,
juillet 25.</small>

<small>Détresse de Constantinople.
A. D.
1395-1402.</small>

instructions secrètes des ambassadeurs chargés de ce message permettaient d'adoucir la rigueur de cette demande, et de proposer un traité que les Grecs acceptèrent avec soumission et reconnaissance : ils accordèrent pour prix d'une trêve de dix ans un tribut annuel de trente mille écus d'or ; ils eurent la douleur de voir tolérer publiquement le culte de Mahomet, et Bajazet eut la gloire d'établir un cadi et de fonder une mosquée dans la métropole de l'Église d'Orient (1). Cependant l'inquiet sultan ne respecta pas long-temps cette trêve ; Bajazet prit le parti du prince de Sélymbrie, le souverain légitime, et environna Constantinople avec son armée. Manuel, dans sa détresse, implora la protection du roi de France ; sa plaintive ambassade en obtint beaucoup de compassion et quelques secours sous les ordres du maréchal de Boucicault (2), dont la pieuse valeur était animée par le souvenir de sa captivité et le désir de s'en venger sur les infidèles. A la tête de quatre vaisseaux de guerre, il cingla d'Aigues-Mortes vers l'Hellespont, força le passage défendu par dix-sept galères turques, descendit six cents hommes d'armes et seize cents archers à Constantinople, et en fit la revue dans la plaine voisine, sans daigner compter

---

(1) Cantemir, p. 50–53. Ducas (c. 13–15) est le seul des Grecs qui avoue l'établissement d'un cadi turc à Constantinople ; encore dissimule-t-il la mosquée.

(2) *Mémoires du bon messire Jean le Maingre, dit Boucicault, maréchal de France*, partie première, c. 30–35.

ni mettre en bataille la multitude des Grecs. Son arrivée fit lever le blocus qui serrait Byzance par terre et par mer. Les escadrons de Bajazet s'éloignèrent précipitamment à une respectueuse distance, et plusieurs forteresses d'Europe et d'Asie furent emportées d'assaut par le maréchal et l'empereur, qui combattirent à côté l'un de l'autre avec la même intrépidité ; mais les Ottomans reparurent bientôt en plus grand nombre, et le brave Boucicault, après s'être maintenu durant une année, résolut d'abandonner un pays qui ne pouvait plus fournir la paye ni la subsistance de ses soldats. Le maréchal offrit à Manuel de le conduire à la cour de France, où il pourrait solliciter lui-même des secours d'hommes et d'argent, et lui conseilla cependant de faire cesser la discorde civile en laissant le trône à son neveu. Manuel accepta la proposition ; il introduisit le prince de Sélymbrie dans la ville, et telle était la misère publique, que le sort de l'exilé parut préférable à celui du souverain. Au lieu d'applaudir aux succès de son vassal, le sultan des Turcs réclama Byzance comme sa propriété ; et, sur le refus de l'empereur Jean, il fit éprouver à la capitale les calamités réunies de la guerre et de la famine. Contre un pareil ennemi on ne pouvait rien espérer des prières ni de la résistance, et le sauvage conquérant aurait dévoré sa proie, si dans cette crise il n'eût pas été précipité du trône par un autre sauvage plus fort que lui. La victoire de Timour ou Tamerlan différa la chute de Constantinople d'environ un demi-siècle, et ce service important, quoique accidentel, donne à l'histoire et au caractère du conquérant mongoul le droit d'occuper une place dans cette histoire.

CHAPITRE LXV.

Élévation de Timour ou Tamerlan sur le trône de Samarcande. Ses conquêtes dans la Perse, la Géorgie, la Tartarie, la Russie, l'Inde, la Syrie et l'Anatolie. Sa guerre contre les Turcs. Défaite et captivité de Bajazet. Mort de Timour. Guerre civile des fils de Bajazet. Rétablissement de la monarchie des Turcs par Mahomet 1er. Siége de Constantinople par Amurath II.

TIMOUR eut pour première ambition le désir de conquérir et de dominer l'univers. Le second vœu de cette âme magnanime fut de vivre dans le souvenir et dans l'estime de la postérité. Ses secrétaires recueillirent soigneusement toutes les transactions civiles et militaires de son règne (1); le récit authentique en fut revu par les hommes les mieux instruits de chaque fait particulier; et on croit généralement

Histoire de Timour ou Tamerlan.

---

(1) On communiqua ces journaux à Sherefeddin ou Cherefeddin-Ali, et il composa en langue persane l'histoire de Timour-Bec, traduite en français par M. Petis de La Croix. *Paris*, 1722, en quatre volumes *in-*12. Je l'ai pris pour mon guide, et je l'ai suivi fidèlement. Sa géographie et sa chronologie sont de la plus grande exactitude, et on peut lui donner confiance pour les faits publics, quoiqu'il loue en esclave la fortune et les vertus de son héros. On peut voir dans les Institutions de Timour le soin qu'il prenait pour se procurer des renseignemens dans son propre pays et chez l'étranger (*Instit. de Timour*, pages 215-217, 349, 351).

dans la famille et dans l'empire de Timour que ce monarque composa lui-même les commentaires (1) de sa vie et les *Institutions* (2) de son gouvernement (3); mais ces soins ne contribuèrent point à conserver sa renommée : ces monumens précieux, écrits en langue mongoule ou persane, restèrent inconnus à l'univers ou au moins à l'Europe. Les

---

(1) Ces commentaires sont encore inconnus en Europe; mais M. White nous fait espérer qu'ils pourront être rapportés par son ami le major Davy, qui a lu en Asie « ce récit fidèle et détaillé d'une époque intéressante et féconde en événemens. »

(2) J'ignore si l'Institution originale, écrite en langue turque ou mongoule, existe encore. Le major Davy, aidé de M. White, professeur de langue arabe, a publié à Oxford, en 1783, in-4°, la traduction persane, et ils y ont joint une traduction anglaise avec un index très-précieux. Cet ouvrage a été traduit depuis du persan en français (*Paris*, 1787) par M. Langlès, très-versé dans les antiquités de l'Orient, qui y a ajouté une Vie de Timour et des Notes très-curieuses.

(3) Shaw Allum, le présent Mogol, lit, estime, mais ne peut imiter les Institutions de son illustre ancêtre : le traducteur anglais croit leur authenticité justifiée par les preuves insérées dans l'ouvrage; mais si l'on concevait quelques soupçons de fraude ou de fiction, la lettre du major Davy ne serait pas susceptible de les détruire. Les Orientaux n'ont jamais cultivé l'art de la critique. La protection d'un prince, moins honorable peut-être, n'est pas moins lucrative que celle d'un libraire; et on ne doit pas regarder comme incroyable qu'un Persan, le véritable auteur, pût renoncer à l'honneur que pourrait lui rapporter son ouvrage, pour en augmenter la valeur et le prix.

nations qu'il asservit exercèrent une vengeance impuissante et méprisable ; et l'ignorance a répété longtemps l'invention de la calomnie (1), qui défigurait sa naissance, son caractère, sa personne et jusqu'à son nom, qu'on avait changé en celui de *Tamerlan* (2). Ce serait cependant un titre de plus à l'estime générale, s'il était réellement passé de la charrue au trône ; et sa jambe boiteuse ne pourrait être un reproche qu'autant qu'il aurait eu la faiblesse de rougir d'une infirmité naturelle ou peut-être honorable.

Les Mongouls, religieusement attachés à la famille de Gengis, le regardaient sans doute comme un sujet rebelle ; cependant il descendait de la noble tribu de Berlass. Carashar Nevian, son cinquième an-

---

(1) On trouve l'original de ce conte dans l'ouvrage suivant, fort estimé pour la pompeuse élégance du style : *Ahmedis Arabsiadæ* (Ahmed-Ebn-Arabshah) *vitæ et rerum gestarum Timuri, arabicè et latinè. Edidit Samuel Henricus Manger. Franequeræ,* 1767, 2 tom. in-4°. On reconnaît dans cet auteur syrien un ennemi toujours malveillant et souvent ignorant ; les titres mêmes de ses chapitres sont injurieux, comme ceux-ci : *Comment le méchant, comment l'impie, comment la vipère,* etc. Le copieux article de Timour inséré dans la *Bibliothèque orientale* présente un mélange d'opinions, parce que d'Herbelot a tiré indifféremment ses matériaux (pag. 877-888) de Khondemir, d'Ebn-Schounah et du Lebtarikh.

(2) *Demir* ou *Timour* signifie en langue turque *fer* ; et *Beg* est la dénomination d'un grand seigneur ou d'un prince. Le changement d'une lettre ou d'un accent produit le mot *lenc* ou *boiteux*, et les Européens ont confondu par corruption les deux mots dans le nom de *Tamerlan*.

cêtre, avait été le visir de Zagataï dans son nouveau royaume de la Transoxiane; et, en remontant à quelques générations, la branche de Timour rejoint, au moins par les femmes (1), la tige impériale (2). Il naquit à quarante milles au sud de Samarcande, dans le village de Sebzar, qui faisait partie du fertile territoire de Cash, dont ses ancêtres étaient les chefs héréditaires; ils commandaient un *toman* de dix mille cavaliers (3). Le hasard le fit naître (4) à une de

---

(1) Après avoir raconté quelques fables ridicules, Arabshah est forcé de reconnaître Timour *Lenc* pour un descendant de Gengis *per mulieres*, et il ajoute avec humeur *laqueos Satanæ* (part. 1, c. 1, p. 25). Le témoignage d'Abulghazi-khan (part. 11, c. 5; part. v, c. 4) est clair, irrécusable et décisif.

(2) Selon une généalogie, le quatrième ancêtre de Gengis et le neuvième de Timour étaient deux frères; ils convinrent que la postérité de l'aîné succèderait à la dignité de khan, et que les descendans du plus jeune exerceraient l'office de ministre et de général. Cette tradition servit du moins à justifier les *premières* entreprises de l'ambitieux Timour (*Institutions*, p. 24, 25, d'après les fragmens manuscrits de l'*Histoire de Timour*).

(3) *Voyez* la *Préface* de Sherefeddin et la *Géographie* d'Abulféda (*Chorasmiæ*, etc., *Descriptio*, p. 60, 61) dans le second volume des *Petits Géographes grecs* d'Hudson.

(4) *Voyez* sur sa naissance et sur l'opinion à cet égard des astrologues de son petit-fils Ulugh-Beg, le docteur Hyde (*Synt. Dissert.*, t. 11, p. 466). Il naquit dans l'année de grâce 1336, avril 9, 11 deg. 57 min., P. M. lat. 36. Je ne sais pas s'ils ont bien constaté la grande conjonction des planètes, d'où il a tiré comme d'autres conquérans le sur-

ces époques d'anarchie qui annoncent la chute des dynasties asiatiques et ouvrent une nouvelle carrière à l'ambition audacieuse. La famille des khans de Zagataï était éteinte, les émirs aspiraient à l'indépendance, et leurs dissensions ne purent être suspendues que par la conquête et la tyrannie des khans du Kashgar, qui, avec le secours d'une armée de Gètes ou de Calmoucks (1), avaient envahi la Transoxiane. Timour avait à peine douze ans lorsqu'il fit ses premières armes ; à vingt-cinq ans, il entreprit de délivrer son pays. Les regards et le vœu des peuples se tournèrent vers un héros qui souffrait pour leur cause; les principaux officiers civils et militaires avaient juré, sur le salut de leur âme, de le soutenir aux dépens de leur fortune et de leur vie ; mais, au moment du danger, ils tremblèrent et gardèrent le silence. Après avoir attendu en vain, durant sept jours, sur les collines de Samarcande, il se retira dans le désert avec soixante cavaliers. Atteint dans

Ses premières aventures.
A. D.
1361-1370.

---

nom de Saheb-Keran, ou Maître des conjonctions (*Bibl. orient.*, p. 878).

(1) Les Institutions de Timour donnent très-improprement aux sujets du khan de Kashgar le nom d'Ouzbegs ou Uzbeks ; ce nom appartenait à une autre race de Tartares qui habitait un pays différent (Abulghazi, part. v, c. 5; part. vii, c. 5). Si j'étais bien sûr que ce nom se trouvât dans l'original turc, je n'hésiterais pas à prononcer que les Institutions furent composées un siècle après la mort de Timour, depuis l'établissement des Uzbeks dans la Transoxiane.

sa fuite par un corps de mille Gètes, il les repoussa avec un carnage incroyable, et ses ennemis furent forcés de s'écrier : « Timour est un homme merveilleux, Dieu et la fortune sont avec lui ! » Mais cette action sanglante réduisit sa petite troupe au nombre de dix, qui diminua encore par la désertion de trois Carizmiens. Il parcourut le désert avec sa femme, ses sept compagnons et quatre chevaux, et passa soixante-deux jours enfermé dans un sombre cachot, dont il se retira par son courage et le remords de son oppresseur. Après avoir traversé à la nage le courant large et rapide du Gihoon ou Oxus, il mena durant plusieurs mois, sur les frontières des États voisins, la vie errante d'un exilé et d'un proscrit. Mais l'adversité donna un nouvel éclat à sa renommée : elle lui apprit à distinguer, parmi les compagnons de sa fortune, ceux qui lui étaient attachés personnellement, et à employer le talent ou le caractère des hommes à leur plus grand avantage, et surtout au sien. Timour, après être rentré dans sa patrie, fut joint successivement par différens partis de confédérés qui l'avaient cherché avec inquiétude dans le désert. Je ne puis me refuser à donner, dans sa touchante simplicité, le récit d'une de ces heureuses rencontres. Il se présenta pour servir de guide à trois chefs suivis de soixante-dix cavaliers. « Lorsqu'ils jetèrent les yeux sur moi, dit Timour, ils furent éperdus de joie; et ils sautèrent à bas de leurs chevaux, et ils vinrent et se mirent à genoux devant moi, et ils baisèrent mes étriers. Je descendis aussi de mon cheval et je les serrai l'un après l'autre dans mes bras; et je mis mon turban sur la tête du premier chef, et je passai autour des reins du second une ceinture entourée de joyaux et travaillée en or, et je revêtis le troisième de mon habit; et ils pleurèrent et je pleurai aussi; et l'heure de la prière était arrivée, et nous priâmes. Et nous remontâmes sur nos chevaux, et nous vînmes à mon habitation; et j'assemblai mon peuple; et je fis un festin. » Les plus braves tribus vinrent bientôt se joindre à ces bandes fidèles; il les mena contre un ennemi supérieur en nombre, et après une guerre mêlée d'événemens divers, les Gètes furent enfin chassés de la Transoxiane. Timour avait déjà fait beaucoup pour sa gloire; mais il lui restait beaucoup à faire, beaucoup d'adresse à employer et de sang à répandre pour forcer ses égaux à reconnaître un maître. La naissance et le pouvoir de l'émir Houssein obligèrent Timour à recevoir en lui un vicieux et indigne collègue, mais dont la sœur était son épouse la plus chérie. La jalousie troubla bientôt leur union; et dans leurs fréquentes querelles, Timour eut toujours l'adresse de faire tomber sur son rival le reproche d'injustice et de perfidie. Enfin, après une dernière défaite, Houssein fut tué par quelques amis de Timour, dont la sagacité osa en cette occasion désobéir, pour la dernière fois, aux ordres de leur chef. Les suffrages unanimes d'une diète ou *couroultai* revêtirent le vainqueur; âgé de

<small>Il est élevé sur le trône du Zagatai. A. D. 1370, avril.</small>

trente-quatre ans (1); du commandement *impérial;* mais il affecta de respecter la maison de Gengis; et tandis que l'émir Timour régnait sur le Zagataï et l'Orient, un khan titulaire servait comme simple officier dans les armées de son serviteur. Un royaume fertile, de cinq cents milles en longueur et en largeur, aurait pu satisfaire l'ambition d'un sujet; mais Timour aspirait au trône du monde, et avant sa mort, il avait ajouté vingt-six couronnes à celle du Zagataï. Sans m'étendre sur les victoires de trente-cinq campagnes ou suivre ses marches continuelles sur le continent de l'Asie, je raconterai succinctement les conquêtes qu'il fit : 1° en Perse, 2° en Tartarie, et 3° dans l'Inde (2), d'où je passerai au récit plus intéressant de sa guerre contre les Turcs.

Ses conquêtes.
A. D.
1370-1400.
1° De la Perse.
A. D.
1380-1393.

I. La jurisprudence des conquérans fournit libéralement à toutes leurs guerres des motifs de sûreté, de vengeance, de gloire, de zèle, de droit ou de convenance. Timour avait à peine réuni le Carizme et le Candahar à son patrimoine du Zagataï, qu'il

---

(1) Le premier livre de Sherefeddin est consacré à la vie privée de son héros, et Timour lui-même ou son secrétaire s'étend avec complaisance (*Instit.*, p. 3-77) sur les treize projets et entreprises qui font le plus d'honneur à son mérite personnel, qu'on aperçoit encore à travers le récit malveillant d'Arabshah (part. 1, c. 1-12).

(2) Le second et le troisième livre de Sherefeddin traitent des conquêtes de la Perse, de la Tartarie et de l'Inde. Ainsi qu'Arabshah (c. 13-55), *voyez* aussi les précieux *Index* des Institutions.

tourna ses regards vers les royaumes de l'Iran ou de la Perse. Le vaste pays qui s'étend de l'Oxus au Tigre ne reconnaissait plus de souverain légitime depuis la mort d'Abousaïd, dernier descendant du grand Holacou. La paix et la justice étaient depuis quarante ans exilées de cette terre ; et Timour, en l'envahissant, semblait répondre à la voix d'un peuple opprimé : les petits tyrans qui l'accablaient auraient pu se défendre en se réunissant ; ils combattirent séparément et succombèrent tous, sans autre différence dans leur destinée que celle qu'y put apporter la promptitude de la soumission ou l'opiniâtreté de la résistance. Ibrahim, prince de Shirwan ou d'Albanie, baisa le marchepied du trône impérial et offrit au souverain des présens de soie, de chevaux et de bijoux, dont chaque article, selon l'usage des Tartares, était composé de neuf objets. Cependant un spectateur observa qu'il n'avait présenté que huit esclaves : « Je suis le neuvième, » répondit Ibrahim, qui s'attendait au reproche, et Timour récompensa cette adulation d'un sourire (1). Shah Mansour, prince du Fars ou de la Perse proprement dite, et le moins puissant de ses ennemis, se montra le plus redoutable. Dans une bataille sous les murs de Shiray, il mit en désordre, avec trois ou quatre mille soldats, le *coul* ou corps de bataille

---

(1) Abulghazi-khan cite la vénération des Tartares pour le nombre mystérieux de neuf, et divise par ce motif son histoire généalogique en neuf parties.

de trente mille hommes de cavalerie, où Timour combattait en personne. Il ne restait autour de celui-ci que quatorze ou quinze gardes. Ferme comme un rocher, il reçut deux coups de cimeterre sur son casque (1). Les Mongouls se rallièrent et firent tomber à ses pieds la tête de Mansour. Le vainqueur rendit hommage à la valeur de son ennemi en exterminant tous les mâles de cette race intrépide. De Shiray, ses troupes s'avancèrent jusqu'au golfe Persique, et la ville d'Ormuz (2) annonça son opulence et sa faiblesse en s'engageant à payer un tribut annuel de six cent mille *dinars* d'or. Bagdad n'était plus la ville de la paix et le séjour du calife; mais

---

(1) Arabshâh (part. 1, c. 28, p. 183) raconte que le lâche Timour s'enfuit dans sa tente, et évita la poursuite de Shah-Mansour en se cachant sous les robes de ses femmes; peut-être Sherefeddin a-t-il exagéré sa valeur (l. III, c. 25).

(2) L'histoire d'Ormuz ressemble à celle de Tyr. La vieille ville, située sur le continent, détruite par les Tartares, fut reconstruite dans une île stérile et manquant d'eau douce. Les rois d'Ormuz, enrichis par le commerce de l'Inde et la pêche des perles, possédaient de vastes territoires en Perse et en Arabie; mais ils furent d'abord tributaires des sultans de Kerman, et furent délivrés, A. D. 1505, de la tyrannie de leurs visirs par celle des Portugais. Marc-Paul (l. 1, c. 15, 16, fol. 7, 8); Abulféda (*Géogr.*, Tab. XI, p. 261, 262); une Chronique originale d'Ormuz, dans l'*Hist. de la Perse* par Stephen (p. 376-416) ou dans Texeira; et les *Itinéraires* insérés dans le premier volume de *Ramusio* ou Ludovico-Barthema (1503, fol. 167), d'André Corsali (1517, fol. 202, 203) et d'Odoardo Barbessa (en 1516, fol. 315-318).

la plus brillante conquête de Houlacou devait exciter l'ambition de son successeur. Depuis les bouches du Tigre et de l'Euphrate jusqu'à leur source, tout le pays qu'arrosent ces deux fleuves fut soumis à son obéissance. Il entra dans Édesse, et châtia les sacriléges Turcomans de la brebis noire, qui avaient pillé une caravane de la Mecque. Les chrétiens de la Géorgie bravaient encore dans leurs montagnes les armes et la loi des mahométans : le succès de trois expéditions lui obtint le mérite de la *gazi* ou guerre sainte, et le prince de Téflis devint son prosélyte et son ami.

II. L'invasion du Turkestan, ou Tartarie orientale, put passer pour une vengeance légitime; l'impunité des Gètes blessait l'orgueil de Timour. Il passa le Gihoon, soumit le royaume de Kashgar et pénétra sept fois dans le cœur de leur pays. Son camp le plus éloigné fut à deux mois de marche ou à quatre cent quatre-vingts lieues au nord-est de Samarcande, et ses émirs, après avoir traversé l'Irtish, gravèrent dans les forêts de la Sibérie un monument grossier de leurs exploits. La conquête du Kipzak (1) ou Tartarie occidentale eut pour motif de secourir les opprimés et de punir les ingrats. Toctamish, prince fugitif, avait obtenu la protection de Timour et un asile à sa cour; il renvoya dédaigneu-

Du Turkestan.
A. D.
1370-1383.

---

(1) Arabshah avait voyagé dans le Kipzak, et acquis de grandes connaissances de la géographie, des villes et des révolutions de ce pays septentrional (part. 1, c. 45-49).

sement les ambassadeurs d'Auruss-khan, qui furent suivis le même jour des armées du Zagataï. Sa victoire rétablit Toctamish dans l'empire septentrional des Mongouls; mais, après dix ans de règne, le nouveau khan oublia les services et la puissance de son bienfaiteur, et ne le regarda plus que comme l'usurpateur des droits sacrés de la maison de Gengis. Il entra en Perse par le défilé de Derbent à la tête de quatre-vingt-dix mille chevaux et de toutes les forces du Kipzak, de la Bulgarie, de la Circassie et de la Russie; il passa le Gihoon, brûla les palais de Timour, et le força de défendre dans le milieu de l'hiver et Samarcande et sa vie. Après quelques doux reproches suivis d'une brillante victoire, l'empereur se résolut à la vengeance. Il envahit deux fois le Kipzak à l'est et à l'ouest de la mer Caspienne et du Volga, avec des forces si considérables, que le front de son armée occupait une étendue de treize milles. Durant cinq mois de marche, ils rencontrèrent à peine une trace d'homme dans leur route, et dépendirent souvent du hasard de la chasse pour leur subsistance. Les armées parurent enfin à la vue l'une de l'autre; mais la trahison de celui qui portait l'étendard du Kipzak, et qui le renversa au milieu de l'action, détermina la victoire en faveur des Zagataïs, et Toctamish, disent les Institutions, abandonna la tribu de Toushi au vent de la désolation (1).

<hr>

(1) *Institut. de Timour*, p. 123-125. M. White, l'éditeur, se plaint du récit insuffisant et superficiel de Sherefeddin

Il se réfugia chez le grand-duc de Lithuanie, revint encore sur les bords du Volga, et, après quinze batailles livrées contre un rival qui s'était élevé dans le sein de ses États, périt dans les déserts de la Sibérie. Timour poursuivit son ennemi jusque dans les provinces tributaires de la Russie ; il fit prisonnier un duc de la maison régnante, au milieu des ruines de sa principale ville ; et la vanité ou l'ignorance orientale put aisément confondre Yeletz avec la capitale de l'empire. L'approche du Tartare fit trembler Moscou, et la résistance n'aurait pas été vigoureuse, puisque les Russes plaçaient toutes leurs espérances dans une image miraculeuse de la Vierge à laquelle ils attribuent la retraite volontaire ou accidentelle du conquérant. La prudence et l'ambition le rappelaient vers le sud ; le pays était épuisé et les soldats mongouls étaient chargés de fourrures précieuses, de toiles d'Antioche (1) et de lingots d'or et d'argent (2). Il reçut, sur les bords du Don ou

---

(l. III, c. 12, 13, 14), qui ignorait les desseins de Timour et le véritable ressort de l'action.

(1) Il est plus aisé de croire aux fourrures de Russie qu'aux lingots ; mais Antioche n'a jamais été fameuse pour les toiles, et cette ville était déjà ruinée. Je soupçonne que ces toiles manufacturées en Europe y avaient été portées par la voie de Novogorod, et probablement par des marchands des villes anséatiques.

(2) M. Lévesque (*Hist. de Russie*, t. II, p. 247 ; *Vie de Timour*, p. 64-67, avant la traduction française des Institutions) a corrigé les erreurs de Sherefeddin, et marqué les

Tanaïs, l'humble députation des consuls et des marchands d'Égypte (1), de Venise, de Gênes, de Catalogne et de Biscaye, qui faisaient le commerce de Tana ou Azof, ville située à l'embouchure de la rivière. Ils lui offrirent des présens, admirèrent sa magnificence et se fièrent de leur sûreté à sa parole; mais une armée formidable suivit promptement la visite paisible d'un émir qui avait examiné soigneusement la situation du port et la richesse des magasins. Les Tartares réduisirent la ville en cendres. Ils pillèrent et renvoyèrent les musulmans; mais tous ceux des chrétiens qui ne s'étaient point réfugiés sur leurs vaisseaux, furent condamnés à la mort ou à l'esclavage (2). Un mouvement de vengeance le porta à brûler les villes d'Astrakhan et de Séraï, mo-

---

véritables limites des conquêtes de Timour ou Tamerlan. Ses argumens sont superflus, et les Annales de Russie suffisent pour constater que Moscou, qui avait été prise six ans avant cette époque par Toctamish, échappa aux armes d'un conquérant plus formidable.

(1) Le *Voyage* de Barbaro à Tana en 1436, après qu'on eut rétabli la ville, cite un consul égyptien du grand Caire (*Ramusio*, t. ii, fol. 92).

(2) On trouve la relation du sac d'Azof dans Sherefeddin (l. iii; c. 55), et plus détaillée encore par l'auteur d'une Chronique italienne (André de Redusiis de Quero, in *Chron. Tarvisiano*, in *Muratori*, *Scriptor. rerum italic.*, t. xix, p. 802-805). Il avait conversé avec les Mianis, deux frères Vénitiens, dont un avait été député au camp de Timour, et l'autre avait perdu à Azof ses trois fils et douze mille ducats.

numens d'une civilisation naissante, et il se vanta d'avoir pénétré dans un pays où règne un jour perpétuel, phénomène extraordinaire d'après lequel ses docteurs mahométans se crurent autorisés à le dispenser de l'obligation de la prière du soir (1).

III. Lorsque Timour proposa à ses princes et à ses émirs la conquête de l'Inde ou l'Indoustan (2), ils firent entendre un murmure de mécontentement: « Et les rivières, s'écrièrent-ils, et les montagnes, et les déserts! et les soldats armés de toutes pièces! et les éléphans destructeurs des hommes! » Mais le ressentiment de l'empereur était plus à craindre que tous ces dangers, et sa raison supérieure lui faisait concevoir la facilité d'une expédition qui leur paraissait si terrible. Ses espions l'avaient informé de la faiblesse et de l'anarchie de l'Indoustan, de la révolte des Soubas dans les provinces, et de l'enfance perpétuelle du sultan Mahmoud, universellement méprisé jusque dans son harem de Delhi. L'armée

De l'Indoustan.
A. D.
1398-1399.

―――――

(1) Sherefeddin dit simplement (l. III, c. 13) qu'on pouvait à peine distinguer un intervalle entre les rayons du soleil levant et ceux du soleil couchant. On peut aisément résoudre ce problème dans la latitude de Moscou au cinquante-sixième degré, à l'aide de l'aurore boréale et d'un long crépuscule: mais un soleil de quarante jours (Khondemir, *apud* d'Herbelot, p. 880) nous resserrerait rigoureusement dans le cercle polaire.

(2) Pour la guerre de l'Inde, *voyez* les *Institut.* (p. 129-139), le quatrième livre de Sherefeddin et l'*Histoire de Ferishta* dans Dow (vol. II, p. 1-20), qui jette une lumière générale sur les affaires de l'Indoustan.

des Mongouls marcha en trois divisions, et Timour observe avec plaisir que ses quatre-vingt-douze escadrons, composés chacun de mille chevaux, correspondaient aux quatre-vingt-douze noms ou qualités du prophète Mahomet. Entre le Gihoon et l'Indus, ils traversèrent une des chaînes de montagnes que les géographes arabes appellent *les ceintures de pierre* de la terre. Les brigands qui les habitaient furent vaincus ou exterminés ; mais un grand nombre d'hommes et de chevaux périt dans les neiges, et l'empereur se fit descendre lui-même dans un précipice sur un échafaud portatif dont les cordes avaient cent cinquante coudées de longueur ; et avant d'atteindre au fond il fallut répéter cinq fois cette opération dangereuse. Timour passa l'Indus à Attock, et traversa successivement, en suivant les traces d'Alexandre, le *Punjab* ou les cinq rivières (1) qui se jettent dans le principal courant. D'Attock à Delhi on ne compte que six cents milles par la route ordinaire ; mais les deux conquérans se détournèrent vers le sud-est, et Timour eut pour motif de rejoindre son petit-fils, qui venait d'achever par son ordre la conquête de Moultan. Le héros macédonien s'arrêta sur le bord oriental de l'Hy-

---

(1) L'incomparable carte que le major Rennel a donnée de l'Indoustan, a fixé pour la première fois avec vérité et exactitude la position et le cours du Punjab ou des cinq branches orientales de l'Indus. Il explique avec discernement et clarté, dans son Mémoire critique, la marche d'Alexandre et celle de Timour.

phase, à l'entrée du désert, et versa des larmes ; mais le Mongoul pénétra dans le désert, réduisit la forteresse de Batnir, et parut à la tête de son armée aux portes de Delhi, ville vaste et florissante, et possédée depuis trois siècles par des rois mahométans. Le siége, et principalement celui de la citadelle, aurait pu exiger beaucoup de temps ; mais, déguisant ses forces, il attira dans la plaine le sultan Mahmoud, suivi de son visir, de dix mille cuirassiers, quarante mille de ses gardes, et cent vingt éléphans dont les défenses étaient armées, dit-on, de lames tranchantes et empoisonnées. Timour daigna prendre quelques précautions contre ces monstres, ou plutôt contre la terreur qu'ils inspiraient à ses troupes. Il fit allumer des feux, creuser un fossé et forma un rempart de boucliers et de pointes de fer : mais l'événement apprit aux Mongouls combien leur frayeur était ridicule, et aussitôt que ces animaux maladroits eurent été mis en fuite, l'espèce inférieure, celle des Indiens, disparut sans combattre. Timour entra en triomphe dans la capitale de l'Indoustan ; il admira l'architecture de la grande mosquée, et annonça le dessein d'en construire une semblable. Mais l'ordre ou la permission d'un pillage et d'un massacre général déshonora les réjouissances de la victoire. Timour résolut ensuite de purifier ses soldats dans le sang des idolâtres ou gentoux, qui surpassaient encore, dans la proportion de dix à un, le nombre des musulmans : il s'avança, pour exécuter cette pieuse intention, à cent milles au nord-est de Delhi, passa le Gange, donna plusieurs batailles sur la terre et sur l'eau, et pénétra jusqu'au fameux rocher de Coupèle, qui, sous la forme d'une vache, semble vomir ce fleuve dont la source descend des montagnes du Thibet (1). Il revint en côtoyant celles du nord; et cette course rapide, d'une seule année, ne put justifier l'étrange crainte des émirs, que les climats du midi ne fissent dégénérer leurs enfans en une race d'Indous.

Guerre de Timour contre le sultan Bajazet.
A. D. 1400,
1er sept.

Ce fut sur les bords du Gange que Timour apprit, par ses rapides messagers, les troubles élevés sur les confins de la Géorgie et de l'Anatolie, la révolte des chrétiens et les desseins ambitieux du sultan Bajazet. Son âge de soixante-trois ans, et d'innombrables travaux, n'avaient altéré ni la vigueur de son corps ni celle de son âme; après quelques mois de repos dans le palais de Samarcande, il annonça une nouvelle expédition de sept ans dans les

---

(1) Les deux grandes rivières, le Gange et le Bourampooter, tirent leur source, dans le Thibet, des flancs opposés de la chaîne des mêmes montagnes, à une distance de douze cents milles l'une de l'autre, et après un cours tortueux de deux mille milles, elles se rejoignent près le golfe du Bengale. Tel est cependant le caprice de la renommée, que le Bourampooter est découvert tout récemment, tandis que le Gange est fameux depuis un grand nombre de siècles dans l'histoire ancienne et moderne. Coupèle, où Timour remporta sa dernière victoire, doit être située près de Loldong, à onze cents milles de Calcutta; les Anglais y campèrent en 1774 (*Mémoire de Rennel*, p. 7-59-90, 91-99).

pays occidentaux de l'Asie (1). Les soldats qui avaient fait les campagnes de l'Inde, eurent le choix de rester chez eux ou de suivre leur prince. Mais toutes les troupes des provinces et des royaumes de la Perse reçurent l'ordre de s'assembler à Ispahan, et d'y attendre l'arrivée de l'empereur. Il attaqua d'abord les chrétiens de la Géorgie, défendus seulement par leurs rochers, leurs forteresses et la rigueur de l'hiver; mais la persévérance de Timour surmonta tous les obstacles. Les rebelles se soumirent soit au tribut, soit au Koran. Les deux religions tirèrent également vanité de leurs martyrs; mais c'est aux prisonniers chrétiens que ce titre est le mieux dû, puisqu'ils pouvaient choisir entre la mort et l'abjuration. En descendant des montagnes, l'empereur donna audience aux premiers ambassadeurs de Bajazet, et entama une correspondance de reproches et de menaces qui s'aigrit insensiblement pendant deux ans avant que la querelle n'éclatât. Deux voisins ambitieux et jaloux manquent rarement de prétextes pour se faire la guerre. Les conquêtes des Mongouls et celles des Ottomans se touchaient aux environs d'Erzeroum et de l'Euphrate; leurs limites incertaines n'étaient établies ni par des traités ni par une longue possession. Chacun de ces deux souverains pouvait accuser son rival d'avoir

---

(1) *Voyez* les *Institutions* (p. 141) jusqu'à la fin du premier livre, et Sherefeddin (l. v, c. 1-16) jusqu'à l'arrivée de Timour en Syrie.

envahi son territoire, menacé ses vassaux ou protégé des rebelles, au nombre desquels ils comprenaient tous les princes fugitifs dont ils possédaient les royaumes, et dont ils poursuivaient encore avec acharnement la vie ou la liberté. L'opposition de leurs intérêts était cependant moins dangereuse que la ressemblance de leurs caractères. Dans la carrière de la victoire, Timour ne voulait point souffrir d'égal, et Bajazet ne connaissait point de supérieur. La première lettre de l'empereur mongoul (1) était propre à irriter plutôt qu'à adoucir le sultan des Turcs; dont il affectait de mépriser la famille et la nation (2). « Ne sais-tu pas que la plus grande partie de l'Asie conquise par nos armes obéit à nos lois ; que nos forces invincibles s'étendent d'une mer à l'autre ; que les potentats de la terre sont rangés en haie devant notre porte, et que nous avons forcé la fortune elle-même à veiller sur la prospérité de notre

---

(1) Nous avons trois différentes copies de ces lettres menaçantes, dans les *Institutions* (p. 147), dans Sherefeddin (l. v, c. 14), et dans Arabshah (t. ii, c. 19, p. 183-201), qui s'accordent plus pour la substance que pour le style. Il y a apparence qu'elles ont été traduites, avec plus ou moins de liberté, du turc en langue arabe et en langue persane.

(2) L'émir mongoul se donne à lui-même et à ses compatriotes le nom de Turcs, et rabaisse Bajazet et sa nation au nom moins honorable de *Turcomans*. Cependant je ne conçois pas comment les Ottomans pouvaient tirer leur origine d'un matelot turcoman. Ces pâtres habitaient bien loin de la mer et de toute affaire maritime.

empire? Sur quoi fondes-tu ton insolence et ta folie? Tu as gagné quelques batailles dans les forêts de l'Anatolie ; méprisables trophées ! Tu as remporté quelques victoires sur les chrétiens d'Europe ; mais ton épée était bénie par l'apôtre de Dieu, et l'obéissance que tu as montrée aux préceptes du Koran, en combattant contre les infidèles, est la seule considération qui nous empêche de détruire ton pays, la frontière et le boulevard du monde musulman. Sois sage tandis qu'il en est temps ; réfléchis, repens-toi, et détourne le tonnerre de notre vengeance, encore suspendu sur ta tête. Toi qui n'es qu'une fourmi, pourquoi veux-tu chercher à irriter les éléphans? hélas! ils t'écraseront sous leurs pieds. » La réponse de Bajazet respirait l'indignation d'une âme profondément blessée d'un mépris auquel elle n'était pas accoutumée. Après avoir traité Timour de brigand et de rebelle du désert, il récapitule ses victoires tant vantées dans l'Iran, le Touran et les Indes, et s'efforce de prouver que Timour n'a jamais triomphé que par la perfidie et les vices de ses adversaires. « Tes armées sont innombrables, je veux le croire ; mais oses-tu comparer les flèches de tes Tartares, toujours fuyans, aux sabres de mes intrépides et invincibles janissaires ? Je défendrai toujours les princes qui ont imploré ma protection ; viens les chercher sous mes tentes. Les villes d'Erzeroum et d'Arzingan m'appartiennent ; et si elles ne me paient pas exactement leur tribut, j'en irai demander les arrérages sous les murs de Tauris et de

Sultanie. » L'excès de la colère arracha au sultan une injure plus personnelle. « Si je fuis devant toi, puissent mes femmes être éloignées de mon lit par trois divorces! mais, si tu n'as pas le courage de m'attendre dans la plaine, puisses-tu recevoir les tiennes après qu'elles auront satisfait trois fois les désirs d'un étranger (1)! ». Chez les Turcs, une injure de fait ou de parole devient une offense impardonnable lorsqu'elle est relative aux mystères du harem (2); et le ressentiment personnel envenima la querelle politique des deux monarques. La première expédition de Timour se borna cependant à détruire la forteresse de Siwas ou Sebaste, située sur les frontières de l'Anatolie; et quatre mille Arméniens, enterrés vifs pour avoir rempli leur devoir avec valeur et fidélité, expièrent l'imprudence du prince ottoman. Timour semblait respecter, comme musulman, la pieuse occupation de Bajazet, atta-

---

(1) Selon le *Koran* (c. 2, p. 27, et les *Discours* de Sale, p. 134), un musulman qui avait répudié trois fois sa femme (qui avait répété trois fois les termes d'un divorce) ne pouvait la reprendre qu'un autre ne l'eût épousée et répudiée. Cette cérémonie est suffisamment humiliante, sans ajouter que le premier mari devait nécessairement souffrir que le second jouît de sa femme en sa présence. (*État de l'Empire ottoman,* par Rycault, l. ii, c. 21).

(2) Arabshah attribue particulièrement aux Turcs la délicatesse commune aux Orientaux de ne jamais parler publiquement de leurs femmes, et il est assez remarquable que Chalcocondyles ait eu quelque connaissance du préjugé et de l'insulte.

ché alors au blocus de Constantinople. Il se contenta de lui donner cette première leçon, et tourna ses armes contre l'Égypte et la Syrie. Dans le récit de ces transactions, les Orientaux, et Timour lui-même, donnent au sultan le titre de *kaissar de Roum*, ou de César des Romains, qu'on pouvait donner légitimement, par une courte anticipation, au monarque qui possédait les provinces des successeurs de Constantin, et menaçait leur capitale (1).

Timour envahit la Syrie.
A. D. 1400.

La république militaire des Mamelucks régnait encore en Égypte et en Syrie; mais la dynastie des Turcs avait été chassée par celle des Circassiens (2); et Barkok, leur favori, avait passé une première fois de l'esclavage, et une seconde fois de la prison sur le trône. Au milieu de la révolte et de la discorde, il brava les menaces du souverain mongoul, entretint une correspondance avec ses ennemis et fit arrêter ses ambassadeurs. Celui-ci attendit avec patience la mort de Barkok pour se venger sur le faible Pharage, son fils et son successeur. Les émirs de Syrie (3)

---

(1) Pour le style des Mongouls, *voyez* les *Institutions* (p. 131, 147), et pour les Persans, consultez la *Bibliothèque orientale* (p. 882). Je ne découvre cependant pas que les Ottomans aient pris le titre de Césars, ou que les Arabes le leur aient donné.

(2) *Voyez* les règnes de Barkok et de Pharage dans M. de Guignes (t. iv, l. xxii), qui a tiré des textes d'Aboul-Mahasen, d'Ebn-Schounah et d'Aintabi, quelques faits que nous avons ajoutés à nos matériaux.

(3) Relativement à ces transactions récentes et inté-

furent assemblés dans Alep, pour repousser l'invasion. Ils fondaient leur confiance dans la discipline et la renommée des Mamelucks, dans la trempe de leurs lances et de leurs épées, du plus pur acier de Damas, dans la force de leurs villes entourées de murs, et dans la population de soixante mille villages. Au lieu de soutenir un siége, ils ouvrirent leurs portes et se déployèrent dans la plaine. Mais leurs forces n'étaient point cimentées par l'union et la vertu, et quelques-uns des plus puissans émirs, séduits par Timour, avaient abandonné ou trahissaient leurs compagnons plus fidèles. Timour avait couvert le front de son armée d'une ligne d'éléphans, dont les tours étaient remplies d'archers et de feux grégeois; les rapides évolutions de sa cavalerie complétèrent la terreur et la déroute. Les Syriens se précipitèrent les uns sur les autres, et furent ou étouffés ou massacrés par milliers à l'entrée de la grande rue d'Alep. Les Mongouls entrèrent dans la ville pêle-mêle avec les fugitifs; et les défenseurs lâches ou corrompus rendirent l'imprenable citadelle après une faible résistance. Parmi les supplians et les captifs, Timour distingua les docteurs de la loi, qu'il admit

Sac d'Alep.
A. D. 1400;
11 nov.

---

rieures, on peut se fier au témoignage d'Arabshah; quoiqu'il montre en d'autres occasions beaucoup de partialité (t. I, c. 64-68; t. II, c. 1-14). Timour devait paraître odieux à un Syrien; mais la notoriété des faits l'aurait obligé de respecter son ennemi et la vérité. Ses reproches servent à corriger la dégoûtante flatterie de Sherefeddin (l. v; c. 17-29).

au dangereux honneur d'une conférence (1). Quoique zélé musulman, le prince des Mongouls avait appris dans les écoles de la Perse à révérer la mémoire d'Ali et d'Hosein, et à considérer les Syriens comme les ennemis jurés du petit-fils de Mahomet. Il fit à ces docteurs une question captieuse que les casuistes de Bochara, de Samarcande et de Hérat, n'étaient point capables de résoudre. « Qui sont, leur demanda-t-il, les véritables martyrs, des soldats qui sont tués de mon côté ou de ceux qui meurent du côté de mes ennemis ? » Mais un des cadis sut adroitement le satisfaire ou lui fermer la bouche, en lui répondant, selon les expressions de Mahomet lui-même, que c'est l'intention qui constitue le martyr, et que les musulmans des deux partis, s'ils ont combattu pour la gloire de Dieu, peuvent également mériter ce titre. La succession légitime du calife paraissait plus difficile à décider; et le vainqueur, irrité de la franchise d'un docteur trop sincère pour sa situation, s'écria : « Tu es aussi faux que ceux de Damas; Mohawiyah n'était qu'un usurpateur, et Yezid un tyran; Ali seul est le véritable successeur de Mahomet. » Une interprétation prudente calma sa colère; et il passa à des sujets de conversation plus

---

(1) Ces intéressantes conversations semblent avoir été copiées par Arabshah (t. 1, c. 68; p. 625-645) du cadi ou historien Ebn-Schounah, un des principaux acteurs; mais comment pouvait-il exister encore soixante-quinze ans après cette époque (d'Herbelot, p. 792)?

familiers : « Quel âge avez-vous ? dit-il au cadi. — Cinquante ans. — Mon fils aîné serait de votre âge. Vous me voyez, continua Timour, je ne suis qu'un misérable mortel, boiteux et décrépit ; cependant il a plu au Tout-Puissant de me choisir pour subjuguer les royaumes d'Iran, de Touran et des Indes. Je ne suis point un homme féroce ; Dieu m'est témoin que dans mes différentes guerres je n'ai jamais été l'agresseur, et que mes ennemis sont eux-mêmes les auteurs de leurs calamités. » Pendant cette paisible conversation, le sang ruisselait dans les rues d'Alep, et l'on entendait de toutes parts les cris des mères et des enfans et ceux des vierges que l'on violait. Le riche pillage abandonné aux soldats put animer leur avidité ; mais leur cruauté fut justifiée par l'ordre absolu qui leur fut donné de présenter un certain nombre de têtes que, selon son ordinaire, il fit arranger avec soin en colonnes et en pyramides. Les Mongouls passèrent la nuit à célébrer leur victoire par des réjouissances, et ce qui restait de musulmans la passa dans les chaînes et dans les larmes. Je ne suivrai point la marche du dévastateur d'Alep à Damas, où les armées d'Égypte l'attaquèrent avec vigueur et le défirent presque entièrement. On attribua un mouvement qu'il fit en arrière à sa détresse et à son désespoir : un de ses neveux passa à l'ennemi ; mais lorsque les Syriens se réjouissaient de sa défaite, la révolte des Mamelucks obligea le sultan de se réfugier précipitamment et honteusement dans son palais du Caire. Quoique abandonnés de leur prince, les habitans de Damas défendirent leurs murs; et Timour offrit de lever le siége, s'ils voulaient se racheter par des présens, dont chaque article serait composé de neuf pièces. Mais dès qu'on l'eut introduit dans la ville sous la foi d'une trève, violant le traité avec perfidie, il exigea une contribution de dix millions en or, et excita ses troupes à châtier la postérité des Syriens, qui avaient exécuté ou approuvé le meurtre du petit-fils de Mahomet. Timour ne réserva du massacre général qu'une famille qui avait honorablement enterré la tête d'Hosein, et une colonie d'ouvriers ou d'artisans qu'il fit passer à Samarcande. Après une existence de sept cents ans, la ville de Damas fut réduite en cendres par le zèle religieux d'un Tartare qui voulait venger le sang d'un Arabe. Les pertes et les fatigues de cette campagne forcèrent Timour de renoncer à la conquête de l'Égypte et de la Palestine; mais, en retournant vers l'Euphrate, il livra la ville d'Alep aux flammes, et constata la piété de ses motifs en accordant la liberté et des récompenses à deux mille sectaires d'Ali, qui se proposaient de visiter la tombe de son fils. Je me suis étendu sur les anecdotes qui servent à faire connaître le caractère personnel du héros mongoul; mais je raconterai brièvement (1) qu'il éleva une pyramide de quatre-vingt-dix mille têtes sur les ruines de

De Damas.
A. D. 1401,
23 janv.

Et de Bagdad.
A. D. 1401,
23 juillet.

---

(1) Sherefeddin (l. v, c. 29-43) et Arabshah (t. ii, c. 15-18) racontent les marches et les conquêtes de Timour entre la guerre de Syrie et celle des Ottomans.

Bagdad, et qu'après avoir encore ravagé la Géorgie, il campa sur les bords de l'Araxe, et annonça la résolution de marcher contre l'empereur ottoman. Sentant l'importance de cette guerre, il rassembla les forces de toutes ses provinces : huit cent mille hommes inscrivirent leurs noms sur le rôle militaire (1); mais le commandement de cinq ou de dix mille chevaux indique plutôt le rang et le traitement des chefs que le nombre effectif des soldats (2). Les Mongouls avaient acquis des richesses immenses dans le pillage de la Syrie, mais la distribution de leur paye et de sept années d'arrérages les attacha plus sûrement à leurs drapeaux.

Timour entre dans l'Anatolie. A. D. 1402.

Tandis que le prince mongoul s'était occupé de ces expéditions, Bajazet avait eu deux années entiè-

---

(1) Ce nombre de huit cent mille est tiré d'Arabshah, ou plutôt d'Ebn-Schounah (*ex rationario Timuri*), qui le rapporte sur le témoignage d'un officier carizmien (t. 1, c. 68, p. 617); et il est assez remarquable que Phranza, historien grec, n'y ajoute que vingt mille hommes. Le Pogge compte un million; un autre contemporain latin (*Chron. Tarvisianum*, ap. Muratori, t. xix, p. 800) en compte un million cent mille; et un soldat allemand qui était à la bataille d'Angora, atteste le nombre prodigieux d'un million six cent mille (Leunclavius, *ad* Chalcocond., l. iii, p. 82). Timour, dans ses Institutions, n'a daigné calculer ni ses troupes, ni ses sujets, ni ses revenus.

(2) Le grand Mogol laissait, par vanité et pour l'avantage de ses officiers, des vides immenses dans les cadres de son armée. Le patron de Bernier, Penge-Hazari, était commandant de cinq mille chevaux, qui se réduisaient à cinq cents (*Voyages*, t. 1, p. 288, 289).

res pour rassembler ses forces : elles consistaient en quatre cent mille combattans, tant cavalerie qu'infanterie (1) ; mais la valeur et la fidélité de ces différens corps ne méritaient pas le même degré de confiance. Nous devons distinguer d'abord les janissaires, qui ont été successivement portés à quarante mille hommes; une cavalerie nationale, connue dans les temps modernes sous le nom de *spahis*; vingt mille cuirassiers d'Europe, couverts d'armures noires et impénétrables ; les troupes de l'Anatolie, dont les princes s'étaient réfugiés dans le camp de Timour, et une colonie de Tartares, qu'il avait chassée du Kipsak, et à laquelle Bajazet avait accordé un établissement dans les plaines d'Andrinople. L'intrépide sultan s'avançait au devant de son rival, et, déployant ses tentes près des ruines de la malheureuse ville de Siwas, il semblait avoir choisi ce poste pour le théâtre de sa vengeance. Timour traversait cependant, depuis l'Araxe, toute l'Arménie et l'Anatolie, sans négliger aucune des précautions dictées par la prudence. La rapidité de sa marche était dirigée avec ordre et avec une exacte discipline : sa cavalerie légère, qui allait en avant et marquait sa route, fouillait avec soin les montagnes, les bois et les ri-

---

(1) Timour lui-même fixe le nombre des Ottomans à quatre cent mille (*Institut.*, p. 153). Phranza les réduit à cent cinquante mille (l. 1, c. 29), et le soldat allemand les porte à un million quatre cent mille. Il paraît évident que l'armée des Mongouls était la plus nombreuse.

vières. Résolu de combattre les Ottomans dans le cœur de leur empire, le prince des Mongouls évita leur camp en se détournant adroitement sur la gauche. Il occupa Césarée, traversa le désert Salé, la rivière Halys, et investit la ville d'Angora. Cependant le sultan, immobile dans son camp et ignorant ce qui se passait, comparait la marche des rapides Tartares à celle d'un limaçon (1). L'indignation lui donna bientôt des ailes pour voler au secours d'Angora; et comme les deux généraux étaient impatiens de combattre, les plaines qui l'avoisinent furent la scène d'une bataille mémorable, qui immortalisa la gloire de Timour et la honte de Bajazet.

Bataille d'Angora.
A. D. 1402, 28 juillet.

L'empereur des Mongouls dut cette victoire à lui-même, au coup d'œil du moment, et à la discipline de trente années. Il avait perfectionné sa tactique sans contrarier l'antique habitude de sa nation (2), dont les forces consistaient encore dans l'adresse de ses archers et les évolutions rapides d'une nombreuse cavalerie. Soit qu'il conduisît au combat une petite troupe ou une grande armée, le mode d'attaque était

(1) Il n'est pas inutile de marquer les distances entre Angora et les villes voisines, par les journées des caravanes, chacune de vingt-cinq milles : d'Angora à Smyrne vingt, à Kiotahia dix, à Bursa dix, à Césarée huit, à Sinope dix, à Nicomédie neuf, à Constantinople douze ou treize. *Voy.* les *Voyages de Tournefort au Levant*, t. II, lettre XXI.

(2) *Voyez* les systèmes de tactique dans les *Institutions*; les éditeurs anglais (p. 373-407) y ont ajouté des plans très-soignés qui en facilitent l'intelligence.

le même. La première ligne chargeait d'abord et était soutenue avec ordre par les escadrons de l'avant-garde. Le général suivait des yeux la mêlée, et, d'après ses ordres, les deux ailes s'avançaient successivement en plusieurs divisions, et se portaient en ligne droite ou oblique où l'empereur jugeait leur secours nécessaire. L'ennemi était pressé par dix-huit ou vingt attaques, dont chacune offrait une chance de victoire; et lorsqu'elles manquaient toutes de succès, l'empereur, jugeant l'occasion digne de lui, faisait avancer son étendard et le corps de bataille, qu'il conduisait en personne (1). Mais à la bataille d'Angora, le corps de bataille fut lui-même soutenu sur les flancs et sur les derrières par les plus braves escadrons de réserve, que commandaient les fils et les petits-fils de Timour. Le destructeur de l'Indoustan déployait orgueilleusement une ligne d'éléphans, trophée plutôt qu'instrument de ses victoires. L'usage des feux grégeois était commun aux Mongouls et aux Ottomans. Mais si l'une des deux nations eût emprunté de l'Europe l'invention récente de la poudre et des canons, ce tonnerre artificiel aurait probablement assuré la victoire à celle qui s'en serait servi (2). Bajazet se distingua dans cette jour-

(1) Le sultan lui-même, dit Timour, doit placer courageusement son pied dans l'étrier de la patience : cette métaphore tartare, omise dans la traduction anglaise, a été conservée par le traducteur français des *Institutions* (p. 156, 157).

(2) Sherefeddin affirme que Timour se servit du feu gré-

née comme général et comme soldat; mais il fallut céder à l'ascendant de son rival. Par différens motifs, la plus grande partie de ses troupes l'abandonnèrent dans le moment décisif. Sa rigueur et son avarice avaient excité une sédition parmi les Turcs, et son fils Soliman se retira lui-même trop précipitamment du champ de bataille. Les forces de l'Anatolie, fidèles dans leur révolte, retournèrent sous les étendards de leurs princes légitimes. Ses alliés tartares s'étaient laissé séduire par les lettres et les émissaires de Timour (1), qui leur reprochait la honte de servir sous les esclaves de leurs ancêtres, et leur offrait l'espérance ou de délivrer leur ancienne patrie, ou même de régner dans la nouvelle. A l'aile droite de Bajazet, les cuirassiers d'Europe chargèrent loyalement et avec une valeur irrésistible : mais la fuite simulée et précipitée des Tartares mit en désordre ces hommes chargés de fer; et leur imprudente poursuite exposa les janissaires, seuls, sans cavalerie et sans armes de trait, à un cercle de chasseurs mongouls. Leur courage fut enfin accablé par la soif, la chaleur et la multitude de leurs ennemis; et l'infortuné Bajazet, qu'un accès de goutte rendait impotent des mains et des jambes, fût transporté hors du champ de bataille

---

geois (l. v, c. 47); mais le silence universel des contemporains réfute l'étrange soupçon de Voltaire, qui suppose que des canons, où sont gravés des caractères inconnus, ont été envoyés à Delhi par ce monarque.

(1) Timour a dissimulé cette importante négociation avec les Tartares; mais elle est évidemment constatée par le té-

par un de ses plus rapides coursiers : le khan titulaire du Zagatai courut à sa poursuite et l'atteignit. Après la défaite des Turcs et la prise du sultan, toute l'A- natolie se soumit au vainqueur, qui planta ses étendards à Kiotahia, et répandit de tous côtés ses ministres de rapine et de destruction. Mirza Méhemmed sultan, l'aîné et le plus chéri de ses petits-fils, courut à Bursa, suivi de trente mille chevaux : transporté par l'ardeur de la jeunesse, il arriva avec quatre mille seulement ; en cinq jours de marche, aux portes de la capitale, et à deux cent trente milles du lieu d'où il était parti. Mais le vol de la terreur est encore plus rapide ; et Soliman, fils de Bajazet, était déjà passé en Europe avec le trésor de son père. Ils trouvèrent cependant des dépouilles immenses dans la ville et dans le palais : les habitans avaient disparu ; mais les maisons, presque toutes construites en bois, furent réduites en cendres. De Bursa, Mehemmed s'avança vers Nicée, ville encore riche et florissante, et les escadrons mongouls ne s'arrêtèrent qu'au bord de la Propontide. Les émirs et Mirza eurent tous le même succès dans leurs excursions. Smyrne, défendue par le zèle et la valeur des chevaliers de Rhodes, mérita seule la présence de l'empereur. Après une résistance opiniâtre, les Mongouls l'emportèrent d'assaut, passèrent tout au fil de l'é-

Défaite et captivité de Bajazet.

moignage des Annales arabes (t. 1, c. 47, p. 391), des Annales turques (Leunclav., p. 321) et des historiens persans (Khondemir, *ap.* d'Herbelot, p. 882).

pée, sans distinction, et leurs machines lancèrent les têtes des héros chrétiens sur deux caraques européennes qui étaient à l'ancre dans le port. Les musulmans d'Asie se réjouirent d'être délivrés d'un dangereux ennemi domestique; et l'on observa, en faisant la comparaison des deux rivaux, que Timour avait réduit en quatorze jours une forteresse qui avait soutenu durant sept années le siége ou du moins le blocus de Bajazet (1).

<small>Histoire de la cage de fer.</small>

Les écrivains modernes rejettent, comme une fable adoptée par la crédulité (2), l'histoire, si long-temps répétée comme une leçon morale, de la cage de fer dans laquelle Tamerlan fit enfermer Bajazet.

<small>Contraire au récit de l'historien persan de Timour.</small>

Ils en appellent avec confiance à l'histoire persane de Sherefeddin-Ali, dont nous avons aujourd'hui une traduction française, et dont je vais extraire et abréger la relation plus vraisemblable de ce mémorable événement. Timour, informé que le sultan captif

---

(1) Dans la guerre de Roum ou de l'Anatolie, j'ai ajouté quelques faits tirés des Institutions au récit de Sherefeddin (l. v, c. 44-65) et d'Arabshah (t. 11, c. 20-35). Pour cette partie seulement de l'histoire de Timour, on peut citer les historiens turcs (Cantemir, p. 53-55; *Annales* de Leunclav., p. 320-322), et les Grecs (Phranza, l. 1, c. 29; Ducas, c. 15-17; Chalcocondyles, l. III).

(2) Le scepticisme de Voltaire, dans son *Essai sur l'Histoire générale* (c. 88), est disposé ici, comme dans toutes les autres occasions, à rejeter ce conte populaire, et à diminuer de l'excès du vice et de la grandeur de la vertu : son incrédulité est souvent raisonnable.

était à l'entrée de sa tente, sortit pour le recevoir, le fit asseoir à ses côtés, et joignant à de justes reproches un ton de considération pour son rang et de pitié pour ses malheurs : « Hélas ! lui dit l'empereur, c'est par votre faute que le décret du destin s'est accompli ; c'est le filet que vous avez tissu ; ce sont les épines de l'arbre que vous avez planté. Je désirais épargner et même secourir le champion des musulmans ; vous avez bravé nos menaces et dédaigné notre amitié ; vous nous avez forcé d'entrer dans vos États à la tête de nos armées invincibles. Considérez l'événement. Je n'ignore point le sort que vous réserviez à moi et à mes soldats, si vous eussiez été vainqueur. Mais je méprise la vengeance ; votre vie et votre honneur sont en sûreté ; je témoignerai ma reconnaissance envers Dieu par ma clémence envers l'homme. » Le sultan captif montra quelques signes de repentir, se soumit au don humiliant d'une robe d'honneur, et embrassa, les larmes aux yeux, son fils Mousa que Timour fit chercher à sa prière, et qu'on trouva sur le champ de bataille parmi les prisonniers. On logea les princes ottomans dans un pavillon magnifique, où ils furent gardés avec presque autant de respect que de vigilance. A l'arrivée du harem de Bursa, Timour rendit au monarque captif sa femme, la reine Despina, et sa fille : mais il exigea pieusement que cette princesse de Servie, qui avait professé librement jusqu'alors la foi chrétienne, acceptât sans délai la religion de Mahomet. Au milieu des réjouissances de la victoire, auxquelles Bajazet fut invité, l'empereur mongoul décora son prisonnier d'un sceptre et d'une couronne, en y ajoutant la promesse de le rétablir sur le trône de ses ancêtres, environné de plus de gloire qu'il n'en avait jamais eu; mais la mort prématurée de Bajazet prévint l'exécution de ce projet. Malgré les soins des plus habiles médecins, il mourut d'une apoplexie à Akshehr, l'Antioche de Pisidie, environ neuf mois après sa défaite. Le vainqueur versa quelques larmes sur sa tombe. Son corps fut transporté avec pompe dans le mausolée qu'il avait fait élever à Bursa; et son fils Mousa, après avoir reçu de riches présens de bijoux, d'or, d'armes et de chevaux, fut investi, par une patente écrite en rouge, de la souveraineté de l'Anatolie.

Tel est le portrait d'un vainqueur généreux, extrait de ses propres mémoires, et dédié à son fils et à son petit-fils dix-neuf ans après sa mort (1). A cette époque où des milliers de témoins connaissaient parfaitement la vérité, un mensonge manifeste aurait été une satire de sa conduite réelle. Ces preuves, adoptées par tous les historiens persans, sont d'un grand poids (2); mais la flatterie, particulièrement

---

(1) *Voyez* l'*Histoire de Sherefeddin* (l. v. c. 49-52; 53-59, 60). Cet ouvrage fut achevé à Shiraz, dans l'année 1424, et dédié à Ibrahim, fils de Sharokh, fils de Timour, qui régnait sur le Farsistan du vivant de son père.

(2) Après avoir lu Khondemir, Ehn-Schounah, etc., le savant d'Herbelot (*Bibl. orient.*, p. 882) peut affirmer qu'on ne trouve cette fable dans aucune histoire authentique;

en Orient, est bien vile et bien audacieuse, et le traitement cruel et ignominieux que reçut Bajazet est attesté par une suite de témoins dont nous citerons quelques-uns par ordre de temps et de pays. 1° Le lecteur n'a pas sans doute oublié la garnison de Français que le maréchal de Boucicault laissa à son départ pour la défense de Constantinople. Ils étaient à portée d'apprendre des premiers, et de la manière la plus exacte, le sort de leur redoutable adversaire, et il est plus que probable que quelques-uns d'eux accompagnèrent les ambassadeurs grecs au camp de Tamerlan. C'est d'après leur récit que l'homme de la suite du maréchal, qui a écrit son histoire, atteste les rigueurs de la prison et de la mort de Bajazet, environ sept ans après l'événement (1). 2° Le nom du Pogge (2) est justement célèbre parmi les restaurateurs de l'érudition dans le quinzième siècle. Il composa son élégant dialogue

Attestée. 1° par les Français.

2° Par les Italiens.

---

mais en niant qu'Arabshah l'ait adoptée d'une manière visible, il fait naître des soupçons sur son exactitude.

(1) « Et fut lui-même (Bajazet) pris et mené en prison, en laquelle mourut de *dure mort*. » (*Mém.* de Boucicault, part. 1, c. 37.) Ces Mémoires furent composés tandis que le maréchal était encore gouverneur de Gênes, d'où il fut chassé en 1409 par une sédition ou émeute du peuple. Muratori, *Ann. d'Ital.*, t. XII, p. 473, 474.

(2) Le lecteur trouvera un récit satisfaisant de la Vie et des OEuvres du Pogge, dans le *Poggiana*, ouvrage intéressant de M. Lenfant, et dans la *Bibliotheca latina mediæ et infimæ ætatis* de Fabricius (t. v, p. 305-308). Le Pogge naquit en 1380, et mourut en 1459.

sur les vicissitudes de la fortune (1) dans la cinquantième année de son âge, et vingt-huit ans après la victoire de Tamerlan (2), qu'il célèbre comme l'égal des illustres Barbares de l'antiquité. Plusieurs témoins oculaires avaient instruit le Pogge de sa discipline et de ses exploits; et il ne néglige point de citer à l'appui de son sujet l'exemple du monarque ottoman que le Tartare enferma dans une cage de fer comme un animal féroce, et donna en spectacle à toute l'Asie. Je pourrais ajouter l'autorité de deux chroniques italiennes peut-être d'une date plus moderne, qui servent au moins à prouver que cette histoire, vraie ou fausse, se répandit dans toute l'Europe avec la première nouvelle de la révolution (3).

3° Par les Arabes.

3°. Dans le temps où le Pogge florissait à Rome, Ahmed-Ebn-Arabshah composait à Damas son élé-

---

(1) Le dialogue *de Varietate fortunæ*, dont on a publié à Paris, en 1723, une édition complète et élégante, *in-4°*, fut composé peu de temps avant la mort du pape Martin v (p. 5), et conséquemment vers l'année 1430.

(2) *Voyez* un éloge brillant et éloquent de Timour, p. 36-39. *Ipse enim novi*, dit le Pogge, *qui fuere in ejus castris.... Regem vivum cepit, caveâque in modum feræ inclusum per omnem Asiam circumtulit egregium admirandumque spectaculum fortunæ.*

(3) *Chronicon Tarvisianum* (*in* Muratori, *Script. rerum ital.*, t. XIX, p. 800) et les *Annales Estenses* (t. XVIII, p. 974). Les deux auteurs, André de Redusiis de Quero et Jacques de Delaito, étaient contemporains et tous deux chanceliers, l'un de Trévise et l'autre de Ferrare. Le témoignage du premier est le plus positif.

gante et malveillante histoire de Timour, dont il avait rassemblé les matériaux dans ses voyages en Turquie et en Tartarie (1). L'écrivain latin et l'arabe, entre lesquels toute correspondance paraît impossible, conviennent l'un et l'autre de la cage de fer, et cet accord annonce évidemment leur véracité. Arabshah raconte encore que Bajazet essuya un autre outrage d'une nature plus sensible. Les expressions indiscrètes d'une de ses lettres sur les femmes et sur les divorces avaient profondément blessé le Tartare jaloux : dans un festin donné en réjouissance de la victoire, ce furent des femmes qui servirent à boire aux convives, et le sultan eut la douleur de voir ses concubines et ses femmes légitimes confondues parmi les esclaves et exposées sans voile à la licence des regards. Pour éviter à l'avenir une humiliation semblable, on prétend que ses successeurs, excepté un seul, se sont abstenus du mariage; et Busbequius (2), ambassadeur de Vienne à la Porte, et observateur attentif, atteste que dans le seizième siècle cette pratique et cette opinion subsistaient encore chez les Ottomans. 4° La différence de langage rend le témoignage d'un Grec aussi indépendant que celui

4° Par les Grecs.

---

(1) *Voy.* Arabshah, t. II, c. 28, 34. Il voyagea *in regiones Rumæas*, A. H. 839 (A. D. 1435, juillet 27), t. II, c. 2, p. 13.

(2) Busbequius, *in legatione turcicâ*, epist. 1, p. 52. Cette autorité respectable est un peu affaiblie par les mariages subséquens d'Amurath II avec une Servienne, et de Mahomet II avec une princesse d'Asie (Cant., p. 83-93).

d'un Arabe ou d'un Latin. En rejetant celui de Chalcocondyles et de Ducas, qui vivaient à une époque moins éloignée, et qui parlent de ce fait d'un ton moins affirmatif, on ne saurait raisonnablement refuser toute confiance à Georges Phranza (1), *protovestiaire* des derniers empereurs, et qui était né un an avant la bataille d'Angora. Vingt-deux ans après l'événement, on l'envoya comme ambassadeur à la cour d'Amurath II; et cet historien put converser avec des janissaires qui avaient partagé la captivité de Bajazet et vu le sultan dans sa cage de fer. 5° La dernière et la meilleure autorité est celle des annales turques, consultées et copiées par Leunclavius, Pococke et Cantemir (2). Ils déplorent unanimement la captivité de la cage de fer; et l'on doit accorder sur ce point quelque confiance à des historiens nationaux, qui ne peuvent inculper le Tartare qu'en découvrant la honte de leur prince et de leur pays.

5° Par les Turcs.

Conclusion probable.

De ces prémisses opposées, on peut tirer une conclusion probable et qui tient un milieu entre les deux opinions. Je veux bien supposer que Sherefeddin-Ali a raconté fidèlement la première entrevue d'apparat dans laquelle le vainqueur, monté par le succès à un ton plus noble, affecta les sentimens de

---

(1) *Voyez* le témoignage de Georges Phranza (l. 1, c. 29) et sa vie dans Hanckius (*de Scriptor. byzant.*, p. 1, c. 40). Chalcocondyles et Ducas parlent vaguement des *chaînes* de Bajazet.

(2) *Annales* Leunclav., p. 321; Pococke, *Prolegom. ad Abulphar.*, *Dynast.*; Cantemir, p. 55.

la générosité. Mais l'arrogance déplacée de Bajazet l'aliéna insensiblement; les princes de l'Anatolie détestaient le sultan, et leurs plaintes étaient justes. On apprit que Timour avait formé le dessein de le conduire en triomphe à Samarcande, et un trou creusé sous sa tente dans le dessein de faciliter sa fuite, obligea l'empereur mongoul à prendre de nouvelles précautions. La cage de fer portée sur un chariot dans des marches continuelles, était peut-être moins destinée à insulter Bajazet qu'à s'en assurer. Timour avait lu dans quelque histoire fabuleuse un traitement semblable infligé à un roi de Perse son prédécesseur. Il condamna Bajazet à représenter la personne de l'empereur romain et à expier son insulte (1). Mais le courage et les forces du sultan ne résistèrent point à cette épreuve, et l'on peut sans injustice attribuer sa mort prématurée à la sévérité de Timour. Celui-ci ne faisait point la guerre aux morts; quelques larmes et un sépulcre, c'était tout ce qu'il pouvait accorder à un captif délivré de son pouvoir; et si Mousa, le fils de Bajazet, obtint la permission de régner sur les ruines de Bursa, la

Mort de Bajazet.
A. D. 1436, 9 mars.

---

(1) Un Sapor, roi de Perse, ayant été fait prisonnier, Maximien ou Galère, César, l'enferma dans une vache artificielle couverte de la peau d'un de ces animaux. Telle est au moins la fable racontée par Eutychès (*Annal.*, t. 1, p. 421, *vers.* Pococke). Le récit de la véritable histoire (*voyez* le deuxième vol. de cette histoire, p. 163), nous apprendra à apprécier l'érudition orientale de tous les siècles qui précédèrent l'hégire.

plus grande partie de l'Anatolie n'en fut pas moins restituée à ses souverains légitimes.

<small>Terme des conquêtes de Timour.</small>

Timour possédait en Asie tout le pays qui s'étend depuis l'Irtish et le Volga jusqu'au golfe Persique, et depuis le Gange jusqu'à Damas et à l'Archipel. Son armée était invincible, et son ambition sans bornes. Son zèle aspirait à subjuguer et convertir les royaumes chrétiens de l'Occident que son nom faisait déjà trembler. Il touchait aux bornes de la terre ; mais une mer étroite, obstacle insurmontable, séparait l'Asie de l'Europe (1), et le maître de tant de *tomans* ou myriades de soldats à cheval ne possédait pas une seule galère. Les deux passages du Bosphore et de l'Héllespont, de Constantinople et de Gallipoli, étaient, l'un entre les mains des chrétiens, et l'autre dans celles des Turcs. Dans ce danger pressant, ils oublièrent la différence de religion pour agir de concert et avec fermeté en faveur de la cause commune. Les deux détroits furent garnis de vaisseaux et de fortifications ; les deux nations refusèrent à Timour les bâtimens de transport qu'il leur demanda successivement sous le prétexte d'attaquer leur ennemi. Elles flattèrent en même temps son orgueil par des

---

(1) Arabshah (t. 11, c. 25) décrit en voyageur curieux et instruit les détroits de Gallipoli et de Constantinople. Pour acquérir une juste idée de ces événemens, j'ai comparé les récits et les préjugés des Mongouls, des Turcs, des Grecs et des Arabes. L'ambassadeur d'Espagne parle de l'union des chrétiens avec les Ottomans pour la défense commune (*Vie de Timour*, p. 96).

tributs, par des ambassades suppliantes, et tâchèrent prudemment de l'engager à la retraite, en lui accordant d'avance tous les honneurs de la victoire. Soliman, fils de Bajazet, implora sa clémence pour son père et pour lui-même, reçut dans une patente écrite en rouge l'investiture du royaume de la Romanie, qu'il possédait déjà par droit de conquête, et témoigna son ardent désir de pouvoir se jeter en personne aux pieds du monarque de l'univers. L'empereur grec, soit Jean ou Manuel (1), se soumit à lui payer le tribut exigé précédemment par le sultan des Turcs, et ratifia ce traité par un serment d'obéissance dont il put se croire absous dès que le Tartare eut évacué l'Anatolie. Mais l'inquiétude et la terreur qui avaient saisi les nations attribuèrent à l'ambitieux Timour le projet romanesque de conquérir l'Égypte et l'Afrique, depuis le Nil jusqu'à l'océan Atlantique, d'entrer en Europe par le détroit de Gibraltar, et de revenir par les déserts de la Russie et de la Tartarie, après avoir subjugué toutes les puissances de la chrétienté. La soumission du sultan d'Égypte détourna ce danger éloigné ou peut-être imaginaire. Au Caire, les honneurs de la prière et le coin des monnaies attestèrent la suprématie du prince mongoul ; et Samarcande

---

(1) Lorsque le titre de César eut été transporté aux sultans de Roum, les princes grecs de Constantinople (Sherefeddin, l. v, c. 54) furent confondus avec les petits souverains chrétiens de Gallipoli et de Thessalonique, sous le titre de Tekkur, dérivé par corruption de του κυριου (Cantemir, p. 51).

scella la soumission de l'Afrique du tribut de neuf autruches et d'une girafe ou caméléopard, présent rare et précieux. L'imagination n'est pas moins étonnée de l'idée d'un conquérant mongoul qui médite et exécute presque de son camp devant Smyrne l'invasion de l'empire chinois (1). Le zèle religieux et l'honneur national l'invitaient à cette entreprise. Le sang des Ottomans qu'il avait versé ne pouvait s'expier que par une destruction proportionnée des infidèles : arrivé aux portes du paradis, il voulait s'y assurer une entrée glorieuse en détruisant les idoles de la Chine, en y fondant des mosquées dans toutes les villes, et en y établissant la croyance en un seul Dieu et en son prophète. L'expulsion récente des descendans de Gengis blessait l'orgueil du nom mongoul; et les troubles de l'empire offraient la plus favorable occasion de vengeance. L'illustre Hongvou, fondateur de la dynastie des *Ming*, était mort quatre ans avant la bataille d'Angora, et son petit-fils, faible et malheureux jeune homme, avait été brûlé dans son palais après une guerre civile qui avait coûté la vie à un million de Chinois (2). Avant d'évacuer l'Anatolie,

---

(1) *Voyez* Sherefeddin (l. v, c. 4), qui décrit dans un Itinéraire exact la route de la Chine, qu'Arabshah (t. II, c. 33) n'indique que d'une manière vague et par des phrases de rhéteur.

(2) *Synopsis Hist. Sinicæ*, p. 74-76, dans la quatrième partie des Relations de Thévenot; Duhalde (*Hist. de la Chine*, t. I, p. 507, 508, édit. *in-fol.*); et pour la chrono-

Timour envoya au-delà du Gihoon une armée ou plutôt une colonie de ses anciens et de ses nouveaux sujets, pour se faciliter l'accès du pays des Calmoucks et des Mongouls, idolâtres qu'il voulait subjuguer, et pour bâtir des villes et des magasins dans le désert; il reçut bientôt, par les soins de son lieutenant, une carte et une description exacte des pays inconnus qui s'étendent depuis les sources de l'Irtish jusqu'au mur de la Chine. Durant ces préparatifs, l'empereur acheva la conquête de la Géorgie, passa l'hiver sur les bords de l'Araxe, apaisa les troubles de la Perse, et retourna lentement dans sa capitale après une campagne de quatre ans et neuf mois.

Dans un court intervalle de repos, Timour déploya sur le trône de Samarcande (1) la magnificence et l'autorité d'un monarque riche et puissant. Il écouta les plaintes des peuples; distribua dans de justes proportions les châtimens et les récompenses, fit élever des temples et des palais, et donna audience aux ambassadeurs de l'Égypte, de l'Arabie, de l'Inde, de la Tartarie, de la Russie et de l'Espagne : ce dernier lui présenta une magnifique tenture de tapisserie qui éclipsait les productions des peintres orientaux. L'empereur célébra les noces de six de

Son triomphe à Samarcande. A. D. 1404, juillet. A. D. 1405, 8 janv.

---

logie des empereurs chinois, de Guignes (*Hist. des Huns*, t. 1, p. 71, 72).

(1) Pour le retour, le triomphe et la mort de Timour, voyez Sherefeddin (l. VI, c. 1-30) et Arabshah (t. II, c. 35-47).

ses petits-fils; ce qui fut regardé comme un acte de religion aussi bien que de tendresse paternelle. Ces fêtes, où reparut toute la pompe des anciens califes, eurent lieu dans les jardins de Canighul, qu'on décora d'un grand nombre de tentes et de pavillons où se déployaient le luxe d'une grande ville et les trophées d'une armée victorieuse. On abattit des forêts entières pour l'usage des cuisines; la plaine était couverte de pyramides de viandes, et de vases remplis de différentes liqueurs; des milliers de convives étaient invités avec courtoisie à participer au festin. Les différens ordres de l'État, les représentans des différentes nations de la terre, furent rangés autour du banquet royal; les ambassadeurs de l'Europe n'en furent point exclus, dit l'orgueilleux historien persan. C'est ainsi, ajoute-t-il, que les *casses*, les plus petits des poissons, trouvent leur place dans l'Océan (1). Le peuple témoigna sa joie par des mascarades et des illuminations. Tous les ouvriers de Samarcande passèrent en revue, et chaque corps de métier tâcha de se distinguer par quelque invention

---

(1) Sheréfeddin (l. vi, c. 24) cite les ambassadeurs d'un des plus puissans souverains de l'Europe : nous savons qu'il est question de Henri III, roi de Castille. La relation curieuse de ses deux ambassades existe encore (Mariana, *Hist. Hispan.*, l. xix, c. 11, p. 329, 330; *Avertissement à l'Histoire de Timour-Bec*, p. 28-33). Il paraît aussi qu'il y eut quelque correspondance entre l'empereur mongoul et la cour de Charles vii, roi de France (*Hist. de France* par Velly et Villaret, p. 336).

ingénieuse, quelque spectacle singulier tiré des moyens de sa profession. Lorsque les cadis eurent ratifié les contrats de mariage, les princes se retirèrent avec leurs épouses dans les chambres nuptiales, où, selon l'usage des Asiatiques, ils changèrent neuf fois de vêtemens. A chaque nouvelle parure, les perles et les pierreries dont ils couvraient leur tête étaient dédaigneusement abandonnées aux gens de leur suite. On proclama un édit d'indulgence générale ; les lois suspendirent leur activité ; tous les plaisirs furent permis ; le peuple se trouva libre et le souverain demeura oisif ; et l'historien de Timour peut observer qu'après avoir dévoué cinquante ans de sa vie à reculer les bornes de son empire, le conquérant ne connut le vrai bonheur que durant les deux mois qu'il cessa d'exercer sa puissance. Mais il ne tarda pas à s'occuper du gouvernement et des préparatifs d'une nouvelle guerre. On déploya l'étendard impérial, et l'expédition contre la Chine fut annoncée. Les émirs firent le relevé des rôles d'une armée composée de deux cent mille hommes, tous soldats choisis, et qui avaient fait les guerres d'Iran et de Touran ; cinq cents vastes chariots et un train immense de chevaux et de chameaux transportèrent les bagages et les provisions ; et les troupes, destinées à faire un trajet que les caravanes les plus heureuses n'achevaient pas en moins de six mois, se préparèrent à une longue absence. Timour ne fut retenu ni par son âge ni par la rigueur de l'hiver ; il monta à cheval, traversa le Gihoon sur la

Timour meurt dans sa marche en Chine. A. D. 1405, 1er avril.

glace, marcha jusqu'à soixante-dix parasanges ou trois cents milles de sa capitale, et prit son dernier camp dans les environs d'Otrar, où l'attendait l'ange de la mort. La fatigue et l'usage imprudent de l'eau à la glace augmentèrent la fièvre qui l'avait saisi; et le conquérant de l'Asie expira dans la soixante-dixième année de son âge, trente-cinq ans après son élévation sur le trône du Zagatai. Ses projets disparurent avec lui, ses armées se débandèrent, la Chine fut sauvée, et le plus puissant de ses fils sollicita, quatorze ans après, par des ambassadeurs, un traité de commerce et d'alliance avec la cour de Pékin (1).

Caractère et mérite de Timour. L'Orient et l'Occident ont retenti du nom de Timour. Ses descendans ont encore le titre d'empereurs; et l'admiration de ses sujets, qui le révéraient presque comme une divinité, est justifiée en quelque façon par les louanges ou l'aveu de ses ennemis les plus acharnés (2). Quoique impotent d'une jambe et d'un bras, sa taille et son maintien n'avaient rien d'ignoble; la sobriété et l'exercice maintenaient la vigueur de sa santé, si nécessaire à lui-même et au monde. Grave et réservé dans ses conversations fa-

---

(1) *Voyez* la traduction de la relation persane de l'ambassade dans la quatrième partie des Relations de Thévenot. Ils présentèrent à l'empereur de la Chine un vieux cheval que Timour avait monté. Ils partirent de la cour de Hérat en 1419, et y revinrent de Pékin en 1422.

(2) Tiré d'Arabshah, t. II, c. 96. Les couleurs plus brillantes ou plus douces sont extraites de Sherefeddin, de d'Herbelot et des Institutions.

milières, il ignorait l'idiome des Arabes, mais parlait avec autant de facilité que d'élégance la langue des Turcs et celle des Persans; il se plaisait à s'entretenir avec des hommes instruits sur des sujets de science ou d'histoire, et s'amusait dans ses heures de loisir au jeu d'échecs, qu'il perfectionna ou défigura en multipliant le nombre des pièces et des combinaisons (1). Il était musulman zélé, quoique peut-être peu orthodoxe (2). Mais la solidité de son jugement peut faire présumer que sa vénération superstitieuse pour les astrologues, les saints de sa religion et les prophéties, n'était qu'une feinte de sa politique. Il gouverna seul et despotiquement son vaste empire. Sous son règne, on ne vit point des rebelles attenter à son autorité, des favoris séduire ses affections, ou des ministres tromper sa justice. Il tenait pour maxime invariable que, quoi qu'il en pût arriver, un prince ne doit jamais révoquer ses ordres ni souffrir qu'on les discute. Mais ses ennemis ont observé que les

---

(1) Il porta son nouveau jeu ou système de trente-deux pièces et soixante-quatre cases, à cinquante-six pièces et cent dix ou cent trente cases; mais, excepté à sa cour, l'ancien jeu a paru suffisamment compliqué. L'empereur mongoul était plutôt satisfait que blessé de perdre contre un de ses sujets, et un joueur d'échecs sentira toute la valeur de cet éloge.

(2) *Voyez* Sherefeddin, l. v, c. 15-25. Arabshah (t. II, c. 96, p. 801-803) accuse d'impiété l'empereur et les Mongouls, qui donnent la préférence au Yacsa ou loi de Gengis (*cui Deus maledicat*), même sur le Koran. Il refuse de croire que l'usage et l'autorité de ce code païen aient été abolis par Sharokh.

ordres de destruction donnés par sa colère s'exécutaient plus exactement que ceux de sa bienfaisance. Ses fils et petits-fils, qui à sa mort se trouvaient au nombre de trente-six, avaient été durant sa vie les premiers et les plus soumis de ses sujets. Lorsqu'ils s'écartaient de leur devoir, on les corrigeait, conformément aux lois de Gengis, par la bastonnade, après laquelle ils reprenaient leurs honneurs et leurs commandemens. Peut-être le cœur de Timour n'était-il pas fermé aux vertus sociales, peut-être n'était-il pas incapable d'aimer ses amis et de pardonner à ses ennemis; mais les règles de la morale sont fondées sur l'intérêt public, et il suffira peut-être d'applaudir à la sagesse d'un prince que ses libéralités n'ont point appauvri, et dont la justice a augmenté ses richesses et sa puissance. Le devoir d'un souverain est sans doute d'entretenir l'harmonie entre l'obéissance et l'autorité, de châtier l'orgueil, de secourir la faiblesse, de récompenser le mérite, de bannir le vice et l'oisiveté de ses États, de protéger le voyageur et le marchand, de contenir la licence du soldat, de favoriser les travaux du laboureur, d'encourager les sciences et l'industrie, et, au moyen d'une répartition modérée, d'augmenter le revenu sans augmenter les taxes. Mais l'exécution de ces devoirs lui procure une ample et prompte récompense. Lorsque Timour monta sur le trône, l'Asie était déchirée par les factions, le brigandage et l'anarchie; sous son règne, un enfant aurait pu porter sans crainte et sans danger une bourse d'or dans sa main de l'orient à l'occident de son fortuné royaume. Timour prétendait que le mérite de cette réforme suffisait pour justifier ses conquêtes et son titre à la souveraineté de l'univers. Mais les quatre observations suivantes feront apprécier ses droits à la reconnaissance des peuples, et conclure peut-être que l'empereur mongoul fut plutôt le fléau du genre humain que son bienfaiteur. 1° Lorsque l'épée de Timour redressait quelques abus ou détruisait quelques tyrannies locales, le remède était infiniment plus funeste que le mal : la discorde, l'avarice et la cruauté des petits tyrans de la Perse, opprimèrent sans doute leurs sujets ; mais le réformateur écrasa sous ses pas des nations entières. Il fit disparaître des villes florissantes, et leur place fut souvent marquée par des colonnes et des pyramides de têtes humaines, abominables trophées de ses victoires. Astrakhan, Carizme, Delhi, Ispahan, Bagdad, Alep, Damas, Bursa, Smyrne et mille autres villes, furent pillées, ou brûlées, ou entièrement détruites par ses troupes et en sa présence. Le restaurateur de l'ordre et de la paix aurait frémi peut-être, si un prêtre ou un philosophe eût osé calculer devant lui les millions de victimes qu'il avait sacrifiées pour les rétablir(1). 2° Ses guerres

---

(1) Outre les passages de ce sanglant récit, le lecteur peut se rappeler la note 1, page 266 du sixième vol. de la présente histoire, où j'ai parlé de ce conquérant ; il y trouvera le calcul de près de trois cent mille têtes qui servirent de monument à sa cruauté. Excepté la tragédie de Rowe, du cinq novembre, je ne m'attendais pas à entendre louer

les plus sanglantes furent plutôt des incursions que des conquêtes. Il envahit successivement le Turkestan, le Kipzak, la Russie, l'Indoustan, la Syrie, l'Anatolie, l'Arménie et la Géorgie, sans avoir l'espérance ou le désir de conserver ces provinces éloignées. Il en sortait chargé de dépouilles, sans laisser après lui ni soldats pour tenir les rebelles en respect, ni magistrats pour protéger les sujets fidèles et soumis. Après avoir renversé l'édifice de leur ancien gouvernement, il les abandonnait à des calamités aggravées ou causées par son invasion, et ces calamités n'étaient compensées par aucun avantage présent ou possible. 3° Il s'occupa surtout du bien-être et de l'éclat intérieur des royaumes de la Transoxiane et de la Perse, qu'il considérait comme les États héréditaires de sa famille. Mais ses fréquentes et longues absences suspendaient et détruisaient souvent ses travaux pacifiques. Tandis qu'il triomphait près du Gange ou du Volga, ses serviteurs et même ses fils oubliaient leur maître et leur devoir. La rigueur tardive des enquêtes et des punitions ne réparait qu'imparfaitement les désordres publics et particuliers, et nous devons nous contenter de louer les Institutions de Timour, comme le projet séduisant d'une monarchie parfaite. 4° Quels que pussent être les bienfaits de son administration, ils disparurent

---

l'aimable modération de Timour (*Préface* de White, p. vij). Cependant on peut excuser l'enthousiasme généreux de la part du lecteur, et encore plus de l'éditeur des *Institutions*.

avec lui. Ses fils et ses petits-fils, plus ambitieux de régner que de gouverner (1), furent ennemis les uns des autres et ennemis du peuple. Sharokh, le plus jeune de ses fils, soutint avec quelque gloire un fragment de l'empire. Mais après sa mort, le théâtre de sa domination fut de nouveau plongé dans le sang et les ténèbres ; et avant la révolution d'un siècle, les Usbeks du nord et les Turcomans de la brebis blanche et de la brebis noire envahirent la Perse et la Transoxiane. La race de Timour aurait cessé d'exister, si un héros, son descendant au cinquième degré, chassé par les Usbeks, n'eût entrepris la conquête de l'Indoustan (2). Les grands mogols, ses successeurs, étendirent leur empire depuis les montagnes de Cachemire jusqu'au cap Comorin, et depuis le Candahar jusqu'au golfe du Bengale. Depuis le règne d'Aurengzeb, cet empire s'est dissous ; un brigand de la Perse a pillé le trésor de Delhi, et une compagnie de marchands chrétiens d'une île de l'Océan septentrional possède aujourd'hui le plus riche de leurs royaumes.

---

(1) Consultez les derniers chapitres de Sherefeddin, Arabshah et M. de Guignes (*Hist. des Huns*, t. IV, l. xx; l'*Histoire de Nadir-Shah* par Fraser, p. 1-62). L'histoire des descendans de Timour est superficiellement racontée, et les seconde et troisième parties de Sherefeddin manquent.

(2) Shah-Allum, le présent mogol, est le quatorzième descendant de Timour par Miran-Shah, le troisième fils de ce conquérant. *Voyez* le deuxième volume de l'*Histoire de l'Indoustan* par Dow.

Il n'en fut pas ainsi de l'empire ottoman ; tel qu'un arbre vigoureux courbé par la tempête, il se releva dès que l'orage fut passé, et reprit une vigueur et une végétation nouvelles. En évacuant l'Anatolie, Timour avait laissé les cités vides de leurs palais, dépouillées de leurs trésors et privées de souverain ; les pâtres et les brigands tartares ou turcomans se répandirent dans les campagnes. Les émirs rentrèrent dans leurs districts, récemment usurpés par Bajazet. L'un d'eux exerça lâchement sa vengeance en démolissant son sépulcre ; et les discordes des cinq fils du sultan consumèrent rapidement les débris de leur patrimoine. Je citerai leurs noms selon l'ordre de leur âge et de leurs actions (1).

1° Il est douteux si celui dont je trace rapidement l'histoire, était le véritable *Mustapha*, ou un imposteur qui prétendait le représenter. Il combattit à côté de son père à la bataille d'Angora ; mais lorsque le sultan captif obtint la permission de faire chercher ses fils, on ne trouva que Mousa ; et les historiens turcs, esclaves de la faction triomphante, assurent que son frère fut compris parmi les morts. En admettant qu'il se soit échappé, il resta caché durant douze ans à ses amis et à ses ennemis, et parut

---

(1) On trouve la relation des guerres civiles depuis la mort de Bajazet jusqu'à celle de Mustapha dans Démétrius Cantemir (p. 58-82), chez les Turcs ; parmi les Grecs dans Chalcocondyles (l. IV et V), Phranza (l. I, c. 30-32) et Ducas (c. 18-27). Ce dernier est le plus détaillé et le mieux instruit.

enfin en Thessalie, où un parti nombreux le reconnut pour le fils et le successeur de Bajazet. Sa première défaite aurait terminé sa vie, si ce vrai ou faux Mustapha n'eût pas été sauvé par les Grecs, qui, après la mort de son frère Mahomet, lui rendirent la liberté et l'empire. Il paraît que la bassesse de ses sentimens attestait son imposture. Après avoir été respecté sur le trône d'Andrinople comme le sultan légitime des Ottomans, sa fuite, des chaînes et un supplice ignominieux, le livrèrent au mépris public. Trente imposteurs jouèrent successivement le même rôle, et eurent tous le même sort. Ces fréquentes exécutions semblent annoncer que la mort du véritable Mustapha n'était pas bien constatée. 2° Lorsque son père eut été réduit en captivité, Isa (1) régna sur les pays voisins d'Angora, de Sinope et de la mer Noire; et Timour renvoya ses ambassadeurs chargés de présens et d'honorables promesses : mais leur maître, victime de la jalousie de son frère, le souverain d'Amasie, perdit bientôt ses provinces et la vie; et l'événement définitif de leur querelle donna lieu d'observer, par une pieuse allusion, que la loi de Moïse et de Jésus, d'*Isa* et de *Mousa*, avait été abrogée par l'autorité supérieure de *Mahomet*. 3° On ne compte point Soliman au nombre des empereurs turcs; il arrêta cependant les progrès des

2° Isa.

3° Soliman.
A. D.
1403-1410.

―――――

(1) Arabshah (t. II, c. 26), dont le témoignage en cette occasion est irrécusable. Sherefeddin atteste aussi l'existence d'Isa, dont les Turcs ne parlent point.

Mongouls, et après leur retraite réunit quelques instans les trônes d'Andrinople et de Bursa. Brave, actif et heureux à la guerre, il joignait la clémence à l'intrépidité ; mais il se laissait entraîner par la présomption et corrompre par l'intempérance et l'oisiveté. Il relâcha la discipline dans un gouvernement où le sujet, s'il ne tremble pas, doit faire trembler le souverain. Ses vices aliénèrent les chefs de l'armée et de la loi ; et l'ivresse dont il faisait habitude, honteuse dans un homme et à plus forte raison dans un prince, était doublement odieuse chez un disciple de Mahomet. Son frère Mousa le surprit à Andrinople, endormi et chargé de vin, l'atteignit dans sa fuite vers Byzance, et le fit périr dans un bain après un règne de sept ans et dix mois. 4° Mais Mousa s'était dégradé en acceptant l'investiture des Mongouls; esclave et tributaire, il ne possédait qu'une faible partie de l'Anatolie ; des milices timides et un trésor épuisé ne suffisaient pas pour repousser les vieilles bandes du souverain de la Romanie. Mousa, déguisé, abandonna le palais de Bursa, traversa la Propontide dans un bateau découvert, parcourut les montagnes de Servie et de Valachie, et parvint, après quelques efforts, à monter sur le trône d'Andrinople, récemment souillé du sang de son frère Soliman. Durant un règne de trois ans et demi, il remporta quelques victoires sur les chrétiens de la Hongrie et de la Morée ; mais il se perdit par sa timidité et sa clémence déplacée. Après avoir renoncé à la souveraineté de l'Anatolie, Mousa fut la victime de ses mi-

4° Mousa.
A. D. 1410.

nistres perfides et de l'ascendant de son frère Mahomet. 5° La victoire définitive que remporta celui-ci fut la récompense de sa prudence et de sa modération. Avant sa captivité, Bajazet avait confié à son fils Mahomet le gouvernement d'Amasie, la barrière des Turcs contre les chrétiens de Trébisonde et de Géorgie, et éloignée d'environ trente journées de Constantinople. La ville, séparée en deux parties égales par la rivière d'Iris, s'élève des deux côtés en amphithéâtre (1), et donne en petit une idée de Bagdad; la citadelle d'Amasie passait chez les Asiatiques pour imprenable. Dans le cours de ses expéditions rapides, Timour paraît avoir négligé ce coin obscur et rebelle de l'Anatolie. Mahomet, sans braver le vainqueur, maintint silencieusement son indépendance, et chassa de sa province les derniers traîneurs tartares. Il se débarrassa du dangereux voisinage d'Isa; ses autres frères, plus puissans, respectèrent dans leurs contestations la neutralité qu'il observa jusqu'au triomphe de Mousa; alors il se déclara le vengeur et l'héritier de Soliman. Mahomet acquit l'Anatolie par un traité, et la Romanie par les armes. Le soldat qui lui présenta la tête de Mousa, fut récompensé comme le bienfaiteur du prince et des peuples. Durant les huit années qu'il régna seul et en paix, il s'occupa d'effacer les suites des discordes

5° Mahomet.
1413-1421.

―――――

(1) Arabshah, *loc. cit.*; Abulféda, *Géog. Tab.* XVII, p. 302; Busbequius, *epist.* 1, p. 96, 97, *in Itinere C. P. et Amasiano.*

civiles, et de rétablir la monarchie ottomane sur une base plus solide. Sur la fin de sa vie, Mahomet fit choix de deux ministres sûrs. Il les chargea de guider l'inexpérience de son fils Amurath; et telles furent la prudence et l'union des deux visirs Ibrahim et Bajazet, qu'ils tinrent la mort de l'empereur secrète durant plus de quarante jours, jusqu'à l'arrivée de son successeur dans le palais de Bursa. Le prince Mustapha, ou un imposteur sous son nom, ralluma en Europe une nouvelle guerre. Le premier visir perdit une bataille et la vie; mais Ibrahim (1) fut plus heureux, et les Turcs révèrent encore le nom et la famille de celui qui termina les guerres civiles par la mort du dernier prétendant au trône de Bajazet.

Règne de l'empereur Amurath II. A. D. 1421, jusqu'au 9 fév. 1451.

Durant ces désordres, les plus sages d'entre les Turcs, et en général le corps de la nation, désiraient vivement la réunion des parties éparses de l'empire. La Romanie et l'Anatolie, déchirées si souvent par l'ambition des particuliers, tendaient fortement à s'y rejoindre. Leurs efforts offraient une leçon aux puissances chrétiennes. Si les flottes de celles-ci s'étaient réunies pour occuper le détroit de Gallipoli, les

Réunion de l'empire des Ottomans. A. D. 1421.

---

(1) Ducas, Grec contemporain, fait l'éloge des vertus d'Ibrahim (c. 25). Ses descendans sont les seuls nobles en Turquie; ils se contentent d'administrer les fondations pieuses de leur ancêtre, avec l'exemption de toutes fonctions publiques. Le sultan leur fait chaque année deux visites (Cantemir, p. 76).

Ottomans auraient été bientôt écrasés, du moins en Europe; mais le schisme de l'Occident, les factions et les guerres de la France et de l'Angleterre, détournèrent les Latins de cette généreuse entreprise. Ils jouirent d'une tranquillité passagère sans penser à l'avenir, et l'intérêt du moment les engagea souvent à servir l'ennemi de leur religion. Une colonie génoise (1) établie à Phocée (2), sur la côte d'Ionie, s'enrichissait par le commerce exclusif de l'alun (3), et assurait, par un tribut, sa tranquillité chez les Ottomans. Dans leur dernière guerre civile, le jeune et ambitieux Adorno, gouverneur des Génois, prit

---

(1) *Voyez* Pachymère (l. v, 29), Nicéphore Grégoras (l. ii, c. 1), Sherefeddin (l. v, c. 57) et Ducas (c. 25). Le dernier de ces écrivains, observateur exact et attentif, mérite particulièrement la confiance pour tout ce qui concerne l'Ionie et les îles. Parmi les nations qui habitaient la nouvelle Phocée, il nomme les Anglais (Ιγγληνοι); cette citation atteste l'ancienneté du commerce de la Méditerranée.

(2) Pour l'esprit de navigation et de liberté de l'ancienne Phocée ou plutôt des Phocéens, consultez le premier livre d'Hérodote et l'Index géographique de son dernier et savant traducteur français, M. Larcher (t. vii, p. 299).

(3) Pline (*Hist. natur.*, xxxv, 52) ne comprend point Phocée parmi les pays qui produisent l'alun. Il nomme d'abord l'Égypte, en second lieu l'île de Melos, dont les mines d'alun ont été décrites par Tournefort (t. i, lettre iv), également recommandable comme voyageur et comme naturaliste. Après avoir perdu Phocée, les Génois découvrirent, en 1459, ce précieux minéral dans l'île d'Ischia (Ismaël Bouillaud, *ad Ducam*, c. 25).

le parti d'Amurath, et arma sept galères pour le transporter d'Asie en Europe. Le sultan, accompagné de cinq cents gardes, s'embarqua à bord du vaisseau amiral, dont l'équipage était composé de huit cents des plus braves Français : sa vie et sa liberté étaient entre leurs mains; et ce n'est pas sans répugnance que nous applaudissons à la fidélité d'Adorno, qui, au milieu du passage, s'agenouilla devant lui, et accepta avec reconnaissance la décharge des arrérages du tribut. Ils débarquèrent à la vue de Mustapha et de Gallipoli; deux mille Italiens, armés de lances et de haches de bataille, accompagnèrent Amurath à la conquête d'Andrinople, et ce service vénal obtint bientôt pour récompense la ruine du commerce et de la colonie de Phocée.

État de l'empire grec.
A. D.
1402-1425. Si Timour avait généreusement marché contre Bajazet à la requête et au secours de l'empereur grec, il aurait mérité la reconnaissance et les éloges des chrétiens (1); mais un musulman qui portait le glaive de la persécution dans la Géorgie, et respectait la

---

(1) De tous les écrivains qui ont vanté la générosité fabuleuse de Timour, celui qui a le plus abusé de cette supposition est sans contredit l'ingénieux sir William Temple, admirateur de toute vertu étrangère. Après la conquête de la Russie, etc., et le passage du Danube, son héros tartare délivre, visite, admire et refuse la capitale de Constantin; son pinceau séduisant s'écarte à chaque ligne de la vérité de l'histoire, mais ses fictions ingénieuses sont encore plus pardonnables que les erreurs grossières de Cantemir. *Voy.* ses *OEuvres,* vol. III, p. 349, 350, éd. *in-8°.*

sainte guerre de Bajazet, n'était point disposé à plaindre ou à protéger les *idolâtres* de l'Europe. Le Tartare n'écouta que son ambition, et la délivrance de Constantinople en fut la conséquence indirecte. Lorsque Manuel abdiqua le gouvernement, il demandait au ciel, plutôt qu'il ne l'espérait, de voir différer jusqu'à la fin de ses misérables jours la ruine de l'Église et de l'empire. Tandis qu'après son retour de l'Occident il s'attendait tous les jours à recevoir la nouvelle de cette catastrophe, il apprit avec autant d'étonnement que de joie le départ, la défaite et la captivité de l'empereur ottoman. Manuel (1) partit sur-le-champ de Modon dans la Morée pour Constantinople, remonta sur son trône, et donna au prince de Sélymbrie un doux exil dans l'île de Lesbos. Les ambassadeurs du fils de Bajazet furent admis en sa présence; mais leur orgueil était abattu, leur ton modeste ; ils étaient contenus dans le respect par la juste appréhension que les Grecs ne facilitassent aux Mongouls l'entrée de l'Europe. Soliman salua l'empereur du nom de père ; il sollicita l'investiture du gouvernement de la Romanie, promit de mériter cette faveur par un attachement inviolable et la restitution de Thessalonique et des plus importantes places situées sur les bords du Strymon, de

---

(1) Pour les règnes de Manuel et de Jean, de Mahomet 1er et d'Amurath II, *voyez* l'*Hist. ottom.* de Cantemir (pag. 70-95) et les trois écrivains grecs Chalcocondyles, Phranza et Ducas, toujours supérieur à ses rivaux.

la Propontide et de la mer Noire. Cette alliance avec Soliman exposa Manuel au ressentiment et à la vengeance de Mousa. Une armée de Turcs parut aux portes de Constantinople, mais ils furent repoussés par terre et par mer ; et si la capitale n'était point gardée par des troupes étrangères, les Grecs durent être étonnés de leur victoire. Mais au lieu de prolonger la division des puissances ottomanes, la politique ou l'inclination engagea Manuel à secourir le plus formidable des fils de Bajazet. Il conclut un traité avec Mahomet, dont les progrès étaient arrêtés par l'insurmontable barrière de Gallipoli. Le sultan et ses troupes traversèrent le Bosphore dans les vaisseaux grecs ; Mahomet fut amicalement reçu dans la capitale, et son heureuse sortie contre son rival fut le premier pas vers la conquête de la Romanie. Après la mort de Mousa, la ruine de Constantinople fut encore suspendue par la prudence et la modération du vainqueur. Fidèle à ses engagemens et à ceux de Soliman, il respecta la paix et les lois de la reconnaissance. A sa mort, il confia la tutelle de ses deux fils à l'empereur grec, dans la vaine espérance de leur assurer un protecteur contre la cruauté de leur frère Amurath ; mais l'exécution de son testament aurait offensé l'honneur et la religion des mahométans. Le divan prononça d'une voix unanime qu'on ne pouvait point abandonner le soin et l'éducation des jeunes princes à un chien de chrétien. Manuel, en apprenant ce refus, assembla ses conseils ; les avis furent partagés, mais la prudence du vieux Manuel céda à la présomption de son fils Jean, et, employant à sa vengeance une arme dangereuse, il rendit la liberté au vrai ou faux Mustapha, qu'il retenait depuis long-temps en ôtage ou en captivité, et pour lequel la Porte ottomane lui payait une pension de trois cent mille aspres (1). Pour sortir d'esclavage, Mustapha consentit à toutes les propositions ; et la reddition des clefs de Gallipoli, c'est-à-dire de l'Europe, fut le prix que l'on mit à sa délivrance ; mais dès qu'il fut assis sur le trône de la Romanie, il renvoya les ambassadeurs grecs avec le sourire du mépris, et leur déclara pieusement qu'au jour du jugement il aimait mieux avoir à rendre compte d'un faux serment, que de la cession d'une ville musulmane entre les mains des infidèles. Manuel devint l'ennemi des deux rivaux, dont l'un lui avait fait une injure, et l'autre en avait reçu une de lui : et Amurath victorieux entreprit dans le printemps suivant le siége de Constantinople (2).

---

(1) L'aspre des Turcs (du mot grec ασπρος) est ou était une pièce blanche ou d'argent, dont le prix est fort baissé aujourd'hui, mais qui valait alors au moins la cinquante-quatrième partie d'un ducat ou sequin de Venise, et les trois cent mille aspres, soit qu'on les regarde comme une pension ou comme un tribut, équivalent à peu près à deux mille cinq cents livres sterling (Leunclavius, *Pandect. turc.*, p. 406-408).

(2) Pour le siége de Constantinople en 1422, *voyez* la *Relation* détaillée et contemporaine de Jean Cananus, publiée par Léon Allatius à la fin de son édition d'Acropolita (p. 188-199).

Siége de Constantinople par Amurath II.
A. D. 1422, 10 juin– 24 août.

Le religieux dessein de soumettre la ville des Césars attira de l'Asie une foule de volontaires qui aspiraient à la couronne du martyre. La perspective de riches dépouilles et de belles esclaves enflammait leur ardeur militaire, et l'empereur vit les projets de son ambition consacrés par les prédictions et la présence de Séid Béchar, descendant du prophète (1), qui arriva au camp monté sur une mule et suivi d'une troupe respectable de cinq cents disciples; mais il dut rougir, si un fanatique rougissait jamais, du démenti donné à ses prophéties. La force des murs de Constantinople résista à une armée de deux cent mille Turcs; les Grecs et les étrangers mercenaires repoussèrent les assauts par d'heureuses sorties; aux nouveaux moyens d'attaque on opposa les anciens moyens de défense: l'enthousiasme du dervis enlevé miraculeusement au ciel pour converser avec Mahomet, fut compensé par la crédulité des chrétiens qui virent la vierge Marie, vêtue de violet, parcourant le rempart pour animer leur courage (2). Après deux mois de siége, une révolte excitée par les Grecs força le sultan de retourner

---

(1) Cantemir, p. 80. Cananus, qui désigne Séid Béchar sans le nommer, suppose que l'ami de Mahomet se donnait dans ses amours la liberté d'un prophète, et qu'on promit au saint et à ses disciples les plus jolies religieuses de Constantinople.

(2) Pour attester cette miraculeuse apparition, Cananus en appelle au témoignage du saint musulman; mais qui nous rendra témoignage pour Séid Béchar?

précipitamment à Bursa, et il l'éteignit promptement dans le sang d'un frère coupable. Tandis qu'Amurath conduisait ses janissaires à de nouvelles conquêtes en Europe et en Asie, Byzance jouit durant trente années du repos précaire de la servitude. Après la mort de Manuel, Jean Paléologue obtint la permission de régner moyennant un tribut de trois cent mille aspres, et la cession de presque tout ce qui excédait les faubourgs de Constantinople.

L'empereur Jean Paléologue II. A. D. 1425, 21 juillet. A. D. 1448, 31 oct.

En considérant que les principaux événemens de cette vie dépendent du caractère d'un seul acteur, on est forcé d'accorder aux qualités personnelles des sultans le premier mérite de la fondation et du rétablissement de l'empire ottoman. On peut remarquer entre eux quelques degrés différens de sagesse et de vertu ; mais depuis l'élévation d'Othman jusqu'à la mort de Soliman, durant une période de neuf règnes et de deux cent soixante-cinq années, le trône, en admettant une seule exception, fut occupé par une suite de princes actifs et courageux, respectés de leurs sujets et redoutés de leurs ennemis. Au lieu de passer leur jeunesse dans l'indolence fastueuse d'un sérail, les héritiers de l'empire étaient élevés dans les camps et dans les conseils. Leurs pères leur confiaient de bonne heure le commandement des provinces et des armées ; et cette noble institution, quoique la source d'une infinité de guerres civiles, a sans doute contribué à la discipline et à la vigueur de la monarchie. Les Ottomans ne peuvent pas s'intituler, comme les anciens califes de

Succession héréditaire et mérite des princes ottomans.

l'Arabie, les descendans ou successeurs de l'apôtre
de Dieu ; et la parenté qu'ils réclament avec les
princes tartares de la maison de Gengis, paraît
moins fondée sur la vérité que sur l'adulation (1).
Leur origine est obscure; mais ils acquirent bientôt,
dans l'opinion de leurs sujets, ce droit sacré et in-
contestable que le temps ne peut effacer et que ne
peut détruire la violence. On dépose, on étrangle un
sultan faible et vicieux ; mais son fils, enfant ou im-
bécile, succède à l'empire, et le plus audacieux rebelle n'a pas encore osé s'asseoir sur le trône de son
souverain (2). Tandis que des visirs perfides ou des
généraux victorieux renversaient les dynasties chan-
celantes de l'Asie, la succession ottomane, confir-
mée par une possession de cinq siècles, fait partie
des principes auxquels est attachée l'existence de la
nation turque.

Éducation et discipline des Turcs.

Cette nation doit en grande partie sa vigueur et

---

(1) *Voyez* Rycault (l. 1, c. 13). Les sultans turcs prennent le titre de khans. Cependant Abulghazi ne semble pas
reconnaître les Ottomans pour ses cousins.

(2) Le troisième grand visir du nom de Kiuperli, qui
fut tué à la bataille de Salankanen en 1691 (Cantemir,
p. 382), osa dire que tous les successeurs de Soliman avaient
été des imbéciles ou des tyrans, et qu'il était temps d'en
éteindre la race (Marsigli, *Stato militare*, etc., p. 28). Cet
hérétique en politique était un zélé républicain, qui justi-
fiait la révolution d'Angleterre contre l'ambassadeur de
France (Mignot, *Hist. des Ottomans*, t. III, p. 434); il ose
ridiculiser la singulière exception qui rend les places et les
dignités héréditaires dans les familles.

sa constitution à une influence assez extraordinaire. Les premiers sujets d'Othman consistaient dans ces quatre cents familles errantes de Turcomans, qui avaient suivi ses ancêtres de l'Oxus au Sangarius, et les plaines de l'Anatolie sont encore couvertes de leurs compatriotes habitant les champs dans des tentes blanches ou noires; mais ce petit nombre se perdit bientôt dans la masse des peuples vaincus, qui, sous le nom de Turcs, sont unis par le lien commun des mœurs, du langage et de la religion. Dans toutes les villes, depuis Erzeroum jusqu'à Belgrade, cette dénomination nationale est celle de tous les musulmans, qui sont considérés comme les premiers et les plus honorables des habitans; mais ils ont abandonné, au moins dans la Romanie, les villages et la culture des terres aux paysans chrétiens. Dans la première vigueur de l'empire ottoman, les Turcs furent eux-mêmes exclus de tous les honneurs civils et militaires; et une classe d'esclaves, un peuple factice, fut formé par la discipline de l'éducation à obéir, à combattre et à commander (1). Depuis Orchan jusqu'au premier Amurath, les sultans tinrent pour maxime qu'un gouvernement militaire devait à chaque génération renouveler ses soldats, et qu'il ne fallait pas chercher ces soldats

---

(1) Chalcocondyles (l. v) et Ducas (c. 23) nous donnent une esquisse grossière de la politique ottomane, et nous font connaître la métamorphose des enfans chrétiens en soldats turcs.

parmi les habitans efféminés de l'Asie, mais chez les belliqueuses nations de l'Europe. Les provinces de Thrace, de Macédoine, d'Albanie, de Bulgarie et de Servie, devinrent les pépinières des armées ottomanes ; et lorsque les conquêtes eurent diminué le cinquième qui revenait au sultan sur le nombre des captifs, on assujettit les chrétiens à une taxe barbare qui leur enlevait chaque cinquième enfant, ou bien se percevait tous les cinq ans. A l'âge de douze ou de quatorze ans, on enlevait les garçons les plus vigoureux à leurs pères ; on enregistrait leurs noms dans le rôle militaire, et dès cet instant ils étaient vêtus, nourris et instruits aux dépens du public, et destinés à le servir. Selon ce que promettait leur extérieur, on les choisissait pour les écoles royales de Bursa, de Péra et d'Andrinople ; on les confiait à la surveillance des pachas, ou bien on les dispersait dans les familles des paysans de l'Anatolie. Le premier soin de leurs maîtres était de leur enseigner la langue turque ; on exerçait leur corps à tous les travaux qui pouvaient le fortifier. Ils apprenaient à lutter, à sauter, à courir, à se servir de l'arc, et dans la suite du mousquet, jusqu'au moment où ils entraient dans les compagnies et les chambrées des janissaires pour y être sévèrement dressés à la discipline monastique ou militaire de l'ordre. Les plus distingués par les talens, la figure ou la naissance, passaient dans la classe des *agiamoglans*, ou au rang supérieur des *ichoglangs*; les premiers étaient attachés au palais, et les autres à la personne du souverain. Ils s'exerçaient dans quatre écoles successives, sous la férule des eunuques blancs, à manier un cheval et à lancer un javelot. Ceux dont le caractère paraissait plus disposé à l'étude, s'appliquaient à celle du Koran et des langues arabe et persane. A mesure qu'ils avançaient en âge et en mérite, on les faisait passer dans les emplois militaires, civils ou ecclésiastiques. Plus on les conservait, plus ils avaient l'espérance d'un rang distingué. A un âge mûr, on les admettait au nombre des quarante agas qui accompagnaient l'empereur, d'où ils étaient élevés, à son choix, au gouvernement des provinces et aux premiers honneurs de l'empire (1). Cette institution s'adaptait admirablement à la forme et à l'esprit d'une monarchie despotique. Les ministres et les généraux, esclaves du prince dans le sens le plus rigoureux, tenaient de sa bonté leur subsistance et leur instruction. Au moment où ils quittaient le sérail, et laissaient croître leur barbe comme un symbole d'affranchissement, ils se trouvaient revêtus d'un office important, sans esprit de parti, sans liaison d'amitié, sans parens et sans héritiers, dépendant

---

(1) Cette esquisse de la discipline et de l'éducation turque est principalement tirée de l'*État de l'Empire ottoman* par Rycault, du *Stato militare del Imperio ottomano* du comte Marsigli (à *la Haye*, 1732, *in-fol.*), et d'une *Description du Sérail*, approuvée par M. Greaves lui-même, voyageur attentif, et publiée dans le second volume de ses OEuvres.

absolument de la main qui les avait tirés de la poussière, et qui pouvait, comme le dit un proverbe turc, briser à sa volonté ces statues de verre (1). Durant le cours d'une éducation lente et pénible, il était facile à un œil pénétrant de juger leur caractère; l'homme se montrait seul, dépouillé, réduit à son mérite personnel; et si le prince avait assez de discernement pour choisir, rien ne le contrariait dans la liberté du choix. On disposait les candidats par les privations aux travaux, et par les habitudes de l'obéissance, à celles du commandement. Les troupes étaient toutes animées du même esprit; et les chrétiens qui ont fait la guerre aux Ottomans, n'ont pu refuser des louanges à la sobriété, à la patience et à la silencieuse modestie des janissaires (2). La victoire ne devait pas paraître douteuse en comparant la discipline et l'éducation des Turcs à l'indocilité des chevaliers, à l'orgueil que leur inspirait leur naissance, à l'ignorance des recrues, au caractère séditieux des vétérans, à l'intempérance et au désordre qui ont régné si long-temps dans les armées de l'Europe.

<small>Invention et usage de la poudre à canon.</small>

L'empire grec et les royaumes voisins n'auraient pu se défendre que par le secours de quelque arme

---

(1) D'après la liste de cent quinze visirs jusqu'au siége de Vienne (Marsigli, p. 13), leur place peut être regardée comme un marché pour trois ans et demi.

(2) *Voyez* les *Lettres* judicieuses et amusantes de Busbecq.

nouvelle, de quelque découverte dans l'art de la guerre, qui leur auraient donné une supériorité décisive sur les Turcs. Ils possédaient cette arme, et cette découverte avait été faite au moment qui devait décider de leur destinée. Les chimistes d'Europe ou de la Chine avaient découvert, soit par hasard, soit par leurs recherches, qu'un mélange de salpêtre, de soufre et de charbon, produisait, à l'aide d'une seule étincelle de feu, une explosion formidable. Ils observèrent bientôt que cette force expansive, comprimée dans un tube solide, pouvait chasser une balle de pierre ou de fer avec une violence et une rapidité irrésistible. L'époque précise de l'invention et de l'application de la poudre à canon (1) se perd dans des traditions douteuses et des expressions équivoques; mais il paraît suffisamment attesté qu'on la connut vers le milieu du quatorzième siècle, et qu'avant la fin de ce même siècle, l'artillerie était d'un usage familier dans les batailles et les siéges, par terre et par mer, chez les peuples de l'Allemagne, de l'Italie, de l'Espagne, de la France et de l'Angleterre (2). Il est assez indifférent de sa-

(1) Le premier et le second volume des *Essais chimiques* du docteur Watson contiennent deux discours précieux sur la découverte et la composition de la poudre à canon.

(2) On ne peut se fier sur cet objet aux autorités modernes. Ducange a recueilli les passages originaux (*Gloss. lat.* t. 1, p. 675, *Bombarda*). Mais dans le jour douteux qui nous parvient de ces premiers écrivains, ce qu'on voit du nom, du bruit, du feu et de l'effet par lesquels ils semblent

voir laquelle de ces nations s'en servit la première. Toutes possédèrent bientôt le même avantage; et le perfectionnement général laissa la balance du pouvoir et de la science militaire dans l'état où elle était auparavant. Cette découverte ne pouvait être long-temps la propriété exclusive des chrétiens; la perfidie des apostats et la politique imprudente de la rivalité la portèrent bientôt chez les Turcs; et les sultans eurent assez de bon sens pour adopter, assez de richesses pour s'approprier les talens des ingénieurs chrétiens. On peut accuser les Génois, qui transportèrent Amurath en Europe, de le lui avoir enseigné; et il est probable qu'ils fondirent et dirigèrent les canons dont il se servit au siége de Constantinople (1). Ils échouèrent dans la première entreprise; mais dans le cours général des guerres de ce siècle, ils eurent nécessairement l'avantage, étant presque toujours les assaillans. Lorsque la première

---

indiquer notre artillerie, peut très-bien s'adapter aux machines des anciens et au feu grégeois. Quant au canon dont les Anglais firent, dit-on, usage à la bataille de Crécy, on doit balancer l'autorité de Jean Villani (*Chron.*, liv. XII, chap. 65) par le silence de Froissard. Cependant Muratori (*Antiq. Italiæ medii ævi*, t. II, *Dissert.* 26, p. 514, 515) a produit un passage décisif de Pétrarque (*de Remediis utriusque Fortunæ dialog.*), qui avant l'année 1344 a maudit ce tonnerre artificiel; *nuper* rara, *nunc* communis.

(1) Le canon des Turcs que Ducas fait paraître (c. 30) pour la première fois devant Belgrade (A. D. 1436), servit, selon Chalcocondyles (l. v, p. 123), dès l'année 1422, au siége de Constantinople.

ardeur de l'attaque et de la défense se ralentit, on pointa cette foudroyante artillerie contre des tours et des murs qui n'avaient été destinés à résister qu'aux efforts moins puissans des machines de guerre inventées par les anciens. Les Vénitiens communiquèrent, sans qu'on puisse leur en faire un reproche, l'usage de la poudre aux sultans de l'Égypte et de la Perse, leurs alliés contre la puissance ottomane. Le secret se répandit bientôt jusqu'aux extrémités de l'Asie, et l'avantage des Européens se trouva borné à des victoires faciles sur les sauvages du Nouveau-Monde. En comparant les rapides progrès de cette invention funeste aux pas lents et pénibles des sciences, de la raison et des arts pacifiques, un philosophe ne pourra s'empêcher de rire ou de pleurer sur la folie du genre humain.

CHAPITRE LXVI.

Sollicitations des empereurs d'Orient auprès des papes. Voyages de Jean Paléologue 1er, de Manuel et de Jean II, dans les cours de l'Occident. Union des Églises grecque et latine proposée par le concile de Bâle, et accomplie à Ferrare et à Florence. État de la littérature à Constantinople. Sa renaissance en Italie, où elle fut portée par les Grecs fugitifs. Curiosité et émulation des Latins.

<small>Ambassade de l'empereur Andronic le Jeune au pape Benoît XII. A. D. 1339.</small>

Durant les quatre derniers siècles de leur empire, on pourrait considérer les marques de haine ou d'amitié des princes grecs à l'égard du pape, comme le thermomètre de leur détresse et de leur prospérité, du succès et de la chute des dynasties barbares. Lorsque les Turcs de la race de Seljouk envahirent l'Asie et menacèrent Constantinople, nous avons vu les ambassadeurs d'Alexis implorer au concile de Plaisance la protection du père commun des chrétiens. A peine les pélerins français eurent repoussé le sultan de Nicée à Iconium, que les empereurs de Byzance reprirent ou cessèrent de dissimuler leur haine et leur mépris naturel pour les schismatiques de l'Occident, et cette imprudence précipita la première chute de leur empire. Le ton doux et charitable de Vataces marque la date de l'invasion des Mongouls. Après la prise de Constantinople, des factions et des ennemis étrangers ébranlèrent le trône du premier Paléologue. Tant que l'épée de Charles fut suspendue sur sa tête, il fit bassement sa cour au pape, et sacrifia au danger du moment sa foi, ses vertus, et l'affection de ses sujets. Après la mort de Michel, le prince et le peuple soutinrent l'indépendance de leur Église et la pureté de leur symbole. Andronic l'Ancien ne craignait ni n'aimait les Latins : dans ses derniers malheurs, l'orgueil servit de rempart à sa superstition ; il ne put décemment rétracter à la fin de sa vie les opinions qu'il avait soutenues avec fermeté dans sa jeunesse: Andronic, son petit-fils, asservi par son caractère et par sa situation, lorsqu'il vit les Turcs envahir la Bithynie, sollicita une alliance spirituelle et temporelle avec les princes de l'Occident. Après cinquante ans de séparation et de silence, le moine Barlaam fut député secrètement vers le pape Benoît XII ; et il paraît que ses insidieuses instructions avaient été tracées par la main habile du grand-domestique (1). « Très-saint père, dit le moine, l'empereur ne désire pas moins que vous la réunion des deux Églises ; mais, dans une entreprise si délicate, il se trouve forcé de respecter sa propre dignité et

---

(1) Cette curieuse instruction a été tirée, je crois, des archives du Vatican, par Odoric Raynald, et insérée dans sa continuation des *Annales* de Baronius (*Rome*, 1646-1677, en dix volumes *in-folio*). Je me suis contenté de l'abbé de Fleury (*Hist. ecclés.*, t. XX, p. 1-8), dont j'ai toujours trouvé les extraits clairs, exacts et exempts de toute partialité.

les préjugés de ses sujets. Les moyens sont de deux sortes, la force ou la persuasion. L'insuffisance du premier est déjà démontrée par l'expérience, puisque les Latins ont subjugué l'empire sans pouvoir ébranler l'opinion des habitans. La persuasion, plus lente, est aussi plus sûre et plus solide. Trente ou quarante de nos docteurs, envoyés chez vous en députation, s'accorderaient probablement avec ceux du Vatican dans l'amour de la vérité et l'unité d'un symbole; mais, à leur retour, quel serait le fruit ou la récompense de leur démarche? Le mépris de leurs confrères et les reproches d'une nation aveugle et opiniâtre. Cependant les Grecs sont accoutumés à révérer les conciles généraux qui ont fixé les articles de notre foi ; et s'ils rejettent les décrets de Lyon, c'est parce qu'on n'a daigné ni entendre ni admettre les représentans de l'Église orientale dans cette réunion arbitraire. Pour accomplir cette pieuse opération, il sera expédient et même nécessaire qu'un légat intelligent parte pour la Grèce, assemble les patriarches de Constantinople, d'Alexandrie, d'Antioche et de Jérusalem, et qu'il prépare avec eux la tenue d'un synode libre et universel. Mais dans ce moment-ci, continua le subtil agent des Grecs, l'empire a tout à craindre de l'invasion des Turcs, qui occupent déjà quatre des principales villes de l'Anatolie. Les habitans annoncent le désir de rentrer sous l'obéissance de leur souverain et dans le sein de leur religion; mais les forces et les revenus de l'empereur sont insuffisans pour cette entreprise; et le légat romain doit se faire accompagner ou précéder d'une armée de Francs, pour chasser les infidèles et ouvrir la route du saint-sépulcre. » En cas que les Latins soupçonneux exigeassent d'avance quelques garans, quelques gages de la fidélité des Grecs, Barlaam avait préparé une réponse raisonnable et convaincante : « 1° Un synode général peut seul consommer la réunion des deux Églises ; il est impossible de l'assembler avant d'avoir délivré les trois patriarches de l'Orient, et un grand nombre d'autres prélats, du joug des mahométans. 2° Les Grecs sont aliénés par d'anciennes injures et une longue tyrannie : on ne peut espérer de les regagner que par quelque acte de fraternité, par quelque secours efficace, qui appuie l'autorité et les argumens de l'empereur et des partisans de l'union. 3° Quand même il resterait quelque légère différence dans la foi ou dans les cérémonies, les Grecs ne sont pas moins les disciples du Christ, et les Turcs sont les ennemis communs de tout ce qui porte le nom de chrétien. L'Arménie, l'île de Rhodes et l'île de Chypre, sont également attaquées, et il convient à la piété des princes français de s'armer pour la défense générale de la religion. 4° Quand même ils regarderaient les sujets d'Andronic comme les plus odieux des schismatiques, des hérétiques ou des païens, l'intérêt des princes de l'Occident devrait les engager à s'acquérir un utile allié, à protéger un empire chancelant qui couvre les frontières de l'Europe, et à se joindre aux Grecs contre les Turcs, sans attendre que ces derniers, après avoir conquis la Grèce, se servent de ses forces et de ses trésors pour porter dans le cœur de l'Europe leurs armes victorieuses. » Les offres, les argumens et les demandes d'Andronic, furent éludés avec une froide et dédaigneuse indifférence. Les rois de France et de Naples rejetèrent les dangers et la gloire d'une croisade. Le pape refusa de convoquer un nouveau concile pour régler les anciens articles de la foi ; et, par égard pour les vieilles prétentions de l'empereur et du clergé latin, il fit usage, dans sa réponse à l'empereur grec, d'une suscription offensante : « Au *Moderator* (1) ou gouverneur des Grecs, et à ceux qui se disent les patriarches de l'Église d'Orient. » On ne pouvait choisir pour cette ambassade une circonstance ou un caractère moins favorables. Benoît XII (2) était un lourd

---

(1) L'ambiguïté de ce titre est heureuse ou ingénieuse; et *moderator*, comme synonyme de *rector*, *gubernator*, est un terme de la latinité classique et même cicéronienne qu'on trouvera non pas dans le *Glossaire* de Ducange, mais dans le *Thesaurus* de Robert Étienne.

(2) La première épître (*sine titulo*) de Pétrarque représente le danger de la *barque* et l'incapacité du *pilote*. *Hæc inter, vino madidus, ævo gravis ac soporifero rore perfusus, jamjam nutitat, dormitat, jam somno præceps atque (utinam solus) ruit.... Heu quantò feliciùs patrio terram sulcasset aratro, quàm scalmum piscatorium ascendisset!* Cette satire engage son biographe à peser les vertus et les vices de Benoît XII, qui ont été exagérés par les guelfes et par les gibelins, par les papistes et les protestans. *Voyez les Mémoires sur la vie de Pétrarque*, tome I, page 259 ; II, not. 15, pag. 13-

paysan, toujours embarrassé de scrupules, et abruti par le vin et la paresse. Sa vanité pût enrichir la tiare d'une troisième couronne; mais il était également inhabile à gouverner un royaume ou l'Église.

Après la mort d'Andronic, les Grecs, en proie aux guerres civiles, ne purent s'occuper de la réunion générale des chrétiens. Mais dès que Cantacuzène eut pardonné à ses ennemis vaincus, il entreprit de justifier ou au moins d'atténuer la faute qu'il avait commise en introduisant les Turcs dans l'Europe, et en mariant sa fille à un prince musulman. Deux de ses ministres, accompagnés d'un interprète latin, se rendirent par ses ordres à la cour du pontife romain, transplantée dans la ville d'Avignon, sur les bords du Rhône, où elle resta durant soixante-dix ans. Ils représentèrent la dure nécessité qui les avait forcés d'embrasser l'alliance des infidèles, et firent entendre par son ordre les mots spécieux et édifians de *croisade* et d'*union*. Le pape Clément vi (1), successeur de Benoît xii, leur fit une réception affa-

Négociation de Cantacuzène avec Clément vi. A. D. 1348.

---

16. Ce fut lui qui donna occasion au proverbe *Bibamus papaliter*.

(1) *Voyez* les Vies originales de Clément vi, dans Muratori (*Script. rerum italicar.*, t. iii, part. ii, p. 550-589); Matthieu Villani (*Chron.*, l. iii, c. 43, *in Muratori*, t. xiv, p. 186); qui le nomme *molto cavallaresco, poco religioso*; Fleury (*Hist. ecclés.*, t. xx, p. 126), et la *Vie de Pétrarque* (t. ii, p. 42-45). L'abbé de Sade lui accorde plus d'indulgence; mais ce dernier auteur était gentilhomme aussi bien que prêtre.

ble et honorable, parut touché des malheurs de Cantacuzène, convaincu de son mérite, persuadé de son innocence, et parfaitement instruit de l'état et des révolutions de son empire. Il avait appris tous ces détails d'une dame de Savoie, de la suite de l'impératrice Anne (1). Si Clément ne possédait pas les vertus d'un prêtre, il avait du moins l'élévation et la magnificence d'un prince, et distribuait les bénéfices et les royaumes avec la même facilité. Sous son règne, Avignon fut le siége du faste et des plaisirs. Il avait surpassé dans sa jeunesse la licence des mœurs d'un baron, et son palais, lorsqu'il fut devenu pape, sa chambre à coucher même, étaient souvent embellis ou déshonorés par la présence de ses favorites. Les guerres de la France et de l'Angleterre ne permettaient pas de penser à une croisade ; mais la vanité de Clément s'amusa de ce projet brillant, et les ambassadeurs grecs s'en retournèrent avec deux prélats latins députés par le pontife. A leur arrivée à Constantinople, l'empereur et les nonces se complimentèrent mutuellement sur leur éloquence et leur piété. Les fréquentes conférences se passèrent en louanges et en promesses, dont ils se laissaient réciproquement amuser sans y donner la moindre

---

(1) On la connaît sous le nom probablement défiguré de Zampea : elle avait accompagné sa maîtresse à Constantinople, où seule elle resta avec elle. Les Grecs eux-mêmes ne purent refuser des louanges à sa prudence, à son érudition et à sa politesse. Cantacuzène, l. 1, c. 42.

confiance. « Je suis enchanté, leur dit le dévot Cantacuzène, du projet de notre guerre sainte; elle fera ma gloire personnelle en même temps que le bien de toute la chrétienté. Mes États offriront aux armées françaises un passage libre et sûr; mes troupes, mes galères et mes trésors, seront consacrés à la cause commune, et mon sort serait digne d'envie si je pouvais mériter et obtenir la couronne du martyre. Je tâcherais en vain de vous peindre l'ardeur avec laquelle je désire la réunion des membres épars de Jésus-Christ. Si ma mort pouvait y servir, je présenterais avec joie ma tête et mon épée. Si ce phénix spirituel devait naître de mes cendres, j'élèverais mon bûcher et je l'allumerais de mes propres mains. » L'empereur grec osa cependant observer que c'était l'orgueil et la précipitation des Latins qui avaient introduit les articles de foi sur lesquels se divisaient les deux Églises. Il blâma la conduite servile et tyrannique du premier Paléologue, et déclara qu'il ne soumettrait sa conscience qu'aux décrets libres d'un synode général. « Les circonstances, continua-t-il, ne permettent ni au pape ni à moi de nous réunir à Rome ou à Constantinople; mais on peut choisir une ville maritime sur les frontières des deux empires, pour assembler les évêques et instruire les fidèles de l'Orient et de l'Occident. » Les nonces parurent satisfaits de ces propositions, et Cantacuzène affecta de déplorer la perte de ses espérances, qui furent bientôt détruites par la mort de Clément et les dispositions différentes de son successeur. Quant à lui, il vécut long-temps encore, mais dans un cloître, d'où l'humble moine ne put, si ce n'est par ses prières, influer sur la conduite de son pupille et les destinées de l'empire (1).

Traité de Jean Paléologue Ier avec Innocent VI. A. D. 1355. Cependant, de tous les princes de Byzance, aucun ne fut si bien disposé que le pupille Jean Paléologue à rentrer sous l'obéissance du pontife romain. Sa mère, Anne de Savoie, avait été baptisée dans le giron de l'Église latine : son mariage avec Andronic l'avait forcée à changer de nom, d'habillement et de culte ; mais son cœur était demeuré fidèle à son pays et à sa religion. Elle avait dirigé elle-même l'éducation de son fils, et l'empereur devenu homme, du moins par sa taille si ce n'est par son esprit, ne cessa point de se laisser gouverner par elle. Lorsque la retraite de Cantacuzène le laissa seul maître de la monarchie grecque, les Turcs commandaient sur l'Hellespont. Le fils de Cantacuzène assemblait des rebelles à Andrinople ; et Paléologue ne pouvait se fier ni à son peuple ni à lui-même. Par le conseil de sa mère, et dans l'espérance d'un secours étranger, il sacrifia les droits de l'Église et de l'État, et cet acte d'esclavage (2), signé d'encre pourpre et scellé

---

(1) *Voy.* toute cette négociation dans Cantacuzène (l. iv, c. 9), qui, à travers les louanges qu'il prodigue à sa propre vertu, trahit l'inquiétude d'une conscience coupable.

(2) *Voyez* ce traité ignominieux dans Fleury (*Histoire ecclés.*, p. 151-154), d'après Raynald, qui l'avait probable-

d'une bulle d'or, fut secrètement porté au pape par un Italien. Le premier article du traité consistait en un serment de fidélité et d'obéissance à Innocent VI et à ses successeurs, les pontifes suprêmes de l'Église catholique et romaine. L'empereur promettait de rendre à leurs nonces ou légats tous les honneurs auxquels ils pouvaient légitimement prétendre, de préparer un palais pour les recevoir, et une église pour leurs cérémonies; enfin de donner Manuel, son second fils, pour ôtage et garant de sa fidélité. Pour toutes ces concessions, il demandait un prompt secours de quinze galères avec cinq cents hommes d'armes et mille archers pour le défendre contre ses ennemis chrétiens et musulmans. Paléologue promit de soumettre ses peuples et son clergé au joug spirituel du pontife romain. Mais pour vaincre la résistance qu'il prévoyait de la part des Grecs, il proposa les deux moyens efficaces de l'éducation et de la séduction. Le légat fut autorisé à distribuer les bénéfices vacans parmi les ecclésiastiques qui souscriraient au symbole du Vatican. On institua trois écoles pour enseigner à la jeunesse de Constantinople la langue et la doctrine des Latins, et le nom d'Andronic, héritier de l'empire, parut le premier sur la liste des étudians. Paléologue déclarait que si tous ses efforts devenaient superflus, si la force et la persuasion se trouvaient insuffisantes, il se croirait in-

---

ment tiré des archives du Vatican. Il ne vaut pas la peine d'avoir été contrefait.

digne de régner. Il transférait dans ce cas à Innocent toute son autorité royale et paternelle, lui donnant plein pouvoir de diriger sa famille et son royaume, et de marier Andronic son fils et son successeur. Mais ce traité n'eut jamais ni exécution ni publicité. Le secours des Romains et la soumission des Grecs n'existèrent que dans l'imagination de leur souverain, que le secret sauva seul du déshonneur de cette inutile humiliation.

<small>Visite de Jean Paléologue à Urbain v, à Rome. A. D. 1369, octob. 9.</small>

Les armées victorieuses des Turcs fondirent bientôt sur lui. Après avoir perdu Andrinople et la Romanie, il se trouva resserré dans sa capitale, vassal de l'orgueilleux Amurath, et réduit à la misérable espérance de n'être que le dernier dévoré par ce sauvage. Dans cet état d'abaissement, Paléologue prit la résolution de s'embarquer pour Venise, d'où il alla se jeter aux pieds du pape. Il fut le premier souverain de Byzance qui eût jamais visité les régions inconnues de l'Occident; mais Paléologue ne pouvait espérer de trouver ailleurs des secours et de la consolation, et sa dignité était moins offensée de paraître dans le sacré collége qu'à la Porte ottomane. Après une longue absence, les papes retournaient alors des bords du Rhône sur ceux du Tibre : Urbain v (1),

---

(1) *Voyez* les deux Vies originales d'Urbain v dans Muratori (*Script. rerum italicar.*, t. III, part. II, p. 623-635), et les *Annales ecclésiastiques* de Spondanus (t. I, p. 573, A. D. 1369, n° 7); et Raynald (Fleury, *Hist. ecclés.*, t. xx, p. 223, 224). Cependant, d'après quelques contradictions,

pontife d'un caractère doux et vertueux, encouragea ou permit le pélerinage du prince grec ; et le palais du Vatican reçut dans la même année les deux fantômes d'empereurs qui représentaient la majesté de Constantin et de Charlemagne. Dans cette visite de supplication le souverain de Constantinople, dont le malheur absorbait la vanité, poussa la soumission des paroles et des formes au-delà de ce qu'on pouvait attendre : obligé de passer d'abord par un examen, il reconnut, en bon catholique, en présence de quatre cardinaux, la suprématie du pape et la double procession du Saint-Esprit. Après cette purification, on l'introduisit à une audience publique dans l'église de Saint-Pierre, où Urbain siégeait sur son trône, environné d'un cortége de cardinaux. Le prince grec, après trois génuflexions, baisa dévotement les pieds, les mains et enfin la bouche du saint père, qui célébra une grand'messe en sa présence, lui permit de tenir la bride de sa mule, et lui donna un repas somptueux dans le Vatican. Malgré cette réception amicale et honorable, Urbain accorda quelque préférence à l'empereur d'Occident (1), et Paléologue n'obtint point le rare privilége de chanter l'évangile en qualité de diacre (2). Urbain tâcha de

---

je soupçonne les historiens des papes d'avoir légèrement exagéré les génuflexions de Paléologue.

(1). *Paulò minùs quàm si fuisset imperator Romanorum.* Cependant on ne lui disputait plus son titre d'empereur des Grecs. *Vit. Urbani* v., p. 623.

(2) Elle était réservée aux successeurs de Charlemagne,

ranimer le zèle du roi de France et des autres souverains de l'Europe en faveur de son prosélyte ; mais ils étaient trop occupés de leurs querelles particulières pour penser à la cause générale. L'empereur fonda son dernier espoir sur un mercenaire anglais, Jean Hawkwood (1) ou Acuto, qui, suivi d'une bande d'aventuriers sous le nom de la *confrérie blanche*, avait ravagé toute l'Italie, depuis les Alpes jusqu'à la Calabre, vendait ses services à ceux qui voulaient les payer, et avait encouru une juste excommunication en attaquant la résidence du pape. Urbain autorisa cependant une négociation avec ce brigand ; mais les forces ou le courage d'Hawkwood se trouvèrent au-dessous de cette entreprise, et ce fut peut-être un bonheur pour Paléologue d'avoir manqué un secours probablement dispendieux, certainement

―――――――

et ils n'en pouvaient jouir que le jour de Noël : à toutes les autres fêtes, ces diacres couronnés se contentaient de présenter au pape le livre et le corporal lorsqu'il disait la messe. Cependant l'abbé de Sade a la générosité de croire qu'il est possible qu'on se soit relâché de cette règle en faveur du mérite de Charles IV, mais non pas le jour précis ; le 1er novembre 1368. L'abbé paraît apprécier au juste l'homme et le privilège. *Vie de Pétrarque*, t. III, p. 735.

(1) A travers la corruption de la dénomination italienne (Matthieu Villani, l. xi, c. 79, dans Muratori, t. xv, pag. 746), l'étymologie de *Falcone in bosco* nous donne le mot anglais Hawkwood, le véritable nom de notre audacieux compatriote (Thomas Walsingham, *Hist. anglican., inter scriptores Camdeni*, p. 184). Après vingt-deux victoires et une seule défaite, il mourut en 1394, général des Floren-

insuffisant, et peut-être dangereux (1). L'infortuné Grec se préparait à quitter l'Italie (2); mais il fût arrêté par un obstacle humiliant. En passant à Venise, il avait emprunté des sommes considérables à une usure exorbitante; ses coffres étaient vides, et ses créanciers inquiets le retinrent pour sûreté de leur paiement. En vain l'empereur pressait Andronic, régent du royaume, et son fils aîné, d'user de toutes les ressources et de dépouiller, s'il le fallait, les autels pour tirer son père d'une captivité ignominieuse. Insensible à la honte de son père, ce fils dénaturé se réjouissait secrètement de sa captivité. L'État était pauvre, le clergé opiniâtre; on ne pouvait même manquer au besoin de quelque scrupule religieux pour servir de masque à une criminelle in-

---

tins; et la république le fit inhumer avec des honneurs qu'elle n'avait point accordés au Dante ni à Pétrarque. Muratori, *Annali d'Italia*, t. XII, p. 212-371.

(1) Ce torrent d'Anglais, soit qu'ils le fussent de naissance ou seulement par la cause qu'ils avaient embrassée, tomba de France en Italie après la paix de Brétigny, en 1360. Muratori s'écrie (*Ann.*, t. XII, p. 197), avec plus de vérité que de politesse : *Ci mancava ancor questo, che dopo essere calpestrata l'Italia da tanti masnadieri Tedeschi ed Ungheri, venissero fin dall' Inghilterra nuovi cani a finire di divorarla.*

(2) Chalcocondyles; liv. 1, p. 25, 26. Le Grec prétend qu'il fit une visite à la cour de France; mais le silence des historiens nationaux le réfute suffisamment. Je ne suis pas beaucoup plus disposé à croire qu'il quitta l'Italie, *valdè benè consolatus et contentus* (*Vit. Urbani* v, p. 623).

différence. Manuel, frère d'Andronic, après lui avoir sévèrement reproché cette négligence si contraire à son devoir, vendit ou engagea ce qu'il possédait, s'embarqua pour Venise, délivra son père, et s'offrit lui-même pour sûreté de la dette. De retour à Constantinople, comme empereur et comme père, Paléologue traita ses deux fils chacun selon leur mérite. Mais le pèlerinage de Rome n'avait réformé ni la foi ni les mœurs de l'indolent Paléologue, et son apostasie ou conversion, dépourvue d'effets comme de sincérité, fut promptement oubliée des Grecs et des Latins (1).

Son retour à Constantinople. A. D. 1370.

Voyage de Manuel en Occident.

Trente ans après le retour de Paléologue, le même motif fit entreprendre, mais avec plus d'étendue, le voyage de l'Occident à Manuel, son successeur. J'ai raconté, dans le chapitre précédent, son traité avec Bajazet, l'infraction du traité, le siége ou blocus de Constantinople, et le secours que les Français envoyèrent sous les ordres du vaillant Boucicault (2). Manuel avait sollicité, par ses ambassadeurs, l'aide des princes latins; mais on imagina que la présence d'un monarque infortuné arracherait des larmes et des secours aux Barbares les plus durs (3);

---

(1) Son retour à Constantinople en 1370, et le couronnement de Manuel, 25 septembre 1373 (Ducange, *Famil. Byzant.*, p. 241), laisse un intervalle pour la conspiration et le châtiment d'Andronic.

(2) *Mém. de Boucicault*, p. 1, c. 35, 36.

(3) Chalcocondyles (l. 11, c. 44-50) et Ducas (c. 14)

et le maréchal, qui lui conseillait ce voyage, le précéda pour préparer sa réception. Les Turcs interceptaient la communication par terre; mais la navigation de Venise était ouverte et sûre. On le reçut en Italie comme le premier, ou du moins comme le second des princes chrétiens. Manuel inspira la compassion comme confesseur et champion de la foi, et la dignité de sa conduite empêcha que cette compassion ne dégénérât en mépris. De Venise, il passa successivement à Padoue et à Pavie. Le duc de Milan, quoique allié secret de Bajazet, le fit conduire honorablement jusqu'aux frontières de ses États (1). Lorsqu'il entra sur les terres (2) de France, les officiers du roi se chargèrent de l'accompagner et de le défrayer. Une cavalcade de deux mille des plus riches citoyens de Paris alla en armes au devant de lui jusqu'à Charenton. Aux portes de Paris, il fut complimenté par le chancelier et le parlement, et

A la cour de France. A. D. 1400, 3 juin.

parlent légèrement; et, à ce qu'il semble, avec répugnance, de son voyage dans l'Occident.

(1) Muratori, *Annali d'Italia*, t. XII, p. 406. Jean Galeazzo fut le premier et le plus puissant des ducs de Milan. Ses liaisons avec Bajazet sont attestées par Froissard; et il contribua à sauver ou à délivrer les prisonniers français de Nicopolis.

(2) Pour la réception de Manuel à Paris, *voyez* Spondanus (*Annal. ecclés.*, t. I, p. 676, 677; A. D. 1400, n° 5), qui cite Juvénal des Ursins et les moines de Saint-Denis, et Villaret (*Hist. de France*, t. XII, p. 331-334), qui ne cite personne, conformément à la nouvelle mode des écrivains français.

Charles vi, suivi des princes et de la noblesse, embrassa son frère avec cordialité. On revêtit le successeur de Constantin d'une robe de soie blanche, et on lui présenta pour monture un superbe cheval blanc. Ce cérémonial n'est point indifférent chez les Français : on y considère la couleur blanche comme le symbole de la souveraineté ; et l'empereur d'Allemagne, après avoir réclamé avec hauteur cette distinction dans sa dernière visite et avoir éprouvé un refus positif, avait été contraint de monter un cheval noir. Manuel logea au Louvre ; les bals et les fêtes se succédèrent avec rapidité ; les Français cherchèrent, en variant ingénieusement les plaisirs de la chasse et de la table, à déployer leur magnificence aux yeux du prince étranger, et à le distraire un instant de sa douleur. On lui accorda l'usage particulier d'une chapelle, et les docteurs de Sorbonne observèrent avec surprise, et peut-être avec scandale, le langage, les cérémonies et les vêtemens du clergé grec. Mais du premier coup d'œil il put apercevoir qu'il n'avait point de secours à espérer de la France : l'infortuné Charles vi ne jouissait que de quelques instans lucides, et retombait sans cesse dans un état de frénésie ou de stupidité. Le duc d'Orléans, son frère, et son oncle le duc de Bourgogne, saisissaient alternativement les rênes du gouvernement ; la guerre civile fut bientôt la suite de leur désastreuse concurrence. Le premier, jeune et d'un caractère ardent, se livrait avec impétuosité à sa passion pour les femmes et pour tous les plaisirs. Le second était père de Jean, comte de Nevers, délivré récemment de sa captivité chez les Turcs. Ce jeune prince intrépide aurait volontiers couru de nouveaux hasards pour effacer sa honte; mais son père, plus prudent, en avait assez des frais et des dangers de la première expérience. Lorsque Manuel eut satisfait la curiosité et peut-être fatigué la patience des Français, il résolut de passer en Angleterre. Sur la route de Douvres à Londres, le prieur et les moines de Saint-Augustin lui firent à Cantorbéry une réception honorable. A Blackheath, il trouva le roi Henri IV, qui, suivi de toute sa cour, vint saluer le roi grec, dit notre vieil historien, dont je transcris exactement les expressions, et fut traité à Londres, durant plusieurs jours, comme l'empereur de l'Orient (1). Mais l'Angleterre était encore moins disposée que la France à entreprendre une croisade. Dans cette même année, le souverain légitime avait été déposé et mis à mort. L'ambitieux usurpateur, Henri de Lancastre, en proie à l'inquiétude et aux remords, n'osait éloigner ses troupes d'un trône con-

A la cour d'Angleterre.
A. D. 1400, décembre.

(1) Le docteur Hody a tiré d'un manuscrit de Lambeth (*de Græcis illustribus*) une note sur le séjour de Manuel en Angleterre. *Imperator, diu variisque et horrendis paganorum insultibus coarctatus, ut pro eisdem resistentiam triumphalem perquireret, Anglorum regem visitare decrevit*, etc. *Rex* (dit Walsingham, p. 364) *nobili apparatu.... suscepit (ut decuit) tantum heroa; duxitque Londonias, et per multos dies exhibuit gloriose, pro expensis hospitii sui solvens, et eum respiciens tanto fastigio donativis*. Il répète la même chose dans son *Upodigma Neustriæ* (p. 556).

tinuellement ébranlé par des révoltes et des conspirations : il plaignit, loua et fêta l'empereur de Constantinople ; mais s'il fit vœu de prendre la croix, ce fut sans doute pour apaiser son peuple et peut-être sa conscience par le mérite ou l'apparence de ce pieux projet (1). Comblé cependant de présens et d'honneurs, le prince grec fit une seconde visite à Paris, et, après avoir passé deux années dans les cours de l'Occident, il traversa l'Allemagne et l'Italie, s'embarqua à Venise, et attendit patiemment dans la Morée le moment de sa ruine ou de sa délivrance. Il avait cependant échappé à la nécessité ignominieuse de vendre sa religion, soit publiquement, soit en secret. Le schisme déchirait l'Église latine : deux papes, l'un à Rome et l'autre à Avignon, se disputaient l'obéissance des rois, des nations et des universités de l'Europe. L'empereur grec, attentif à ménager les deux partis, s'abstint de toute correspondance avec ces deux rivaux, tous deux indignes et peu favorisés de l'opinion. Il partit au moment du jubilé, et traversa toute l'Italie sans demander ou mériter l'indulgence plénière, qui efface les péchés des fidèles et les dispense de la pénitence. Cette négligence offensa le pape de Rome ; il accusa Manuel d'irrévérence pour l'image du Christ, et exhorta les

---

(1) Shakspeare commence et termine la tragédie de *Henri IV* par le vœu que fit ce prince de prendre la croix, et le pressentiment qu'il avait de mourir à Jérusalem.

princes de l'Italie à abandonner un schismatique obstiné (1).

A l'époque des croisades, les Grecs avaient contemplé avec autant de terreur que de surprise le cours perpétuel des émigrations qui ne cessaient de s'écouler des pays inconnus de l'Occident. Les visites de leurs derniers empereurs déchirèrent le voile de séparation, et leur découvrirent les puissantes nations de l'Europe, qu'ils n'osèrent plus insulter du nom de barbares. Un historien grec de ce siècle (2) a conservé les observations du prince Manuel et des observateurs plus curieux qui l'accompagnaient. Je vais rassembler ces idées éparses et les présenter en raccourci à mon lecteur. Peut-être ne verra-t-il pas sans plaisir ce tableau grossier de l'Allemagne, de la

Connaissances et descriptions des Grecs.

---

(1) Ce fait est rapporté dans l'*Historia politica*, A. D. 1391-1478, publiée par Martin Crusius (*Turco-Græcia*, p. 1-43). L'image du Christ, à laquelle l'empereur refusa ses hommages, était probablement un ouvrage de sculpture.

(2) Laonicus Chalcocondyles termine son histoire des Grecs et des Ottomans à l'hiver de 1463, et sa conclusion précipitée semble annoncer qu'il cessa d'écrire dans cette même année. Nous savons qu'il était d'Athènes, et que quelques contemporains du même nom contribuèrent à la renaissance de l'idiome grec dans l'Italie. Mais dans ses nombreuses digressions, cet historien a toujours eu la modestie de ne jamais parler de lui-même. Leunclavius, son éditeur, et Fabricius (*Bibl. græc.*, t. VI, p. 474) paraissent ignorer tout-à-fait son état et l'histoire de sa vie. Pour ses descriptions de l'Allemagne, de la France et de l'Angleterre, *voyez* l. II, p. 36, 37, 44-50.

De l'Allemagne.

France et de l'Angleterre, dont l'état ancien et moderne nous est si bien connu. « 1° L'Allemagne, dit Chalcocondyles, offre un vaste pays, et s'étend depuis Vienne jusqu'à l'Océan, depuis Prague en Bohême jusqu'à la rivière Tartessus et aux (1) Pyrénées (cette géographie paraîtra sans doute un peu extraordinaire). Le sol est assez fertile, quoiqu'il ne produise ni figues ni olives ; l'air y est sain, les hommes sont robustes et d'une santé vigoureuse. On éprouve rarement, dans ces contrées septentrionales, les calamités de la peste ou des tremblemens de terre. Après les Scythes ou les Tartares, on peut regarder les Allemands ou Germains comme la nation la plus nombreuse. Ils sont braves et patiens ; et si toutes leurs forces obéissaient à un seul chef, elles seraient irrésistibles. Ils ont obtenu du pape le privilége d'élire l'empereur des Romains (2), et le patriarché latin n'a point de sujets plus zélés et plus soumis. La plus

---

(1) Je ne relèverai point les erreurs de la géographie de Chalcocondyles. Dans cette description il a peut-être suivi et mal compris Hérodote (l. II, c. 33), dont on peut interpréter le texte (*Hérodote* de Larcher, t. II, p. 219-220) ou excuser l'ignorance. Ces Grecs modernes n'avaient-ils donc jamais lu Strabon ni aucun de leurs géographes?.

(2) Un citoyen de la nouvelle Rome, tant que cette nouvelle Rome subsista, n'aurait pas daigné honorer le ρηξ allemand du titre de βασιλευς ou αυτοκρατωρ Ρωμαιων ; mais Chalcocondyles avait dépouillé toute vanité, et il désigne le prince de Byzance et ses sujets sous les dénominations exactes et humbles de Ελληνες et βασιλευς Ελληνων.

grande partie de ces pays est divisée entre des princes et des prélats ; mais Strasbourg, Cologne, Hambourg, et plus de deux cents villes libres forment autant de républiques confédérées, régies par des lois sages et justes, conformes à la volonté et à l'intérêt général. Les duels, ou combats singuliers à pied, y sont d'un usage familier en temps de paix et de guerre. Les Allemands excellent dans tous les arts mécaniques ; c'est à leur industrie que nous devons l'invention de la poudre et des canons, connus aujourd'hui de la plus grande partie des nations. 2° Le royaume de France s'étend environ à quinze ou vingt jours de marche depuis l'Allemagne jusqu'à l'Espagne, et depuis les Alpes jusqu'à la mer, qui la sépare de l'Angleterre : on y trouve un grand nombre de villes florissantes. Paris, la résidence des rois, surpasse toutes les autres en luxe et en richesses. Un grand nombre de princes et de seigneurs se rendent alternativement dans le palais du monarque, et le reconnaissent pour leur souverain. Les plus puissans sont les ducs de Bretagne et de Bourgogne : le dernier possède les riches provinces de Flandre, dont les ports sont fréquentés par nos commerçans et par les négocians des pays les plus éloignés. La nation française est ancienne et opulente ; sa langue et ses mœurs, bien qu'avec quelque différence, ne s'éloignent pas entièrement de celles des Italiens. La dignité impériale de Charlemagne, leurs victoires sur les Sarrasins, et les exploits de leurs héros Olivier et Ro-

De la France.

land (1), les enorgueillissent au point qu'ils se regardent comme le premier peuple de l'Occident; mais cette vanité insensée a été récemment humiliée par l'événement malheureux de leur guerre contre les Anglais qui habitent l'île de la Bretagne. 3° On peut considérer la Bretagne au milieu de l'Océan, et vis-à-vis les côtes de la Flandre, comme une ou comme trois îles réunies par l'uniformité de mœurs et de langage sous le même gouvernement. Sa circonférence est de cinq mille stades; le pays, couvert d'un grand nombre de villes et de villages, produit peu de fruits et point de vin, mais il abonde en orge, en froment, en miel et en laines. Les habitans fabriquent une grande quantité de draps et d'étoffes; Londres (2), leur capitale, l'emporte, pour le luxe, la richesse et la population, sur toutes les villes de

De l'Angleterre.

---

(1) On traduisait dans le quatorzième siècle la plupart des vieux romans en prose française, et ils devinrent la lecture favorite des chevaliers et des dames de la cour de Charles VI. Un Grec est sûrement plus excusable d'avoir cru aux exploits d'Olivier et de Roland, que les moines de Saint-Denis d'avoir inséré dans leur Chronique de France les fables de l'archevêque Turpin.

(2) Λονδινη.... δε τε πτολις δυναμει τε προεχουσα των εν τη νησω ταυτη πασων πολεων, ολϐω τε και τη αλλη ευδαιμονια ουδεμιας των προς εσπεραν λειπομενη. Dès le temps de Fitz-Stephen ou le douzième siècle, Londres paraît avoir joui de cette supériorité en richesse et en grandeur; elle l'a conservée depuis en augmentant son étendue progressivement, au moins dans la même proportion que les autres capitales de l'Europe.

l'Occident. Elle est située sur la Tamise, rivière large et rapide., qui, à la distance de trente milles, se jette dans la mer des Gaules. Le flux et le reflux offrent tous les jours aux vaisseaux de commerce la facilité d'entrer et de sortir sans danger de son port. Le roi est le chef d'une puissante et turbulente aristocratie. Ses premiers vassaux possèdent leurs fiefs en franc-aleu héréditaire; et les lois fixent les limites de son autorité et de leur obéissance. Ce royaume a été souvent déchiré par des factions, et conquis par des étrangers; mais les habitans sont courageux, robustes, renommés dans les armes et victorieux à la guerre. Leurs boucliers ressemblent à ceux des Italiens, et leur épée à celle des Grecs. Leurs principales forces consistent dans la supériorité de leurs archers. Leur langage n'a aucune affinité avec celui du continent; mais leurs habitudes de vie diffèrent peu de celles des Français. On peut regarder le mépris de la chasteté des femmes et de l'honneur conjugal comme la principale singularité de leurs mœurs. Dans leurs visites réciproques, le premier acte d'hospitalité est de permettre à leurs hôtes les embrassemens de leurs femmes et de leurs filles. Entre amis, ils les empruntent et les prêtent sans honte, sans que personne soit blessé de cet étrange commerce et de ses suites inévitables (1). » Instruits

---

(1) En admettant que le double sens du verbe κύω (*osculor* et *in utero gero*) fût susceptible d'une équivoque, on ne pourrait pas douter de l'erreur et du sens de Chalco-

comme nous le sommes des usages de la vieille Angleterre, et sûrs de la vertu de nos mères, nous pouvons sourire de la crédulité, ou nous indigner de l'injustice de l'historien grec, qui a confondu sans doute un baiser (1) décent de réception, avec des familiarités criminelles ; mais cette injustice ou cette crédulité peuvent nous être utiles en nous apprenant à nous méfier des détails donnés par des voyageurs sur des nations étrangères et éloignées, et à ne pas croire légèrement des faits qui répugnent au caractère de l'homme et aux sentimens de la nature (2).

<small>Indifférence de Manuel pour les Latins.
A. D. 1402-1417.</small>

Après son retour et la victoire de Timour, Manuel régna plusieurs années heureux et paisible. Tant que les fils de Bajazet recherchèrent son amitié et ménagèrent ses faibles États, il se contenta de son ancienne religion, et composa dans ses loisirs vingt dialogues théologiques pour sa défense. L'arrivée des ambassa-

---

condyles, d'après la pieuse horreur qu'il annonce pour cet usage barbare (p. 49).

(1) Érasme (*epist. Fausto Andrelino*) parle d'une manière agréable de la mode anglaise de baiser les étrangers à leur arrivée et à leur départ, mais n'en tire aucune mauvaise supposition.

(2) Nous pourrions peut-être appliquer cette observation à la communauté des femmes que César et Dion-Cassius supposent avoir existé parmi les anciens Bretons (l. LXII, t. II, p. 1007). *Voyez* Dion, avec les remarques judicieuses de Reimar. Les *Arreoy* d'Otahiti, qu'on regardait d'abord comme de la plus grande évidence, nous paraissent moins criminels à mesure que nous acquérons la connaissance des mœurs de ce peuple amoureux et pacifique.

deurs grecs au concile de Constance (1), annonça le rétablissement de la puissance ottomane en même temps que celle de l'Église latine : les conquêtes d'Amurath et de Mahomet rapprochèrent l'empereur du Vatican ; le siége de Constantinople fit presque acquiescer à la double procession du Saint-Esprit ; et lorsque, débarrassé de ses rivaux, Martin v occupa seul la chaire pontificale, il se rétablit entre l'Orient et l'Occident un commerce amical de lettres et d'ambassades. L'ambition d'une part, et de l'autre l'infortune, dictaient un même langage de paix et de charité. Manuel affectait le désir de marier les six princes ses fils à des princesses italiennes, et le pape, non moins rusé, fit passer à Constantinople la fille du marquis de Montferrat avec un cortége séduisant de jeunes filles de haute naissance, dont les charmes lui paraissaient propres à vaincre l'obstination des schismatiques. Sous l'extérieur du zèle, on pouvait cependant apercevoir que tout était faux à la cour et dans l'Église de Constantinople. Selon que le danger paraissait plus ou moins pressant, l'empereur précipitait ou prolongeait ses négociations, autorisait ou désavouait ses ministres, et échappait à des instances trop pressantes en alléguant la néces-

Ses négociations.
A. D. 1417-1425.

---

(1) *Voyez* Lenfant (*Hist. du Concile de Constance*, t. II, p. 576), et pour l'histoire ecclésiastique du temps, les *Annales* de Spondanus, la bibliothèque de Dupin (t. XII) et les vingt-un et vingt-deuxième volumes de l'histoire ou plutôt de la continuation de Fleury.

sité de consulter les patriarches et les prélats, et l'impossibilité de les assembler dans un moment où les Turcs environnaient la capitale. D'après l'examen des transactions publiques, il paraît que les Grecs insistaient sur trois opérations successives, un secours, un concile et enfin la réunion, tandis que les Latins éludaient la seconde, et ne voulaient s'engager à la première que comme une suite et une récompense volontaire de la troisième ; mais l'extrait d'une conversation particulière de Manuel nous expliquera plus clairement l'énigme de sa conduite et ses véritables intentions. Sur la fin de ses jours, l'empereur avait revêtu de la pourpre Jean Paléologue II, son fils aîné, sur lequel il se reposait de la plus grande partie du gouvernement. Dans un de ses entretiens avec son collègue, où il n'avait pour témoin que l'historien Phranza, son chambellan favori (1), Manuel développa à son successeur les vrais motifs de ses négociations avec le pontife de Rome (2).

<small>Conversation particulière de l'empereur Manuel.</small>

---

(1) Dès sa première jeunesse Georges Phranza ou Phranzès fut employé au service de l'État et du palais ; et Hanckius (*de Script. byzant.*, part. 1, c. 40) a recueilli sa vie de ses propres écrits. Il n'était âgé que de vingt-quatre ans lorsque Manuel, en mourant, le recommanda à son successeur dans les termes les plus forts. *Imprimis verò hunc Phranzen tibi commendo, qui ministravit mihi fideliter et diligenter* (Phranza, l. II, c. 1). L'empereur Jean lui montra cependant de la froideur, et préféra le service des despotes du Péloponèse.

(2) *Voyez* Phranza, l. II, c. 13. Tandis qu'il existe tant

« Il ne nous reste, dit Manuel, pour toute ressource contre les Turcs, que la crainte de notre réunion avec les Latins, la terreur que leur inspirent les belliqueuses nations de l'Occident, qui pourraient se liguer pour notre délivrance et leur destruction. Dès que vous serez pressé par les infidèles, faites-leur envisager ce danger. Proposez un concile, entrez en négociations; mais prolongez-les toujours et éludez la convocation de cette assemblée, qui ne vous serait d'aucune utilité spirituelle ou temporelle. Aucun des deux partis ne voudra reculer ou se rétracter; les Latins sont orgueilleux, les Grecs sont obstinés. En voulant accomplir la réunion, vous ne feriez que confirmer le schisme, aliéner les Églises, et nous exposer sans ressource et sans espoir à la merci des Barbares. » Peu satisfait de cette sage leçon, le jeune prince se leva et sortit en silence. Le prudent monarque, continue Phranza, me regarda, et reprit ainsi son discours : « Mon fils se croit grand et héroïque; mais, hélas! ce siècle misérable n'offre aucun champ à l'héroïsme ni à la grandeur. Son esprit audacieux pouvait convenir dans les temps plus heureux de nos ancêtres. Notre situation présente exige moins un empereur qu'un économe circonspect des

---

de manuscrits grecs dans les bibliothèques de Rome, de Milan, de l'Escurial, c'est une honte que nous soyons réduits à des traductions latines et aux extraits de Jacques Pontanus (*ad calcem Theophylact. Simocattæ;* Ingolstadt, 1604) qui manquent également d'élégance et d'exactitude. Fabricius, *Bibl. græc.*, t. VI; p. 615-620.

débris de notre fortune. Je n'ai point oublié les vastes espérances qu'il fondait sur notre alliance avec Mustapha, et je crains que sa témérité imprudente ou même sa piété ne précipite la ruine de notre maison et de la monarchie. » L'expérience et l'autorité de Manuel éludèrent cependant le concile et conservèrent la paix jusqu'à la soixante-dix-huitième année de son âge ; dans laquelle il expira revêtu d'un habit monastique, après avoir distribué ses meubles précieux à ses enfans, aux pauvres, à ses médecins et à ses domestiques favoris. Andronic (1), son second fils, eut pour sa part la principauté de Thessalonique, et mourut de la lèpre peu de temps après avoir vendu cette ville aux Vénitiens, qui en furent promptement dépouillés par les Turcs. Quelques succès avaient réuni le Péloponèse ou Morée à l'empire, et dans des temps plus heureux, Manuel avait fortifié l'isthme, dans une étendue de six milles (2), d'un mur solide, flanqué de cent cinquante-trois tours, qui disparut à la première irruption des Ottomans. La fertile péninsule aurait pu suffire aux quatre jeunes princes, Théodore, Constantin, Démétrius et

Mort de l'empereur Manuel.

---

(1) *Voyez* Ducange, *Fam. byzant.*, p. 243-248.

(2) L'étendue exacte de l'Hexamilion entre les deux mers était de trois mille huit cents orgyiæ ou toises de six pieds grecs (Phranza, l. 1, c. 38), ce qui produit un mille grec plus court que celui de six cent soixante toises de France, que d'Anville prétend être en usage dans la Turquie. On évalue communément la largeur de l'isthme à cinq milles. *Voyez* les *Voyages* de Spon, Wheeler et Chandler.

Thomas; mais ils épuisèrent les restes de leurs forces en guerres civiles, et les vaincus se réfugièrent dans le palais de Constantinople, où ils vécurent sous la protection et la dépendance de leur frère Jean Paléologue II.

Ce prince, l'aîné des fils de Manuel, fut reconnu, après la mort de son père, pour seul empereur des Grecs. Il s'occupa d'abord de répudier son épouse et de contracter un nouveau mariage avec la princesse de Trébisonde. La beauté était à ses yeux la plus indispensable qualité d'une impératrice. Il obtint l'aveu de son clergé, en le menaçant de se retirer dans un cloître, et d'abandonner le trône à son frère Constantin, si on refusait de consentir à son divorce. La première, ou pour mieux dire la seule victoire de Paléologue, fut celle qu'il remporta sur un Juif (1), qu'après une longue et savante dispute, il convertit à la foi chrétienne : cette importante conquête a été soigneusement consignée dans l'histoire du temps; mais il renouvela bientôt le projet de réunir les deux Églises, et, sans égard pour les avis de son père, prêta l'oreille, à ce qu'il paraît de bonne foi, à la proposition de s'aboucher avec le pape dans un concile général au-delà de la mer Adriatique. Martin v

Zèle de Jean Paléologue II.
A. D.
1425-1437.

---

(1) La première objection des Juifs est sur la mort de Jésus-Christ : si elle fut volontaire, le Christ est coupable de suicide ; à quoi l'empereur oppose un mystère. Ils disputent ensuite sur la conception de la Vierge, sur le sens des prophéties, etc. Phranza, l. II, c. 12, jusqu'à la fin du chapitre.

encourageait ce dangereux projet, et son successeur Eugène s'en occupa faiblement, jusqu'à ce qu'enfin, après une négociation languissante, l'empereur reçut une sommation de la part d'une assemblée revêtue d'un caractère différent, celle des prélats indépendans de Bâle, qui s'intitulaient les représentans et les juges de l'Église catholique.

<small>Corruption de l'Église latine.</small>

Le pontife romain avait défendu et gagné la cause de la liberté ecclésiastique; mais le clergé victorieux se trouva bientôt exposé à la tyrannie de son libérateur, que son caractère sacré mettait à l'abri des armes qu'il employait si efficacement contre les magistrats civils. Les appels anéantissaient leur grande charte où le droit d'élection; on l'éludait par des *commendes*, on le déjouait par des survivances, et il était obligé de céder à des réserves arbitraires (1). La cour de Rome institua une vente publique qui enrichissait les cardinaux et les favoris du pape des dépouilles de toutes les nations; celles-ci voyaient les principaux bénéfices de leur territoire s'accumuler sur la tête des étrangers et des absens. Durant leur résidence à Avignon, l'ambition des papes se

---

(1) Dans le Traité *delle Materie Beneficiarie* de Fra Paolo (quatrième volume de la dernière et la meilleure édition de ses OEuvres), il développe avec autant de liberté que de profondeur tout le système politique des papes. Quand Rome et sa religion seraient anéanties, ce volume précieux leur survivrait comme une excellente histoire philosophique et un avertissement salutaire.

convertit en avarice et en débauche (1). Ils imposaient rigoureusement sur le clergé le tribut des dîmes et des premiers fruits ; mais ils toléraient ouvertement l'impunité des vices, des désordres et de la corruption. Ces scandales multipliés furent aggravés par le grand schisme d'Occident, qui dura plus d'un demi-siècle. Dans leurs fougueuses querelles, les deux pontifes de Rome et d'Avignon publiaient réciproquement les vices de leur rival; leur situation précaire avilissait leur autorité, relâchait leur discipline et multipliait leurs besoins et leurs exactions. Les synodes de Pise et de Constance (2) furent successivement tenus pour guérir les maux de l'Église et rétablir son autorité; mais, sentant leurs forces, ces grandes assemblées résolurent de rétablir les privilèges de l'aristocratie chrétienne. Les pères de Constance prononcèrent une sentence personnelle contre deux pontifes qu'ils refusaient de reconnaître;

<small>Schisme.
A. D.
1377-1429.

Concile de Pise.
A. D. 1409;
de Constance.
A. D.
1414-1418.</small>

---

(1) Le pape Jean XXII, lorsqu'il mourut à Avignon en 1334, laissa dix-huit millions de florins d'or, et la valeur de sept millions de plus en argenterie et en bijoux. *Voyez* la *Chronique* de Jean Villani (l. XI, c. 20, dans la Collection de Muratori, t. XIII, p. 765), dont le frère apprit ces détails des trésoriers du pape. Un trésor de six ou huit millions sterling, dans le quatorzième siècle, paraît énorme et presque incroyable.

(2) M. Lenfant, protestant instruit et éclairé, a donné une *Histoire des Conciles de Pise, de Constance et de Bâle*, en six volumes *in-quarto;* mais la dernière partie est faite à la hâte, et ne traite complétement que des troubles de la Bohême.

et déposèrent par une troisième celui qu'ils avaient avoué pour leur souverain. Ils procédèrent ensuite à limiter l'autorité du pape, et ne se séparèrent point qu'ils ne l'eussent soumis à la suprématie d'un concile général. On statua que pour la réforme et le maintien de l'Église, on convoquerait régulièrement ces assemblées à une époque fixe, et que chaque synode indiquerait, avant de se dissoudre, le temps et le lieu de l'assemblée suivante. La cour de Rome éluda facilement la convocation du concile de Sienne; mais la vigoureuse fermeté de celui de Bâle (1) pensa être fatale à Eugène IV, le pontife régnant. Les pères, qui pressentaient ses desseins, se hâtèrent de publier, par leur premier décret, que les représentans de l'Église militante étaient revêtus d'une juridiction spirituelle ou divine sur tous les chrétiens, sans en excepter le pape, et qu'on ne pouvait dissoudre, proroger ni transférer un concile général, qu'après la délibération libre de ses membres, suivie de leur consentement. Eugène n'ayant pas moins fulminé sa bulle de dissolution, ils osèrent sommer, répri-

De Bâle.
A. D.
1431-1443.

---

(1) Les actes originaux ou minutes du concile de Bâle composent douze volumes *in-folio*, que l'on conserve dans la bibliothèque publique. Bâle était une ville libre, avantageusement située sur le Rhin, et défendue par la confédération des Suisses ses voisins. Le pape Pie II, qui, sous le nom d'Æneas Sylvius, avait été secrétaire du concile, fonda en 1459 l'université. Mais qu'est-ce qu'un concile ou une université, en comparaison des presses de Froben, ou des études d'Érasme?

mander et menacer le rebelle, successeur de saint
Pierre : après lui avoir accordé par de longs délais
le temps du repentir, ils déclarèrent finalement que
s'il ne se soumettait pas avant le terme fixe de
soixante jours, il demeurerait suspendu de toute
autorité temporelle et ecclésiastique ; et pour établir
leur juridiction sur le prince comme sur le prêtre, ils
s'emparèrent de l'administration du gouvernement
d'Avignon, annulèrent l'aliénation du patrimoine
sacré, et défendirent de lever à Rome de nouvelles
contributions. Leur hardiesse fut justifiée, non-seulement par l'opinion générale du clergé, mais par
l'approbation et la protection des premiers monarques de la chrétienté. L'empereur Sigismond se déclara le serviteur et le défenseur du synode ; l'Allemagne et la France en firent autant ; le duc de Milan
était l'ennemi personnel d'Eugène ; et une émeute du
peuple romain força le pontife à fuir du Vatican.
Rejeté à la fois par ses sujets spirituels et temporels,
il ne lui resta d'autre parti à prendre que celui de la
soumission. Eugène se rétracta dans une bulle humiliante, qui ratifiait tous les actes du concile, in-
corporait ses légats et les cardinaux à cette assemblée
vénérable, et semblait annoncer sa résignation aux
décrets d'une législature suprême. Leur renommée
s'étendit jusque dans l'Orient, et ce fut en présence
des pères du concile que Sigismond reçut les ambassadeurs ottomans (1), qui mirent à ses pieds douze

Ils se dé-
clarent
contre Eu-
gène IV.

---

(1) L'annaliste Spondanus (A. D. 1433, n° 25, t. 1, p. 824.)

grands vases remplis de robes de soie et de pièces d'or. Les pères de Bâle aspiraient à la gloire de ramener les Grecs et les Bohémiens dans le giron de l'Église; leurs députés pressèrent l'empereur et le patriarche de Constantinople de se réunir à une assemblée qui possédait la confiance des nations de l'Occident. Paléologue n'était point éloigné d'accepter cette proposition, et le sénat catholique reçut honorablement ses ambassadeurs; mais le choix du lieu parut un obstacle insurmontable : il refusait obstinément de traverser les Alpes ou la mer de Sicile, et exigeait qu'on assemblât le concile dans quelque ville de l'Italie ou dans les environs du Danube. Les autres articles éprouvèrent moins de difficultés : on convint de défrayer l'empereur et une suite de sept cents personnes durant son voyage (1), de lui faire remettre sur-le-champ une somme de huit mille ducats (2) pour aider son clergé, et

Négociations avec les Grecs.
A. D.
1434-1437.

---

raconte, d'une manière peu affirmative, cette ambassade ottomane, qui n'est attestée que par Crantzius.

(1) Syropulus, p. 19. Il paraît par cette liste que les Grecs exagérèrent le nombre des laïques et des ecclésiastiques qui suivirent réellement l'empereur et le patriarche; mais le grand ecclésiarque n'en donne point le compte exact. Les soixante-quinze mille florins qu'ils demandaient au pape, dans cette négociation (p. 9), formaient une somme au-dessus de leurs besoins, et qu'ils ne pouvaient espérer d'obtenir.

(2) Je me sers indifféremment des mots *ducat* ou *florin*, qui tirent leur dénomination, les premiers, des ducs de

d'accorder dans son absence un secours de dix mille ducats, de trois cents archers et de quelques galères, pour la sûreté de Constantinople. La ville d'Avignon fit les fonds des premières avances, et l'on prépara l'embarquement à Marseille, quoique avec un peu de lenteur et de difficulté.

Dans sa triste situation, Paléologue jouissait du plaisir de voir les puissances ecclésiastiques de l'Occident rechercher à l'envi son amitié. Mais l'artificieuse activité d'un monarque l'emporta sur la lenteur et l'inflexibilité qui forment le caractère des républiques. Les décrets de Bâle tendaient continuellement à limiter le despotisme du pape, et à élever dans l'Église un tribunal suprême et permanent. Eugène portait le joug avec impatience, et l'union des Grecs lui fournissait un prétexte décent pour transporter du Rhin sur le Pô un synode indocile et factieux. Au-delà des Alpes, les pères n'espéraient plus de conserver leur indépendance. La Savoie ou Avignon, qu'ils acceptèrent avec répugnance, étaient regardés à Constantinople comme situés fort au-delà des colonnes d'Hercule (1). L'empereur et son clergé redou-

Jean Paléologue s'embarque sur les galères du pape. A. D. 1437, 24 nov.

Milan, et les seconds, de la république de Florence. Ces pièces d'or, les premières qui furent frappées en Italie et peut-être dans le monde latin, peuvent être comparées, pour le poids et la valeur, au tiers d'une guinée d'Angleterre.

(1) A la fin de la traduction latine de Phranza on trouve une longue épître grecque, ou déclamation de George de Trébisonde, qui conseille à Paléologue de préférer Eugène

taient les dangers d'une longue navigation; ils s'offensèrent de l'orgueilleuse déclaration par laquelle le concile annonça qu'après avoir anéanti la nouvelle hérésie des Bohémiens, il déracinerait bientôt l'ancienne hérésie des Grecs (1). Du côté d'Eugène, tout était douceur, complaisance et respect. Il invitait le souverain de Constantinople à faire cesser, par sa présence, le schisme des Latins comme celui des Grecs. Il proposa pour le lieu de leur entrevue amicale, Ferrare, située sur les bords de la mer Adriatique; et à l'aide d'une surprise ou de quelque artifice, il se procura un faux décret du concile qui approuvait sa translation dans cette ville de l'Italie. Neuf galères furent équipées pour cette expédition à Venise et dans l'île de Candie : elles devancèrent les vaisseaux de Bâle ; l'amiral romain reçut ordre de ceux-ci de les couler à fond, de les brûler et de les détruire (2) : ces escadres ecclésiastiques auraient pu

---

et l'Italie. Il parle avec mépris de l'assemblée schismatique de Bâle, des Barbares de la Gaule et de l'Allemagne, qui s'étaient ligués pour transporter la chaire de saint Pierre au-delà des Alpes : οι αθλιοι (dit-il) σε και την μετα σου συνοδον εξα των Ηρακλειων στηλων και περα Γαδηρων εξαξουσι. N'y avait-il donc point de carte géographique à Constantinople?

(1) Syropulus (p. 26-31) exprime son indignation et celle de ses compatriotes. Les députés de Bâle tâchèrent d'excuser cette imprudence, mais ils ne pouvaient nier ni changer l'acte du concile.

(2) Condolmieri, neveu et amiral du pape, déclare expressément, οτι ορισμον εχει παρα του παπα ινα πολεμηση οπου αν

se rencontrer dans les mêmes mers où Sparte et Athènes s'étaient disputé jadis la gloire de la prééminence. Alternativement assailli par les deux factions, qui semblaient toujours prêtes à en venir aux mains pour la possession de sa personne, Paléologue hésita encore, avant de quitter son palais et son pays, de tenter cette dangereuse entreprise. Il se rappelait les conseils de son père, et le bon sens devait lui suggérer que les Latins, divisés entre eux, ne s'accorderaient pas pour une cause étrangère. Sigismond essaya de le détourner de son voyage. On ne pouvait le soupçonner de partialité, puisqu'il adhérait au concile, et ce conseil recevait encore du poids de l'étrange opinion où l'on était que Sigismond nommerait un Grec pour successeur à l'empire (1). Le sultan des Turcs était encore un conseiller qui ne méritait pas sa confiance, mais qu'il craignait d'offenser. Amurath ne comprenait rien aux querelles des chrétiens. Bien qu'il redoutât leur union, il offrit d'ouvrir ses trésors aux besoins de Paléologue, en déclarant toutefois, avec une apparence de généro-

---

ευρη τα κατεργα της συνοδου, και ει δυνηθη καταδυση και αφανιση. Les pères du synode donnèrent à leurs marins des ordres moins péremptoires, et jusqu'au moment où les deux escadres se rencontrèrent, les deux partis tâchèrent de cacher aux Grecs cette animosité.

(1) Syropulus parle des espérances de Paléologue (p. 36) et du dernier avis de Sigismond (p. 57). L'empereur grec apprit à Corfou la mort de son ami, et s'il en eût été instruit plus tôt, il serait retourné à Constantinople (p. 79).

sité, que Constantinople serait inviolablement respectée durant l'absence de son souverain (1). Les plus riches présens et les plus belles promesses achevèrent de décider le prince grec. Il désirait s'éloigner pour quelque temps d'une scène de malheur et de danger. Après s'être débarrassé des députés du concile par une réponse équivoque, il annonça la résolution de s'embarquer sur les galères du pape. Le grand âge du patriarche Joseph le rendait plus susceptible de crainte que d'espoir; effrayé des dangers qu'il allait courir sur l'Océan, le pontife observa que dans un pays étranger sa faible voix et celle d'une trentaine de ses prélats seraient étouffées par le nombre et le pouvoir des évêques qui composaient le synode latin. Il céda cependant à la volonté de Paléologue, à la flatteuse assurance qu'on l'écouterait comme l'oracle des nations, et au désir secret d'apprendre de son frère de l'Occident à rendre l'Église indépendante des souverains (2). Les cinq porte-croix

---

(1). Phranza lui-même, quoique par des motifs différens, était de l'avis d'Amurath (l. II, c. 13). *Utinam ne synodus ista unquam fuisset, si tantas offensiones et detrimenta paritura erat!* Syropulus parle aussi (p. 58) de l'ambassade ottomane. Amurath tint sa parole. Il menaça peut-être (p. 125-219), mais n'attaqua point la ville.

(2) Le lecteur sourira de l'ingénuité avec laquelle il fit part de cette espérance à ses favoris : Τοιαυτην πληροφοριαν σχησειν ηλπιζε και δια του παπα εθαρρει ελευθερωσαι την εκκλησιαν απο της αποτεθεισης αυτου δουλειας παρα του βασιλεως (p. 92); cependant il lui aurait été difficile de pratiquer les leçons de Grégoire VII.

ou dignitaires de Sainte-Sophie furent attachés à sa suite; et l'un d'eux, le grand ecclésiarque ou prédicateur, Sylvestre Syropulus (1), a composé (2) une histoire curieuse et sincère de la *fausse* union (3). Le clergé obéit malgré lui aux ordres de l'empereur et du patriarche; mais la soumission était son premier devoir, et la patience sa plus utile vertu : on trouve dans une liste choisie de vingt prélats, les métropolitains d'Héraclée, Cyzique, Nicée, Nicomé-

---

(1) Le nom chrétien de Sylvestre est tiré du calendrier latin. En grec moderne πουλος s'ajoute à la fin d'un mot pour exprimer un diminutif; et aucun des argumens de l'éditeur Creyghton ne peut l'autoriser à substituer *Sguropulus* (Sguros, fuscus) au Syropulus de son propre manuscrit, dont le nom est signé par lui-même dans les actes du concile de Florence. Pourquoi l'auteur ne serait-il pas d'extraction syrienne?

(2) D'après la conclusion de cette histoire, j'en fixerais la date à l'année 1444, quatre ans après le synode. Lorsque le grand ecclésiarque abdiqua son office (sect. XII, p. 330-350), le temps et la retraite avaient calmé ses passions; et Syropulus, quoique souvent partial, n'est jamais emporté.

(3) *Vera historia unionis non veræ inter Græcos et Latinos* (*Hagæ Comitis*, 1660, *in-fol.*) Robert Creyghton, chapelain de Charles II durant son exil, la publia le premier avec une traduction pompeuse et peu fidèle. Le titre polémique est sûrement de l'invention de l'éditeur, puisque le commencement de l'ouvrage manque. Pour le mérite de la narration et même du style, Syropulus peut être classé parmi les meilleurs écrivains de Byzance; mais il est exclus des collections orthodoxes des conciles.

die, Éphèse et Trébisonde, et deux nouveaux évêques, Marc et Bessarion, élevés à cette dignité sur la confiance qu'inspiraient leur savoir et leur éloquence. On nomma quelques moines et quelques philosophes pour donner plus d'éclat à l'érudition et à la sainteté de l'Église grecque, et une troupe de chanteurs et de musiciens pour le service de la chapelle impériale. Les patriarches d'Alexandrie, d'Antioche et de Jérusalem, envoyèrent des députés ou on leur en supposa; le primat de Russie représentait une Église nationale, et les Grecs pouvaient le disputer aux Latins pour l'étendue de leur empire spirituel. On exposa les précieux vases de Sainte-Sophie aux dangers de la mer, afin que le patriarche pût officier avec la pompe ordinaire; et l'empereur employa tout l'or qu'il put rassembler, à décorer son char et son lit d'ornemens massifs (1). Mais tandis que les Grecs tâchaient de soutenir l'extérieur de leur ancienne magnificence, ils se disputaient le partage des quinze mille ducats que le pape leur avait donnés pour aumône préliminaire. Lorsque tous les préparatifs furent terminés, Paléologue, suivi d'un train nombreux, accompagné de son frère Démétrius et des premiers personnages de l'État et de l'Église,

---

(1) Syrop. (p. 63) exprime franchement son intention : ιν'ουτω πομπαων εν Ιταλοις μεγας βασιλευς παρ' εκεινων νομιζοιτο; et la traduction latine de ce passage par Creyghton peut donner une idée de ses brillantes paraphrases. *Ut pompâ circumductus noster imperator Italiæ, populis aliquis deauratus Jupiter crederetur, aut Cræsus ex opulentâ Lydiâ.*

s'embarqua sur huit vaisseaux à voiles et à rames, cingla par le détroit de Gallipoli dans l'Archipel, et passa dans le golfe Adriatique (1).

Après une longue et fatigante navigation de soixante-dix-sept jours, cette escadre religieuse jeta l'ancre devant Venise, et la réception qui lui fut faite attesta la joie et la magnificence de cette république. Souverain du monde, le modeste Auguste n'avait jamais exigé de ses sujets les honneurs que les Vénitiens indépendans prodiguèrent à son faible successeur. Du haut d'un trône placé sur la poupe de son vaisseau, Paléologue reçut la visite, ou, pour parler à la grecque, les adorations du doge et des sénateurs (2). Ils montaient le Bucentaure suivi de douze puissantes galères : la mer était couverte d'innombrables gondoles destinées, les unes à la pompe du spectacle, les autres au plaisir des spectateurs ; l'air retentissait des sons de la musique et du bruit des acclamations ; les vêtemens des mate-

Son entrée triomphante à Venise. A. D. 1438, 9 février.

---

(1) Sans m'asservir à citer Syropulus pour chaque fait particulier, j'observerai que la navigation des Grecs, depuis Constantinople jusqu'à Venise et Ferrare, se trouve dans sa quatrième section (p. 67-100); et que cet historien a le rare talent de mettre chaque scène sous les yeux de son lecteur.

(2) Durant la tenue du synode, Phranza était dans le Péloponèse ; mais le despote Démétrius lui fit un récit exact de la manière honorable dont l'empereur et le patriarche furent accueillis à Venise et à Ferrare (*dux..... sedentem imperatorem adorat*). Les Latins en parlent plus légèrement (l. II, c. 14, 15, 16).

lots et même les vaisseaux brillaient de soie et d'or; et tous les emblêmes présentaient les aigles romaines unies aux lions de Saint-Marc. Ce brillant cortége remonta le grand canal et passa sous le pont de Rialto. Les Orientaux contemplaient avec admiration les palais, les églises et l'immense population d'une ville qui semblait flotter sur les vagues (1); mais ils soupirèrent en apercevant les dépouilles et les trophées du sac de Constantinople. Après avoir séjourné quinze jours à Venise, Paléologue continua sa route alternativement par terre et par eau jusqu'à Ferrare. La politique du Vatican l'emporta dans cette occasion sur son orgueil, et le prince grec reçut tous les anciens honneurs accordés à l'empereur d'Orient. Il fit son entrée sur un cheval *noir;* mais on conduisait devant lui un superbe cheval blanc dont le harnois était décoré d'aigles en broderie d'or. Il marcha couvert d'un dais soutenu par les princes de la maison d'Este, les fils ou les parens de Nicolas, marquis de la ville et souverain plus puissant que Paléologue (2). Le prince grec ne descendit de che-

<small>A Ferrare. 28 février.</small>

---

(1) La surprise qu'éprouvèrent le prince grec et un ambassadeur de France à la vue de Venise (*Mém. de Philippe de Comines,* l. vii, c. 18), prouve incontestablement qu'elle était, dans le quatorzième siècle, la première et la plus belle ville du monde chrétien. Relativement aux dépouilles de Constantinople que les Grecs y aperçurent, *voy.* Syporulus (p. 87).

(2) Nicolas iii, de la maison d'Este, régna quarante-huit ans (A. D. 1393-1441); il posséda Ferrare, Modène, Reggio,

val qu'au pied de l'escalier ; le pape s'avança jusqu'à la porte de son appartement, releva le prince au moment où il fléchissait le genou, et, après l'avoir embrassé paternellement, le conduisit à un siége placé à sa gauche. Le patriarche grec ne voulut point descendre de sa galère avant d'être convenu d'un cérémonial qui mît une apparence d'égalité entre l'évêque de Rome et celui de Constantinople ; celui-ci reçut du premier un embrassement fraternel, et tous les ecclésiastiques grecs refusèrent de baiser les pieds du pontife romain. A l'ouverture du synode, les chefs ecclésiastiques et temporels se disputèrent le centre ou la place d'honneur ; et Eugène n'éluda l'ancien cérémonial de Constantin et de Marcien, qu'en alléguant que ses prédécesseurs ne s'étaient trouvés en personne ni à Nicée ni à Chalcédoine. Après de longs débats, on convint que les deux nations occuperaient, à droite et à gauche, les deux côtés de l'église ; que la chaire de saint Pierre serait élevée à la première place devant le rang des Latins, et que le trône de l'empereur grec, à la tête de son clergé, serait à la même hauteur, en face de la seconde place ou du siége vacant de l'empereur d'Occident.(1).

Parme, Rovigo et Commachio. *Voyez* sa vie dans Muratori (*Antichità Estense*, t. II, p. 159-201).

(1) Le peuple des villes latines rit beaucoup des vêtemens des Grecs, de leurs longues robes, de leurs manches et de leur barbe. L'empereur n'était distingué que par la couleur pourpre et par son diadème ou tiare, dont la

<small>Concile des Grecs et des Latins à Ferrare, le 8 octob. A. D. 1438; et à Florence, le 6 juillet A. D. 1439.</small>

Mais dès que les réjouissances et les formalités firent place à des discussions sérieuses, les Grecs, mécontens du pape et d'eux-mêmes, se repentirent de leur imprudent voyage. Les émissaires d'Eugène l'avaient représenté à Constantinople comme au faîte de la prospérité, à la tête des princes et des prélats européens, prêts à sa voix à croire et à prendre les armes. L'assemblée peu nombreuse du concile de Ferrare dissipa l'illusion: Les Latins ouvrirent la première session avec cinq archevêques, dix-huit évêques et dix abbés, dont le plus grand nombre étaient sujets ou compatriotes du pontife italien. Excepté le duc de Bourgogne, aucun des souverains de l'Occident ne daigna paraître ou envoyer des ambassadeurs; et il n'était pas possible de supprimer les actes judiciaires de Bâle contre la personne et la dignité d'Eugène, qui se terminèrent par une nouvelle élection. Dans ces circonstances, Paléologue demanda et obtint un délai qui pût lui donner le temps d'obtenir des Latins quelque avantage temporel pour prix d'une union désapprouvée de ses sujets; après la première séance, les débats publics furent remis à six mois. L'empereur, suivi d'une troupe de favoris et de janissaires, passa l'été

---

pointe était ornée d'un magnifique diamant (Hody, *de Græcis illustribus*, p. 31); un autre spectateur convient cependant que la mode grecque était *più grave e più degna* que l'italienne (Vespasiano, *in Vit. Eugen.* VI, Muratori, t. XXV, p. 261).

dans un vaste monastère situé agréablement, à six milles de Ferrare. Oubliant dans les plaisirs de la chasse les querelles de l'Église et les calamités de l'État, il ne s'occupa qu'à détruire le gibier, sans écouter les justes plaintes du marquis et des laboureurs (1). Pendant ce temps, ses malheureux Grecs souffraient tous les maux de l'exil et de la pauvreté. On avait assigné à chaque étranger, pour sa dépense, trois ou quatre florins d'or par mois; et quoique la somme entière ne montât pas à plus de sept cents florins, l'indigence ou la politique du Vatican laissait toujours beaucoup d'arrérages (2). Ils soupi-

(1) Pour les chasses de l'empereur, voy. Syropulus (p. 143; 144-191): Le pape lui avait envoyé onze mauvais faucons; mais il acheta un excellent coureur amené de Russie. On sera peut-être surpris de trouver ce nom de *janissaires;* mais les Grecs adoptèrent ce nom des Ottomans sans en imiter l'institution, et on en fit souvent usage dans le dernier siècle de l'empire grec.

(2) Les Grecs obtinrent, après beaucoup de difficultés, qu'au lieu de provisions on leur ferait une distribution d'argent. On donna quatre florins par mois aux personnes d'un rang honorable, et trois florins pour chaque domestique. L'empereur en reçut trente-quatre, le patriarche vingt-neuf, et le prince Démétrius vingt-quatre. La paye entière du premier mois ne monta qu'à six cent quatre-vingt-onze florins. Cette somme annonce que le nombre total des Grecs n'excédait pas deux cents (Syropulus, p. 104, 105). Au mois d'octobre 1438, on devait les arrérages de quatre mois: on devait encore trois mois en avril 1439, et cinq et demi dans le mois de juillet, à l'époque de l'union (p. 172-225-271).

vaient après leur délivrance; mais un triple obstacle s'opposait à leur fuite. On ne souffrait pas qu'ils sortissent de Ferrare sans un passe-port de leurs supérieurs : les Vénitiens avaient promis d'arrêter et de renvoyer les fugitifs; et en arrivant à Constantinople ils ne pouvaient échapper à l'excommunication, aux amendes, et à une sentence qui condamnait même les ecclésiastiques à être dépouillés nus et fouettés publiquement (1). La faim put seule décider les Grecs à ouvrir la première conférence; et ce ne fut qu'avec une répugnance extrême qu'ils consentirent à suivre à Florence le synode fugitif. Mais cette nouvelle translation était inévitable. la peste était à Ferrare : on soupçonnait la fidélité du marquis ; les troupes du duc de Milan approchaient de la ville; et comme elles occupaient la Romagne, ce ne fut pas sans peine et sans danger que le pape, l'empereur et les prélats, trouvèrent un chemin à travers les sentiers peu fréquentés de l'Apennin (2).

Mais la politique et le temps surmontèrent tous ces obstacles. La violence des pères de Bâle contri-

(1) Syropulus (p. 141, 142-204-221) déplore l'emprisonnement des Grecs qu'on retenait de force en Italie, et se plaint de la tyrannie de l'empereur et du patriarche.

(2) On trouve une relation claire et exacte des guerres d'Italie dans le quatrième volume des *Annales* de Muratori. Il paraît que le schismatique Syropulus (p. 145) a exagéré les craintes et la précipitation du pape, dans sa retraite de Ferrare à Florence. Les actes prouvent qu'elle fût assez tranquille, et qu'elle se fit d'une manière convenable.

bua au succès d'Eugène. Les nations de l'Europe
détestèrent le schisme, et rejetèrent l'élection de
Félix v, successivement duc de Savoie, ermite et
pape. Les plus puissans des princes se rapprochèrent de son rival, et passèrent insensiblement de la
neutralité à un attachement sincère. Les légats, suivis de quelques membres respectables, désertèrent
vers les Romains, qui virent augmenter chaque jour
leur nombre et ramener l'opinion publique. Le concile de Bâle se trouva réduit à trente-neuf évêques
et trois cents membres du clergé inférieur (1); tandis
que les Latins de Florence réunissaient à la personne
du pape huit cardinaux, deux patriarches, huit archevêques, cinquante-deux évêques et quarante-
cinq abbés ou chefs d'ordres religieux. Les travaux
de neuf mois et les débats de vingt-cinq séances
opérèrent enfin la réunion des Grecs. Les deux Églises avaient agité quatre questions principales : 1° l'u-
sage du pain azyme dans la communion; 2° la
nature du purgatoire; 3° la suprématie du pape;
4° la procession simple ou double du Saint-Esprit.
La cause des deux nations fut discutée par dix habiles théologiens. Le cardinal Julien employa son
éloquence inépuisable en faveur des Latins; et les

---

(1) Syropulus compte sept cents prélats dans le concile de
Bâle; mais l'erreur est palpable et peut-être volontaire.
Les ecclésiastiques de toutes les classes qui furent présens à
ce concile, et tous les prélats absens qui adhéraient expressément ou tacitement à ses décrets, n'auraient pas suffi
pour composer ce nombre.

Grecs eurent pour principaux champions Marc d'Éphèse et Bessarion de Nicée. Nous ne passerons point sous silence une observation qui fait honneur aux progrès de la raison humaine. On traita la première de ces questions comme un point peu important qui pouvait varier sans conséquence selon l'opinion des temps ou des nations; quant à la seconde, les deux partis convinrent qu'il devait y avoir un état intermédiaire de purification pour les péchés véniels. Quant à savoir si cette purification s'opérait par le feu élémentaire, c'était un point que dans peu d'années les contestans devaient avoir la commodité de décider sur le lieu même. La suprématie du pape paraissait plus importante et plus contestable ; cependant les Orientaux avaient toujours reconnu l'évêque de Rome pour le premier des cinq patriarches; ils ne firent point difficulté d'admettre qu'il exercerait sa juridiction conformément aux saints canons, condescendance vague qui pouvait se définir ou s'éluder selon les circonstances. La procession du Saint-Esprit, du père seul, ou du père et du fils, était un article de foi plus profondément enraciné dans l'opinion des hommes. Dans les sessions de Ferrare et de Florence, on divisa l'addition latine de *filioque* en deux questions : 1° celle de la légalité; 2° et celle de l'orthodoxie. Il n'est peut-être pas nécessaire de protester sur un pareil sujet de mon impartiale indifférence ; mais il me semble que les Grecs avaient en leur faveur un argument victorieux dans la défense, faite par le concile de Chalcédoine,

d'ajouter aucun article, quel qu'il fût, au symbole
de Nicée, ou plutôt de Constantinople (1). Dans les
affaires de ce monde, il n'est pas aisé de concevoir
qu'une assemblée de législateurs puisse lier les mains
à des successeurs revêtus de la même autorité ; mais
une décision dictée par l'inspiration divine doit
être vraie et immuable ; l'avis d'un évêque ou d'un
synode provincial ne peut prévaloir contre le jugement universel de l'Église catholique. Quant au fond
de la doctrine, les argumens étaient égaux des deux
côtés, et la dispute paraissait interminable : la procession d'un Dieu confond l'intelligence humaine.
L'Évangile, placé sur l'autel, n'offrait rien qui pût
résoudre cette question ; les textes des pères pouvaient avoir été falsifiés par supercherie ou em-
brouillés par des argumens captieux ; et les Grecs ne
connaissaient ni les écrits des saints latins, ni leurs
caractères (2). Nous pouvons du moins être assurés
que les argumens de chacun des deux partis parurent impuissans à ceux du parti opposé. La raison
peut éclairer le préjugé ; une attention soutenue peut

---

(1) Les Grecs opposés à l'union ne voulaient pas sortir
de ce poste avantageux (Syropulus, p. 178-193-195-202).
Les Latins n'eurent pas honte de produire un vieux manuscrit du second concile de Nicée, dans lequel on avait
ajouté le *filioque* au symbole, supposition évidente (p. 173).

(2) Ὡς εγω (dit un Grec célèbre) οταν εις ναον εισελθω
Λατινων ου προσκυνω τινα των εκεισε αγιων, επει ουδε γνωριζω τινα
(Syropulus, p. 109). *Voyez* l'embarras des Grecs (p. 217,
218, 252, 253, 273).

rectifier l'erreur du premier coup d'œil, lorsque l'objet est à notre portée : mais les évêques et les moines avaient appris dès leur enfance à répéter une formule de mots mystérieux ; ils attachaient leur honneur national et personnel à la répétition des mêmes mots, et l'aigreur d'une dispute publique acheva de les rendre intraitables.

<small>Négociations avec les Grecs.</small> Tandis qu'ils se perdaient dans un labyrinthe d'argumens obscurs, le pape et l'empereur désiraient également une apparence d'union qui pouvait seule remplir le but de leur entrevue : l'obstination ne résista point à des négociations personnelles et secrètes. Le patriarche Joseph avait succombé sous le poids de l'âge et des infirmités ; ses dernières paroles avaient été des paroles de paix et de charité. L'espoir d'occuper sa place tentait l'ambition du clergé ; et la prompte soumission des archevêques de Russie et de Nicée, Isidore et Bessarion, fut achetée et récompensée par une prompte promotion à la dignité de cardinal. Dans les premiers débats, Bessarion s'était montré le plus ferme et le plus éloquent champion de l'Église grecque ; et, si sa patrie le rejeta comme apostat et comme enfant illégitime (1), il présenta, si l'on peut en croire l'histoire ecclésiastique, l'exemple rare d'un patriote qui se recom-

---

(1) *Voyez* la dispute polie de Marc d'Éphèse et de Bessarion, dans Syropulus (p. 257), qui ne dissimule jamais les vices de ses compatriotes, et rend un hommage impartial aux vertus des Latins.

mande à la cour par une résistance marquante et une soumission placée à propos. Aidé de ses deux coadjuteurs spirituels, l'empereur sut employer vis-à-vis de chacun des évêques les argumens les plus appropriés à leur situation générale et à leur caractère particulier. Tous cédèrent successivement à l'exemple ou à l'autorité. Prisonniers chez les Latins, et dépouillés de leurs revenus par les Turcs, trois robes et quarante ducats formaient leur trésor qui se trouva bientôt épuisé (1). Ils dépendaient, pour leur retour, des vaisseaux de Venise et de la générosité du pape; et telle était leur indigence, qu'il suffit pour les gagner de leur offrir le paiement des arrérages qui leur étaient dus (2). Le secours qu'exigeait le danger de Constantinople pouvait excuser une prudente et pieuse dissimulation; mais on y ajouta de vives inquiétudes pour leur sûreté personnelle, en insinuant que les hérétiques opiniâtres

---

(1) Relativement à l'indigence des évêques grecs, *voyez* un passage de Ducas (c. 31). Un de ces prélats possédait pour tout bien trois vieilles robes, etc. Bessarion avait gagné quarante florins d'or à enseigner pendant vingt-un ans dans son monastère; mais il en avait dépensé vingt-huit dans son voyage du Péloponèse, et le reste à Constantinople (Syropulus, p. 127).

(2) Syropulus prétend que les Grecs ne reçurent point d'argent avant d'avoir signé l'acte d'union (p. 283); il raconte cependant quelques circonstances suspectes, et l'historien Ducas affirme qu'ils se laissèrent corrompre par des présens.

seraient abandonnés en Italie à la justice ou à la vengeance du pontife romain (1). Dans l'assemblée particulière des Grecs, vingt-quatre membres de cette Église approuvèrent la formule d'union, et il n'y eut que douze opposans. Mais les cinq porte-croix de Sainte-Sophie qui prétendaient à remplacer le patriarche, furent repoussés par les règles de l'ancienne discipline; leur droit de voter fut transmis à des moines, à des grammairiens, à des laïques, dont on attendait plus de complaisance; et la volonté du monarque produisit une fausse et lâche unanimité. Deux fidèles patriotes osèrent seuls déclarer leurs sentimens personnels et ceux de la nation. Démétrius, frère de l'empereur, se retira à Venise pour n'être pas témoin de cette union; et Marc d'Éphèse, prenant peut-être son orgueil pour sa conscience, traita les Latins d'hérétiques, rejeta leur communion, et se déclara hautement le champion de l'Église grecque et orthodoxe (2). On essaya de rédiger le traité d'union en termes qui pussent satisfaire les Latins sans trop humilier les Grecs; mais, en pesant

(1) Les Grecs expriment douloureusement leurs craintes d'un exil ou d'un esclavage perpétuel (p. 196), et furent extrêmement frappés des menaces de l'empereur (p. 260).

(2) J'oubliais un autre opposant d'un rang moins élevé, mais très-orthodoxe, le chien favori de Paléologue, qui, ordinairement tranquille sur le marchepied du trône, aboya avec fureur durant la lecture du traité d'union. On employa inutilement les caresses et les coups de fouet pour le faire taire (Syropulus, p. 265, 266).

les mots et les syllabes, on laissa cependant un peu incliner la balance en faveur du Vatican. On convint (je demande ici l'attention du lecteur) que le Saint-Esprit procède du père et du fils comme d'un même principe et d'une même substance; qu'il procède par le fils étant de la même nature et de la même substance, et qu'il procède du père et du fils par une *spiration* et une production. On comprendra plus facilement les articles du traité préliminaire. Eugène s'engageait vis-à-vis des Grecs à payer tous les frais de leur retour; à entretenir dans tous les temps deux galères et trois cents soldats pour la défense de Constantinople; à fournir dix galères pour un an, ou vingt pour six mois, toutes les fois qu'il en serait requis; à solliciter dans une occasion pressante les secours des princes d'Europe, et à faire mouiller dans le port de Byzance tous les vaisseaux qui transporteraient des pèlerins à Jérusalem.

Dans la même année et presque dans le même jour, on déposait Eugène à Bâle, tandis qu'il terminait à Florence la réunion des Grecs avec les Latins. Le premier de ces synodes, que le pontife romain appelait à la vérité une assemblée de démons, le déclara coupable de simonie, de parjure, de tyrannie, d'hérésie et de schisme (1), incorrigible de ses vices

Eugène est déposé à Bâle, le 25 juin 1438.

——————————

(1) Les Vies des papes, recueillies par Muratori (t. III, part. II, t. xxv), représentent Eugène IV comme un pontife de mœurs pures et même exemplaires. Sa situation difficile, en attachant sur lui les regards du monde et ceux

Réunion des Grecs avec les Latins, le 6 juillet 1438.

et indigne de remplir aucune fonction ecclésiastique. Le second, au contraire, le révérait comme le vicaire légitime et sacré de Jésus-Christ, comme celui dont la piété et les vertus avaient réuni, après une séparation de six siècles, les catholiques de l'Orient et de l'Occident en un seul troupeau et sous un seul pasteur. L'acte d'union fut signé par le pape, l'empereur et les principaux membres des deux Églises, sans excepter même ceux qu'on avait exclus, comme Syropulus (1), du droit de donner leur suffrage. Deux copies semblaient suffire, l'une pour l'Orient, et l'autre pour l'Occident; mais Eugène en fit transcrire et signer quatre, afin de multiplier les monumens de sa victoire (2). Le 6 juillet, jour mémorable,

---

de ses ennemis, était un motif et est un garant de sa circonspection.

(1) Syropulus crut qu'il était moins honteux d'assister à la cérémonie de l'union que d'en signer l'acte; mais il fut obligé de faire l'un et l'autre, et s'excuse mal sur son obéissance à l'empereur (p. 290-292).

(2) Il n'existe plus aujourd'hui aucun de ces actes originaux de l'union. Des dix manuscrits dont on conserve cinq à Rome, et les autres à Florence, Bologne, Venise, Paris et Londres, neuf ont subi l'examen d'un critique habile, M. de Bréquigny, qui les rejette à raison de la différence des signatures grecques et des fautes dans l'écriture. On en peut cependant regarder quelques-uns comme des copies authentiques qui furent signées à Florence avant le 26 août, époque à laquelle le pape et l'empereur se séparèrent (*Mém. de l'Académie des Inscriptions*, tom. XLIII, p. 287-311).

les successeurs de saint Pierre et de Constantin montèrent sur leurs trônes, en présence des deux nations assemblées dans la cathédrale de Florence. Les représentans de ces nations, le cardinal Julien, et Bessarion, archevêque de Nicée, parurent dans la chaire, et après avoir lu à haute voix l'acte d'union, chacun dans sa langue nationale, ils se donnèrent publiquement le baiser de paix et de réconciliation au nom et aux applaudissemens de leurs compatriotes présens. Le pape et son clergé officièrent conformément à la liturgie romaine; on chanta le symbole avec l'addition du *filioque*. Les Grecs déguisèrent assez gauchement leur approbation, en prétextant l'ignorance où ils étaient du sens de ces mots harmonieux, mais mal articulés (1); et les Latins, plus scrupuleux, refusèrent avec fermeté d'admettre aucune des cérémonies de l'Église d'Orient. L'empereur et son clergé n'oublièrent pas cependant tout-à-fait l'honneur national. Ils ratifièrent volontairement le traité, sous la clause tacite qu'on n'entreprendrait point de rien innover dans leur symbole ou leurs cérémonies; ils ménagèrent et respectèrent la généreuse fermeté de Marc d'Éphèse, et refusèrent, après la mort de Joseph, de procéder à l'élection d'un nouveau patriarche, ailleurs que dans la cathédrale de Sainte-Sophie. Eugène surpassa ses promesses et leurs espérances par la libéralité de ses récompenses générales et particulières. Les Grecs s'en

---

(1) Ημιν δε ως ασημοι εδοκουν φωναι (Syropulus, p. 297).

retournèrent par Ferrare et Venise avec moins de pompe et plus de modestie (1). J'instruirai mon lecteur, dans le chapitre suivant, de la réception qu'on leur fit à Constantinople. Le succès de la première entreprise encouragea Eugène à renouveler cette scène édifiante; les députés des arméniens et des maronites, les jacobites d'Égypte et de Syrie, les nestoriens et les Éthiopiens, successivement admis à baiser les pieds du pape, annoncèrent l'obéissance et l'orthodoxie de l'Orient. Leurs ambassadeurs, inconnus chez les nations qu'ils prétendaient représenter (2), répandirent dans l'Occident la pieuse renommée d'Eugène, et des clameurs adroitement semées accusèrent les schismatiques de la Suisse et de la Savoie d'être les seuls opposans à la parfaite union du monde chrétien. A leur vigoureuse opposition succéda enfin la lassitude d'un effort inutile. Le concile de Bâle fut insensiblement dissous, et Félix, renonçant à la tiare, retourna dans son dévot ou délicieux ermitage de Ripaille (3). Des actes mu-

(1) En retournant à Constantinople, les Grecs conversèrent à Bologne avec les ambassadeurs d'Angleterre, qui, après quelques questions et quelques réponses désintéressées dans cette affaire, se moquèrent de l'union prétendue de Florence (Syropulus, p. 307).

(2) Les réunions des nestoriens et des jacobites, etc., sont si insignifiantes ou si fabuleuses, que j'ai inutilement feuilleté, pour en trouver des traces, la *Bibliothèque orientale* d'Assemani, fidèle esclave du Vatican.

(3) Ripaille est situé près Thonon dans la Savoie, au midi

tuels d'oubli et d'indemnité établirent la paix générale : on laissa tomber les projets de réforme ; les papes continuèrent à exercer leur despotisme spirituel et à en abuser, et les élections de Rome ne furent troublées depuis par aucune contestation (1).

Les voyages consécutifs des trois empereurs ne leur produisirent pas de grands avantages dans ce monde ni peut-être dans l'autre; mais les suites en furent heureuses. Ils portèrent l'érudition grecque en Italie, d'où elle se répandit chez toutes les nations de l'Occident et du Nord. Dans l'esclavage abject où étaient réduits les sujets de Paléologue, ils possédaient encore la clef précieuse des trésors de l'antiquité, cette langue harmonieuse et féconde qui donne une âme aux objets des sens, et un corps aux

État de la langue grecque à Constantinople.
A. D.
1300-1453.

---

du lac de Genève : c'est aujourd'hui une chartreuse. M. Addison (*Voyage d'Italie*, vol. II, p. 147, 148, édition de ses OEuvres par Baskerville) a célébré le lieu et son fondateur. Æneas Sylvius et les pères de Bâle prodiguent des louanges à la vie austère du duc ermite; mais malheureusement le proverbe italien et le proverbe français font foi de l'opinion généralement répandue de son luxe.

(1) Relativement aux conciles de Bâle, Ferrare et Florence, j'ai consulté les actes originaux qui forment les dix-sept et dix-huitième volumes de l'édition de Venise, et sont terminés par l'histoire claire, mais partiale, d'Augustin Patrice, Italien du quinzième siècle. Ils ont été rédigés et abrégés par Dupin (*Bibl. ecclés.*, t. XII) et le continuateur de Fleury (t. XXII); le respect de l'Église gallicane pour les deux partis les a contenus dans une circonspection qui les rend presque ridicules.

abstractions de la philosophie. Depuis que les Barbares, après avoir forcé les barrières de la monarchie, s'étaient répandus jusque dans la capitale, ils avaient sans doute corrompu la pureté du dialecte, et il a fallu d'abondans glossaires pour interpréter une multitude de mots tirés des langues arabe, turque, esclavonne, latine ou française (1). Mais cette pureté se soutenait à la cour, et on l'enseignait encore dans les colléges. Un savant Italien (2), qu'une longue résidence et une alliance honorable (3) avaient naturalisé à Constantinople environ trente ans avant la

(1) Meursius, dans son premier Essai, rassembla trois mille six cents mots *græco-barbares*; il en ajouta mille huit cents dans une seconde édition, et laissa cependant encore beaucoup à faire à Portius, Ducange, Fabrotti, les Bollandistes, etc. (Fabr., *Bibl. græc.*, tom. x, pag. 101, etc.) On trouve des mots persans dans Xénophon; et des mots latins dans Plutarque; tel est l'effet inévitable du commerce et de la guerre : mais cet alliage n'altéra point le fond de la langue.

(2) François Philelphe était un sophiste ou philosophe vain, avide et turbulent. Sa Vie a été composée avec soin par Lancelot (*Mém. de l'Acad. des Inscr.*, t. x, p. 691-751), et Tiraboschi (*Istoria della Letteratura italiana*, t. vii, p. 282-294), en grande partie d'après ses propres Lettres. Ses ouvrages fort travaillés et ceux de ses contemporains sont oubliés; mais leurs Épîtres familières peignent encore les hommes et les temps.

(3) Il épousa et avait peut-être séduit la fille de Jean, petite-fille de Manuel Chrysoloras. Elle était jeune, riche et belle, et d'une famille noble, alliée à celle des Doria de Gênes et aux empereurs de Constantinople.

conquête des Turcs, nous a laissé sur le langage des Grecs quelques détails embellis peut-être par sa partialité. « La langue vulgaire, dit Philelphe (1), a été altérée par le peuple et corrompue par la multitude de marchands ou d'étrangers qui arrivent tous les jours à Constantinople et se mêlent avec les habitans. C'est des disciples de cette école que les Latins ont reçu les traductions plates et obscures de Platon et d'Aristote. Mais nous ne nous attachons qu'aux Grecs qui méritent d'être imités parce qu'ils ont échappé à la contagion. On retrouve dans leurs conversations familières la langue d'Aristophane et d'Euripide, des philosophes et des historiens d'Athènes, et le style de leurs écrits est encore plus soigné et plus correct. Ceux qui sont attachés à la cour par leur place et leur naissance, sont ceux qui conservent le mieux, sans aucun mélange, l'élégance et la pureté des anciens; on retrouve toutes les grâces naturelles du langage chez les nobles matrones, qui n'ont aucune

---

(1) *Græci quibus lingua depravata non sit..... ita loquuntur vulgo hâc etiam tempestate ut Aristophanes comicus, aut Euripides tragicus, ut oratores omnes, ut historiographi, ut philosophi.... litterati autem homines et doctius et emendatius....*. *Nam viri aulici veterem sermonis dignitatem atque elegantiam retinebant, imprimisque ipsæ nobiles mulieres; quibus cùm nullum esset omninò cum viris peregrinis commercium, merus ille ac purus Græcorum sermo servabatur intactus* (Philelp., epist. ad ann. 1451, ap. Hodium, p. 188, 189). Il observe dans un autre passage : *Uxor illa mea Theodora locutione erat admodum moderata et suavi et maximè atticâ.*

communication avec les étrangers; que dis-je? les étrangers! elles vivent retirées et éloignées des regards même de leurs concitoyens. Elles paraissent rarement dans les rues, et ne sortent de leurs maisons que le soir, pour aller à l'église ou visiter leurs plus proches parens. Dans ces occasions, elles vont à cheval couvertes d'un voile, accompagnées de leurs maris, environnées de leur famille ou de leurs domestiques (1). »

Parmi les Grecs, un clergé opulent et nombreux se dévouait au service des autels : les moines et les évêques se distinguèrent toujours par l'austérité de leurs mœurs, et ne se livrèrent jamais, comme les ecclésiastiques latins, aux intérêts et aux plaisirs de la vie séculière et même de la vie militaire. Après avoir perdu une partie de leur temps dans les dévotions, la discorde et l'oisiveté de l'église ou du cloître, les esprits actifs et curieux se livraient avec ardeur à l'étude de l'érudition grecque, sacrée et profane. Les ecclésiastiques présidaient à l'éducation de la jeunesse; les écoles d'éloquence et de philosophie se perpétuèrent jusqu'à la chute de l'empire; et l'on peut affirmer que l'enceinte de Constantinople contenait plus de sciences et de livres qu'il n'y en avait de répandus dans les vastes contrées de l'Occident (2).

---

(1) Philelphe cherche ridiculement l'origine de la jalousie grecque ou orientale dans les mœurs de l'ancienne Rome.

(2) *Voyez* l'état de la littérature des treizième et quator-

Mais nous avons déjà observé que les Grecs s'étaient arrêtés ou rétrogradaient, tandis que les Latins s'avançaient par des progrès rapides. Ces progrès étaient animés par l'esprit d'indépendance et d'émulation; et même le petit univers renfermé dans les bornes de l'Italie contenait plus de population et d'industrie que l'empire expirant de Byzance. En Europe, les dernières classes de la société s'étaient affranchies de la servitude féodale; et la liberté amène le désir de s'instruire et les lumières qui en sont la suite. La superstition avait conservé l'usage à la vérité grossier et corrompu de la langue latine; des milliers d'étudians peuplaient les universités répandues depuis Bologne jusqu'à Oxford (1), et leur ardeur mal dirigée pouvait se tourner vers des études plus libérales et plus nobles. Dans la résurrection des sciences l'Italie fut la première qui jeta pour ainsi dire son linceul, et Pétrarque a mérité, par ses leçons et son exemple, d'être considéré comme le premier qui en

Comparaison des Grecs avec les Latins.

zième siècles, dans les OEuvres du savant et judicieux Mosheim (*Instit. Hist. eccles.*, p. 434-440, 490-494).

(1) A la fin du quinzième siècle, il existait en Europe environ cinquante universités; plusieurs avaient été fondées avant l'année 1300. Elles étaient peuplées en raison de leur petit nombre. Bologne comptait dix mille étudians, principalement de jurisprudence. Dans l'année 1357, les étudians d'Oxford diminuèrent de trente mille à six mille (*Hist. de la Grande-Bretagne*, par Henry, vol. IV, p. 478). Cependant ce reste était encore fort supérieur au nombre qui compose aujourd'hui cette université.

ralluma le flambeau. L'étude et l'imitation des écrivains de l'ancienne Rome produisirent un style plus pur, des raisonnemens plus justes et des sentimens plus nobles. Les disciples de Virgile et de Cicéron s'approchèrent avec un empressement respectueux des Grecs, maîtres de ces grands écrivains. Dans le sac de Constantinople, les Français et même les Vénitiens avaient méprisé et détruit les ouvrages de Lysippe et d'Homère : un seul coup suffit pour anéantir irrévocablement les chefs-d'œuvre de l'art; mais la plume renouvelle et multiplie par la copie les œuvres du génie, et posséder et comprendre ces copies fut l'ambition de Pétrarque et de ses amis. La conquête des Turcs hâta sans doute le départ des muses, et nous ne pouvons nous défendre d'un mouvement de terreur en réfléchissant que les écoles et les bibliothèques de la Grèce auraient pu être détruites avant que l'Europe sortît de sa barbarie, et que les germes des sciences auraient été dispersés avant que le sol de l'Italie fût suffisamment préparé pour leur culture.

Renaissance de l'érudition grecque en Italie.

Les plus savans Italiens du quinzième siècle avouent et célèbrent la renaissance de l'érudition grecque (1), ensevelie depuis plusieurs siècles dans

---

(1) Les écrivains qui ont traité le plus à fond la restauration de la langue grecque en Italie, sont le doct. Homph. Hody (*de Græcis illustribus, linguæ græcæ litterarumque humaniorum instoratoribus*, Londres, 1742, grand in-8°) et Tiraboschi (*Istoria della Letteratura italiana*, t. v, p. 364-377; t. VII, p. 112-143). Le professeur d'Oxford est un

l'oubli. On cite pourtant dans cette contrée, et au-delà des Alpes, quelques hommes savans, qui, dans les siècles d'ignorance, se distinguèrent honorablement par la connaissance de la langue grecque, et la vanité nationale n'a point négligé les louanges dues à ces exemples d'érudition extraordinaire. Sans examiner trop scrupuleusement leur mérite personnel, on doit remarquer que leur science était sans motif et sans utilité ; qu'ils pouvaient aisément se satisfaire eux-mêmes ainsi que des contemporains encore plus ignorans ; qu'il existait chez eux très-peu de manuscrits écrits dans la langue qu'ils avaient apprise si miraculeusement, et qu'on ne l'enseignait dans aucune université de l'Occident. Il en restait quelques vestiges dans un coin de l'Italie, comme langue vulgaire, ou du moins comme langue ecclésiastique (1). L'ancienne influence des colonies doriennes et ioniennes n'était pas totalement détruite : les églises de la Calabre avaient été long-temps attachées au trône de Constantinople, et les moines de Saint-Basile faisaient encore leurs études au mont Athos et dans les écoles de l'Orient. Le moine Barlaam,

Leçons de Barlaam. A. D. 1339.

savant laborieux; mais le bibliothécaire de Modène jouit des avantages d'un historien national et moderne.

(1) *In Calabriâ quæ olim magna Græcia dicebatur, coloniis græcis repleta, remansit quædam linguæ veteris cognitio* (docteur Hody, p. 2). Si les Romains la firent disparaître, elle fut restaurée par les moines de Saint-Basile, qui possédaient sept couvens dans la seule ville de Rossano (Giannone, *Istoria di Napoli*, t. 1, p. 520.)

qu'on a déjà vu paraître comme sectaire et comme ambassadeur, était Calabrois de naissance, et ce fut lui qui ressuscita le premier, au-delà des Alpes, la mémoire ou les écrits d'Homère (1). Pétrarque et Boccace (2) le représentent comme un homme de petite taille, très-étonnant par son génie et son érudition, qui avait un discernement juste et rapide, mais une élocution lente et difficile. Ils attestent que, dans le cours de plusieurs siècles, la Grèce n'avait pas produit son égal pour la connaissance de l'histoire, de la grammaire et de la philosophie. Les princes et les docteurs de Constantinople reconnurent, par leurs attestations, la supériorité de son mérite. Il en existe encore une : l'empereur Cantacuzène, le protecteur de ses adversaires, avoue que ce profond et subtil logicien (3) était versé dans la lecture d'Euclide, d'Aristote et de Platon. A la cour d'Avignon il se lia d'intimité avec Pétrarque (4), le plus savant des Latins, et le désir mutuel de s'instruire fut le motif de

Études de Pétrarque.
A. D.
1339-1374.

---

(1) *Ii Barbari*, dit Pétrarque en parlant des Allemands et des Français, *vix, non dicam libros, sed nomen Homeri audierunt*. Peut-être le treizième siècle était-il, à cet égard, moins heureux que celui de Charlemagne.

(2) *Voy.* le caractère de Barlaam dans Boccace (*de Geneal. deorum*, l. xv, c. 6).

(3) Cantacuzène, l. ii, c. 36.

(4) Relativement à l'intimité entre Pétrarque et Barlaam, et à leurs deux entrevues à Avignon en 1339, et à Naples en 1342, *voy.* les excellens *Mémoires sur la vie de Pétrarque* (t. i, p. 406-410; t. ii, p. 75-77).

leur commerce littéraire. Le Toscan suivit avec ardeur l'étude de la langue grecque; après avoir laborieusement combattu contre la sécheresse et la difficulté des premières règles, Pétrarque parvint à sentir les beautés des poëtes et des philosophes dont il possédait le génie; mais il ne jouit pas long-temps de la société et des leçons de son nouvel ami. Barlaam abandonna une ambassade inutile, et provoqua imprudemment, à son retour en Grèce, le fanatisme des moines, en tâchant de substituer la lumière de la raison à celle de leur *nombril*. Après une séparation de trois ans, les deux amis se rencontrèrent à la cour de Naples; mais le généreux écolier, renonçant à l'occasion de se perfectionner, obtint pour Barlaam, à force de recommandations, un petit évêché (1) dans la Calabre, sa patrie. Les différentes occupations de Pétrarque, l'amour, l'amitié, ses correspondances et ses voyages, le laurier qu'il reçut à Rome, et ses compositions soignées en vers et en prose, en latin et en italien, le détournèrent de l'étude d'un idiome étranger; et en avançant en âge, il lui resta moins d'espoir que de désir d'apprendre la langue grecque. Il avait environ cinquante

---

(1) L'évêché dans lequel se retira Barlaam, était primitivement l'ancienne Locries, Seta Cyriaca dans le moyen âge, et par corruption Hieracium, Gerace (*Dissert. chorograph. Italiæ medii ævi*; p. 312). Là *dives opum* du temps des Normands fut bientôt réduite à l'indigence, puisque l'Église même était pauvre; la ville contient cependant encore trois mille habitans (Swinburne, p. 340).

ans, lorsqu'un de ses amis, ambassadeur de Byzance, également versé dans les deux langues, lui fit présent d'une copie d'Homère. La réponse de Pétrarque atteste également sa reconnaissance, ses regrets et son éloquence. Après avoir célébré la générosité du donateur et la valeur d'un don plus précieux à ses yeux que l'or et les rubis, il continue ainsi : « Le présent du texte original de ce divin poëte, source de toute invention, est digne de vous et de moi : vous avez rempli votre promesse et satisfait mes désirs. Mais votre générosité est imparfaite ; en me donnant Homère, il fallait aussi vous donner vous-même, devenir mon guide dans ce champ de lumière, et découvrir à mes yeux étonnés les séduisantes merveilles de l'Iliade et de l'Odyssée. Mais hélas ! Homère est muet pour moi, ou je suis sourd pour lui, et il n'est pas en mon pouvoir de jouir de la beauté que je possède. J'ai placé le prince des poëtes à côté de Platon, le prince des philosophes, et je m'enorgueillis à les contempler. J'avais déjà tout ce qui a été traduit en latin de leurs écrits immortels ; mais, sans en tirer du profit, j'éprouve de la satisfaction à les voir, ces Grecs respectables, dans leur véritable costume national. La vue d'Homère m'enchante ; et, quand je tiens dans mes mains ce silencieux volume, je m'écrie avec un soupir : Poëte illustre, avec quelle joie j'écouterais tes chants, si la mort d'un ami et la douloureuse absence d'un autre n'ôtaient pas à mon ouïe toute sa sensibilité ! Mais l'exemple de Caton m'encourage, et je ne désespère pas encore, puisqu'il ne parvint que sur la fin de sa vie à la connaissance des lettres grecques (1). »

La science à laquelle Pétrarque tâchait en vain d'atteindre, ne résista point aux efforts de son ami Boccace, le père de la prose toscane (2): Cet écrivain populaire, qui doit sa célébrité au *Décameron*, c'est-à-dire, à une centaine de contes d'amour et de plaisanterie, peut être considéré, à juste titre, comme celui qui ranima en Italie l'étude abandonnée de la langue grecque. En 1360, il parvint à retenir auprès de lui, par ses conseils et son hospitalité, Léon ou Léonce Pilate, disciple de Barlaam, qui allait à Avignon. Boccace le logea dans sa maison, lui obtint une pension de la république de Florence, et dévoua tous ses loisirs au premier professeur grec qui eût

De Boccace.
A. D. 1360,
etc.

―――――――――――

(1) Je transcrirai un passage de cette lettre de Pétrarque (*Famil.* ix, 2): *Donasti Homerum non in alienum sermonem violento alveo derivatum, sed ex ipsis Græci eloquii scatebris, et qualis divino illi profluxit ingenio...... Sine tuâ voce Homerus tuus apud me mutus, immò verò ego apud illum surdus sum. Gaudeo tamen vel adspectû solo, ac sæpe illum amplexus atque suspirans dico : O magne vir,* etc.

(2) Pour la vie et les écrits de Boccace, né en 1313, et mort en 1375, le lecteur peut consulter Fabricius (*Bibl. lat. medii ævi,* t. 1, p. 248, etc.) et Tiraboschi (t. v, p. 83-439-451). Les éditions, les traductions et les imitations de ses Nouvelles ou Contes, sont innombrables. Il avait honte cependant de communiquer cet ouvrage frivole et peut-être scandaleux à son respectable ami Pétrarque, dans les Lettres et Mémoires duquel il paraît d'une manière honorable.

enseigné cette langue dans les contrées occidentales de l'Europe. L'extérieur de Léon aurait dégoûté un disciple moins ardent. Il était enveloppé du manteau d'un philosophe ou d'un mendiant ; son maintien était repoussant, ses cheveux noirs rabattus sur son visage, sa barbe longue et malpropre, ses manières étaient grossières, son caractère inconstant et sombre ; et il ne réparait cet extérieur rebutant, lorsqu'il parlait latin, ni par les grâces ni même par la clarté de l'élocution. Mais son esprit renfermait un trésor d'érudition grecque. Il était également versé dans la fable et l'histoire, dans la grammaire et la philosophie : il expliqua les poëmes d'Homère dans les écoles de Florence. Ce fut sur ses instructions que Boccace composa, en faveur de son ami Pétrarque, une traduction littérale en prose de l'Iliade et de l'Odyssée, dont il est probable que Laurent Valla se servit secrètement pour composer, dans le siècle suivant, sa version latine. Boccace recueillit dans la conversation de Léon les matériaux de son traité sur la généalogie des dieux du paganisme, que son siècle regarda comme un prodige d'érudition. L'auteur le parsema de caractères et de passages grecs pour exciter la surprise et l'admiration de ses ignorans contemporains (1). Les premiers pas de

Léonce Pilate, premier professeur de la langue grecque à Florence et dans l'Occident. A. D. 1360-1363.

---

(1) Boccace se permet une honnête vanité : *Ostentationis causâ græca carmina adscripsi.... jure utor meo ; meum est hoc decus, mea gloria scilicet inter Etruscos græcis uti carminibus. Nonne ego fui qui Leontium Pilatum*, etc. (de

l'instruction sont lents et pénibles ; l'Italie entière ne fournit d'abord que dix disciples d'Homère : Rome, Venise et Naples, n'ajoutèrent pas un seul nom à cette liste. Mais les étudians se seraient multipliés et les progrès auraient été plus rapides, si l'inconstant Léon n'eût pas abandonné, au bout de trois ans, une situation honorable et avantageuse. En passant à Padoue, il s'arrêta quelques jours chez Pétrarque, qui fut aussi blessé de son caractère sombre et insociable que satisfait de son érudition. Mécontent des autres et de lui-même, dédaignant le bonheur dont il pouvait jouir, Léon ne portait jamais son imagination avec plaisir que sur les personnes et les objets absens. Thessalien en Italie, et Calabrois en Grèce, il méprisait, en présence des Latins, leurs mœurs, leur religion et leur langage, et ne fut pas plus tôt arrivé à Constantinople qu'il regretta la richesse de Venise et l'élégance des Florentins. Ses amis d'Italie furent sourds à ses importunités : comptant sur leur curiosité et leur indulgence, il s'embarqua pour un second voyage ; mais, à l'entrée du golfe Adriatique, le vaisseau qu'il montait fut assailli d'une tempête ; et l'infortuné professeur, qui s'était attaché comme Ulysse à un mât, périt frappé de la foudre. Le sensible Pétrarque donna des larmes à sa mort ; mais il s'informa surtout soigneusement si quelque copie de

---

Genealog. deorum, l. xv, c. 7). Cet ouvrage, oublié aujourd'hui, eut treize ou quatorze éditions.

Sophocle ou d'Euripide n'était point tombée entre les mains des mariniers (1).

Établissement de la langue grecque en Italie par Manuel Chrysoloras.
A. D.
1390-1415.

Les faibles germes recueillis par Pétrarque et semés par Boccace, se desséchèrent bientôt. La génération suivante se borna d'abord à perfectionner l'éloquence latine ; elle abandonna l'érudition grecque, et ce ne fut que vers la fin du treizième siècle que cette étude se renouvela d'une manière durable en Italie (2). Avant d'entreprendre son voyage, Manuel avait député des orateurs aux souverains de l'Occident, pour émouvoir leur compassion. Parmi ces envoyés, Manuel Chrysoloras (3) était le plus considérable par son rang ou par son savoir. Sa nais-

---

(1) Léonce ou Léon Pilate est suffisamment connu par ce qu'en disent le docteur Hody (p. 2-11) et l'abbé de Sades (*Vie de Pétrarque*, t. III, p. 625-634-670-673). L'abbé de Sades a très-habilement imité le style dramatique et animé de son original.

(2) Le docteur Hody (p. 54) blâme aigrement Léonard Arétin, Guarin, Paul Jove, etc., d'avoir affirmé que les lettres grecques avaient été restaurées en Italie, *post septingentos annos;* comme si, dit-il, elles avaient fleuri jusqu'à la fin du septième siècle. Ces écrivains dataient probablement de la fin de l'exarchat, et la présence des militaires et des magistrats grecs à Ravenne devait avoir conservé en quelque façon l'usage de leur langue nationale.

(3) *Voy.* l'article de Manuel ou Emmanuel Chrysoloras, dans Hody (p. 12-54) et Tiraboschi (t. VII, p. 113-118). La date précise de son arrivée flotte entre les années 1390 et 1400, et n'a d'autre époque sûre que le règne de Boniface IX.

sance était noble, et on prétendait que ses ancêtres avaient quitté Rome à la suite du grand Constantin. Après avoir visité les cours de France et d'Angleterre, où il obtint quelques contributions et beaucoup de promesses, le député fut invité à faire publiquement les fonctions de professeur, et Florence eut encore tout l'honneur de cette seconde invitation. Chrysoloras, également versé dans les langues grecque et latine, mérita le traitement que lui faisait la république, et surpassa ses espérances. Des écoliers de tout âge et de tout rang accoururent à son école; et l'un d'eux composa une histoire générale, dans laquelle il rend compte de ses motifs et de ses succès.

« A cette époque, dit Léonard Arétin (1), j'étudiais la jurisprudence; mais mon âme était enflammée de l'amour des lettres, et je donnai quelque temps à l'étude de la logique et de la rhétorique. A l'arrivée de Manuel, je balançai en moi-même si j'abandonnerais l'étude des lois ou si je laisserais échapper l'occasion précieuse qui se présentait; et, dans l'ardeur de ma jeunesse, je raisonnai ainsi avec moi-même : Te manqueras-tu à toi-même et à ta fortune? Refu-

---

(1) Cinq ou six citoyens nés à *Arezzo*, ont pris successivement le nom d'*Arétin*; le plus célèbre et le moins digne de l'être, vécut dans le seizième siècle. Léonard Bruni l'Arétin, disciple de Chrysoloras, fut savant dans les langues, orateur, historien, secrétaire de quatre papes et chancelier de la république de Florence, où il mourut, A. D. 1444, âgé de soixante-quinze ans. Fabr., *Bibl. medii ævi*, t. 1, p. 190, etc.; Tiraboschi, t. VII, p. 33-38.

seras-tu d'apprendre à converser familièrement avec Homère, Platon et Démosthènes, avec ces poëtes, ces philosophes et ces orateurs, dont on raconte tant de merveilles, et que toutes les générations ont reconnus pour les grands maîtres des sciences? Il se trouvera toujours dans nos universités un nombre suffisant de professeurs du droit civil; mais un maître de langue grecque, et un maître comme celui-ci, si on le laisse échapper, on ne le remplacera peut-être jamais. Convaincu par ce raisonnement, je me livrai tout entier à Chrysoloras, et mon ardeur était si vive, que les leçons que j'avais étudiées dans la journée étaient la nuit le sujet constant de mes songes (1). »
Dans le même temps, Jean de Ravenne, élevé dans la maison de Pétrarque (2), expliquait les auteurs latins à Florence. Les Italiens qui illustrèrent leur siècle et leur pays, se formèrent à cette double école; et cette ville devint l'utile séminaire de l'érudition des Grecs et des Romains (3). L'arrivée de

---

(1) *Voy.* ce passage dans l'Arétin. *In Commentario rerum suo tempore in Italiâ gestarum, apud Hodium*, p. 28-30.

(2) Pétrarque, qui aimait ce jeune homme, se plaint souvent de la curiosité trop avide, de l'activité indocile et du penchant à l'orgueil, qui annonçaient le génie et les talens futurs de son disciple (*Mém. sur Pétrarque*, t. III, p. 700-709).

(3) *Hinc græcæ latinæque scholæ exortæ sunt, Guarino, Philelpho, Leonardo Aretino, Caroloque, ac plerisque aliis tanquam ex equo Trojano prodeuntibus, quorum emulatione multa ingenia deinceps ad laudem excitata sunt* (*Platina*

l'empereur rappela Chrysoloras de son école à la cour; mais il enseigna dans la suite à Pavie et à Rome avec le même succès et les mêmes applaudissemens. Les quinze dernières années de sa vie se partagèrent entre l'Italie et Constantinople; tantôt envoyé, et tantôt professeur, l'honorable emploi d'éclairer par ses talens une nation étrangère ne lui fit jamais oublier ce qu'il devait à son prince et à son pays. Manuel Chrysoloras mourut à Constance, où il avait été député vers le concile par son souverain.

D'après cet exemple, une foule de Grecs indigens et instruits au moins de leur langue, se répandirent en Italie et hâtèrent ainsi les progrès des lettres grecques. Les habitans de Thessalonique et de Constantinople fuirent loin de la tyrannie des Turcs dans un pays riche, libre, et où on les accueillit généreusement. Le concile introduisit dans Florence les lumières de l'Église grecque et les oracles de la philosophie de Platon : les fugitifs qui adhéraient à l'union avaient le double mérite d'abandonner leur patrie non-seulement pour la cause du christianisme, mais plus particulièrement pour celle du catholicisme. Un patriote qui sacrifie son parti et sa conscience aux séductions de la faveur, peut cependant n'être pas

Les Grecs en Italie.
A. D.
1400-1500.

---

in Bonifacio ix). Un autre auteur italien ajoute les noms de *Paulus Petrus Vergerius, Omnibonus Vincentius, Poggius, Franciscus Barbarus,* etc. Mais je doute qu'une chronologie exacte accordât à Chrysoloras l'honneur d'avoir formé tous ces savans disciples. Hody, p. 25-27, etc.

privé des vertus sociales d'un particulier. Loin de son pays, il est moins exposé aux noms humilians d'esclave et d'apostat, et la considération qu'il acquiert parmi ses nouveaux associés peut le rétablir insensiblement dans sa propre estime. Bessarion obtint la pourpre ecclésiastique pour prix de sa docilité; il fixa sa résidence en Italie, et le cardinal grec, patriarche titulaire de Constantinople, fut considéré à Rome comme le chef (1) et le protecteur de sa nation. Il exerça ses talens dans les légations de Bologne, de Venise, de France et d'Allemagne ; et dans un conclave il fut presque désigné un moment pour la chaire de saint Pierre (2). Ses honneurs ecclésiastiques illustrèrent son mérite et ses travaux littéraires. Il fit de son palais une école, et dans ses visites au Vatican le cardinal était toujours suivi d'un cortége nombreux de disciples des deux nations (3), de savans qui s'ap-

Le cardinal Bessarion, etc.

---

(1) *Voyez* dans Hody l'article de Bessarion (p. 136-177). Théodore Gaza, George de Trébisonde, et les autres Grecs que j'ai nommés ou omis, sont cités dans les différens chapitres de ce savant auteur. *Voyez* aussi Tiraboschi dans les première et seconde parties de son sixième tome.

(2) Les cardinaux frappèrent à sa porte, mais son conclaviste refusa d'interrompre l'étude de Bessarion. « Nicolas, lui dit-il lorsqu'il en fut instruit, ton respect me coûte la tiare, et à toi le chapeau. »

(3) Tels que Georges de Trébisonde, Théodore Gaza, Argyropule et Andronic de Thessalonique, Philelphe, le Pogge, Blondus, Nicolas, Perrot, Valla, Campanus, Platina, etc. : *viri* (dit Hody avec le zèle d'un disciple) *nullo œvo perituri* (p. 136).

plaudissaient eux-mêmes et qu'applaudissait le public, et dont les écrits, aujourd'hui couverts de poussière, furent répandus de leur temps et utiles à leurs contemporains. Je n'entreprendrai point de compter tous ceux qui contribuèrent dans le quinzième siècle à restaurer la littérature grecque. Il suffira de citer avec reconnaissance les noms de Théodore Gaza, de Georges de Trébisonde, de Jean Argyropule et de Démétrius Chalcocondyles, qui enseignèrent leur langue nationale dans les écoles de Florence et de Rome. Leurs travaux égalèrent ceux de Bessarion, dont ils révéraient la dignité, et dont la fortune était l'objet de leur secrète envie ; mais la vie de ces grammairiens fut humble et obscure ; ils s'étaient écartés de la carrière lucrative de l'Église, leurs mœurs et leurs vêtemens les séquestraient de la société, et puisque le mérite de l'érudition leur suffisait, ils devaient aussi se contenter de sa récompense. Jean Lascaris (1) mérite une exception. Son affabilité, son éloquence et sa naissance illustre, recommandèrent à la cour de France un descendant des empereurs : on

Leur mérite et leurs défauts.

---

(1) Il était né avant la prise de Constantinople, mais il poussa son honorable carrière jusqu'en 1535. Léon X et François Ier furent ses plus illustres patrons. Il fonda sous leurs auspices les colléges grecs de Rome et de Paris (Hody, p. 247-275). Lascaris laissa en France de la postérité; mais les comtes de Vintimille et leurs nombreuses branches n'ont d'autre droit à ce nom qu'une alliance douteuse avec la fille de l'empereur grec dans le treizième siècle (Ducange, *Fam. byzant.*, p. 224-230).

l'employa alternativement dans les mêmes villes, comme professeur et comme négociateur. Par devoir et par intérêt, ces savans cultivèrent l'étude de la langue latine, et quelques-uns parvinrent à écrire et à parler une langue étrangère avec élégance et facilité; mais ils ne dépouillèrent jamais la vanité nationale. Leurs louanges ou au moins, leur admiration était réservée exclusivement aux écrivains de leur pays, aux talens desquels ils devaient leur réputation et leur subsistance. Ils trahirent quelquefois leur mépris par des critiques irrévérentes ou plutôt des satires contre la poésie de Virgile et les harangues de Cicéron (1). Ces habiles maîtres avaient dû leur supériorité à la pratique habituelle d'une langue vivante; et leurs premiers disciples ne pouvaient plus discerner combien ils avaient dégénéré de la science et même de la pratique de leurs ancêtres. Le bon sens de la génération suivante proscrivit dans les écoles la prononciation vicieuse (2) qu'ils y avaient

---

(1) François Floridus a conservé et réfuté deux épigrammes contre Virgile, et trois contre Cicéron. Il traite l'auteur de *Græculus ineptus et impudens* (Hody, p. 274). Un critique anglais a accusé de nos jours l'Énéide de contenir *multa languida, nugatoria, spiritu et majestate carminis heroïci defecta*, et beaucoup de vers que lui, Jérémie Markland, aurait rougi d'avouer (*Præfat. ad Statii Sylvas*, p. 21, 22).

(2) Emmanuel Chrysoloras et ses collègues ont été accusés d'ignorance, d'envie et d'avarice (*Sylloge*, etc., t. II, p. 235). Les Grecs modernes prononcent le β comme le *v*

introduite. Ils ne connaissaient point la valeur des
accens grecs ; et ces notes musicales qui, prononcées
par une langue attique, renfermaient pour une oreille
attique le secret de l'harmonie, n'étaient à leurs
yeux, comme aux nôtres, que des marques muettes
et insignifiantes, inutiles en prose et gênantes dans
la poésie. Ils possédaient les véritables principes de
la grammaire ; les précieux fragmens d'Apollonius et
d'Hérodien furent fondus dans leurs leçons, et leurs
traités de la syntaxe et des étymologies, quoique dépourvus d'esprit philosophique, sont encore aujour-
d'hui d'un grand secours aux étudians. Lorsque les
bibliothèques de Byzance furent détruites, chaque
fugitif saisit un fragment du trésor, une copie de
quelque auteur qui, sans lui, aurait été perdu. Ces
copies furent multipliées par des plumes laborieuses,
quelquefois élégantes ; ils corrigèrent le texte, et y

---

consonne, et confondent les trois voyelles η ι υ et plusieurs
diphthongues. Telle était la prononciation commune que le
sévère Gdiner maintint dans l'université de Cambridge,
par des lois pénales ; mais le monosyllabe βη représentait
à une oreille attique le bêlement d'une brebis, et un bélier
aurait été à cet égard un meilleur témoignage qu'un évêque ou un chancelier. On trouvera les traités des savans qui
rectifièrent la prononciation, et particulièrement d'Érasme,
dans le *Sylloge* d'Havercamp (deux volumes *in-8°, Lugd.
Bat.*, 1736-1740). Mais il est difficile de peindre des sons
par des mots ; et en renvoyant à l'usage moderne, ils ne
peuvent se faire entendre que de leurs compatriotes res-
pectifs. Nous observerons qu'Érasme a donné son approbation à notre prononciation du θ, *th*. (Érasme, tom. II, p. 130.)

ajoutèrent leurs interprétations ou celles des anciens scholiastes. Les Latins connurent, sinon l'esprit, du moins le sens littéral des auteurs classiques de la Grèce. Les beautés du style disparaissent dans une traduction ; mais Théodore Gaza eut le bon esprit de choisir les solides ouvrages de Théophraste et d'Aristote. Leurs histoires naturelles des plantes et des animaux ouvrirent un vaste champ à la théorie et aux expériences.

<small>Philosophie platonicienne.</small>

On poursuivit cependant toujours par préférence les nuages incertains de la métaphysique. Un Grec vénérable ressuscita en Italie le génie de Platon, condamné depuis long-temps à l'oubli, et l'enseigna dans le palais des Médicis (1). Cette élégante philosophie pouvait être de quelque avantage dans un temps où le concile de Florence ne s'occupait que de querelles théologiques. Son style est un précieux modèle de la pureté du dialecte attique ; il adapte souvent ses plus sublimes pensées au ton familier de la conversation, et les enrichit quelquefois de tout l'art de l'éloquence et de la poésie. Les Dialogues de ce grand homme présentent un tableau dramatique de la vie et de la mort d'un sage ; et quand il daigne

---

(1) Georges Gemistus Pletho, qui a composé de volumineux ouvrages sur différens sujets ; il fut le maître de Bessarion et de tous les platoniciens de son siècle. Dans sa vieillesse, Georges visita l'Italie, et retourna promptement finir ses jours dans le Péloponèse. *Voyez* une curieuse *diatribe* de Leo Allatius *de Georgiis*, dans Fabricius (*Bibl. græc.*, t. x, p. 639-756).

descendre des cieux, son système moral imprime dans l'âme l'amour de la vérité, de la patrie et de l'humanité. Socrate, par ses préceptes et son exemple, avait recommandé un doute modeste et de libres recherches; et l'enthousiasme des platoniciens, qui adoraient aveuglément les visions et les erreurs de leur divin maître, pouvait servir à corriger la méthode sèche et dogmatique de l'école péripatéticienne. Aristote et Platon offrent des mérites si égaux, quoique très-différens, qu'on trouverait, en les balançant, la matière d'une controverse interminable; mais quelque étincelle de liberté peut jaillir du choc de deux servitudes opposées. Ces deux sectes divisèrent les Grecs modernes, qui combattirent sous l'étendard de leurs chefs avec moins d'intelligence que de fureur : les fugitifs de Constantinople choisirent Rome pour leur nouveau champ de bataille; mais les grammairiens mêlèrent bientôt à cette contestation philosophique la haine et les injures personnelles; et Bessarion, quoique partisan zélé de Platon, soutint l'honneur national en interposant les avis et l'autorité d'un médiateur. La doctrine de l'Académie faisait, dans les jardins des Médicis, les plaisirs des hommes polis et éclairés; mais cette société philosophique fut bientôt détruite; et si le sage d'Athènes fut encore étudié dans le cabinet, son puissant rival resta seul l'oracle de l'école et de l'Église (1).

---

(1) Boivin (*Mém. de l'Acad. des Inscript.*, t. II, p. 715.

Émulation et progrès des Latins.

J'ai représenté avec impartialité le mérite littéraire des Grecs ; mais on doit avouer que l'ardeur des Latins les seconda et les surpassa peut-être. L'Italie était alors partagée en un grand nombre de petits États indépendans ; les princes et les républiques se disputaient l'honneur d'encourager et de récompenser la littérature. Nicolas v (1), dont le mérite fut infiniment supérieur à sa réputation, se tira, par son érudition et ses vertus, de l'obscurité où l'avait placé sa naissance. Le caractère de l'homme l'emporta toujours sur l'intérêt du pape, et Nicolas aiguisa de ses propres mains les armes dont on se servit bientôt pour attaquer l'Église romaine (2). Il avait été l'ami des principaux savans de son siècle ; il devint leur protecteur, et telle était la rare simplicité de ses mœurs, qu'eux ni lui ne s'aperçurent presque pas de ce changement. Lorsqu'il pressait

Nicolas v. A. D. 1447-1455.

---

729) et Tiraboschi (t. vi, part. 1, p. 259-288) ont éclairci l'état de la philosophie platonicienne en Italie.

(1) *Voyez* la *Vie de Nicolas* v par deux auteurs contemporains, Janottus Manettus (t. iii, part. ii, p. 905-962) et Vespasien de Florence (t. xxv, p. 267-290), dans la Collection de Muratori. *Consultez* Tiraboschi (t. vi, p. 1-46, 52-109) et Hody, aux articles de Théodore Gaza, de Georges de Trébisonde, etc.

(2) Le lord Bolingbroke observe, avec autant d'esprit que de justesse, que les papes furent à cet égard moins politiques que le mufti, et qu'ils rompirent eux-mêmes le talisman qui enchaînait depuis si long-temps le genre humain. *Lettres sur l'étude de l'Hist.*, l. vi, p. 165, 166, édit. *in-8°*, 1779.

d'accepter un présent, il ne l'offrait pas comme une mesure du mérite, mais comme une marque de son affection ; et lorsque la modestie hésitait à profiter de sa faveur : « Acceptez, disait-il avec le sentiment de ce qu'il valait, vous n'aurez pas toujours un Nicolas parmi vous. » L'influence du saint-siége se répandit dans toute la chrétienté, et le vertueux pontife en profita plus pour acquérir des livres que des bénéfices. Il fit chercher dans les ruines des bibliothèques de Constantinople et dans tous les monastères de l'Allemagne et de la Grande-Bretagne, les manuscrits poudreux de l'antiquité, dont il faisait tirer des copies exactes lorsqu'on refusait de lui vendre l'original. Le Vatican, ancien dépôt des bulles et des légendes, des monumens de la superstition et de la fraude, se remplit d'un mobilier plus intéressant ; et telle fut l'activité de Nicolas, que, dans les huit années de son règne, il parvint à composer une bibliothèque de cinq mille volumes. C'est à sa munificence que le monde latin fut redevable des traductions de Xénophon, Diodore, Polybe, Thucydide, Hérodote et Appien ; de la Géographie de Strabon, de l'Iliade, des plus précieux ouvrages de Platon, d'Aristote, de Ptolémée, de Théophraste, et des pères de l'Église grecque. Un marchand de Florence, qui gouvernait la république sans titre et sans armes, imita l'exemple du pontife romain. Côme de Médicis (1) fut la tige d'une suite

Côme et Laurent de Médicis. A. D. 1428-1492.

---

(1) *Voyez* l'histoire littéraire de Côme et de Laurent.

de princes; son nom et son siècle sont intimement liés avec l'idée du rétablissement des sciences. Son crédit devint de la renommée ; ses richesses furent consacrées à l'avantage du genre humain; ses correspondances s'étendaient du Caire à Londres, et le même vaisseau lui rapportait souvent des livres grecs et des épiceries de l'Inde. Le génie et l'éducation de son petit-fils Laurent en firent non-seulement le protecteur, mais un membre et un juge de la littérature. Le malheur trouvait dans son palais un secours, et le mérite une récompense; l'académie platonicienne faisait le charme de ses loisirs; il encouragea l'émulation de Démétrius Chalcocondyles et d'Ange Politien; et Jean Lascaris, son zélé missionnaire, rapporta de l'Orient deux cents manuscrits, dont quatre-vingts étaient inconnus alors aux bibliothèques de l'Europe (1). Le même esprit anima

---

de Médicis dans Tiraboschi (t. vi, p. 1, l. 1, c. 2), qui distribue de justes éloges à Adolphe d'Aragon, roi de Naples, aux ducs de Milan, de Ferrare, d'Urbin, etc. La république de Venise est celle qui a le moins de droits à la reconnaissance des savans.

(1) Tiraboschi (t. vi, part. 1, p. 104), extrait de la Préface de Jean Lascaris à l'Anthologie grecque, imprimée à Florence en 1494. *Latebant* (dit Alde dans sa Préface aux Orateurs grecs, *apud* Hody, p. 249) *in Atho Thraciæ monte; eas Lascaris..... in Italiam reportavit. Miserat enim ipsum Laurentius ille Medices in Græciam ad inquirendos simul et quantovis emendos pretio bonos libros.* Il est assez digne de remarque que cette recherche ait été facilitée par le sultan Bajazet II.

toute l'Italie, et les progrès des nations payèrent les princes de leur libéralité. Les Latins se réservèrent la propriété exclusive de leur propre littérature; et ces disciples de la Grèce devinrent bientôt capables de transmettre et de perfectionner les leçons qu'ils avaient reçues. Après une courte succession de maîtres étrangers, l'émigration cessa; mais le langage de la Grèce s'était répandu au-delà des Alpes, et les étudians de France, d'Allemagne et d'Angleterre (1), propagèrent dans leur patrie le feu sacré qu'ils avaient reçu dans les écoles de Rome et de Florence (2). Dans les productions de l'esprit comme dans celles de la terre, l'art et l'industrie surpassent les dons de la nature : les auteurs grecs, oubliés sur les bords de l'Ilissus, ont été mis en lumière sur ceux de l'Elbe et de la Tamise; Bessarion et Gaza auraient pu porter envie à la supériorité des Bar-

---

(1) Grocyn, Linacer et Latimer, qui avaient étudié à Florence sous Démétrius Chalcocondyles, introduisirent la langue grecque dans l'université d'Oxford, dans les dernières années du quinzième siècle. *Voyez* la *Vie* curieuse d'Érasme, composée par le docteur Knight; bien qu'un zélé champion de son académie, il est forcé d'avouer qu'Érasme apprit à Oxford le grec qu'il enseigna à Cambridge.

(2) Les jaloux Italiens désiraient se réserver le monopole de l'instruction grecque. Lorsque Alde fut sur le point de publier ses Commentaires sur Sophocle et Euripide, *Cave*, lui dirent-ils, *cave hoc facias, ne Barbari, istis adjuti, domi maneant, et pauciores in Italiam ventitent* (Docteur Knight, dans sa *Vie d'Érasme*, p. 365, extrait de Beatus Rhenanus).

bares, à l'exactitude de Budé, au goût d'Érasme, à l'abondance d'Étienne, à l'érudition de Scaliger, au discernement de Reiske ou de Bentley. Ce fut le hasard qui mit du côté des Latins l'avantage de l'invention de la presse ; mais Alde Manuce et ses innombrables successeurs employèrent cet art précieux à perpétuer et à multiplier les ouvrages de l'antiquité (1). Un seul manuscrit apporté de la Grèce produisait dix mille copies, toutes plus belles que l'original. Sous cette forme, Homère et Platon liraient leurs propres ouvrages avec plus de satisfaction, et leurs scholiastes doivent céder le prix à nos éditeurs occidentaux.

Usage et abus de l'ancienne érudition.

Avant la renaissance de la littérature classique, les Barbares de l'Europe étaient plongés dans la plus épaisse ignorance ; et la pauvreté de leur langue annonçait la grossièreté de leurs mœurs. Ceux qui étu-

(1) La presse d'Alde Manuce, Romain, fut établie à Venise vers l'année 1494. Il imprima au-delà de soixante ouvrages volumineux de littérature grecque, dont la plupart étaient encore en manuscrit, et dont plusieurs contenaient des Traités de différens auteurs ; il fit de quelques-uns deux, trois et jusqu'à quatre éditions. (Fabricius, *Bibl. græc.*, t. XIII, p. 605, etc.) Sa gloire ne doit pas cependant nous faire oublier que le premier livre grec, la *Grammaire de Constantin Lascaris*, fut imprimé à Milan en 1476, et que l'Homère imprimé à Florence, en 1488, est enrichi de tout l'art de la typographie. *Voy.* les *Annales typographiques de Maittaire* et la *Bibliographie instructive de Deburc*, imprimeur-libraire de Paris, distingué par ses connaissances.

dièrent les idiomes plus parfaits de Rome et de la
Grèce, se trouvèrent transplantés dans un nouveau
monde de sciences et de lumières. Ils se virent admis dans la société des nations libres et polies de
l'antiquité, et à la conversation familière de ces
hommes immortels qui avaient parlé le langage sublime de l'éloquence et de la raison. De tels rapports devaient nécessairement élever l'âme et perfectionner le goût des modernes ; cependant on peut
croire, d'après les premiers essais, que l'étude des
anciens avait donné à l'esprit humain des chaînes
plutôt que des ailes. L'esprit d'imitation, quelque
louable qu'il soit, tient toujours de l'esclavage ; et
les premiers disciples des Grecs et des Romains semblaient former une colonie d'étrangers au milieu de
leur pays et de leur siècle. Le soin minutieux apporté à pénétrer dans les antiquités des temps reculés, aurait pu être employé à perfectionner l'état
présent de la société : les critiques et les métaphysiciens suivaient servilement l'autorité d'Aristote ; les
poëtes, les historiens et les orateurs, répétaient orgueilleusement les pensées et les expressions du siècle d'Auguste ; ils observaient les ouvrages de la nature avec les yeux de Pline et de Théophraste, et
quelques-uns d'eux, dévots païens, rendaient secrètement hommage aux dieux d'Homère et de Platon (1). Les Italiens, dans le siècle qui suivit la

---

(1) Je choisirai trois exemples singuliers de cet enthousiasme classique : 1° au synode de Florence, Gemistus

mort de Pétrarque et de Boccace, se trouvèrent écrasés sous le nombre et la puissance de leurs anciens auxiliaires. On vit paraître une foule d'imitateurs latins que nous laissons convenablement reposer sur les rayons de nos bibliothèques ; mais on citerait difficilement, à cette époque d'érudition, la découverte d'une science, un ouvrage d'invention ou d'éloquence dans la langue (1) nationale. Cependant, aussitôt que le sol eut été suffisamment pénétré de cette rosée céleste, la végétation et la vie parurent de toutes parts ; les idiomes modernes se perfectionnèrent ; les auteurs classiques de Rome

---

Pletho dit à Georges de Trébisonde, dans une conversation familière, que toutes les nations renonceraient bientôt à l'Évangile et au Koran, pour embrasser une religion ressemblante à celle des gentils (Leo Allatius, *apud* Fabricium, t. x, p. 751). 2º Paul II persécuta l'Académie romaine, fondée par Pomponius-Lætus, et les principaux membres furent accusés d'hérésie, d'impiété et de *paganisme* (Tiraboschi, t. vi, part. 1, p. 81, 82). 3º Dans le siècle suivant, des étudians et des poëtes célébrèrent en France la fête de Bacchus, et immolèrent, dit-on, un bouc en réjouissance des succès que Jodelle avait obtenus par sa tragédie de *Cléopâtre* (*Dictionnaire de Bayle*, art. *Jodelle*; Fontenelle, t. III, p. 56-61). A la vérité, l'esprit de bigoterie a souvent découvert une impiété sérieuse dans ce qui n'était qu'un jeu de l'imagination et du savoir.

(1) Boccace ne mourut que dans l'année 1375, et nous ne pouvons placer la composition du *Morgante maggiore* de Louis Pulci et de l'*Orlando innamorato* du Bojardo, avant l'année 1480. Tiraboschi, t. vi, part. II, pag. 174-177.

et d'Athènes inspirèrent un goût pur et une noble émulation. En Italie, comme ensuite en France et en Angleterre, au règne séduisant de la poésie et des fictions succédèrent les lumières de la philosophie spéculative et expérimentale. Le génie peut quelquefois luire prématurément ; mais dans l'éducation d'un peuple comme dans celle d'un individu, il faut que sa mémoire soit exercée avant de mettre en mouvement les ressorts de sa raison ou de son imagination, et ce n'est qu'après les avoir imités long-temps que l'artiste parvient à égaler et quelquefois à surpasser ses modèles.

FIN DU TOME DOUZIÈME.

TABLE DES CHAPITRES

CONTENUS DANS LE DOUZIÈME VOLUME.

Pages

Chapitre LX. Schisme des Grecs et des Latins. État de Constantinople. Révolte des Bulgares. Isaac l'Ange détrôné par son frère Alexis. Origine de la quatrième croisade. Alliance des Français et des Vénitiens avec le fils d'Isaac. Leur expédition navale à Constantinople. Les deux siéges et la conquête définitive de cette ville par les Latins. 1

Chap. LXI. Partage de l'empire entre les Français et les Vénitiens. Cinq empereurs latins des maisons de Flandre et de Courtenai. Leurs guerres contre les Bulgares et contre les Grecs. Faiblesse et pauvreté de l'empire latin. Les Grecs reprennent Constantinople. Conséquences générales des croisades 87

Chap. LXII. Les empereurs grecs de Nicée et de Constantinople. Élévation et règne de Michel Paléologue. Sa fausse réunion avec le pape et l'Église latine. Projets hostiles du duc d'Anjou. Révolte de la Sicile. Guerre des Catalans dans l'Asie et dans la Grèce. Révolutions et situation présente d'Athènes. 160

Chap. LXIII. Guerres civiles et ruine de l'empire grec. Règnes d'Andronic l'Ancien, d'Andronic le Jeune et de Jean Paléologue. Régence, révolte, règne et abdication de Jean Cantacuzène. Établissement d'une colonie génoise à Péra et à Galata. Leurs guerres contre l'empire et contre la ville de Constantinople. 216

Chap. LXIV. Conquêtes de Gengis-khan et des Mongouls depuis la Chine jusqu'à la Pologne. Danger des Grecs et de Constantinople. Origine des Turcs ottomans en Bithynie. Règnes et victoires d'Othman, Orchan, Amurath 1er et Bajazet 1er. Fondation et progrès de la monarchie des Turcs en Asie et en Europe. Situation critique de Constantinople et de l'empire grec. 265

Chap. LXV. Élévation de Timour ou Tamerlan sur le trône de Samarcande. Ses conquêtes dans la Perse, la Géorgie, la Tartarie, la Russie, l'Inde, la Syrie et l'Anatolie. Sa guerre contre les Turcs. Défaite et captivité de Bajazet. Mort de Timour. Guerre civile des fils de Bajazet. Rétablissement de la monarchie des Turcs par Mahomet 1er. Siége de Constantinople par Amurath II 333

Chap. LXVI. Sollicitations des empereurs d'Orient auprès des papes. Voyages de Jean Paléologue 1er, de Manuel et de Jean II, dans les cours de l'Occident. Union des Églises grecque et latine proposée par le concile de Bâle, et accomplie à Ferrare et à Florence. État de la littérature à Constantinople. Sa renaissance en Italie, où elle fut portée par les Grecs fugitifs. Curiosité et émulation des Latins. 406

FIN DE LA TABLE DES CHAPITRES.

TABLE DES MATIÈRES

CONTENUES DANS CE VOLUME.

	Pages
Schisme des Grecs.	1
Leur aversion pour les Latins.	2
Procession du Saint-Esprit.	3
Variations dans la discipline ecclésiastique.	4
Querelles ambitieuses de Photius, patriarche de Constantinople, avec les papes. A. D. 857-886.	6
Les papes excommunient le patriarche de Constantinople et les Grecs. A. D. 1054.	9
Inimitié des Grecs et des Latins. A. D. 1000-1200.	10
Les Latins à Constantinople.	12
Règne et caractère d'Isaac l'Ange. A. D. 1185-1195.	15
Révolte des Bulgares. A. D. 1186.	17
Usurpation et caractère d'Alexis l'Ange. A. D. 1195-1203.	19
Quatrième croisade. A. D. 1198.	21
Les barons français se croisent.	24
État des Vénitiens. A. D. 697-1200.	26
Alliance des Français et des Vénitiens. A. D. 1201.	31
Assemblée de la croisade et départ de Venise. A. D. 1202.	34
Siége de Zara. Nov. 10.	37
Alliance des croisés avec le jeune Alexis.	39

	Pages
Départ de Zara pour Constantinople. A. D. 1203, avril 7.	42
Arrivée. Juin 24.	Ibid.
L'empereur tente inutilement une négociation.	46
Passage du Bosphore. Juillet 6.	48
Premier siége et conquête de Constantinople par les Latins. Juillet 7-18.	52
Rétablissement de l'empereur Isaac l'Ange et de son fils Alexis.	57
Querelle entre les Grecs et les Latins.	61
La guerre recommence. A. D. 1204.	64
Alexis et son père sont déposés par Mourzoufle. Fév. 8.	66
Second siége de Constantinople.	Ibid.
Pillage de Constantinople.	72
Partage du butin.	75
Misère des Grecs.	76
Sacriléges et railleries.	78
Destruction des statues.	79
Élection de l'empereur Baudouin 1er. A. D. 1204.	87
Partage de l'empire grec.	92
Révolte des Grecs. A. D. 1204, etc.	97
Théodore Lascaris, empereur de Nicée. A. D. 1204-1222.	99
Guerre des Bulgares. A. D. 1205.	103

TABLE DES MATIÈRES.

	Pages
Défaite et captivité de Baudouin. A. D. 1205.	107
Règne et caractère de Henri. A. D. 1206-1216.	110
Pierre de Courtenai, empereur d'Orient. A. D. 1217.	115
Sa captivité et sa mort. A. D. 1217-1219.	117
Robert, empereur de Constantinople. A. D. 1221-1228.	118
Baudouin II et Jean de Brienne, empereurs de Constantinople. A. D. 1228-1237.	121
Baudouin II. A. D. 1237-1261.	122
La sainte couronne d'épines.	127
Succès des Grecs. A. D. 1237-1261.	130
Les Grecs reprennent Constantinople. A. D. 1261, juillet 25.	133
Conséquences générales des croisades.	138
Origine de la famille de Courtenai. A. D. 1020.	145
1° Les comtes d'Édesse. A. D. 1101-1152.	147
2° Les Courtenai de France.	149
Leur alliance avec la famille royale. A. D. 1150.	Ibid.
3° Les Courtenai d'Angleterre.	154
Les comtes de Devon.	155
Rétablissement de l'empire grec.	160
Théodore Lascaris. A. D. 1204-1222.	161
Jean Ducas Vatacès. A. D. 1222-1255.	Ibid.
Théodore Lascaris II. A. D. 1255-1259.	164
Minorité de Jean Lascaris. A. D. 1259.	166
Famille et caractère de Michel Paléologue.	168
Son élévation au trône.	171
Michel Paléologue, empereur. A. D. 1260.	175
Conquête de Constantinople. A. D. 1261.	175
Retour de l'empereur grec. A. D. 1261.	177
Paléologue bannit le jeune empereur après lui avoir fait crever les yeux. A. D. 1261.	179
Paléologue est excommunié par le patriarche Arsène. A. D. 1262-1268.	181
Schisme des arsénites. A. D. 1266-1312.	182
Règne de Michel Paléologue. A. D. 1259-1282.	184
Règne d'Andronic l'Ancien. A. D. 1273-1332.	185
Son union avec l'Église latine. A. D. 1274-1277.	186
Il persécute les Grecs. A. D. 1277-1282.	190
L'union dissoute. A. D. 1283.	192
Charles d'Anjou s'empare de Naples et de la Sicile. A. D. 1266, fév. 26.	193
Il menace l'empire grec. A. D. 1270, etc.	195
Paléologue excite les Siciliens à se révolter. A. D. 1280.	197
Service et guerre des Catalans dans l'empire grec. A. D. 1303-1307.	202
Révolutions d'Athènes. A. D. 1204-1456.	209
Situation présente d'Athènes.	212
Superstition d'Andronic et du siècle. A. D. 1282-1320.	216
Premières querelles entre les deux Andronic. A. D. 1320.	220
Trois guerres civiles entre les deux empereurs. A. D. 1321-1328.	224
Couronnement d'Andronic le Jeune. A. D. 1325.	225
Andronic l'Ancien abdique l'empire. A. D. 1328.	226
Sa mort. A. D. 1332, fév. 13.	228

TABLE DES MATIÈRES.

	Pages
Règne d'Andronic le Jeune. A. D. 1328-1341.	229
Ses deux épouses.	Ibid.
Règne de Jean Paléologue. A. D. 1341-1391.	232
Bonheur de Jean Cantacuzène.	Ibid.
Il est nommé régent de l'empire.	234
Sa régence est attaquée. A. D. 1341.	Ibid.
Par Apocaucus.	235
Par l'impératrice Anne de Savoie.	Ibid.
Par le patriarche.	236
Cantacuzène prend la pourpre. A. D. 1341, oct. 26.	237
Guerre civile. A. D. 1341-1347.	240
Victoire de Cantacuzène.	Ibid.
Cantacuzène rentre dans Constantinople. A. D. 1347.	243
Règne de Cantacuzène. A. D. 1347-1355.	245
Jean Paléologue prend les armes contre Cantacuzène. A. D. 1353.	247
Abdication de Cantacuzène au mois de janvier. A. D. 1355.	249
Dispute concernant la lumière du mont Thabor. A. D. 1341-1351.	Ibid.
Établissement des Génois à Péra ou Galata. A. D. 1291-1347.	253
Commerce et insolence des Génois.	256
Guerre des Génois contre l'empereur Cantacuzène. A. D. 1348.	257
Défaite de la flotte de Cantacuzène.	259
Victoire des Génois sur les Grecs et les Vénitiens. A. D. 1352.	260
Zingis-khan ou Gengis-khan, premier empereur des Mongouls et des Tartares. A. D. 1206-1227.	266
Lois de Gengis-khan.	269
Son invasion de la Chine. A. D. 1210-1214.	273
De Carizme, de la Transoxiane et de la Perse. A. D. 1218-1224.	275
Sa mort. A. D. 1227.	278
Conquêtes des Mongouls sous les successeurs de Gengis. A. D. 1227-1295.	279
De l'empire septentrional de la Chine. A. D. 1234.	Ibid.
De la Chine méridionale. A. D. 1279.	282
De la Perse et de l'empire des califes. A. D. 1258.	283
De l'Anatolie. A. D. 1242-1272.	285
Du Kipzak, de la Russie, de la Pologne, de la Hongrie, etc. A. D. 1235-1245.	286
De la Sibérie. A. D. 1242.	290
Les successeurs de Gengis. A. D. 1227-1259.	291
Ils adoptent les mœurs de la Chine. A. D. 1259-1368.	293
Division de l'empire des Mongouls. A. D. 1259-1300.	295
Danger de Constantinople et de l'empire grec. A. D. 1240-1304.	296
Déclin des empereurs ou khans mongouls de la Perse. A. D. 1304.	299
Origine des Ottomans. A. D. 1240, etc.	300
Règne d'Othman. A. D. 1299-1326.	301
Règne d'Orchan. A. D. 1326-1360.	303
Il fait la conquête de la Bithynie. A. D. 1326-1339.	304
Division de l'Anatolie entre les émirs turcs. A. D. 1300, etc.	305

TABLE DES MATIÈRES.

	Pages
Perte des provinces asiatiques. A. D. 1312, etc.	306
Les chevaliers de Rhodes. A. D. 1310-1523.	307
Premier passage des Turcs en Europe. A. D. 1341-1347.	Ibid.
Mariage d'Orchan avec une princesse grecque. A. D. 1346.	310
Établissement des Ottomans en Europe. A. D. 1353.	311
Mort d'Orchan et de son fils Soliman.	314
Règne d'Amurath 1er, et ses conquêtes en Europe. A. D. 1360-1389.	Ibid.
Les janissaires.	316
Règne de Bajazet 1er ou Ilderim. A. D. 1389-1403.	318
Ses conquêtes depuis l'Euphrate jusqu'au Danube.	Ibid.
Bataille de Nicopolis. A. D. 1396.	320
Croisade et captivité des princes français. A. D. 1396-1398.	321
L'empereur Jean Paléologue. A. D. 1355-1391.	326
Discorde des Grecs.	327
L'empereur Manuel. A. D. 1391-1425.	329
Détresse de Constantinople. A. D. 1395-1402.	Ibid.
Histoire de Timour ou Tamerlan.	333
Ses premières aventures. A. D. 1361-1370.	337
Il est élevé sur le trône du Zagatai. A. D. 1370, avril.	339
Ses conquêtes. A. D. 1370-1400.	340
De la Perse. A. D. 1380-1393.	Ibid.
Du Turkestan. A. D. 1370-1383.	343
Du Kipzak, de la Russie, etc. A. D. 1390-1396.	344
De l'Indoustan. A. D. 1398-1399.	347
Guerre de Timour contre le sultan Bajazet. A. D. 1400.	350
Timour envahit la Syrie. A. D. 1400.	355
Sac d'Alep. A. D. 1400.	356
De Damas. A. D. 1401.	359
Et de Bagdad. A. D. 1401.	Ibid.
Timour entre dans l'Anatolie. A. D. 1402.	360
Bataille d'Angora. A. D. 1402.	362
Défaite et captivité de Bajazet.	365
Histoire de la cage de fer.	366
Contraire au récit de l'historien persan de Timour.	Ibid.
Attestée, 1° par les Français.	369
2° Par les Italiens.	Ibid.
3° Par les Arabes.	370
4° Par les Grecs.	371
5° Par les Turcs.	372
Conclusion probable.	Ibid.
Mort de Bajazet. A. D. 1403, 9 mars.	373
Terme des conquêtes de Timour.	374
Son triomphe à Samarcande. A. D. 1405.	377
Timour meurt dans sa marche en Chine. A. D. 1405.	379
Caractère et mérite de Timour.	380
Guerres civiles des fils de Bajazet. A. D. 1403-1421.	386
1° Mustapha.	Ibid.
2° Isa.	387
3° Soliman. A. D. 1403-1410.	Ibid.
4° Mousa. A. D. 1410.	388
5° Mahomet. A. D. 1413-1421.	389
Règne de l'empereur Amurath II. A. D. 1421-1451.	390
Réunion de l'empire des Ottomans. A. D. 1421.	Ibid.

TABLE DES MATIÈRES.

	Pages
État de l'empire grec. A. D. 1402-1425.	392
Siége de Constantinople par Amurath II. A. D. 1422.	396
L'empereur Jean Paléologue II. A. D. 1425-1448.	397
Succession héréditaire, et mérite des princes ottomans.	Ibid.
Éducation et discipline des Turcs.	398
Invention et usage de la poudre à canon.	402
Ambassade de l'empereur Andronic le Jeune au pape Benoît XII. A. D. 1339.	406
Négociation de Cantacuzène avec Clément VI. A. D. 1348.	411
Traité de Jean Paléologue Ier avec Innocent VI. A. D. 1355.	414
Visite de Jean Paléologue à Urbain V à Rome. A. D. 1369.	416
Son retour à Constantinople. A. D. 1370.	420
Voyages de Manuel en Occident.	Ibid.
A la cour de France. A. D. 1400.	421
A la cour d'Angleterre. A. D. 1400.	423
Son retour en Grèce. A. D. 1402.	424
Connaissances et descriptions des Grecs.	425
De l'Allemagne.	426
De la France.	427
De l'Angleterre.	428
Indifférence de Manuel pour les Latins. A. D. 1402-1417.	430
Ses négociations. A. D. 1417-1425.	431
Conversation particulière de l'empereur Manuel.	432
Mort de l'empereur Manuel.	434
Zèle de Jean Paléologue II.	435
Corruption de l'Église latine.	436
Schisme. A. D. 1377-1429.	437
Concile de Pise. A. D. 1409.	Ibid.
De Constance. A. D. 1414-1418.	Ibid.
De Bâle. A. D. 1431-1443.	438
Ils se déclarent contre Eugène IV.	439
Négociations avec les Grecs. A. D. 1434-1437.	440
Jean Paléologue s'embarque sur les galères du pape. A. D. 1437.	441
Son entrée triomphante à Venise. A. D. 1438.	447
A Ferrare.	448
Concile des Grecs et des Latins à Ferrare. A. D. 1438.	450
A Florence. A. D. 1439.	Ibid.
Négociations avec les Grecs.	456
Eugène est déposé à Bâle. A. D. 1438.	459
Réunion des Grecs avec les Latins. A. D. 1438.	460
Leur retour à Constantinople. A. D. 1440.	462
Paix définitive de l'Église. A. D. 1449.	Ibid.
État de la langue grecque à Constantinople. A. D. 1300-1453.	463
Comparaison des Grecs avec les Latins.	467
Renaissance de l'érudition grecque en Italie.	468
Leçons de Barlaam. A. D. 1339.	469
Études de Pétrarque. A. D. 1339-1374.	470
De Boccace. A. D. 1360.	473
Léonce Pilate, premier professeur de la langue grecque à Florence et dans l'Occident. A. D. 1360-1363.	474

	Pages		Pages
Établissement de la langue grecque en Italie par Manuel Chrysoloras. A. D. 1390-1415.	476	Philosophie platonicienne.	484
		Émulation et progrès des Latins.	486
		Nicolas v. A. D. 1447-1455.	Ibid.
Les Grecs en Italie. A. D. 1400-1500.	479	Côme et Laurent de Médicis. A. D. 1428-1492.	487
Le cardinal Bessarion, etc.	480		
Leur mérite et leurs défauts.	481	Usage et abus de l'ancienne érudition.	490

FIN DE LA TABLE DES MATIÈRES.

ON TROUVE CHEZ LE MÊME LIBRAIRE:

Petit (le) Conteur de poche, ou l'Art d'échapper à l'ennui, choix amusant et portatif d'anecdotes historiques, curieuses, galantes et comiques; de bons mots, saillies, naïvetés, réparties ingénieuses, calembours; quatrième édition, revue, corrigée et considérablement augmentée; 1 vol. in-18, orné d'une jolie figures. 1 fr. 50 c.

Précis de l'Histoire des Empereurs romains, depuis Auguste jusqu'à la translation de l'empire à Constantinople; avec des anecdotes historiques sur les principaux personnages qui ont vécu à cette époque, et un détail curieux des mœurs et usages des Romains; ouvrage destiné à l'instruction de la jeunesse; 1 fort vol. in-12, orné de 12 jolies gravures. 3 fr.

Le Présent maternel, ou la Semaine amusante et instructive; ouvrage consacré à la jeunesse, traduit de l'anglais, par T.-P. Bertin, seconde édition; 2 vol. in-18, ornés de 8 figures en taille-douce. 3 fr.

Religion (la), poëme, suivi de la Grâce et d'un choix de poésies sacrées, par Louis Racine; 1 vol. in-18, très-gros, orné d'une jolie figure. 1 fr. 50 c.

Repaires (les) du Crime, ou Histoire des Brigands fameux en Espagne, en Italie, en Angleterre, et dans les principales contrées de l'Europe; troisième édition, revue, corrigée et augmentée d'un Coup d'œil sur les Bandes de Schinderhannes et autres associés des bords du Rhin; 1 vol. in-18, orné d'une très-jolie figure. 1 fr. 50 c.

Six mois a Paris, ou le Guide sentimental de la jeunesse dans la société, par l'auteur d'une Année de Bonheur; 1 fort vol. in-12, orné de 6 figures. 4 fr.

Tableau de l'Amour conjugal, par Nicolas Venette, docteur en médecine, nouvelle édition, ornée de 12 figures; 2 vol. in-12. 5 fr.

Le même, avec les fig. col. 7 fr.

Les Vertus du Christianisme, ou Recueil de Traits sublimes inspirés par la religion; 1 v. in-12, orné de 4 figures, troisième édition. 3 fr.

Voyages en France et autres Pays, en prose et en vers, par Racine, La Fontaine, Regnard, Chapelle et Bachaumont, Hamilton, Voltaire, Piron, Gresset, Fléchier, Lefranc de Pompignan, Bertin, Desmahis, Béranger, Bret, Bernardin de Saint-Pierre, Parny, Boufflers, etc.; troisième édition. Paris, 1818; 5 vol. in-18, ornés de 36 jolies planches gravées et dessinées par les meilleurs artistes. 15 fr.

Voyage sentimental en France, par Sterne, suivi des Lettres d'Yorick à Élisa, d'Élisa à Yorick; nouvelle édition, d'après les meilleures traductions, ornée de 4 figures; 2 vol in-18. 3 fr.

Œuvres d'Homère, avec des remarques, précédées de réflexions sur Homère et sur la traduction des poètes, par Bitaubé, membre de l'Institut et de la Légion-d'Honneur; 4 volumes in-12, ornés de 4 jolies figures. 12 fr.